INTRODUCTION TO MICROECONOMICS

SECOND EDITION

Stanley Fischer
Rudiger Dornbusch
Richard Schmalensee

PROFESSORS OF ECONOMICS
MASSACHUSSETTS INSTITUTE
OF TECHNOLOGY

McGRAW-HILL BOOK COMPANY
New York   St. Louis   San Francisco   Auckland   Bogotá
Caracas   Colorado Springs   Hamburg   Lisbon   London
Madrid   Mexico   Milan   Montreal   New Delhi
Oklahoma City   Panama   Paris   San Juan   São Paulo
Singapore   Sydney   Tokyo   Toronto

INTRODUCTION TO MICROECONOMICS

Copyright © 1988, 1983 by McGraw-Hill, Inc. All rights reserved.
Printed in the United States of America. Except as permitted under
the United States Copyright Act of 1976, no part of this publication
may be reproduced or distributed in any form or by any means, or
stored in a data base or retrieval system, without the prior written
permission of the publisher.

1234567890 HALHAL 89210987

ISBN 0-07-021009-8

This book was set in Clearface Regular by Better Graphics, Inc.
The editors were Elisa Adams, Scott D. Stratford, and Larry Goldberg;
the designer was Hermann Strohbach;
the production supervisor was Salvador Gonzales.
Drawings were done by Fine Line Illustrations, Inc.
Cover photograph was provided by David F. Hughes, © 1982.
Arcata Graphics/Halliday was printer and binder.

Library of Congress Cataloging-in-Publication Data

Fischer, Stanley.
    Introduction to microeconomics.
    Includes bibliographical references and index.
    1. Microeconomics.   I. Dornbusch, Rudiger.
II. Schmalensee, Richard.   III. Title.
HB172.F48   1988   338.5   87-29666
ISBN 0-07-021009-8   CIP

ABOUT THE AUTHORS

Stanley Fischer (*right*) was an undergraduate at the London School of Economics and has a Ph.D. from MIT. He taught at the University of Chicago while Rudi Dornbusch was a student there, starting a long friendship and collaboration. Since 1973 he has taught at MIT and spent several leaves at the Hebrew University in Jerusalem. His main research interests are in monetary theory, macroeconomic policy, and economic growth and development. He has published widely in these areas and participates regularly in scholarly meetings. He is the editor of the *NBER Macroeconomics Annual*, initiated by the National Bureau of Economic Research to bridge the gap between theory and policy in the macroeconomic area.

Rudiger Dornbusch (*center*) did his undergraduate work in Switzerland and holds a Ph.D. from the University of Chicago. He has taught at Chicago, Rochester, and since 1975 at MIT. His research is primarily in international economics, with a major macroeconomic component. His special research interests are the behavior of exchange rates, high inflation and hyperinflation, and the international debt problem. He visits and lectures extensively in Europe and in Latin America, where he takes an active interest in problems of stabilization policy, and has held visiting appointments in Brazil and Argentina. His writing includes *Open Economy Macroeconomics* and, with Stanley Fischer, *Macroeconomics*. His interests in public policy take him frequently to testify before Congress and to participate in international conferences. He regularly contributes newspaper editorials on current policy issues here and abroad.

Richard Schmalensee (*left*) was born in Belleville, Illinois, where he attended the public schools. He was an undergraduate at MIT, from which he also holds a Ph.D. He has taught at the University of California, San Diego, and, since 1977, at MIT and has held visiting appointments at the University of Louvain in Belgium. His main research interests are in microeconomics, with special emphasis on imperfect competition, regulation, and antitrust policy. His many publications include *The Economics of Advertising* and *The Control of Natural Monopolies*, and he is coeditor of *The Handbook of Industrial Organization*. He consults regularly on regulatory and antitrust issues.

TO: MICHAEL, DAVID, AND JONATHAN
    SERGIO
    ALEXANDER AND NICHOLAS

Contents

	Preface	xix
PART ONE	**INTRODUCTION**	1
Chapter 1	**An Introduction to Economics**	3
	1. The Dismal Science?	4
	Is Economics Dismal? Is Economics a Science?	
	2. The Production Possibility Frontier	7
	Models and Reality Opportunity Cost Cost and Choice Growth Efficiency	
	3. Economic Systems	11
	Prices and Markets The Extreme Cases Mixed Economies	
	4. The Road Ahead	14
	Micro and Macro Economic Jargon	
	Summary	15
	Key Terms	16
	Problems	16
	Appendix: Understanding Graphs	16
	What Is a Graph? Drawing a Graph Linear Relations Nonlinear Relations	
Chapter 2	**Basic Concepts and Techniques**	22
	1. Economic Models and Theories	23
	The Circular Flow of Income Models in General Models and Data	
	2. Measuring Economic Variables	27
	Prices, Quantities, and Values Average Price Level Dollar Value of Aggregate (Total) Output Quantity of Aggregate Output	
	3. Comparing Economic Variables	31
	Ratios in Economics Percentage Changes	
	4. Developing Economic Laws	34
	Time Series and Cross Section Data Scatter Diagrams and Econometrics Limits to Understanding	

	Summary	38
	Key Terms	39
	Problems	39

Chapter 3   **Supply, Demand, and the Market**   41

1. Markets   42

2. The Demand Curve   42

3. The Supply Curve   44

4. The Interaction of Supply and Demand: Market Equilibrium   45
   Movement to Equilibrium   Quantity Demanded versus Quantity Bought

5. Behind the Demand Curve   48
   *Prices of Related Goods   Consumers' Incomes   Consumers' Tastes
   Expected Future Prices*

6. Shifts of the Demand Curve   50
   An Increase in the Price of a Substitute   The Effects of a Reduction in Income

7. Behind the Supply Curve   52
   Durable Productive Assets   Available Technology   Prices of Variable Inputs

8. Shifts of the Supply Curve   54

9. Do Buyers and Sellers Respond to Prices?   54
   Consumer Response to Prices: The VCR   Producer Response to Prices: Oil and Coal

10. What, How, and For Whom   55

Summary   56
Key Terms   56
Problems   57

Chapter 4   **Government in the Mixed Economy**   59

1. What Do Governments Do?   59
   *Create Laws, Rules, and Regulations   Buy and Sell Goods and Services
   Make Transfer Payments   Impose Taxes   Try to Stabilize the Economy
   Affect the Allocation of Resources*

2. What Should Governments Do?   64
   The Business Cycle   Public Goods   Externalities   Information-Related Problems   Monopoly and Market Power   Income Redistribution and Merit Goods   Summary

3. How Do Governments Decide?   69
   Voting and Consistency   Logrolling   Concentrated Interests   Spending, Taxes, and Deficits

	Summary	74
	Key Terms	74
	Problems	74

PART TWO — SUPPLY, DEMAND, AND PRODUCT MARKETS — 77

Chapter 5 — Elasticities and Market Adjustment — 79

1. The Price Elasticity of Demand — 80
2. Demand Elasticity and Sellers' Revenue — 83
   How to Maximize Total Revenue
3. Demand Elasticity: Extreme Cases — 87
4. Substitutes and Price Elasticity — 87
5. Other Demand Elasticities — 88
   Cross Price Elasticity of Demand   Income Elasticity of Demand
6. The Price Elasticity of Supply — 91
7. Demand and Supply in the Short Run and the Long Run — 92
   Demand Adjustment   Supply Adjustment

Summary — 97
Key Terms — 98
Problems — 98

Appendix: More on Demand Curves and the Price Elasticity of Demand — 99
   Different Demand Curves   Arc Elasticity

Chapter 6 — Consumer Behavior and Market Demand — 101

1. Individual and Market Demand Curves — 101
2. Diminishing Marginal Utility and Demand Curves — 103
   The Budget Constraint   Marginal Utility and Demand   Relative Prices and Consumer Decisions
3. Utility and Behavior — 108
   Measurable Utility and Revealed Preference   Economic Man
4. Must All Demand Curves Slope Downward? — 109
   Income and Substitution Effects of a Price Change   The Law of Demand
5. Consumer's Surplus — 111

Summary — 114
Key Terms — 114
Problems — 115

x Contents

        Appendix: Consumer Behavior without Measurable Utility   116
           The Budget Constraint   Income and Substitution Effects   Indifference Curves

Chapter 7   Business Organization and Behavior   123

    1. Industries and Firms in the U.S. Economy   123

    2. Forms of Business Organization   125
        Proprietorships and Partnerships   Corporations   The Common Denominator: Profits

    3. Profit Maximization   129
        Do Businesses Maximize?   What Are Managers' Goals?

    4. Accounting and Economic Reality   131
        The Income Statement   The Balance Sheet   Accounting and Market Values   Accounting Cost and Opportunity Cost

    Summary   134
    Key Terms   137
    Problems   137

Chapter 8   Production and Costs   138

    1. Production and the Firm's Time Horizon   138
        Technical and Economic Efficiency   The Production Function   The Short Run and The Long Run

    2. Production in the Short Run   141
        Total Product   Marginal Product   Average Product

    3. Short-Run Cost Curves   144
        Fixed and Variable Costs   Total and Marginal Costs   Average Costs   Changes in Cost Conditions

    4. Production and Costs in the Long Run   149
        Long-Run Average Cost   Long-Run Marginal Cost

    5. Economies and Diseconomies of Scale   151
        Economies of Scale   Diseconomies of Scale   Returns to Scale in Practice

    Summary   155
    Key Terms   155
    Problems   156

Chapter 9   Supply in a Competitive Industry   157

    1. Perfectly Competitive Firms and Markets   158
        The Perfectly Competitive Firm   Perfectly Competitive Markets   An Important but Extreme Case

2. The Firm's Short-Run Supply Decision ... 160
Finding the Optimal Positive Output   Deciding Whether to Produce   The Two-Step Procedure

3. Firm and Market Short-Run Supply Curves ... 164
The Firm's Short-Run Supply Curve   The Market's Short-Run Supply Curve   Shifts of Short-Run Supply Curves

4. Long-Run Supply Curves ... 168
The Firm's Long-Run Supply Decision   The Firm's Long-Run Supply Curve   The Market's Long-Run Supply Curve   Shapes of Long-Run Market Supply Curves   Shifts of Long-Run Supply Curves   Supply Curves and Industry Marginal Cost

Summary ... 174
Key Terms ... 174
Problems ... 175

Chapter 10 The Invisible Hand: Competition and Economic Efficiency ... 176

1. Efficient Resource Allocation ... 177
Efficiency and Equity   Efficiency and Value Judgments

2. The Price System and Efficiency ... 179
Marginal Cost and Marginal Valuation   Social Optimality   The Role of Prices

3. Consumers' and Producers' Surplus ... 181
Consumers' Surplus   Producers' Surplus   Efficiency of Competitive Equilibrium   Efficiency and Equity

4. Economywide Competition and Pareto Efficiency ... 186
Consumer Behavior and Efficiency in Consumption   Competitive Supply and Production Efficiency   Exchange Efficiency and Pareto Optimality   The Role of Prices   The Distribution of Income

Summary ... 190
Key Terms ... 191
Problems ... 191

PART THREE MARKET IMPERFECTIONS AND GOVERNMENT REGULATION ... 193

Chapter 11 Imperfect Competition: Monopoly ... 195

1. Imperfectly Competitive Markets ... 196
Monopoly and Monopoly Power   Monopolistic Competition   Oligopoly   Markets with Large Buyers

2. Marginal Revenue and Monopoly Output ... 198

*Marginal Revenue   Optimal Monopoly Output   Monopoly Profits
Demand Elasticity*

    3. Monopoly versus Competition   203
        Price and Output   Social Cost of Monopoly

    4. Why Do Monopolies Exist   206
        Natural Monopoly   Essential Resources and Government Policy

    5. Extensions of the Basic Monopoly Model   208
        Price Discrimination   Dominant Firms

    6. Monopoly and Progress   210

    Summary   211
    Key Terms   212
    Problems   212

Chapter 12   Oligopoly and Monopolistic Competition   214

    1. Concentration and Differentiation in the U.S. Economy   215
        Seller Concentration   Why Are Markets Concentrated?   Product Differentiation

    2. Collusion and Rivalry in Oligopoly   218
        The Oligopolist's Dilemma   When Does Collusion Occur?

    3. Varieties of Oligopoly Behavior   221
        *Explicit Collusion: Cartels   Tacit Collusion: Leadership and Stability
Noncollusive Oligopoly Behavior   Entry Deterrence and Predation*

    4. Monopolistic Competition   226
        Short-Run Equilibrium   Long-Run Equilibrium   Monopolistic versus Perfect Competition

    5. Nonprice Competition: Variety and Advertising   228
        Variety   Advertising

    Summary   230
    Key Terms   231
    Problems   231

Chapter 13   Regulation of Economic Activity   233

    1. Market Failure, Politics, and Regulation   234
        Market Failure

    2. Regulation in Practice   235
        Economic Regulation   Social Regulation

3. Externalities and the EPA ... 238
*Externalities and Optimal Regulation   Pollution Control by the EPA
Is There a Better Way?*

4. Information and Protection ... 243
*Information, Standards, and Paternalism   Regulatory Failures
Regulatory Reform*

5. Airlines and the Deregulation Movement ... 247
Airline Deregulation   Effects of Deregulation

Summary ... 249
Key Terms ... 250
Problems ... 250

Chapter 14 Government and the Monopoly Problem ... 251

1. The Monopoly Problem ... 252
*Monopoly Losses and Antitrust   Natural Monopoly and Regulation
The Costs of Monopoly Power*

2. Antitrust and Unnatural Monopoly ... 254
*Antitrust Laws and Their Enforcement   Government Policy and Judicial
Interpretation   Should Antitrust Policy Change?*

3. Natural Monopoly and Economic Regulation ... 262
The Regulatory Task   Regulatory Performance

Summary ... 265
Key Terms ... 266
Problems ... 266

PART FOUR FACTOR MARKETS AND INCOME DISTRIBUTION ... 269

Chapter 15 Production and Derived Demand ... 271

1. Firm Demand for a Single Variable Input ... 272
Marginal Revenue Product   Optimal Labor Demand   Real Input Price

2. Firm Demand for Multiple Inputs ... 275
The Fundamental Rule for Input Demands   Capital-Labor Substitution

3. Changes in Firms' Input Demands ... 278
Input Price Changes   Output Price Changes   Productivity Changes

4. The Industry's Demand for Inputs ... 279
The Industry Demand Curve   Industry-Level Input Demand Elasticities

xiv Contents

Summary	282
Key Terms	282
Problems	282
Appendix: Isoquants and the Firm's Choice of Production Technique	282
Properties of Isoquants Producing at Lowest Cost	

Chapter 16 Labor Supply and Wage Determination — 286

1. Wage Differentials	286
2. The Supply of Labor	287
The Individual's Labor Supply Decision The Supply of Labor to the Economy The Supply of Labor to an Industry	
3. Industry Labor Market Equilibrium	292
4. The Determination of the Average Real Wage	294
5. The Minimum Wage	295
6. Supply Limitations and Economic Rent	296
Summary	298
Key Terms	298
Problems	298
Appendix: Income and Substitution Effects of a Wage Increase	299

Chapter 17 Human Capital and Unions — 301

1. Human Capital	301
Education and Age-Earnings Profiles Signaling versus Training	
2. Education and Training	303
Investing in Education The Returns on Investment in College The Market for Educated Workers On-the-Job Training and Age-Earnings Profiles Human Capital in Arts and Sports	
3. Unions in the U.S. Economy	309
Origins of U.S. Unions The Great Depression and Legal Changes Declining Union Membership	
4. What Do Unions Do?	311
Protection and Company Towns Unions as Monopolists Union Wages as Compensating Differentials Unions and Profitability Bargaining and Strikes	
Summary	317
Key Terms	318
Problems	318

3. Externalities and the EPA — 238
*Externalities and Optimal Regulation   Pollution Control by the EPA
Is There a Better Way?*

4. Information and Protection — 243
*Information, Standards, and Paternalism   Regulatory Failures
Regulatory Reform*

5. Airlines and the Deregulation Movement — 247
Airline Deregulation   Effects of Deregulation

Summary — 249
Key Terms — 250
Problems — 250

Chapter 14 Government and the Monopoly Problem — 251

1. The Monopoly Problem — 252
*Monopoly Losses and Antitrust   Natural Monopoly and Regulation
The Costs of Monopoly Power*

2. Antitrust and Unnatural Monopoly — 254
Antitrust Laws and Their Enforcement   Government Policy and Judicial Interpretation   Should Antitrust Policy Change?

3. Natural Monopoly and Economic Regulation — 262
The Regulatory Task   Regulatory Performance

Summary — 265
Key Terms — 266
Problems — 266

PART FOUR   FACTOR MARKETS AND INCOME DISTRIBUTION — 269

Chapter 15 Production and Derived Demand — 271

1. Firm Demand for a Single Variable Input — 272
Marginal Revenue Product   Optimal Labor Demand   Real Input Price

2. Firm Demand for Multiple Inputs — 275
The Fundamental Rule for Input Demands   Capital-Labor Substitution

3. Changes in Firms' Input Demands — 278
Input Price Changes   Output Price Changes   Productivity Changes

4. The Industry's Demand for Inputs — 279
The Industry Demand Curve   Industry-Level Input Demand Elasticities

	Summary	282
	Key Terms	282
	Problems	282
	Appendix: Isoquants and the Firm's Choice of Production Technique *Properties of Isoquants Producing at Lowest Cost*	282

Chapter 16 Labor Supply and Wage Determination — 286

1. Wage Differentials — 286

2. The Supply of Labor — 287
   The Individual's Labor Supply Decision   The Supply of Labor to the Economy   The Supply of Labor to an Industry

3. Industry Labor Market Equilibrium — 292

4. The Determination of the Average Real Wage — 294

5. The Minimum Wage — 295

6. Supply Limitations and Economic Rent — 296

Summary — 298
Key Terms — 298
Problems — 298

Appendix: Income and Substitution Effects of a Wage Increase — 299

Chapter 17 Human Capital and Unions — 301

1. Human Capital — 301
   Education and Age-Earnings Profiles   Signaling versus Training

2. Education and Training — 303
   Investing in Education   The Returns on Investment in College   The Market for Educated Workers   On-the-Job Training and Age-Earnings Profiles   Human Capital in Arts and Sports

3. Unions in the U.S. Economy — 309
   Origins of U.S. Unions   The Great Depression and Legal Changes   Declining Union Membership

4. What Do Unions Do? — 311
   Protection and Company Towns   Unions as Monopolists   Union Wages as Compensating Differentials   Unions and Profitability   Bargaining and Strikes

Summary — 317
Key Terms — 318
Problems — 318

	2. The Firm's Short-Run Supply Decision *Finding the Optimal Positive Output Deciding Whether to Produce The Two-Step Procedure*	160
	3. Firm and Market Short-Run Supply Curves *The Firm's Short-Run Supply Curve The Market's Short-Run Supply Curve Shifts of Short-Run Supply Curves*	164
	4. Long-Run Supply Curves *The Firm's Long-Run Supply Decision The Firm's Long-Run Supply Curve The Market's Long-Run Supply Curve Shapes of Long-Run Market Supply Curves Shifts of Long-Run Supply Curves Supply Curves and Industry Marginal Cost*	168
	Summary	174
	Key Terms	174
	Problems	175
Chapter 10	**The Invisible Hand: Competition and Economic Efficiency**	176
	1. Efficient Resource Allocation *Efficiency and Equity Efficiency and Value Judgments*	177
	2. The Price System and Efficiency *Marginal Cost and Marginal Valuation Social Optimality The Role of Prices*	179
	3. Consumers' and Producers' Surplus *Consumers' Surplus Producers' Surplus Efficiency of Competitive Equilibrium Efficiency and Equity*	181
	4. Economywide Competition and Pareto Efficiency *Consumer Behavior and Efficiency in Consumption Competitive Supply and Production Efficiency Exchange Efficiency and Pareto Optimality The Role of Prices The Distribution of Income*	186
	Summary	190
	Key Terms	191
	Problems	191
PART THREE	**MARKET IMPERFECTIONS AND GOVERNMENT REGULATION**	193
Chapter 11	**Imperfect Competition: Monopoly**	195
	1. Imperfectly Competitive Markets *Monopoly and Monopoly Power Monopolistic Competition Oligopoly Markets with Large Buyers*	196
	2. Marginal Revenue and Monopoly Output	198

*Marginal Revenue   Optimal Monopoly Output   Monopoly Profits
Demand Elasticity*

   3. Monopoly versus Competition   203
       Price and Output   Social Cost of Monopoly

   4. Why Do Monopolies Exist   206
       Natural Monopoly   Essential Resources and Government Policy

   5. Extensions of the Basic Monopoly Model   208
       Price Discrimination   Dominant Firms

   6. Monopoly and Progress   210

Summary   211
Key Terms   212
Problems   212

Chapter 12 Oligopoly and Monopolistic Competition   214

   1. Concentration and Differentiation in the U.S. Economy   215
       Seller Concentration   Why Are Markets Concentrated?   Product Differentiation

   2. Collusion and Rivalry in Oligopoly   218
       The Oligopolist's Dilemma   When Does Collusion Occur?

   3. Varieties of Oligopoly Behavior   221
       *Explicit Collusion: Cartels   Tacit Collusion: Leadership and Stability
Noncollusive Oligopoly Behavior   Entry Deterrence and Predation*

   4. Monopolistic Competition   226
       Short-Run Equilibrium   Long-Run Equilibrium   Monopolistic versus Perfect Competition

   5. Nonprice Competition: Variety and Advertising   228
       Variety   Advertising

Summary   230
Key Terms   231
Problems   231

Chapter 13 Regulation of Economic Activity   233

   1. Market Failure, Politics, and Regulation   234
       Market Failure

   2. Regulation in Practice   235
       Economic Regulation   Social Regulation

	Appendix: The Algebra of Present Values and Rates of Return *Interest and Present Value Perpetuities Rate of Return*	319
	Appendix Problems	320
Chapter 18	**Tangible Wealth: Capital and Land**	321
	1. Tangible Wealth: The Facts	322
	2. Rentals, Interest Rates, and Asset Prices *Stocks and Flows Interest and Present Value Calculating the Value of an Asset Real and Nominal Interest Rates Why Are Real Interest Rates Positive?*	323
	3. Land Rents and Land Prices *Land Services Land Prices Rents in General*	329
	4. The Supply of Capital Services *Short-Run Supply Costs and Long-Run Supply The Long-Run Supply of Capital to the Economy The Long-Run Supply to an Industry*	330
	5. Equilibrium in the Market for Capital Services *Demand for Capital Services Long-Run Equilibrium Short-Run Adjustment Adjustment in the Long Run Capital and Rates of Return in the U.S. Economy*	333
	6. The Prices of Capital Assets	337
	Summary	338
	Key Terms	339
	Problems	339
Chapter 19	**Uncertainty in Economic Life**	340
	1. Individual Attitudes toward Risk	341
	2. Insurance Markets *Risk Aversion Risk Pooling Risk Spreading Moral Hazard and Adverse Selection*	341
	3. Risk and Capital *Risk and Return Risk Spreading in the Capital Markets Risk Pooling and Diversification Efficient Markets*	345
	4. Hedging and Futures Markets *Hedgers and Speculators Futures Prices as Forecasts*	351
	Summary	354
	Key Terms	354
	Problems	354

Chapter 20 Inequality, Poverty, and Discrimination in the United States — 356

1. The Functional Distribution of Income — 357
    The Theory   The U.S. Experience

2. The Personal Distribution of Income — 360
    The Lorenz Curve   Qualifications   The Distribution of Wealth

3. Economic Mobility — 363
    Measuring Mobility   Family, Merit, and Luck

4. Discrimination — 365
    Who Has the Good Jobs?   Equal Pay for Equal Work?   Toward Equal Opportunity

5. Poverty — 369
    Relative and Absolute Poverty   The Incidence of Poverty   The Poverty Pool

Summary — 372
Key Terms — 373
Problems — 373

PART FIVE TAXES, TRANSFERS, AND GOVERNMENT SPENDING — 375

Chapter 21 Taxes and Government Purchases — 377

1. Taxation in the U.S. Economy — 378
    The VAT

2. Principles of Taxation — 379
    How to Tax Fairly   Taxation, Efficiency, and Waste   Deadweight Burdens and Efficient Taxation

3. Tax Reform — 586
    Income versus Consumption Tax   Corporate Income Tax   Tax Simplification

4. Government Purchases — 387
    Provision of Public Goods   Government Provision of Goods   Cost-Benefit Analysis

5. Local Government — 391
    Zoning and the Invisible Foot   Education

Summary — 393
Key Terms — 394
Problems — 394

Chapter 22 Welfare Programs, Poverty, and Income Distribution — 396

1. The Equity-Efficiency Trade-Off — 397

		Contents	xvii

	2. Welfare Programs in the United States	398
	Government Retirement Programs Other Social Insurance Cash Assistance In-Kind Benefits The Safety Net Effects on Poverty The Return of Poverty	
	3. Disincentive Effects of Transfers	403
	Social Security Welfare Programs Welfare and the Tax System	
	4. What Can Be Done?	405
	Workfare The Negative Income Tax Private Charity	
	5. Government and Income Distribution: The Results	408
	Summary	409
	Key Terms	410
	Problems	410

PART SIX   THE WORLD ECONOMY — 413

Chapter 23   Gains from Trade and Problems of Trade — 415

1. Comparative Advantage and Gains from Trade — 416
   Who Produces What under Free Trade?   Gains from Trade   Many Goods

2. Differences in Factor Endowments — 420
   Differences in Capital-Labor Ratios   Some Evidence on Factor Endowments and Trade Patterns

3. Intra-Industry Trade — 422

4. Gainers and Losers — 423
   Refrigeration   The U.S. Automobile Industry

5. The Economics of Tariffs — 424
   The Free-Trade Equilibrium   Equilibrium with a Tariff   Costs and Benefits of a Tariff

6. Arguments for Tariffs — 428
   Second-Best Arguments   Cheap Foreign Labor   Foreign Subsidies and Dumping   Exploiting National Market Power   National Defense

7. Other Commercial Policies — 431
   Quotas   Nontariff Barriers   Export Subsidies

8. Why Is There Protection? — 432
   Protection over Time   Politics, Economics, and Protection

Summary — 436
Key Terms — 436
Problems — 437

Glossary — 439

Index — 447

Preface

Our aim in the second edition of *Introduction to Microeconomics* is to present the essential core of the field in a way that enables students to use economics to understand the world in which we live. After this course, students can expect both to have learned the basic facts about markets and the microeconomic role of government and to have mastered principles they can use to understand many of the economic changes, controversies, and policy debates they will encounter throughout their lives.

This edition follows the first edition in broad outline and approach, emphasizing the basics and applications throughout. However, it has been totally rewritten. Chapters have been moved, added, and removed; material has been moved among chapters and within chapters; and each chapter has undergone a complete revision.

Overview

The four introductory chapters in Part 1 present essential material on the nature of economics (Chapter 1); the use of graphs, data, and models in economic analysis (Chapter 2); the basic model of market supply and demand (Chapter 3); and—in an essentially new chapter (Chapter 4)—the role of government in the economy. Chapter 4 reviews how governments actually affect the economy, what economic theory says about the ideal role of government, and how governments in practice make decisions.

By the end of these first four chapters, the student should have a good idea of what economics is about, know how to read diagrams and use data, understand how markets work, and know the facts about the mixed economy. By tying the operation of markets in Chapter 3 to the economy's solution of its fundamental "how," "what," and "for whom" problems, we quickly introduce the student to the extraordinary power of markets. By describing the potential role of the government in dealing with externalities and affecting the distribution of income in Chapter 4, we alert students to the fact that market solutions are not necessarily optimal; by describing the political economy of government decision making, we make the student aware that government solutions may also be far from optimal.

After this general introduction, we switch to microeconomics, starting with the basic material and going on to more applied areas. By starting with and emphasizing the basics and avoiding gimmicks, we ensure that the student is well equipped to handle and, we hope, enjoy the applications. We develop the competitive model fully in Part 2 and move on to imperfect competition and regulation in Part 3, the factor markets in Part 4, and the microeconomics of government in Part 5. We conclude in Part 6 with a chapter on the gains from trade and the problems of trade, thus providing an introduction to the increasingly important issues surrounding the role of the United States in the world economy.

In More Detail

We start Part 2 with Chapter 5, which develops the definitions and uses of the price and income elasticities of demand, along with cross elasticities. Here, as elsewhere in the book, we draw frequently on real-world data and examples—from oil to medical care to sporting goods—to clarify concepts and make sure that students know the material is useful. Chapter 6 goes behind the demand curve to show how market demand curves are built up from individual demand curves and how utility theory can be used to derive the properties of demand curves. The idea of consumer's surplus is developed, and an appendix presents indifference curve analysis.

Chapters 7 through 9 deal with business organization and accounting and with the supply side of the market. Here we have improved the order of the material by presenting Chapter 9, which deals with supply in a competitive industry, before introducing imperfect competition. We now allow the student to develop a thorough understanding of the competitive model of the firm and market before encountering the varieties and ambiguities of imperfect competition. Chapter 10, on competition and economic efficiency, shows why competitive markets are efficient and equips the student to undertand the distortions caused by imperfect competition. By simplifying the material, we have been able to present it earlier, enabling the student to develop a far deeper understanding of the problems of monopoly than was possible in the first edition.

In Part 3 we cover both imperfect competition and the government policies that deal with it. We start in Chapter 11 with the polar case of monopoly, giving examples of monopolies, discussing their origins and effects, and introducing the natural monopoly problem. In Chapter 12, we move on to oligopoly and other forms of imperfect competition. Chapter 13 provides an overview of government regulation, and Chapter 14 discusses government's role in dealing with monopoly. These two chapters stress both the principles determining the role government could play in improving the allocation of resources and its actual role. We illustrate the principles throughout with real-world examples, describing the origins and operation of regulatory agencies, the effects of airline deregulation, the government's merger guidelines, the partial deregulation of the telephone industry, and more.

Part 4, covering Chapters 15 to 20, deals with the factor markets, starting with a short chapter on the principles of derived demand. This new chapter allows students to see the principles of factor demand more clearly. Even here, we draw on real-world data on capital-labor ratios to illustrate factor substitution.

Chapters 16 and 17 discuss labor markets, examining labor supply and demand and wage determination and then considering human capital and labor unions, using plentiful data and examples. The labor markets are of special interest to students, who are preparing to enter them. We have found in our teaching that the material on human capital in Chapter 17 is of particular interest to students; they will appreciate the calculations involved in deciding whether to pursue an education and can also be relied on to challenge the view that only pecuniary returns matter.

The economics of capital and land presented in Chapter 18 is also fascinating. Present-value calculations (already introduced in Chapter 17 in discussing human capital) and discussions of when an investment is worthwhile come easily to students. By building the theory of capital around present-value calculations, we present capital theory in a way that is logical, manageable, and intuitively understandable. We extend the discussion to consider uncertainty in Chapter 19. This important area is not generally covered in introductory texts, but it is entirely accessible and extremely interesting to students because the problems of insurance and the prospects of investing in the stock market are familiar to many.

We conclude the section on factor markets with a discussion of the distribution of income, poverty, and discrimination in the United States in Chapter 20. We define the Lorenz curve and present facts on the distribution of income and wealth, the incidence of poverty, and the extent of discrimination. Although this chapter is largely descriptive, we use the theory of the factor markets developed in Part 4 to discuss the effects of changes in labor supply on wages and the distribution of income.

The two chapters in Part 5 examine the role of government both in taxing and producing and purchasing goods and services (Chapter 21) and in making transfer payments that are intended, among other things, to alleviate poverty (Chapter 22). The discussion is again a combination of description and analysis, including a careful evaluation of the current debate about the effects of welfare programs and possible reforms.

In Chapter 23 (Part 6) we turn briefly to the international economy, examining the potential gains from trade—surely one of the highlights of an introductory course—and the reasons why trade appears in practice to be as much a problem as a benefit for the economy. This chapter provides students with a good introduction to the microeconomics of trade and protection and should give them guidance through the continuing controversies over free trade and open markets that dominate the headlines today and will continue to do so for years to come.

Special Features

Stressing the Fundamentals

The teachers we remember most fondly gave us conceptual tools that we could use on our own after the course was over—along with the confidence and understanding necessary to use those tools well. We try to emulate those teachers here by developing microeconomics cumulatively, making sure that the student understands the core material before moving on to more advanced topics. For instance, we make sure that the student understands supply and demand thoroughly before we discuss noncompetitive market structures. Similarly, we set out the principles of derived demand before going on to more detailed examinations of the factor markets.

We want the student who uses this book to be able to *do* economics, that is, to use the principles presented here effectively to analyze new problems. That is why we emphasize mastery of fundamental material so heavily and why we keep recent developments—such as game theory and public choice—in perspective rather than seeking to recast economics into a new framework. That is also why we shy away from all but the briefest of biographical details about economists, dead or alive.

Data and Applications

Economics is not studied for the logical beauty of its theory but rather for what it can tell us about the real world. From the start we emphasize that economics is motivated by and can be used to understand and analyze the world in which students live. We thus present a blend of theory, applications, and policy discussions that brings economics across as the relevant and live social science that it is.

Whenever possible—and it is almost always possible—we illustrate the usefulness of the principles developed in each chapter by applying them to an example from the U.S. economy or the economy of a foreign country. For example, in discussing the mixed economy in Chapter 4, we draw on data from a wide range of countries. In discussing protection in Chapter 23, we can unfortunately draw on many recent examples, from textiles to automobiles, and we do.

We not only discuss examples to illustrate theory but also present a good deal of data from the United States and abroad to make sure that the student has an idea of the basic facts of economic life: How unequal is the distribution of income? How concentrated are U.S. industries? We discuss critical measurement problems and empirical uncertainties rather than pretending omniscience and stress the dual roles of theory and empirical analysis in resolving controversies and determining desirable policy.

Comparative International Data

Our data and examples are drawn from abroad as well as from the United States. By opening up the foreign dimensions we give students a broader perspective—quite appropriate in the increasingly integrated world economy—and give the teacher an opportunity to draw on a far wider set of data and experiences to illustrate the principles he or she is developing.

Boxes

There is a box or two in most chapters, presenting either case studies or material that is of interest but not necessarily in the main line of development of the chapter.

The Bottom Line

We conclude the text of each chapter with a single paragraph that succinctly summarizes its central theme, points the way to the next chapter, or both. In addition, we present a detailed summary at the end of each chapter.

Glossary

We warn students in Chapter 1 that economics has a language of its own that uses familiar words in precise but unfamiliar ways. To help them master this language, the most important definitions are collected in a glossary at the end of the book.

Additional Material

Instructor's Manual, Test Bank, and Study Guide

Professor Michael Morgan of the College of Charleston has prepared a comprehensive instructor's manual to accompany the text, an expanded test bank, and a very useful study guide.

Also available from your McGraw-Hill representative or from the Economics Editor, College Division—27th

Floor, McGraw-Hill, 1221 Avenue of the Americas, New York, NY 10020, are overhead masters, overhead transparencies, and a computerized graphics-based tutorial that reviews fundamental microeconomic and macroeconomic concepts.

Acknowledgments

In writing this book we have been helped by friends and colleagues, by many professors who read through earlier drafts and the first edition of the book and through their advice gave us the benefit of their own teaching experiences, by the McGraw-Hill team, and by our assistants.

We owe special thanks to colleagues who were willing to provide us with information and with feedback. We would like to mention especially David Begg, Eliana Cardoso, Henry Farber, Kathleen Feldstein, Martin Feldstein, Nan Friedlaender, Zvi Griliches, Jerry Hausman, Paul Joskow, Thomas Moore, Michael Morgan, Robert Pindyck, James Poterba, and Yoram Weiss.

Our acknowlegments to the many professors who offered advice and suggestions for improving the manuscript of both the first and second editions appear on pages xxv–xxvii. These individuals will recognize the major differences that have resulted from their comments. For their suggestions, we would like to thank also Jeff Rigsby, Robert Shaw, Mike Tamada, Alice Tufel, and Jean Therese Wenzel.

We were fortunate to have the assistance of Susan Collins, Donald Deere, Mike Gavin, Andy Kaufman, Betty Krier, Jeff Miron, and Alex Zanello. Tere Bautista, Carol McIntire, and Elizabeth Walb helped type the first edition, and Brian Corbin and Lisa Funaro managed the second.

For this second edition we want to acknowledge the members of the McGraw-Hill team, especially Elisa Adams, whose professionalism, thoroughness, and good humor have kept us going. Larry Goldberg managed the book through the press with impressive efficiency. This book is much the better for their help and for the help of the many others we have mentioned and thanked above.

Finally, we should make it clear that we are each fully and equally implicated in the virtues and faults of this book and the companion volumes, *Economics* and *Introduction to Macroeconomics*.

Stanley Fischer
Rudiger Dornbusch
Richard Schmalensee

Postscript

With this edition we have been fortunate to add Richard Schmalensee as a third author. Dick's touch, insights, and experience are evident throughout the book, but especially in the microeconomics sections. It has been a pleasure for us to work with him.

Rudiger Dornbusch
Stanley Fischer

To the Student

Welcome! We wrote this book to help *you* learn the fundamental principles on which all economics is built. You can use these principles to understand the changing economic world in which you will live the rest of your life. This book introduces theories, facts, and examples that will help you think systematically about economic issues and problems that you read about and encounter directly every day.

Microeconomics is not a field in which there is always an argument in favor of every possible viewpoint. There *are* right and wrong answers to some questions, but there is uncertainty about others. One of our aims is to show why economists understand some issues and to explain the disagreements about others. In choosing the examples and applications, and especially in policy discussions of often controversial topics, we have tried to develop this perspective, first making the issue clear and then analyzing the different viewpoints, not hesitating to say which of them do not make sense. For instance, our discussion of protection in Chapter 23 shows that there are some—very few, to be sure—economic arguments that do favor protection of domestic industry against foreign competition; it also shows that many of the most common arguments cannot be supported by logic or evidence.

We hope that by the end of the course you will understand how economists analyze policy issues and problems and that you will be able to analyze economic controversies on your own. Fortunately, the fundamental economic principles presented in this text generally give the essentially correct answers to most economic problems. More advanced material in economics usually refines but does not reverse the conclusions that are reached on the basis of basic principles.

How to Study

There is a world of difference between reading about economics and actually *doing* and understanding economics. Doing economics means using the theories and facts you have learned to answer for yourself questions about the economy that you encounter in your daily life, in reading, and in thinking about the economy around you. We hope that by the end of the course you will be able to use economics by yourself to understand the real world.

To do economics, you have to learn *actively*. Reading is not enough. Question the text at every step. If we say, "Thus X must be true," be sure you see why. If the text makes three points, be sure after reaching the third that you remember the first. Above all, when we apply theory, follow the application with care: The applications reinforce the text both by taking you through the theory again and by showing how it relates to the real world.

In learning actively, put in some of your own input. When a line is drawn one way, ask why. See whether it can be drawn differently and what happens when it is. Solve the problems at the end of each chapter. At the end of each section ask yourself what the point was and what you have learned. To make sure, you may want to jump ahead to the chapter summary.

Study Guide

Professor Michael Morgan of the College of Charleston has prepared an excellent *Study Guide* that accompanies the textbook. It briefly reviews each chapter and then provides many questions that reinforce the material of the chapter and help you learn it actively. The questions in the *Study Guide* in effect take you through the analysis of the chapter step by step.

Anyone who works through the *Study Guide* in conjunction with the text can be sure that she or he understands the material in this book.

Dig in and enjoy!

Stanley Fischer
Rudiger Dornbusch
Richard Schmalensee

Acknowledgments

Reviewers for Economics, Second Edition

Bradley Billings
Georgetown University
Donald L. Bumpass
Texas Tech University
Arthur Butler
SUNY-Buffalo
Donald T. Butler
Central College
Dennis Byrne
University of Akron
Joseph P. Cairo
LaSalle University
Larry A. Chenault
Miami University
Cletus C. Coughlin
Federal Reserve Bank of St. Louis
Albert L. Danielsen
University of Georgia
Ernest R. Diedrich
St. John's University
Robert C. Dolan
University of Richmond
Patricia J. Euzent
University of Central Florida
Louis M. Falkson
Cornell University
Paul G. Farnham
Georgia State University
Gary A. Gigliotti
Rutgers University
Clyde Haulman
College of William & Mary

Ann Helwege
Tufts University
William R. Henry
University of Mississippi
Catherine Hofmann
University of Idaho
Monte Juillerat
Indiana University/Purdue University-Indianapolis
James Kearl
Brigham Young University
Phil J. Lane
Fairfield University
William W. Lang
Rutgers University
William Leifert
Kent State University
Richard Long
Georgia State University
Jerome L. McElroy
Saint Mary's College
Janet Mitchell
University of Southern California
Milton G. Mitchell
University of Wisconsin
Michael J. Moore
Duke University
Robert M. Mulligan
Providence College
C. Louise Nelson
Davidson College
Lucjan T. Orlowski
Sacred Heart University

Alannah Orrison
New York University
James Price
Syracuse University
Ali Rassuli
Indiana University/Purdue University-Fort Wayne
William Rogerson
Northwestern University
Bernard Saffran
Swarthmore College
Fabio Sdogati
Marquette University
Stephen D. Soderlind
St. Olaf College
William E. Spellman
Coe College
James Starkey
University of Rhode Island
Richard Tresch
Boston College
Steven J. Weiss
University of Toledo
Arthur L. Welsh
Pennsylvania State University
Mark Wheeler
Bowling Green State University
Edgar W. Wood
University of Mississippi
Yung Y. Yang
California State University

Acknowledgments

Reviewers for Economics, First Edition

Norman D. Aitken
University of Massachusetts
James W. Albrecht
Columbia University
Joseph Alexander
Babson College
Kenneth O. Alexander
Michigan Tech
Roy Andersen
Knox College
Richard Anderson
Texas A & M University
Mostapha H. Baligh
Bergen Community College
Maurice B. Ballabon
Baruch College
Richard Ballman
Augustana College
Robert Barry
College of William and Mary
Peter S. Barth
University of Connecticut
R. C. Battalio
Texas A & M University
G. C. Bjork
Claremont Men's College
Dwight M. Blood
Colorado State University
Frank J. Bonello
University of Notre Dame
Allan J. Braff
University of New Hampshire
Philip E. Brotherton
Los Angeles Pierce College
M. Northrup Buechner
St. John's University
P. D. Burdett
University of Wisconsin
H. Richard Call
American River Community College
Thomas F. Cargill
University of Nevada

Mabel Chang
Bronx Community College
F. C. Child
University of California–Davis
Robert Christiansen
Colby College
Donald Coffin
Illinois State University
Donald R. Connell
University of Nebraska–Omaha
C. S. Cox
St. Louis Community College
Donald Cummings
University of Northern Iowa
J. Ronnie Davis
University of South Alabama
Ernest M. DeCicco
Northeastern University
David Denslow
University of Florida
George M. Eastham
California Polytechnic State University
Kenneth G. Elzinga
University of Virginia
Yiu-Kwan Fan
University of Wisconsin–Stevens Point
Paul G. Farnham
Georgia State University
Claude H. Farrell
University of North Carolina–Wilmington
Charles Fischer
Pittsburg State University
James Frew
University of North Carolina–Greensboro
George Garman
Loyola University
Otis Gilley
University of Texas–Austin
Richard M. Gillis

Williamette University
Frank W. Glodek
Denison University
Jack Goddard
Northeastern State University
Rae Jean B. Goodman
U.S. Naval Academy
Craufurd D. Goodwin
Duke University
A. R. Gutowsky
California State University–Sacramento
U. B. Henderson
Central State University
William L. Holahan
University of Wisconsin
Robert Holland
Illinois State University
Phyllis W. Isley
Norwich University
Habib Jam
Glassboro State College
George Jensen
California State University–Los Angeles
John H. Kagel
Texas A & M University
Timothy Keely
Tacoma Community College
Ziad K. Keilany
University of Tennessee
Greg Kilgariff
Marist College
James T. Kyle
Indiana State University
Kathleen M. Langley
Boston University
Allen Larsen
Florida Southern College
Gary Lemon
DePauw University
Alan C. Lerner
New York University

Lester E. Levy
  Northern Illinois University
Francis McGrath
  Iona College
Allan Mandelstamm
  Virginia Polytechnic Institute
James Marlin
  Western Illinois University
David A. Martin
  *State University of
  New York–Geneseo*
Walther P. Michael
  Ohio State University
Gerald M. Miller
  Miami University
D. Morawetz
  Boston University
J. Michael Morgan
  College of Charleston
John S. Murphy
  Canisius College
Frank Musgrave
  Ithaca College
Karen Nelson
  Smith College
R. D. Norton
  Mount Holyoke College
John Olienyk
  Colorado State University
Henry Orion
  Fairleigh Dickinson University
Mack Ott
  Penn State University
D. Ounjian
  Tufts University
Patricia L. Pacey
  University of Colorado
Peter Parker
  Lafayette College
George M. Perkins
  *University of
  Wisconsin–Milwaukee*

Martin M. Perline
  Wichita State University
H. Craig Petersen
  Utah State University
Carol Pfrommer
  *University of
  Alabama–Birmingham*
James V. Pinto
  Central State University
Bette Polkinhorn
  California State University
Lawrence B. Pulley
  Brandeis University
Rama Ramachandran
  Southern Methodist University
Michael Reed
  University of Nevada–Reno
Christopher C. Rhoden
  Solano Community College
Roberto Rios
  Lehman College
Steven M. Rock
  Illinois Institute of Technology
Allen Sanderson
  Princeton University
Todd Sandler
  University of Wyoming
Hyman Sardy
  Brooklyn College
Leslie Seplaki
  Rutgers University
John C. Shannon
  Suffolk University
Richard U. Sherman, Jr.
  Ohio State University
Marvin Slowbarger
  San Jose State University
Clifford Sowell
  Eastern Kentucky University
George A. Spiva
  University of Tennessee

Lawrence Steinhauer
  Albion College
Alan C. Stockman
  University of Rochester
Houston H. Stokes
  University of Illinois
Robert C. Stuart
  Douglass College
Eugene M. Swann
  *University of
  California–Berkeley*
Michael K. Taussig
  Rutgers University
Lloyd B. Thomas
  Kansas State University
William O. Thweatt
  Vanderbilt University
Timothy D. Tregarthen
  University of Colorado
John Vahaly
  University of Louisville
Dale W. Warnke
  College of Lake County
Bernard Wasow
  New York University
Michael W. Watts
  *Indiana University–Purdue
  University at Indianapolis*
J. Wetzel
  *Virginia Commonwealth
  University*
Samuel Williamson
  University of Iowa
Jeffrey Wolcowitz
  Harvard University
Mahmood Yousefi
  University of Northern Iowa
William J. Zahka
  Widener College

PART ONE
INTRODUCTION

Chapter 1
An Introduction to Economics

Every society must solve three basic problems every day:

- *What* goods and services should be produced and in what amounts?
- *How* should those goods and services be produced?
- *For whom* should the goods and services be produced?

What, how, and for whom to produce are universal problems because human wants are practically unlimited, but all societies have only limited quantities of *resources* that can be used to produce goods or services. (Productive resources include labor, land, buildings, machinery, and raw materials.) If resources were not scarce, we could all have everything we ever wanted: continuous vacations, fine paintings, fast sports cars, elegant fur coats, or whatever else our dreams are made of. Even in the United States, the richest country in the world, almost everyone wants more than he or she has or is ever likely to have.

The central economic problem faced by all societies is the conflict between people's essentially unlimited desires for goods and services and the limited resources that can be used to satisfy those desires. Hence our definition of economics.

● ***Economics* is the study of how societies with limited, scarce resources decide what gets produced, how, and for whom.**

The great nineteenth-century English economist Alfred Marshall (1842–1924) described economics as "the study of mankind in the ordinary business of life." This description reflects the fact that economic choices—that is, decisions about how to use scarce resources to satisfy people's wants and desires—are so common that often we do not notice that we are making them. Virtually every minute you decide how best to use your scarce time. For instance, you choose between work, play, and sleep. If you choose to work, you still have to decide whether to go to class, read a textbook, or do a problem. If you choose to go shopping, you may have to decide between an expensive pair of shoes on the one hand and an inexpensive pair but a larger bank account on the other.

Businesses and governments also make economic choices every day. A farmer must decide when and what to plant and how much to invest in new machinery. General Motors must decide which cars to manufacture, how many of each to produce, whether to invest in robots or hire more workers, whether to produce here or abroad, and how much to charge for the cars. The government must choose how much to spend on education, defense, research, and many other programs; how much to raise in taxes of various kinds; and how much to borrow. These choices all arise because resources are scarce. In this book we describe how consumers, businesses, and governments make economic choices and how those choices interact to determine the overall allocation of scarce resources in society.

1. The Dismal Science?

Early in the nineteenth century, economics came to be called "the dismal science."[1] This label is still frequently applied today. It raises two important questions which this section addresses: Is economics dismal? Is it a science?

Is Economics Dismal?

Our definition of economics begins with the notion of *scarcity*, and this does sound dismal and depressing. However, scarcity does not imply shortages or poverty. Pure water is not costless to produce in most places, and supplies are limited. Water is therefore scarce, but most of us can easily afford much more of it than we need to survive. To say that a resource is scarce is merely to assert that increased supplies of it could be put to worthwhile uses.

Moreover, as Marshall's description indicates, economics has something to say about much of our lives and the world in which we live them. In this book you will study a wide range of decisions—from a student's allocation of time between work and play to a President's decisions about the size of the federal government—and their effects. You will learn about the operation of the large and small businesses whose products you buy, and you will understand the key issues in debates about government policy in a host of areas. To paraphrase Samuel Johnson's description of London in the seventeenth century, if you're tired of economics, you're tired of life. Like Johnson's London, economics is exciting—though sometimes challenging.

But there is a grain of truth in the "dismal" label. Economics used to be called political economy because economists spend a lot of time analyzing the effects of actual and proposed government policies. Also, economists are often the ones who perform the dismal but important chore of reminding politicians that resources are scarce, so that most choices involve *trade-offs*. Trade-offs are situations in which more of one good thing can be obtained only by giving up some of another good thing.

Is Economics a Science?

Economists are notorious for their disagreements. George Bernard Shaw, for instance, asserted that "if all economists were laid end to end, they would not reach a conclusion."[2] If the word "economists" were replaced by the word "physicists" in this quote, nobody would laugh. But if physicists agree on everything and economists agree on nothing, why is the Nobel Prize in economic *science* awarded in the same ceremony as the Nobel Prize in physics?

Disagreements among economists are of two sorts. The first has to do with positive economics.

● **Positive economics** seeks objective or scientific explanations of the workings of an economy; it deals with what is or could be.

Much of positive economics, on which this book concentrates, is not controversial. Here are three examples you will encounter in later chapters. All economists agree that if the government imposes a tax on a good, its price

---

[1] In 1798 the English economist Thomas Malthus (1766–1834) published a best-selling book entitled *Essay on the Principle of Population*. He argued that because land suitable for growing food was limited, the pressure of population growth would tend to keep most people on the edge of starvation most of the time. This truly dismal view is not held by many economists today since it is not consistent with recent history.

[2] Quoted in Simon James, *A Dictionary of Economic Quotations*, Barnes and Noble, New York, 1981, p. 74.

will rise. Any economist would predict that superb weather conditions producing a bumper crop of wheat will lead to a fall in the price of wheat—and to a reduction in farmers' incomes. No economist would disagree with the assertion that prolonged rapid increases in the money supply will cause prices to rise.

When they practice positive economics, economists behave like scientists in other fields. Like chemists and physicists, they sometimes argue about facts and their interpretation. For instance, many economists think high budget deficits cause high interest rates; others believe the evidence does not support that view. This debate receives more publicity than physicists' disagreements about subatomic particles, since the outcome is likely to affect government decisions that matter to many people. Disagreements of this sort, like arguments about why the dinosaurs died out, can in principle be settled by further research and evidence. The Nobel Prize is awarded for advances in positive economics.

The most visible disagreements among economists involve normative economics.

● *Normative economics* **offers prescriptions for action based on personal value judgments; it deals with what should be.**

When an economist argues that increasing income taxes will reduce inflation a lot and increase unemployment a little, she is making a positive statement. If she goes on to argue that taxes *should* be increased, she is making a normative statement. Even if another economist agrees with the first statement, he will disagree with the second if his own values lead him to think that reducing inflation is much less important than avoiding unemployment. Because economists, like other people, disagree about what is fair and about what society's goals and priorities should be, no amount of research can settle disagreements about normative economics.

In reading what economists have to say about the issues of the day, it is important to distinguish between positive and normative statements. Two examples will serve to illustrate both this point and the kinds of problems raised by the need to allocate scarce resources among competing uses.

THE FEDERAL BUDGET IN THE EARLY 1980s. Figure 1-1 shows defense spending by the U.S. federal government since 1972.[3] Defense spending is shown as a percentage

[3] The appendix to this chapter discusses graphs and their interpretation.

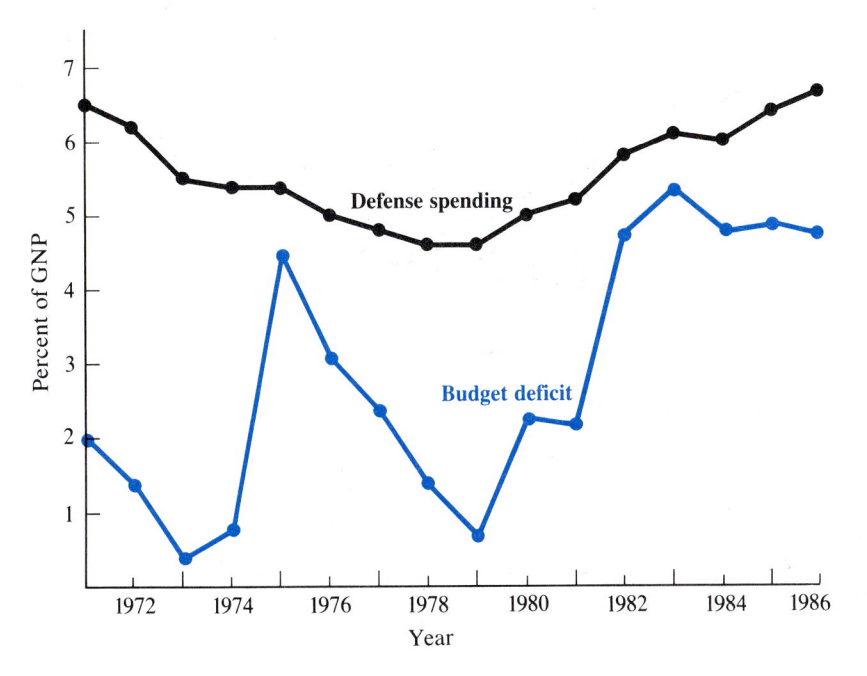

FIGURE 1-1. Defense Spending and the Government Budget Deficit. The figure shows spending for national defense by the U.S. federal government and the U.S. federal government's budget deficit (spending minus taxes), both expressed as a percentage of total production in the U.S. economy (GNP), for the years 1971 through 1986.

of the total value of goods and services produced in the United States—the gross national product, or GNP—for the same year.[4] Defense spending as a percentage of GNP began falling in 1972, as the Vietnam war wound down, and reached a low point in 1978–1979. A major defense buildup began in 1980. By 1986 defense spending had increased to 6.6 percent of U.S. income, up sharply from approximately 4.5 percent in the late 1970s.

The defense buildup reflected an economic decision: After 1979 the United States decided, through the political process, to allocate a larger share of its scarce resources to defense and a smaller share to nondefense uses. The resources that went into the defense buildup could have been used instead for food production, cancer research, housing, or new machinery to lower the cost of making automobiles. Society chose instead to strengthen the national defense. Economists participated in this decision by making both positive statements (analyzing the effects of the defense buildup) and normative statements (arguing that those effects were on balance good or bad).

During the defense buildup, the federal government reduced the percentage of GNP it spent for nondefense purposes only slightly, so that total government spending as a percentage of GNP rose. Moreover, income tax rates were cut, and tax receipts (the government's main source of revenue) did not rise as fast as government spending. The difference between spending and taxes—the federal government's budget deficit—rose to the highest levels in U.S. peacetime history. Figure 1-1 shows the federal government budget deficit (also expressed as a percentage of U.S. GNP) since 1972. The deficit increased from under 1 percent of GNP in 1979 to over 5 percent in 1984, growing far more rapidly than defense spending did.

The size of the budget deficit worries many economists and other citizens. In 1985 seven former chairmen of the Council of Economic Advisers, the President's White House economists, expressed their concern as follows:

> Despite our different views on some matters, as professional economists we are of one mind about the fundamental dangers which the continued existence of such deficits poses for the nation. Most seriously, continued Federal deficits of the amounts now projected would erode the long-term vitality and stability of the nation's economy. . . .

This statement is a subtle mix of positive and normative economics. Its conclusions about the probable effects of continued large deficits are positive, but the implication that it would be desirable to reduce deficits by raising taxes or reducing spending is normative. By the end of this course you will be able to distinguish between positive and normative statements. You will also learn to analyze both how society should decide whether to spend more on defense and less on other things and whether and why the budget deficit matters to the economy as a whole.

THE YOUTH EMPLOYMENT OPPORTUNITY WAGE. It is illegal in the United States to pay an employee in most jobs less than the minimum wage, which in 1986 was $3.35 per hour. The minimum wage has a simple appeal: People should have a reasonable standard of living, and $134 a week for 40 hours of work is certainly not excessive.

But almost all economists agree that the minimum wage actually hurts some of the people it was designed to help. They argue that the minimum wage makes it more expensive for businesses to hire inexperienced and unskilled workers. The higher the minimum wage, the fewer such workers will be hired as firms make more use of skilled labor and automated machinery. If the minimum wage is high enough to matter, it thus reduces the number of low-wage jobs available. Some of those who would earn very low wages without the minimum wage earn nothing at all with it, because there are no jobs for them. From the point of view of society as a whole, the resulting unemployment is a waste of scarce (human) resources.

In the early 1980s, the Reagan administration proposed changing the minimum wage law to provide for a "Youth Employment Opportunity Wage." They noted that many low-wage workers are students who want summer jobs and that (as we have just argued) the minimum wage law reduces the number of summer jobs available, making it harder for young people to get work experience. To deal with this problem, the administra-

---

[4] The precise definition and measurement of GNP is discussed in Chapter 2.

tion implemented a special summertime minimum wage equal to 75 percent of the regular minimum wage, payable only during the period between May 1 and September 30 each year and only to people under age 22. The idea was to make it easier for young people to get summer jobs without lowering the wages paid to year-round workers.

Was this change desirable? Positive economics can help answer this question by determining how many summer jobs the program created, how the earnings of students were affected, and the effects (if any) on other workers. But to say whether the proposal *should* have been adopted, one must make a normative, or value, judgment by deciding whether the benefits received by those whom the change helped outweighed the costs imposed on those whom it harmed.

2. The Production Possibility Frontier

At this point you should have at least a rough idea of what economics, particularly positive economics, is *about*. This section will give you an idea of what it is *like* by introducing and discussing an important economic idea that is used frequently in this book: the production possibility frontier, or PPF.

● *The production possibility frontier* **(PPF) shows the maximum possible amount of some specified good or service that can be produced by a particular economy, given the resources and knowledge it has available and the amounts of other goods and services it also produces.**

Imagine an economy that has limited amounts of two resources—tractors and labor—and that can use these resources to produce food, entertainment, or both. Figure 1-2 shows a graph of the PPF for this hypothetical economy. For each possible level of food production, the PPF shows the maximum amount of entertainment that can also be produced with the resources available. For instance, at point B the economy is producing 275 tons of food. Given this level of food output, the maximum amount of entertainment that can be produced is 100 units.

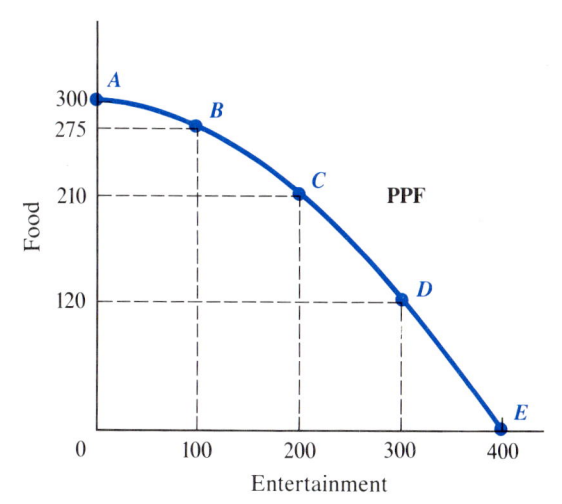

FIGURE 1-2. The Production Possibility Frontier. The curve labeled PPF is the production possibility frontier for an imaginary economy that can produce only two goods: food and entertainment. For each possible level of entertainment production, the curve shows the maximum possible output of food that the economy can produce using the resources and knowledge available to it. This PPF is bowed out, reflecting the fact that the higher the output of entertainment, the more food must be given up for any given increase in entertainment production.

Point A on the PPF indicates that if this economy were to allocate all its resources to food production, 300 tons would be produced. At the other extreme, if all resources were allocated to producing entertainment, with the tractors providing joyrides or trips to and from the beach, the total output of entertainment would be 400 units. This is shown by point E in Figure 1-2.

Models and Reality

In real economies millions of people with different skills and abilities use many types of tools and machines to produce millions of different goods and services. Why, then, should we spend time talking about a purely imaginary and unrealistic economy with only two inputs and two outputs? As you will see in later chapters, much of economics is concerned with the analysis of *models* of this general sort—that is, with the analysis of imaginary economies that are unrealistically simple. Why do economists do this, and what can they hope to learn about the real world in this manner?

The main reason for working with simple model economies is that real economies are much too complex to analyze in complete detail. It would take many volumes the size of this one to describe fully what is produced in the U.S. economy at any time, how it is produced, and for whom it is produced. Many more volumes would be necessary to describe all the possible alternative decisions that could have been made by businesses, consumers, and governments. The largest computers would strain to use all this information to compute the actual PPF of the U.S. economy at any instant.

It is not clear what could be done with the results. We would certainly be unable to describe the PPF of the United States with a graph; there are too many actual and possible goods. And if we insisted on being perfectly realistic, these computations would have to be redone with new data every time a new hammer was produced or a worker learned a new skill or fell sick. Moreover, all this effort would tell us nothing at all about the possibilities open to other economies or the principles that describe their operation.

By working with simple models that can be relatively easily analyzed, economists seek to uncover *general principles* that apply in more complex, realistic situations. Simplification is necessary in order to avoid being drowned in irrelevant detail; the trick is to exclude only the details that really are irrelevant to the problem or issue being studied. As we will discuss in Chapter 2, economists do use evidence about the real world both to suggest what sorts of models will be useful and instructive and to see whether the implications of their models are consistent with the facts. Accordingly, we devote considerable attention in this book to the facts of economic life. But let us first see how the particular model economy we have described can be used to develop some important general principles that will reappear often in later chapters.

Opportunity Cost

Suppose the simple economy whose PPF is illustrated in Figure 1-2 is initially producing only food so that its choice of what to produce is described by point A. If people and tractors are shifted into the entertainment industry, the output of food must fall. Because resources are scarce, society must eat less if it is to consume more entertainment.

The opportunity cost of any increase in the consumption of entertainment is the reduction in food consumption that must accompany it.

● **The *opportunity cost* of any good or service is the amount of other goods or services that must be given up to obtain it.**

The opportunity cost of attending college includes both the out-of-pocket costs of books and tuition *and* the wages you would be earning if you were working full time instead.[6] By deciding to attend college you have given up the *opportunity* to work full time. Similarly, if resources in our model economy are shifted into entertainment, the economy must give up the *opportunity* of having the food which those resources could have produced. For instance, if the economy decides to produce 100 units of entertainment, the new allocation of resources is described by point B in Figure 1-2. The figure then shows that the opportunity cost of producing 100 units of entertainment is the 25 units of food production (the difference between 300 and 275) that must be sacrificed in moving from point A to point B.

However resources were initially allocated, if more people and tractors are withdrawn from the food industry and are put to work producing entertainment, entertainment output will increase and food production will fall. Thus the PPF slopes downward in Figure 1-2; it has a negative slope.[7]

When the PPF is bowed out, as in Figure 1-2, opportunity costs *increase* as resources are moved from one industry to the other. Opportunity costs for our model economy are shown in the third column of Table 1-1. For instance, if the economy shifts from the resource allocation described by point A to that described by point B, the opportunity cost of increasing the output of entertainment by 100 units will be 25 (= 300 − 275) units of food; between D and E the opportunity cost of the 100

---

[6] This point is explored at length in Chapter 15.
[7] Slopes, positive and negative, are explained in the appendix to this chapter.

TABLE 1-1. The Model Economy's Production Possibilities

Point	Output (units) of Entertainment	Food	Opportunity cost of 100 units of entertainment (units of food)
A	0	300	
B	100	275	25
C	200	210	65
D	300	120	90
E	400	0	120

added units of entertainment will be much higher: 120 units of food (= 120 − 0).

The opportunity cost of entertainment in terms of food increases in our model economy the more entertainment is produced, because different methods of production are used in the two industries. Food production uses relatively more tractors and less labor than entertainment. To produce the first 100 units of entertainment (moving from A to B), society can move a lot of labor and a few tractors into entertainment without having much of an effect on food production. By the time the economy is at point D, it can produce the last 100 units of entertainment only by taking the remaining tractors (which are used relatively more than labor in food production) and labor and putting them to work to produce entertainment—and using lots of tractors and a small amount of labor is not a very sensible way of producing entertainment.

Because different industries in fact generally use different methods of production, opportunity costs increase in the fashion shown in Figure 1-2. Thus PPFs are generally drawn as "bowed-out" to reflect this important feature of the menu of output combinations available to real economies.

Cost and Choice

Suppose the economy is currently producing 210 units of food and 200 units of entertainment. This allocation of resources is described by point C in Figure 1-2. The czar, who is considering a reallocation of resources, asks you for the cost of entertainment. If you understand him to mean the opportunity cost, how should you reply?

One answer might be as follows. In order to produce 200 units of entertainment, the economy has to give up 90 units of food (300 − 210). Thus the average cost of 100 units of entertainment at point C is 45 units of food (90/2). This is a sensible answer as far as it goes, but it is not likely to be very useful to the czar or anyone else.

The problem is that this answer tells the czar only about the consequences of shutting down the entertainment industry completely; it doesn't help him choose among the many other possible resource allocations. The best reply would be, "How will you use my answer?" If he says, "To decide whether to reduce entertainment production by 100 units," the answer, from Table 1-1, is 65 units of food. But if he says, "To decide whether to *increase* entertainment production by 100 units," Table 1-1 indicates that the answer is 90 units of food.

There are two related lessons here. First, there is no single correct answer to questions like "What is the cost of entertainment?" The correct measure of cost depends on the choice being considered. Second, to evaluate any possible action, one must focus carefully on its consequences—on the costs and benefits it would produce. In order to decide whether to produce one more car this month, for instance, a firm must compare the *increase* in revenue it would receive with the *increase* in cost it would incur. The average cost of all the cars produced this month is irrelevant, just as the average cost of entertainment is irrelevant to the czar. This is an example of what economists call *the principle of choice at the margin*: Only those (marginal) things which would be changed by a particular action are relevant to deciding whether to take that action.

Growth

The PPF is defined for given supplies of resources and a given knowledge of how to use them to produce output. Suppose more tractors are suddenly available to our model economy. How will its PPF change as a consequence?

Figure 1-3 shows the answer. The initial PPF is AE, as before. An increase in the supply of tractors would increase the amount of food that could be produced for any level of entertainment production. The menu of production possibilities from which society could choose would thus expand. This is represented in Figure 1-3 by an

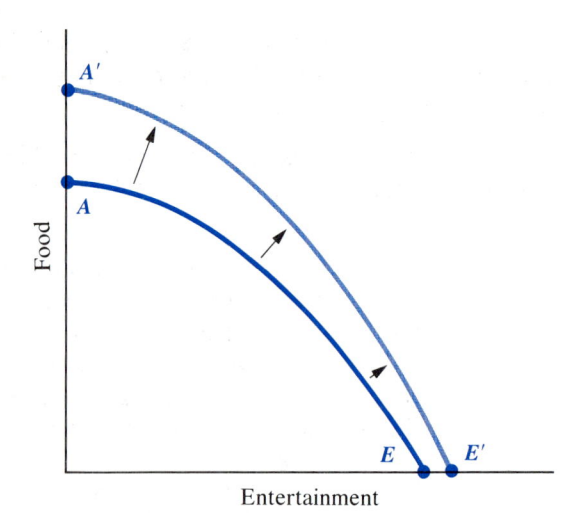

FIGURE 1-3. The PPF: Economic Growth. If the supply of tractors available to our imaginary economy is increased, it will be possible to produce more of both food and entertainment. This is shown by an outward shift of the PPF, as indicated by the arrows, from AE to $A'E'$. Note that the increase in the maximum possible food production (shown on the food axis) is larger than the increase in the maximum possible entertainment output (shown on the entertainment axis), because tractors are better suited to producing food than entertainment.

outward shift in the PPF from AE to $A'E'$. (Note that the figure reflects the fact that tractors are better suited to producing food than to producing entertainment.)

Many other changes would also expand this society's menu of choices. If all workers became experts in farming, singing, or tap dancing, or if movies or weed killers were invented, the effect would be shown graphically as an outward shift in the PPF.

Clearly, any society would like the largest possible menu of production possibilities from which to choose. Three major forces have fueled economic growth and dramatically expanded the choices available to most real economies over time: increases in productive assets, increases in the skill and education of the labor force, and advances in knowledge.[8] All these desirable develop-

---

[8] PPFs also shift outward as populations grow, but this may or may not increase the average production possibilities per person, and that is our main concern here.

ments have an important common feature: Society can obtain more of them only by consuming less today.

In our model economy, the supply of tractors can be expanded only by taking resources away from the food and entertainment industries and using them to produce tractors. In order to increase the skill of the labor force, resources would have to be devoted to education and training. And knowledge is unlikely to advance unless resources that could have produced food or entertainment are instead devoted to research. Like real economies, our model economy faces an important choice between consumption today and consumption in the future. In order to grow rapidly, it must reduce consumption today and make investments (in tractors, education, and research) that will pay off only in the future.

Trade-offs that involve incurring costs today in order to receive benefits tomorrow arise for businesses, consumers, and government decision makers. We analyze the key choices involved and their implications in several of the chapters that follow.

Efficiency

The PPF for any economy is a frontier between two regions: a region where the economy is wasting resources, inside the PPF; and a region the economy cannot reach, outside the PPF.

Points such as W, which is inside the PPF in Figure 1-4, represent *inefficient* allocations of resources. With the given resources, the economy could produce more food and as much entertainment as at W, or it could produce more entertainment and no less food. Any reallocation of resources from W to a point in the region bounded by the arrows would yield more of both goods.

● **An allocation of resources is *inefficient* if it is possible for the economy to produce more of any one good or service from its available resources without reducing the output of another good or service.**

Efficient use of resources implies that it is impossible for society to have more of one good without having less of another. Points on the PPF are thus efficient. Points inside the PPF correspond to situations in which the economy is wasting resources. This doesn't necessarily mean that they are idle; hard but poorly managed work may produce much less output than is possible, for instance.

By contrast, limited supplies of resources make it impossible to produce at points outside the PPF, such as U. Scarcity thus limits the economy's choices to points on or inside the PPF.

Economists often say that "there is no such thing as a free lunch," meaning that more of anything can be produced only by giving up something else.[9] Of course, if the economy were producing inefficiently, at a point such as W, there could be a free lunch; we would be able to have more food without losing any entertainment by moving to the PPF. Once production is efficient, however, the economy faces a trade-off: More of one good means less of another.

3. Economic Systems

In principle, every society at every instant has a PPF which shows the maximum amount of any one good or service it can produce for every possible level of production of all other goods and services. But while we can thus think of any society as choosing a point on or inside its PPF at each instant, this does not help us understand how decisions about what to produce, how to produce, and for whom to produce are made in practice. *People* make choices, not convenient abstractions such as "society."

Prices and Markets

In most countries outside the Soviet bloc and China, *markets* and the *prices* determined in them play the central role in allocating resources among competing uses. Some markets are particular places where people bring goods to sell and others come to buy, for example, the New York Stock Exchange and the wholesale fruit and vegetable markets found in many cities. In other markets, such as the markets for the services of professional basketball players and government bonds, a few people conduct most of the business over the telephone.

[9] Or, as the science fiction writer Robert Heinlein put it, TANSTAAFL: "There ain't no such thing as a free lunch."

Other markets, such as those for used cars and the services of professors of economics, are less tightly organized. However, a general definition covers all cases.

● A *market* is a set of arrangements by which buyers and sellers of a good or service are in contact to trade that good or service.

Much of economics (and of this book) is devoted to studying how prices are determined in markets; how prices serve to coordinate the decisions of firms, households, and governments; and how the answers to "what," "how," and "for whom" questions emerge from this process. We begin this enterprise in Chapter 3 with the study of supply and demand.

To get a feeling for how markets and prices work, think back to the last time you bought a hamburger at a fast-food restaurant. You probably chose the restaurant in part because it charged low prices. Perhaps you preferred steak, but steak was more expensive and your bank account was limited. Thus the price of steak relative to hamburger ensured that "society" answered the "for whom" question about lunchtime steaks in favor of someone else.

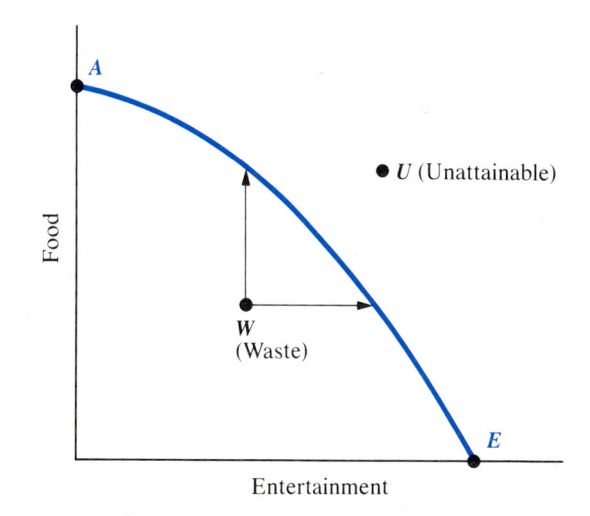

FIGURE 1-4. The PPF: Waste and Efficiency. If society's outputs correspond to a point *on* the PPF, resources are being used efficiently in production. Inside the PPF (as at point W) there is waste. Points outside the PPF (such as U) correspond to outputs that are unattainable because resources are scarce.

Now consider the seller. The restaurant owner is in the business because, given the price of hamburger meat, the rent, and the wages she has to pay, she can sell hamburgers for a price high enough to produce a profit. If only a few people in the neighborhood liked hamburgers or if her rent were much higher, she would not be able to operate a hamburger restaurant at her current location. She might try to operate the same sort of restaurant somewhere else, set up another sort of business, work for someone else, or go to law school. As it is, though, the prices at which she can sell hamburgers and buy the resources she needs to produce them are at levels that lead her to operate this business.

The student behind the counter is probably working there because he's receiving the best wage he can get for the type of part-time work he wants to do. The best wage he can get is still pretty low because many people are willing and able to do this sort of work. If the wage were much lower, he might stop working altogether and try to borrow money to pay his way through college. If the wage were much higher, the restaurant might not be able to stay in business.

Prices, determined in many markets, are guiding your decision to buy a hamburger, the owner's decision to sell it, and the other student's decision to work. Society is allocating scarce resources—including hamburger meat, a building, and the counter help's time—into the production of hamburgers through the *price system*. If nobody liked hamburgers, they couldn't be sold at a price that covered costs, the owner of the restaurant wouldn't be in the hamburger business, and society wouldn't be devoting any resources to hamburger production. If the price of beef doubled (perhaps because a rise in the cost of grain made it more expensive to feed cattle), the price of hamburgers would increase, and people would begin to eat more tuna fish sandwiches. If the market-determined wage for counter help fell, your favorite fast-food restaurant might decide to hire more students and stay open all night. When consumers' desires or supplies of resources change, prices change, and these changes lead to shifts in the allocation of resources.

The Extreme Cases

Markets play a role in allocating resources in all economies, but no economy relies only on markets. To get an idea why, it is useful to consider two extreme cases: an economy with no markets and an economy with only markets.

THE COMMAND ECONOMY. In theory, scarce resources could be allocated among alternative uses without the employment of markets or prices.

● **In a *command economy* the government makes all decisions about production and consumption.**

In a command economy the government would decide what would be produced, how it would be produced, and for whom it would be produced. It would allocate resources among industries, tell those in charge of each industry exactly how much to produce and how to do the job, and specify how much of each good and service would be consumed by each person in the society.

To appreciate what this description implies, think about how you would begin to run by command the city in which you live. How would you decide where each person should live, what clothing he should wear, and what food he should eat? (Who gets the Brussels sprouts?) How would you decide exactly how each person should spend every minute of the day? Who should distribute groceries, who should program computers, and who should be in school? How many buildings of what types should be built, what materials should be used, and how should each construction job be managed? Of course, all these decisions and more are being made every day, mainly through the interaction of individual choices through markets.

Even with the best computers, the government would have an impossible task in a command economy. It is hard to imagine that such an economy could ever produce anything close to an efficient allocation of resources. Not surprisingly, no such economies exist. However, in some countries the government owns all factories, land, and housing and makes many of the basic decisions about where people live, what work they do, and what goods and services they consume.

FREE MARKETS AND THE INVISIBLE HAND. At the opposite extreme from the command economy, in which the government does everything, is the free-market economy, in which the government does nothing.

● **In a *free-market economy* the government plays no role in allocating resources.**

In a free-market economy all decisions about resource allocation are made by households and businesses interacting in markets free of any sort of government intervention. Individuals in free-market economies pursue their own interests, trying to do as well for themselves as they can, without government interference.

At first it might seem that an economy in which everyone pursued his or her self-interest with no government direction at all would be at least as chaotic and inefficient as a command economy. Adam Smith (1723–1790), a Scottish philosophy professor and one of the founders of economics, argued strongly against this view in his classic book *The Wealth of Nations* (1776). Smith contended that individuals pursuing their self-interest in a free-market economy would be led, "as if by an invisible hand," to do things that are in the interests of others and of society as a whole. Much of modern economics rests on Smith's insight, and much of this book is accordingly devoted to exploring its implications and limitations.

We can easily convey the flavor of Smith's argument by returning to the hamburger restaurant discussed previously. The restaurant owner is more likely to be interested in her profits than in the efficient use of society's scarce resources. She is led by her self-interest to hold down her costs—and thus decides how to produce in a way that avoids wasting resources. She tries to adjust her menu in order to maximize profit—and thus decides what to produce in a way that responds to consumers' wants and desires. If she invents a popular new sandwich or a better way to cook hamburgers, she will make more money—but her customers will also be better off, and the choices available to society as a whole will have increased. Prices play the central role in all this: The prices of what she sells reflect the value of her products to consumers, while the prices of what she buys reflect the costs of her suppliers.

In a free-market economy, prices determine not only what is produced and how but also for whom. The people who own valuable resources—inherited as wealth or talent or accumulated through hard work or luck—will receive more of society's output. Those who have fewer resources to begin with or who choose to work less hard will receive less.

Despite the strength and elegance of Adam Smith's argument, no pure free-market economies exist. As Chapter 4 discusses in detail, governments intervene in the operation of markets in many ways and for many reasons. Most governments play an important role in the "for whom" decision—by giving food to those who would otherwise starve, for instance—and attempt to deal with economywide problems such as inflation and unemployment. Governments typically produce some goods and services (such as education and national defense) and regulate the operation of many markets (by controlling both the price of electricity and the purity of hamburger meat, for instance). Taxes are imposed both to pay for government purchases and to affect the operation of markets.

Mixed Economies

Command and free-market economies are thus both unrealistic extreme cases. They are interesting mainly because they help us understand the operation of real economies, which are complex mixtures of these two extremes.

● **In a *mixed economy* both the government and the private sector (businesses and consumers) play important roles in answering the "what," "how," and "for whom" questions for society as a whole.**

All countries have mixed economies, though some are close to the command extreme while others rely mainly on markets.

Figure 1-5 gives some examples. The government plays a much more important role in the socialist economies of the Soviet bloc than it does in the United States and elsewhere. But even in Albania, where the government's role may be the most important, consumers can choose some of the goods they buy and private agricultural markets exist to some extent. Even in Hong Kong, perhaps the economy closest to the free-market extreme, the government levies taxes, provides education, prevents starvation, and regulates the operation of

FIGURE 1-5. Degrees of Market Orientation. In a pure command economy, all decisions about resource allocation are made by the government. At the other extreme, in a pure free-market economy, all resources are allocated through markets. All real economies are mixed: Both government decisions and markets matter. The relative importance of government and the market varies considerably among nations, however.

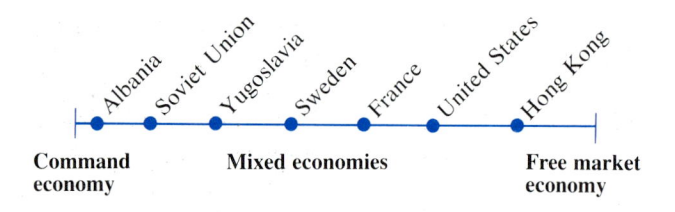

many markets. In many societies, including the United States, the optimal amount of government intervention is a matter of intense, ongoing controversy.

Since both government and private-sector decisions are important in real economies, both are analyzed extensively in this book. The focus is on the United States, an economy in which most (but not all) production is done by privately owned firms that do not receive detailed "what" and "how" instructions from the government. You will learn how markets work and when their operation leads toward or away from the efficient use of resources. You will learn about government intervention in market economies both in theory and in practice. And you will learn how to analyze economic arguments for and against particular government actions.

4. The Road Ahead

Where do we go from here? The next three chapters provide the foundation for all that follows. They discuss the methods and techniques used by economists, the way supply and demand interact in markets to determine prices, and the role of governments in mixed economies. After learning these fundamentals, you may study either microeconomics or macroeconomics.

Micro and Macro

*Micro*economics deals with the economic behavior of individual economic agents—mainly households and firms—and of *particular* markets and industries. The focus is on the prices and outputs of particular goods and services and on how markets interact to determine the allocation of scarce resources among millions of alternative uses. Typical microeconomic questions include the following: Why does a gallon of gasoline cost less than a gallon of milk but more than a gallon of water? What is the effect of rent controls on the supply of housing? What is the effect of a youth minimum wage on the employment of the young and the old? Why is the price of electricity always set by the government?

*Macro*economics, by contrast, studies the operation of the economy as a whole. In macroeconomics the focus is on the economy's *total* production of all goods and services and on changes in the *average* level of prices. Why are there booms and recessions? Why do prices rise more rapidly at one time than another; that is, why is the inflation rate sometimes high and sometimes low? Why is the total number of unemployed persons in the economy sometimes low and sometimes high? What effect does the government's budget deficit have on inflation and unemployment? How do changes in the value of the dollar relative to other currencies affect the U.S. economy?

Despite these differences in focus, microeconomics and macroeconomics are not fundamentally different subjects. The same concepts and the same basic ideas appear in both areas, and understanding one will help you understand the other.

Economic Jargon

Most academic subjects use specialized languages—or *jargons*—to make it easier for those in the know to communicate with one another. Physicists, for instance, use odd words such as "neutron" and "proton." But the jargon of physics also contains familiar words such as "force" and "mass" that are used in precise, special ways. In order to do well in physics, you must learn both the definitions of unfamiliar words (such as "neutron") *and* the special definitions of familiar words (such as "force") in the jargon of physics.

Definitions of both sorts are important in economics as well. "Opportunity cost" is a new term to most readers of this book, for instance, while "efficiency" is a familiar word that has a precise, special meaning in the jargon of economics. Most of the definitions you need to learn in order to master economics and its jargon involve familiar words and phrases. Students have a natural tendency to skip over definitions of words they use every day and to use terms in the same ways when "speaking economics" and when using ordinary discourse. Be warned: This way lies big trouble. When an economist speaks of "money," for instance, he means neither "income" nor "wealth," even though there is often no distinction made among these terms in ordinary speech.

■ President Truman is said to have begged his closest advisers to find him a one-handed economist. He meant that he was tired of hearing economists tell him that if he took almost any action, "On the one hand, some good things will happen, but on the other hand, so will some bad things." But most real-life economic decisions require exactly this sort of analysis, and in this sense there are no one-handed economists. Economics is about choices that are made difficult by scarcity—the sorts of choices we, as individuals and as members of society, have to make every day.

Summary

1. Economics studies how societies faced with the central problem of reconciling unlimited desires for goods and services with scarce resources that limit output decide what gets produced, how it is produced, and for whom it is produced.
2. Economists deal with both positive and normative questions. Positive economics seeks a scientific understanding of the workings of the economy; it deals with what is or could be. Normative economics offers prescriptions for action based on personal value judgments; it deals with what should be. The deepest disagreements among economists have to do with normative questions; most of positive economics is not controversial.
3. The production possibility frontier (PPF) shows the maximum amount of one good or service that can be produced for each given level of outputs of other goods and services. The PPF of any society will change if the quantity or quality of productive resources changes or if useful knowledge advances.
4. The PPF of an imaginary simple economy with only two possible outputs illustrates a number of basic economic principles. The opportunity cost of increasing the output of one of the goods is the amount of the other good that must be given up. Only the changes that a particular action would cause should be considered in evaluating its desirability; decisions should be made on the margin. In order to shift out the PPF, or make possible greater production tomorrow, society must reduce consumption today. Society is wasting resources if it is producing inside the PPF; it produces efficiently on the PPF. Points outside the PPF are unattainable because resources are scarce.
5. In a command economy, all decisions on "what", "how", and "for whom" would be made by the government. The government's task in such an economy would almost certainly be impossible; at any rate, there are no real command economies.
6. At the other extreme, in a free-market economy, the government would play no role in the allocation of resources; the decisions of firms and households would interact through markets to make all the "what," "how," and "for whom" decisions. Adam Smith argued that individuals pursuing their own interests in free markets are led "as if by an invisible hand" to advance the interests of society as a whole. But there are no completely free-market economies; all real governments affect decisions about resource allocation in many ways and for many reasons.
7. All modern economies are mixed—intermediate between the command and free-market extremes. In mixed economies, both government decisions and market forces affect the allocation of resources. The actual roles of the government and the market vary considerably among nations, with the market playing the lead in the United States. The roles each should play are frequently intensely controversial.
8. There are two main branches of economics. Microeconomics concentrates on the operation of individual markets and the interactions among them. Macroeconomics studies the economy as a whole, concentrating on such issues as inflation, unemployment, and growth in total output. The same basic principles apply in both branches.

Key Terms

Scarcity
"What," "how," and "for whom" questions
Trade-offs
Positive versus normative economics
Production possibility frontier (PPF)
Opportunity cost
Choice at the margin
Economic growth
Efficient production
Markets
Prices
Command economy
Free-market economy
Invisible hand
Mixed economy
Microeconomics and macroeconomics

Problems

1. (a) Suppose you lived by yourself on an island. Which of the three basic economic problems would you not have to solve? (b) Why is there no economic problem when people already have everything they want? (c) Do you think that people have virtually unlimited wants, or do you think that one day we will be producing so much that people will all have as much as they want of everything?
2. How are the "what," "how," and "for whom" problems settled within your family?
3. There are five workers in an economy. A worker can make either four cakes or three shirts per day. (a) Draw society's production possibility frontier. (b) How much cake could society consume if it was willing to do without shirts? (c) Indicate which points on your diagram represent inefficient methods of production. (d) Explain why points outside the frontier are unattainable.
4. The economy is as in Problem 3, but a new method of producing shirts has been invented. Now one worker can make five shirts per day. There has been no improvement in the making of cakes. (a) Show society's new production possibility frontier. (b) How does it relate to the old frontier? (c) If consumers like both shirts and cakes, what is likely to happen to society's choice of what to produce?
5. Economists often say that there is no free lunch. But when society is producing inefficiently, it is possible to produce more of all goods. In that sense there is a free lunch; nothing need be lost by producing one more lunch. Explain when there is no free lunch and why.
6. Even in Soviet-bloc economies, workers earn incomes that they can, at least in part, spend in stores to buy whatever they like. Why do you think Soviet planners don't go all the way to a command economy and directly allocate all goods and services to individual citizens?
7. Explain, using the principle of choice at the margin, how a fast-food restaurant should decide whether to hire another person to serve behind the counter.
8. Describe how the invisible hand would work if a large number of college students decided to drop out and look for full-time jobs.
9. Which of the following statements is positive and which is normative? Explain. (a) The rate of inflation has fallen to close to zero. (b) The rate of inflation has fallen to close to zero, and it's time to get the economy moving again. (c) The level of income is higher in the United States than in the Soviet Union. (d) Americans are happier than Russians. (e) Because people should not drink, we should tax liquor more. (f) If we tax liquor more, we will reduce the amount of drinking in society.
10. Explain whether the following are statements about macroeconomics or microeconomics. (a) The price of bananas is down this month. (b) The oil-price shock in 1973-1974 caused a great deal of both inflation and unemployment in the United States. (c) Farmers' plantings of wheat are high and the weather looks good, so there should be a large harvest. (d) Unemployment in Michigan is high relative to the level in the rest of the country.

Appendix: Understanding Graphs

Graphs are the hammers and saws of introductory economics, the basic analytical tools. Graphs such as those in this book appear even in advanced treatises, since a picture is often better than a thousand words. This appendix is designed to teach you how to interpret and use the graphs you will encounter in this text and in life.

What Is a Graph?

● **A *graph* is a picture of a relation between two or more variables, all of which are described by numbers.**

Table 1-1, for instance, contains information on two variables described by numbers: food production and entertainment production for an imaginary economy. The relation between these variables is that each pair of numbers in the table gives the maximum possible food output for the indicated level of entertainment production. In any picture of this relation, each pair of numbers in the table is represented by a point in the picture, as in Figure 1-2. Figure 1-2 also shows many output pairs satisfying this relation that are not listed in Table 1-1. The figure thus contains more information than the table. The figure also reveals at a glance key features of the relation involved—such as the fact that increasing the output of entertainment requires reducing the output of food—that are much harder to see in columns of numbers.

TYPES OF GRAPHS. There are two basic types of graphs in this book; examples of both are present in this chapter. In the first type of graph, the relation connecting the variables is *empirical*. Graphs of this type, such as Figure 1-1, present facts. Each dot on the curve labeled "defense spending," for instance, corresponds to two numbers: a year, and defense spending as a percentage of GNP in that year. Later years correspond to dots farther to the right; higher levels of defense spending correspond to dots farther above the bottom of the graph. The dots are connected by lines in Figure 1-1 to make it easier to see changes over time.

Some graphs of empirical relations are not designed to illustrate changes over time and thus do not have "time" as one of the variables shown. If one wanted to show that GNP and defense spending generally rise together, for instance, one might draw a graph in which each dot showed the values of GNP and of defense spending (both in billions of dollars, say) in a particular year. (Chapter 2 has examples of graphs of this sort.) In all graphs of empirical relations, each point shows the values of variables *observed together*.

In the second type of graph, the relation connecting the two variables is *theoretical*. Graphs of this type are used to illustrate the workings of imaginary economies or parts of imaginary economies and thus to develop general principles that help us understand the operation of real economies. Figure 1-2 is a graph of this type. Graphs of theoretical relations generally involve complete curves rather than sets of dots.

Drawing a Graph

Suppose we are interested in the relation between the use of fertilizer and the output of strawberries in a particular field. To simplify the discussion, let *X* stand for "tons of fertilizer used" and let *Y* stand for "tons of strawberries produced." Suppose someone argues that the following theoretical relation connects these two variables:

$$Y = f(X) = 100X + 100 \qquad (A1)$$

The notation $Y = f(X)$ means that *Y* depends on (or is a function of) *X* according to the relation (or function, or schedule) *f*. The second part of equation (A1) describes the relation *f* exactly. Figure 1A-1 shows a graph of this

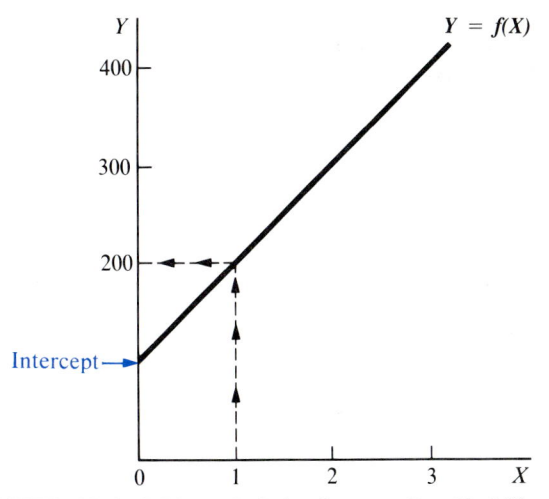

FIGURE 1A-1. A Linear Relation between Two Variables, *X* and *Y*. The figure shows a straight-line, or linear, relation $Y = f(X)$ between two variables, *X* and *Y*. All points along the line correspond to values of *X* and *Y* that satisfy the specified relation.

relation. Each point on the line labeled "$Y = f(X)$" corresponds to a pair of numbers that satisfy the relation in equation (A1).

The line across the bottom of Figure 1A-1 is the *horizontal* axis. It is labeled with the name of the variable it describes, X in this case, and with numbers that indicate the values of X that correspond to points on the axis. Only some possible X values are shown; the point on the axis corresponding to $X = 1.5$ is halfway between the points labeled 1 and 2, for instance. Similarly, the line along the side of Figure A1-1 is the *vertical* axis. Its labels indicate that each point on it corresponds to a particular value of Y. The point where the axes cross is called the *origin* of the graph; it corresponds to zero values of both variables.

The theoretical relation in equation (A1) says that if $X = 1$, Y must equal 200 ($= 100 \times 1 + 100$). You can verify that Figure 1A-1 depicts this fact by starting at the value 1 on the X axis, drawing an arrow up to the curve labeled "$Y = f(X)$," and then going across to the Y axis to read off the value $Y = 200$. Similarly, if $X = 3$, the graph shows that $Y = 400$, as the theoretical relation requires ($400 = 100 \times 3 + 100$).

To draw any graph, one must begin by drawing and labeling the axes. To graph an empirical relation, one then puts a dot on the graph corresponding to each observed pair of values of the two variables involved. To graph a theoretical relation, one must compute the values of Y implied by each of several values of X and then put a dot on the graph corresponding to each pair of numbers (each X and the corresponding Y implied by the relation). If the relation is theoretical, the dots are usually connected by a smooth curve. It may or may not be instructive to draw such a smooth curve on the graph of an empirical relation. Sometimes, as in Figure 1-1, no simple smooth curve provides a good summary of the observed points.

Linear Relations

The relation graphed in Figure 1A-1 is *linear*, meaning that the curve that represents it is a straight line. In order to graph any linear relation, we need to know only two numbers: the *intercept* and the *slope*. If a relation is graphed with X on the horizontal axis and Y on the vertical axis, as in Figure 1A-1, the *intercept* is the value of Y corresponding to $X = 0$. Graphically, the intercept is thus the point at which the graphed line intersects the vertical axis, since X is zero at this point. The intercept of the relation f graphed in Figure 1A-1 is 100. In the strawberry example, this is the production that would result if no fertilizer were used.

The *slope* of a straight line is the change in Y corresponding to a 1-unit increase in X. The theoretical relation graphed in Figure 1A-1 implies that if X increases by 1 unit (1 more ton of fertilizer is used), Y will increase by 100 units (100 additional tons of strawberries will be produced). The slope of the line in Figure 1A-1 that depicts this relation must thus be 100. In our example, the larger the slope is, the more responsive or sensitive strawberry output will be to the use of fertilizer. A slope of 200, for instance, implies that each additional ton of fertilizer will increase strawberry production by 200 tons; output will be twice as sensitive to applications of fertilizer.[10]

The slope of a linear relation can also be calculated directly from its graph. Figure 1A-1 shows that if $X = 0$, $Y = 100$, while if $X = 3$, $Y = 400$. The change in Y between these two points is 300 ($400 - 100$), and the increase in X is 3 ($3 - 0$). The change in Y per unit increase in X is thus 100 (300/3). Any pair of points used in this fashion to calculate the slope of a *linear* relation will produce the same answer.

SLOPE AND STEEPNESS. Given the *scales* of the horizontal and vertical axes—that is, the amount by which X and Y, respectively, increase per inch on the page—the slope of a rising line is greater as the line becomes steeper. For instance, the colored line in Figure 1A-2 has a slope of 200 because Y increases by 200 units for every 1-unit increase in X, while the solid line has a slope of 100. In the strawberry example, that colored line might describe the relation of fertilizer to output for a field with poor soil, so that at least a ton of fertilizer is required to produce any strawberries at all (How does the graph show this?), but with drainage conditions that make fertilizer especially effective.

---

[10] Chapter 5 shows that the slope of a relation is not necessarily the best measure of responsiveness in all situations.

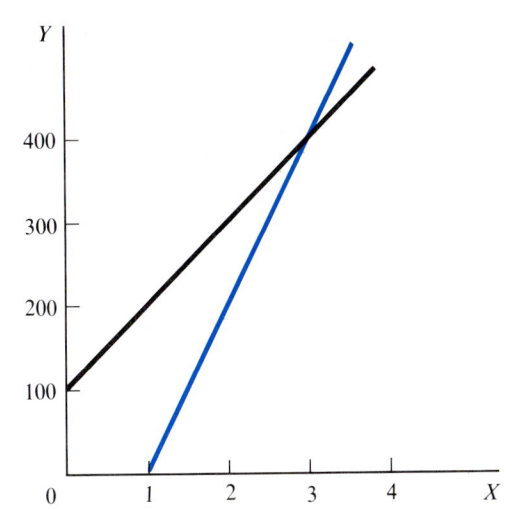

FIGURE 1A-2. The Steeper Line Has the Greater Slope. The black line in this figure graphs the relation $Y = f(X)$ shown in Figure 1A-1; it has a slope of 100. The steeper, colored line has a slope of 200.

It is important to understand clearly that slope and steepness are related only when the scales of the axes are held constant. If the vertical axis in Figure 1A-2 were relabeled so that 100 became 200, 200 became 400, and so on, the slopes of the relations shown would double (Why? Because for an increase in X of 1, Y now increases by 200 along the black line—whereas before Y increased only by 100 for an increase in X of 1), even though the lines would not be any steeper. Similarly, the graph of one linear relation may be steeper than the graph of another even though their slopes are the same, simply because different scales were used to draw them.

POSITIVE AND NEGATIVE SLOPES. All the lines in Figures 1A-1 and 1A-2 are rising. Along a rising line, any increase in X is associated with a positive change—an increase—in Y. Thus a rising line has a *positive slope*, and we accordingly say that the variables involved are *positively, or directly, related*.

Now consider Figure 1A-3, which shows a falling line. The relation g shown in the figure implies that increases in X are associated with negative changes—decreases—in Y. These two variables are thus said to be *negatively, or inversely, related*. We can compute the slope of the line in Figure 1A-3 directly from the graph. When $X = 1$, $Y = 300$, as shown by the arrows on the figure. You should be able to show similarly that when $X = 3$, $Y = 100$. The increase in X between these two points is 2 (3 − 1), while the associated change in Y is −200 (100 − 300). The slope of this line is thus −100 (−200/2). Falling lines like this one always have *negative slopes*, since the change in Y associated with any increase in X is always negative. You should be able to show that if the scales of the axes are fixed, the steeper a falling line is, the more negative is its slope. A slope of −200 corresponds to a steeper falling line than a slope of −100, for instance.

What does a line look like if its slope is zero? A slope of zero means that increases in X are associated with no change at all in Y. This means that the line must be perfectly flat, parallel to the horizontal axis.

Nonlinear Relations

Figures 1A-1 through 1A-3 shows straight-line, or linear, relations between the two variables X and Y. Linear

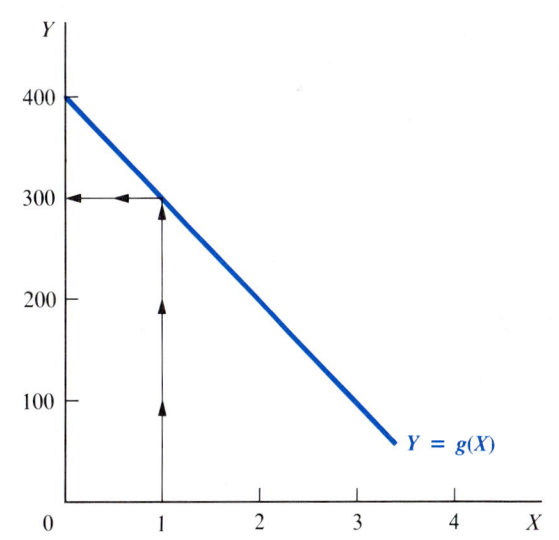

FIGURE 1A-3. A Negative Linear Relation between Two Variables, X and Y. This diagram portrays the relation $Y = g(X)$, which associates decreases in Y with increases in X. For instance, when $X = 0$, $Y = 400$ (the intercept), but when X increases to 1, Y falls to 300. The slope of the line is −100.

relations are particularly easy to analyze, since they are completely described by two numbers: the slope and the intercept. Unfortunately, many relations encountered in economics, such as the PPF in Figure 1-2, are not linear.

To return to the strawberry example, the linear relation depicted in Figure 1A-1 may provide a fairly good description of the relation between fertilizer used and strawberries produced for low levels of fertilizer use. However, as more and more fertilizer is applied, one would expect the increase in output produced by yet another ton of fertilizer to fall. One would also expect there to be some upper limit to the tonnage of strawberries that can be grown in a particular field, no matter how much fertilizer is used. Moreover, if too much fertilizer is applied, output may decrease. Output would surely drop to zero if a thick layer of fertilizer cut off all sunlight.

Figure 1A-4 shows the graph of a *nonlinear* relation between fertilizer use (X) and strawberry production (Y) that is consistent with this discussion.[11] If no fertilizer is applied ($X = 0$), 100 tons of strawberries are produced, so that the *intercept* of this curve is 100, as in Figure 1A-1. If 1 ton of fertilizer is applied, 200 tons of strawberries are obtained, as before. But according to Figure 1A-4, if a second ton of fertilizer is used, strawberry output rises by only 80 tons. The maximum production of strawberries, just over 400 tons, is produced if 5.5 tons of fertilizer are used. Beyond this point, further increases in X are associated with decreases in Y. The output of strawberries falls to zero if just under 12 tons of fertilizer are applied.

For X between zero and 5.5, X and Y are positively (or directly) related along the curve shown in Figure 1A-4, while for larger values of X, they are negatively (or inversely) related. Clearly, the *slope* of a nonlinear curve is not constant, as it is for a straight line. For some increases in X the change in Y is positive, for some it is negative, and for some (compare $X = 4$ and $X = 7$) it is zero. This means that we cannot speak of the slope of a nonlinear curve as a whole, as we can speak of the slope of a straight line.

But we can define the slope of a nonlinear curve *at each point* along it. In order to do this, we must first define the *tangent* to a curve at any point as the straight line that just touches but does not cut the curve at that point. As some geometry teachers put it, the tangent just kisses the curve; it doesn't embrace it. To draw a tangent to a nonlinear curve at some point, slide a ruler up to the curve, stopping when the ruler just touches the curve at

[11] In equation form, the relation shown in Figure 1A-4 is $Y = f(X) = 100 + 110X - 10X^2$.

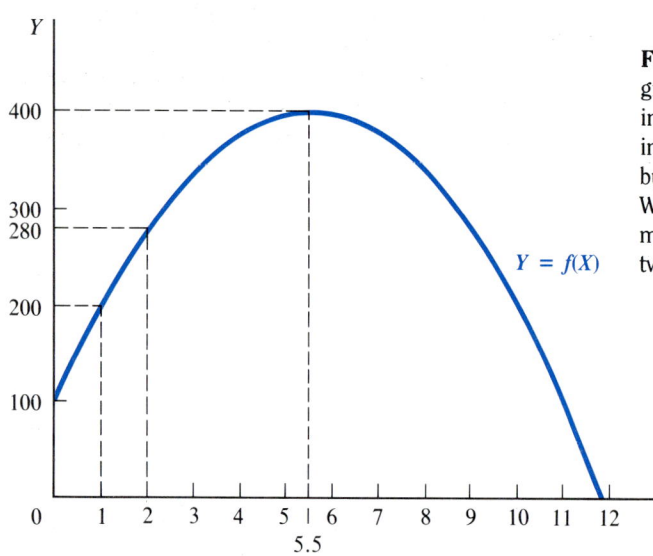

FIGURE 1A-4. A Nonlinear Relation. The relation $Y = f(X)$ graphed here is nonlinear; the change in Y produced by a 1-unit increase in X depends on the initial value of X. When X is increased from 0 to 1, Y rises from 100 (the intercept) to 200, but when X increases from 2 to 3, Y rises by only 80 units. When X is less than 5.5, X and Y are positively related; Y is maximized when $X = 5.5$; and when X is greater than 5.5, the two variables are inversely related.

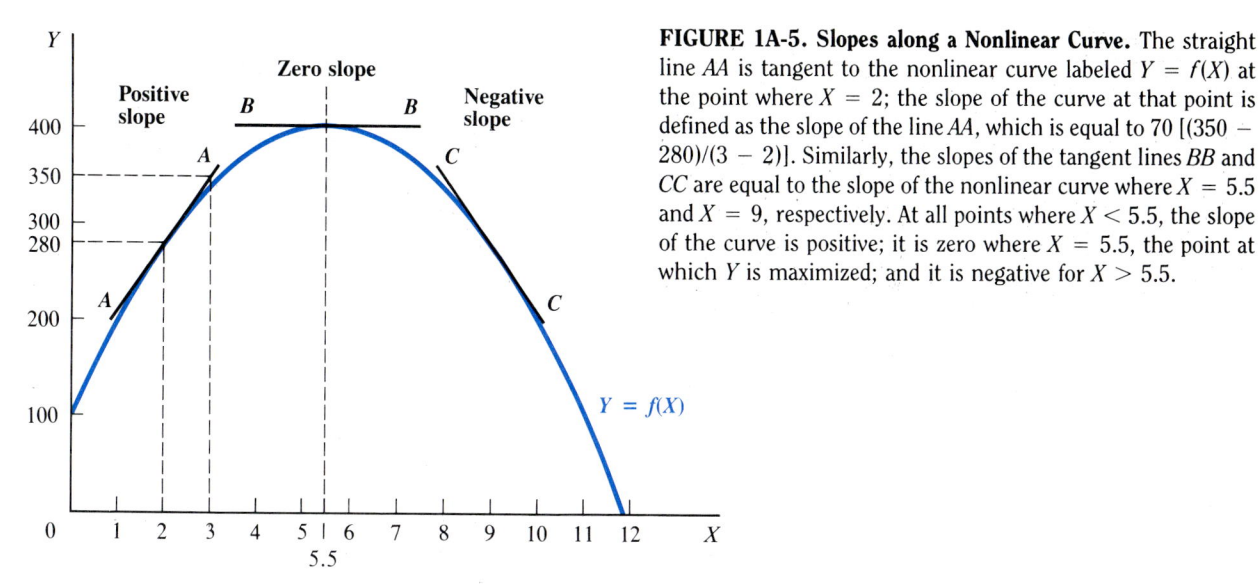

FIGURE 1A-5. Slopes along a Nonlinear Curve. The straight line AA is tangent to the nonlinear curve labeled $Y = f(X)$ at the point where $X = 2$; the slope of the curve at that point is defined as the slope of the line AA, which is equal to 70 [(350 − 280)/(3 − 2)]. Similarly, the slopes of the tangent lines BB and CC are equal to the slope of the nonlinear curve where $X = 5.5$ and $X = 9$, respectively. At all points where $X < 5.5$, the slope of the curve is positive; it is zero where $X = 5.5$, the point at which Y is maximized; and it is negative for $X > 5.5$.

the point of interest. Rotate the ruler around the point so that all nearby points on the curve are visible. The ruler can then be used to draw the tangent.

The slope of a nonlinear curve at any point is defined as the *slope of the line tangent to it at that point*. This definition is illustrated in Figure 1A-5, using the same relation depicted in Figure 1A-4. The straight line AA is tangent to the nonlinear curve $Y = f(X)$ where $X = 2$. Along AA, $Y = 350$ when $X = 3$, and so the slope of AA is equal to 70 [(350 − 280)/(3 − 2)]. The slope of the nonlinear curve is thus equal to 70 when $X = 2$.

Line BB is tangent to the curve where $X = 5.5$, where Y takes on its maximum value. This line is perfectly flat, so that its slope, and thus the slope of the nonlinear curve where $X = 5.5$, is zero. This is an example of a general principle: The slope of a smooth curve is always zero where Y is either larger or smaller (turn Figure 1A-5 upside down) than at all nearby points. (To see why we must limit ourselves to nearby points, draw a curve that rises, then falls, and then rises above its previous peak.)

Finally, CC is tangent to the curve where $X = 9$. Since CC slopes downward, the slope of the nonlinear curve is negative when $X = 9$. (In fact, a very good ruler will show that the slope is equal to −70.) As these examples indicate, the slope of a nonlinear curve is positive when the curve is rising (increases in X are associated with increases in Y) and negative when it is falling (increases in X are associated with decreases in Y), just as with a straight line.

Chapter 2
Basic Concepts and Techniques

It is more fun to play baseball if you know how to catch, and cutting lumber is much easier with a saw than without. Every activity or academic discipline, be it baseball, carpentry, dentistry, or economics, involves the use of a basic set of tools. The tools may be tangible, like the carpenter's saw or the dentist's drill, or intangible, like the ability to catch a baseball or, as in economics, a set of basic concepts and techniques that aid in understanding, communication, and thinking.

This chapter sets out some of the basic concepts and ideas in every economist's toolbox. (You read about some others in Chapter 1.) You may be studying economics to understand the society in which you live, prepare for a career in business, or make the world a better place. Whatever the reason, there is no way to make progress without a working knowledge of the tools of the trade.

Economics makes more use of numbers, graphs, and (in more advanced courses) equations than other social sciences, such as sociology and anthropology. The main reason is that the material side of life, on which economics concentrates, is easily and naturally described by numbers. The financial pages of the daily newspaper, for instance, are filled with numbers—stock prices, the numbers of shares bought and sold, the prices of foreign currencies, interest rates, and much more.

Happily for most of us, economics is more than playing with numbers: Economists try to understand what they observe, predict what will happen in the future, and analyze the consequences of proposed changes in government policy. All these tasks require the use of models or theories.

● A *model* or *theory* **is a simplified description of reality or, equivalently, an exact description of a simple imaginary economy.**

Section 1 of this chapter discusses the role of theory in economics and presents an important illustrative model—the circular flow of income—that serves as the foundation of all macroeconomic analysis. Section 1 also describes the use of evidence to develop and evaluate economic models.

Economic models describe relations among economic variables.

● **An** *economic variable* **is anything that influences the** "what," "how," and "for whom" decisions with which economics is concerned or anything that describes the results of those decisions.

Consumers' attitudes about the future are thus economic variables, since they may affect spending and saving decisions; so are the numbers of tractors and workers available to an economy, and so are the prices of hamburgers and jet fuel.

We use *data* to measure and analyze economic variables and to examine the relations predicted by economic models.

● *Economic data* are facts, most often expressed as numbers, that provide information about economic variables.

Thus surveys of consumer attitudes, counts of tractors, and stock prices are economic data.[1] Section 2 discusses the main types of numerical measures used in economics, and sections 3 and 4 present some of the main techniques employed in using data to develop and evaluate economic models.

1. Economic Models and Theories

Economists measure and describe the material side of life, but their main goal is to understand how economies operate. In economics, as in other fields, understanding is valuable because it enables us to use logic to answer "what if" questions.

For instance, if you understand how a car operates, you can predict what will happen to any car if it runs out of gas. To make such a prediction, you apply basic logic to a simple description or model of automobile operation. The simpler the model, the easier it is to use it to give general answers to "what if" questions but the less detailed the predictions it yields. Thus the simplest theory of auto operation would predict only that any car's engine will stop if it runs out of gas, while a more complex model might enable you to predict how far a particular car would coast, depending on the road and its speed, when the gas ran out.

Real economies are too complex to think about logically in full detail; there are too many different goods, services, firms, workers, and consumers to keep track of. In order to develop understandable descriptions of reality that can be used to answer "what if" questions, we must simplify drastically. But it then follows that *all* economic theories are, strictly speaking, wrong—since they leave out some aspects of reality. The ultimate test of a model or theory is not whether it provides a fully realistic description of reality, since none do, but rather whether it is useful: Does it provide generally correct answers to questions of interest?[2] Another way to put this is that the predictions of economic models should be consistent with the available evidence.

Chapter 1 presented and discussed a simple economic model: an imaginary economy that could allocate labor and tractors to produce food and entertainment. In this section we introduce another important economic model and use it to discuss the roles of theory and evidence in economics.

The Circular Flow of Income

The decisions of over 85 million households, over 17 million firms, and over 80,000 government units together determine the total output produced in the U.S. economy, the number of workers employed to produce it, and the total income of the households in the economy. The amount of goods firms produce depends on how much they think they can sell and at what prices. The amount they sell is the amount people buy, which depends on household income, which in turn depends on how much firms are producing and selling.

Systematic thinking about these interactions begins with the *circular flow diagram*, as shown in Figure 2-1. The figure presents an overview of the economy, empha-

---

[1] As a matter of grammar, the word "data" is plural and denotes a collection of facts; a single fact is a "datum."

[2] An old story that economists hear often tells about a physicist, a chemist, and an economist stranded on a desert island with a single can of stew. The physicist and chemist try to open the can using the techniques of their disciplines, but they fail. The economist announces that he knows how to do the job. When he has the others' attention, he begins, "Assume a can opener." This story gets a laugh because economic theories are often clearly unrealistic; our response is that they *must* be unrealistic to be simple enough to be understood and employed.

Part One: Introduction

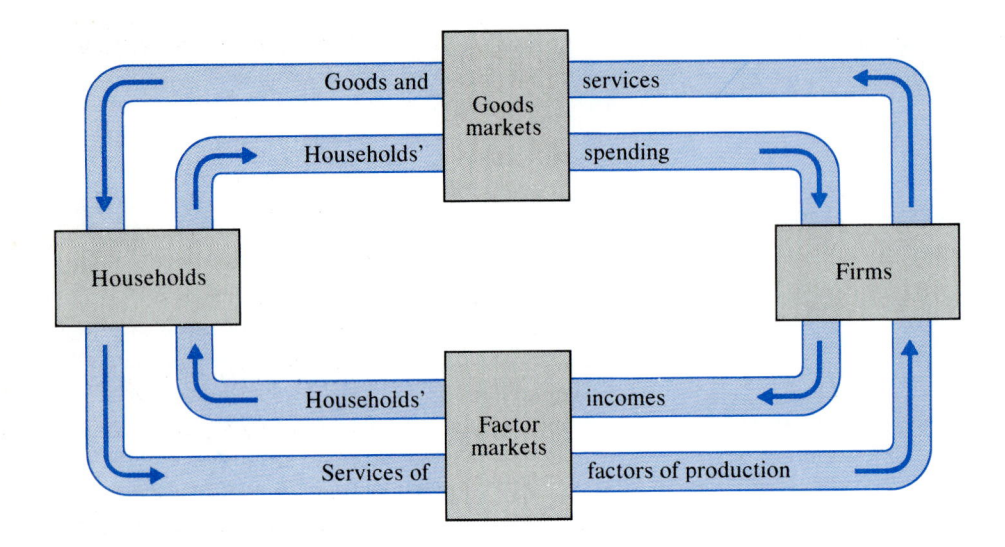

```
                 Goods and    services
                        ┌─────────┐
                        │  Goods  │
                        │ markets │
              Households'│         │spending
                        └─────────┘

    ┌──────────┐                              ┌──────────┐
    │Households│                              │  Firms   │
    └──────────┘                              └──────────┘

              Households'│         │incomes
                        ┌─────────┐
                        │ Factor  │
                        │ markets │
                        └─────────┘
                Services of    factors of production
```

sizing the interactions between firms and households that determine the economy's level of production. The diagram simplifies reality by leaving out government taxation and spending as well as purchases and sales made abroad.

Households are represented by the block on the left of the diagram. They own the factors of production used by firms to produce goods and services.

● *Factors of production* are the inputs—including labor services, land, machines, tools, buildings, and raw materials—used to produce goods and services.

Households obtain income by selling raw materials and labor services and renting out their land and capital goods (machines, tools, and buildings).[3] That is, they sell the services (the use) of their factors of production to firms. They use their income—composed of wages, rents, and profits—to buy goods and services produced by firms.

Firms are represented by the block on the right of the diagram. They are organizations that use factors of production to produce goods and services, which they then sell to households. Firms pay out profits to the households that own them.

Flowing between households and firms are goods and factors of production as well as payments for the goods and the use of the factors. The outer loop shows the physical movements of goods and factors of production between households and firms. The services of factors of production flow from the households to the firms in the lower outer loop. The goods and services made using those factors of production flow in the opposite direction, from firms to households, in the upper outer loop.

The inner loop shows the corresponding flows of dollar payments. Wages, rents for the use of land and machines, and profits flow from firms to households in the lower inner loop. Together these payments make up households' incomes. Flowing out of the household sector is a stream of payments for goods. The payments received by firms are the total dollar value of their sales of goods.

The flows of factors and goods are conducted through markets. Firms sell their products in *goods markets*, which are shown in the upper loop. Households sell the use of their factors of production in the *factor markets*, which are shown in the lower loop. Table 2-1 provides a verbal summary of the circular flow of goods and factors. Parts 2 and 3 of this book focus on goods markets, and Part 4 concentrates on factor markets. (Parts 3 and 5 cover the interactions of government and the marketplace.)

---
[3] Much of the land, buildings, and equipment in the economy is owned by business firms, but all business firms are ultimately owned by households.

TABLE 2-1. Transactions by Households and Firms in the Circular Flow

Market	Households	Firms
	Supply factors of production to firms and use their income to buy goods and services.	Use factors of production to produce goods and services
Factor markets	Supply services of factors of production and receive income	Pay profits to households and pay them for the use of factors of production
Goods markets	Spend on goods and services produced by firms	Sell goods and services to households

INCOME AND OUTPUT. One important implication of the circular flow model is that the total value of sales of goods by firms is equal to the total value of households' incomes. That is, in an economy without government or foreign trade, the dollar value of total output is equal to the dollar value of household income. Here is the reasoning. Households receive wages for their labor and payments for the use of their land and machines from firms. If firms make profits, those too are paid out to households and make up the rest of household income. The sum of the firms' costs of production (wages and rents for the use of land and machines) plus profits is thus the total dollar value of household income. But that same sum—costs plus profits—is also equal to firms' total revenue, or, equivalently, the dollar value of firms' output. Therefore, the total value of firms' output is equal to households' total income. Graphically, the value of the payments in both the upper and the lower inner loops in Figure 2-1 is the same.[4]

The circular flow diagram implies that income is equal to spending for goods and services. Does that mean that if *you* decide to spend more, *your* income will rise?

Unfortunately, no. The equality of income and spending applies only to the economy as a whole.

Models in General

The circular flow diagram shown in Figure 2-1 is an economic model. Like all models, it is a highly simplified description of reality. (For instance, it simplifies by leaving out the government and ignoring transactions with foreigners and among firms.[5]) Simplification is essential for understanding and insight. Thinking about the circular flow model, for example, reveals that income and output are always equal for an economy as a whole. Hours of computer analysis might have revealed that this equality holds for a particular real economy in a particular period, but only if the data used had absolutely no errors. Moreover, finding that income equaled output for a particular real economy would by itself give one no reason to suspect that this equality would also hold for other economies at other times. Theoretical analysis, or the application of the rules of logic to simplified descriptions of reality, is necessary to develop general principles.

Like most models, Figure 2-1 answers some questions and raises others. The circular flow diagram shows that total income is equal to the dollar value of total output, but it does not show why the levels of income and employment of factors of production are at one particular level rather than another. It describes the economy in the deep recession of 1982, when 10 percent of the labor force could not find jobs, just as well as it describes the booming economy of 1969, when less than 4 percent of the labor force was out of work. Other questions the circular flow diagram suggests include the following: What happens to the level of production when households decide they want to spend less and save more? What happens when firms discover new ways of making goods with less labor—can everyone still find a job?

It takes a more complete model to show how the level of production and total income of the economy are determined. Building such a model is one of the central tasks of macroeconomics. The circular flow diagram is the

---

[4] A warning note: Once a government and foreign trade are brought in, total output and household income are no longer exactly equal—because we spend some of our income on goods produced abroad, for instance, and because the government takes some of it as taxes. The essential idea of the interaction between households' spending decisions and firms' production decisions remains, however.

[5] We assumed, for instance, that firms sell their outputs to households, whereas many firms sell only to other firms.

right starting point, for it draws attention to the interactions among firms' production decisions that generate income for households and households' spending decisions that generate sales for firms. It also draws attention to the goods and factor markets in which firms and households interact.

Models and Data

While simplified models must be used to develop general principles and answer "what if" questions, models that are not consistent with the real world will not yield valid principles or useful answers. Economists, like other scientists, use data both to build models and to evaluate them, as shown in Figure 2-2.

Someone interested in a problem often starts thinking about it by collecting data on the economic variables that seem likely to be involved. These data may suggest either a relationship that should be investigated further or the main features that should be included in a model that helps explain the problem.

For instance, suppose you want to know whether college education is likely to pay off by raising your annual income. The first step in analyzing this problem might

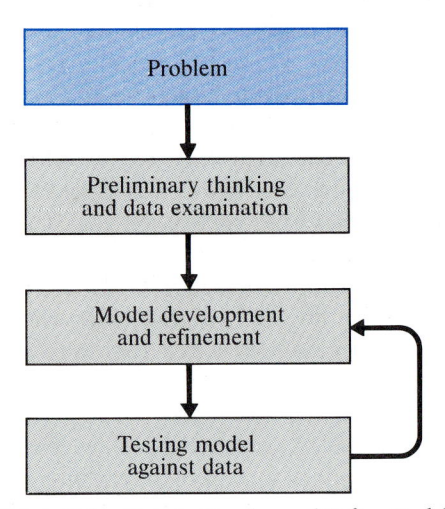

FIGURE 2-2. Using Data to Develop and Refine Models. Work on an economic problem usually begins by examining data and developing one or more models consistent with it. Additional data are then used to test the models' predictions. These tests may support a single proposed model, suggest refinements, or indicate the need for an entirely new model.

TABLE 2-2. Income and Education in the United States, 1984*

Educational attainment	Median income
Less than 8 years of elementary school	10.1
8 years of elementary school	11.9
1–3 years of high school	14.8
4 years of high school	22.4
1–3 years of college	25.8
4 years or more of college	37.1

* Educational attainment of householders and median annual household income in thousands of dollars.
Source: *Statistical Abstract of the United States, 1986*, p. 446.

be to collect data on the typical incomes of individuals who received different amounts of education before starting work. For this purpose you would probably use *median* rather than *mean* income.

We compute the *median* of any set of numbers (for instance, incomes of college graduates) by first putting the numbers in order of increasing size and then selecting the number in the middle. Thus 4 is the median of the following set of numbers: 3, 3, 4, 5, 100. The *mean* of these numbers, or their sum divided by the number of elements summed, is 23 (115/5). As this example suggests, the median is used instead of the mean when the aim is to show a typical situation and when extreme data might distort the picture. The median is generally used to analyze income data, since mean incomes are often strongly affected by a few high observations. The word "average" is sometimes used to signify both mean and median; it is often important to know which is meant.

Table 2-2 shows that those with more education typically earn higher incomes. The most obvious model of the effects of college education suggested by these data is that college teaches useful skills that employers reward with higher pay.

However, a little more thought suggests alternative models in which college teaches nothing useful that are also consistent with these data. One such model is the following: Rich parents are more likely than poor parents to send their offspring to college, and individuals' incomes are mainly determined by their parents' incomes. Another alternative is that colleges simply accept the most able people, those who will do well in later life no matter what.

As in this example, a first look at the data often suggests several plausible models. The next step is to test these alternatives in order to see whether any are consistent with all the relevant evidence. This step usually involves thinking logically about what the alternative models predict about the world and then gathering more data in order to see whether those predictions are correct. In this example, the first alternative model predicts that if a person's parents are rich, she will be rich whether or not she attends college. The second alternative predicts that identical twins who have the same level of inherited ability will have nearly identical incomes, even if one goes to college and the other does not.

2. Measuring Economic Variables

Most economic variables are more like tractors and stock prices than like attitudes; they can be easily and completely described by numbers. Government agencies collect and publish tons of numerical data each year, as do private sources such as the American Newspaper Publishers Association and the National Association of Manufacturers. The *Statistical Abstract of the United States*, published each year by the U.S. Department of Commerce, contains an extraordinary range of facts and indicates where even more can be found. Economists do not rely exclusively on data published by others; they gather data from many sources, including corporations' annual reports, medieval church records, interviews with businesspeople, surveys of consumers, and, from time to time, experiments.

Questions about quantities of productive inputs, outputs of goods and services, prices of particular goods, and levels of household incomes can usually be answered fairly completely with numbers. The most common numbers used in economics are prices, quantities, and dollar values.

Prices, Quantities, and Values

Markets matter in all economies, and most decisions concerning resource allocation in the United States are made in markets. Accordingly, most economic data describe transactions in markets. When you buy hamburgers, you are engaging in a typical market transaction: the exchange of some quantity of money for some quantity of a particular good or service. Your purchase of hamburgers can be described by three related numbers: the price per hamburger, the number of hamburgers bought, and the total dollar amount of the purchase. Similarly, most economic data provide information about prices, quantities, or dollar amounts.

Prices are of course stated as so many dollars per unit of a good or service: $1.95 per hamburger, $6.50 per haircut, or $3.37 per bushel of wheat.[6] Quantities are physical measures of goods or services: numbers of hamburgers or haircuts, bushels of wheat, tons of coal, barrels of imported oil. Dollar amounts are obtained by multiplying a price and a related quantity, as follows:

$$\text{Price} \times \text{quantity} = \text{dollar amount} \quad (1)$$

The terms "dollar amount of" and "dollar value of" are used interchangeably, and often they are even omitted—for instance, when instead of saying "the dollar value of spending on imported cars" we say "spending on imported cars."

Prices, quantities, and dollar values describe transactions in the market for any single good or service. Real economies are composed of millions of markets, and a complete description of the economy would require an extraordinary amount of detail, far beyond the comprehension of any individual. Thus to analyze the economy as a whole, we have to summarize transactions in individual markets and use *economywide* measures of price, quantity, and dollar value. To summarize prices, we use a measure of the *average* price in different markets. To summarize quantities and the total dollar value of production, we use measures of the *total* quantity and value of goods produced.

The rest of this section describes the main measures of the economywide average price level, the quantity of output, and total dollar value of output.

Average Price Level

From one year to the next, some prices will rise, some will stay the same, and some will fall. Because there are millions of prices, we cannot analyze the economy keep-

---

[6] In other countries, prices are stated in the local currency: Canadian dollars, British pounds, French francs, Japanese yen, or German marks, for example.

ing all these details in view. Instead, we have to use a measure of the average price level.

● The *average price level*, or simply the price level, is a weighted average of the prices of different goods and services in the economy, with more important prices receiving larger weights.

Changes in the price level thus reveal whether prices on average are rising or falling.[7]

The price level is generally measured by a price index.

● A *price index* is 100 times the ratio of the dollar cost of a specified collection of goods and services (the market basket) in a given period to the cost of the same collection in a specified base period.

The basic idea is that if you buy the same things every week at the grocery store, the amount you pay for that collection of goods serves as a measure or index of the average level of prices in the store.

Table 2-3 illustrates the computation of a price index for which the market basket consists of one apple and four oranges. The first step is to compute the cost of the market basket in each year. We then obtain the index by dividing the cost in each year by the cost in the base year and multiplying the result by 100. Thus the price index for year 2 is computed as $120 = (18/15) \times 100$. Note that the value of a price index in its base period is always

[7] When the price level changes, the quantity of goods that can be bought with a dollar changes. Thus when the price level rises, a dollar buys fewer goods; when the price level falls, a dollar buys more goods. For instance, if prices double, a dollar buys half as many goods as it used to. It is often said that the *purchasing power of money* falls when prices rise; these are just two different ways of saying the same thing.

TABLE 2-3. Computation of a Price Index

	Quantities in market basket	Prices in year 1	Prices in year 2
Apples	1	3	2
Oranges	4	3	4
Cost of market basket		15	18
Price Index (base = year 1)		100	120

TABLE 2-4. Weights in the Consumer Price Index

Goods or service	Weight, %
Housing	42.6
Transportation	18.7
Food and beverages	17.8
Apparel and upkeep	6.5
Medical care	4.8
Entertainment	4.4
Other goods and services	5.1

Source: Bureau of Labor Statistics.
Note: Weights do not sum to 100 because of rounding.

100. When a price index is above 100, prices are on average higher than in the base period, while values below 100 indicate that prices are on average lower. In the example in Table 2-3, one price rose between year 1 and year 2 and one price fell. Since the price that rose was more important (that is, there were four oranges in the basket compared with one apple), it had a larger weight in the price index, and the index increased.

CONSUMER PRICE INDEX. The consumer price index (CPI) is the most widely used price index. The CPI, which is calculated and reported each month by the federal government, is based on the cost of a market basket of goods and services designed to represent the purchases of a typical urban household. The basket includes specified quantities of over 250 different categories of goods and services. Table 2-4 shows the shares, or weights, of the major categories in the CPI market basket. These weights reflect the relative importance of the goods in the spending of urban households. They are based on surveys of spending habits in the period 1982–1984.

The base period for the CPI is 1967. Thus the 1987 CPI, for instance, is calculated as follows:

$$\text{CPI} = \frac{\text{cost of CPI market basket in 1987}}{\text{cost of CPI market basket in 1967}} \times 100 \quad (2)$$

Values of the CPI for different years are given in Table 2-5. The CPI is equal to 100 in 1967 because that is the base year. By 1986 the CPI was more than three times the 1967 value, meaning that the cost of the typical collection of goods bought by an urban consumer more

TABLE 2-5. CPI for Selected Years, 1960–1986

Year	1960	1967	1972	1977	1982	1984	1986
CPI	88.7	100	125.3	181.5	289.1	311.1	328.4

Source: *Economic Report of the President, 1987*, Table B-55.

than tripled over those 19 years.[8] Going backward, the index was less than 100 in 1960, indicating that the price level in 1960 was lower than the price level in 1967.

USING THE CPI. Why bother to calculate price indices? One answer is suggested by the fact that the CPI is often called *the cost of living index*. Here "living" means the lifestyle (that is, the purchases) of a typical urban consumer in the United States. Changes in the CPI can be used to see whether increases in incomes or wages have been wiped out by increases in prices.

To do this, we use the CPI to calculate how much *real income* changes over time.

● **Nominal income is the value of income measured in dollars; *real income* is the value of income measured in terms of the goods it will buy.**

The higher the price level, the less that can be bought with any given nominal or dollar income. A price index is accordingly used to convert nominal income to real income by adjusting for changes in the price level since a given base period. Table 2-6 shows per person dollar income[9] and real income in the United States in selected

[8] Equivalently, a dollar bought less than one-third the amount of goods in 1986 than it bought in 1967.

[9] The income data are *disposable personal income*, that is, the income individuals have left to spend after taxes.

TABLE 2-6. Dollar and Real Income, United States, Selected Years

Year	1960	1967	1977	1986
Dollar income	1986	2828	6262	12312
CPI	88.7	100	181.5	328.4
Real Income (1967 dollars)	2239	2828	3450	3749

Source: *Economic Report of the President, 1987*.
Note: Income is per capita disposable income.

years, where the CPI has been used to convert dollar income to real income.

For example, real income in 1977 is calculated by recognizing that prices in 1977 were 1.815 times their level in 1967. Real income in 1977 (measured in 1967 dollars) is the dollar income in 1977 ($6262) divided by 1.815. The resultant measure of real income, $3450, is real income *in 1967 dollars*—or in other words, the value, using the prices of 1967, of the goods that could have been bought in 1977 with 1977 income. Whereas the dollar value of income in 1977 was more than double the 1967 level of dollar income, real income increased by only 22 percent ([(3450 − 2828)/2828] × 100 percent) over that period.

Any time it is necessary to compare the *real* value of dollar figures in two different years, a price index is used to reduce those dollar numbers to a common real basis.

Dollar Value of Aggregate (Total) Output

The dollar value of total production in the economy, called GNP, is estimated on a quarterly basis (that is, for each quarter of the year) by the federal government.

● **Nominal gross national product, or nominal GNP, is the dollar value of all goods and services produced in the economy in a given period, computed using the prices of that period.**

Here, as we have explained, "nominal" means "measured in dollars." Note the use of the terms "goods" and "services" in this definition. Goods are tangible; services are not. Automobile production is included in GNP, as are the outputs of bread, clothes, power plants, and other goods. GNP also includes the value of all haircuts produced by Americans. Haircuts are services, as are economics lectures, TV performances, and the services provided by a bank or a real estate broker.

Nominal GNP is calculated as the sum of the dollar values (price times quantity) of the outputs of all the millions of goods and services produced in the economy. The value of GNP can accordingly change for two reasons. First, the physical volume of production can change because more or fewer people are employed or because each worker becomes more or less productive.

Second, the value of GNP can change because the prices of goods have changed with physical output unchanged.

In practice, of course, both prices and physical output change over time. Any particular increase in nominal GNP may mean that more has been produced or that prices have risen—or both. As the rest of this section shows, an economywide version of equation (1) is used to sort out the effects of changes in outputs and changes in prices.

Quantity of Aggregate Output

Because the total value of production, or nominal GNP, can change both because prices change and because quantities change, it is not a good measure of the economy's total physical output of goods and services. For instance, nominal GNP would increase if all prices went up even though the quantity of each good produced was unchanged.

To obtain a measure of physical production in the economy, we calculate the value of output using constant prices.

● *Real GNP* **is the dollar value of all goods and services produced in the economy in a given period, calculated using the prices of a fixed base year.**

Since the same set of prices is used to value outputs in different years, changes in real GNP reflect only changes in physical quantities. Real GNP thus measures the aggregate level of physical production in the economy.

Currently the government uses the prices of 1982 to compute real GNP. Thus each car that is produced in 1987 is given a value equal to that of an equivalent car (with the same horsepower and options) in 1982,[10] and each 1987 haircut is given the price of a 1982 haircut. The value of production of each good or service is calculated using the prices of 1982, the components are added, and the result is real GNP in 1982 dollars. Nomi-

TABLE 2-7. Nominal and Real GNP in Billions of Dollars and the GNP Deflator

Year	Nominal GNP, current $	Real GNP, 1982 $	GNP deflator, 1982 = 100
1972	1213	2609	46.5
1980	2732	3187	85.7
1982	3166	3166	100.0
1984	3765	3490	107.9
1986	4209	3677	114.5

Source: *Economic Report of the President*, *1987*, Tables B-1 through B-3.

nal GNP, in contrast, is computed by using the prices in force in each year to value production. It is said to be measured in *current* dollars, while real GNP is measured in *constant* dollars.

Table 2-7 shows nominal and real GNP for some recent years. Note that for 1982, real and nominal GNP are the same. The reason is that the prices of 1982 are used as base year prices to calculate real GNP. Between 1972 and 1982, nominal GNP nearly tripled while real GNP did not even double. This reflects the substantial increase in the price level over this decade. Between 1980 and 1982, nominal GNP rose while real GNP fell. This means that on average prices rose substantially while total physical production actually fell. Real GNP thus gives a better picture than nominal GNP of the level of output or activity in the economy.

THE GNP DEFLATOR. Nominal GNP is different from real GNP in that different prices are used to value the level of output in a given year. For instance, if prices have risen, nominal GNP will be above real GNP. Nominal and real GNP data can thus be combined to give an alternative measure of the price level—the *GNP deflator*[11]—as follows:

$$\text{GNP deflator} = \frac{\text{nominal GNP}}{\text{real GNP}} \times 100 \qquad (3)$$

---

[10] This is not a simple chore in practice because products change over time. For instance, some electronic gadgets on 1987 cars were simply not available in 1982, and there is no fully satisfactory way of figuring out what they would have cost in that year. The U.S. Department of Commerce uses a lot of ingenuity in trying to produce the best possible estimates of real GNP.

[11] The formula for the GNP deflator is basically an aggregate version of equation (1): price × quantity = dollar value. Nominal GNP is the *dollar value* of total output; real GNP is the *quantity* of output. The GNP deflator, a measure of the *price* level, is therefore given by equation (3) as the ratio of dollar value to quantity.

Values of the deflator for selected recent years are given in Table 2-7.

The GNP deflator is, after the CPI, the most widely used measure of the economywide price level. The main difference between the CPI and the GNP deflator is that the GNP deflator is based on *all* goods and services produced in the economy, not just those typically purchased by urban households. The market basket used to compute the deflator thus includes office buildings, locomotives, guided missiles, and other products not covered by the CPI.[12] The CPI is accordingly a slightly better measure of the cost of living, while the GNP deflator is a slightly better measure of the economywide price level. Over periods of a year or more, however, they generally give similar pictures of changes in price levels.

3. Comparing Economic Variables

In order to use economic data to describe the world as clearly as possible, search for relationships among economic variables, or test economic models, it is often necessary to make comparisons over time or across space—among firms, households, or nations, for instance. This section presents two key tools used in comparisons of these sorts: ratios and percentage changes.

Ratios in Economics

The ratio of any one variable to any other variable is unchanged if both variables are doubled or halved; that is, ratios are independent of factors that make both variables large or small. For instance, a commonly used measure in examining saving behavior is the saving ratio, which is the ratio of savings to income. If we want to know whether the typical person living in Switzerland is more thrifty than the average American, we examine the saving rate or ratio in each country. The saving ratio in Switzerland is higher than the saving ratio in the United States. That means the average Swiss saves a higher proportion of income than the average American. Even so, because the U.S. economy is so large, total saving in the United States far exceeds total saving in Switzerland. By using the ratio, we make sure that the effects of the large size of the U.S. economy are taken into account in comparing saving behavior.

SHARES. The discussion of U.S. defense spending in Chapter 1 employed data about the share of defense spending in GNP—that is, the ratio of defense spending to GNP—rather than the absolute level of defense spending. This procedure serves to adjust automatically for changes in the size of the economy over time and to focus on the fraction of the nation's total output that is allocated to defense.

Shares are also used for comparisons at the same point in time. It would be meaningless to compare defense spending in the United States with defense spending in Belgium, for example, since the United States is so much larger. The shares of GNP each devotes to defense can be usefully compared, however. Similarly, we would not be surprised to know that rich people generally spend more dollars on food than poor people; it is more interesting to learn that on average the rich spend a smaller share of their incomes on food than do the poor.

RELATIVE PRICES. In 1960, southern pine timber sold in the United States for $34.50 per 1000 board feet while sugar pine sold for $29.00. By 1984 these prices had risen to $139.40 and $84.30, respectively.[13] Both prices rose substantially over this period, but so did most prices in the economy. From the point of view of a buyer of pine (a furniture company, for instance), what matters more is that the price of southern pine rose substantially relative to the price of sugar pine.

● **The price of good or service A *relative* to the price of some other good or service B is equal to the ratio of the price of A to the price of B.**

The price of southern pine relative to the price of sugar pine was 1.19 (34.50/29.00) in 1960 and 1.65

---

[12] There is a more subtle reason why the behavior of the two indices is different. The CPI is based on the prices of a fixed basket of goods, while each year's GNP deflator is based on the quantities of goods and services produced that year. Thus the GNP deflator for 1986 is calculated using the basket of goods produced in 1986, the 1987 deflator is based on the basket produced in 1987, and so forth.

[13] These numbers are from the *Statistical Abstract of the United States, 1986*, Table 1206.

(139.40/84.60) in 1984. Over this period southern pine became more expensive relative to sugar pine. In 1960, 1000 board feet of southern pine cost as much as 1190 board feet [(34.50/29.00) × 1000] of sugar pine, while in 1984, 1000 board feet of southern pine cost as much as 1650 board feet of sugar pine. Price ratios automatically adjust for changes in the general price level, just as shares of GNP automatically adjust for changes in the scale of the economy.

REAL PRICES. To find out whether the price of, say, southern pine rose more rapidly than the general price level in the United States, we compute its real price.

● The *real price* of any good or service at any time is its dollar price relative to the price level.

Recall that southern pine cost $34.50 (per 1000 board feet) in 1960 and $139.40 in 1984. From Table 2-5, the CPI in 1960 was 88.7 and was 311.1 in 1984. The CPI thus rose by a factor of 3.51 (311.1/88.7) from 1960 to 1984. To get the real price of southern pine in 1984, we divide $139.40 by 3.51, giving $39.72 as the 1984 price of southern pine *expressed in 1960 dollars*.

Thus the real price of southern pine in 1960 dollars increased from $34.50 in 1960 to $39.72 in 1984. The price of southern pine rose more rapidly than the average level of prices over the period 1960–1984.[14]

Percentage Changes

Like ratios, percentage changes are used to eliminate factors that affect both numbers being compared. For instance, Table 2-8 shows percentage changes in real GNP over decades. The percentage change in real GNP over the period 1950–1960 is calculated as follows:

$$\text{Percentage change in real GNP} = \frac{\text{real GNP in 1960} - \text{real GNP in 1950}}{\text{real GNP in 1950}} \times 100\%$$

$$= \frac{1665 - 1204}{1204} \times 100\%$$

$$= 0.383 \times 100\%$$

$$= 38.3\%$$

Percentage changes serve to adjust for differences in units of measurement. They do not use any units (pounds, feet, tractors) and therefore provide comparable measures of changes in two different series of data. We might compare the percentage change in U.S. beef production to the percentage change in the U.S. population. Such a comparison would normally be more informative than a comparison of the absolute increase in population (say, 2 million people) to the absolute increase in beef production (say, 900,000 cattle).

To further illustrate the computation and use of percentage changes, suppose we want to know whether the U.S. economy grew more rapidly in the 1950s, the 1960s, or the 1970s. Table 2-8 shows real GNP at the beginning and end of each of these decades. One simple but misleading way to compare the decades is to compute the *absolute* change in real GNP in each by means of simple subtraction. Thus the absolute change in real GNP from 1950 to 1960 was 1665 − 1204 = 461. Table 2-8 shows that the absolute change in real GNP was greater in the 1970s than in the 1960s, and greater in the 1960s than in the 1950s. This comparison might suggest that the economy grew most rapidly in the 1970s and least rapidly in the 1950s.

However, it is highly misleading to compare absolute changes here. The economy was more than twice as large in 1970 as in 1950, so that a $1 increase in real GNP was *relatively* more important in 1950 than in 1970. A $1204 billion increase in real GNP would have doubled the

TABLE 2-8. Changes in U.S. Real GNP

Year	Real GNP*	Absolute change*	Percentage change
1950	1204		
		461	38.3
1960	1665		
		751	45.1
1970	2416		
		771	31.9
1980	3187		

* In billions of 1982 dollars.
Source: Economic Report of the President, 1987, Table B-2.

---

[14] In Problem 6 we ask you to calculate the change in the real price of sugar pine over the same period.

output of the 1950 economy but would not have come close to doubling the 1970 economy.

In order to make meaningful comparisons, we must adjust for differences in the size of the economy at the start of each decade. We do this by dividing the absolute change in real GNP by its initial value, thus obtaining the *percentage* change (or *relative* change) in aggregate output. The last column in Table 2-8 shows the percentage changes in U.S. real GNP in each of the last three decades. It indicates that the economy in fact grew most rapidly in the 1960s and least rapidly in the 1970s.

Note that the formula for percentage change involves a ratio. As this suggests, percentage changes and changes in ratios are directly related. If beef production increases at a greater percentage rate than population, for instance, beef production per person rises.

GROWTH RATES. In studying changes in economic variables over time, it is useful to look at increases per period of time. We might want to ask whether GNP grew more rapidly between 1983 and 1984 than between 1982 and 1983. To make this comparison, we would have to compute the growth rate of real GNP for each period.

● The *growth rate* of an economic variable is the percentage rate per period (typically per year) by which the variable is increasing or decreasing.

A growth rate is also a percentage change, but it is the percentage change *per period*.

To compute the growth rates of U.S. real GNP from 1982 to 1983 and from 1983 to 1984, we obtain the data for real GNP for the 3 years (in billions of 1982 dollars, real GNP was 3166 in 1982, 3279 in 1983, and 3490 in 1984) and then use the formula for a percentage change from one year to the next. For example, the growth rate of real GNP from 1982 to 1983 is

$$\text{Growth rate of real GNP} = \frac{\text{real GNP in 1983} - \text{real GNP in 1982}}{\text{real GNP in 1982}} \times 100\%$$

$$= \frac{3279 - 3166}{3166} \times 100\%$$

$$= 3.6\%$$

A similar calculation shows that the growth rate of real GNP from 1983 to 1984 was 6.4 percent—higher than the growth rate the previous year and, incidentally, one of the highest on record.[15]

INFLATION RATES. Another frequently used growth rate is the inflation rate.

● The *inflation rate* is the growth rate of the average price level, expressed as the percentage increase or decrease per period (usually a year).

For instance, to calculate the inflation rate of the CPI from January 1984 to January 1985, we need to know the price index in each month. The CPI for January 1984 was 305.2; a year later, in January 1985, it was 316.1. Then we use the usual formula for a percentage change, as follows:

$$\text{Inflation rate} = \frac{\text{CPI in January 1985} - \text{CPI in January 1984}}{\text{CPI in January 1984}} \times 100\%$$

$$= 3.6\%$$

The inflation rate per year can also be calculated for inflation over periods other than a year. For instance, the CPI is announced each month, and the corresponding annual inflation rate is often announced at the same time. Suppose the CPI rose from 316.1 in January 1985 to 317.4 in February 1985. This is an increase of 0.41 percent, or an inflation rate of 0.41 percent per month. If the inflation rate were 0.41 percent per month each month for a year, the price level would rise by 5.0 percent that year.[16] We thus say that inflation from

---

[15] Growth rates *per year* are often calculated from the change in a variable over some period other than a year. This makes it possible to compare rates of change over periods of different lengths, just as always computing the speed of a car in miles per hour makes possible speed comparisons for trips of different lengths. For instance, real GNP increased 31.9 percent over the *decade* 1970–1980, which implies an annual growth rate of 2.8 percent. That is, if GNP had grown at a steady rate of 2.8 percent per year over the period 1970–1980, its total increase over the decade would have been 31.9 percent. For the student with some math, if a variable grows y percent over a period of x years, its annual growth rate is $[100 \times ([1 + (y/100)]^{1/x} - 1)]$ percent.

[16] For the mathematically inclined, the annual inflation rate is obtained by using the formula $[(1.0041)^{12} - 1] \times 100$ percent. This is a special case of the formula introduced in footnote 15.

January to February 1985 was at an annual rate of 5 percent.[17]

4. Developing Economic Laws

Economic theories predict general relations that should hold among economic variables. Data are employed to test those predictions and measure the economic laws that appear to hold. Theory might predict that a fall in the price of fish will increase fish consumption, for instance. One can use data to test this prediction and, if it is found to be correct, to measure how much consumption increases when prices fall. This section explores the use of data in this fashion and discusses limits on our ability to develop universal economic laws.

Time Series and Cross Section Data

The data in Table 2-7 are time series data, showing the values of real and nominal GNP for different years.

● **A *time series* is a collection of measurements of a variable at different points or intervals of time.**

Individual time series can be presented in tables, such as Table 2-7, or in graphs, such as Figure 2-3.[18] Trends and other patterns in the data are usually much easier to see in a graph than in a table. For instance, the fall in real

---

[17] Another useful formula decomposes the growth rate of nominal GNP. As we noted previously, changes in nominal GNP reflect both changes in prices and changes in real output. Expressed in terms of growth rates, the growth rate of nominal GNP is equal to the inflation rate (as measured by the growth rate of the GNP deflator) plus the growth rate of real GNP. Thus if real GNP grows 2 percent per year and the GNP deflator rises 3 percent, nominal GNP increases 5 percent.

[18] If you have not read the appendix to Chapter 1, you should do so before reading the rest of this section.

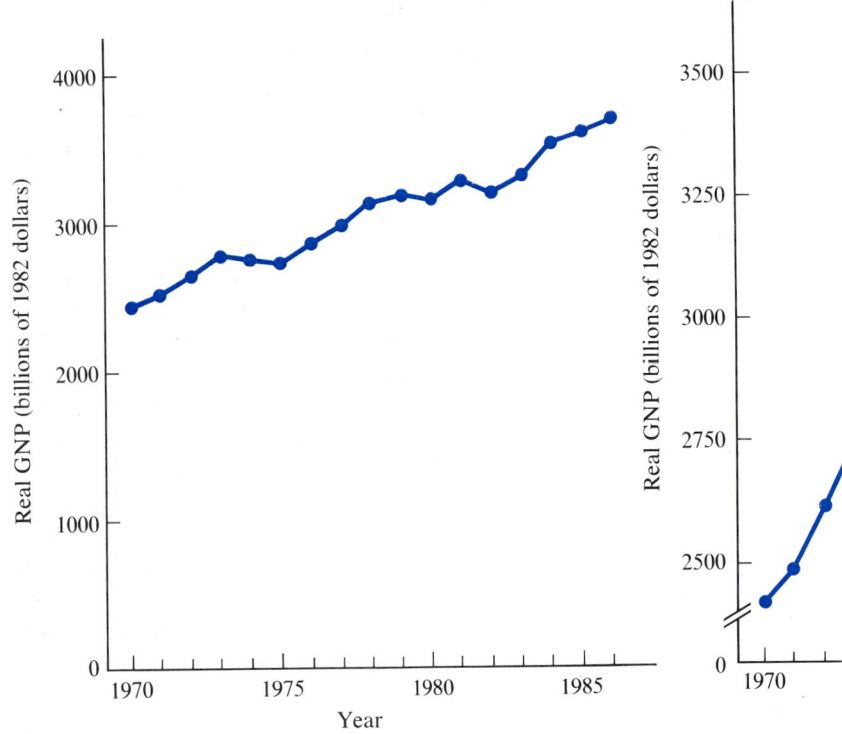

FIGURE 2-3. U.S. Real GNP, 1970–1986. (*Source: Economic Report of the President, 1987*, Table B-2.)

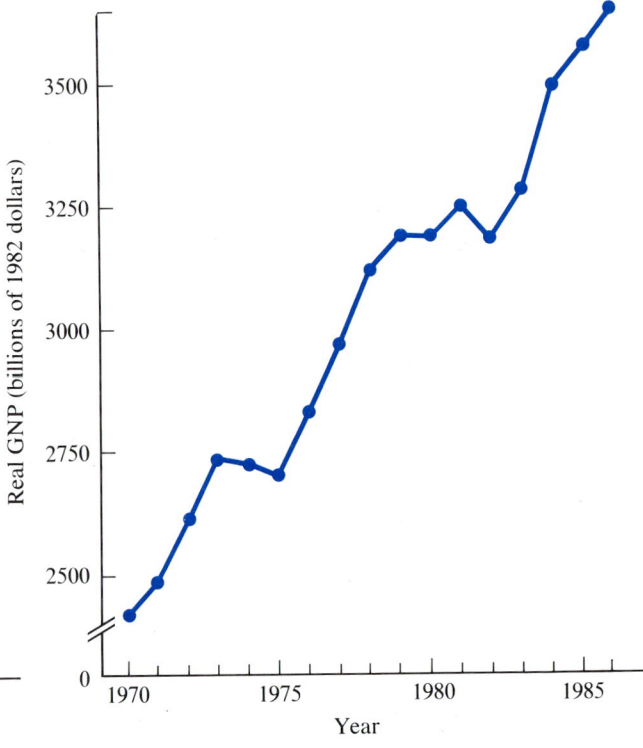

FIGURE 2-4. U.S. Real GNP, 1970–1986. (*Source: Economic Report of the President, 1987*, Table B-2.)

GNP in 1982 stands out clearly in Figure 2-3. On the other hand, it is easier to read exact data values (such as real GNP in 1982) in a table.

Interpreting graphs of economic data can be tricky, since the eye can be misled by simple changes in presentation. Figure 2-4 shows exactly the same data that are shown in Figure 2-3, except that the scale on the vertical axis is much larger. Because the vertical axis in Figure 2-4 has been stretched, real GNP seems to grow faster and to fluctuate more than in Figure 2-3, even though the data are precisely the same. Illusions like this are well known in advertising and politics.[19] Note that there is a gap in the vertical axis in Figure 2-4, indicating that the scale is not continuous and that most of the area between 0 and $2500 billion has been left out. Such a warning should always be present when a special scale of this sort is used.

While time series data allow comparisons over time, cross section data permit comparisons at a single point in time.

● *Cross section data* **are measurements of a variable for different economic units (such as households, firms, states, or nations) at the same point in time.**

Table 2-2 contains cross section data, with households as the economic units, on two variables: income and education. Cross section data can also be shown graphically; Figure 2-5 presents the same information as Table 2-2.[20] The overall positive relation between income and education is easier to see in the graph than in the table, while the table makes the details clearer.

Scatter Diagrams and Econometrics

Figure 2-5 also serves as an example of a scatter diagram.

● **A** *scatter diagram* **is a graph showing the values of two economic variables for several different economic units or time periods.**

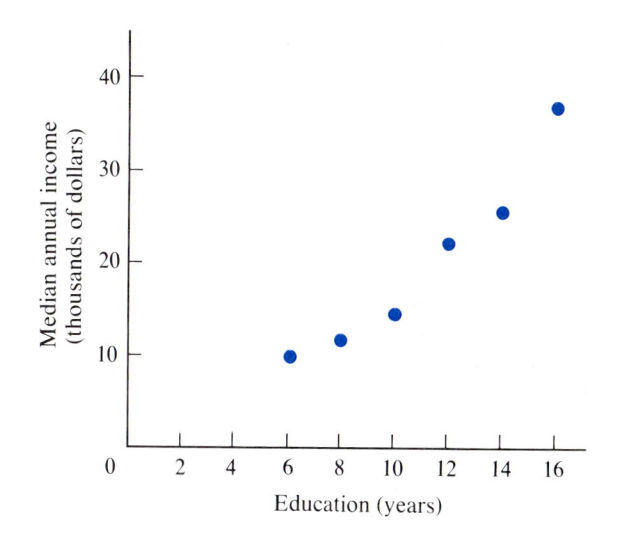

Scatter diagrams reveal at a glance whether there is an obvious relation between the two variables plotted.

Time series data can also be displayed on a scatter diagram. Figure 2-6, for instance, shows some of the recent history of inflation and unemployment that economists and policymakers were trying to understand in 1978. Each dot shows the values of the annual inflation rate (using the GNP deflator to measure the price level) and the annual rate of growth of real GNP for a single year. Each of the 10 black dots corresponds to a year in the 1958–1967 period; each of the 10 colored dots corresponds to a year in the 1968–1977 period. Over the whole 20-year period covered by the figure, no useful relation between the two variables is apparent, especially if the two years with the highest inflation rates are excluded. (These are 1974 and 1975, and world oil prices quadrupled in late 1973.) But the figure does suggest an interesting pattern: It appears that no matter how rapidly real GNP grew, the inflation rate was higher in the second decade than in the first.[21]

---

[19] For examples of the deceptive use of graphs and percentage changes, see Darrell Huff and Irving Geis, *How to Lie with Statistics*, W.W. Norton, New York, 1954, and "Playing with Numbers," *The Economist*, May 31, 1986.

[20] In drawing the figure, we assumed that those with less than 8 years of primary school had on average 6 years of eduction, that those with 1 to 3 years of high school had on average 10 years of education, that those with 1 to 3 years of college had on average 14 years of education, and that all college graduates had 16 years of education.

[21] In the problem section we present more recent data on inflation and unemployment and ask you to relate them to this pattern.

Part One: Introduction

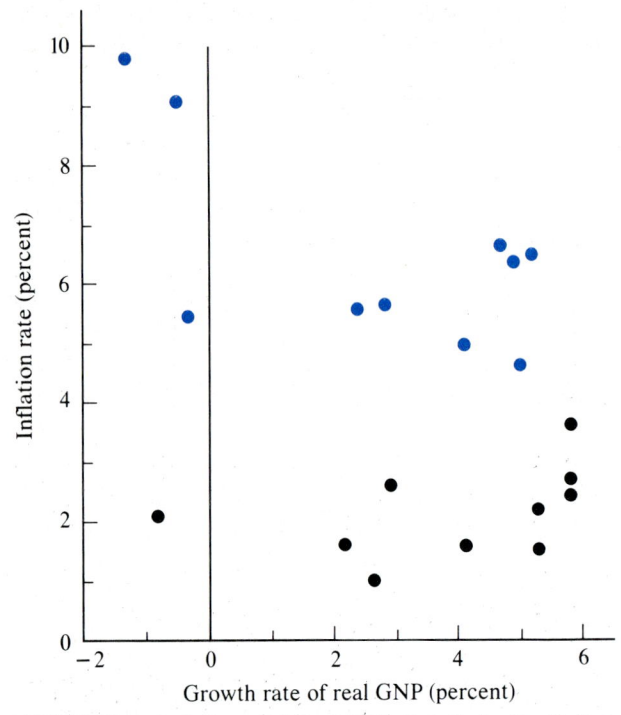

FIGURE 2-6. Inflation and Real GNP Growth in the United States, 1958–1977. The inflation rate (based on the GNP deflator) and the growth rate of real GNP are percentage changes per year. Black dots depict observations for the years 1958–1967; colored dots correspond to the years 1968–1977. (*Source*: *Economic Report of the President, 1986*, Tables B-2 and B-3.)

While scatter diagrams can be used to search for simple relations between pairs of variables, econometric techniques are employed to measure and search for more complex relationships among economic variables. These relationships are expressed in terms of numbers and equations.

● *Econometrics* **is the branch of economics that develops and uses statistical methods to measure relationships among economic variables.**

We do not present econometric techniques in this text, but we do rely on econometric results in describing the facts of economic life. It is thus worthwhile to spend a few paragraphs discussing econometric descriptions of relations among economic variables.

Econometric techniques imply that the data on income and education graphed in Figure 2-5 can be summarized by the following equation:

Median annual
    income   = −8.61 + 2.63 × education
($ thousands)   (years)   (4)

This equation was selected (by a computer) to describe the relation as well as possible on average, but it does not predict median annual income exactly at any level of educational attainment. According to this equation, for instance, the median income of people with 12 years of education should be $22,950 [(−8.61 + 2.63 × 12) × 1000], slightly above the true value (from Table 2-6) of $22,400.

Figure 2-7 is identical to Figure 2-5, except that line *EE* is drawn so that all points on it satisfy equation (4). Figure 2-7 makes it clear that equation (4) is not an exact representation of the relation between income and education in the United States in 1984. But the offsetting advantage is that for any level of education, the equation tells us what is approximately or on average the associated level of income. It thus summarizes the relationship between income and education in numerical terms.

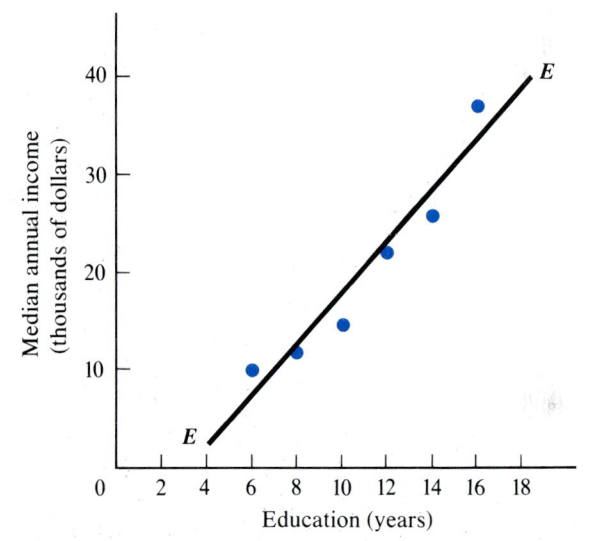

FIGURE 2-7. Median Income and Education, 1984. The fitted line *EE* describes the average relationship between median annual income and educational attainment. (*Source*: Table 2-2.)

Equation (4) tells us that on average each extra year of education was associated with an extra $2630 of household income in 1984. This numerical measure of the relation between income and education cannot easily be obtained by looking at Table 2-2, Figure 2-5, or even Figure 2-7. Numerical measures of this sort are essential for deciding which economic relations are important. If equation (4) had implied that each extra year of education was associated with only an extra $20 of income, for instance, most people would conclude that the relation between income and education is not very important.

There is information not only in the line in Figure 2-7 but also in the position of the individual points relative to the line. Note in particular that the point for those with some college (14 years of education on average) is below the line, while the point for college graduates (16 years of education) is well above the line. Thus people who drop out of college get less return for each extra year of education than those who graduate.

Limits to Understanding

Economics, like medicine, engineering, or any other live field of study, does not yet have a full understanding of everything with which it is concerned. Understanding in economics is limited particularly by the need to rely mainly on nonexperimental data and by the variability of human behavior.

NONEXPERIMENTAL DATA. Scientific theories often predict a relationship between two variables, *given that everything but those two variables remains the same*. For instance, it is reasonable to predict that an individual who studies for an extra year will obtain a higher income when she eventually begins to work, other things equal. "Other things equal" here means that the *only* change that is being considered is that the individual studies for an extra year. It is assumed, for instance, that she does not change her major from accounting to sociology.

In many sciences "other things equal" predictions can be tested by means of controlled experiments. One can see how fertilizer affects corn growth, for instance, by applying different amounts of fertilizer to different rows of corn in the same field. Some experiments have been used in economics. For example, in the 1970s the U.S. Department of Health, Education and Welfare funded large-scale experimental studies in Denver and Seattle concerning the effects of different types of income maintenance (welfare) payments. A less expensive and increasingly popular alternative is to experiment with students, setting up classroom experiments designed to approximate real market situations.[22]

But most data used by economists are not derived from controlled experiments. The data on education and income in Figures 2-5 and 2-7 provide a good illustration. It is clear that the observed differences in income do not reflect only differences in education. Those who graduate from college differ in many other ways from those who don't: On average they got higher Scholastic Aptitude Test (SAT) scores, received better grades in high school, and had wealthier parents. Accordingly, we cannot conclude from the data on education and income that individuals who continue their studies for an extra year should expect to earn an extra $2630 per year as a result. All that the data actually show is that, on average, individuals with an extra year of education had an income in 1984 that was higher by $2630.

Economists must often use sophisticated econometric techniques to attempt to test "other things equal" predictions with real-world data of this sort, and they must search for evidence from the United States and abroad that sheds light on difficult problems. For instance, in Germany in 1923 prices rose by a factor of *10 billion*. That was almost a laboratory experiment in how economies behave when there is inflation.

Nonetheless, there is no guarantee that the real world will always generate data that can discriminate between particular competing theories. From the end of World War II until the mid-1970s, for instance, household incomes in constant dollars generally increased in the United States, the real price of electricity fell steadily, and electricity consumption per household rose steadily.

---

[22] On the income maintenance experiments, see Gary Burtless and Robert H. Haveman, "Policy Lessons from Three Labor Market Experiments," Brookings Institution Reprint #410, 1985. Experiments with students are discussed by Vernon L. Smith, "Experimental Economics: Induced Value Theory," *American Economic Review*, May 1976.

Using these data, economists found it difficult to determine the effects of price changes on electricity consumption, other things equal. Thus, when the real price of electricity began rising rapidly in the mid-1970s, it was not clear whether the use of electricity would fall a lot or a little as a consequence.

In many areas of economics more than one plausible model is consistent with the available evidence. A really good debater can often make his favorite model seem best in such cases. The only defenses against skillful argument are healthy skepticism and a willingness to take an independent look at the data. Eventually, as new evidence is uncovered, the truth will emerge.

HUMAN BEHAVIOR. Geology and astronomy are not experimental sciences either, yet they have established many laws that seem to hold universally. However, people are more complex than rocks, and people, unlike stars, change their behavior as they learn.

It seems to be essentially impossible to predict the response of each and every firm or household to most economic changes—if only because people sometimes make mistakes. It is thus easy to find an individual exception to almost any economic principle, even when average or total behavior can be fairly well predicted.

Economic theory, for instance, predicts that if the price of orange juice goes up slightly, consumers will decide to drink a bit less orange juice, other things equal. In fact, if the price of orange juice goes up from one week to the next, some households will drink more orange juice, not less, because they will find themselves suddenly craving it. And other households will find themselves suddenly bored with orange juice and will stop drinking it altogether. Luckily, these individual idiosyncrasies tend to cancel out on average so that the average response of households to a change in the price of orange juice may be quite predictable.

A more fundamental obstacle to the development of economic laws is that the laws and relations that describe the economy change over time. For instance, sales of bicycles in the United States had been declining for years until, much to everyone's surprise, sales increased rapidly in the early 1970s as people learned about the benefits of exercise. Not only do people change their behavior as they learn, they sometimes learn from economists. If people realize that the government generally cuts taxes when unemployment rises, for instance, they may come to expect a tax cut when they see unemployment creeping up. Or if most economists agree that the government can't stop inflation, firms and households may believe them and start to behave as if prices will continue to rise rapidly for a long time.

■ Economists study human behavior in the world around them. This makes economics both fascinating and difficult. Of all the basic tools discussed in this chapter, the hardest to master is probably the use of simple and to some extent unrealistic models to learn about the complex real world. There is something of an art to this, since one must give up literal realism without losing touch with the main features of reality. However, as the rest of this book illustrates, economists have nonetheless managed to develop models that are simple enough to be understandable yet powerful enough to reveal the basic forces that govern economic life.

Summary

1 Economic variables either influence or describe the allocation of scarce resources. Data are facts, usually numerical, that provide information about economic variables.
2 Models or theories, which are simplified descriptions of reality, are used in economics and other fields to aid understanding and to answer "what if" questions. All models are necessarily unrealistic; good models are those which give correct answers to questions of interest. Data are used both to suggest relationships that should be taken into account by models and to test and evaluate models after they have been developed.
3 The circular flow diagram provides an overview of the organization and working of the economy. Households obtain income by selling to firms the services of the factors of production they own. Firms use the factors of production to produce goods and services for sale to households, whose

income makes it possible for them to buy the goods. Households and firms deal with each other in both the goods and factor markets.

4 Prices and quantities are the basic units of measurement in economics. The product of price and quantity is a dollar amount, or value.

5 The price level is the weighted average level of prices in the economy as a whole. A price index expresses the cost of a given market basket or collection of goods relative to the cost of the same goods in a base year.

6 The consumer price index (CPI) is based on the cost of a market basket of goods that reflects the purchases of a typical urban household. It is the most widely used price or cost of living index.

7 Nominal gross national product (GNP) is the total dollar value of the goods and services produced in the economy within a given period. Nominal GNP can change either because prices change or because physical production changes. Real GNP is the value of the output produced in a given year, calculated using the prices of a given base year. Real GNP is a measure of the economy's physical quantity of production. The GNP deflator is equal to 100 times nominal GNP divided by real GNP. The GNP deflator is a measure of the price level that is based on all goods and services produced in the economy.

8 Ratios (particularly shares, relative prices, and real prices) and percentage changes (particularly growth rates and inflation rates) are widely used in economics to make comparisons over time or among economic units (such as firms, households, states, or nations) at the same time.

9 Graphs of economic data, particularly scatter diagrams, are used to reveal trends, patterns, and possible relations between economic variables. Econometric techniques are used to describe relations between economic variables in terms of numbers and equations.

10 Most economic data are not generated by controlled experiments, and so it is often difficult to test the "other things equal" predictions of theory. Moreover, economics studies human behavior, which varies among people and over time.

Key Terms

Model
Theory
Economic variable
Data
Circular flow of income
Factors of production
Median versus mean
Price
Quantity
Dollar amount
Price level
Price index
Consumer price index (CPI)
Nominal gross national product (GNP)
Real gross national product
Current versus constant dollars
GNP deflator
Relative and real prices
Percentage change
Growth rate
Inflation rate
Time series
Cross section
Scatter diagram
Econometrics

Problems

1 Suppose the weights in the CPI are exactly those given in Table 2-4. (*a*) Suppose that between 1986 and 1990 housing prices go up 20 percent and all other prices are unchanged. By what percentage does the CPI rise between those years? (*b*) Suppose that between 1986 and 1990 the prices of food and beverages, transportation, apparel, and upkeep all go up 20 percent while all other prices remain unchanged. By what percentage does the CPI rise over those 4 years? (*c*) Suppose you are a person who especially loves entertainment and you spend 18 percent of your income on entertainment. Explain why the CPI might not give an accurate measure of your personal cost of living.

2 Suppose the only goods produced in an economy are ice cream and cabbage: The following table shows data on the quantities and prices of output in 1972 and 1986:

	1972		1986	
Good	Price	Quantity	Price	Quantity
Cabbage	0.40	1.2	1.00	2.2
Ice cream	0.25	1.4	1.25	3.0

Prices are in dollars per unit, ice cream output is measured in millions of gallons, and cabbage output is measured in millions of pounds.

(a) Calculate nominal GNP for 1972 and 1986. (b) Calculate real GNP in 1986 with 1972 as the base year. (c) Calculate the GNP deflator for 1986. (d) Which increased by a larger percentage between 1972 and 1986, the deflator for the hypothetical economy in this problem or that for the United States? (Use the data in Table 2-5.)

3 (a) Using the data in Problem 2, calculate the percentages by which the prices of the two goods individually increased over the period; explain why your answer is consistent with the GNP deflator being a price average. (b) Calculate the percentages by which the two quantities increased; explain why your answer is consistent with real GNP being a quantity total.

4 This chapter discusses the relationship between median income and educational attainment extensively. The main "other things equal" variable discussed in the text is the ability level of those who obtain more education. (a) Can you think of other things that should be taken into account but were not? (b) How do you think the fact that those who study longer are older before they get a job affects the data in Table 2-2 and Figure 2-5? (c) Suppose five individuals earn incomes (measured in thousands of dollars) of 2.5, 15.3, 16.5, 17.4, and 19.3, respectively. What is the mean income? What is the median?

5 In 1980, fishermen in Massachusetts received an average of 27.3 cents per pound for cod, 42.4 cents per pound for flounder, and 38.7 cents per pound for haddock. By 1984, these prices had become 37.9 cents, 96.5 cents, and 71.5 cents, respectively. (a) Compute the percentage changes in each of these three prices over this period. (b) Compute the price of cod relative to the price of flounder, the price of flounder relative to that of haddock, and the price of haddock relative to that of cod in 1980 and in 1984. (c) Relate the changes in the relative prices to differences in the percentage changes you computed in (a). (d) Using data on the GNP deflator from Table 2-7, compute the real 1984 prices of cod, flounder, and haddock in 1980 cents per pound

6 (a) Write down from the text the CPI and the price of sugar pine lumber in the years 1960 and 1984. (b) Calculate the real price of sugar pine in 1984, measured in 1960 dollars. (c) Did the real price of sugar pine rise or fall over that period? (d) Consider people building a house and considering whether to use southern or sugar pine in 1960 and in 1984. How would the price changes between those years be likely to affect their decision to use sugar as opposed to southern pine?

7 You have the idea that crime may be related to economic factors. In particular, you believe it may have something to do with people not getting jobs. (a) How would you test your idea? What data would you want and why? (b) Where would you look for the data? (c) What "other things equal" problem would you want to keep in mind?

8 You are on the university football stadium advisory board and have to help set the price for tickets. You want to take in the maximum possible revenue for the football team. Bearing in mind that revenue is equal to price times the quantity of seats sold, describe your "model" of the relationship between the price of tickets and total revenue. (*Note*: This question does not have only one correct answer.)

9 The following data refer to total consumption (spending by households) and total income (after taxes) received by households in the United States, each measured in trillions of current dollars.

	1978	1979	1980	1981	1982	1983	1984	1985
Consumption	1.40	1.57	1.73	1.92	2.05	2.23	2.42	2.58
Income	1.55	1.73	1.92	2.13	2.26	2.42	2.67	2.80

Source: *Economic Report of the President*, *1986*, Table B-25.

(a) Plot the two time series on a graph with time on the horizontal axis. (b) Plot the scatter diagram of the data. (c) Use a ruler to plot a line on the scatter diagram to summarize the relation between these variables. (d) What do (b) and (c) suggest about the relationship between households' income and their spending?

10 Figure 2-6 shows rates of inflation and real GNP growth in the United States through 1977. Data for more recent years are as follows:

Rate of	1978	1979	1980	1981	1982	1983	1984	1985	1986
Inflation	7.3	8.9	9.0	9.7	6.4	3.9	3.8	3.3	2.7
Real growth	5.3	2.5	−0.2	1.9	−2.5	3.6	6.4	2.7	2.5

Source: *Economic Report of the President*, *1987*, Tables B-2 and B-3.

How do these data modify the pattern shown in Figure 2.6? (It will probably be useful to trace Figure 2-6 and plot these additional data on the result.)

11 Discuss the following argument. "Economics starts from an assumption that we know to be wrong, that people behave predictably. We really cannot tell how people will respond to changes in economic variables such as prices or incomes because the response depends very much on individual psychology. It is thus very likely that economists' predictions will be extremely inaccurate. We simply cannot expect anything useful to come out of the field, and out of this course." (Obviously, there is no "correct" answer.)

Chapter 3
Supply, Demand, and the Market

In the United States and in other mixed economies, most decisions about resource allocation are made through *the price system*, in which supply and demand interact in numerous markets for goods and services. Here and in economics generally, "demand" is a shorthand way of describing the behavior of buyers, and "supply" refers to the behavior of sellers.

In this chapter you will learn how the buyers and sellers in a market determine how much of a good or service is produced and sold as well as the price at which purchases and sales occur. The model of demand and supply developed here is very general and can be applied, for example, to the markets for cars, labor, banana splits, haircuts, and baseball players. This chapter will give you the basic tools necessary to analyze the determinants and effects of changes in supply and demand in almost any market.

The general ideas of supply and demand are already part of our everyday language and experience. When there is a bumper wheat crop, the price of wheat falls. When a dealer has too many cars on the lot, she cuts the price. In both these cases we say that price has fallen because the supply of the good on the market has increased. On the other hand, house rentals and hotel rates are higher at the seashore in the summer than in the winter. We usually say that this occurs because demand is higher in summer than in winter. When ticket prices are higher for playoff games than they are during the regular season, we blame it on the greater demand for seats during the playoffs.

But everyday language is too vague to be used in the analysis of market behavior. The term "demand," for instance, is commonly applied to a variety of economically distinct concepts and variables. As Chapter 1 noted, economists use a special vocabulary (or jargon) with precisely defined terms in order to avoid errors and misunderstandings. This chapter presents some of that vocabulary.

After reviewing the notion of a market, we examine buyers' and sellers' behavior in markets for goods and services and show how the interaction of buyers and sellers determines prices and allocates scarce resources. (Since everything in this chapter applies to markets for goods and for services, we shorten our sentences most of the time by speaking of "goods" rather than "goods and services.") We begin by setting out the determinants of demand and supply and then study their interaction using the model of supply and demand analysis. When you have mastered the basic theory of supply and demand presented in this chapter, you will have taken the single most important step toward understanding how mixed and free-market economies work.

1. Markets

The notion of a *market* is central to the analysis of resource allocation through the price system. As you learned in Chapter 1, this term has a broad meaning: A market is any set of arrangements by which buyers and sellers of a good are in contact to trade that good. Usually in any category of goods or services traded in real markets, the goods are not all exactly alike—consider cars, banana splits, and baseball players. However, markets are always defined over an aggregate of similar products. The best aggregate to use in any particular case is determined by the problem to be solved. Thus to explain shortstops' salaries, we would focus on the supply of and demand for shortstops, while to explain the general level of wages and salaries in the economy, we would work with the broader market for all labor services.

Markets may be specific places where buyers and sellers meet to trade, such as the produce markets in most large cities, but buyers and sellers in a single market may also be widely dispersed. In the market for used cars, for instance, dealers and private sellers are on the selling side. Buyers come into contact with sellers by reading newspaper advertisements, visiting dealers, looking at notices on bulletin boards or on the cars themselves, and hearing from friends about people who want to sell.

Some markets, such as the New York Stock Exchange, operate through intermediaries or traders. Buyers and sellers of stocks call in their orders from all over the country—indeed, from all over the world—and can have those orders carried out within minutes. The markets for internationally traded commodities such as wheat and copper work largely over the telephone, with potential buyers and sellers talking to one another, and making deals, from all around the world.

Market prices are set in many different ways. In the used car market the buyer and seller bargain with each other over the price. In auctions buyers compete against each other until the final price is reached. In supermarkets sellers fill the shelves and post prices, which buyers in turn decide to take or leave.

Despite these apparent differences, all markets have a common, basic economic core. The supply and demand model simplifies reality by concentrating on these core features.

2. The Demand Curve

"Demand" is a general term describing the behavior of buyers and potential buyers of a good. To understand how markets operate, it is necessary to work with more precise definitions. The first of these is the quantity demanded.

● **The *quantity demanded* of a good is the amount that buyers are willing to buy in some period (day or year, for example). Quantity demanded depends on the price of the good and on other factors, including the prices of other goods and buyers' incomes and tastes.**

"Willing to buy" here means that buyers would actually be willing and able to pay for the quantity demanded if it were available.

It is important to distinguish between the quantity *demanded* and the quantity actually *bought*. If some government agency set the price of blue jeans at $1 per pair, the quantity *demanded* in any period would probably be very large. But since few sellers would supply jeans at this price, the quantity actually *bought* by consumers would probably be very small, since buyers would be unable to find as many jeans as they were willing to buy. The quantity demanded is determined only by buyers' behavior, while, as we discuss later in this chapter, both buyers and sellers determine the quantity bought.

Price plays the leading role in the supply-demand model. Experience suggests that typically the quantity of a good demanded increases when its price goes down and decreases when its price goes up, all other things equal. There are two main reasons for this. First, the lower the price, the greater the number of people likely to buy the good. Second, the lower the price, the more any one person is likely to buy within any given period.

The relationship between price and quantity demanded for any good may be summarized in the demand schedule for that good.

● The *demand schedule* **is the relationship between the quantity of a good demanded and the price of that good. Other factors that may affect the quantity demanded, such as the prices of other goods, are held constant in drawing up the demand schedule.**

The demand schedule shows how much buyers would want to purchase at each of a set of prices.

Table 3-1 shows the demand schedule for a hypothetical example: fish in the Chicago area. The first and second columns together define the demand schedule for fish by showing the relationship between the quantity demanded and price.

The first column in Table 3-1 shows a range of prices, from $0, when fish is free, to $5 per pound of fish. The second column shows the quantity demanded at each price. The higher the price, the smaller the quantity demanded. The quantity demanded is obviously largest when fish is free. If fish were free, most households would choose a diet with plenty of fish and relatively little meat or poultry. The quantity demanded of fish would be high, but it would not be unlimited. Nobody would want to eat only fish or have huge amounts of fish lying around the house, possibly spoiling. Table 3-1 shows a hypothetical quantity demanded of 15 million pounds per week when fish is free.

At $4 per pound, the quantity demanded is only 3 million pounds. As fish becomes more expensive, households substitute other foods, such as chicken and pizza, for fish in their diets. At a yet higher price of $5 per pound, the quantity demanded goes down to zero. People are no longer eating fish.[1]

Figure 3-1 shows the same relationship as Table 3-1 in the form of a graph called a demand curve.[2] Such graphs are the most common way of showing the relationship between quantity demanded and price.

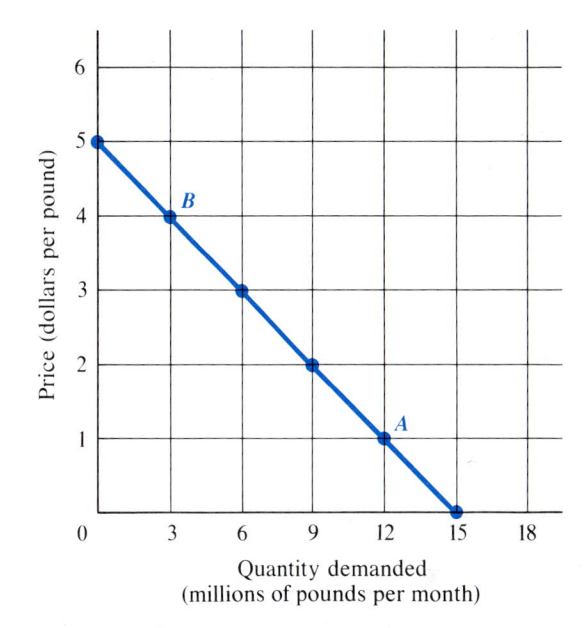

FIGURE 3-1. The Demand Curve. The diagram shows how the prices and quantities demanded in Table 3-1 are translated into a demand curve. The vertical axis measures price, and the horizontal axis measures quantity demanded. We can pick a price in the table, say, $1, and observe the corresponding quantity demanded: 12 million pounds per month. Point A shows that particular price-quantity combination. Similarly, point B shows a price of $4 per pound and the corresponding quantity demanded: 3 million pounds per month. Plotting all the data in the table and connecting the resulting points yields the demand curve, which is downward-sloping because quantity demanded falls when price rises.

TABLE 3-1. The Demand Schedule for Fish in the Chicago Area

Price, $/lb	Quantity demanded, millions of lb/month
0	15
1	12
2	9
3	6
4	3
5	0

---

[1] In practice it would take a much higher price than $5 to drive the quantity of fish demanded all the way down to zero. The quantity demanded of caviar is positive even at a price of several hundred dollars per pound, for instance.

[2] Because the demand curve contains exactly the same information as the demand schedule, economists sometimes refer to it also as the demand schedule.

● The *demand curve* shows graphically the quantity of a good demanded at each price, with other factors that affect quantity demanded held constant. The demand curve is typically downward-sloping.

In Figure 3-1 prices, corresponding to the first column of Table 3-1, are measured on the vertical axis. Quantities, in millions of pounds per month, are measured on the horizontal axis. Each combination of price and quantity in Table 3-1 is shown by a dot in Figure 3-1. For instance, point A shows that at a price of $1, quantity demanded is 12 million pounds. Point B shows that quantity demanded is 3 million pounds when price is $4.

3. The Supply Curve

Just as "demand" is a general term describing the behavior of buyers, "supply" is a general term describing the behavior of actual and potential sellers of a good. We define quantity supplied, the supply schedule, and the supply curve by analogy to the case of demand.

● The *quantity supplied* of a good is the amount sellers are willing to sell in some period (day or year, for example). Quantity supplied depends on the price of the good and on other factors, primarily the prices of the inputs used in production and the techniques of production available to sellers.

"Willing to sell" here means that sellers would actually be willing and able to deliver the quantity supplied if there were enough buyers.

Just as it is important to distinguish between the quantity demanded and the quantity bought, so it is important to distinguish here between the quantity *supplied* and the quantity *sold*. To return to the blue jeans example, suppose the price of jeans were fixed by law at $100 per pair. Then the quantity *supplied* would probably be large, since jeans can be produced for much less than $100, and at that price profits would be high. But because few consumers would be willing to buy jeans at this price, the quantity actually *sold* would probably be much smaller. The quantity supplied is determined by seller behavior alone, while buyers and sellers together determine the quantity sold.

Quantity supplied usually increases with the price of the good. The higher the price at which fish can be sold, the more resources—ships, electronic equipment, and labor—will be used in fishing, and the more fish will be offered for sale. As the price of fish rises, fishermen use their boats more intensively and new fishermen come into the market. At higher prices it may be profitable for sellers to import fish from other parts of the country and even from abroad. If the price of fish falls, fishermen become less willing to incur the costs and put forth the effort necessary to catch fish, so that quantity supplied falls.

The supply schedule summarizes the relation between price and the quantity supplied. It describes sellers' behavior in the same way that the demand schedule describes buyers' behavior.

● The *supply schedule* is the relationship between the quantity of a good supplied and its price. Other factors that may affect the quantity supplied, such as the prices of inputs and available production techniques, are held constant in drawing up the supply schedule.

The supply schedule shows how much sellers will want to sell at each of a set of prices.

Table 3-2 shows a hypothetical supply schedule for fish in the Chicago area. The quantity of fish supplied rises as price increases. No fish are offered for sale at a price of zero; indeed, the price has to rise above $1 before any fish appear on the market. At $2 per pound, the quantity supplied is already 3 million pounds per month. Quantity supplied continues rising as price increases.

As in the study of buyers' behavior, it is useful to represent sellers' behavior graphically. The most widely used representation is the supply curve, which is simply a graph of the supply schedule.

TABLE 3-2. The Supply Schedule for Fish in the Chicago Area

Price, $/lb	Quantity supplied, millions of lb/week
0	0
1	0
2	3
3	6
4	9
5	12
6	15

- **The *supply curve*** shows graphically the quantity of a good supplied at each price, with other factors that affect quantity supplied held constant. The supply curve is typically upward-sloping.

The position and slope of the supply curve are determined mainly by the costs of producing the good. Firms will not be willing to supply goods unless the price covers the cost of production. The supply curve slopes upward because more resources have to be drawn into an industry to increase quantity supplied, and this generally increases costs. In order to catch more fish, fishermen have to work longer hours and must be rewarded for doing so with overtime pay or higher wages. If more fishermen must be hired, it may be necessary to raise wages. As fishing boats and equipment are worked harder, more breakdowns occur, and more maintenance is required.

Figure 3-2, which is based on Table 3-2, shows the supply curve for fish in the Chicago area. Once again, price is on the vertical axis and quantity per month is on the horizontal axis. Each dot on the supply curve represents a combination of price and quantity supplied, as shown in Table 3-2. For example, point *A* shows that at a price of $4 per pound, 9 million pounds of fish will be supplied per month.

TABLE 3-3. Demand and Supply Schedules and Market Equilibrium

Price ($/lb)	(2) Quantity demanded	(3) Quantity supplied	(4) = (2) − (3) Excess demand	Direction of price change
0	15	0	15	Rising
1	12	0	12	Rising
2	9	3	6	Rising
3	6	6	0	Constant
4	3	9	−6	Falling
5	0	12	−12	Falling
6	0	15	−15	Falling

(all in millions of pounds per month)

4. The Interaction of Supply and Demand: Market Equilibrium

The actual price in any market and the quantity actually bought and sold are determined by the interaction of supply and demand. To show how this works, Table 3-3 combines the demand and supply schedules of Tables 3-1 and 3-2. At low prices the quantity demanded exceeds the quantity supplied; people want to buy more fish than suppliers are willing to sell. At high prices quantity demanded is less than quantity supplied; suppliers would like to sell a lot of fish, but buyers are not willing to buy large quantities at high prices.

Column (4) shows the difference between columns (2) and (3). That difference—the excess of quantity demanded over quantity supplied—is called the *excess demand* for fish. Excess demand is positive at low prices, meaning that quantity demanded exceeds quantity supplied. That is, if the price were somehow fixed at a low level, there would be a *shortage* of fish; buyers would not be able to find all the fish they would want to buy. Excess demand is negative at high prices, meaning that quantity demanded is less than quantity supplied. When excess demand is negative, we say there is an *excess supply* in

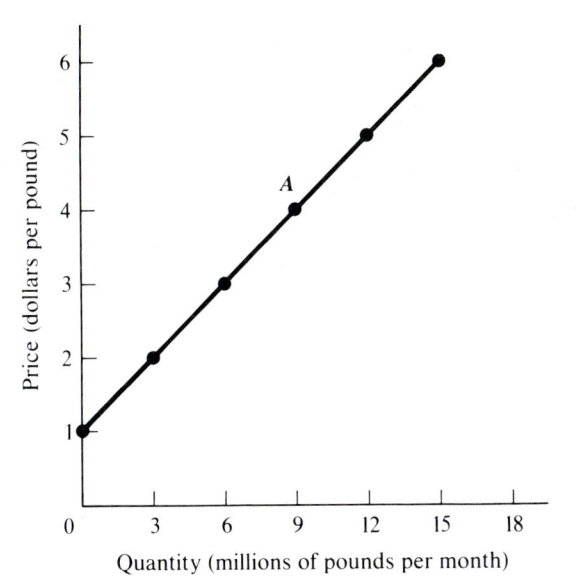

FIGURE 3-2. The Supply Curve. The prices and corresponding quantities supplied in Table 3-2 can be plotted to yield the supply schedule shown here. Point *A*, for instance, shows that if the price is $4 per pound, 9 million pounds per month will be supplied. The supply schedule is upward-sloping, showing that as price increases, so does the quantity supplied.

the market. If the price were somehow fixed at a high level, there would be a *surplus* of fish; sellers would not be able to find enough buyers to take all the fish they would want to supply.

Table 3-3 shows that at a price of $3 per pound, quantity supplied is equal to quantity demanded. At that price there is neither an excess demand nor an excess supply of fish. Sellers can find customers for all the fish they want to supply, and buyers can obtain all the fish they want to buy.

● **The *equilibrium price* is the price at which the quantity demanded is equal to the quantity supplied. This quantity is accordingly the *equilibrium quantity*.**

Thus Table 3-3 shows that $3 per pound is the equilibrium price and 6 million pounds per month is the equilibrium quantity. At any price below the equilibrium price, there is an excess demand, or a shortage. At any price above the equilibrium price, there is an excess supply, or a surplus.

Figure 3-3 puts together the demand and supply curves of Figures 3-1 and 3-2 in order to illustrate graphically the determination of market equilibrium. The demand curve, *D*, is to the right of the supply curve, *S*, for prices below $3 per pound. This shows graphically that there is excess demand at low prices. At prices above $3 per pound, the supply curve is to the right of the demand curve, indicating that there is excess supply. The curves intersect at point *E*, showing that the quantity demanded equals the quantity supplied at a price of $3 per pound. Point *E* is accordingly called the equilibrium point. Point *E* shows both the equilibrium price—$3, read off the vertical axis—and the equilibrium quantity—6 million pounds of fish per month, read off the horizontal axis—in the Chicago-area fish market.

Movement to Equilibrium

An economist using the supply-demand analysis described here would predict that the price of fish in Chicago will be $3 per pound and that 6 million pounds of fish will be bought and sold per month. The reason is that if price is not equal to $3 per pound, market forces will move it to that level.

To see how this occurs, suppose first that the price of fish is $2 per pound. As Figure 3-4 shows, there will be an excess demand for fish at that price, shown graphically as the distance *AB*—the excess of quantity demanded over quantity supplied. At a price of $2, the excess demand will be 6 million pounds. (This can also be seen in Table 3-3.)

When quantity demanded exceeds quantity supplied, sellers find themselves running out of fish. Customers show up to buy but cannot do so. Sellers soon realize that they can raise the price and still sell as much as they want to supply (that is, they can actually sell the quantity *supplied*) at the new higher price. Thus any time there is excess demand, price will rise. The upward-pointing vertical black arrow shows that the price rises whenever there is excess demand—whenever the price is below $3.

Suppose alternatively that price is above the equilibrium level, say, $4 per pound. In this situation there will be an excess supply, shown by the distance *CF* in Figure 3-4, equal to 6 million pounds. Sellers want to sell 12 million pounds of fish per month at this price, but quantity *demanded* is only 6 million pounds. Suppliers must cut price to get rid of the excess fish. Thus price will tend to fall, as the downward-pointing black vertical arrow shows, whenever there is excess supply.

Thus if the market price is not equal to the equilibrium price, the actions of buyers and sellers move it toward the equilibrium price. When price is equal to $3, in equilibrium, sellers have no reason to change price because they are selling as much as they want, neither more nor less. Buyers are buying exactly the amount they want, so there is no pressure from buyers that will tend to change price. At equilibrium, and only there, forces tending to bring about price changes are exactly balanced.

The details of price and quantity changes out of equilibrium may be affected in complex ways by differences in market organization of the sort discussed in section 1; auction markets for rare paintings will move toward equilibrium differently from the way markets for used cars do. But we need not worry about these complexities in order to understand the determination of market equilibrium. The equilibrium point is what we expect to observe. The supply-demand model is thus used in practice to forecast market behavior by forecasting equilibrium prices and quantities.

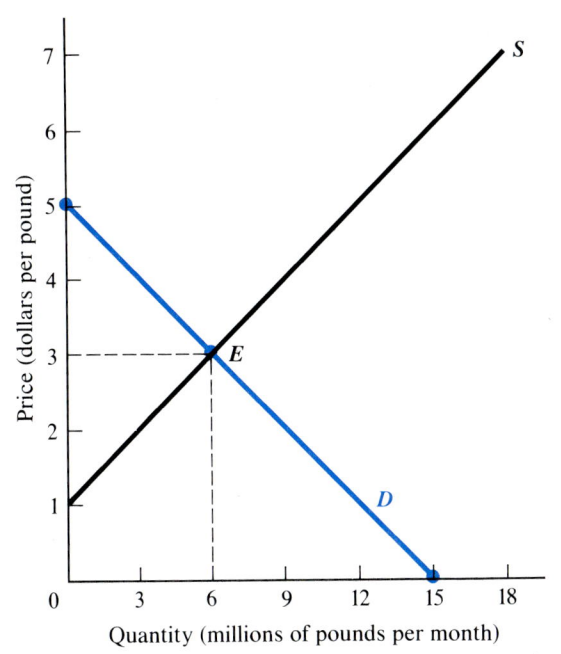

FIGURE 3-3. Demand, Supply, and Equilibrium. The figure shows the demand curve, D, from Figure 3-1 and the supply curve, S, from Figure 3-2. The equilibrium point is labeled E. At that point quantity supplied is equal to quantity demanded; the equilibrium quantity is thus 6 million pounds per month. The equilibrium price is $3 per pound.

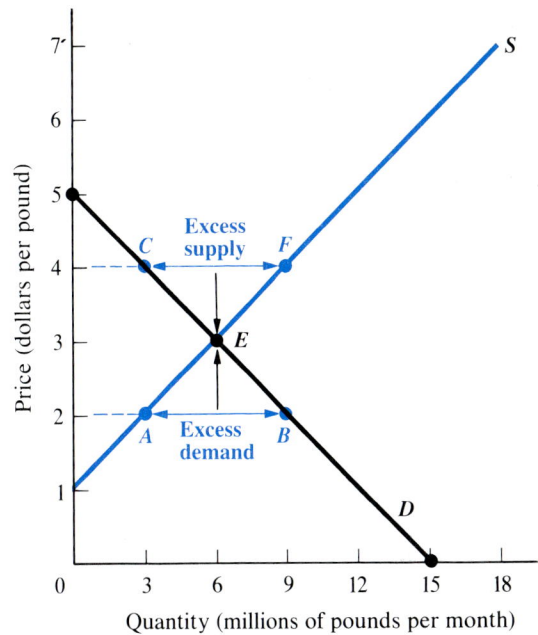

FIGURE 3-4. Excess Demand, Excess Supply, and Price Adjustment. At prices above the equilibrium price of $3, there is an excess supply of goods (a surplus), and this causes sellers to cut price. At prices below $3, there is an excess demand (a shortage), and the price is raised. These price changes are shown by the vertical arrows. Only at the equilibrium point does the price remain constant.

Quantity Demanded versus Quantity Bought

A market is in equilibrium when quantity demanded is equal to quantity supplied. It is easy to confuse quantity demanded with the quantity bought, and quantity supplied with the quantity sold. Suppose the price of fish were $2. Suppliers would bring only 3 million pounds to market each month. Demanders would rush to buy all the fish available. (They would want to buy more.) Quantity bought and quantity sold would each be equal to 3 million pounds per month.

Indeed, quantity bought is always equal to quantity sold at any price, since in every sale there is always a buyer and a seller, and the amount bought in each transaction is equal to the amount sold. But that does not mean the market is in equilibrium at any price.

For instance, when price is $2, buyers would like to buy 9 million pounds of fish, not 3 million. Quantity *demanded* is 9 million pounds while quantity *bought* is only 3 million pounds per month, since no more is offered for sale. The fact that quantity bought is always equal to quantity sold thus says nothing whatsoever about whether a market is in equilibrium. A market is in equilibrium whenever quantity demanded is equal to quantity supplied, not whenever quantity bought is equal to quantity sold.

Stock market reports on the evening news provide a familiar example of the confusion between quantities bought and sold and quantities demanded and supplied. These reports often explain that the price of a stock fell that day because there was "heavy selling." Such statements make no sense, because just as many shares are bought as are sold every day; heavy selling implies heavy buying and vice versa. What such a report means to say is that prices fell, say, from $50 per share to $49, because *at the original price* ($50) there was an excess supply of the stock. Price went down to the equilibrium level ($49) at which quantity demanded was equal to quantity supplied.

5. Behind the Demand Curve

Demand and supply curves are drawn holding everything but market price constant. When other factors that affect quantities demanded and supplied change, the quantities demanded and supplied at each price change, and the equilibrium price and quantity also change. This is shown graphically as shifts in the demand and supply curves, which change the equilibrium point. Thus to understand why prices and quantities observed in real markets change, we have to go "behind" the demand and supply curves and consider the factors other than price that determine quantities demanded and supplied.

Four such factors are important determinants of buyer behavior; economists describe these as "demand side" influences.

- Prices of related goods
- Consumers' incomes
- Consumers' tastes
- Expected future prices

In the rest of this section we discuss each of these determinants in turn.

Prices of Related Goods

The quantity demanded of any particular good will be affected by changes in the prices of related goods. Changes in the prices of alternative foods such as beef and chicken will affect the quantity of fish demanded, for instance.

An increase in the price of chicken causes some consumers to eat fish more often and chicken less often than before; they *substitute* fish for chicken in their diets. This means that at any price of fish, the quantity of fish demanded increases. This change in the demand schedule is shown graphically in Figure 3-5.

The new demand curve for fish, D', lies everywhere to the right of the old demand curve, D, reflecting the in-

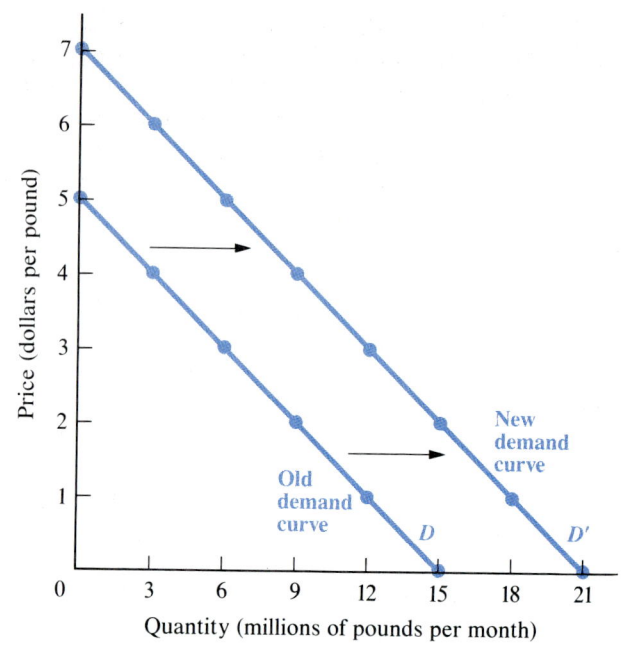

FIGURE 3-5. An Increase in the Price of Chicken Shifts the Demand Curve for Fish. An increase in the price of chicken increases the quantity of fish demanded at each price. Thus the entire demand curve for fish shifts to the right. The old demand curve is D, and the new demand curve, which corresponds to a higher price of chicken, is D'.

crease in quantity demanded caused by the rise in the price of chicken. For instance, at a price of $1, the quantity of fish demanded is now 18 million pounds per month instead of the 12 million pounds it was when chicken was cheaper. An increase in the price of chicken is thus shown graphically as *shifting* the demand curve for fish to the right.

The effect of a change in the price of one good on the demand schedule of another depends on whether the goods are substitutes or complements.

● **Goods are *substitutes* if an increase in the price of one good raises the quantity demanded of the other at every price. Goods are *complements* if an increase in the price of one good lowers the quantity demanded of the other.**[3]

---

[3] These definitions are not technically precise, but they give the basic meanings of the concepts and are adequate for most applications.

In the chicken-fish case, fish is a substitute for chicken. Beef is also a substitute for fish. Movies are a substitute for television. Taxis are substitutes for buses. There is an almost endless number of possible pairs of substitutes.

On the other hand, gasoline and cars are complements. When the price of gasoline goes up, the quantity of cars demanded falls. Other complements are coffee and nondairy creamer, hammers and nails, shoes and shoelaces, beer and pretzels. These are goods that tend to be used together. While an increase in the price of a substitute shifts the demand curve for a good to the *right*, an increase in the price of a complement shifts the demand curve to the *left*.

Aside from tartar sauce, there seem to be few complements for fish in the United States. That is, it is hard to think of many goods for which the quantity demanded would increase noticeably if the price of fish fell. The difficulty of thinking of a complement for fish suggests correctly that goods are typically substitutes and that complementarity, while present in some instances, is less often important.

The invention of new products changes the quantities demanded of existing complements and substitutes. The invention of the compact disk player, the personal computer, and light beer affected quantities demanded in related markets. When a new good or service appears, it is as if its price had fallen from infinity (making it effectively impossible to buy) to an affordable range. Thus the demand curve for substitute goods shifts to the left. The demand curve for complements will shift to the right—unless the innovation reduces the need for the complement. For instance, an invention that makes cars more fuel-efficient may shift the demand curves for both motorcycles and gasoline to the left.

Consumers' Incomes

When a consumer's income rises, he will typically want to spend more. He will demand more of most—but not all—goods.

● A *normal good* is a good for which the quantity demanded at every price increases when income rises. An *inferior good* is a good for which quantity demanded falls when income rises.

Inferior goods are typically goods for which there are alternatives of higher quality or greater convenience. For instance, intercity bus travel is an inferior good. As their incomes rise, people generally switch from riding buses to driving their own cars or traveling by air. Plain white bread is another inferior good, at least in the United States today.[4] As incomes rise, households buy fancier breads or buy rolls, or else they get their calories from more expensive foods such as meat.

Because an increase in the incomes of consumers who are potential buyers in a market raises quantity demanded at each price, it is shown graphically as shifting the demand curve for normal goods to the right. Similarly, an increase in consumers' incomes has the effect of shifting the demand curve for inferior goods to the left, since quantity demanded is lower at each price.

THE NUMBER OF CONSUMERS. Holding constant the average income of potential buyers, the greater the number of consumers in a market, the greater the quantity demanded of any good at each price. Thus an increase in the number of consumers will shift the demand curve to the right. A reduction in the number of consumers will shift the demand curve to the left.

Consumers' Tastes

Consumers' tastes or preferences are a major factor determining the quantity of any good demanded. Consumers' preferences are shaped in part by society, habit, education, and advertising. For instance, the quantity of haircuts demanded is determined in part by social conventions about how long hair should be worn. The quantity of textiles demanded to produce skirts depends in part on fashion. Increasing health and fitness consciousness has increased the quantities demanded of jogging equipment, exercise centers, and natural foods while reducing the quantities demanded of pastries and other high-calorie foods.

Habits and conventions typically change quite slowly. Fashions may change rapidly. Whatever the reason,

---

[4] In the Middle Ages in Europe, when incomes were very low by current standards, white bread made from wheat was a luxury for most people. When their incomes fell, people switched to whole wheat bread or to bread made from other, less nourishing grains.

when consumers' tastes or preferences for any good change, the demand curve for that good shifts accordingly.

Expected Future Prices

The quantity of a good demanded within any given period depends not only on prices in that period but also on prices expected in future periods. For instance, the quantity of cars demanded this month will be higher at any given price if car prices are expected to rise next month. Similarly, the quantity of cars demanded this month depends also on the prices consumers expect to pay for gasoline in the future. If gasoline prices are expected to be much higher in the future, the quantity of cars demanded at any given price this month will be lower than it would be if gas prices were not expected to rise.

Expected future incomes will also affect quantities demanded in the current period. If people believe their incomes will rise in the near future, they will increase the quantity of goods they want to buy at any given price this period.

6. Shifts of the Demand Curve

Changes in the factors that determine the demand schedule alter that schedule or, in graphic terms, shift the demand curve. Changes in the demand schedule for any good in turn change the equilibrium price and the equilibrium quantity of the good produced. Two examples will show how the the supply-demand diagram can be used to analyze this process.

An Increase in the Price of a Substitute

What happens to the price of fish when the price of chicken rises? This may sound like a riddle, but it is a serious question in economics. If the price of chicken increases, the quantity of fish demanded at every price will rise. Buyers will want to consume more fish. But the costs of producing fish will not have changed, and the quantity of fish supplied will increase only if its price rises. Thus an increase in the price of chicken will raise

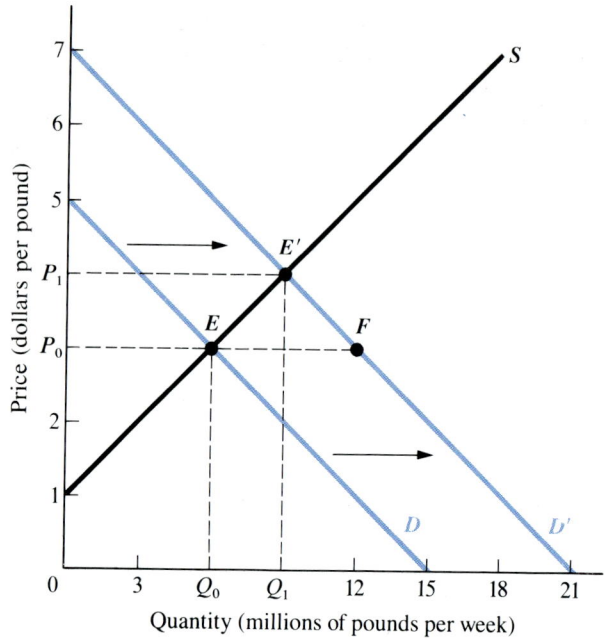

FIGURE 3-6. An Increase in the Price of Chicken Raises the Equilibrium Price of Fish. The increase in the price of chicken shifts the demand curve for fish from D to D'. At each price, the quantity of fish demanded increases. At the initial equilibrium price of \$3 (P_0) there is now an excess demand of 6, equal to the distance EF. Price therefore rises, and the quantity of fish supplied increases. The new equilibrium is at point E', with the equilibrium price equal to \$4 (P_1) and the equilibrium quantity equal to 9 million pounds per month (Q_1).

both the equilibrium price of fish and the equilibrium quantity of fish bought and sold.

Let us now show this graphically. Figure 3-6 adds the supply curve to Figure 3-5, which showed how an increase in the price of chicken shifts the demand curve for fish. Before the price of chicken increases, the demand curve is D, and equilibrium is represented by point E, with the equilibrium price equal to P_0 (\$3 per pound) and the equilibrium quantity equal to Q_0 (6 million pounds per month).

Now the price of chicken rises. The effect is shown as a shift of the demand curve for fish to the right, to D'. At each price, quantity demanded on D' is 6 (million lb) greater than on D. At the initial equilibrium price, P_0, there is thus an excess demand for fish of 6. This is shown as the distance EF in Figure 3-6. If the price of fish does not change, buyers will be unable to find all the fish they want to purchase, since sellers will not be willing to supply that much. As we mentioned earlier, sellers will react to the resulting shortages by raising price.

Price will rise until quantity demanded equals quantity supplied; at that point the market is in equilibrium again. Figure 3-6 shows graphically that the new market equilibrium is depicted by point E', which is to the northeast of E. Sellers have raised price to P_1, the new equilibrium level, and the price increase has reduced the quantity demanded from 12 (at price P_0) to Q_1. From Figure 3-6 we see that P_1 is \$4 (per pound) and Q_1 is 9 (million lb); after the demand curve has shifted, quantity demanded is equal to quantity supplied at a price of \$4. The equilibrium price is higher than it was before the increase in the price of chicken, and the equilibrium quantity is also higher.

The price rise from P_0 to P_1 does two things. First, it reduces the quantity of fish demanded as consumers in effect move up along the new demand curve D'. (Box 3-1 emphasizes the importance of the distinction between a *shift of* a demand curve and a *movement along* a given demand curve.) Second, it increases the quantity supplied as producers respond to the increased price. The shift in the demand curve thus results in consumers obtaining more fish, but to do so they must pay a higher price in order to persuade suppliers to produce more.

This example hints at why economists refer to the price *system*: An increase in one price leads to an increase in another, suggesting—correctly—that prices in many different markets are interrelated. When the price of chicken goes up, the price of fish goes up, and so do the prices of other substitutes, such as beef and pork.

These interconnections among markets become very clear when disease or bad weather affects a major crop or foodstuff. Suppose, for example, that the price of chicken increased because a disease killed many chickens. Consumers would substitute other foods, such as fish, pizza, and beef, increasing the quantities of those goods they demanded. But this would lead to increases in the prices of substitutes for chicken. Graphically, this is depicted as shifts of the demand curves for these other foods to the right. Although the disease affected only chickens, prices would rise in many other markets as well, reflecting a general increase in the scarcity of meat.

This example also suggests how prices allocate resources. If a central planner in a command economy were faced with a reduction in the number of chickens with which to feed the population, she would use alternative food sources—and would send out orders to fishermen, ranchers, and others to increase their production to make up for the lost chicken meat. That is precisely what the price system achieves. The increased prices of substitute goods tell sellers to produce more fish, beef, and other chicken substitutes. Market prices act in exactly the same way as the orders of a central planner, but they operate without central direction, "as if by an invisible hand."[5]

Figure 3-6 shows how an increase in the price of a substitute shifts the demand curve for a good to the

---

[5] As Chapter 1 noted, this famous phrase is from Adam Smith's classic *Wealth of Nations*, published in 1776.

Box 3-1. Movements along the Demand Curve versus Shifts of the Demand Curve

The demand curve *shifts* when any of the factors that affect quantity demanded (other than the price of the good) change. Such shifts show the responses of consumers to changes in the prices of other goods, income, tastes, and so forth. Figure 3-6, for instance, shows the demand curve for fish shifting from D to D' when the price of chicken rises.

In contrast, a movement *along* a demand curve shows the response of quantity demanded to a change in the price of the good itself. In Figure 3-6 the movement from F to E' is a movement along the demand curve as consumers respond to the price increase from \$3 to \$4 per unit by cutting back the quantity of fish demanded.

Why does the difference matter? A *shift* of the demand curve causes equilibrium price and quantity to change, but *movements along* the demand curve are just part of the process by which the market comes into equilibrium.

right, causing both its price and its quantity to increase. You should be able to show that an increase in the price of a complement is depicted as a shift in the demand curve to the left and that it causes both price and quantity to fall.

The Effects of a Reduction in Income

When consumers' incomes fall, the quantity of a normal good demanded is reduced at all prices. Graphically, this is shown as a shift of the demand curve to the left. Figure 3-7 depicts the impact of a fall in income on the demand for a normal good: The demand curve shifts to the left from D to D'.

At the initial equilibrium price in the market depicted in Figure 3-7, P_0, the quantity demanded, has fallen, implying an excess supply of the good. This is shown as the distance AE in the figure. Suppliers find themselves with unsold goods, and they cut price and production.

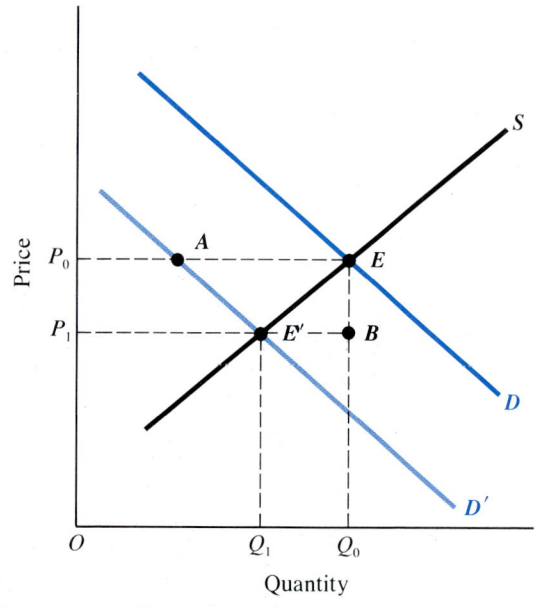

FIGURE 3-7. Effects of a Reduction in Income. When consumers' incomes fall, the demand curve shifts to the left, from D to D'. The supply curve, S, does not shift, so that there is excess supply at the initial price equal to the distance AE. The equilibrium point moves from E to E', and equilibrium price and quantity both fall.

The reduction in price continues until excess demand is zero, so that the new equilibrium price is P_1. The point representing equilibrium moves from E to E', and equilibrium quantity accordingly falls from Q_0 to Q_1. In this example, as in the previous one, price and quantity change in the same direction. This is the case because both the initial and final equilibrium points lie on the unchanged, rising supply curve.

Note that in both of the examples in this section, the change in the equilibrium price partially offsets the initial shift in quantity demanded. In Figure 3-6, quantity demanded increased by 6 million pounds at the initial price of $3 per pound. In the new equilibrium at a price of $4, quantity demanded was 9 million pounds, 3 (instead of 6) million more than in the initial equilibrium. The price rise necessary to induce sellers to increase the quantity supplied reduces quantity demanded, thus absorbing some of the impact of the increase of 6 million pounds in quantity demanded at each given price. Similarly, in Figure 3-7 quantity demanded falls at the initial price by an amount equal to the distance AE. But in the new equilibrium the quantity purchased falls not by the amount AE but by the smaller amount $E'B$. The price fall necessary to reduce quantity supplied acts as a shock absorber, partially offsetting the impact of the initial shift in demand.

A change in *any* of the factors held constant when drawing the demand curve may cause the quantity demanded at every price to change. Such a change is shown graphically as a shift of the demand curve. *Anything* that causes the demand curve to shift to the right produces a rise in both price and quantity; *anything* that causes the demand curve to shift to the left produces a fall in both price and quantity.

7. Behind the Supply Curve

The supply curve is drawn holding constant the determinants of sellers' costs. To go "behind" the supply curve, we now discuss three major influences on these costs. These "supply side" factors are important determinants of sellers' behavior.

- Durable productive assets

- Available technology
- Prices of variable inputs

Changes in any of these factors will change the quantity supplied at all prices and thus will be depicted as a shift of the supply curve.

Durable Productive Assets

Supply curves are often drawn taking as given the durable productive assets—or physical capital—owned by sellers of the good. These include such things as fishing boats, stores, assembly lines, delivery trucks, computers, and printing presses. The more physical capital sellers own, all else equal, the greater the quantity supplied at any price level.

The quantity of physical capital is often taken as given because it usually takes some time to adjust productive inputs such as the number of fishing boats. That is, they are fixed in the short run, though in the long run they can be changed. Because of this, the change in quantity supplied produced by a change in market price may be different in the short run from what it is in the long run. This difference is an important topic in later chapters.

Available Technology

By technology we mean the set of known techniques or methods for producing any particular good or service. Any improvement in technology that makes it possible to produce and market a given quantity of a good more cheaply will tend to increase the quantity supplied of that good at any price. That is, advances in technology generally shift supply curves to the right. For example, the introduction of new sonar equipment makes it easier to track fish and therefore increases the catch of each boat. Firms will be willing to sell more fish at any given price since they can land that quantity of fish at a lower cost than they could before.

Prices of Variable Inputs

In general, changes in the prices of inputs affect production costs and therefore the quantity of output firms are willing to supply at each price. A change in any input cost, including the cost of labor or of fishing boats, will shift the supply curve if the quantity of that input can be varied. Such inputs are called *variable*. If labor becomes cheaper, the cost of supplying any given quantity of fish falls and firms will hire more labor and increase the quantity of fish supplied at every price. If the cost of fishing boats falls, the quantity of fish supplied will increase in the long run, when the number of boats can also be increased.

If the price of any variable input falls, firms will be willing to supply a larger quantity of output at every price. This increase in quantity supplied at all prices is depicted as a shift of the supply curve to the right. Figure 3-8 illustrates the opposite case, in which higher input prices shift the supply curve to the left, from S to S'.

While physical capital, technology, and variable input costs are the most important factors determining the position of the supply curve in any market, other factors may also matter. The weather is important in some

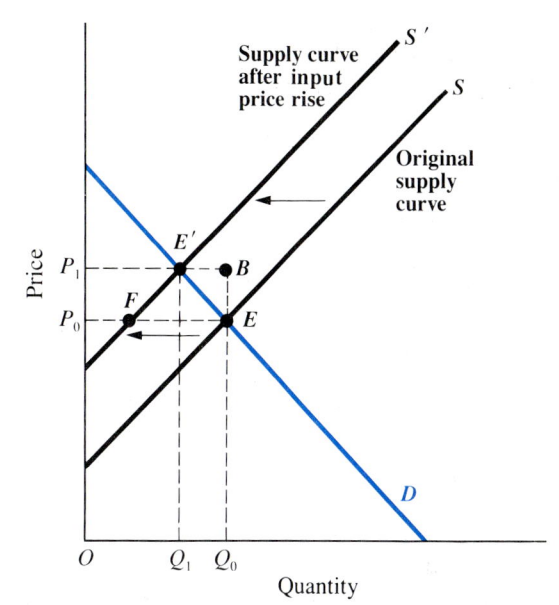

FIGURE 3-8. Effects of an Increase in the Price of an Input. When the cost of a variable input rises, the supply curve shifts to the left, from S to S'. The demand curve, D, does not shift. Equilibrium price rises because of the cost increase, and equilibrium quantity falls.

industries, for instance. Also, the government frequently affects costs by regulating the way firms operate. When the government requires firms to limit their discharges of chemicals into rivers, for example, firms' costs will rise, and the corresponding supply curves will shift to the left.

8. Shifts of the Supply Curve

If the price of diesel fuel, an important input in the fishing industry, increases, fishermen will be willing to supply less fish at each price. This decrease in quantities supplied is shown in Figure 3-8 as a shift of the supply curve to the left, from S to S'. What happens to equilibrium price and quantity?

Since the quantity supplied at the initial equilibrium price, P_0, has fallen while the quantity demanded has not changed, there is now an excess demand for fish. Figure 3-8 shows that at price P_0 firms no longer want to supply the amount Q_0 but rather a smaller amount corresponding to point F. As sellers observe buyers scrambling to find fish, they will increase price. Price will thus rise, reducing quantity demanded, until the quantities demanded and supplied are again equal, now at a higher price.

In the figure, the leftward shift of the supply curve moves the equilibrium point from E to E'. Equilibrium price thus rises from P_0 to P_1, and equilibrium quantity falls from Q_0 to Q_1. An increase in the cost of production thus causes price to rise and quantity to fall. Price and quantity must move in opposite directions, since the old and new equilibrium points both lie on the unchanged, negatively sloped demand curve.

As in the case of demand, the price change partially offsets the effects of the initial shift; total output falls by less than the supply curve shifted. At the initial price, quantity supplied fell by the amount EF. But the total reduction in production is only $E'B$, which is smaller than EF. The price system acts here too as a shock absorber.

A change in *any* of the factors held constant when drawing the supply curve may cause quantity supplied to change at every price. Such a change is represented graphically as a shift of the supply curve. *Anything* that shifts the supply curve to the left produces a rise in price and a fall in quantity; *anything* that shifts the supply curve to the right produces a fall in price and a rise in quantity.

9. Do Buyers and Sellers Respond to Prices?

Let us step back from the model of supply and demand we have just examined and ask whether it is broadly consistent with the relevant evidence. The key feature of this model is that quantity supplied and quantity demanded both respond to price. Is there evidence that buyers and sellers really do respond to price? Indeed there is. Some comes from the effects of common changes in supply or demand conditions. Bad weather generally increases food prices, for instance, as the model predicts. Some evidence comes from econometric analysis of time series and cross section data concerning particular markets. And sometimes evidence that prices matter can be obtained from market data without having to use econometric techniques, as in the two examples that follow.

Consumer Response to Prices: The VCR

The videocassette recorder (VCR) is a comparatively new product. As is typical of such products, its price was originally very high and then began to fall as producers mastered the technology and mass production got under way. Consumers responded to the falling price by increasing the quantity demanded. Table 3-4 shows how the quantity demanded increased as price fell.

Producer Response to Prices: Oil and Coal

In late 1973 the Organization of Petroleum Exporting Countries (OPEC) sharply raised the world price of oil.[6] Table 3-5 shows that as a result the price of oil in the United States increased by about 60 percent. In response to this, firms and households shifted from oil to coal as a source of energy. That is, the quantity of coal demanded

---

[6] This episode and the behavior of OPEC since 1973 are discussed in Chapter 12.

TABLE 3-4. Consumer Response to Prices: The VCR

Year	1979	1980	1981	1982	1983	1984
Average real price*	1291	1097	908	712	597	482
Quantity (thousands/yr)	478	804	1330	2030	4020	7142

* In 1984 dollars; calculated by dividing each year's actual current dollar price by that year's CPI and then multiplying by the 1984 CPI. (See Chapter 2 if this is mysterious.)

Source: *Statistical Abstract of the United States, 1985,* p. 777, and *1986,* p. 770.

TABLE 3-5. Oil Prices, Coal Prices, and Coal Production (Indices, 1972 = 100)

	1973	1974	1975	1976	1977
Real oil price*	106	156	163	159	160
Real coal price*	108	156	163	142	143
Coal production	99	101	109	114	116

* Computed using the GNP deflator.

Source: *Business Statistics, 1982,* pp. 115–116

at every price rose, the demand curve for coal shifted to the right, and the price of coal *also* increased. The increased coal price brought about an increase in coal production, as shown in Table 3-5.

Table 3-5 shows that coal production increased slowly in response to the increase in the price of coal. This is not surprising, since it takes some time to open new coal mines. Because of this slow response, the short-run increase in the coal price exceeds the long-run increase. This pattern, which is visible in the second row, is called *overshooting*; price initially overshoots its eventual level. In the short run, with the quantity of coal supplied increasing relatively little, the shift in the demand curve leads to a sharply higher price. Then as the quantity supplied increases further because new mines are opened, the price of coal declines.

10. What, How, and For Whom

The example of the effects of an increase in the price of chicken on the price and output of fish illustrates how the price system, operating through markets, allocates resources. By allowing a free market, society in effect decides how much of a particular good to produce by finding the price at which the quantity demanded is equal to the quantity supplied.

If there is a rightward shift of the demand curve, the market typically ensures that more is produced.[7] But price has to rise to provide incentives for suppliers to sell more of the good. If there is a rightward shift in the supply curve, for example, because a new and more efficient production technology has been invented, quantity produced will increase and price will fall. Price falls to provide the incentive for buyers to purchase more.

Production levels for most of the thousands of goods and services in the U.S. economy are decided in markets by the interaction of the supply and demand schedules for those goods. Quantities demanded and supplied in various markets are interrelated. The price of one good affects not only the quantity of that good demanded but also the quantities demanded of other goods. Similarly, a change in the cost of a widely used input, such as oil, will have repercussions in many markets.

In free markets, *what* is decided by supply and demand, as we have seen. The free market also determines *how* goods are produced. In order to understand that choice, we analyze production and firm behavior, that is, the supply side of the economy, in several of the chapters in Part 2.

Finally, the free market determines *for whom* goods are produced. Goods and services are produced for all those willing and able to pay the equilibrium price to obtain the quantity they demand. Their ability to pay is in turn determined by the market price at which they can sell their labor and by the value the market puts on the wealth they have accumulated or inherited. Part 3 discusses markets for these factors of production.

■ As we noted in Chapter 1, there are no actual free-market economies. In part this is because the free market's answers to the basic economic questions are sometimes unappealing. The free market does *not* automatically provide enough food for everyone not to be

---

[7] In some situations it is impossible to produce more of a good, and then the only way quantity demanded can be made equal to quantity supplied is through a price increase. An example would be a shift in the demand for Picasso paintings. We examine such cases in Chapter 5.

hungry, nor does it provide adequate shelter, clothing, or medical care for everyone. It provides food, medical care, and all other goods for those willing *and able* to pay. Society, operating through the political process, may want to modify or totally reject the free-market solutions. This is one of the reasons why government intervention in the free market through regulation, taxation, and the redistribution of income is so pervasive throughout the world. We begin the study of government in the economy in the next chapter.

Summary

1. Most decisions concerning resource allocation in the United States and other mixed economies are made through the price system. Prices are determined in markets; these markets take many different forms, but their operation can be summarized with the basic model of demand and supply.
2. Quantity demanded is the amount of a good buyers are willing to buy per period (day or year, for example) in a given market. Quantity demanded depends on the price of the good and on other factors. Chief among these are the prices of alternative goods, the incomes of buyers, their tastes, and expected future prices.
3. The demand schedule is the relationship between the quantity of a good demanded and its price, other factors held constant. The demand curve is the graphic representation of the demand schedule. Demand curves are typically downward-sloping, showing that quantity demanded increases as price falls.
4. Quantity supplied is the amount of a good sellers want to sell per period in a given market. Quantity supplied depends on the price of the good and on other factors. Chief among these are the durable productive assets (physical capital) and technology available to suppliers and the prices of variable inputs, all of which determine sellers' costs.
5. The supply schedule is the relationship between the quantity of a good supplied and its price, other factors held constant. The supply curve—the graphic representation of the supply schedule—is typically upward-sloping, showing that quantity supplied increases when price rises.
6. The market is in equilibrium when price is at the level at which quantity demanded is equal to quantity supplied. At any price below the equilibrium price there is excess demand (or a shortage), with quantity demanded exceeding quantity supplied. At any price above the equilibrium price there is excess supply (or a surplus), with quantity supplied exceeding quantity demanded.
7. Price moves towards the equilibrium level if the market is not in equilibrium. When there is excess demand, suppliers can raise price and still sell as much as they would like to at the higher price. When there is excess supply, the pressure of unsold output leads firms to cut price. Because markets move to equilibrium, economists generally concentrate on equilibrium price and quantity when analyzing markets' responses to changes in supply or demand.
8. Changes in the factors other than the price of the good that determine quantity demanded shift the demand curve, causing equilibrium price and quantity to change. An increase in the price of a substitute good shifts the demand curve to the right, increasing both price and quantity. Similarly, an increase in the number of consumers, a shift in tastes toward this good, or the expectation that price will rise in the next period shifts the demand curve to the right. An increase in the price of a complementary good shifts the demand curve to the left, reducing price and quantity.
9. An increase in consumers' incomes increases the quantity demanded of a normal good, shifting the demand curve to the right and raising price and quantity. An increase in consumers' incomes shifts the demand curve for an inferior good to the left, reducing price and quantity.
10. The position and slope of the supply curve are determined mainly by costs of production. These in turn are determined by technology and the costs of inputs. An improvement in technology, reducing the costs of production, will typically shift the supply curve to the right, causing equilibrium price to fall and output to rise. So will a reduction in the cost of an input.
11. The price system helps solve the "what," "how," and "for whom" problems in a free-market economy. *What* is determined by supply and demand in the markets for different goods. *How* is determined by firms' decisions about the best way to produce. *For whom* is determined by the ability and willingness of consumers to pay for different goods, which is determined in turn by the prices at which they can sell their labor and the value of their wealth.

Key Terms

Market
Demand
Quantity demanded

Quantity bought
Demand schedule
Demand curve
Supply
Quantity supplied
Quantity sold
Supply schedule
Supply curve
Excess demand (shortage)
Excess supply (surplus)
Equilibrium quantity
Substitutes
Complements
Normal good
Inferior good
Shift of a curve
Movement along a curve
Price system

Problems

1 Hypothetical supply and demand schedules for toasters are shown in the accompanying table. Plot the supply and demand curves for toasters and find the equilibrium price and quantity.

Supply and Demand Schedules for Toasters

Price, $	Quantity demanded, millions/yr	Quantity supplied, millions/yr
10	10	3
12	9	4
14	8	5
16	7	6
18	6	7
20	5	8

2 Using the same data, what is the excess supply or demand (a) when price is $12? (b) when price is $20?
3 Explain why and in what direction the price of toasters will change in (a) and (b) in Problem 2.
4 What happens to the demand curve for toasters when the price of bread rises? Show in a supply-demand diagram how the equilibrium price and quantity of toasters change. Explain why price will not remain at its original level.
5 How is the demand curve for toasters affected by the invention of the toaster oven, which to many people seems like a new and better way of toasting? What effect will this have on the equilibrium quantity of toasters bought and sold and on the price of toasters? Why?
6 Returning to the toaster data, suppose the quantity supplied at each price rises by 1 million. Calculate the new equilibrium price and quantity. Does the equilibrium quantity increase more or less than 1 million, that is, more or less than the increase in the quantity supplied at each price? Why?
7 (a) Suppose cold weather makes it more difficult to catch fish. What happens to the supply curve for fish? What happens to equilibrium price and quantity? (b) Suppose the cold weather also reduces the quantity of fish demanded because people do not go shopping. Show what happens to the demand curve for fish. (c) What happens to the equilibrium quantity of fish when cold weather sets in and both these effects occur? (d) Can you say what happens to the equilibrium price of fish?
8 Using demand and supply schedules, show how an increase in income will affect the demand curve for an inferior good. What happens to price and quantity?
9 Explain why the price of a good starts rising this month when people expect that its price will go up next month. (Use a supply-demand diagram and ask yourself how an increase in the expected price affects the curves.)
10 What is wrong with the following argument? "The cold weather reduced the quantity of seaside hotel rooms demanded, thereby reducing both the equilibrium price of renting a hotel room and the number of rooms rented. The fall in the price of hotel rooms in turn stimulated demand so that in the end price returned to its original level." (Use Box 3-1.)
11 When the federal government gave away 300 million pounds of cheese at the end of 1981, some supermarkets were upset, claiming this would affect their business badly. How would the supermarkets' business have been affected?
12 Suppose the supply curve of fish shifts to the left as a result of overfishing. (a) Show graphically what happens to the price and quantity of fish. (b) Building on your answer to (a), show how the overfishing affects the price of chicken. (c) Using your answers to (a) and (b), explain why economists speak of the price *system*.
13 Referring to the discussion of the oil and coal markets in section 9, use supply and demand curves to show graphically the changes in the coal market caused by increased oil prices. First show the short-run effect of higher oil prices and then show the impact of the opening of new coal mines, which can be thought of as shifting the supply curve to the right.

14 *Extra credit*. Using the toaster data, suppose a tax of $1 is put on toasters. For convenience, assume that the seller pays the tax. Thus if the seller charges $16 for the toaster, he receives only $15, and the government gets the other $1. Similarly, if he charges $18, he receives only $17, and the government gets $1. What happens to the quantity of toasters sold when the tax is imposed? What happens to the price the consumers pay? What happens to the price the sellers receive after paying the tax? [*Suggestion*: There is now a difference between the amount the buyers pay and the amount (net of tax) the sellers receive. Interpret the demand schedule as describing the amount buyers want at the price they have to pay, and the supply schedule as describing the amount suppliers want to sell at the price they receive. There is a gap of $1 between the amount buyers pay and the amount sellers receive.]

Chapter 4
Government in the Mixed Economy

Most resources in the United States are allocated through markets in which individuals and privately owned firms trade with other individuals or firms. However, governments play a major role in the U.S. economy and in other mixed economies as well. They set the legal rules; they buy goods and services—from paper clips to aircraft carriers—through markets; they produce some services, such as defense; and they make large-scale transfer payments such as Social Security benefits. In financing themselves through taxation and borrowing, governments exert a major influence on prices, interest rates, and production.

Governments in modern industrial economies collect between one-quarter and one-half of GNP in taxes each year and typically spend a little more than they receive in taxes. Because governments play so large a part in economic life, to understand the operation of a modern economy we have to understand not only how markets work but also how government affects the operation of the economy.

This chapter addresses three basic questions about the government's role in economic life. What do governments *actually do*? How can governments *in principle* improve the allocation of resources in the economy? How do governments *decide* what to do? Our aim here is to develop an overview of the role of government as a basis for our continuing discussion of government policy in later chapters.

1. What Do Governments Do?

There are over 80,000 governments—federal, state, and local—in the United States. Their combined budgets total 35 percent of GNP, and they directly employ 16 percent of the labor force. What do they do?

Create Laws, Rules, and Regulations

Governments determine the legal framework that sets the basic rules for the ownership of property and the operation of markets. If the legal framework outlaws private ownership of businesses, the economy is socialistic; if businesses are owned by individuals and operated for private profit, the economy is capitalistic.[1] Even in the most capitalistic economies, there are limits to the rights of ownership. Not everyone can own a handgun, for instance. Nor are people entirely free to use their property as they please; for example, it is usually illegal to build a factory on land in a residential area.

In addition, governments at all levels *regulate* economic behavior, setting detailed rules for the operation of businesses. Regulations range from zoning requirements—limiting how land can be used and where businesses can locate—through job health and safety regulations and building codes to attempts to entirely prevent some types of business, such as the sale of heroin. Some regulations apply to all businesses; examples include laws against fraud and racial discrimination in hiring as well as the antitrust laws that (among other things) prohibit competitors from agreeing to fix prices. Some regulations apply only to certain industries, such as requirements that barbers and doctors have appropriate training and laws that prohibit competition with the local electric company. Government regulation and its effects on the operations of markets in the U.S. economy are the subjects of Chapters 20 and 21.

Buy and Sell Goods and Services

Governments buy and produce many goods and services, such as defense, education, parks, and roads, which they provide to firms and households. Most of these goods, such as defense and education, are provided to users free of direct charge. Some, such as local bus rides, the use of turnpikes, and government publications, are paid for directly by the user.

Governments, like private firms, must decide what to buy and what to produce themselves. For instance, governments typically buy computers but write the programs they need to operate them. In order to do this, governments must act as buyers in the markets for the services of computer programmers.

Governments also produce and sell goods. In many countries, the phone company is government-owned, as

---

[1] The extent of private ownership is always a matter of degree, however. Governments own some businesses even in the most capitalistic economies; some farms are private in even the most socialistic economies.

TABLE 4-1. Composition of Government Spending in the United States, 1983
(Percentages of Total Government Spending)

Function	Federal	State	Local	Total
Total	58.2	17.3	24.6	100.0
National defense and international relations	16.9	—	—	16.9
Education	0.9	3.3	8.8	13.1
Health and hospitals	0.9	1.5	1.7	4.2
Transportation and highways	0.4	1.6	1.4	3.4
Police	0.2	0.2	1.1	1.5
Social Security, welfare, etc.	20.6	6.6	1.4	28.7
Interest on debt	8.0	0.8	1.0	9.8
Other	10.2	3.3	9.2	22.4

Note: The totals for the components may not total 100.0 because of rounding.
Source: *Facts and Figures on Government Finance, 1986*, (Washington, D.C.: Tax Foundation Inc.)

is the electric system. In some states in the United States, only state-owned stores can sell liquor. In some foreign countries, the government is the monopoly seller of tobacco products.

Make Transfer Payments

Governments also make transfer payments, such as Social Security and unemployment benefits, to individuals.

● **Transfer payments are payments for which no current direct economic service is provided in return.**

A firefighter's salary is not a transfer payment; a Social Security check is, and so are unemployment and welfare benefits.

Government spending is the sum of government purchases of goods and services and transfer payments. Table 4-1 gives a breakdown of government spending in the United States. The big categories are defense, education, and Social Security and welfare.

Impose Taxes

Governments pay for the goods they buy and for the transfer payments they make mostly by levying taxes.

(The rest is financed by borrowing.) Table 4-2 shows the major sources of government revenues. Over 60 percent of all government revenue in the United States is collected by the federal government and only about 40 percent by state and local governments. But the federal government transfers large amounts to state and local governments, leaving itself with only 54 percent of total revenue.

The largest fraction of total and federal tax revenue comes from personal income taxes, followed by contributions for Social Security. Taxes on corporate income accounted for less than 8 percent of total government revenue in 1984, though the tax reform act of 1986 will probably raise corporate taxes to more than 10 percent of total government revenue. State and local governments rely heavily on general sales taxes (often with some categories of goods, such as food and clothing, exempted) and property taxes for revenue. In all, taxes total about 30 percent of GNP, meaning that the government—federal, state, and local—takes nearly a third of total income in taxes. The microeconomics of government taxation and spending is studied in more detail in Chapters 21 and 22.

SPENDING, TAXES, AND DEFICITS. In 1929 federal government spending was 3 percent of GNP; in 1985 it was nearly 25 percent of GNP. Over the same period state and

TABLE 4-2. Sources of Government Revenue in the United States, 1984
(Percentages of Total Net Government Revenue)

Source	Federal government	State and local government	Total
Taxes on income and property			
Personal income taxes	27.2	5.7	32.9
Social insurance	23.2	3.7	26.9
Corporate profits taxes	6.2	1.7	7.9
Property taxes	—	8.7	8.7
Taxes on goods			
Excise and sales taxes	3.2	13.2	16.4
Customs duties (tariffs)	1.0	—	1.0
Other (including nontaxes)	1.3	4.9	6.2
Total	62.1	37.9	100.0
Federal grants to state and local governments	−8.2	+8.2	—

Source: *Survey of Current Business,* August 1985.

local government spending increased from under 9 percent of GNP to nearly 13 percent of GNP.

Government spending has increased faster than GNP all around the world. Figure 4-1 shows total government spending as a percentage of GNP for the United States and for the other major developed market economies

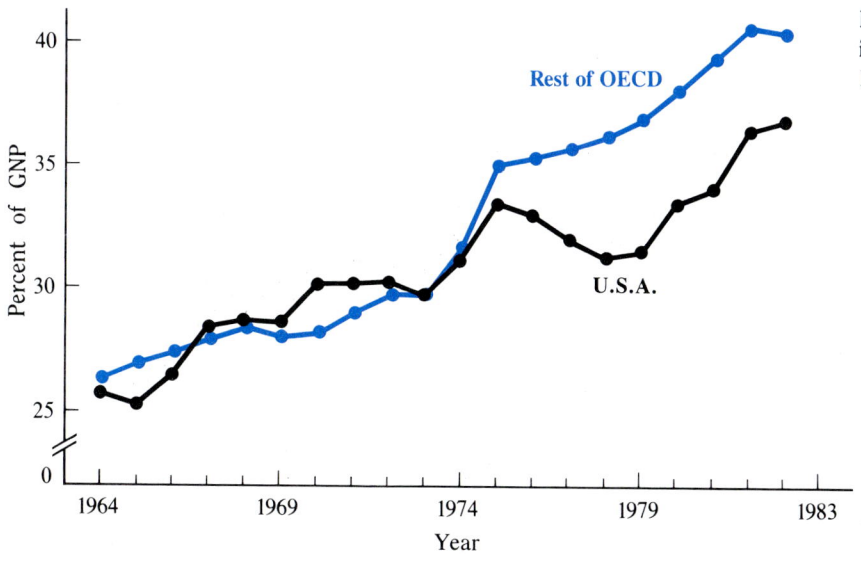

FIGURE 4-1. Total Government Spending as a Percentage of GNP, 1964–1983.

FIGURE 4-2. The Federal Budget Surplus as a Percentage of GNP, 1950–1987.

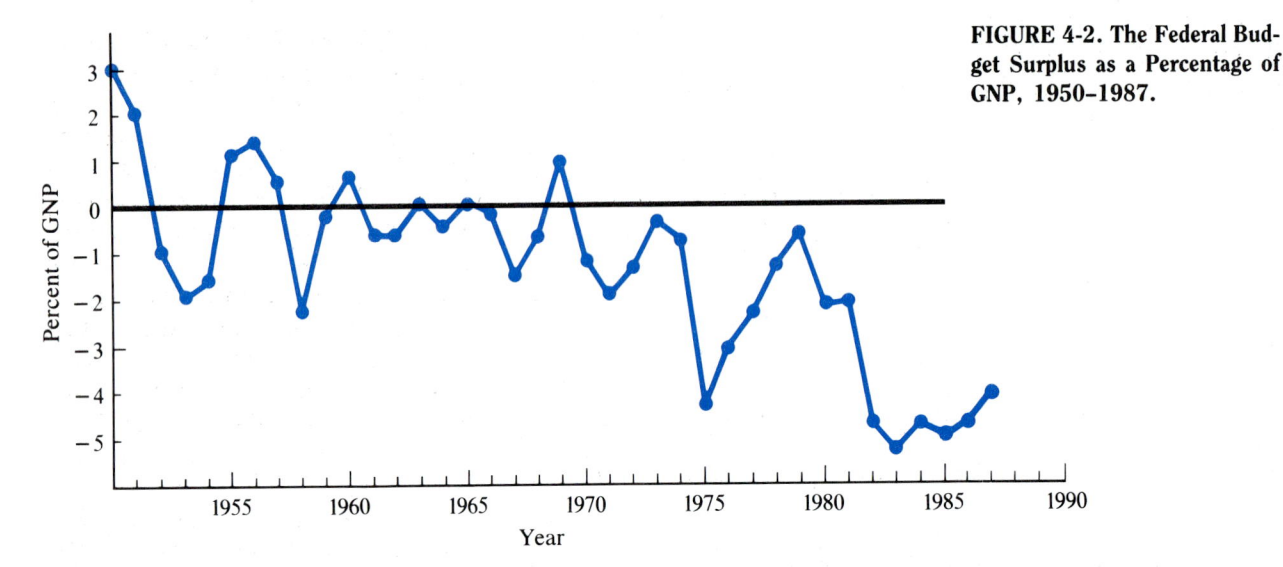

(i.e., the other members of the Organization for Economic Cooperation and Development, or OECD) since 1964.[2] The increase in U.S. government outlays has been significantly slower than that of the other countries, particularly in recent years, but there has been an apparently irreversible increase in this area in all the countries in the OECD.

In the last few years the increase in government outlays in the United States has been accompanied by a sharp increase in the federal government budget deficit (spending minus taxes) measured as a share of GNP, as Figure 4-2 shows. (Figure 4-2 shows the budget surplus, which is equal to minus the deficit.) Nor is there much prospect of significant deficit reduction soon.

The trends in Figures 4-1 and 4-2 raise several questions. Why has government spending increased? Is this increase necessarily a bad thing? Will it continue? Are deficits also bound to increase? We discuss these issues in section 3, where we consider how governments make the decisions that create these trends.

Try to Stabilize the Economy

Every market economy suffers from business cycles.

● The *business cycle* consists of fluctuations of total production, or GNP, accompanied by fluctuations in the level of unemployment and the rate of inflation.

Governments, through their control of taxes and government spending and through their ability to control the quantity of money in the economy, often attempt to modify fluctuations in the business cycle. The federal government may reduce taxes in a recession in the hope that people will increase spending and thus raise the GNP. The Federal Reserve Board, or the Fed, which controls the quantity of money, may increase the quantity of money more rapidly in a recession to help bring the economy out of the recession. When inflation is high, the Fed may reduce the rate of money growth with the aim of reducing inflation.

These are macroeconomic policies through which the government attempts to *stabilize* the economy, keeping it as close as possible to full employment with low inflation. The 1946 Employment Act gave the federal government the legal responsibility of promoting maximum employment, production, and "purchasing power."[3]

---

[2] The OECD is a Paris-based group of 24 free-world industrialized countries. The large members (listed in descending size of GNP) are the United States, Japan, Germany, France, the United Kingdom, Italy, Canada, and Australia.

[3] Promoting maximum purchasing power is taken to mean keeping the rate of inflation low.

Affect the Allocation of Resources

By spending and taxing, the government of course plays a major part in allocating resources in the economy. In terms of what, how, and for whom, government chooses much of *what* gets produced, from defense expenditures to education to its support for the arts. It affects *how* goods are produced through regulation and through the legal system. It affects *for whom* goods are produced through its taxes and transfers, which take income away from some people and give it to others.

Beyond these direct effects, the government also affects the allocation of resources indirectly through taxes (and subsidies, which are negative taxes) on the price and level of production in individual markets. When government taxes a good, such as cigarettes, it generally reduces the quantity of that good produced; when it subsidizes a good, such as milk, it generally increases the quantity of the good produced.

Figure 4-3 depicts the market for cigarettes and shows the effects of an *excise* tax of 30 cents a pack.[4] An excise tax applies to a single good or service, such as tobacco, liquor, or long-distance telephone calls. The price paid by purchasers is on the vertical axis. The demand curve for cigarettes, D, shows the quantity demanded at each price *that buyers pay*. Before any taxes are imposed, the supply curve is S. This curve shows the quantity supplied at each price *that sellers receive*.

Now suppose the government imposes a 30-cent tax on cigarettes. Purchasers will now pay 30 cents more per pack than suppliers receive, with the difference going to the government. For instance, if buyers pay $1.00, sellers receive only $0.70; the other 30 cents goes to the government.[5]

The demand curve shows the amount buyers want to buy at each price they pay. The tax does not change the amount buyers are willing to buy at any given price, and it therefore does not shift D. (Recall that the price on the vertical axis in Figure 4-3 is the price paid *by buyers*.)

But S does shift. Sellers are willing to sell the same amount as before for each price *they receive*. But they now receive less than buyers pay; the difference is the tax. The supply curve S in Figure 4-3 shifts upward to S' by an amount exactly equal to the tax; thus at each level of output, firms receive after taxes exactly the amount they receive on S at that level of output. This ensures that at any quantity supplied, the amount sellers retain after the tax is paid is exactly the same as it is on S—which shows the quantity supplied at each price received by sellers. The tax is the distance between S and S'.[6]

So far we have been asking how the tax shifts the

---

[4] The federal government currently imposes a tax of 16 cents a pack, and state and local taxes add just over 15 cents on average. These taxes account for about a third of the retail price of cigarettes and contribute over $9 billion per year to government revenues.

[5] The tax on cigarettes is said to be a *specific* tax, because the amount paid depends only on the quantity of cigarettes sold, not on the price. A tax of 30 percent of the sellers' revenue, which would depend on the price, would be an *ad valorem* tax. Sales taxes are the most familiar ad valorem taxes.

[6] To be sure you understand the analysis of the tax, you could draw supply and demand curves with the price received by the seller on the vertical axis. In this case the supply curve will not shift when a tax is imposed. What happens to the demand curve?

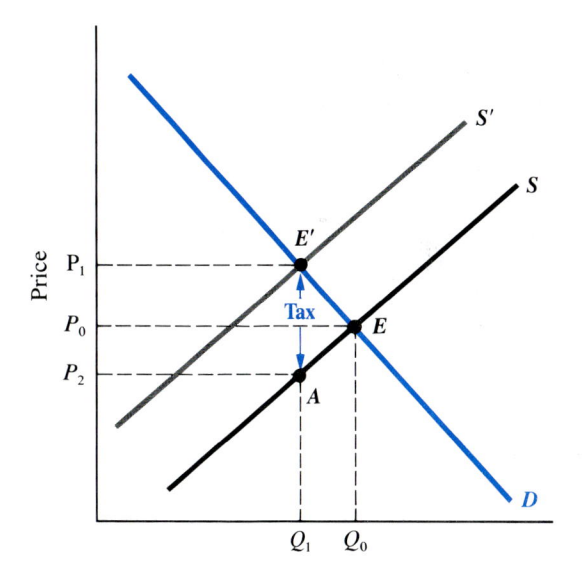

FIGURE 4-3. A Tax Raises Price and Lowers Quantity Produced. The vertical axis shows the price paid by buyers of the good. Before the tax, the equilibrium is at E. The imposition of a tax shifts the supply curve upward because part of the amount paid by sellers now goes to the government. S shifts upward to S' by an amount exactly equal to the per unit tax imposed. The price paid by buyers rises, that received by sellers (at point A) falls, and quantity falls.

demand and supply curves. It does not shift the demand curve at all. It shifts the supply curve upward by the amount of the tax, from S to S'. As a result of the shift in the supply curve, the market equilibrium will change. The tax moves the market equilibrium from point E to point E' in Figure 4-3. In the new equilibrium at E', buyers pay P_1 for each pack, more than the original price of P_0. Sellers receive P_2 for each pack of cigarettes, less than before. The government takes the difference. Amount Q_1 is sold, less than the amount sold previously, Q_0. By creating a gap or wedge between the price paid by buyers and that received by sellers, the tax reduces consumption and production.

Note that the tax makes both buyers and sellers worse off, at least in economic terms. Buyers pay a higher price, and sellers receive a lower price. (Buyers may be healthier as a consequence of the tax, of course.) Box 4-1 shows how the distribution of this burden depends on the responsiveness of buyers and sellers to price changes, as reflected in the shapes of the demand and supply curves.

The power to tax is thus the power to affect the allocation of the economy's resources, or to change what gets produced. By taxing cigarettes, the government can reduce the amount of cigarettes smoked and thereby improve health. By taxing income earned from work, the government affects the amount of time people want to work. Because they affect the allocation of resources indirectly, through their effects on relative prices, as well as directly, taxes loom large in the workings of the market system and have a profound effect on the way society allocates its scarce resources.

2. What Should Governments Do?

Why should governments intervene in a market economy? Adam Smith, the father of economics, argued in his 1776 classic, *The Wealth of Nations*, that people pursuing their own interests are led as if by "an invisible hand" to promote the interests of society.[7] If there is an invisible hand, if markets allocate resources efficiently so that consumers' wants are satisfied at minimum cost, why should governments intervene in the economy at all?

In this section we discuss theoretical justifications for government intervention in a market economy. The general argument for government intervention is *market failure*. Sometimes markets do not allocate resources efficiently, and government intervention may improve economic performance. Economic theory identifies six broad types of market failure, which we describe below.

Very few economists dispute the idea that the government could in theory improve the allocation of resources by correcting market failures, but many dispute the idea that government in fact improves the allocation of resources. Conservative economists, including Nobel Prize winners Milton Friedman of the Hoover Institution and James Buchanan of George Mason University, argue that in practice the government is even more likely to fail to allocate resources efficiently than are markets. We take up their arguments in section 3, but first we discuss the six reasons why government intervention may at least in principle improve the allocation of resources.

[7] Modern Library, New York, 1973, p. 423.

Box 4-1. Who Really Pays an Excise Tax?

The answer to the question of who really pays an excise tax seems simple: It's whoever sends the money to the government. But that is a superficial answer. If an excise tax on cigarettes raises the price of cigarettes—the amount paid by buyers—by an amount equal to the tax, economists say that the tax is effectively paid by buyers, even if it is the sellers who send the checks to the government. And if a tax does not at all affect the price paid by buyers, instead reducing the price received by sellers by an amount equal to the tax, we say that the tax is effectively paid by the sellers.

Suppose the price of cigarettes was $1.00 before the tax was imposed. Suppose the government imposes a tax of $0.30 per pack, and the price of cigarettes rises to $1.30. Then the entire burden of the tax is on the buyers; in effect they pay the entire tax. Alternatively, suppose the market price remains at $1.00, and now sellers receive only $0.70 after paying the tax. Then the entire burden of the tax is on the suppliers.

In general the price of the good will rise by less than the amount of the tax, as in Figure 4-3. This means that both buyers and sellers bear part of the burden: The buyers are paying more than they did before, and the sellers are receiving less than before. We now show how the distribution of the burden of the tax between buyers and sellers depends on the slopes of the supply and demand curves.

Figure 4B-1 illustrates this point. In both panels, a tax shifts the supply curve upward from S to S', just as in Figure 4-3. As a consequence, the price paid by buyers rises from P_0 to P_1 and the price received by sellers falls from P_0 to P_2. The difference between P_1 and P_2 is the amount of the tax per unit of the good. This difference is the same in the two panels.

In (a), the demand curve is relatively steep, meaning that buyers change quantity demanded very little when price changes. The supply curve is relatively flat. As a consequence, buyers bear most of the burden of the tax. That is, the rise in the price paid by buyers, $(P_1 - P_0)$, exceeds the fall in the price received by sellers, $(P_0 - P_2)$. The burden falls on buyers because they change quantity demanded very little when price rises. If the supply curve were perfectly flat, the entire burden of the tax would fall on buyers.

In (b), by contrast, the demand curve is relatively flat and the supply curve is relatively steep. The flat demand curve means that buyers are willing to reduce the quantity demanded a lot when price rises a little. In this case sellers bear most of the burden of the tax. The fall in the price they receive is greater than the rise in the price that buyers pay. If the demand curve were perfectly flat, the entire burden of the tax would fall on sellers.

In both cases, the side of the market (buyers or sellers) that is less responsive to price bears most of the cost of the tax. In (b), for instance, most buyers find it easy to do without the good, and they will switch to substitutes when a tax is imposed rather than pay a higher price. On the other hand, if the supply curve is relatively steep, this means that sellers will accept a lower price per unit before making large reductions in the quantity supplied. Thus buyers can avoid the tax by switching to substitutes, and sellers are the ones who bear most of the tax burden.

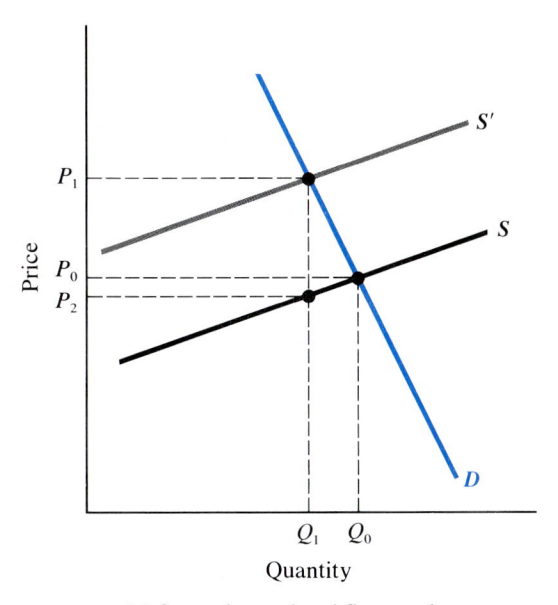

(a) Steep demand and flat supply

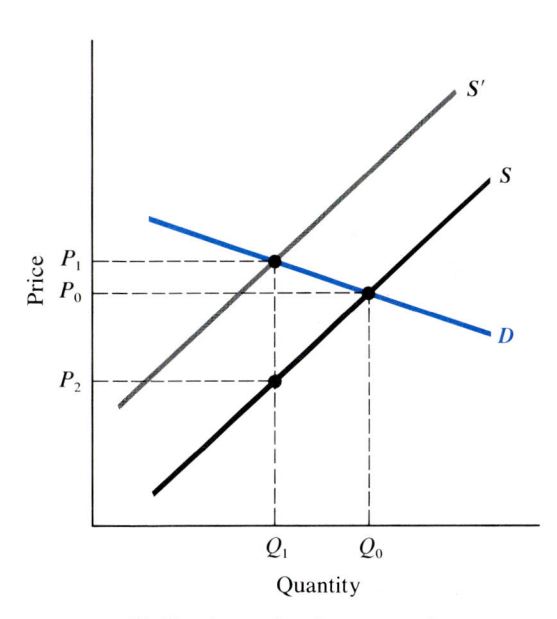

(b) Flat demand and steep supply

FIGURE 4B-1. The Burden of a Tax. In both panels, an excise tax shifts the supply curve from S to S'. The difference between P_1, the price paid by buyers, and P_2, the price received by sellers, is the same in both panels. This difference is equal to the per unit tax. In (a), buyers bear most of the burden of the tax, because the demand curve is steep and the supply curve is flat. In (b), on the other hand, sellers bear most of the burden of the tax, because the demand curve is steep and the supply curve is flat.

The Business Cycle

The business cycle has many external causes, from wars to oil-price changes to bursts of new inventions. Government policies also affect the business cycle. Increases in taxes and reductions in government spending generally reduce GNP; increases in the money stock increase GNP and prices. Government policy can make the business cycle worse, lengthening recessions and creating inflation, or it can reduce economic fluctuations.

There are major controversies in macroeconomics over whether and to what extent the government can stabilize the economy. Obviously, the government cannot control the economy perfectly or we would not have severe recessions and inflation. But since the government does control a large share of total spending and the quantity of money, it must make its decisions with their effect on the business cycle in mind. And it does: Taxes may be cut when the economy is in a recession, and the growth rate of money may be reduced when the inflation rate is too high or be increased when the economy is in a recession.

Public Goods

Most of the goods supplied by businesses and demanded by consumers are private goods.

● A *private good* is a good that, if consumed by one person, cannot be consumed by another.

Ice cream is a private good. When you eat your ice cream cone, your friend doesn't get to consume it. Your clothes are also private goods. When you wear them, everyone else is precluded from wearing them at the same time.

But there are goods we can all consume simultaneously, without anyone's consumption reducing anyone else's. These are called public goods.

● A *public good* is a good that, even if it is consumed by one person, is still available for consumption by others.

Clean air is a public good. So is national defense, or public safety. If the armed forces are protecting the country from danger, your being safe in no way prevents anyone else from being safe.

It is no coincidence that most public goods are not provided in private markets. Because of the *free-rider* problem, private markets have trouble ensuring that the right amount of a public good will be produced. A free rider is someone who gets to consume a good that is costly to produce without paying for it. The free-rider problem applies particularly to public goods because if anyone were to buy the good, it would then be available for everyone else to consume.

For instance, suppose a market were set up for national defense. Even if each of us felt that we needed defense, we would not have the right incentives to buy our share of defense. Since the amount of national defense I will have is the same as the amount everyone else has, I have a strong incentive to wait for someone else to buy it rather than contribute my fair share. I will have a free ride on everyone else's purchases. But of course if everyone is waiting for someone else to buy national defense, there will be no defense.

To get around the free-rider problem, the country has to find some way of deciding *together* how much to spend on defense. Governments are set up to make such *collective* decisions. Many of the goods provided by the government are in fact public goods. National defense and police services are certainly public goods. National parks are a mixed case, since the views in the parks are a public good, at least until congestion sets in, but use of the eating facilities is not.

GOVERNMENT PRODUCTION. It may seem from this discussion that the government *should* produce public goods and *should not* produce any other goods. Neither conclusion is correct. The government does not have to produce public goods; it only has to specify how much of each should be produced. It may rely on private contractors to do the actual production, as it does, say, with regard to defense equipment. Indeed, it used to be common for countries to have private contractors provide armies on a commercial basis. It is increasingly common for municipalities to hire private contractors to remove garbage.

On the other hand, there is no general economic reason why governments should not produce private goods. There are government-owned firms in many countries, including the United States. About 20 percent of electricity generation in the United States is accounted for by government firms and other nonbusiness enterprises; the figure is close to 100 percent in most other countries. Telephone service in most countries is provided by the government or a government-owned firm.

Some government enterprises appear to be commercially successful and efficient. Nonetheless, the general presumption from experience is that government is less likely to produce efficiently than is the private sector. In part this happens because government-owned companies are often given financial aid when they lose money rather than being closed down as they would be if they were run privately. In addition, government enterprises are often required to hire more workers than would be efficient—in part to combat unemployment.

Externalities

Markets work well when the price of a good equals society's cost of producing that good and when the value of the good to the buyer is equal to the benefit of the good to society. However, the costs and benefits of production are sometimes not fully reflected in market prices.

Consider the problem of pollution. A firm produces chemicals and discharges the waste into a lake. The discharge pollutes the local water supply, kills fish and birds, and creates an offensive smell. These adverse side effects represent costs to society of producing the chemical, and they should accordingly be reflected in its market price—but they may not be. Unless the chemical company is charged for the damages caused by its pollution, the market price of its output will understate the true cost of production to society. In this case there is an externality in the production of the chemical.

● An *externality* exists when the production or consumption of a good directly affects businesses or consumers not involved in buying and selling it and when those spillover effects are not fully reflected in market prices.

Externalities are not all negative. The homeowner who repaints her house provides spillover benefits for the neighbors; they no longer have to look at a peeling or dilapidated house. In all externalities, there exists something that affects firms' costs or consumers' welfare (such as pollution or views of newly painted houses) but that is not traded in a market. Economists often speak of externalities as caused by "missing markets."

When externalities are present, market prices do not reflect all the social costs and benefits of the production of a good. Government intervention may improve the functioning of the economy, for example, by requiring firms to treat their waste products in certain ways before dumping them. Since externalities involve missing markets, they can also be handled in principle by market-type solutions. The government might charge firms (an estimate of) the damages their pollution causes, for instance, or might permit a certain amount of total pollution and allow firms to buy and sell rights to pollute. There has been little experience with such market-type solutions, however.

The presence of externalities can provide the justification for a number of government activities besides pollution control. Examples range from control of broadcasting (interference is an externality) to zoning and other restrictions on land use.

Information-Related Problems

Unless firms and consumers are well informed, they may take actions that are not in their own interests. Unless decisions are made on the basis of good information, markets will not work well. But in a free-market economy, particularly a modern, complex free-market economy, firms and consumers are not likely to be well informed about the consequences of all their decisions.

Private markets may not produce the right kinds and amounts of information. Firms have little incentive to study the long-term health hazards to which their workers are exposed, for instance, and if there were no penalties for fraud, producers of unsafe goods would have every incentive to conceal the flaws in their products. Furthermore, modern economies are so complex that few individuals can digest and evaluate all the information necessary to make fully informed decisions all the time. It may be efficient to have the government process some complex information on behalf of its citizens.

Governments have long recognized a need to protect poorly informed consumers from actions they would regret. Laws against fraud have been around for centuries. Modern governments generally regulate working conditions, inspect and grade foods, regulate the design and safety of consumer products, and require that certain products (such as foods and dangerous chemicals) have informative labels.

Monopoly and Market Power

Competitive markets generally work well, but markets where either buyers or sellers can manipulate prices generally do not. In particular, too little output will be produced and price will be too high in a market where a single seller controls supply.

● A *monopolist* **is the single seller of a good or service.**

Monopolists can earn high profits by restricting the quantity sold and raising price. Because they are the only sellers, they have no fear of being undercut by competitors—and consumers end up paying more than they should.

Some monopolies are almost unavoidable. Most public utilities—such as the gas company and the electric company—are local monopolies. The government can regulate such companies by controlling the prices they are allowed to charge, or it may elect to supply the products involved itself. (Most telephone service in the United States is supplied by regulated private firms; most water is supplied by governments.) Other monopolies may be artificial, brought about through manipulation by firms. Here governments intervene with antitrust laws, seeking to make competition more vigorous and to prevent monopolies or other attempts to control supply.

Any buyer or seller who has the ability to affect market price significantly is described as having *market power* or *monopoly power*. Government intervention to limit market power, for instance, by preventing firms with market power from charging high prices, can improve the allocation of resources.

Income Redistribution and Merit Goods

The distribution of income that is generated by free markets has no ethical claim to being just or fair, as we noted at the end of Chapter 3. Depending on who starts out with what resources, private markets can produce many different final distributions—different "for whoms"—of resources and welfare. Private markets may produce a distribution in which the top 1 percent of income earners receive 40 percent of total income in the economy, or they may produce an even distribution of income. Either way government may want to intervene to affect the distribution of income—by taxing some and giving to others.

In practice, modern governments engage in large-scale redistribution of income. The share of transfers in government spending has increased not only in the United States but all over the world in the period since 1960. The 11 percent of GNP spent by government in the United States on transfer payments represents government redistribution of income—toward the elderly (through Social Security), the unemployed (through unemployment benefits), tobacco farmers (through tobacco price supports), and other beneficiaries. The rapid growth of transfer spending has been a source of real controversy, with critics arguing that many government welfare programs have harmed the people they were designed to help.

There is a difference between government intervention to affect the distribution of income and intervention to ensure the right level of production of public goods or to make market prices reflect externalities. In the latter cases the government is taking actions that at least in principle can make everyone in society better off. But when the government intervenes to affect the income distribution, it makes some people better off by making others worse off.

Governments are concerned not just with the distribution of income but also with the consumption of particular goods and services.

● *Merit goods* **are goods that society thinks people should consume or receive, no matter what their incomes are.**

Merit goods typically include health, education, shelter, and food. Thus we—society—might think that everyone should have adequate housing and take steps to provide it. Is there an economic justification for government intervention in regard to merit goods? In a sense there always is, because the sight of someone who is homeless creates an externality, making everyone else unhappy. By providing housing or shelter for those who would otherwise be on the streets, the government makes the rest of us feel better.

Society's concern over merit goods is closely related to its concern over the distribution of income. The difference in the case of merit goods is that society wants to ensure an individual's consumption of *particular* goods rather than goods in general. Some of the goods provided by the government and listed in Table 4-1—for instance, health and education—are merit goods.

With merit goods, as with public goods, government concern with consumption does not justify government production. Economic theory justifies policies that ensure that individuals consume the specified amounts of merit goods. It does *not* say that the government should produce these goods itself, nor does it say exactly how the government should intervene.

One way would simply be to require that the right amounts of the goods be consumed. In the case of education, everyone has to go to school up to a certain age. But nobody has to go to a government school—any accredited school will do. In the case of housing, the government can build low-income houses and rent them at a subsidized rate, provide rent supplements, or simply specify minimum housing standards.

The most difficult question that has to be answered in discussing both merit goods and the distribution of income is how society or the government decides who should get what. Any one person can have a perfectly sensible viewpoint on these issues—for instance, that the more even the distribution of income the better, that the distribution of income we have is best, that people who work harder should be rewarded, that people who need more should get more, or that everyone should have decent housing and no one should starve. Translating these different opinions into a consistent view that is taken by the government and implemented in taxation and transfer policy is the impossible task of politics.

Summary

The discussion in this section provides some theoretical justification for government intervention in a market economy. However, governments do not make their tax and spending decisions on the basis of what economists say their role should be. Only by a huge stretch of the imagination could we say that in fact all government purchases of goods and services are purchases of public goods or merit goods or that interventions in any particular market are designed only to remove externalities. It would take even more imagination to see government intervention that affects the distribution of income as resulting from a consistent view of the optimal distribution. We now discuss the mechanisms that democratic societies use to make their actual decisions about taxation and government spending.

3. How Do Governments Decide?

The motivations economists ascribe to individuals and firms are simple. Firms are in business to make profits for their owners. Individuals are assumed to choose those combinations of goods which make them best off. These simple assumptions permit economists to explain most consumer and business decision making.

Government decision making cannot be explained so simply. The typical process by which governments tax, spend, and make other decisions is shown in Figure 4-4. Voters express their preferences for decision makers. These are legislators and elected members of the executive branch, such as the President and state governors. Their job is to make the basic decisions on spending and taxing, pass new laws, and establish new regulatory programs. Each individual who is elected has offered the

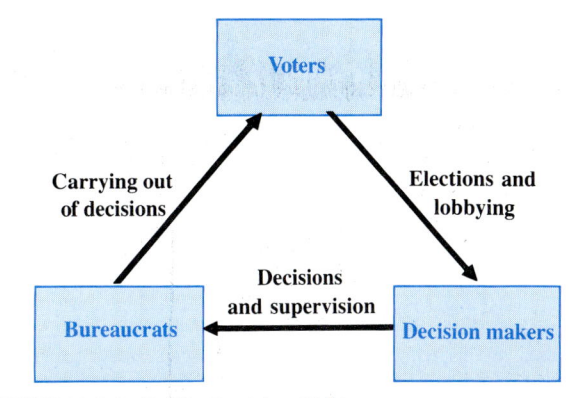

FIGURE 4-4. Public Decision Making.

electorate a package of policies and attitudes that she will support. Thus by voting, the electorate gets to express its preferences among alternative policy packages, though not on each issue.

The legislators in turn tell bureaucrats (including the chief executive) what to do, and the bureaucrats collect the revenues, administer government spending, enforce the laws, and devise and implement regulations, such as health and safety regulations, mandated by the legislature. Throughout the process of making and implementing any government decision, interested voters and organizations will be lobbying—trying to persuade the legislators and bureaucrats—to move the decision their way.

The people who run the government—legislators, elected officials, and bureaucrats—are not mere ciphers who simply do the bidding of society. They have their own objectives, in some sense trying like everyone else to maximize their own well-being. They may maximize their own well-being by doing what they believe is good for the public, or they may have much narrower goals, such as getting reelected or advancing up the hierarchy. A well-designed system is one in which the people who run the government are led to pursue the interests of society as they pursue their own goals, just as the invisible hand in competitive markets leads individuals pursuing their own interest to pursue society's interests.

Modern theories of public choice[8] try to understand and predict how people in the political system end up allocating resources, given the structure of the system and given their own aims.[9] The key question is how and to what extent the outcome of the process represented in Figure 4-4 reflects the preferences of voters. Certainly there is a widespread feeling among voters that the government is often unresponsive to their wishes. As we now show, there are indeed difficulties in making decisions through the political process.

---

[8] Among the most important developers of this theory are Nobel Prize winners Kenneth Arrow of Stanford and James Buchanan of George Mason University.

[9] A similar issue arises in the theory of the firm. Firms are run by managers on behalf of stockholders, and there is a question (discussed in Chapter 7) of whether the managers always act in the stockholders' best interests—just as there is a question of whether the government always acts in the public's interest.

Voting and Consistency

Public decision making would be easy if everyone were identical. The most important problem that a society solves through the political process is how to reconcile the different views and interests of its members. Obviously the difficult issues are not the ones on which everyone agrees about what should be done but the issues on which voters have different views.

Arriving at a choice through the political system poses very special problems. One of them is the paradox of voting described in Box 4-2. Three or more people may not be able to use majority voting to make consistent choices.[10] In practical terms, this means that decisions made by voting can depend on what seem to be mere details of procedure, such as the order in which votes are taken.

Logrolling

The possibility of logrolling is another problem with majority voting. In logrolling, groups get together to decide how they will vote on a package of issues rather than taking one issue at a time. Table 4-3 shows how logrolling can affect voting.

There are two issues, A and B, and three voters, 1, 2, and 3. The table shows the dollar values of gains and losses from each proposal for each voter. Assume that a person votes for a measure only if he gains from doing so. Thus voter 1 would vote against both A and B, while voter 2 would vote against A but in favor of B.

---

[10] Stanford's Kenneth Arrow won the Nobel Prize in economics in part for his work showing that society cannot find a procedure for making choices that are consistent unless the choices are effectively always left to one person's tastes. The demonstration is based on the paradox of voting.

TABLE 4-3. Logrolling

	Issues	
Voters	A	B
1	−6	−1
2	−3	4
3	5	−1

Box 4-2. The Paradox of Voting

Society may be unable to rank policy choices consistently through majority voting, as Table 4B-1 illustrates. Society must choose among three possibilities: A, B, and C. The table shows how the three voters, 1, 2, and 3, rank the possibilities. Voter 1, for example, likes A best, B next, and C least.

TABLE 4B-1. The Paradox of Voting: Voters' Rankings

	Ranking of Possible Choices		
Voters	A	B	C
1	1	2	3
2	3	1	2
3	2	3	1

Now let the group choose between A and B *by majority vote*. The result is two votes to one in favor of A, since both voters 1 and 3 prefer A to B. Similarly the vote will be two to one in favor of B over C, since both voter 1 and voter 2 prefer B to C. Thus with majority voting the group prefers A to B and B to C. For the sake of consistency, we should then expect the vote to favor A over C. But as you can confirm from the table, C wins in a vote against A. The conclusion is that majority voting cannot lead to consistent choice among the three alternatives in the table.[11]

Is this a serious problem or merely a curiosity? It is a serious problem because it means that majority voting cannot always be relied on to produce consistent decisions. For instance, will society prefer A to C if individuals have the preferences shown in Table 4B-1? The answer is that it depends on whether the choice is made in a direct vote between A and C, in which case majority voting leads to the choice of C, or in two successive votes between A and B and between B and C, in which case society chooses A.

Is there any mechanism that can be relied on to make consistent choices for society that reflect the underlying preferences of people in society? The answer is no, unless the preferences of individuals are reasonably similar.

Both issues would be defeated two to one in a straight majority vote. But now consider a coalition between any two voters: Each agrees to vote favorably on the other's preferred issue. Voters 2 and 3 can agree to vote favorably on the two issues. Voter 2 will be ahead by $1, losing $3 on A but making up by winning $4 on issue B. Similarly, voter 3 will lose $1 on issue B but will more than recover on issue A. Both measures are rejected with majority voting; both pass with a coalition assembled by logrolling.

Note that the total value placed by all voters on the two issues in Table 4-3 is negative. But both of them pass. Is logrolling a theoretical curiosity or a real-world problem? It is a way of life in legislatures, where members have to get support for their favorite projects from colleagues who will later bring up their own favorite projects for a vote.

Concentrated Interests

Free international trade brings benefits to consumers, as evidenced by their buying imported cars, textiles, and shoes. But on the other side, the domestic producers of cars, textiles, and shoes lose jobs and profits and are damaged by the imports. As we will see in Chapter 23, the benefits to society as a whole from free trade generally outweigh the costs.

Politically, however, those opposed to free trade—called protectionists—frequently succeed in having Congress reduce or cut off the flow of imports. Sometimes legislators impose tariffs, which are taxes on imports. Sometimes the pressure on Congress and the executive branch translates into pressure on foreign governments to impose quotas, limiting the amount they export to the United States. For instance, from 1981 to 1984 Japan

---

[11] Economists usually assume that *individual* consumers do have consistent preferences. Of course, that may not be entirely true; we often wonder today why we bought something yesterday, even when we knew perfectly well what we were buying. Furthermore, many of the problems of voting reappear when we think of the family as the basic consuming unit. Families tend to "solve" the paradox of voting by heeding only the preferences of the parents. (Show that the paradox of voting cannot emerge unless there are at least three decision makers.)

imposed quotas on the number of cars exported to the United States, and there are quotas on textiles and other goods.

Why does protectionism frequently succeed even though free trade benefits consumers and society as a whole? Because the costs of free trade to the losers are highly concentrated, while the benefits to consumers are not. Competition from imports hits particular workers and firms very hard: A worker who loses a high-paying job in the automobile industry bears a large cost. The benefits to consumers are more widely diffused and thus less obvious. After all, consumers can buy domestic cars, and the loss from not being able to buy a foreign auto is not nearly so painful as the loss of a good job.

Because the costs of imports are concentrated, the losers are both more visible and more easily organized. It takes only four chief executives of the automobile manufacturers and the president of the Autoworkers' Union testifying before Congress to make it absolutely plain what their losses are from imports. It is much harder for the millions of potential purchasers of foreign cars to get together and convincingly testify what their losses would be if imports were cut off.

Similarly, consider milk price supports. The dairy industry is small and very productive—so much so that it cannot sell as much as it produces at existing prices. The government therefore buys and stores a lot of milk.[12] The subsidization of milk is costly for taxpayers and milk consumers. Why does it continue? Because dairy farmers are a politically powerful, geographically concentrated group, whereas milk consumers are not. Furthermore, the dairy farmers' organization finds it easy to make political contributions to those who vote for their interest, whereas it would be extremely difficult for the general public to get together on the issue of the milk subsidy in order to make contributions to politicians opposed to the subsidy. Simply asking for voluntary contributions from those who want milk prices reduced runs up against the free-rider problem, as everyone recognizes that his or her small contribution will *by itself* make no real difference.

---

[12] It is no accident that U.S. foreign aid to poor countries often includes shipments of evaporated milk.

The fact that concentrated particular interests are more influential politically than diffused general interests helps one understand many government decisions. Government intervention in the economy cannot be viewed as simply correcting inefficiencies in the operation of markets. Although market failures provide a general theoretical justification for government intervention, the actual reasons for and the effects of government policy may have little to do with correcting market failures.

This discussion of the imperfections of government decision making in a democratic society should not be read to indicate that there is a better way. There is no perfect way to make society's decisions. The question is which system *best*, rather than perfectly, reflects the preferences of the people. As many are reputed to have said, "Democracy is the worst form of government, except for all the others."

Spending, Taxes, and Deficits

In section 1 we observed that government spending as a percentage of GNP has risen rapidly over the last 20 years in all developed market economies. Is this trend likely to continue?

Most of the increase in government spending in the United States and the other OECD countries over the past 20 years has been in social expenditures, particularly old age pensions, unemployment benefits, and health care. In part this change reflects the changing composition of the population. As the baby boom generation has matured, the population has aged. In the seven largest OECD countries, 27 percent of the population was age 14 or under in 1960, but only 20 percent was in 1985. Over that same period the percentage of the population above age 65 increased from under 10 percent to 13 percent. With present trends, the aging of the population will continue well into the twenty-first century.

Taking care of the old and sick has been increasingly viewed as an obligation of government rather than of the individuals themselves, their families, or private charities. And there is no reason why richer societies—as the OECD countries have become in the past 25 years—should not provide relatively more for the old than do poorer societies. No doubt, though, the growing political power of the old has played its part in increasing transfer payments to the aged. Presidential candidates in the United States have repeatedly pledged not to reduce Social Security benefits.

Whether society should devote an increasing share of its resources to the old and the sick is primarily a matter for political and ethical consideration. Economic analysis can reveal the effects of alternative means of doing so. What are the effects of reducing Social Security payments for older people who work? What are the effects of allowing people to retire and begin receiving benefits at age 60 instead of 62? Are there better ways than Medicare of providing health care to the elderly? Those are all questions on which economics can be brought to bear.

It is unlikely that the rising share of government spending shown in Figure 4-1 will continue. Certainly in the United States there has been a strong political reaction against this trend, suggesting that government will not command a larger share of resources in the near future than it does now. In many other OECD countries, conservative governments seeking to limit expenditures have come to power.

The problem of *large* U.S. deficits is relatively recent. These date from the tax cuts of 1981–1983, which were not accompanied by reductions in government expenditure. That decision was partly based on the argument that Congress would spend whatever revenues it had and that cutting revenue was therefore the way to cut spending. By 1987 it had not worked out that way. The deficit has been a major political and economic issue, but not much has been done about it. Why? Because Congress and the administration have not found programs to cut to make expenditures fit revenues. The political pressure against spending cuts has been too strong.

This could be the case because the benefits of many spending programs are concentrated, while the costs of paying for those programs are spread over the whole population. But it could also be the case because society genuinely prefers the government spending levels it has.

Controversy continues over the economic effects of deficits. When the government runs a deficit, spending more than it receives in taxes, it has to borrow to make up the difference. Government borrowing increases the national debt. Deficits are commonly believed to cause inflation, and the existence of the national debt is believed to impose a burden on future generations, who will have to pay taxes to pay off that debt.

Because it has been so difficult to cut government spending and because budget deficits in the United States have recently been large, there have been many proposals for laws that would make balanced budgets mandatory or would limit the share of government spending in GNP. Several states have passed laws that limit the level and/or growth of local taxes and spending.

There have also been attempts to pass laws to balance the budget at the federal level. Some want a constitutional amendment; others simply want a law passed by Congress. In 1985 Congress passed the Gramm-Rudman-Hollings bill, which required the deficit to be cut year by year until the budget was balanced by 1991. The bill was declared unconstitutional, but a replacement law was passed. Nonetheless, it is uncertain that Gramm-Rudman-Hollings will succeed in reducing the deficit, for it contains loopholes. Many ask why Congress should be expected to balance the budget as a result of the Gramm-Rudman-Hollings bill when it has had the power to balance the budget by cutting spending or raising taxes all along.

Why would a constitutional amendment or a general law limiting deficits help cut the deficit or spending when Congress cannot cut spending now? The answer is that because of logrolling and the paradox of voting, spending levels determined within the constraint of an overall total may well be different from those resulting from a series of piecemeal decisions.

■ The government plays a central role in modern mixed economies. Resources are allocated not only through markets but also through the political process. There are strong theoretical reasons why government intervention can help improve the allocation of resources, and much government action takes place in areas where markets work badly—for instance, in the provision of public goods such as defense and in regulation. Other government action redistributes income, transferring income from some people to others. Here the argument for government intervention involves judgments about ethics or fairness. But just as markets may work badly, so too may the political process. We will study not only how government can improve the performance of the economy in principle but also whether its actions actually do so in practice.

Summary

1. Governments play a major role in modern mixed economies. Total spending by all levels of government—federal, state, and local—in the United States exceeds 35 percent of GNP.
2. The role of government extends beyond purchasing goods and services and making transfer payments. Governments set the legal framework in which economic activity takes place, regulate economic activity, and attempt to stabilize the business cycle.
3. The taxes that governments raise to finance their activities have effects on the allocation of resources. By taxing a good, the government raises the price to the buyer and reduces the price received by the seller, thereby reducing the output of the good.
4. The more responsive quantity demanded (supplied) is to changes in price, the smaller the share of the burden of an excise tax borne by buyers (sellers), all else equal.
5. Government intervention in the economy can be justified on economic grounds by market failures. Stabilization of business cycles, deciding on the amount of public goods to produce, responding to externalities, correcting information-related problems, preventing the exercise of market power, and intervening to create a socially desired distribution of income and merit goods are all economic grounds for a government role in the economy.
6. Government decisions should represent the interests of society, but there is often no simple way of ascertaining the true interests or preferences of society as a whole. Voting procedures may produce inconsistent decisions, and logrolling may cause the costs of government actions to outweigh the benefits. The political process may give excessive weight to the preferences of concentrated interests.
7. The share of government spending in GNP has risen sharply over the past half century and even over the past 20 years. Much of that increase has been caused by increased transfer payments, partly as a result of the aging of the population. The increase in the government's share of total spending is slowing and may even be reversed. Laws to limit government spending and deficits have been passed at the state and federal levels in the United States.

Key Terms

Transfer payment
Stabilization policy
Market failure
Business cycle
Public goods
Private goods
Free rider
Externality
Information problems
Monopoly
Market Power
Merit goods
Public choice
Paradox of voting
Logrolling
Concentrated interests
Protectionism

Problems

1. In Table 4-1, specify the categories of spending that reflect (a) the government's provision of public goods, (b) a concern with merit goods, (c) a concern with the distribution of income.
2. Discuss what distinguishes Disneyland from a national park. Which of the two, if either, is a public good? Should either or both be publicly provided? Could the national parks be run by private enterprise?
3. Why does society try to make sure that every child receives an education? Discuss different ways this could be done and give reasons for choosing one method rather than another.
4. Which of the following qualify as public goods? (a) fire protection, (b) clean streets, (c) garbage collection, (d) ambulance service, (e) the U.S. Marine Corps Marching Band, (f) the postal service. Explain and discuss alternative ways of providing these goods.
5. Do you buy any goods or services from a monopoly? Specify

which, and explain why that product is sold by a monopoly and why government intervention may be needed to control the prices it charges.

6 In the 1970s government set strict rules about the amount of pollutants cars were permitted to emit. Does this fit any of the categories that justify government intervention in markets? Explain.

7 What reason is there for thinking that the distribution of income produced by private markets would be desirable or undesirable? What is your view on the desirability of government intervention to affect the distribution of income?

8 What is the basic difference between private and government decision making that makes it necessary to study the principles of public choice?

9 Discuss the following statement: "The problem with public decisions is that people hate taxes so much that the government never is willing to undertake all the spending it should for fear of offending those who have to pay the bill."

10 Suppose the government wanted to encourage the consumption of milk. Show, using a diagram like Figure 4-3, how a subsidy (the opposite of a tax) to milk producers could increase milk consumption. (You should show supply and demand curves with the price paid by consumers on the vertical axis.) When the government gives a subsidy, it pays a certain amount per gallon to the producer. Thus to answer the question, you have to show what happens to the supply curve of milk (drawn with the price paid by consumers on the axis) when the government pays a subsidy.

PART TWO
SUPPLY, DEMAND, AND PRODUCT MARKETS

Chapter 5
Elasticities and Market Adjustment

Chapter 3 analyzed the responses of supply, demand, and market equilibrium to changes. It showed, for instance, that increases in the price of any good or service reduce the quantity demanded and that increases in consumer income raise equilibrium price and quantity demanded for a normal good. In many situations, however, knowing the direction of the response to change is not enough; the *magnitude* of the response is often very important.

Events in the world oil market illustrate this point. At the end of 1973 the Organization of Petroleum Exporting Countries (OPEC), the main oil exporters, tripled the price of oil. (Recall that this is an increase of 200 percent.) Having read Chapter 3, you should expect that this price increase reduced the quantity of oil demanded, and the quantity of oil demanded did fall. If it had fallen to zero, the price increase would have also cut OPEC revenues to zero. Even a somewhat less drastic fall in the quantity of oil demanded would have lowered OPEC revenues. But in fact quantity demanded fell very little in the first few years after the price increase. Because OPEC member nations sold nearly unchanged amounts of oil at much higher prices, their revenues were immensely higher.

This chapter introduces the concept of *elasticity*, which economists use to deal with many situations in which magnitudes matter, and uses it to deepen our understanding of market adjustment to changes in the determinants of demand and supply. The discussion begins with the *price elasticity of demand*, a measure of the responsiveness of the quantity of a good demanded to a change in its price. Chapter 3 showed that quantity demanded depends not only on a good's own price but also on the prices of other goods and on consumers' incomes. For instance, an increase in the price of tea raises the quantity of coffee demanded. The *cross price elasticity of demand* measures the responsiveness of the quantity of one good demanded to a change in the price of another. The *income elasticity of demand* measures the response of the quantity of a good demanded to a change in income. These concepts are introduced and discussed in this chapter.

The focus then shifts to the supply side. The *price elasticity of supply*, which measures the responsiveness of the quantity of a good supplied to a change in its price, is central here. The chapter concludes with a discussion of the importance of time in the analysis of supply and demand: Price elasticities of demand and supply differ depending on *how long* demanders and suppliers have had to adjust to a price change. As we will see, this principle helps explain why OPEC no longer has the same power in the world oil market that it had in the early 1970s.

1. The Price Elasticity of Demand

Suppose the price of an input used to produce two goods increases, thus increasing suppliers' costs in both markets. Figure 5-1 illustrates the effects on the markets for the two goods involved. The effect of the input price rise is represented as an upward shift of the supply curve from S to S' in both panels. Since the determinants of demand have not changed, quantities demanded at all prices are not affected by the increase in sellers' costs, and the demand curves do not shift. As the figure shows, equilibrium prices rise from P_0 to P_1 and equilibrium quantities fall from Q_0 to Q_1. Both the old equilibrium points, labeled E, and the new equilibrium points, labeled E', are on the original, unchanged demand curves, D_a and D_b, respectively.

Inspection of Figure 5-1 certainly suggests that the price increase is more important in the market depicted in (*a*) than in that shown in (*b*), while the reduction in output appears less important in (*a*) than it is in (*b*). These differences reflect the fact that quantity demanded is less responsive to price changes in (*a*) than it is in (*b*). We now develop measures of the responsiveness of quantity demanded to changes in price that can support these impressions with numbers.

The first two columns of Table 5-1 present a hypothetical demand schedule for football tickets, and Figure 5-2 shows the corresponding demand curve. (For now ignore the third column in Table 5-1.) One obvious measure of the responsiveness of the quantity of tickets demanded to price changes is the increase in the number of tickets bought when price is cut by $1.[1] In this case that is 4000 tickets per dollar of price cut.

But this obvious measure cannot be used to make

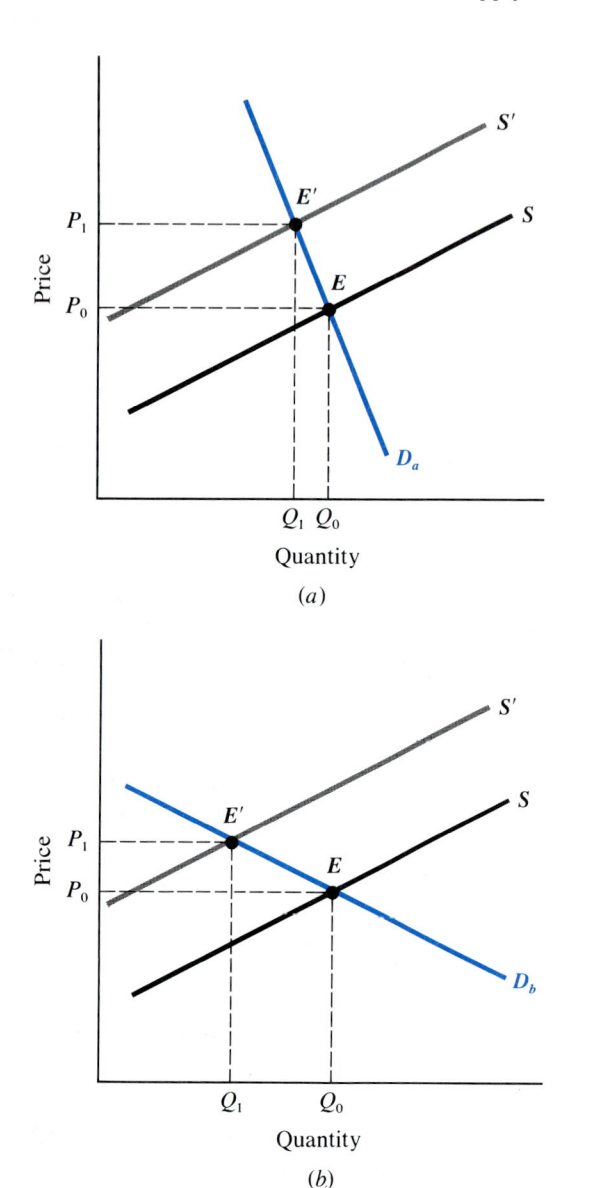

FIGURE 5-1. Effects of a Supply Shift on Price and Quantity. The supply curve shifts from S to S' in both panels. Price changes relatively more and quantity relatively less in (*a*) than in (*b*) because quantity demanded is less sensitive to price in (*a*) than it is in (*b*).

---

[1] The increase in the quantity of tickets demanded when the price is cut by $1 is greater the flatter the demand curve in Fig. 5-2.

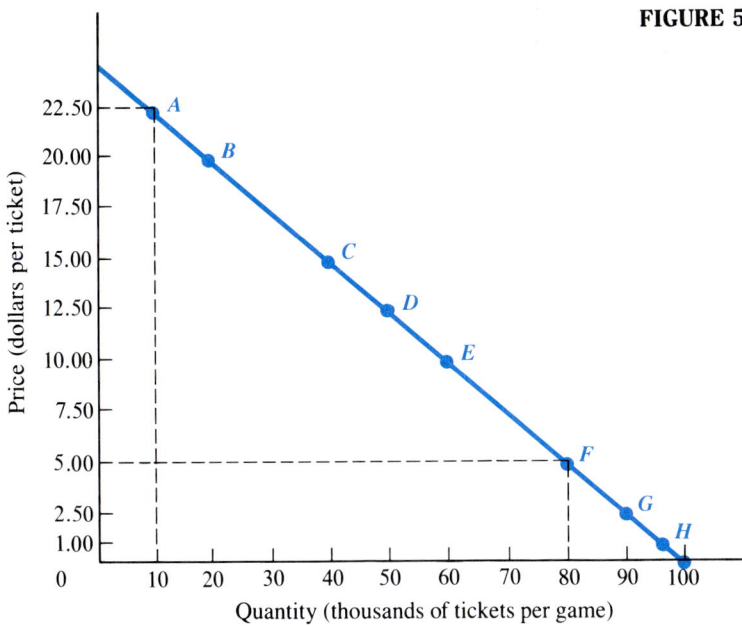

FIGURE 5-2. The Demand Curve for Football Tickets.

comparisons between different markets, since whether 4000 is a large or a small change in quantity demanded depends on the initial size of the market and the units of measurement used. An increase of 4000 in the quantity of compact disks demanded per year in the United States would be trivial; the same increase in the quantity of large office buildings demanded in Boston would be very important indeed. This same comparison makes it clear that whether a price change of $1 is large or small depends on the initial level of price. On the other hand, if we measured office space in Boston in square feet instead of buildings, an increase of 4000 in quantity demanded would be negligible while an increase in price of $1 would be important.

Chapter 2 noted that percentage changes are commonly used in economics to adjust for differences in initial levels and in units of measurement. Thus we can avoid the problems associated with the slope of the demand curve by instead relating the *percentage* change in quantity demanded to the *percentage* change in price. This produces the most useful measure of the responsiveness of quantity demanded to price changes.

● The *price elasticity of demand* is the percentage change in quantity demanded of a good produced by a 1 percent change in its price, holding constant all other factors that affect quantity demanded.

Economists frequently refer simply to the elasticity of demand when they mean the *price* elasticity of demand. The larger the price elasticity of demand, the more responsive quantity demanded is to changes in price and the *more elastic* demand is said to be.

In Figure 5-1, the price increase in (*a*) appears more important than that in (*b*) because the percentage in-

TABLE 5-1. The Demand Schedule and Price Elasticity of Demand for Football Tickets

Price, $/ticket	Quantity demanded, thousands per game	Price elasticity of demand
22.50	10	9.00
20.00	20	4.00
15.00	40	1.50
12.50	50	1.00
10.00	60	0.67
5.00	80	0.25
2.50	90	0.17
1.00	96	0.04

crease in (a) is clearly larger than that in (b). Similarly, the percentage decrease in quantity is clearly smaller in (a) than it is in (b). The price elasticity of demand is the relevant measure of the responsiveness of quantity demanded to price changes when the percentage change in price or quantity is used to measure the importance of changes in price or quantity. Thus the elasticity of demand is less at the initial equilibrium in Figure 5-1a than it is in Figure 5-1b, even if (a) depicts the market for records and (b) depicts the market for office buildings in Boston.

The following formula can be used to calculate the price elasticity of demand.[2]

$$\text{Price elasticity of demand} = \frac{\text{percentage change in quantity demanded}}{\text{percentage change in price}} \quad (1)$$

[2] The formula applies for any size of price change for linear demand curves and for small price changes for any shape of demand curve. The linear case serves to illustrate all the main elasticity concepts as simply as possible. The appendix to this chapter discusses the general (nonlinear) case.

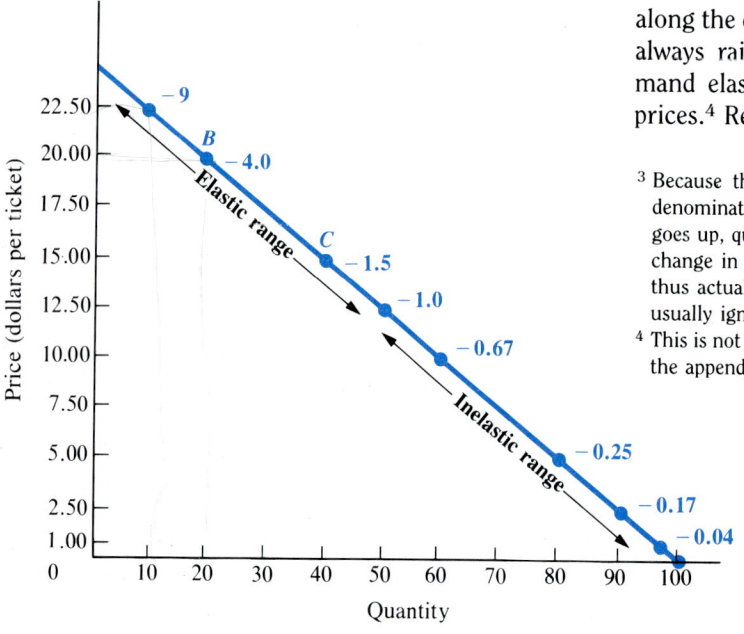

The last column of Table 5-1 shows the price elasticity of demand for football tickets at different prices. Here is a typical calculation for the price elasticity when price is cut from $22.50 to $20.00 and quantity demanded increases from 10 to 20 (thousand seats per game). The numerator in equation (1) is

$$\text{Percentage change in quantity demanded} = \frac{(20 - 10)}{10} \times 100\% = 100$$

The denominator is

$$\text{Percentage change in price} = \frac{(22.50 - 20.00)}{22.50} \times 100\%$$
$$= 11.1$$

Accordingly, the price elasticity of demand when price is $22.50 is given as follows:

$$\text{Price elasticity of demand} = \frac{100}{11.11} = 9.0$$

The price elasticities of demand shown in Table 5-1 are all calculated in this manner.[3] Figure 5-3 again shows the demand curve for football tickets, this time with the price elasticities of demand at different points indicated. Notice that the elasticity in Figure 5-3 is not constant along the demand curve even though a cut in price by $1 always raises quantity demanded by 4000 tickets. Demand elasticity is high at high prices and low at low prices.[4] Referring to equation (1), this happens because

[3] Because the demand curve slopes downward, the numerator and denominator in equation (1) have opposite signs—that is, when price goes up, quantity demanded goes down. The ratio of the percentage change in quantity demanded to the percentage change in price is thus actually negative. By convention, though, the negative sign is usually ignored.

[4] This is not necessarily true for demand curves that are not linear; see the appendix to this chapter.

FIGURE 5-3. The Elasticity of Demand along the Demand Curve for Football Tickets. Price elasticity of demand on this linear demand curve is high at high prices and low at low prices.

an increase in quantity demanded of 4000 tickets represents a smaller *percentage* increase when price is initially low and quantity demanded is already high, and a $1 price decrease is a larger *percentage* decrease in these conditions.

2. Demand Elasticity and Sellers' Revenue

Suppose the information in Table 5-1 has been computed by the stadium manager, who is interested in the total revenue the university receives from football tickets. Looked at from the buyers' viewpoint, total spending on football tickets (or any other good or service) is the product of price and quantity demanded.

Total spending = price × quantity demanded   (2)

Total spending by purchasers is also the amount of revenue received by sellers.

Table 5-2 shows total spending on football tickets at each price in the fourth column. For example, at a price of $20 per ticket, the quantity demanded is 20 (thousand), and hence total spending on tickets is 400 ($20 × 20). Note that in Table 5-2 total spending first rises and then declines as price falls.

Equation (2) points to the two effects of a change in price on total spending. When price falls, the first term on the right-hand side of equation (2) falls, tending to reduce total spending. But when price falls, quantity demanded *rises*, tending to raise total spending. Whether total spending actually rises or falls depends on whether quantity goes up enough to offset the effect of the lower price.

Table 5-2 exhibits the following important general result:

● **When the elasticity of demand for any good is greater than 1, a small reduction in price increases spending on that good; when demand elasticity is less than 1, a small reduction in price reduces total spending on the good.**

This result is certainly plausible. In order for the rise in quantity demanded to outweigh the effect of a price reduction on total revenue, quantity demanded must be sufficiently responsive to price. The greater the demand elasticity, the more responsive quantity demanded is to changes in price.

The relation between demand elasticity and changes in revenue is so important that it has determined the terminology used to describe demand elasticities.

● **Demand is said to be *elastic* if the price elasticity of demand is greater than 1. Demand is *inelastic* if the price elasticity is less than 1. Demand is *unit-elastic* if the elasticity equals 1.**

In Figure 5-3, demand is elastic at all prices above $12.50 and inelastic at all prices below $12.50. Demand is unit-elastic at a price of $12.50.

Figure 5-4 shows graphically how total spending changes as price changes when the demand curve is linear. In all three cases, the initial price, P_A, is reduced to P_B. As a consequence, quantity demanded rises from Q_A to Q_B. Initial spending is equal to price times quantity demanded, $P_A \times Q_A$, or the rectangle OP_AAQ_A. At the new, lower price, total spending is equal to $P_B \times Q_B$, or the rectangle OP_BBQ_B.

What is the change in spending? The reduction in price implies that spending falls by the gray area marked with a minus sign, but increased quantity demanded raises spending by the colored area marked with a plus sign. The net result in Case A is an increase in spending, since the (+) area is larger than the (−) area. In other

TABLE 5-2. Price Elasticity of Demand and Total Spending on Tickets

Price, $/ticket	Quantity demanded, thousand per game	Elasticity	Total spending (price × quantity), $ thousand per game
22.50	10	9.00	225
20.00	20	4.00	400
15.00	40	1.50	600
12.50	50	1.00	625
10.00	60	0.67	600
5.00	80	0.25	400
2.50	90	0.17	225
1.00	96	0.04	96
0.00	100	0.00	0

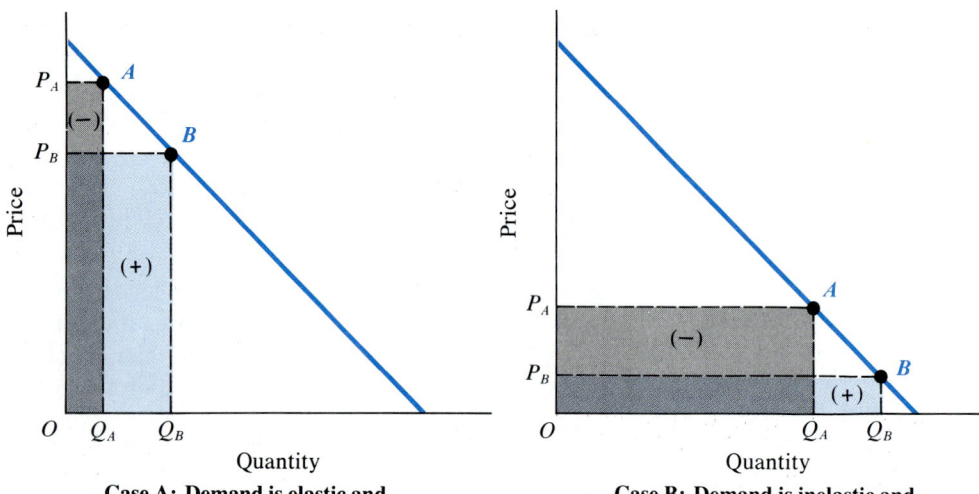

Case A: Demand is elastic and expenditure increases when price falls

Case B: Demand is inelastic and expenditure falls when price falls

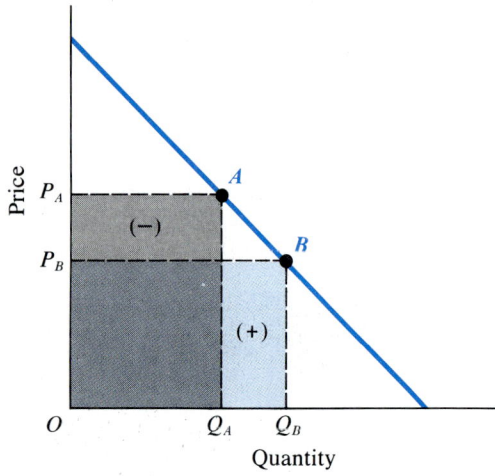

Case C: Demand elasticity is 1 and expenditure stays the same when price falls

FIGURE 5-4. The Relationship between Elasticity of Demand and the Effects of Price Changes on Total Spending. Total spending on the good is the product of price and quantity, equal to the rectangle OP_AAQ_A when price is P_A. When price falls to P_B, total spending on the good changes by the difference between the colored (+) area and the gray (−) area.

words, in the elastic range of the demand curve (toward the upper end) a cut in price raises not only quantity demanded but also total spending. The increase in quantity demanded more than outweighs the decline in price.

Case B shows the opposite result in the inelastic part of the demand curve. Here a cut in price, while of course raising quantity demanded, leads to a fall in total spending. The (+) area is smaller than the (−) area because the quantity demanded is not sufficiently responsive to price, and total spending thus is lower at the lower price.

Case C depicts the borderline case, in which the extra spending due to higher quantity demanded exactly balances the effect of the lower price. In this case, demand is unit-elastic. To see why, recall the definition of total spending in equation (2): total spending = price × quantity demanded. Now if price falls by 1 percent and

TABLE 5-3. Demand Elasticities and Total Spending

	Price elasticity of demand		
Change in price	Above 1 (elastic)	Equal to 1 (unit-elastic)	Below 1 (inelastic)
Price increase	Spending falls	Spending is unchanged	Spending rises
Price decrease	Spending rises	Spending is unchanged	Spending falls

quantity demanded rises, as a consequence, by 1 percent, then the product of price times quantity demanded remains unchanged.[5] If quantity demanded increases by more than 1 percent, total spending rises; if it rises by less than 1 percent, total spending falls. Thus the unit-elastic point on the demand curve is the dividing point below which further price cuts reduce total spending.

Table 5-3 summarizes how the relationship between price changes and consumer spending on a good depends on the price elasticity of demand.

How to Maximize Total Revenue

As we have noted, total spending on a good by consumers is also equal to total revenue received by sellers. Demand elasticity is thus a very useful concept for sellers who want to figure out the effects of price changes on their revenues.

For instance, suppose the manager of the football stadium whose demand schedule is presented in Tables 5-1 and 5-2 is trying to decide what price to charge to maximize ticket revenue per game. Table 5-2 shows that the answer is $12.50, the point of unitary elasticity. At any higher price, the manager can increase revenue by cutting price; at any lower price, she can increase revenue by increasing price. *The conclusion is that spending and revenue are maximized at the point where demand is unit-elastic.*

Figure 5-5 shows the total revenue data from Table 5-2 graphically. The amount spent on football tickets—total ticket revenue per game—is shown at each price. From the diagram, total spending, or total revenue, reaches a maximum at the price of $12.50, at which the demand elasticity is 1. This confirms the conclusion that revenue or total spending is maximized when the price elasticity of demand is equal to 1.[6]

Box 5-1 shows how knowing the relation between demand elasticity and sellers' revenue helps us understand an interesting feature of agricultural markets. Any individual farmer's income will be higher, the better is his harvest, all else equal. But farmers' total income is usually *lower* when all harvests are good than when they are bad. Here and in many other settings it is important

---
[5] Because the price elasticity of demand is different at every point on the demand curve in Figure 5-4, a 1 percent fall in price from the point of unitary elasticity will actually *slightly* reduce total spending. Why? As the price is cut, the consumer moves along the demand curve to points where elasticity is slightly below 1, and spending therefore falls with further cuts in price. The price elasticity relationships described above and summarized in Table 5-3 apply *exactly* only for infinitesimally small changes in price.

[6] Note that sellers are usually more interested in maximizing profit—the difference between revenue and costs—than in maximizing revenue. We consider profit maximization in Chapters 9 and 11.

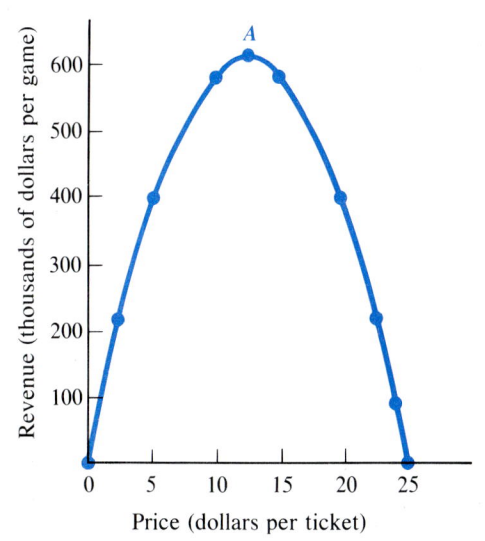

FIGURE 5-5. Price and Total Revenue from Football Tickets. As price is cut from high levels, total spending by buyers (and therefore total revenue of sellers) increases. It continues increasing so long as demand is elastic. When price hits $12.50, at point A, demand is unit-elastic. Further cuts in price then reduce revenue because demand is inelastic at lower prices.

Box 5-1. Farmers and Bad Harvests—And the Fallacy of Composition

Are farmers better off when the weather is good or when it is bad? The natural tendency is to think that farmers will be better off if the weather is good and crops are large. Paradoxically, however, farmers may be better off when the weather is bad and there is a poor harvest.

Figure 5B-1 shows the demand curve for food, D. The demand for food is typically inelastic, as is D in the range P_A to P_B. (Section 4 discusses why.)

After farmers have planted their seed, the size of the harvest depends largely on the weather. If the harvest is small, as shown by supply curve S', the price will be high. If the crop is large as a result of good weather, as shown by supply curve S, the price will be low.

When do farmers earn more? Because demand is inelastic, total spending on food falls when the price of food falls. Because price is higher when S' is the supply curve, farmers receive more revenue when the weather is bad. Bad weather is thus good for farmers.

The fact that large crops reduce sellers' revenue when demand is inelastic leads sellers in such markets sooner or later to try to limit the total quantity supplied. By restricting supply they can prevent collapses in revenue caused by bumper crops.

For instance, Brazil has been the most important coffee-growing nation in the world for many years. Before the Brazilian government stepped in, a bumper crop of coffee in Brazil would lead to a collapse of prices and revenues in the world market, because the demand for coffee is inelastic. The government decided to help Brazilian coffee producers by preventing bumper crops from coming on the market. How? Any time there was a bumper crop, the government would buy up supplies (at low prices) and simply burn them.

Figure 5B-1 shows that all farmers *taken together* will be better off if the weather is bad and the harvest is small so long as demand is inelastic. But what if any *one* farmer experiences a disaster, such as a fire, that reduces his harvest alone? That individual farmer will indeed be worse off as a result of the disaster. The reduction in the amount he sells will have very little impact on the market price, which is unaffected by his bad luck. He therefore loses from his own fire but would have gained had everyone's crops been reduced.

This example warns us to beware of an error of logic called the *fallacy of composition* by keeping the following principle in mind:

● **What is true for a single individual is not necessarily true for everyone taken together, and what is true for everyone taken together does not necessarily hold for a single individual.**

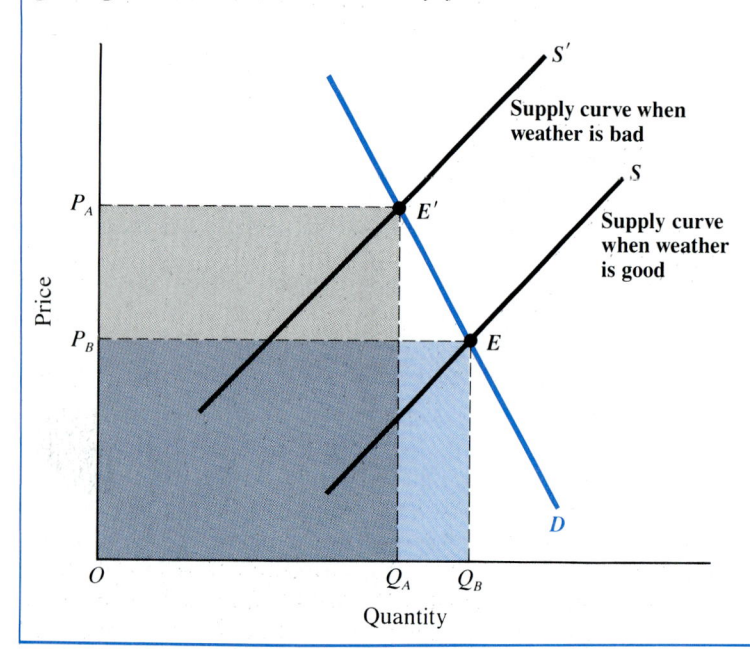

FIGURE 5B-1. Bad Weather Helps Farmers. Demand for food is inelastic at points E and E'. Thus a poor harvest, which corresponds to supply curve S' and leads to a high price (P_A), gives farmers as a group more revenue than a good harvest, which corresponds to supply curve S and leads to a lower price (P_B).

to recognize that what is true for a single individual is not necessarily true for everyone taken together.

3. Demand Elasticity: Extreme Cases

We now look at what is implied for price elasticities when the demand curve takes on two important extreme shapes, as illustrated in Figure 5-6.[7] The vertical demand curve D shows absolutely no response of quantity demanded to price changes. In this case the elasticity of demand is zero; an economist would say that demand is completely, or *perfectly*, *inelastic*. Someone who says, "I *must* have that, whatever the price," claims that his demand for some good is perfectly inelastic. Of course, since everyone has limited resources, there is always some price increase that will reduce the quantity demanded of any good. But someone's demand elasticity for a particular good could well be zero over a wide range of prices.

The elasticity of demand is infinite on the *perfectly elastic* horizontal demand curve D' in Figure 5-6. Here purchasers are not willing to pay more than P_0 for any amount of the good; quantity demanded is zero at higher prices. The way the curve is drawn, individuals are willing to buy unlimited amounts at price P_0. This too is not believable, again because resources are limited. But it is quite possible that demand is perfectly elastic over some range of quantities, so that consumers are willing to purchase any amount within that range at price P_0.

Demand curve D' is an important case, because it represents the demand curve faced by a small competitive firm in a large market. If such a firm tries to charge more than the other sellers, it will lose all its customers. But because it is small relative to the market as a whole, it can sell as much as it wants to produce at the prevailing price. We return to this important special case in Chapter 9.

Table 5-4 summarizes the concepts developed so far in connection with the price elasticity of demand.

[7] More on shapes of demand curves (for example, that they need not be straight lines) and on measuring elasticities appears in the appendix at the end of this chapter.

TABLE 5-4. Demand Elasticity Concepts

Elasticity	Technical term	Description
Infinite	Perfectly elastic Infinitely elastic	Demand curve is horizontal
Greater than one	Elastic	Demand curve is negatively sloped
One	Unit-elastic	
Less than one	Inelastic	
Zero	Perfectly inelastic Completely inelastic	Demand curve is vertical

4. Substitutes and Price Elasticity

What determines whether the price elasticity of demand for any particular good or service will be large or small? The most important factor is the availability of good substitutes. Consider two examples.

First, take the market for all foods: meat, bread, fish, poultry—everything edible. Suppose the prices of *all* foods rise by 1 percent. Will the overall quantity demanded change by a large amount, such as 10 percent, or a small amount, such as 0.5 percent? The answer is more nearly 0.5 percent. The reason is that consumers have no good substitutes for food in general and cannot really do without it. They can adjust their diets, using food more efficiently and getting slimmer, but most

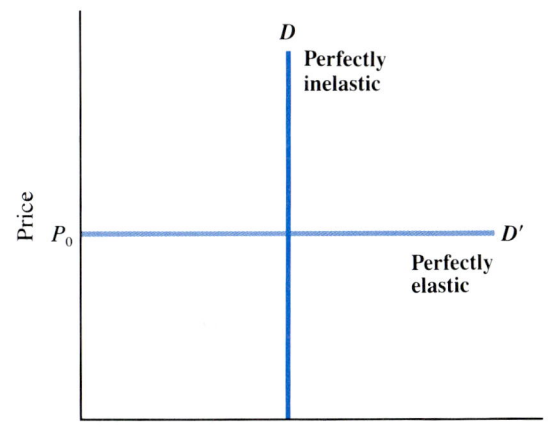

FIGURE 5-6. Perfectly Elastic (D') and Inelastic (D) Demand Curves.

people will find it very painful to reduce the quantity of food demanded very much.

Second, suppose there is a 1 percent rise in the price of a particular brand of cornflakes, and no other prices change. In this case, most consumers will find plenty of good substitutes available. They can consume other cornflakes, other breakfast cereals, or any of a variety of alternative breakfast foods, including eggs, steak, pastries, fruit, or simply bread and butter. Some consumers, of course, may have such strong preferences for a particular brand of cornflakes that they will not view any of these alternatives as good substitutes, and their individual demand schedules may be inelastic. But since most consumers have many relatively good substitutes available, the overall price elasticity of demand for a particular brand of corn flakes may well be 3 or 5 or more.

The principle that the availability of substitutes determines demand elasticity implies that a more narrowly defined commodity (a particular brand of cornflakes as opposed to cornflakes in general, cornflakes as opposed to breakfast foods, or oil as opposed to energy) typically has a larger price elasticity of demand than a more broadly defined product.

Table 5-5 lists some estimates of price elasticities from two empirical studies of consumer behavior. These estimates confirm that the demand for groups of basic commodities, such as food and shelter, is inelastic. By contrast, the price elasticity of demand can be quite large for more narrowly defined products, such as sporting goods and toilet articles. An interesting comparison is between the elasticity of demand for all forms of transportation, which is 0.60, and the elasticity of demand for a very particular form, namely, taxicab rides, which is 1.24. The fact that the demand elasticity for taxicabs is so much larger reflects the availability of substitute forms of transportation, including buses, private cars, and rental cars. In contrast, the only alternative to consuming transportation services is not traveling.

5. Other Demand Elasticities

The quantity of a good demanded is affected not only by its own price but also by the prices of other goods and by consumers' incomes, as was discussed in Chapter 3. The responsiveness of quantity demanded to these influences is also generally measured by elasticities.

Cross Price Elasticity of Demand

We saw in Chapter 3 that the quantity of a good demanded increases when the price of a substitute rises and falls when the price of a complement rises. Thus the quantity of fish demanded will increase when the price of beef rises, for instance, while the quantity of cars demanded will fall when the price of gasoline rises.

● The *cross price elasticity of demand* is the percentage change in the quantity of a good demanded when the price of another good increases by 1 percent.

The cross price elasticity of demand for good *i* (e.g., fish) with respect to the price of good *j* (e.g., beef) is calculated from the following formula, which closely resembles equation (1):

TABLE 5-5. Estimates of Price Elasticities of Demand

Good or Service	Price elasticity of demand
Food	0.63
Clothing	0.51
Transportation	0.60
Shelter	0.56
Medical care	0.80
Toilet articles	2.42
Sporting goods	2.40
Taxicab services	1.24
Flowers, seeds, plants	2.70

Sources: E. Lazear and R. Michael, "Family Size and the Distribution of Real Per Capita Income," *American Economic Review*, March 1980, Table 2, for rows 1-4; and H. Houthakker and L. Taylor, *Consumer Demand in the United States*, Harvard University Press, 1970, Table 3.2, for rows 5-9.

$$\begin{array}{c}\text{Cross price elas-}\\\text{ticity of demand of}\\\text{good } i \text{ with respect}\\\text{to good } j\end{array} = \frac{\begin{array}{c}\text{percentage change}\\\text{in quantity}\\\text{of good } i \text{ demanded}\end{array}}{\begin{array}{c}\text{percentage change}\\\text{in price of good } j\end{array}} \quad (3)$$

The expressions "good *i*" in the numerator and "good *j*" in the denominator emphasize that the cross price elasticity measures the effect of a change in the price of *one* good on the quantity of *another* good demanded. Note also that the cross price elasticity of good j with respect to the price of good i is not in general equal to the quantity defined by equation (3).

The definitions of complements and substitutes given in Chapter 3 can be expressed in terms of cross price elasticities.

● **Goods are *substitutes* when the cross price elasticities of demand between them are positive; goods are *complements* when the cross price elasticities are negative.**[8]

The larger the positive cross price demand elasticities between any pair of goods, the more easily buyers substitute between them. Thus one would expect the cross price elasticities between two brands of diet cola to exceed those between bread and apples, even though bread and apples are probably also substitutes to some extent. Similarly, large negative cross price elasticities reveal important instances of complementarity.

Table 5-6 shows estimates of the price elasticities and cross price elasticities of demand for some goods. By convention we show the elasticity of demand for each good with respect to its own price as positive, even though an increase in the price of the good reduces quantity demanded. The cross price elasticities of demand are shown with the measured signs.

The estimates in Table 5-6 show that an increase in the price of either fish or meat increases the quantity of the other good demanded; meat and fish are therefore sub-

---

[8] As we noted in Chapter 3, this definition is not perfectly satisfactory in theory (though it is usually fine in practice); a slightly different definition is given in more advanced courses.

TABLE 5-6. Price Elasticities and Cross Price Elasticities

	Elasticity of demand with respect to the price of		
	Meat	Fish	Tobacco products
Meat	0.48	0.01	−0.04
Fish	0.06	0.72	−0.03

Source: A. P. Barten, "Consumer Demand Functions under Conditions of Almost Additive Preferences," *Econometrica*, January–April 1964, Table XV.

stitutes. The table also implies that tobacco products are a complement for both meat and fish—perhaps because some people like to smoke during meals. Note that the quantity demanded of both meat and fish is more responsive to a change in each good's own price than to a change in the price of the other good. Note also that the cross price elasticity of demand for fish with respect to the price of meat is not equal to the cross price elasticity for meat with respect to the price of fish.

Income Elasticity of Demand

Changes in the level of consumers' income change the quantity of any good or service demanded at all prices and thus shift the demand curve, as we discussed in Chapter 3. The responsiveness of quantity demanded to changes in income—that is, the extent to which a change in income shifts the demand curve—is measured by the income elasticity of demand.

● **The *income elasticity of demand* is the percentage change in quantity demanded caused by a 1 percent increase in income.**

The income elasticity of demand is calculated as follows:

$$\text{Income elasticity of demand} = \frac{\text{percentage change in quantity demanded}}{\text{percentage change in income}} \quad (4)$$

In Chapter 3 we discussed the difference between *normal* and *inferior* goods. The quantity of a normal good demanded increases when income rises, while the demand for an inferior good falls when income rises. These classes of goods can be defined by their income elasticities of demand.

● **A *normal good* is a good for which the income elasticity of demand is positive. An *inferior good* is a good for which the income elasticity of demand is negative.**

Which goods are inferior? As income increases, consumers tend to shift toward higher-quality models of all kinds of goods—from cheap shoes toward more expensive ones, from cheap cuts of meat toward steaks, from cloth coats to fur coats. Low-quality variants of any good are thus likely to be inferior in the economic sense. As

TABLE 5-7. The Demand Response to Income Changes: Summary

Type of good	Defining characteristic	Income elasticity	Income growth implies budget share	Example
Normal goods	Quantity demanded rises with income	Positive	May rise or fall	Clothing
Luxuries	Quantity demanded rises proportionately more than income	Greater than 1	Rises	Sporting goods
Necessities	Quantity demanded rises proportionately less than income	Less than 1	Falls	Food
Inferior goods	Quantity demanded falls when income rises	Negative	Falls	Low-quality shoes

income rises, the quantity of those goods demanded actually declines.

The income elasticity of demand is useful for making another important distinction, between luxuries and necessities.

● A *luxury* has an income elasticity of demand greater than 1. A *necessity* has an income elasticity of demand less than 1.

If the income elasticity of demand exceeds 1, a 1 percent increase in income raises quantity demanded by more than 1 percent, all else equal. With prices fixed, this means that total spending on the good also rises by more than 1 percent. Thus the *share* of consumer spending accounted for by luxuries rises with income. The terminology here reflects the fact that rich people spend a larger fraction of their incomes on luxuries than poor people do. Fur coats and steak are luxuries. By the same reasoning, the share of consumer spending devoted to necessities such as socks and bread falls with a rise in income. This means that the poor generally spend a larger part of their income on necessities than do the rich. As a country becomes wealthier, industries producing inferior goods decline, industries producing necessities grow less rapidly than average, and industries producing luxury goods grow more rapidly than average.

"Necessity" and "luxury" are examples of words that are used in everyday language to mean many things but that have precise meanings in the language of economics. To avoid confusion, keep in mind that in economics the meanings of these terms do not extend beyond the definitions we have just given. Thus beer and cigarettes are necessities to an economist, even though they are hardly necessary for physical survival.

Table 5-7 presents a summary of the relationships between changes in quantity demanded and changes in income that were defined in this section.

Table 5-8 gives estimates of income elasticities for a variety of goods and services. Note that transportation here appears as a luxury good; this reflects, among other things, the possibility of graduating from a bus to a Rolls-Royce. Food and shelter are normal, nonluxury goods, since their income elasticities are positive but less than 1.[9] The table shows that a number of goods have quite high income elasticities, including such obvious

[9] Food has been known to be a necessity in the economic sense, i.e., a good with income elasticity positive but less than 1, since the nineteenth-century studies of Ernst Engel, a German statistician and economist. Engel's finding continues to hold in regard to later experience. For instance, in the United States, 27 percent of consumers' spending was for food in 1954, compared with only 19 percent in 1984.

TABLE 5-8. Income Elasticities of Demand

Good	Income elasticity
Food	0.77
Clothing	0.82
Transportation	1.10
Shelter	0.89
Medical care	1.90
Toilet articles	3.6
Sporting goods	3.7
Taxicab services	2.8

Sources: E. Lazear and R. Michael, "Family Size and the Distribution of Real Per Capita Income," *American Economic Review*, March 1980, Table 2, for rows 1–4; and H. Houthakker and L. Taylor, *Consumer Demand in the United States*, Harvard University Press, 1970, Table 3.2, for rows 5–8.

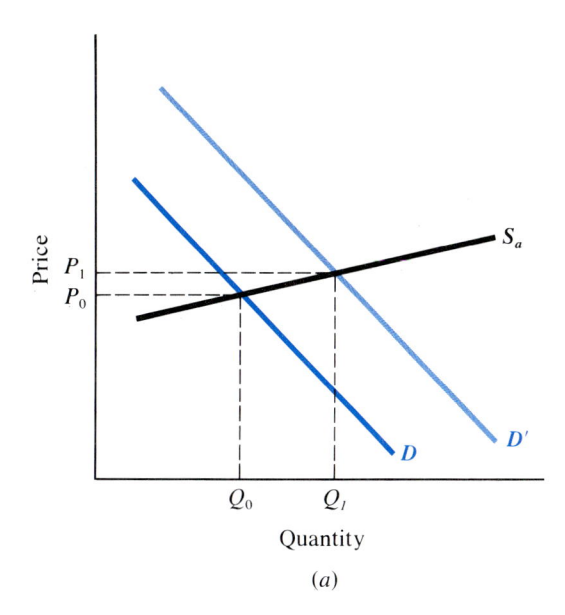

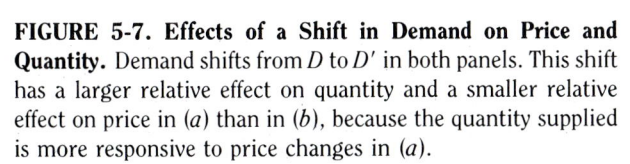

FIGURE 5-7. Effects of a Shift in Demand on Price and Quantity. Demand shifts from D to D' in both panels. This shift has a larger relative effect on quantity and a smaller relative effect on price in (a) than in (b), because the quantity supplied is more responsive to price changes in (a).

luxury items as jewelry, taxicab rides, and sporting goods. An income elasticity of 3.7 for sporting goods, for example, implies that for every rise in income of 1 percent, the quantity demanded of sports equipment rises by 3.7 percent. As this finding indicates, the sporting goods industry has grown rapidly in recent years.

6. The Price Elasticity of Supply

The price elasticity of supply (often called just the elasticity of supply) is as important as the elasticity of demand in determining how markets respond to changes in the economy. When consumer income increases or some other change occurs that has the effect of shifting the demand curve, price and quantity will adjust *along* the supply curve. Then the magnitudes of the changes in price and production are determined by the shape of the supply curve, as Figure 5-7 illustrates. (The next two paragraphs parallel our earlier discussion of Figure 5-1.)

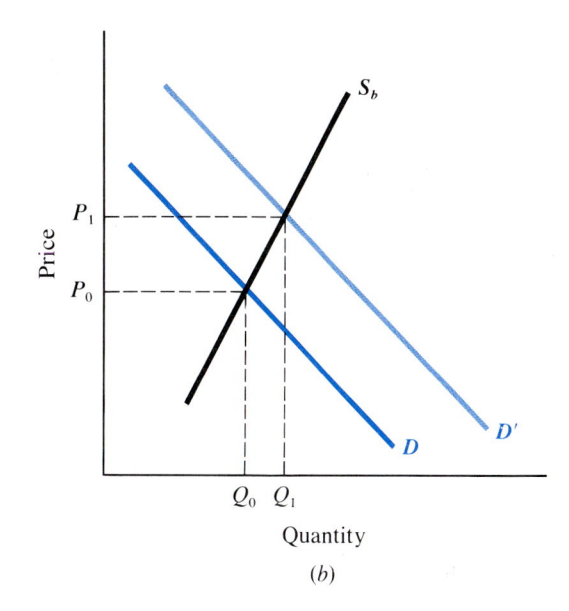

Figure 5-7 shows the effect of an increase in consumer income on two markets. The increase in income has the effect of shifting the demand curve from D to D' in both markets. As a consequence, the equilibrium price rises from P_0 to P_1, and the equilibrium quantity rises from Q_0 to Q_1. Both the old and new equilibrium points are on the fixed supply curves, S_a in Figure 5-7a and S_b in Figure 5-7b. The figure suggests to the eye that the increase in quantity is more important in the market depicted in (a), while the price increase appears more important in (b). It is also visually apparent that this difference arises because quantity supplied is more responsive to price along supply curve S_a than it is along S_b.

But exactly as in the case of the demand curve, the slope of the supply curve cannot be used to compare supply responsiveness between these two markets. Because we don't know the scales used to draw Figure 5-7, the dollar increase in price in (a) could well exceed that in (b). (Figure 5-7a might describe the market for yachts, and Figure 5-7b the market for shrimp, for instance.) Inspection of Figure 5-7 does show that the *percentage* increase in price is larger in (b), while the *percentage* increase in quantity is smaller. Accordingly, as in the case of demand, an elasticity measure, which relates these percentage changes, gives the most useful measure of the responsiveness of quantity supplied to changes in price.

- The *price elasticity of supply* (or, more commonly, *elasticity of supply*) is the percentage change in the quantity supplied of a good produced by a 1 percent change in its price, holding constant all other factors that affect quantity supplied.

Because the supply curve slopes upward, the elasticity of supply is always positive. The more elastic supply is, the easier it is for sellers to increase their outputs to take advantage of an increase in price, and the larger the (percentage) increase in the quantity supplied in response to any given (percentage) increase in price. At the initial equilibria in Figure 5-7, the supply curve S_a in (a) is more elastic than S_b in (b), regardless of the industries depicted. The following formula can be used to compute the elasticity of supply.[10]

$$\text{Elasticity of supply} = \frac{\text{percentage change in quantity supplied}}{\text{percentage change in price}} \quad (5)$$

We noted previously that whether a small price increase raises or lowers sellers' total revenue depends on whether the elasticity of demand is below or above 1. But a *supply* elasticity of 1 does *not* provide an important dividing point, because the total revenue received by suppliers always increases as price rises along the supply curve—since price and quantity increase together.

The elasticity of supply is zero when the supply curve is vertical, as it is in S' in Figure 5-8. There is no increase in quantity supplied no matter how much the price rises; supply is said to be perfectly inelastic. The supply curve of Leonardo da Vinci's painting of Mona Lisa is perfectly inelastic; there is a fixed quantity available (one) that cannot be increased no matter how high the price rises.

The elasticity of supply is infinite when the supply curve is horizontal, as in the case of S in Figure 5-8. In this case there is no supply at all unless price is at least P_0, but suppliers are willing to sell any amount de-

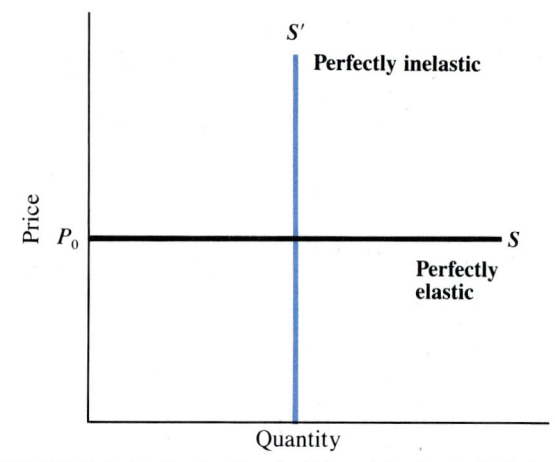

FIGURE 5-8. Perfectly Elastic (S) and Inelastic (S') Supply Curves.

manded at price P_0. This supply curve is said to be perfectly elastic. Because resources are limited, no real supply curve can be perfectly elastic at all quantity levels, but a supply curve can have infinite elasticity over a considerable range of quantities if the good can be produced at a constant cost per unit. The supply curve of pins is probably horizontal over the range of quantities that are likely to be demanded in practice, for instance.[11]

7. Demand and Supply in the Short Run and the Long Run

So far we have described how to measure the responsiveness of buyers and sellers to changes in prices, but we have said nothing about the time over which their responses occur. Events in the oil market after the 1973

---

[10] As in the case of the demand curve, the formula applies exactly for a change in price of any size if the supply curve is linear and for small price changes for any shape of supply curve, linear or nonlinear.

[11] Because sellers can often shift from producing one good to producing another—consider red wine and white wine—it is sometimes useful to work with cross price elasticities of supply. These are defined by changing equation (3) so that "supply" replaces "demand." Cross price elasticities of supply are generally negative: An increase in the price of red wine, all else equal, will reduce the quantity of white wine supplied. Large negative cross price supply elasticities between two goods arise when it is easy, on average, for sellers to shift from supplying one to supplying the other.

OPEC price increase discussed at the start of this chapter make clear the importance of timing in practice.

Having tripled oil prices in 1973, with effects discussed at the start of the chapter, OPEC again raised the price of oil sharply at the end of 1979, this time by 250 percent. But over the decade starting in 1973, firms and households had time to respond to the higher price in many ways. People bought smaller, more fuel-efficient cars. They insulated their homes better. Some oil users switched to coal for heating fuel. In the case of oil, quantity demanded responds far more to a change in price over 10 years than it does to a change over 1 year. This is one reason why OPEC was in trouble in the mid-1980s, no longer planning further price rises but rather trying in vain to keep the price of oil from falling.

Another reason for OPEC's problems is that the quantity of oil supplied by nonmembers of OPEC increased substantially during the 1970s. The quantity of oil supplied by nonmembers is, like the quantity of oil demanded, far more responsive to a change in price over a long period, when there has been time to explore for oil, drill wells, and build new refineries, than it is in a short period of a few years.

As this experience illustrates, the response of both quantity demanded and quantity supplied to a change in price depends on how long buyers and sellers have to adjust to the change. Both demand and supply elasticities are typically greater in the long run than in the short run.

Demand Adjustment

The response of the quantity of gasoline demanded to the dramatic increase in its price during the early 1970s provides an example of the difference between short-run and long-run responses to a price change. In 1973 most Americans had big cars that got poor mileage. They had few ways of economizing on gasoline when its price shot up. Many consumers decided to buy smaller cars in the future, but in the meantime they still had their big cars and still had to use them to go to work and run errands. Thus the quantity of gasoline demanded fell very little in the first few months after its price increased. But as consumers replaced big cars with small cars, the demand curve for gasoline gradually shifted.

● **The *long-run demand curve* shows how quantity demanded depends on price when buyers have been able to adjust fully to price changes. A *short-run demand curve*, in contrast, applies when consumers have not fully adjusted to price changes.**

In general there is a set or family of short-run demand curves, differing in the extent to which buyers have been able to adjust to price changes. Because consumers respond more to a change in price in the long run than in the short run, the long-run demand curve is generally more elastic than any short-run demand curve.[12]

In the case of gasoline, the long-run demand curve may describe buyer behavior 5 or 6 years after a price increase. That is how long it takes for most people to buy more fuel-efficient cars.[13] In the case of cornflakes, full adjustment to a price increase may take only a few weeks, as people use up the small amounts they have in the closet and move on to buy other breakfast foods.

SUPPLY SHIFTS. The general difference between the short-run and long-run responses to a supply shift are illustrated in Figure 5-9. The initial equilibrium in the market for beef is described by point E. Suppose there is then a permanent shift in the supply curve, from S to S', caused by government policies that raise the price of the grain used to feed cattle. In the short run the price of beef rises a lot, from P_0 to P_1, while the quantity demanded adjusts relatively little, from Q_0 to Q_1, as the equilibrium point moves from E to E' along the short-run demand curve, D_S. When beef becomes noticeably more expensive, consumers begin to experiment with other meats and alter their eating habits. As they discover alternatives to beef that they like, they gradually reduce the quantity of beef demanded at the new, higher

---

[12] Durable goods present a complication here. When the price of cars goes down, the quantity of cars that people want to *own* rises, and the long-run change in the quantity owned will exceed the short-run change. But the quantity of cars *purchased* may increase more in the short run than in the long run as people adjust their ownership patterns.

[13] Complete adjustment to the price change of gasoline takes as long as it takes the last gas guzzler to die—and that could be decades. Although the definition of the long run says "fully" adjust to price changes, the long run is in practice defined as a period long enough for most of the adjustment (say, 95 percent) to take place.

94 Part Two: Supply, Demand, and Product Markets

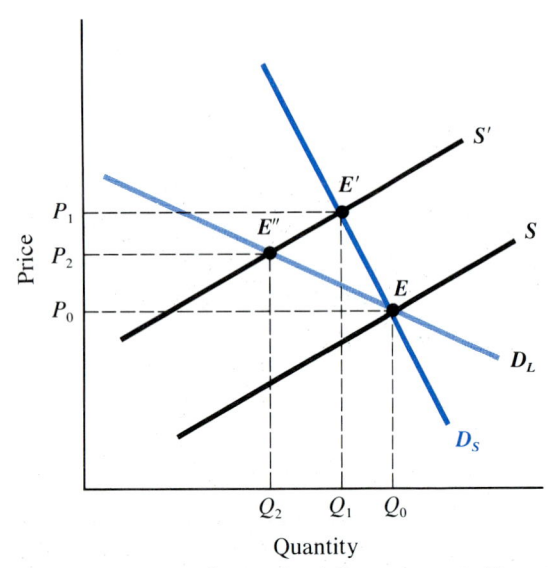

FIGURE 5-9. Price and Quantity Adjustment over Time to a Supply Shift. When the supply curve shifts upward from S to S', equilibrium moves in the short run from E to E' with price rising sharply and quantity not falling much. Then, over time, as consumers adjust to the rise in price, the long-run demand curve D_L becomes relevant, the equilibrium moves to E''' with price falling below P_1, and quantity continuing to fall to Q_2.

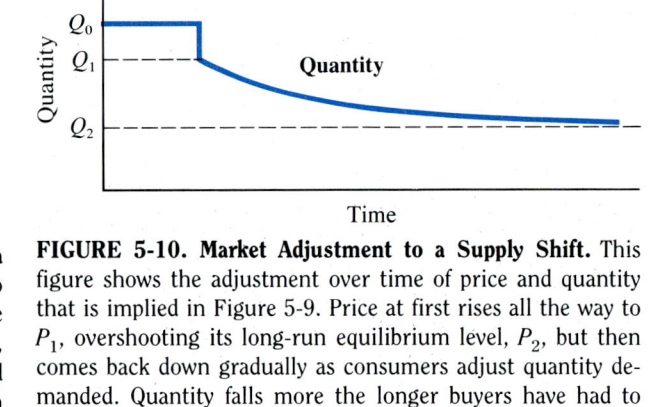

FIGURE 5-10. Market Adjustment to a Supply Shift. This figure shows the adjustment over time of price and quantity that is implied in Figure 5-9. Price at first rises all the way to P_1, overshooting its long-run equilibrium level, P_2, but then comes back down gradually as consumers adjust quantity demanded. Quantity falls more the longer buyers have had to adjust their behavior.

prices. In the long run, when consumers have fully adjusted their eating habits in response to higher prices, the demand curve becomes D_L, and the long-run equilibrium is at point E'''. The change from E' to E''' is a movement along the new supply curve. At the final equilibrium point, E''', price (P_2) is higher than at E but lower than at E', and quantity (Q_2) is lower than at both E and E'.

The point describing equilibrium does not shift all at once from E' to E'''. Rather, the adjustment takes time, with the demand curve shifting gradually from D_S to D_L as more and more consumers become accustomed to eating less beef and more of other meats. Equilibrium price and quantity thus adjust gradually over time. Figure 5-10 shows how price and quantity respond over time to the shift in the supply curve in Figure 5-9. The price rises rapidly to P_1, then gradually falls back from that high level to P_2. Price exceeds the initial level, P_0, at all times. Price is described as *overshooting* the long-run equilibrium level. Quantity, in contrast, adjusts in the same direction all the time. As Figure 5-9 illustrates, it is because quantity demanded adjusts slowly (consumers take time to alter their eating habits) that price overshoots the new long-run equilibrium level P_2 by first going beyond it to P_1.

Note how the price system is sending signals to demanders. The sharp rise in price to P_1 sends a clear signal that there is a benefit to adjusting to the supply shift. The sharp initial increase in price gives consumers a strong incentive to adjust their eating habits and reduce the importance of beef in their diets.

Supply Adjustment

The supply curve, like the demand curve, is more elastic in the long run than in the short run.

- **A *long-run supply curve*** shows how quantity supplied depends on price when firms have had time to adjust fully to price changes. A ***short-run supply curve***, in contrast, applies when sellers have not fully adjusted to price changes.

Firms are limited in their short-run supply response because they cannot adjust all their inputs quickly. The size of a shop or factory is not quickly adjustable, nor is the machinery available for production. Firms can and do expand output through overtime work and by hiring more workers, but that is relatively expensive. Thus quantity supplied is less responsive to price in the short run than it is in the long run, when the firm has time to move to a new factory and obtain the machinery it needs as well as to train the new labor it needs.

DEMAND SHIFTS. Figure 5-11 shows how the slow adjustment of supply affects the responses of equilibrium price and output to a shift in demand. S_S is the short-run supply curve of exercise equipment, and S_L is the corresponding long-run curve. Assume that the demand curve shifts from D to D' as people worry more about health and fitness. In the short run, equilibrium moves from E to E' along the short-run supply curve. As sellers fully adjust to the price rise by further increasing the output of exercise equipment, the market moves along the new demand curve to its long-run equilibrium at E''. Prices rise a lot in the short run, sending a signal to suppliers that it is profitable to adjust to the demand shift by producing more exercise equipment.

Comparing the preceding paragraph with our earlier discussion of supply shifts, a useful general proposition emerges.

- **A shift in either the supply curve or the demand curve has its greatest impact on price in the short run but its greatest impact on quantity in the long run.**

Box 5-2 discusses an example of dynamic responses to price changes that illustrates several of the concepts developed in this chapter.

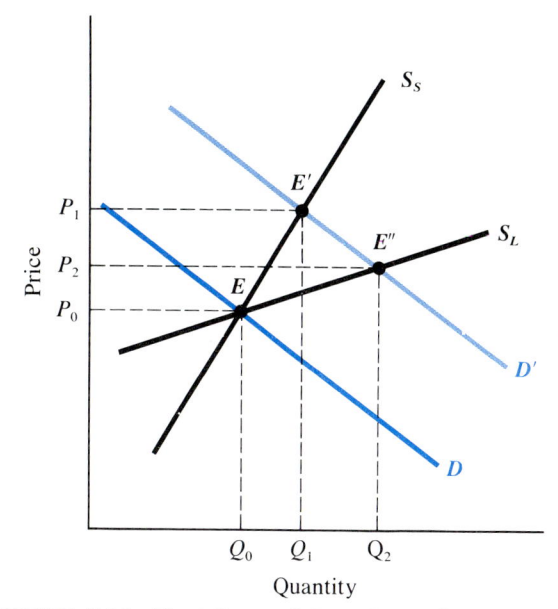

FIGURE 5-11. Short-Run and Long-Run Adjustment to a Demand Shift. When the demand curve shifts from D to D', equilibrium shifts initially from E to E', because the short-run supply curve is S_S. The long-run supply curve is S_L, so that the long-run equilibrium is at E''. As in Figure 5-9, price initially overshoots its new long-run level and quantity again adjusts gradually toward the long-run equilibrium level, Q_2.

■ The concepts presented in this chapter can be thought of as tools that greatly enhance the power and usefulness of the supply and demand model introduced in Chapter 3. In fact, there is really not much more to be said, even in the most advanced courses, about the use of supply and demand curves to analyze the determination of equilibrium price and output. However, there is a lot more to be said about exactly how the locations of those curves are determined and how they relate to the behavior of households and firms. We turn next to this task and begin by studying how the behavior of individual consumers and households determines the market demand curves for goods and services.

Box 5-2. OPEC and the Price of Coal

As we discussed in Chapter 3, the massive rise in the price of oil in 1973 and 1974 set off an increase in the prices of other sources of energy, such as coal and natural gas. The price of oil went up because OPEC, which at that time was able to set the price, decided to raise it. But the price of coal was not set by OPEC. Why, then, did it rise soon after the price of oil rose?

Using Figure 5B-2, we can employ the concepts developed in this chapter to analyze the increase in the price of coal. Figure 5B-2a shows the market for oil; Figure 5B-2b shows the market for coal. In (a) OPEC raises the price from P_0 to P_1. Because coal and oil are substitutes, an increase in the price of oil shifts the demand curve for coal to the right in (b), from D to D'. Because the short-run supply elasticity of coal is small, the price of coal increases substantially in the short run, and quantity supplied rises relatively little.

Referring back to Figure 5-11, after the initial shift in the demand curve for coal, its price should fall gradually over time because the long-run supply curve is more elastic than the short-run supply curve; quantity supplied increases as price falls during this movement along the new demand curve. Figure 5B-3 shows that the actual pattern in the coal market was consistent with this picture. The real price of coal nearly doubled from 1972 to 1975 and then slowly fell. Meanwhile coal production kept increasing. (The low output of coal in 1978 was caused by a coal miners' strike.)

The increase in the price of oil should have led consumers to reduce oil consumption over time as they moved to smaller cars and found other ways of economizing on petroleum products, and the shift in the demand curve for coal implies that coal consumption should have increased. Table 5B-1 provides evidence that is consistent with this prediction. The ratio of petroleum consumption to coal consumption fell substantially after 1973. Indeed, while the consumption of petroleum actually fell, that of coal increased substantially.

TABLE 5B-1. Ratio of Petroleum to Coal Consumption, 1972–1983

Years	1972–74	1975–77	1978–80	1981–83
Ratio	2.70	2.62	2.48	1.96

Source: *Statistical Abstract of the United States, 1985*, Table 950. Petroleum and coal consumption are measured by their energy content.

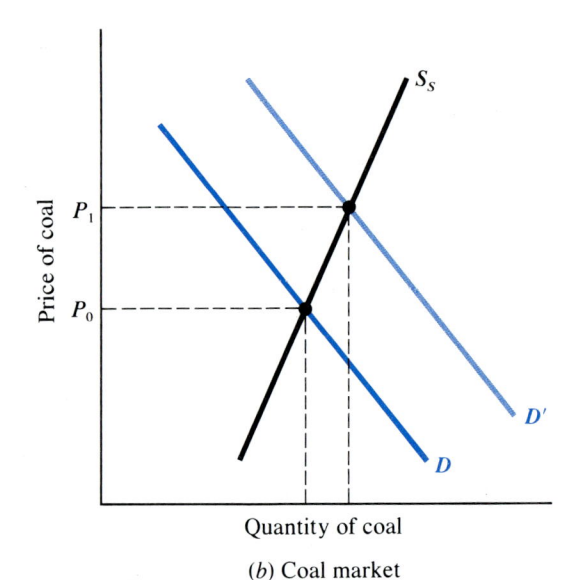

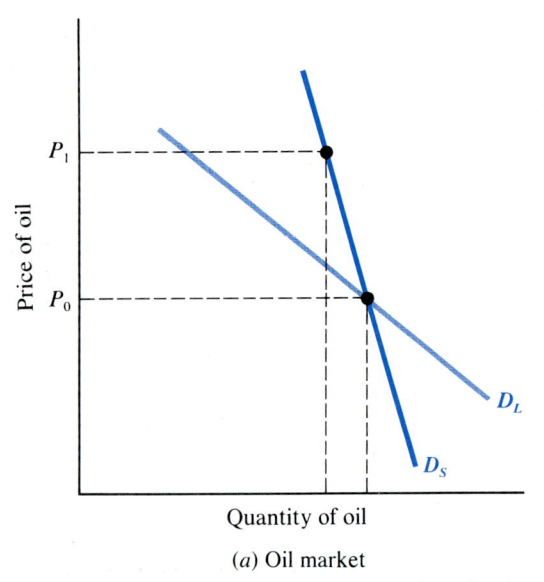

FIGURE 5B-2. Effects of OPEC on the Price of Coal. When OPEC raised the price of oil from P_0 to P_1 [shown in (a)], it thereby shifted the demand curve for coal, a substitute for oil, to the right, from D to D' [shown in (b)]. The price of coal rose substantially, and quantity did not change much in the short run. But because the long-run supply curve of coal was more elastic, the quantity of coal supplied rose substantially over time, as shown in Figure 5-11.

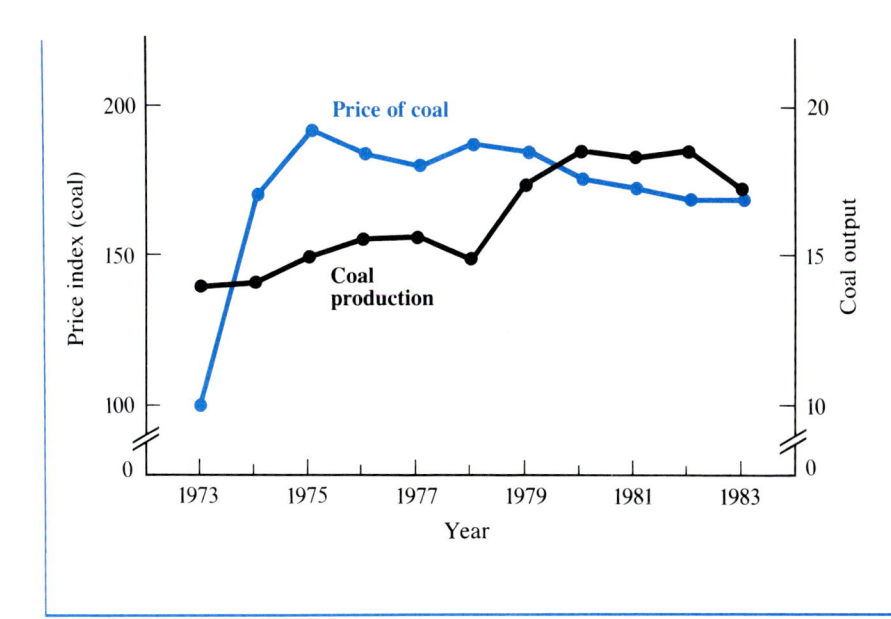

FIGURE 5B-3. Coal Price and Production, 1973–1983. The real price of coal (expressed as an index with 1973 = 100) is measured on the left-hand vertical axis, and coal production (in energy units (quadrillions of Btu) is measured on the right-hand vertical axis. A near doubling of the real price of coal from 1973 to 1975 led to a slow increase in the production of coal (interrupted by a strike in 1978) while price slowly came down from its peak level. The adjustment pattern is similar to that described in Figure 5-11. (Source: *Statistical Abstract of the United States, 1985*, Tables 950 and 961. Output is in quadrillion Btu; price index is for price of bituminous coal relative to GNP deflator.)

Summary

1. The price elasticity of demand, or elasticity of demand, measures the responsiveness of the quantity of a good demanded to a change in its price. It is defined as the ratio of the percentage change in quantity to the percentage change in price.
2. The price elasticity of demand changes along a linear (straight-line) demand curve. It is high when price is high and low when price is low.
3. If the elasticity of demand exceeds 1, demand is said to be elastic. In this case, total spending on the good increases as price falls. Since total spending is equal to the total revenue of sellers, sellers' revenue rises as price falls in this case. The demand elasticity is infinite in the perfectly elastic case of a horizontal demand curve.
4. If the elasticity of demand is less than 1, demand is said to be inelastic. In this case sellers' revenue falls when price falls. The demand elasticity is zero in the perfectly inelastic case of a vertical demand curve.
5. Sellers' revenue is maximized when the elasticity of demand is 1. Demand is then said to be unit-elastic.
6. The elasticity of demand for a good is determined chiefly by the availability of good substitutes. This implies that the demand elasticity will be lower for a large group of goods (e.g., food) than for any particular good in that group (e.g., cornflakes).
7. The cross price elasticity of demand measures the responsiveness of the quantity of a good demanded to a change in the price of another good. Goods are substitutes if the cross price elasticity of demand is positive and complements if it is negative.
8. The income elasticity of demand measures the responsiveness of quantity demanded to a change in income. It is equal to the percentage change in quantity demanded divided by the percentage change in income. Goods for which the income elasticity of demand is positive are normal; a good is inferior if the income elasticity of demand is negative. A good is a luxury if the income elasticity of demand exceeds 1 and a necessity if the income elasticity is less than 1. Consumers spend a larger share of their income on luxuries as income increases.
9. The price elasticity of supply, or elasticity of supply, is the percentage increase in quantity supplied divided by the percentage increase in price. Supply elasticity is greater than or equal to zero; it is zero when the supply curve is vertical and infinite when the supply curve is horizontal.
10. Both the elasticity of demand and the elasticity of supply are typically larger in the long run than in the short run. This implies that a shift in either the supply curve or the demand

curve produces a large change in price and a small change in quantity in the short run and a smaller change in price and a larger change in quantity in the long run.

Key Terms

Price elasticity of demand
Elastic demand
Perfectly (infinitely) elastic demand
Inelastic demand
Perfectly (completely) inelastic demand
Unit-elastic demand
Fallacy of composition
Cross price elasticity of demand
Substitutes and complements
Income elasticity of demand
Normal and inferior goods
Luxuries and necessities
Price elasticity of supply
Short-run demand and supply curves
Long-run demand and supply curves
Short-run and long-run adjustment
Overshooting

Problems

1. Consider the market for potatoes. The supply curve is assumed to be vertical—farmers supply a given quantity of 1000 tons at each level of price. The demand schedule is downward-sloping. The initial price is $120 per ton. (a) Suppose a harvest failure reduces the available supply by 10 percent to 900 tons. Show diagrammatically the effect of the supply reduction on equilibrium price. (b) Suppose the elasticity of demand at the initial equilibrium price is 0.5. By how much must price increase to restore market equilibrium? [You don't have to use a diagram to answer (b). Equation (1) will be enough.]

2. Consider the following goods: (a) milk, dental services, beverages; (b) candy, chewing gum, food; (c) entertainment, movies, travel. For each of these goods, state whether you expect demand to be price-elastic or price-inelastic. In addition, rank the elasticities of demand within each group of goods, where possible. Explain your answers.

3. The subway system has been losing money and decides to raise the price of a ride to try to increase its revenue and reduce losses. What determines whether this is the right move?

4. (a) Explain where, on a straight-line demand curve, consumer spending is at a maximum and explain why. (b) What use could this information be to the manager of the football stadium, the demand schedule for which appears in Table 5-1?

5. The accompanying table gives estimates of price and income elasticities for food and for consumer durable items such as toys, sports equipment, boots, and pleasure aircraft. Characterize the demand for each good as elastic or inelastic and say whether the good is a necessity or a luxury.

| | Elasticities of demand ||
	Price	Income
Food	0.5	0.7
Consumer durables	2.4	3.7

6. Suppose the weather has been good, and a big harvest has been predicted. Explain why individual farmers will continue to work hard to bring in the largest possible crop even though they know they would all have been better off if the weather had not been good.

7. When costs go up, automobile manufacturers usually raise prices to help cover the higher costs. Explain whether this makes sense if the demand for their products is elastic.

8. The accompanying table shows hypothetical levels of income and spending on clothing and shoes and on housing, respectively, for years 1 and 10. Calculate the share of income spent on each of the goods in the two years. Then say whether the goods are necessities or luxuries. (Assume that the real prices of these goods did not change over the period and that real income rose from year 1 to year 10.)

Income and Spending on Clothing and Shoes and on Housing

| | Income, | Spending ($ billion) on ||
Year	$ billion	Clothing and shoes	Housing
1	600	50	100
10	1500	100	240

9. Explain the following: If the elasticity of demand for a good is not 1 and if consumer income is fixed, then a change in the price of the good must affect the demand for at least one other good.

10. Compare two countries: Mexico (where income is lower) and Canada (where income is higher). In which country

would you expect a higher fraction of consumer spending to be devoted to (a) food? (b) electricity? (c) cosmetics?

11 Movie tickets are currently sold at $4, and the Golden Twenties movie theater attracts 200 customers per day at that price. The manager has reason to believe that demand for seats in his theater is highly elastic, with a price elasticity of demand of 4, and therefore decides to cut price to $3.50 to fill the 100 seats that are currently vacant. (a) Is there any reason to believe that the demand elasticity facing the Golden Twenties movie house might be as high as 4? Explain. (b) If the demand elasticity is indeed 4 and price is cut from $4 to $3.50, by how much will quantity demanded rise? (c) What will happen to total revenue? (d) *Extra credit.* What would happen to quantity demanded if other movie houses in the area followed the Golden Twenties' move and reduced their prices too?

12 Use the data in the accompanying table to calculate the price elasticity of demand for good 1 and the cross price elasticity of demand for good 1 with respect to the price of good 2. Are goods 1 and 2 substitutes or complements?

	Price of good 1	Price of good 2	Consumption of good 1
Situation A	16	10	40
Situation B	12	10	50
Situation C	12	12	52

Appendix: More on Demand Curves and the Price Elasticity of Demand

This appendix takes up two questions. First, what are the possible shapes of demand curves? Second, how can demand elasticities be measured consistently?

Different Demand Curves

All the demand curves in this chapter are linear (i.e., straight lines). The elasticity of demand varies along these curves, starting out high when price is high, reaching 1 at the midpoint, and then falling to zero when price reaches zero. But demand curves certainly are not all linear. The main advantage of linear demand curves is that they are easy to draw and analyze.

Elasticity is constant and equal to 1 all along the specially shaped demand curve D in Figure 5A-1a.[14] In

[14] To measure price elasticity at any point on a nonlinear demand curve, one must first draw the tangent to that curve at the point considered, as discussed in the appendix to Chapter 1. Then the elasticity of the (linear) tangent at the point of tangency is equal to the elasticity of the (nonlinear) demand curve at that point.

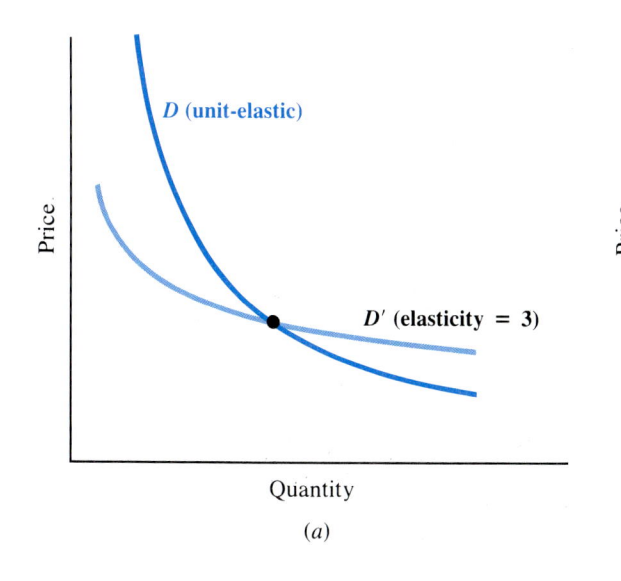

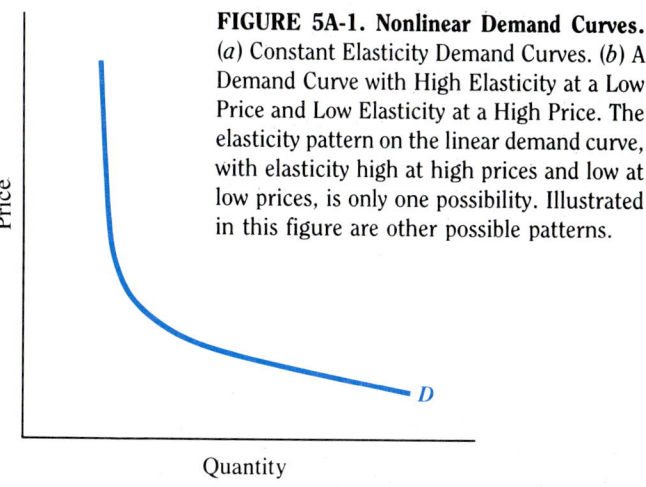

FIGURE 5A-1. Nonlinear Demand Curves. (a) Constant Elasticity Demand Curves. (b) A Demand Curve with High Elasticity at a Low Price and Low Elasticity at a High Price. The elasticity pattern on the linear demand curve, with elasticity high at high prices and low at low prices, is only one possibility. Illustrated in this figure are other possible patterns.

this special case, total spending on the good is the same no matter what the price. Demand curve D' in (a) also has constant elasticity. This time the elasticity is 3, and so total spending on the good rises as price is cut, no matter whether the price is high or low. Thus Figure 5A-1a shows two demand curves, D and D', one of which (D) has higher elasticity than the other (D') at all prices.[15]

Figure 5A-1b depicts another possibility. In the demand curve, D, shown here, which is more sharply curved than those in (a), elasticity is low at high prices and high at low prices.

What actual demand curves look like is a matter of *fact*. Shapes of demand curves vary from good to good, but it is often difficult to distinguish between plausible alternative shapes on the basis of available data. Both linear demand curves and demand curves with constant elasticity often turn out to be useful in practice.

Arc Elasticity

The elasticity of demand is usually defined with reference to a single point on the demand curve. Thus elasticity is different at every point on the straight-line demand curve in Figure 5-3, and equation (1) can be used to compute the elasticity at any point.

For some problems, however, one is interested in the elasticity of demand associated with a substantial change in price. For this purpose, the formula shown in equation (1) has the awkward implication that the demand elasticity appears to differ depending on whether price is being raised or lowered, even if the demand curve is linear.

To see the problem, consider price and quantity changes between points B and C on the curve shown in Figure 5-3. The elasticity of demand at point B is shown as 4.0 in Tables 5-1 and 5-2. This is because when price falls from $20 at B to $15 at C, quantity demanded rises by 100 percent from 20,000 to 40,000 and price falls by 25 percent.[16] Elasticity is thus equal to 4, (100/25).

But now consider the reverse direction, from C to B. Starting at C, price rises by 33.3 percent when it goes up from $15 to $20 [($5/$15) × 100 percent]. Quantity falls by 50 percent [(20,000/40,000) × 100 percent]. Now elasticity seems to be 1.5 (50/33.3). This is, of course, the elasticity at point C.

These calculations indicate that if equation (1) is used to measure the price elasticity associated with a substantial change, such as that between points B and C, the calculated elasticity will depend on the direction in which price is changing. The concept of *arc elasticity* was invented to avoid this difficulty.

● **The *arc elasticity* measures the elasticity of demand between two points using the average price between those two points and the average quantity to compute percentage changes.**

The formula for the arc elasticity is

$$\text{Arc elasticity of demand} = \frac{\text{change in quantity demanded}}{\text{average quantity}} \div \frac{\text{change in price}}{\text{average price}}$$

Let us use this formula to calculate the arc elasticity of demand between points B and C. The change in quantity demanded is 20,000. Average quantity is 30,000 [(20,000 + 40,000)/2]. The change in price is $5, and the average price is $17.50 [(20 + 15)/2]. Thus

$$\text{Arc elasticity} = \frac{20{,}000}{30{,}000} \div \frac{5}{17.5}$$

$$= \frac{(2)(17.5)}{(3)(5)}$$

$$= 2.33$$

This calculation does not depend on whether we begin at point B or at point C. As might be expected, the arc elasticity (2.33) falls between the elasticities at points B (4.0) and C (1.5).

---

[15] For students who are familiar with logarithms, we note that along both these curves there is a linear relation between the *logarithms* of price and of quantity demanded.

[16] To check the calculations, the percentage change in quantity demanded is ([(40,000 − 20,000)/20,000] × 100 percent) and the percentage change in price is ([(20 − 15)/20] × 100 percent).

Chapter 6
Consumer Behavior and Market Demand

In Chapters 3 and 5 we described demand curves, the elasticity of demand, and the factors that shift demand curves. For instance, if apples are a normal good, an increase in consumers' income shifts the demand curve for apples to the right. Our goal in this chapter is to go behind the demand curve to learn why and how it shifts and why it slopes downward.

We begin by showing how market demand curves summarize the demand curves of individual consumers. We then develop the economic model of consumer behavior, which explains how consumers' tastes and incomes, along with all prices, determine their demand schedules for all goods and services.[1] We then use the model of consumer behavior to answer a number of questions about demand curves. Two in particular are important: How do we know that demand curves *must* slope downward? How is consumer demand theory used in the cost-benefit analyses of government decisions?

The economic model of consumer behavior is useful and interesting both in its own right and because it is an instructive example of *marginal analysis* of the type discussed in Chapter 1. The same sort of analysis is employed in later chapters and in fact is used every day in business decision making.

1. Individual and Market Demand Curves

Individual consumers and households are the units that make spending decisions and thus determine the quantity demanded of any good or service. But it is the *market*, not the individual demand curve, that (along with the supply curve) determines price and thus quantities bought and sold. Thus we begin our analysis of demand by describing the relationship between the market demand curve and the demand curves of individuals.

The market demand *schedule*, which was introduced in Chapter 3, is related to the demand schedules of all the individual buyers in a simple way.

---

[1] Business firms are important buyers in some markets. Both consumers and businesses buy paper clips, for instance, but businesses buy more of them. Similarly, consumers are important sellers in some markets, notably those for labor services. This chapter deals only with consumer buying behavior. Business buying behavior and consumer selling behavior are discussed in Part 4, which deals with markets for inputs used by firms.

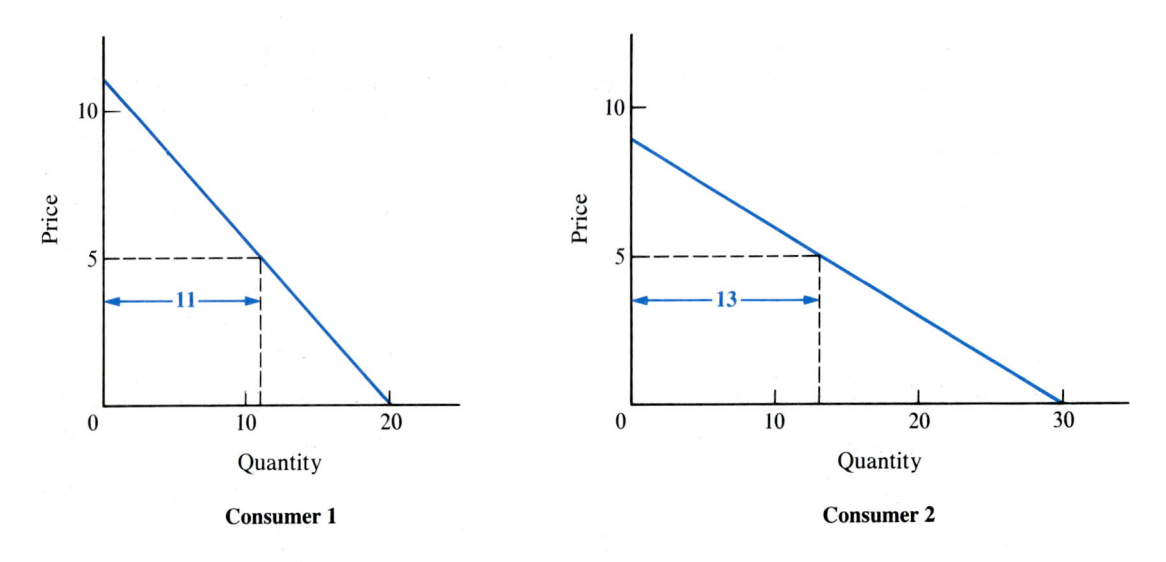

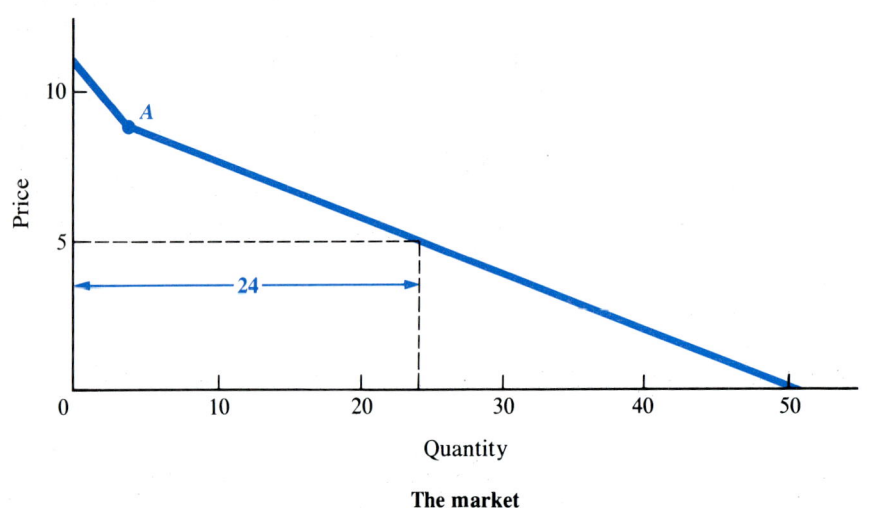

FIGURE 6-1. Individual Demand Curves and the Market Demand Curve. The market demand curve is the horizontal sum of the individual demand curves. For instance, if the price is $5, the quantity demanded by consumer 1 is 11 units and the quantity demanded by consumer 2 is 13 units. The total quantity demanded at a price of $5 is thus 24 units, as shown on the market demand curve.

● The *market* demand schedule, which gives the total quantity demanded at each price, holding constant all other influences on demand, is obtained by adding the quantities demanded by all buyers at each price. That is, the *market* demand schedule is the sum of buyers' *individual* demand schedules.

Similarly, the market demand *curve* is the sum of the demand curves of all the individuals in the market. Figure 6-1 shows how the market demand curve is constructed by adding the quantities demanded at each price by all individuals (in this case, just two of them) in the market. This process is known as *adding the demand curves horizontally*. The market demand curve is kinked at point A because it is there, at a price of $9, that consumer 2 comes into the market. At higher prices, the quantity demanded by consumer 2 is zero, and the entire market demand comes from consumer 1.

● The *market* demand curve is obtained by adding the *individual* demand curves of all buyers horizontally.

In Chapter 3 we argued that market demand curves slope downward. This is often referred to as the *law of demand*: Increases in price reduce the quantity demanded. But can we *prove* that this law must hold in all markets? Figure 6-1 makes it clear that if all individual demand curves slope downward, so will the market demand curve. To see whether we can prove that individual demand curves slope downward, let us develop a model that describes the behavior of individual consumers.

2. Diminishing Marginal Utility and Demand Curves

In the nineteenth century, some economists believed that there exists a definite numerical indicator of each person's happiness or *utility*. In this section we assume for the sake of simplicity that they were right and thus suppose that each consumer has, somewhere in her head, a *utility meter* that measures how happy she is. According to this model of consumer behavior, each consumer chooses quantities demanded of all goods and services in order to maximize her utility, given the limits imposed by available income. The farther to the right the needle on her utility meter is at any instant, the happier she is. The units marked on this meter are traditionally called *utils*.

This is a strange description of human behavior in two important respects. First, it is hard to believe that there really is some measure of happiness that can be used to support statements such as, "Dick's happiness would double if he ate one more chocolate." Second, most of us don't think about maximizing anything when we decide how many chocolates to eat or how many concerts to attend. However, we show in section 3 that the utility meter assumption simplifies our argument without misleading us.

We first describe the way in which available income and prevailing prices limit the choices available to a consumer. We then develop the notion of *marginal utility* and use it to show how individuals' demands for goods and services reflect preferences, prices, and income.

The Budget Constraint

Consider the economic problem facing Fred, a young consumer with an income of $12 per week. He can divide his income between hamburgers and concerts, both of which he likes. Hamburgers cost $1 each, while concert tickets cost $2.[2] In deciding how many hamburgers to eat and how many concerts to attend, Fred has to take into account the fact that he can spend only $12 per week. His income and the prices of the goods and services he is interested in buying determine his budget constraint.

● **The *budget constraint* specifies the combinations of goods the consumer can afford to buy.**

Table 6-1 and Figure 6-2 show some of the possible combinations of goods that Fred can buy with his available income. Each row in the table shows an affordable combination of the two goods, which economists call a *consumption bundle*. If Fred devotes his entire income to hamburgers, he will eat 12 of them a week but will attend no concerts. This is shown in the last row in the table and by point *A* in Figure 6-2.

Alternatively, if he spends all his income on concerts, he will attend six of them but will eat no hamburgers. This is shown in the first row in the table and by point *D* in Figure 6-2. The entries in between all satisfy Fred's budget constraint, which can be expressed as follows:

$$\text{Spending on hamburgers} + \text{spending on concerts} = \text{income (\$12)} \quad (1)$$

The budget constraint *ABCD* in Figure 6-2 shows all the combinations of goods Fred can buy with his income.

[2] We assume throughout this chapter that each consumer takes the prices of all goods and services as given and independent of his choices. (In the terminology of Chapter 5, each consumer faces perfectly elastic supply curves in all markets.) Since most markets involve many, many consumers, this is a reasonable assumption.

TABLE 6-1. Alternative, Affordable Consumption Bundles for Fred

Hamburgers		Concerts		
Quantity (Q_H)	Spending ($1 × Q_H)	Quantity (Q_C)	Spending ($2 × Q_C)	Total spending
0	$ 0	6	$12	$12
4	4	4	8	12
8	8	2	4	12
12	12	0	0	12

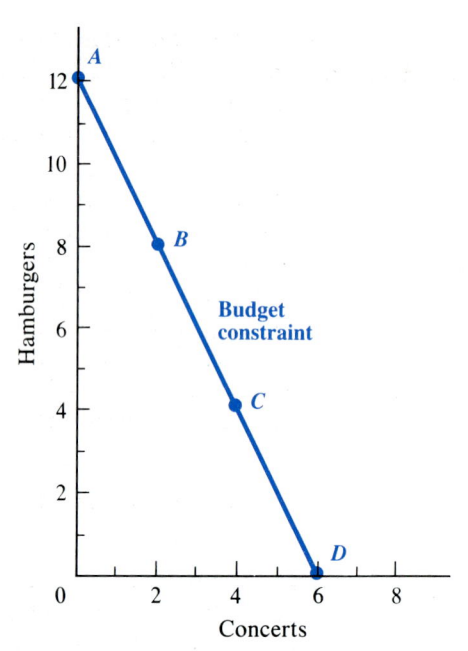

FIGURE 6-2. The Consumer's Budget Constraint. With income of $12 and with hamburgers costing $1 and concerts $2, the budget constraint, the line *ABCD*, shows the combinations of goods the consumer can afford to buy.

Table 6-1 and Figure 6-2 show the *trade-off* that Fred must make between hamburgers and concerts. The more hamburgers he demands, the fewer concerts he can attend. Trade-offs occur in general because resources are scarce; here scarcity appears because Fred's income is limited. Because there is a trade-off, Fred faces a problem of choice.

In Chapter 1 the *opportunity cost* of any good was defined as that which has to be given up to obtain it. Here the opportunity cost of one extra concert is two hamburgers. That opportunity cost can be seen in the slope of the budget constraint in Figure 6-2, where two hamburgers have to be given up to obtain one extra concert.

Marginal Utility and Demand

Now let us see how Fred's preferences or tastes determine which consumption bundles he will select among those he can afford. Recall that his utility meter measures his happiness. Table 6-2 presents part of Fred's *utility function*, which describes how the reading on that meter depends on his consumption of hamburgers and concerts. The utility that Fred derives from any consumption bundle is the sum of the utility he receives

TABLE 6-2. Utility and Marginal Utility

	Utility from hamburgers				Utility from concerts		
Quantity (Q_H)	Total utility (utils)	Marginal utility (MU_H)	MU per $	Quantity (Q_C)	Total utility (utils)	Marginal utility (MU_C)	MU per $
0	0			0	0		
		14	14			30	15
1	14			1	30		
		12	12			20	10
2	26			2	50		
		10	10			18	9
3	36			3	68		
		8	8			16	8
4	44			4	84		
		7	7			14	7
5	51			5	98		
		6	6			13	6.5
6	57			6	111		
		5	5			12	6
7	62			7	123		
		4	4			11	5.5
8	66			8	134		

from hamburgers and the utility he receives from concerts.[3] Thus if Fred consumes two hamburgers and attends five concerts in a week, his utility meter shows 124 utils, equal to 26 utils from hamburgers plus 98 from concerts.

The columns headed "marginal utility" in Table 6-2 give the increase in Fred's utility produced by an extra hamburger or concert. Thus the marginal utility of attending one more concert if he has already been to seven is equal to 11: total utility from eight concerts (134) minus total utility from seven concerts (123).[4]

● The *marginal utility* of any good is the increase in total utility that is obtained by consuming an additional unit of that good.

---
[3] The assumption that the utility derived from any one good does not depend on the amount of the other good consumed is rather strong. In fact, Fred would probably not get much pleasure from a concert if he were starving. But this assumption simplifies the analysis here considerably, and nothing fundamental changes if it does not hold.

[4] In Table 6-2 we show marginal utility on the row between two other rows to reflect the fact that marginal utility comes from the purchase of the extra unit. For instance, the marginal utility of 14 utils from the first hamburger—going from zero hamburgers to one—is recorded between the row showing zero hamburgers and the row showing one hamburger.

Figure 6-3a shows the total utility that Fred obtains from eating hamburgers, and Figure 6-3b shows the corresponding marginal utility. The more hamburgers he eats, the greater his *total* utility, so the curve in Figure 6-3a is rising. Eating one hamburger a week gives him 14 utils; this means that the marginal utility of the first hamburger is 14 utils. But the *marginal* utility of each hamburger is lower than that of the previous one, so the curve of marginal utility in Figure 6-3b is falling. For instance, if he has already eaten seven hamburgers, the marginal utility of the eighth is only 4 utils, compared with 14 for the first hamburger. Fred's utility function is said to exhibit diminishing marginal utility.

● A consumer has *diminishing marginal utility* from a good if each extra unit of the good consumed adds less to total utility than the unit before.

People's preferences for most goods seem consistent with the principle of diminishing marginal utility. For instance, the first cookie eaten on any occasion usually tastes better than the tenth, and we understand that a second mink coat is generally less exciting than the first. Graphically, diminishing marginal utility is reflected in Figure 6-3a by the decreasing slope (the flattening out)

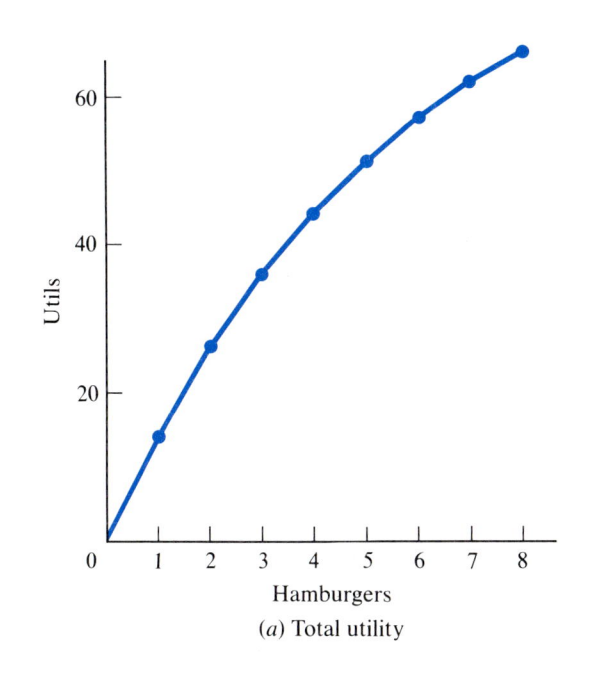

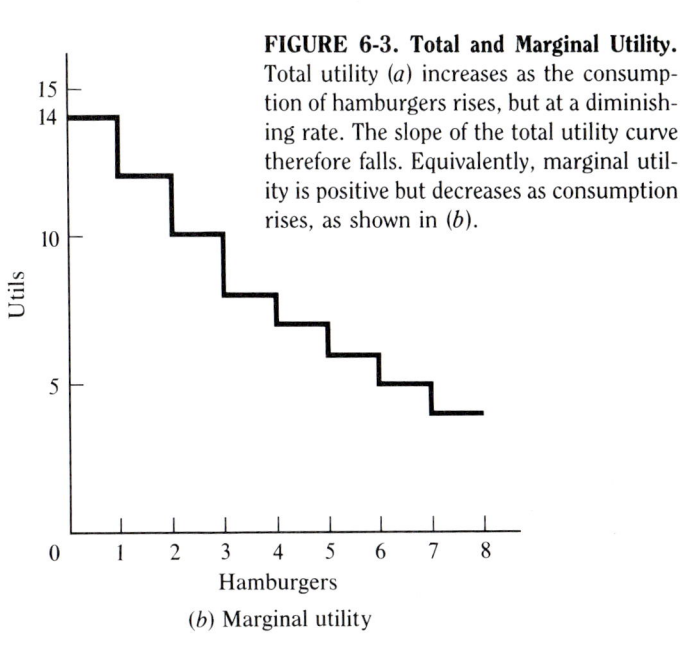

FIGURE 6-3. Total and Marginal Utility. Total utility (*a*) increases as the consumption of hamburgers rises, but at a diminishing rate. The slope of the total utility curve therefore falls. Equivalently, marginal utility is positive but decreases as consumption rises, as shown in (*b*).

(a) Total utility

(b) Marginal utility

of the total utility curve and in Figure 6-3*b* by the negative slope of the marginal utility curve.

What quantities of hamburgers and concerts should Fred demand to maximize his utility (or happiness)? To solve this problem, Fred should pick an affordable consumption bundle and ask himself whether he could increase his utility by spending a dollar more on one good and a dollar less on the other. If so, his utility is not as high as it could be, and he should change his demands accordingly. If not—if he cannot increase utility by shifting spending from one good to the other—his utility is at a maximum, and he should leave his demands unchanged. This approach, which we now develop in detail, is an application of marginal analysis and, in particular, of the concept of marginal utility.

Suppose to start with that Fred is buying six hamburgers (cost = $6) and three concerts (cost = $6). He can afford this consumption bundle, and it will yield a total utility of 125 utils (57 + 68). But this bundle is not optimal. By switching $2 of spending from hamburgers to concerts, Fred can attend one more concert, with the gain in utility—the marginal utility—from the fourth concert equal to 16. The opportunity cost of the extra concert is the loss in utility from reducing hamburger consumption by 2 units; the loss in utility from cutting hamburger consumption from six to four is 13 utils (6 utils on the sixth hamburger + 7 utils on the fifth). By switching $2 of spending from hamburgers to concerts, Fred loses 13 utils but gains 16 utils. He therefore comes out ahead by 3 utils.

How about going even further, from four hamburgers and four concerts to two hamburgers and five concerts? As we ask you to show in Problem 2 at the end of the chapter, Fred should not do it. He would have lower utility than when he buys four hamburgers and four concert tickets. Only with the combination of four hamburgers and four concerts, at point *C* in Figure 6-2, is utility as high as possible given the budget constraint.

This bundle satisfies both Fred's budget constraint and the following condition for an optimal allocation of his income between the two available goods.

$$\frac{MU_H}{P_H} = \frac{MU_C}{P_C} \quad (2)$$

The symbols MU_H and MU_C are defined in Table 6-2; P_H and P_C are the prices of hamburgers and concerts respectively. The general principle that underlies equation (2) is the following.[5]

● **The consumer maximizes utility by choosing the consumption bundle satisfying the budget constraint at which the ratio of marginal utility to price is the same for all goods.**

The *MU/P* ratio shows marginal utility *per dollar* spent to increase the consumption of any good. If Fred has attended two concerts already, for instance, the marginal utility of attending one more concert is 18. But, since each concert costs $2, the marginal utility per dollar is only 9 (18/2).

The column headed "*MU* per $" in Table 6-2 shows the *MU/P* ratio for each good at each level of consumption. With hamburgers costing $1, the marginal utility of one more dollar spent on hamburgers is just the marginal utility of one more hamburger; thus the "*MU* per $" and "*MU*" columns are equal. But with concerts costing $2, the marginal utility per dollar for a concert is half the marginal utility of each concert. If 4 units of each good are consumed, marginal utility per dollar is equal to 8 for both goods. Equation (2) is not satisfied at any other consumption bundle that Fred can afford. Hence 4 units of each is the optimal, or utility-maximizing, choice.

What about Fred's demand curves for these goods? When, given Fred's income, we find that combination of goods at which marginal utility per dollar is equalized, we have determined a point on Fred's demand curve for hamburgers and a point on his demand curve for concerts. We know that when Fred's income is $12, the price of hamburgers is $1, and the price of concerts is $2, Fred will demand four hamburgers and four concerts. Thus

---

[5] Condition (2) comes from the following argument. At the optimal point, Fred cannot come out ahead by shifting a dollar of spending from one good to the other—if he could, he would not already be at an optimal point. How much of the first good, say, *H*, can he buy by shifting $1 of spending to it? The answer is $1/P_H$. For instance, if the price is 50 cents, or $0.5, he can buy 2 units of *H* with a dollar. Similarly, he loses $1/P_C$ units of good *C* by shifting a dollar of spending away from *C*. How much utility does he gain by using a dollar to buy more of *H*? He gets marginal utility—the gain from an extra unit—times the number of units he buys, or MU_H/P_H; similarly he loses MU_C/P_C by reducing spending on *C* by a dollar. Only if those amounts are equal has he chosen the optimal combination of goods.

we have a model that describes the decisions that lie behind individual demand curves.

The data on Fred's utility function given in Table 6-2 can be used, along with equation (2), to predict the changes in the quantities of hamburgers and concerts Fred would demand if prices changed or if his income changed. For instance, if Fred's income goes up to $15, he will increase both hamburger and concert demand by 1 unit. Hamburgers and concerts are thus both normal goods at this point.

The model of consumer behavior presented here thus makes it possible to *derive* an individual's demand curves from information about his income and preferences and the prices he faces. The key step in our analysis was the recognition that *marginal* utility, not total utility, is what matters to an individual seeking to derive as much satisfaction as possible from a limited income. As Box 6-1 indicates, the recognition that marginal utility determines spending also helps us understand why goods that are essential to life (such as water) are often less expensive than others (such as diamonds) that are merely pretty to look at.

Conditions such as equation (2), in which marginal benefits from alternative actions (in this case, marginal utilities from spending a dollar on different goods) are compared, keep coming up in situations where people are trying to do as well as possible—trying to maximize profits, minimize costs, or in this case maximize utility. The logic here extends to profit maximization and cost minimization—topics we develop in Chapters 9 and 13, respectively.

Relative Prices and Consumer Decisions

Suppose Fred's income doubles, to $24 per week, but the prices of hamburgers and concerts also exactly double, to $2 and $4, respectively. How does Fred's spending pattern change? It does not change at all.

To see this, note first that Fred can still afford all the consumption bundles listed in Table 6-1 and shown in Figure 6-2. Consumption bundles he couldn't afford before are still not feasible for him. That is, doubling his income *and all prices* leaves his budget constraint unchanged.

Similarly, equation (2) is still satisfied at the consumption bundle consisting of four hamburgers and four concerts per week. To see this clearly, note that the following equation can be obtained by rearranging equation (2):

$$\frac{MU_H}{MU_C} = \frac{P_H}{P_C} \qquad (3)$$

Similarly, the general rule stated below equation (2) can be restated as follows:

Box 6-1. Marginal Utility and the Water-Diamond Paradox

In the nineteenth century, many economists were puzzled by the following problem: Why is the price of water, which is essential to human life, so much lower than that of diamonds, which are merely decorative? One simple answer is that diamonds are scarce and water is plentiful. But that cannot be the whole answer, because it is still true that consumers get more total utility from water (without it they die) than from diamonds. The concept of marginal utility solves the problem.

Consumers keep buying a good until the ratio of its *marginal* utility to price is equal to that for other goods. *At the margin* the last gallon of water we drink or use in the shower gives very little extra utility. At the margin, though, the last diamond that someone buys generally makes him very happy. Thus it is no surprise that people are generally willing to pay more for additional diamonds than for additional water.

But how does this solve the problem? The point is that the *total* utility an individual receives from all the water he uses may be very large and is almost certainly larger than the total utility received from diamonds. But one extra gallon of water gives much less extra utility to most people than one extra carat of diamond—and it is the *marginal*, not the total, utility that is relevant to the price people are willing to pay for goods. As the analysis of Fred's choice makes clear, total utility is basically irrelevant to market behavior.

To see the point another way, suppose someone who had a one-carat diamond was dying of thirst and was given the opportunity of buying a gallon of water with the diamond. You can be sure he would eagerly make the trade—because in those conditions the marginal utility of the water would greatly exceed that of the diamond.

● **In order to maximize total utility subject to a budget constraint, the ratio of the marginal utilities of any pair of goods must equal the ratio of their prices.**

As long as the *ratio* of the price of hamburgers to the price of concerts does not change and the budget constraint does not shift, Fred's best choice remains the same: 4 units of each good. This example illustrates the following general principle.

● **Changing all prices and income in the same proportion leaves the consumer's demands for all goods unchanged.**

One way to convince yourself that this principle must hold is to ask yourself whether you would behave any differently if all prices and incomes were quoted in pennies rather than in dollars.

Economists express this point by saying that only *relative* prices and *real* incomes matter in consumer decision making. If you know the ratios of Fred's income to the prices of hamburgers and concerts, you can figure out how much of each good he will demand. The absolute or dollar levels of his income and of the prices of the two goods are irrelevant.[6]

3. Utility and Behavior

We agreed that the model developed in the preceding section involves an odd description of consumer behavior. Nobody really has a utility meter or computes marginal utilities before deciding whether to buy a hamburger. But these odd features can in fact be eliminated without affecting the model's predictions or its usefulness.

Measurable Utility and Revealed Preference

Modern economists recognize that there is no observable measure of human happiness that corresponds to the utility function used in section 2. Neither total nor marginal utility can ever be observed.

An economist studying Fred can only observe his behavior: how his spending changes when his income and prices change. Doubling all the total utilities shown in Table 6-2 would also double all the marginal utilities shown there but, as equation (3) indicates, would not change Fred's behavior in any way. Thus we can never learn the values of total or marginal utility by observing consumer behavior.

But it *is* possible to tell whether any particular individual prefers one consumption bundle to another. Such a preference is revealed by our observing which of the two bundles the individual chooses when she can afford both. It turns out that this is enough information about consumer tastes to construct a model of consumer behavior with all the important implications of the model presented in section 2.[7] This is the *revealed preference* approach to consumer theory.[8]

The revealed preference approach builds the theory of consumer behavior on the assumption that consumers make *consistent* choices among the goods they can buy. To illustrate what is meant here by consistent behavior, suppose a consumer selects consumption bundle A when she can also afford B. She has thus revealed a preference for A over B. Now suppose that later, when prices and income have changed so that she can no longer afford A, she selects B even though she can also afford C. She has thus revealed a preference for B over C. The consumer is then said to be consistent if she never selects C in any situation in which she can afford both A and C. If she did, she would be acting contrary to the preferences she had revealed by her earlier behavior. In general, consistency means that the consumer's decisions are stable over time. The theory of revealed preference shows that any consumer who is consistent in this sense behaves *as if* she were maximizing utility.

The basic reason why nothing more than consistency is required is that *ratios* of marginal utilities, like the ratio appearing in equation (3), can be observed by observing quantities demanded at various prices and income levels. The condition for maximizing utility subject to a budget constraint stated after equation (3) is still

---

[6] This principle raises a troubling question, however. If, say, a 10 percent increase in all prices and incomes does not affect consumer behavior or utility in any way, why are people so concerned about inflation?

[7] This point is developed in detail in the appendix to this chapter.
[8] This theory was invented in the 1930s by MIT's Paul Samuelson, Nobel Prize winner and textbook author.

valid: The ratio of the prices of any pair of goods must equal the ratio of their marginal utilities.

INTERPERSONAL COMPARISONS OF UTILITY. People are sometimes tempted to compare the utility or happiness of different people, saying things such as, "Ron is twice as happy as Fritz." Such comparisons would be difficult to make even if we could somehow measure utility for Ron and Fritz individually—since Ron's utils might not be the same as Fritz's. But since there is no way to measure utility for either of them, their happiness certainly cannot be compared—at least not on any scientific basis.[9]

Economic Man

An additional criticism of the model developed in section 2 is that it is a silly description of the way humans behave. Some have argued that the "economic man" described in section 2 is a selfish, calculating creature unlike most real humans—or at least unlike any humans one would care to know.

The first adjective reflects a misunderstanding. The economic model of consumer behavior does not assume selfishness. The "goods" that enter the utility function can be anything at all. Fred may be choosing between donations to two worthy charities or between sending food to famine victims and taking the Boy Scouts on an outing.

The second adjective is more serious. Nobody, not even an economist, goes through life calculating ratios of marginal utilities. But as we noted previously, the modern theory of revealed preference shows that all we really need to assume is that consumers behave consistently.

Even the assumption of consistency may seem strong, however. Most people like variety. Fred attends both rock and classical concerts, for instance, and sometimes even listens to country music. The assumption of consistency is most likely to be valid when applied to average behavior over fairly long periods of time. That is, if Fred attends 10 rock concerts and 2 classical concerts this year and neither prices nor his income changes, we would expect him to attend approximately 10 rock and 2 classical concerts next year.

New products can alter behavior without changing tastes. If Fred discovers a new group that plays exactly the sort of rock he likes best, he may give up classical music entirely. But of course individuals' tastes change as well, and the assumption of consistent behavior is always to some extent unrealistic.[10] Fred is likely to attend fewer rock concerts and more classical concerts as he gets older. When an individual's tastes change, the economic model of consumer behavior can be used to figure out the bundle of goods he will choose given his new tastes. Economics has less to say about the precise causes of changes in tastes, though we do discuss the role of advertising in Chapter 12.

In short, the economic model of consumer behavior is useful even though consumers do not consciously maximize anything or even compute ratios of marginal utilities. The theory of revealed preference shows that utility maximization can be used to describe the *results* of consistent consumer decision making, if not the process by which decisions are made.

4. Must All Demand Curves Slope Downward?

Can we prove that individual demand curves must slope downward? As this section shows, the answer is no. Theory raises the intriguing possibility that demand curves can slope upward under certain conditions, but no such exception to the law of demand has ever been discovered.

It is useful to begin by analyzing an increase in the price of hamburgers in the example given in section 2. Figure 6-4 shows how an increase in the price of hamburgers from $1 to $2 affects Fred's budget constraint. Now he can at most buy only 6 hamburgers instead of 12. He can no longer consume at point *C*. The budget constraint shifts from *ABCD* to *A'B'C'D*.

If he keeps going to four concerts, he will be able to eat only two hamburgers a week, at point *C'*. And if he keeps eating four hamburgers, he will be able to attend only

---

[9] We all know people who have a happy outlook on life and others who don't. Even so, we can't say that one's happiness is greater than the other's—the miserable person may enjoy suffering.

[10] Recall the argument in Chapter 2 that models in general must be "unrealistic" in order to be useful.

FIGURE 6-4. The Effects of a Price Increase on the Budget Constraint. An increase in the price of hamburgers reduces the maximum number of hamburgers that can be consumed, rotating the budget constraint from ABCD to A'B'C'D. The maximum number of concerts that can be attended, shown at point D, remains unchanged.

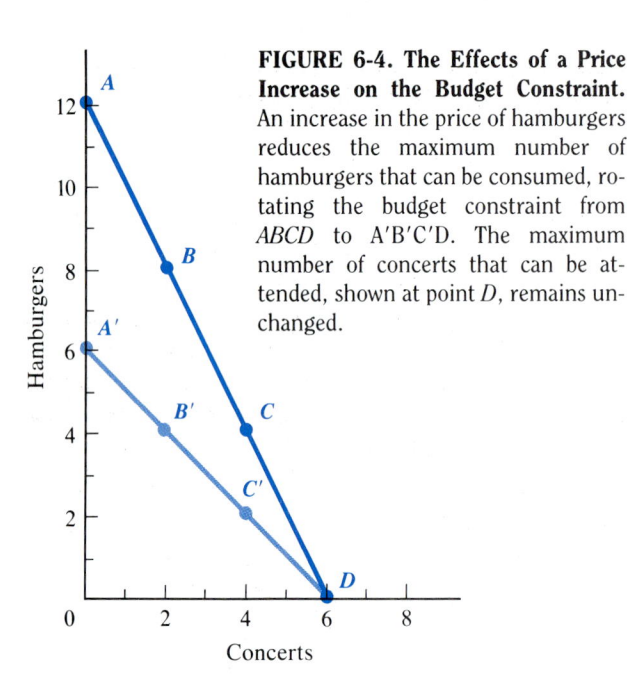

two concerts, at point B'. In fact, by comparing total utility (from Table 6-2) for all affordable consumption bundles, you should be able to show that Fred will cut back to one hamburger per week.[11] In this case Fred buys fewer hamburgers when their price rises. His demand curve for hamburgers is therefore downward-sloping and thus satisfies the law of demand.

Income and Substitution Effects of a Price Change

In order to see how and why changes in price affect the quantity demanded, it is useful to divide the effects of a price change into two parts. For the sake of concreteness, let us focus on an increase in the price of hamburgers.

The first effect of an increase in the price of hamburgers is that Fred cannot afford to buy what he used to.

[11] Note that the MU/P ratios are not exactly equal at this point, though they are closer than at any other feasible point. This arises because we consider only the utilities of integer numbers of commodities, such as 0, 1, 2, and 3. But these are not really the only possibilities: By attending 3 concerts every 2 weeks, for instance, Fred could consume 1.5 concerts a week. If all possible (integer and noninteger) levels of consumption are possible, the MU/P ratios must be exactly equal at the point that maximizes utility.

Now his budget constraint in Figure 6-4 has moved to A'B'C'D, and he can no longer afford point C. If prices were unchanged but his dollar income fell, he would also be unable to afford that bundle. Economists say that a price increase reduces a consumer's *real* income, defined as the amount of goods his income can buy. Thus there is an income effect from a price change.

● **Price increases lower real income; price decreases raise real income. The *income effect* of a price change is the adjustment of quantity demanded to the resulting change in real income.**

In response to the reduced purchasing power of his income, Fred has to reduce consumption of at least some and maybe all goods when the price of hamburgers rises.

The second effect of a price increase is to change the relative prices of all goods. Even if Fred were able to continue consuming the same amount as before, he would not want to. Hamburgers are more expensive relative to concerts than they were before. Their "MU per $" in Table 6-2 falls when their price rises. Accordingly, Fred would want to reduce his consumption of hamburgers, substituting concert going for hamburger eating. This second effect—the effect of the change in the *relative* price of the goods—is the substitution effect.

● **The *substitution effect* of a price change is the adjustment of quantities demanded to the change in relative prices.**

When the price of any good goes up, the consumer tends to substitute other goods, so that the substitution effect of a price increase always involves a reduction in the quantity demanded.[12]

The Law of Demand

Income and substitution effects can now be used to show why, at least in theory, demand curves don't necessarily slope downward. If price changes had only substitution effects, all demand curves would slope downward. As any particular good becomes more expensive relative to others, all else equal, consumers demand less of it. In other words, the substitution effect of a price increase on the

[12] This prediction of the theory of consumer behavior is established in the appendix to this chapter.

quantity demanded is always negative. But price increases also have income effects. A price increase of any good reduces each consumer's real income. If the good is normal, so that a reduction in income will reduce the quantity demanded, the income effect is also negative.

Our first conclusion follows: *If a good is normal, its demand curve must slope downward*. Why? Because both the income and substitution effects of a price rise are negative: A higher price reduces quantity demanded through both income and substitution effects.

● **The *law of demand* must always hold for normal goods. The income and substitution effects of an increase in the price of a normal good are both negative, so that an increase in price must reduce the quantity of a normal good demanded by any consumer.**

On the assumption that concerts are a normal good, we show in Table 6-3 why the demand curve for concerts must have a negative slope.

But not all goods are normal. Suppose, contrary to what we have assumed so far, hamburgers are an inferior good; that is, the consumption of hamburgers goes up when income falls, all else equal. Then decreases in real income will also raise the demand for hamburgers, and the income effect of a price increase on the quantity of hamburgers demanded will be *positive*. Table 6-3 shows why in that case it is theoretically possible for the demand curve for an inferior good to slope upward. The negative substitution effect of a price increase could in theory be outweighed by a positive income effect. While steak becomes more attractive relative to hamburgers (the substitution effect), the consumer can be made so much poorer by an increase in the price of hamburgers (the income effect) that he gives up steak entirely and eats more hamburgers on balance. This possibility describes what is called a *Giffen good*.[13]

TABLE 6-3. Income, Substitution, and Total Effects of Price Increases on Quantities Demanded

Good	Assumed type	Income effect	Substitution effect	Total effect
Concerts	Normal	Negative	Negative	Negative
Hamburgers	Inferior	Positive	Negative	?

Should we expect to find Giffen goods, or goods with upward-sloping demand curves, in the real world? Not really. No such good has ever been found. And, since any economist who found a Giffen good would instantly become famous, this has not been for lack of effort.[14]

● **In fact, the law of demand also holds for inferior goods. Individual and market demand curves for inferior goods also slope downward in practice, even though the theory of consumer behavior does not require this.**

5. Consumer's Surplus

Suppose that, as often happens, Congress is considering policies to reduce imports of sugar. The reduction in imports would reduce the supply of sugar to the U.S. market. This would raise the price of sugar, thereby helping domestic producers and hurting consumers. The gain to producers can be measured in dollar terms by the change in their profit. The harm to consumers can also be measured in dollar terms, using the concept of consumer's surplus. Once these dollar values have been computed, one can compare producers' gains with consumers' losses to see whether import restrictions would produce a net gain or loss for society as a whole, and one can ask whether other ways of aiding domestic sugar producers (cash payments financed by higher income taxes, for instance) would be better for consumers.

---

[13] Sir Robert Giffen, a nineteenth-century British economist, is often said to have raised the possibility of the demand curve for an inferior good—specifically potatoes—sloping upward. The suggestion is said to have been made at the time of the Irish famine in 1846. Potatoes, which made up a large fraction of Irish diets in this period, were an inferior good. If their price rose substantially, consumers would be made much poorer and might be forced to give up other food almost entirely and to increase the quantity of potatoes demanded. But despite a search by economists interested in the question, no record of such a suggestion by Giffen has been found.

[14] Despite the theoretical possibility shown in Table 6-3, the failure to find a Giffen good in the real world should not come as a great surprise. The income effect of a change in the price of an inferior good would have to be large to offset the substitution effect. But most goods account for only a small share of consumers' budgets, so that the effects of changes in their prices on consumers' real incomes are not large. Similarly, it is hard to think of inferior goods for which the quantity demanded is highly sensitive to changes in income. Thus the links from the change in price to an increase in demand via the income effect are relatively weak.

The definition of consumer's surplus is straightforward.

● The *consumer's surplus* associated with any good is the difference between the maximum amount a consumer would pay for the quantity of that good he or she demands and the actual amount paid.

What makes this concept useful in practice is that it can be directly related to consumers' demand curves.

To show this, we again use the example of hamburgers, with Figure 6-5 showing Fred's demand curve for hamburgers. For convenience, the demand curve has steps in it, but this is not essential. Suppose the price of hamburgers is P, equal to $1. Here is the key result: *Consumer's surplus is the shaded area under the demand curve and above the price line PP.* We now show that this area measures the difference (in dollars) between the maximum amount Fred would be willing to pay for the four hamburgers he consumes each week and the amount he actually pays.

The first step in the argument is to establish that Fred's demand curve shows the *maximum* amount he would be willing to pay for each hamburger he consumes; one can thus think of it as showing the marginal dollar value of each additional hamburger eaten. Note first that if the price were above P_1, Fred would not demand any hamburgers. When the price drops to P_1, he buys one hamburger, so that he is willing to pay as much as P_1 for the first hamburger he demands. Similarly, the fact that Fred demands a second hamburger when the price falls to P_2 shows that the second hamburger is worth P_2 to him.

But while Fred is willing to pay up to P_1 for the first hamburger each week, he actually pays only P. He thus enjoys a *surplus* of $(P_1 - P)$ on that first hamburger, the difference between its value to him and its cost. This is shown by the shaded area labeled A. Similarly, he enjoys a surplus of $(P_2 - P)$ on the second hamburger, which is shown by the shaded area labeled B. Proceeding in this fashion for the third and fourth hamburgers, we have shown that *the total shaded area in Figure 6-5 is the dollar value of Fred's consumer's surplus from hamburgers.*

The notion of consumer's surplus can be used to put a dollar value on price changes. Suppose this surplus is $10 per week. This means that Fred would be willing to pay up to $10 for the right to buy hamburgers at price P rather than do without them entirely. Now consider two alternative changes that make Fred worse off. First, suppose that the price of hamburgers rises to P_2 and that Fred's surplus falls by $4, to $6 per week. Second, suppose that instead of raising the price, the producer asks Fred to pay $4 per week for a card that would entitle him to buy hamburgers at the low price P. Fred would have exactly the same surplus (and exactly the same utility) in both cases.

He would thus be willing to pay up to $4 to prevent the price increase to P_2. The cost of the price rise to P_2 is $4 per week for Fred—that is the maximum amount he'd be willing to pay to prevent the price increase. We have thus shown that the fall in Fred's consumer's surplus produced by the price increase gives a dollar measure of the cost of that price increase to him.

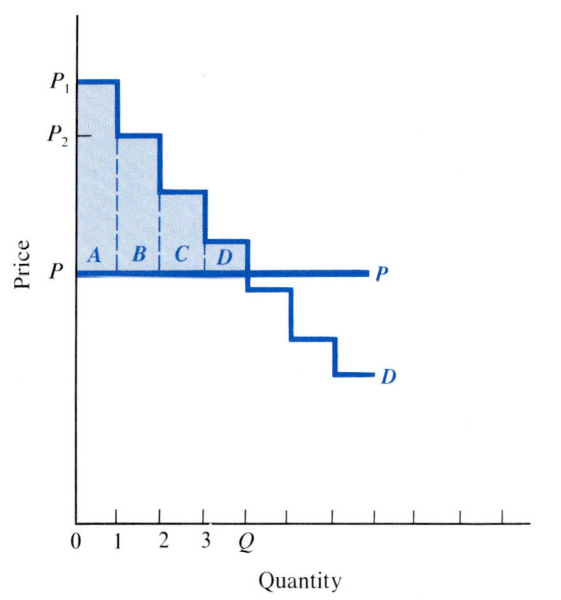

FIGURE 6-5. Consumer's Surplus. Fred's demand curve for hamburgers, D, shows at each level of consumption the maximum price that he is willing to pay for an additional hamburger. He is willing to pay P_1 for the first hamburger of the week, but at market price P he has to pay only P. Therefore $(P_1 - P)$, shown as the shaded area labeled A, represents his consumer's surplus on the first hamburger. He is willing to pay up to P_2 for his second hamburger but has to pay only P. Thus area B represents Fred's surplus on his second hamburger, and so on. The entire shaded area represents Fred's total consumer's surplus associated with a market price of P.

- **The fall in consumer's surplus produced by a price increase is equal to the maximum amount the consumer would be willing to pay to prevent the price increase; the surplus rise produced by a price decrease is equal to the maximum amount the consumer would be willing to pay to bring about the price decrease.**

The change in consumer's surplus produced by a price change thus gives a dollar measure of the (positive or negative) value of the price change to the consumer.[15]

Box 6-2 provides an example of the use of this measure to evaluate an actual proposed change in federal policy that would have raised the price of sugar. In this example, a market demand curve is used to compute the change in surplus. Because market demand curves are

[15] In advanced courses one learns that this measure is only an approximation, though a very useful one in practice.

Box 6-2. The Cost of an Increase in the Price of Sugar

In 1976, the federal government was considering tripling the tariff on sugar imports. (A tariff is a tax that must be paid whenever a particular product is brought into the country.[16]) This action would have raised the domestic price of sugar from $12.00 per hundredweight (cwt) to $13.20 (a hundredweight equals 100 pounds). The Council on Wage and Price Stability (COWPS), which has since been abolished, was asked to measure the cost this price increase would impose on consumers. Such measures are regularly calculated to evaluate proposed government actions.

The COWPS analysis of this particular proposal is summarized in Figure 6B-1 (not drawn to scale). Consumer's surplus at the initial price is equal to the sum of the areas A, B, and C. Because the demand curve for sugar is extremely inelastic, the quantity of sugar demanded was expected to fall only slightly, from 220.0 million cwt per year to 218.9 million cwt per year, in response to the price increase. At the higher price, consumer's surplus would be equal to the area A. The price increase considered would thus reduce total consumer's surplus by the sum of the shaded areas B and C. This amounts to $263.34 million per year.

Area B represents the increased cost of the sugar that would be purchased at the higher price. It is equal to $262.68 million per year ($1.20 × 218.9). At the new, higher price, sugar consumption would fall by 1.1 million cwt. Because consumers enjoyed a surplus on this sugar before the price cut, the cut in consumption involves a second loss, which is measured by area C. The average surplus that would have been enjoyed on this sugar is $0.60 per cwt ($1.20/2), and area C is equal to $0.66 million ($0.60 × 1.1). (If the demand curve for sugar had been more elastic, C would have been larger relative to B.)

The sum of areas B and C, $263.34 million, is the total loss of consumer's surplus and a measure of the loss consumers would suffer from the higher tariff. Because of these costs to consumers, and for other reasons, COWPS argued against the proposed tariff increase.

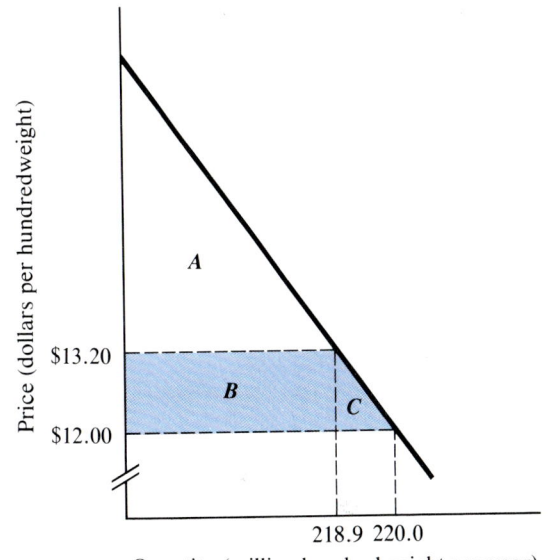

[16] The general effects of tariffs are considered in Chapter 23.

Note: For more details, see Thomas M. Leonard, "Domestic Sugar Producers and International Competition," in J.C. Miller III and B. Yandle, editors, *Benefit-Cost Analyses of Social Regulation*, Washington, DC, American Enterprise Institute, 1979.

obtained as the horizontal sum of individual demand curves (see Figure 6-1), this yields the sum of the dollar values of the price change to all buyers. One problem with this approach is that it weights all consumers equally. A reduction of $1 in a billionaire's surplus counts just as much as a $1 reduction in the surplus of a poor family. The only way to get around this problem is to work directly with the demand curves of individuals or groups of consumers.

■ In Chapter 3 we argued that a good's own price, the prices of other goods, consumers' income, and consumers' tastes all affect the quantity demanded. In this chapter we have developed an economic model of consumer behavior which shows exactly how these influences interact to affect spending. By moving from a list of influences to a model, we have been able to uncover fundamental relations between price changes and income changes: All price changes have income effects, and their impacts on consumers can be given dollar values when we use the concept of consumer's surplus. We begin in the next chapter to go more deeply into the supply side of the market. Our task is to see exactly how the influences listed in the discussion of business behavior in Chapter 3 interact to determine the quantity supplied. The marginal analysis used here to maximize utility will prove useful in that setting as well.

Summary

1. The market demand schedule is obtained by adding the quantities demanded by all buyers at each price. The market demand curve is the horizontal sum of the demand curves of all individuals in the market.
2. The budget constraint specifies the combinations of goods (or consumption bundles) the consumer can afford to buy. Because no consumer can afford everything she wants, consumers face trade-offs summarized by the negative slope of the budget constraint.
3. In economics, utility denotes the satisfaction or happiness a consumer obtains from the goods and services he purchases. The marginal utility of any good is the increase in total utility that results from consuming an additional unit of that good. Marginal utility is usually assumed to be diminishing, meaning that marginal utility is less the more of a good the consumer already is purchasing.
4. A consumer adjusts spending to maximize utility by choosing a consumption bundle satisfying the budget constraint at which the ratio of marginal utility to price is the same for all goods. At this point the last dollar's worth of spending on each good yields the same increase in utility, so that no reshuffling of the spending pattern can increase utility.
5. An alternative way of describing utility maximization is to say that the ratio of the prices of any pair of goods must equal the ratio of their marginal utilities.
6. Changing all prices and income in the same proportion leaves the consumer's demands for all goods unchanged.
7. The theory of revealed preference shows that if consumers behave consistently, their spending behavior will be described by the model of utility maximization.
8. The income effect of a price change is the adjustment of quantities demanded to the change in the purchasing power of income. The substitution effect of a price change is the adjustment of quantities demanded to the change in relative prices.
9. The substitution effect of an increase in the price of any good leads to a reduction in the quantity of that good demanded.
10. The income effect of an increase in the price of a normal good leads to a reduction in the quantity of that good demanded. Thus demand curves for normal goods must satisfy the law of demand: They slope downward. In practice, demand curves for inferior goods also slope downward.
11. The consumer's surplus associated with any good is the difference between the maximum amount a consumer would pay for the quantity of that good she demands and the actual amount paid. Consumer's surplus can be measured by the area between the demand curve and the price line.
12. The change in consumer's surplus produced by a price change gives a dollar measure of the (positive or negative) value of the price change to the consumer.

Key Terms

Market demand curve
Individual demand curve
Budget constraint
Consumption bundle

Utility function
Total utility
Marginal utility
Diminishing marginal utility
Relative prices
Income effect

Substitution effect
Law of demand
Giffen good
Consumer's surplus
Value of a price change

Problems

1 Explain whether the following statement is true or false. There are two reasons the market demand curve slopes downward. First, the demand curve of each individual slopes downward; second, the lower the price, the more people there are actually buying the good. (Use Figure 6-1 in answering.)

2 Referring to Table 6-2, show that it would not be optimal for Fred to consume two hamburgers each week and attend five concerts. Use the concept of marginal utility in your answer.

3 Alex has an income of $200 per week. She lives in a simple world in which there are only two scarce goods: beef and shirts. Beef costs $5 a pound, and shirts cost $20 each. (a) Make a table, like Table 6-1, showing five consumption bundles that Alex can afford. (b) Graph those points and use your graph to describe Alex's budget constraint. (c) If Q_B is the quantity of beef Alex demands and Q_S is the quantity of shirts she demands, write down an equation similar to equation (1) that describes the set of consumption bundles Alex can buy. (d) What is Alex's opportunity cost of buying two additional shirts? (e) How would Alex's budget constraint change if the price of beef fell to $1 a pound, the price of shirts fell to $4, and her income fell to $40?

4 Carl's utility from the consumption of cookies (per day) is as follows.

Cookies consumed	Total utility from cookies
0	100
1	143
2	180
3	200
4	216
5	226
6	235

(a) Carl argues that he gets 100 utils from cookies each day just from knowing that there are cookies in the world. As long as the world contains cookies, is there any way his behavior could ever be inconsistent with this argument? (b) Calculate Carl's marginal utility of cookies at each level of cookie consumption. (c) Does his utility function exhibit diminishing marginal utility of cookies?

5 Betty has a weekly allowance of $6, which she spends on comic books and candy bars. Comic books cost $2 each, and candy bars cost $1 each. Betty's utility each week is the sum of her utility from comics and her utility from candy. The two parts of her utility function are as follows.

Comics consumed	Total utility from comics	Candy consumed	Total utility from candy
0	0	0	0
1	12	1	8
2	22	2	13
3	30	3	17
4	36	4	20
5	41	5	22
6	45	6	23

(a) Does Betty show diminishing marginal utility from comics? From candy bars? (b) Show that it is not optimal for Betty to devote her entire allowance to comics. (c) Show that it is not optimal for her to spend her entire allowance on candy. (d) What combination of goods will Betty choose?

6 Use the example in Problem 5. (a) How would Betty's spending change if her allowance were raised to $9 per week? (b) How would your answer to Problem 5(d) change if all the total utilities in the table in Problem 5 were doubled? Relate your answer to the discussion of measurable utility in section 3.

7 John loves to buy videotapes of movies and audio tapes. Videotapes cost $30 each, and the type of audio tapes he buys cost $12 each. (a) John announces that his marginal utility of videotapes is 10 utils, while his marginal utility of audio tapes is 20 utils. Is he maximizing utility? Explain your answer so that John will understand it. (b) How should he change his spending in order to increase his utility? (c) Suppose John announces instead that he doesn't know what a util is but does know that the marginal utility of a videotape for him is equal to the marginal utility of an audio tape. How would your answers to (a) and (b) change?

8 Melissa has two exams tomorrow, one in economics and one in history. She feels confident about economics but is worried about history. Melissa would like to maximize the sum of her scores on the two exams. It is getting late, and she can spend only 1 more hour studying. Depending on

how many additional minutes she spends on each exam, she expects the following scores.

Minutes spent on economics	Expected score in economics	Minutes spent on history	Expected score in history
0	70	0	50
10	76	10	58
20	81	20	65
30	85	30	71
40	88	40	76
50	90	50	80
60	91	60	83

(a) What does "diminishing marginal utility" mean here? Is it present? (b) Explain to Melissa why she shouldn't spend the whole hour on her weaker subject, history. (c) How should she spend the hour? (d) How would the optimal use of Melissa's time change if all the economics scores were 20 points lower and all the history scores were 10 points higher? (e) Relate your answer to (d) to the discussion of measurable utility in section 3.

9 We observe that when Florence's income increases, the quantity of apples she demands also increases. Using this information, prove that the quantity of apples she demands will decrease if the price of apples rises.

10 Greg will buy no record albums if they cost more than $6 each. If the price is between $6 and $5, he will buy one each month. If the price is between $5 and $3, he will buy two per month. If the price is between $3 and $1, he will buy three per month. (a) What is Greg's consumer's surplus from albums if they cost $2 each? (b) Suppose the price rises to $4. By how much does Greg's consumer's surplus from records decline? (c) Indicate why your answer to (b) gives a dollar measure of the cost to Greg of the increase in the price of record albums.

11 The supply curve of widgets is perfectly elastic at a price of $4 per widget. The demand curve is downward-sloping. The government imposes a tax of $1 on widgets. (a) What is the new equilibrium price of widgets? (You may want to refer to Chapter 4 to see how a tax affects the market price.) (b) Using a diagram, show that the government revenue from this tax is less than the loss of consumer's surplus it produces. (*Note*: The difference between surplus lost and revenue gained is often called the *deadweight loss* of a tax.)

Appendix: Consumer Behavior without Measurable Utility

The theory of consumer behavior in section 2 of this chapter made the assumption that an individual consumer's utility or happiness can be measured numerically. This implausible assumption is not strictly necessary (though it did simplify the analysis), since all we really need to know about a consumer's preferences is which consumption bundles are preferred to which others. This appendix supports that assertion and provides a graphic analysis of consumer spending behavior.

We begin by reviewing the graphic representation of the budget constraint and of changes in prices and income. We show graphically why proportional changes in income and all prices must leave consumer demands unaffected. The second section shows how the income and substitution effects of a price increase operate. It proves that the substitution effect of a price change is always negative. We then complete the model of consumer behavior using *indifference curves* to describe preferences and show that consumer spending can be analyzed completely without assuming that utility is measurable.

The Budget Constraint

Margie has an income of $100, which she can spend on food and entertainment. Food costs $5 per pound, and entertainment costs $10 per hour. Using this information, we can prepare a table, such as Table 6-1, listing alternative, affordable consumption bundles.

Equivalently, we can show the budget constraint in a diagram, as in Figure 6A-1. The graphic representation of the budget constraint is often called the budget line.

● **The *budget line* shows the maximum combinations of goods a consumer can afford, given her income and the prices she must pay.**

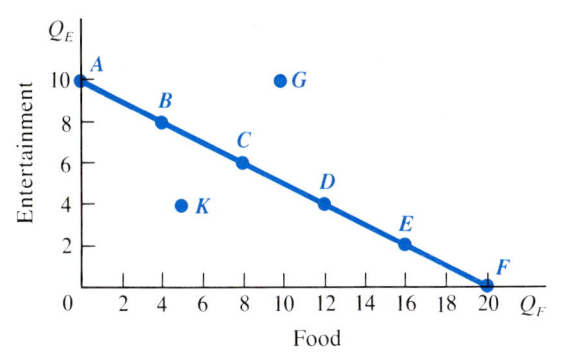

FIGURE 6A-1. Margie's Budget Line. *AF* is the consumer's budget line, given income of $100, a price of entertainment of $10, and a price of food of $5. Line *AF* shows the possible consumption bundles (such as *A*, *B*, and *C*) that use up Margie's entire budget. She cannot afford points above and to the right of the line (such as *G*). Points inside the budget line, such as *K*, are affordable—but points on the budget line allow her to buy more of both goods than she would buy at *K*.

The position of the budget line is determined by the two intersections with the axes, points *A* and *F*, respectively. Point *A* shows the maximum amount of entertainment Margie's budget can buy, in this case 10 units of entertainment [total income ($100)/price of entertainment ($10 per hour)]. The other extreme is point *F*, where all the income is devoted to food. Here Margie's budget buys a maximum of 100/5 = 20 pounds of food. The budget line is drawn by connecting these two points. Points between *A* and *F*, such as *B* and *C*, describe alternative combinations of food and entertainment that Margie can afford.

The budget line shows the *trade-offs* the consumer can make between food and entertainment. The flatter the budget line, the lower its slope, and the more food that must be given up to obtain an extra unit of entertainment. In fact, *the slope of the budget line is the ratio of the prices of the two goods*.[17] The higher the price of entertainment *relative* to the price of food, the more units of food Margie must forgo to buy one extra unit of entertainment and, accordingly, the flatter the budget line. If a unit of entertainment cost $25 rather than $10, for instance, Margie would have to forgo 5 pounds of food rather than only 2 pounds of food to buy an extra hour of entertainment.

Points to the right of the budget line, such as *G*, depict consumption bundles Margie cannot afford. Points to the left of the budget line, such as *K*, are affordable but irrelevant. Margie would prefer to consume more of both goods than at point *K*, and she can afford to do so, so Margie will choose her purchases from points on the budget line.

We now show in detail how changes in income and prices shift the budget line.

INCOME CHANGES. Suppose Margie's income rises from $100 to $160 per week, but the prices of food and entertainment remain unchanged at $5 and $10, respectively. How does her budget line change?

With a higher income, some consumption bundles that were unaffordable are now within her reach. The budget line must shift outward, from *AF* to *A'F'* in Figure 6A-2. *A'* is the point at which the entire income of $160 is spent on entertainment; at a price of $10, it is possible to buy a maximum of 16 units of entertainment. Similarly, at *F'* Margie can consume 32 units of food per week. Connecting *A'* and *F'* gives the new budget line.

● **An increase in income shifts the budget line outward; a decrease in income shifts the budget line inward. In both cases the new budget line is parallel to the old line.**

Suppose Margie's initial consumption is represented by point *e* on her old budget line. How will she alter her spending behavior in response to the increase in her income? If both food and entertainment are normal goods, she will increase the quantities demanded of both. This corresponds to a move to the northeast of point *e*. But we also know that the new consumption point will lie on the new budget line, *A'F'*. Therefore, the new consumption point will lie on the stretch *bc* defined by the vertical and horizontal dashed lines through point *e*—that is, to the northeast of *e* and on the new budget line. (You should be able to see that if entertainment

---

[17] Since Margie can increase her food consumption only by decreasing her consumption of entertainment, the slope of the budget line is in fact negative. Just as it is standard to ignore the negative slope of the demand curve when defining the price elasticity of demand, we simply work with the (positive) ratio of the two prices here.

118 Part Two: Supply, Demand, and Product Markets

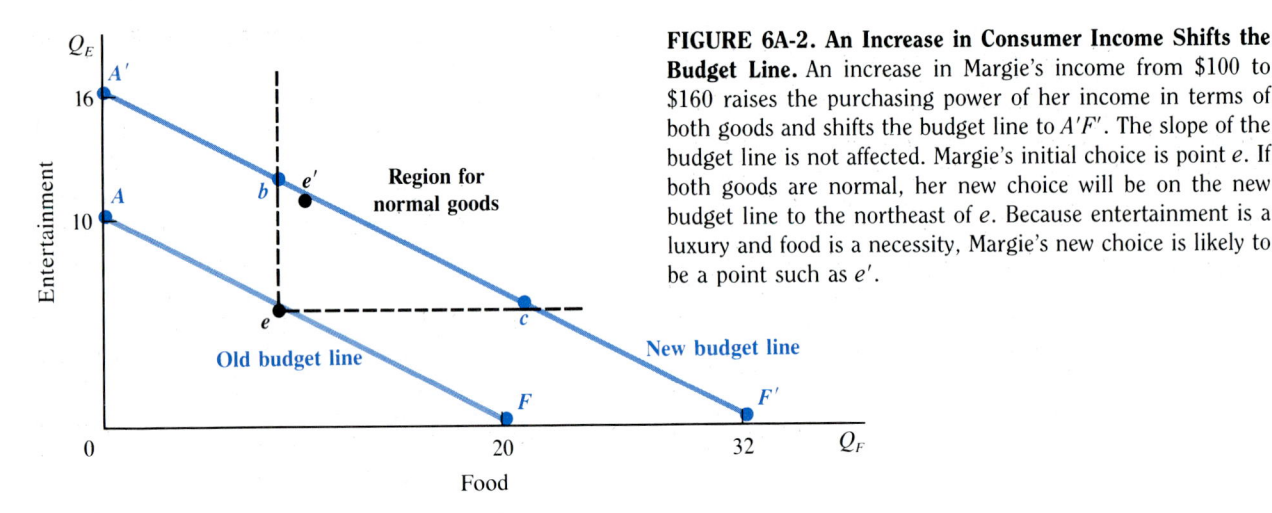

FIGURE 6A-2. An Increase in Consumer Income Shifts the Budget Line. An increase in Margie's income from $100 to $160 raises the purchasing power of her income in terms of both goods and shifts the budget line to $A'F'$. The slope of the budget line is not affected. Margie's initial choice is point e. If both goods are normal, her new choice will be on the new budget line to the northeast of e. Because entertainment is a luxury and food is a necessity, Margie's new choice is likely to be a point such as e'.

were an inferior good, the new consumption point would be to the right of point c on the new budget line.)

We can say a bit more than this in general. Since food is a necessity for most consumers, we would expect the income elasticity of Margie's demand for food to be less than 1.[18] Thus the quantity of food demanded should rise proportionally less than income rises. Entertainment, in contrast, is generally a luxury, so we would expect the quantity of entertainment demanded to rise proportionally more than income rises. We would therefore expect Margie's new equilibrium to be at a point such as e', where the ratio of entertainment to food is greater than it is at e.

PRICE CHANGES. Figure 6A-3 again shows Margie's initial budget line, AF. Suppose that, given this budget line, she chooses point e as the optimal consumption bundle. At this point she consumes 6 hours of entertainment and 8 pounds of food each week.

Now let the price of food double, from $5 to $10 per pound. In Figure 6A-3 we show, as we did in Figure 6-4,

[18] Recall from Chapter 5 that this result was established by Ernst Engel in the nineteenth century.

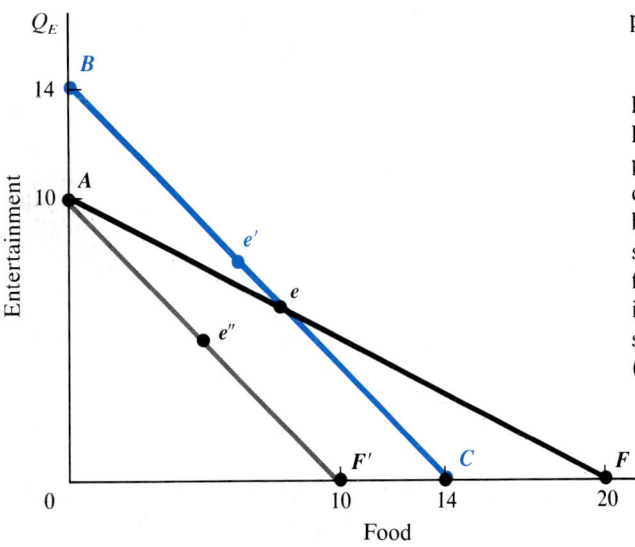

FIGURE 6A-3. The Income and Substitution Effects of a Price Increase. When the food price doubles from $5 to $10 per pound, Margie's budget line shifts from AF to AF', and her consumption bundle changes from e to e''. The hypothetical budget line BC goes through the initial point e but has the same slope as AF'. BC corresponds to an income of $140 and a food price of $10. The shift from e to e'' can be broken down into two steps: the reaction to a shift from AF to BC (the substitution effect) and the reaction to a shift from BC to AF' (the income effect).

that the budget line rotates around point A and that the new intersection with the food axis is at point F'. Margie's new budget line therefore is the line AF'.

● **An increase in the price of a good rotates the budget line inward; a decrease in the price of a good rotates the budget line outward. In both cases the maximum quantity of the good with the unchanged price remains constant.**

Notice that every point on Margie's new budget line except point A lies *inside* her old budget line. This means that Margie's standard of living has fallen because she can no longer afford her initial consumption bundle, point e on AF. Indeed, point A is the only point on AF that she can still afford.

PROPORTIONAL CHANGES IN INCOME AND PRICES. Proportional changes in income and prices leave the position of the budget line unchanged. For example, if all prices and money income double, the consumer can afford exactly the same combinations of goods as before. If the consumption bundles the consumer can afford haven't changed (that is, if the budget line hasn't moved) and her tastes haven't changed, her choices won't change.

Income and Substitution Effects

The graphic techniques we have developed help illustrate the income and substitution effects of a price increase and prove that the substitution effect of a price increase is always negative. Figure 6A-3 shows an increase in the price of food from $5 to $10, which shifts the budget line from AF to AF'. Suppose that, as a consequence, Margie's consumption bundle changes from e (6 hours of entertainment and 8 pounds of food) to e''.

To break down this move into the substitution and income effects of the price increase, we first construct the hypothetical colored budget line BC, which is parallel to the new budget constraint (AF') but passes through the point describing the old consumption bundle (e). Thus BC describes a hypothetical situation in which food and entertainment both cost $10, as is the case along AF'. The graph shows that the maximum quantity of food that can be purchased along BC is 14 units. At a food price of $10, this implies that income along BC must be $140 (14 × $10).

We now imagine the change in Margie's budget line from AF to AF' occurring in two steps. The *substitution effect* of the increase in the price of food is the change in demand caused by a shift in the budget line from AF to BC, and the *income effect* is the response Margie would make to a shift in the budget line from BC to AF'. Let us consider these in turn.

The first shift, from AF to BC, involves a change in relative prices along with a *compensating* change in dollar income so that the original bundle, at point e, is still affordable. We now show that as long as Margie behaves consistently, she will react to this shift by moving to a point such as e', to the left of e.

Margie could have bought any of the consumption bundles represented by points to the right of e, between e and C, when her budget line was AF, but she chose to buy the bundle represented by e instead. She has thus revealed that she prefers e to all points to the right of it on BC, and it would be inconsistent for her to choose one of those points now, when she can still afford e. Margie must accordingly move to a point such as e', to the left of e along BC. We have thus shown that regardless of Margie's preferences, the substitution effect of an increase in the relative price of food leads to a reduction in the quantity of food demanded. In the language of this chapter, *the substitution effect of an increase in the price of any good on the demand for that good is negative*.

The second step in the shift from AF to AF' is a shift from BC to AF'. But this second step simply represents a fall in income from $140 to $100, with both prices held constant at $10. The response to this shift is therefore clearly the income effect of the increase in the price of food. Since both food and clothing are normal goods, less of both are demanded at the final optimal point, e'', than at e'. Since both income and substitution effects are negative, the net effect of an increase in the price of food must be to reduce the quantity of food demanded.

Indifference Curves

Consumer preferences can be graphically represented in a way that avoids the assumption that utility can always

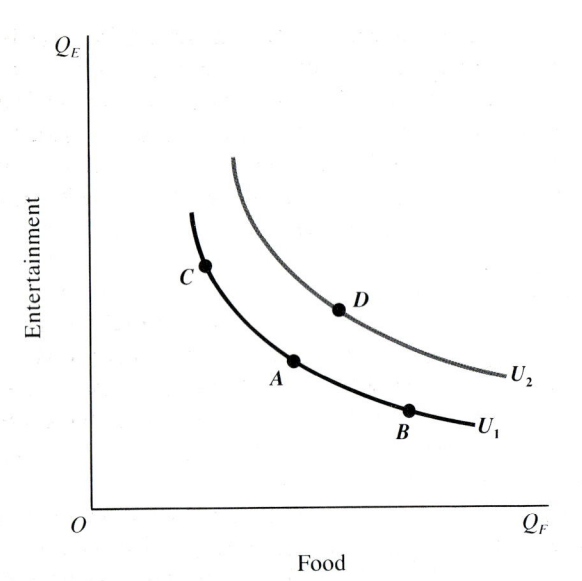

FIGURE 6A-4. Indifference Curves. The schedule U_1 is an indifference curve. It shows all the combinations of food and entertainment, such as points B and C, among which Margie is indifferent because they yield the same level of utility as the combination at point A. U_2 is another indifference curve. It must correspond to a higher level of utility, since Margie prefers more of both goods to less, and she consumes more food and more entertainment at point D than she does at point A. Any point on U_2 is accordingly preferred to any point on U_1.

be measured by a single number. The curves U_1 and U_2 shown in Figure 6A-4 are two of Margie's indifference curves.

● An *indifference curve* shows a set of consumption bundles among which a consumer is indifferent. That is, all consumption bundles on an indifference curve yield the consumer the same level of utility.

Along U_1 we have different combinations of food and entertainment. For example, point C is a bundle with lots of entertainment and little food. Point A by contrast involves a more balanced mix, and point B is richer in food but has less entertainment.

Indifference curves provide a graphic representation of the utility function introduced in section 2 of this chapter. According to the model presented there, Margie assigns a utility value (in utils) to all possible consumption bundles. The curve connecting all bundles that yield some particular value of utility (such as 124 utils per week) is an indifference curve. Thus U_1 shows one set of equal-utility bundles.

Point D is on another indifference curve, U_2. Since more is better than less, utility is higher on U_2 than it is on U_1. All points on U_2 yield the same level of utility; this level is higher than that yielded by all points on U_1.

We have not drawn more indifference curves, but in fact there is a whole family of them. Some lie below U_1, since they correspond to lower levels of utility than the consumption bundles along U_1. Others lie between U_1 and U_2, and still others lie above U_2. Indeed, since every point in the diagram represents a consumption bundle and accordingly can be assigned a utility value, every point lies on some indifference curve.

DRAWING INDIFFERENCE CURVES. Four rules about consumer tastes or preferences are reflected in the way we draw indifference curves.

First, *indifference curves cannot cross*, because each indifference curve corresponds to a particular level of utility. If they crossed, this would imply that the consumption bundle at the crossing point in fact had not one level of utility but two, one corresponding to each of the indifference curves. Since that does not make sense, indifference curves cannot cross.

Second, *higher indifference curves correspond to higher levels of utility or satisfaction*, because the consumer can have more of both goods on higher indifference curves than on lower indifference curves. In the model discussed in section 2 we assumed that utility can be measured, so that a definite number could be assigned to each indifference curve. But such numbers are not necessary to describe behavior, because the consumer simply attempts to reach the highest indifference curve possible. To do this she does not need to assign numbers to any of the curves.

Third, *indifference curves are negatively sloped*. Moving along an indifference curve, Margie is willing to give up some entertainment if in exchange she receives more food. If she consumes less of one good, then, to be indifferent, she must consume more of the other.

Fourth, *as one moves from left to right along an indifference curve, the curve flattens out*. The indifference curve first is very steep and then becomes flatter. At point C, for example, Margie is not eating much and is willing to give up a lot of entertainment to acquire another pound of food. At point *B*, by contrast, where she is consuming lots of food, she is willing to sacrifice only a very small amount of entertainment for another pound of food.

This flattening out of the indifference curve reflects the *diminishing marginal rate of substitution* of entertainment for food. "Diminishing marginal rate of substitution" means that Margie's willingness to give up entertainment in exchange for extra units of food declines as she consumes more and more food and less and less entertainment, that is, as she moves from *C* toward *B*. In the indifference curve analysis of consumer behavior, the assumption of diminishing marginal rates of substitution replaces the assumption of diminishing marginal utility employed in section 2 in this chapter.

INDIFFERENCE CURVE SLOPES. The slope of any of the indifference curves at any point thus tells us how many units of entertainment Margie can give up to get 1 unit of food and leave utility unchanged.[19] Suppose the slope is 3 at some point. That means she is willing to give up 3 units of entertainment to get 1 unit of food. Then the ratio of the marginal utility of food to the marginal utility of entertainment at that point must be 3. Why?

Suppose 1 extra unit of food brings in 30 utils. We have just said that Margie is willing to give up 3 units of entertainment to get 30 utils. Therefore, the marginal utility of entertainment must be 10 (30/3). Accordingly, *the slope of any indifference curve, which is equal to the marginal rate of substitution, is equal to the ratio of the marginal utilities of the goods*,[20] as follows:

$$\begin{array}{c}\text{Slope of}\\ \text{indifference}\\ \text{curve}\end{array} = \begin{array}{c}\text{marginal rate}\\ \text{of substitution}\\ \text{of food for}\\ \text{entertainment}\end{array} = \frac{\text{marginal utility}}{\text{of food}}\\ \frac{\text{marginal utility}}{\text{of entertainment}} \quad (A1)$$

Equation (A1) shows that the assumption of diminishing marginal utility implies that indifference curves have the shape shown in Figure 6A-4. As we move to the right along an indifference curve, the consumption of food

---

[19] Slopes of nonlinear curves such as these indifference curves were defined in the appendix to Chapter 1.
[20] To be consistent with our treatment of the budget line, we ignore the fact that all indifference curve slopes are also in fact negative.

increases and the consumption of entertainment decreases. Therefore, according to the assumption of diminishing marginal utility, the marginal utility of food decreases and the marginal utility of entertainment increases. Equation (A1) then shows that the marginal rate of substitution declines. The slope of the indifference curve accordingly decreases also.

THE CONSUMER'S SPENDING BEHAVIOR. We now demonstrate how we can use indifference curves to predict consumer demands for food and entertainment. It is not necessary to assign a definite utility value to each curve, as in effect we did in section 2. It is only necessary to know that Margie would rather be on a higher indifference curve than a lower one.

Given that she must select a consumption bundle represented by a point on (or inside) budget line *AF* in Figure 6A-5, the best Margie can do is to reach indifference curve U_2. In order to do this, she must select the

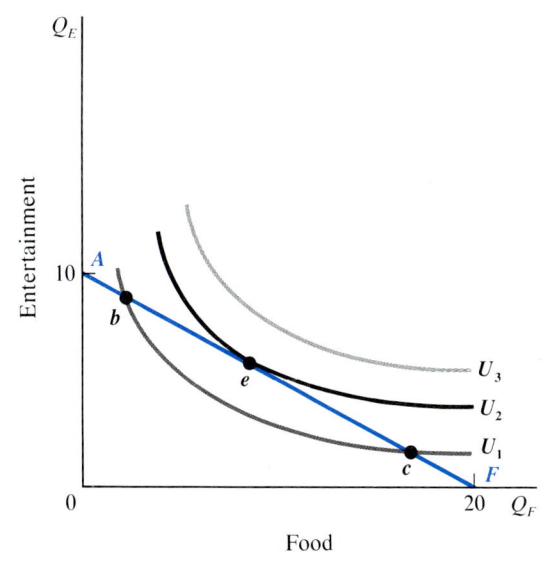

FIGURE 6A-5. Margie's Optimal Consumption Bundle. This diagram shows Margie's budget line, *AF*, and three of her indifference curves. She can reach any point on the budget line but cannot reach any point above it. Among the points on the budget line is point *e*. It represents the consumption bundle that yields the highest possible level of utility, because it is on the highest possible indifference curve. At the optimal point the budget line is tangent to an indifference curve.

consumption bundle at point e, as this is the only point on U_2 she can afford. There is no reason for her to choose a point on a lower indifference curve, such as U_1, because she can do better. She cannot reach any points on indifference curves such as U_3 that lie above U_2—because she does not have enough income to do so.

We now relate the graphic representation of consumer spending behavior in Figure 6A-5 to the analysis of utility maximization presented in section 2. Note first that at Margie's best consumption point, e, *the budget line is tangent to (just touches) the indifference curve*. This means that the slope of the indifference curve equals the slope of the budget line at this point. We have argued that the slope of the budget line is the price ratio and that the slope of the indifference curve is the marginal rate of substitution. Margie is thus on the highest possible indifference curve (that is, she is maximizing her utility) if she has chosen the consumption bundle on her budget line at which the following condition is satisfied:

$$\begin{matrix} \text{Marginal rate} \\ \text{of substitution} \\ \text{of food for} \\ \text{entertainment} \end{matrix} = \frac{\text{marginal utility of food}}{\text{marginal utility of entertainment}} = \frac{\text{price of food}}{\text{price of entertainment}} \quad (A2)$$

But this is just equation (3) in Chapter 6 plus the definition of the marginal rate of substitution we have just given.

THE EFFECTS OF A PRICE INCREASE. Indifference curves can be used to show the effects of a price increase on demand. In Figure 6A-6, the price of food doubles, shifting the budget line from AF to AF'. Margie can no longer attain point e. How will she alter her spending behavior?

The diagram shows that she will select the bundle represented by point e' on AF'. This is the point where an indifference curve is tangent to the new budget line, or,

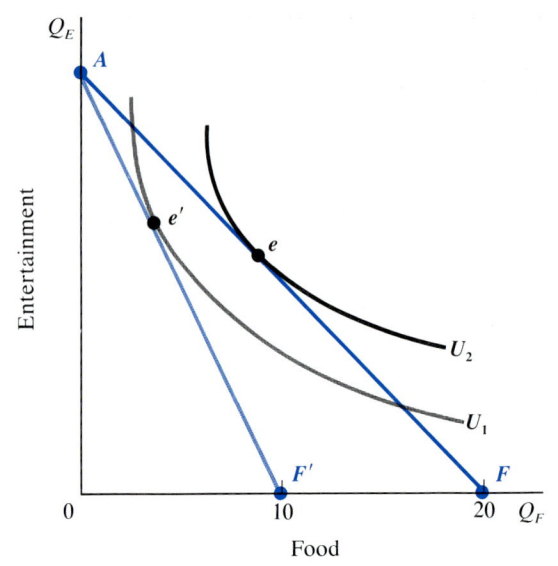

FIGURE 6A-6. The Effect of an Increase in the Price of Food on Margie's Demands for Food and Entertainment. Margie selects point e on budget line AF, which corresponds to a $100 income and prices of $10 for entertainment and $5 for food. When the food price increases to $10, she must choose a point on the new budget line, AF'. Indifference curve U_1 is now the highest indifference curve she can reach, given the new budget line. Therefore, point e' represents her new consumption bundle.

to put it differently, where the budget line to which the consumer must stick just touches the highest indifference curve. At this point the consumer maximizes utility (reaches the highest possible indifference curve) while still satisfying the budget constraint (being on the budget line).

At e' the quantity of entertainment demanded has risen compared with e. You should now draw an example in which the quantity of entertainment demanded falls as a consequence of an increase in the price of food.

Chapter 7
Business Organization and Behavior

In Chapter 3 we saw that the behavior of buyers (demand) and that of sellers (supply) together determine the amount of a good produced and its price. In Chapter 6 we presented the economic theory of consumer behavior, which shows how quantities demanded are determined by prices, incomes, and consumers' tastes. This chapter begins an in-depth analysis of the supply side of the economy. In this and the next five chapters we study the behavior of business firms, concentrating on how they decide what quantities of goods and services to supply.

We look first at the structure of the supply side of the U.S. economy. Business firms differ in many ways. They operate in different industries. They range in size from giant corporations such as General Motors, IBM, and Exxon, with hundreds of thousands of employees and owners, to small shops in which the owner is the only worker. They also have different legal structures; some have stockholders, but most do not. Before we can talk about business behavior in general, we must discuss both how businesses differ and how they are all alike.

We then consider a critical element of the economic theory of business behavior: the assumption that firms maximize profit. In the chapters that follow we show that this is a powerful assumption that enables us to understand much of what businesses actually do. However, like the assumption of utility maximization discussed in Chapter 6, profit maximization has frequently been questioned. Is it sensible to assume that real firms maximize anything? If so, can we be sure that profit is what is maximized?

Finally, we discuss exactly what economists mean by "profit." To do this, we introduce some key concepts from accounting, which has been called "the language of business." To apply economic models of business behavior to the real world, economists must understand how and why the languages of accounting and economics differ. Especially important is the difference between economic and accounting concepts of profit, since it is economic profit that firms are assumed to maximize.

1. Industries and Firms in the U.S. Economy

Our discussion of the supply side of the economy starts with a look at the menu of goods and services produced

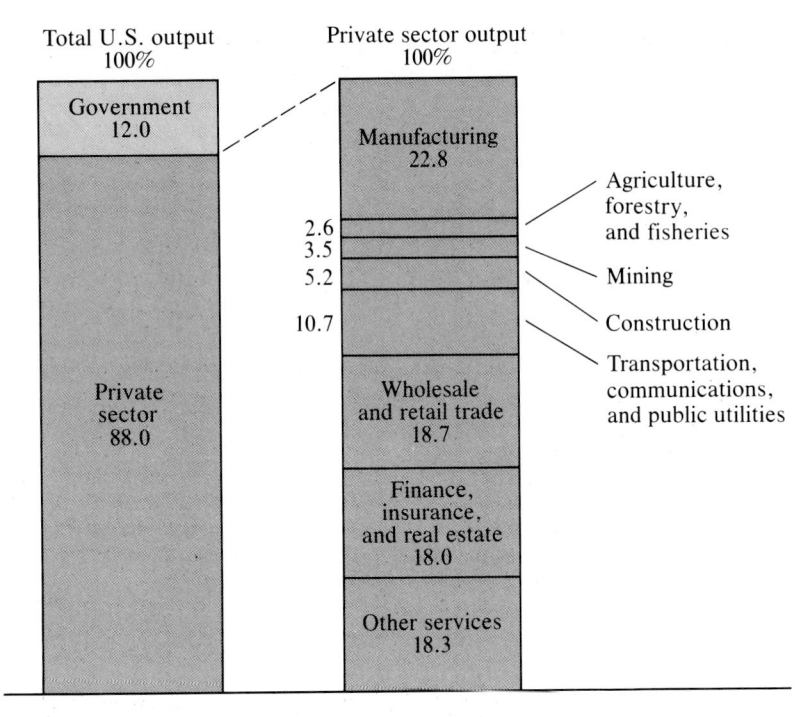

FIGURE 7-1. The Composition of Output in the U.S. Economy, 1985. Figures shown are percentages of total U.S. output (on the left) and total U.S. private sector output (on the right). Components do not total exactly 100 percent because of rounding and statistical discrepancies. (*Source*: *Survey of Current Business*, July 1986, Table 6.1)

Total U.S. output 100%:
- Government 12.0
- Private sector 88.0

Private sector output 100%:
- Manufacturing 22.8
- Agriculture, forestry, and fisheries 2.6
- Mining 3.5
- Construction 5.2
- Transportation, communications, and public utilities 10.7
- Wholesale and retail trade 18.7
- Finance, insurance, and real estate 18.0
- Other services 18.3

in the United States. Figure 7-1 shows the main sectors or industries in the economy and the fraction of total output (GNP) produced by the public and private sectors and the fraction of total private-sector output for which each major industry accounts. Their share of output is a guide to the economic importance of different industries in the U.S. economy.

The first point to note is that in the United States most goods are produced by the private sector. Government contributes only about 12 percent of total output.[1] This is quite different from many other countries where the government sector includes airlines, banks, steel mills, automobile plants, railroads, tobacco stores, and other enterprises. The U.S. government sector produces services ranging from education to national defense, along with goods ranging from water supply to government publications, but most output is produced in the private sector.

Figure 7-1 makes the idea of "goods and services" more concrete by showing the different industries that produce these outputs. Most of the industries in Figure 7-1 are easily recognized. For example, banking or a stock brokerage business would fall in the group "finance, insurance, and real estate." But what is included in "other services"? There we have a wide array of activities including education, recreation, hotels, health care, automobile repair, and business consulting.

There have been significant shifts in the composition of U.S. private output over time. In 1920, agriculture alone accounted for over 14 percent of private output; its share has been declining steadily for well over a century as agricultural productivity has increased phenomenally, and U.S. agriculture can now feed the United States and much of the rest of the world while employing less than 3 percent of the labor force. More recently, the relative importance of manufacturing has declined, from around 32 percent in 1965 to 23 percent in 1985. This has been essentially offset by growth in finance, insurance, and real estate and in other services. Their combined share of U.S. private output has increased from 28 percent in 1965 to 36 percent in 1985.

---

[1] Recall from Chapter 4 that government expenditure is equal to a third of GNP in the United States. The difference between government expenditures and government production is made up of (1) transfer payments and (2) purchases by government of goods and services produced by the private sector.

Those who expect this shift toward services to continue argue that we have entered a "postindustrial" era in which the United States will become a "service economy"—as opposed to an industrial economy centered on manufacturing. As our economy shifts from producing goods to producing services, the composition of employment shifts from "blue-collar" factory jobs to "white-collar" office jobs. Some welcome these changes as the wave of the future; others are upset that Japan and other countries are becoming the world's industrial giants and fear that the U.S. economy cannot survive merely by means of our taking in each other's laundry, or looking after each other's health, and attending each other's lectures.

Looking within these broad sectors, we see that goods and services in the U.S. economy are produced by about 19 million firms.[2] Some of them are well-known sellers of familiar products: producers of cars including GM and Ford, restaurant and hotel chains such as McDonalds and Holiday Inn, communications companies such as AT&T and CBS, oil companies such as Gulf and Exxon, food producers such as Kellogg and General Foods, and financial service businesses such as American Express and Citibank. However, most firms in the U.S. economy are small and little known.

Table 7-1 shows how firms are distributed across different sectors of the economy. It also shows the differences among industries in terms of average annual receipts per firm, which is an indicator of average firm size. (Average receipts are simply revenues from the sale of goods and services; costs are not deducted.)

The differences in average receipts per firm shown in Table 7-1 are striking. Average receipts are lowest in agriculture, forestry, and fisheries—largely because there are almost 2 million farm proprietorships in the United States, with average business receipts of only $40,000. Two-thirds of the firms in the United States are in the three industries at the bottom of the list, all of which produce services. These firms also tend to be relatively small as measured by their average receipts. There are many small grocery stores, insurance agencies, and automobile repair shops. At the other extreme, there

---

[2] Authors' estimate for 1987. There were 16.5 million firms in 1982, the latest year for which official data are available.

TABLE 7-1. Industrial Distribution and Average Receipts of Firms in the U.S. Economy, 1982

Industry	Firms, percentage	Average receipts per firm, thousands of dollars
All industries	100.0	419.5
Agriculture, forestry, and fisheries	14.9	61.8
Mining	1.4	955.0
Construction	9.4	218.4
Manufacturing	3.2	4487.4
Transportation, communications, and public utilities	3.5	1086.0
Wholesale and retail trade	21.4	633.7
Finance, insurance, and real estate	13.0	478.0
Other services	32.6	98.5

Source: Statistical Abstract of the United States, 1986, Tables 876 and 1126. Percentages do not total 100 because of rounding.

are relatively few manufacturing firms, but they tend to be large. The average receipts here are $4.5 million.

Corresponding to these differences in the sizes of firms are differences in the ways they are organized.

2. Forms of Business Organization

There are three main types of business firms in the United States: *individual proprietorships*, *partnerships*, and *corporations*. Figure 7-2 shows that the vast majority of the 16.5 million firms in the United States in 1982 were individual proprietorships. It also shows that on average the annual revenue of an individual proprietorship was only $42,400 and that of a partnership was nearly four times as much, while corporations on average sold over $2 million worth of goods and services.

Proprietorships and Partnerships

Suppose you decide to open a corner health food store. You will have to rent space for the store, buy food to put on the shelves, and perhaps hire someone to stand at the cash register while you are in class. You will keep what-

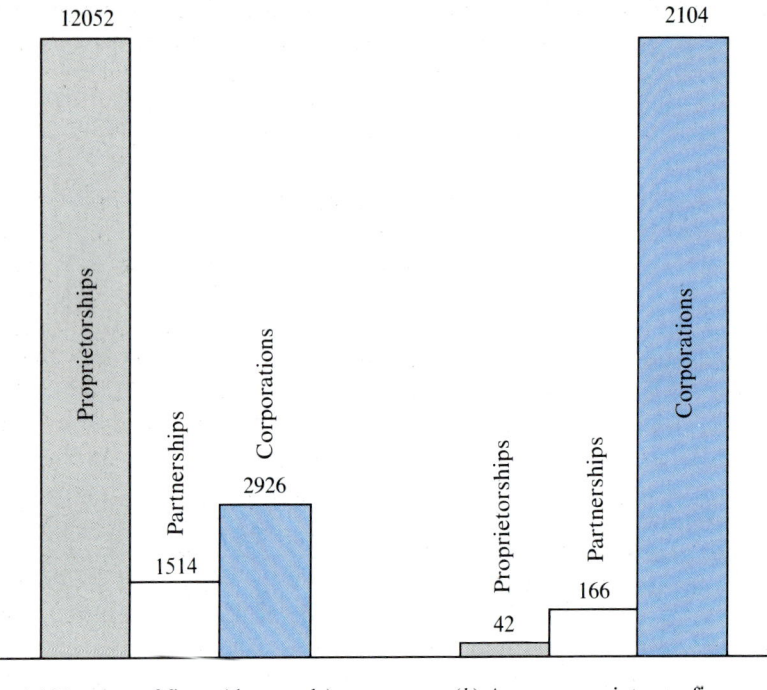

FIGURE 7-2. Business Firms in the United States, 1982. Panel (*a*) shows the number of firms in the United States in 1981 by organizational type, and (*b*) shows the average receipts of each type of firm in 1981. (*Source*: *Statistical Abstract of the United States, 1986*, Tables 876 and 1126.)

(*a*) Number of firms (thousands)

(*b*) Average receipts per firm (thousands of dollars)

ever profits remain after your business expenses have been paid.

● An *individual proprietorship* **is a business owned by an individual, who is fully entitled to the profit earned by the business and fully responsible for any losses the business incurs.**

Perhaps your store will show a loss, as many individual proprietorships do. If it does, you will have to pay the losses out of your own pocket. If the losses are large, you may be unable to pay. You will then have to go into bankruptcy and allow all your cash and other personal assets to be divided among the people to whom you owe money.

But individual proprietorships do not always fail. More often, they provide a tough living for their owners, who work long hours, frequently earning less than the average wage earner. Sometimes they provide handsomely for their owners.

If your health food store prospers, you may want to expand. To do so, you may have to move to bigger premises, buy bigger stocks of goods to have available for sale, and perhaps buy a delivery truck, hire more clerks, and buy office furniture. You will need *financial capital*, or money up front, to pay for all the new equipment and stock. Where will that come from? If you don't have enough money yourself, you will probably try to obtain the necessary financial capital from a friend or relative, who will then become your partner.

● A *partnership* **is a business jointly owned by two or more people who share its profit. Each of the owners, or *partners*, is jointly responsible for any losses the business incurs.**

Sometimes one of the partners runs the business and the other merely puts up money; sometimes both or all are active in the business. There are some very large partnerships, with hundreds of partners, particularly among law and accounting firms.

But the partnership form has two important disadvantages. First, partnerships (like individual proprietorships) have unlimited liability. This means that if the business loses money, each partner is individually responsible for its debts, whether or not he or she was actually active in the business. If there are two partners, for instance, and one of them goes bankrupt, the other is responsible for all the debts of the firm. A partner in a firm puts all his or her own wealth on the line, not just the assets of the firm.[3]

The second important disadvantage of this form of organization is that partnership agreements are very inflexible. If a new partner is taken in or if an existing partner dies or wants to get out, lawyers must be brought in to draw up a new partnership agreement. This inflexibility makes it inconvenient to raise the financial capital necessary to begin operating a business and finance its growth. In some businesses, such as law firms, in which little equipment is required and there is no need to have large amounts of goods on the shelves for sale, the necessary funds can be obtained from the wealth of the individual owner or the partners—perhaps with the aid of loans from banks or other individuals. But the larger the business and the more equipment and supplies it needs to operate, the more difficult it is to provide the necessary funds in these ways. A rapidly growing business also must be able to raise large amounts of funds on a more or less regular basis. It is very inconvenient to do this by repeatedly taking on new partners.

Corporations

Because of these disadvantages of the partnership form, if your health food business becomes large and its prospects for growth look good, you will probably *incorporate* it. That is, you will form a corporation.

● A *corporation* **is an organization legally permitted to carry on certain activities, such as running a railroad or producing a newspaper. The owners of a corporation are liable only for their investments in the corporation, even if these are not sufficient to cover the losses it incurs.**

A corporation, unlike an individual proprietorship or a partnership, has a legal existence separate from that of the people who own it at any particular time. Thus a corporation does not go out of existence when one of its owners—called a *shareholder* or *stockholder*—dies or when new owners are brought in.

Ownership of a corporation is divided among its shareholders. The original shareholders are the people who contribute money or other resources (such as work without pay or the idea for the product the company is producing) when the corporation is set up. In return they are given rights to a share of the company's earnings. This is done by distributing pieces of paper, called stock certificates, that specify the type of income those who own them are entitled to receive.[4] The shareholders of each corporation (those who own its stock certificates) elect a board of directors, which is responsible for hiring top management and supervising its work.

As a firm grows, it can raise money by printing more stock certificates and selling them. In exchange for rights of ownership, the corporation obtains the resources it needs to operate and grow. Shareholders in turn can typically resell their shares for cash to anyone who can buy them. Thus the current owners of a corporation are not necessarily the people who bought the original shares. Most likely, the current owners bought their stock from previous owners through a broker working in the stock market. In some small companies, there are restrictions on the rights of an owner to sell shares in order to prevent outsiders from acquiring control of the firm.[5] But outsiders can acquire control of large firms without such restrictions by buying their shares. Box 7-1 illustrates this process.

The earnings of a corporation may be paid out to the

---

[3] For this reason firms that need their clients' trust—such as law and accounting firms—are often partnerships. The partnership form indicates to potential customers that the people running the firm are willing to put their own personal fortunes behind the firm's work.

[4] While there are many different kinds of stock, the main distinction is between *common* and *preferred* stock. Preferred stock specifies a fixed dividend payment, while common stock does not. No dividends can be paid on common stock until all holders of preferred stock have received the specified dividends to which they are entitled. On the other hand, there is no upper limit on the size of the dividend that may be paid on common stock.

[5] If a group of shareholders owns a majority of the shares of a corporation, the group is said to control that corporation. Such a group can select the members of the firm's board of directors, and the board can then fire the existing management or force the corporation to merge with another firm.

Box 7-1 Proxy Fights, Takeovers, and GAF Corporation

In 1968, Samuel J. Heyman, then a young lawyer, took over his family's real estate business in Connecticut when his father died. The business prospered, and Heyman began to collect modern art and invest in stocks. By late 1981 he had acquired 3 percent of the stock of GAF Corporation, a producer of chemicals and building materials. Heyman thought that GAF was a sound but badly managed firm, and he expected a management change that would increase the value of his stock.

But the chairman of GAF's board of directors did not resign as Heyman had expected, and Heyman's efforts to persuade the firm to change its policies failed. In March 1983, Heyman launched a *proxy fight* in an attempt to gain control of GAF. He wrote to the firm's shareholders directly and took out full-page ads in newspapers, trying to persuade them to elect his candidates as the firm's board of directors instead of re-electing the existing board. The firm's management also wrote to the shareholders and took out ads stressing Heyman's lack of management experience. Most attempts to gain control of large corporations in this fashion fail, but in April 1983, Heyman succeeded.

In the first 9 months after he was elected chairman of the board by GAF's shareholders, Heyman cut GAF's expenses by 23 percent, in part by closing three plants and firing 700 of the firm's 4700 employees. He moved the company's headquarters from Manhattan to Wayne, New Jersey, to save on rent. GAF's profits increased sharply over the next 3 years.

On December 9, 1985, GAF attempted to take over the Union Carbide Corporation, a producer of chemicals and consumer products that was about 10 times the size of GAF. In December 1984, a leak at a Carbide plant in Bhopal, India, had killed over 2000 people, and a year later it was still unclear how much Carbide would have to pay as a consequence. Since the Bhopal tragedy, Carbide had been engaged in a vigorous program of cost reduction. But the general impression in the financial community was that, as one analyst put it, "Carbide is fat, and a lot of people think it has been mismanaged for years."

GAF already owned 10 percent of Carbide's shares when it began its takeover attempt. It made a *tender offer* to Carbide shareholders, offering to buy the rest of Carbide's stock at $68 a share. On the day of the offer, Carbide stock was selling at $63 a share. This was a *hostile takeover*, since Carbide's management opposed it. This time Heyman failed to get control. He was forced to withdraw his offer on January 8, 1986, since he could not match an $85-per-share counteroffer by Carbide management. (To pay for this, Carbide decided to sell all its consumer products businesses.) On the other hand, by selling most of its Carbide holdings for $85 per share, GAF made $81 million after taxes.

Note: For more details, see "The Proxy Fighter Who's Turning around GAF," *Fortune*, February 3, 1985; "Union Carbide Is Target of Takeover Bid by GAF," *New York Times*, December 10, 1985; and "GAF Ends Carbide Bid; Gain Put at $81 Million," *New York Times*, January 9, 1986.

---

shareholders as dividends or kept in the firm as retained earnings.

● **Dividends are more or less regular (usually quarterly) payments made by a corporation to its stockholders.** *Retained earnings* **are the part of earnings that a firm does not pay out to its stockholders as dividends. These earnings are kept in the firm.**

Dividend payments represent a direct return on shareholders' investments. Corporations are not obliged to pay dividends, but most do. Large firms typically try to maintain a steady flow of dividend payments to their owners. The rate at which dividends are paid out, both as a percentage of the firm's profits and as a percentage of the price of the stock, varies substantially from firm to firm.

Profits that are kept in a firm as retained earnings are usually employed to finance investment and thus increase the value of the firm's shares. Eventually retained earnings provide a return to shareholders in the form of capital gains.

● **Capital gains are earned when an asset, such as a share of stock, is sold and the seller receives more than was originally paid for the asset.**

A corporation may use its retained earnings in many ways to increase its ability to make profits. It may finance new investment in equipment or factories, buy another company, or add to its bank account or other financial assets. As a company retains earnings and uses them to build up assets that generate earnings, the value of its shares is likely to rise because actual and potential shareholders will expect it to pay larger dividends in the future. Thus retained earnings generally benefit existing shareholders by making it possible for them to realize capital gains if they sell their shares.

The shareholders who own any part of a corporation have *limited liability*, which means they are not liable for more money than they have committed to the corporation. If one of us buys shares in your newly incorporated health food business, the worst that can happen to us is that our shares will become worthless when your business fails. If we are partners, however, and your business owes $10 million more than it can pay, all of our wealth can be taken to pay off the firm's debts—no matter how little each of us initially invested. A shareholder in a corporation clearly has much less to worry about than a partner does.

Two important advantages of the corporate form of organization are that ownership shares can be quickly and cheaply bought and sold and that shareholders have limited liability. These advantages have made the corporation the main form of organization of big business. The firms whose names are household words are corporations. The largest U.S. firm in terms of employment in 1985 was General Motors, a corporation with 811,000 employees, or nearly 1 percent of the total U.S. work force.[6] In 1986, 40 U.S. firms—all corporations—employed over 100,000 workers each and 8.7 million workers together. Thus a few large corporations account for a very substantial portion of total employment (and output) in the United States. By contrast, the roughly 12 million individual proprietorships in the United States today produce less than 20 percent of GNP and, despite their number, are far less important economically than the corporations.

The Common Denominator: Profits

Can we really hope to have a theory of business behavior that applies to firms as different as a health food store organized as an individual proprietorship, a law firm organized as a partnership, and a giant corporation that manufactures automobiles? Yes, because businesses of all three types have one feature in common: All have one or more *owners* whose wealth depends on the earnings of the firm.

The owners of all three forms of business want the firms to maximize profits in order to make themselves as wealthy as possible. In most situations, the decision that maximizes owners' wealth is the same whether the firm involved is organized as an individual proprietorship, a partnership, or a corporation. Economists accordingly assume that all businesses are run so as to maximize profits. While this may seem a natural assumption, it has not escaped criticism.

3. Profit Maximization

The assumption that businesses maximize profit has been subjected to two serious criticisms. First, some have argued that real business decisions are so complex and often are made on the basis of so little information that it is not realistic to assume that businesses are *able* to maximize anything. Second, it has been argued that the thousands of shareholders of large corporations cannot effectively control corporate management. Under these conditions, it is contended that managers may be free to pursue their own goals at the expense of shareholders' wealth. Let us examine these criticisms in turn.

Do Businesses Maximize?

Is it realistic to assume that managers always and everywhere make exactly the right decisions to maximize profits? Plainly not: Everybody makes mistakes. But this does not make the economic theory of business behavior incorrect.

Suppose all snark producers are trying to make as much money as possible but none can figure out the best way to produce snarks. Different firms will probably adopt different production methods. Those which are lucky will select the best method and will prosper. The others will have higher costs and will decline. The unlucky firms may imitate the lucky ones and thus produce optimally, or they may be driven from the market. Either

---

[6] The 1986 assets of General Motors ($63 billion) were less than those of Exxon ($69 billion), but Exxon had only 146,000 employees. Which of these firms was larger thus depends on exactly how "larger" is defined.

way, the market will come to be dominated by firms producing snarks optimally, even though no manager consciously maximized anything.

One can thus describe the *outcome* of this competitive process at least approximately as profit maximization, even though, just as in the case of consumer behavior, maximization does not describe the *process* of decision making. Economists often say that competition forces firms to act *as if* they were maximizing profits, even though executives may not consciously maximize anything when they make decisions.

What Are Managers' Goals?

Most large corporations are not run by their owners.[7] Such corporations are owned by many shareholders who in principle control the firm through the board of directors, whose members they elect. The board of directors in turn appoints the managers and is supposed to make sure they run the firm in the interests of the ultimate owners, the shareholders.

However, in a large firm the board of directors actually has little direct control over management decisions. A large corporation is a very complex organization, and it is difficult for a part-time board of directors to control the full-time managers who make all the day-to-day decisions. If managers cannot be directly compelled to maximize shareholders' wealth, what goals might they pursue?

Managers' salaries are usually higher the larger the firm. Therefore, it is sometimes argued that managers aim to make the firms they run grow bigger rather than trying to maximize the wealth of their shareholders. If a firm does not have any very good investments to make, the best thing to do with its profits might be to give them back to the shareholders by increasing dividend payments so that the shareholders could then invest elsewhere. But to make the company grow, managers might instead retain the earnings and use them to build more factories.

There are other situations in which managers might want to act in ways that are not in the interests of shareholders. For instance, when an outsider attempts to take over a badly run firm, the existing management may oppose the takeover even though the shareholders would benefit—since the managers would lose their jobs.

To deal with these problems, shareholders usually try to give managers an interest in maximizing the firm's profits. Bonus schemes increase management salaries when profits increase. Senior managers are often paid in part with stock in the company in the hope that they will act in a way that keeps its value high and therefore maximizes all shareholders' wealth. If such devices fail, the shareholders of a poorly run firm are likely to support takeover attempts by outsiders, and such attempts often succeed despite the opposition of managers. Managers who do not serve shareholders' interests are thus less likely to retain their jobs than are those who do.

FIRMS' SOCIAL OBJECTIVES. Businesses, particularly large corporations, sometimes make donations to charity, provide funds for public television, or act in other philanthropic ways that do not directly increase their profits. This raises two related questions: Do such actions end up benefitting shareholders? Should large corporations think only of their shareholders?

Philanthropic activities may in fact indirectly increase profits in the long run, because they cause the community in which the firm operates to think well of it. Perhaps the firm will find it easier to get the city to approve a new building, or perhaps there will be an accidental discharge of pollution that will be forgiven because the corporation has been a good citizen.

Even if corporate philanthropy does not benefit shareholders, some observers argue that businesses really are more like citizens than profit-maximizing machines and should have social consciences. Others argue that corporations should limit themselves to maximizing their owners' wealth. They argue that the money corporations give away belongs to their shareholders and that the shareholders should decide for themselves what charities to support.

While these are interesting questions, it is good to keep in mind that corporations rarely spend a large fraction of their shareholders' money on charity. Philanthropic contributions by even the largest U.S. corporations average well below 1 percent of pretax income.

---

[7] Adolf A. Berle, Jr., and Gardiner C. Means, in their 1932 classic, *The Modern Corporation and Private Property*, argued that managements often pursue aims that differ from those of the stockholders.

4. Accounting and Economic Reality

Economists assume that firms are operated so as to maximize *economic profit*, or the difference between revenue and cost.

● **A firm's *revenue* is the amount it receives from the sale of goods or services during a given period (say, a year). The firm's *costs* are the expenses of producing the goods or services sold during the period. *Profit*, or *net income*, is the excess of revenue over costs.**

These definitions are simple in principle, but it is not at all simple to measure costs and profits accurately in practice. Businesses use the tools of accounting for this purpose, and most of the information we have about businesses and their behavior is based on accounting data. A knowledge of basic accounting principles is thus useful in a wide range of situations.

Unfortunately, accounting systems were not designed to provide data for economic analysis. They were initially developed so that shareholders in corporations and partners who were not active in partnership businesses could obtain honest and reliable information about the profits to which they were entitled. To meet this goal, it was important to compute profits in such a way that the work of accountants could be checked by outsiders unfamiliar with the details of any particular business.[8] As a consequence and as we shall see, accounting systems do not generally reflect things that are hard to measure precisely, even if they are very important. This means in particular that accounting measures of profit differ from the economic profit that firms are assumed to maximize. We will discuss the main differences between these concepts of profit after presenting the basic principles of accounting.

The Income Statement

Let us begin by considering the accounting measurement of profit for a simple firm. Rent-a-Clerk, Inc., is a firm that does what its name suggests. It hires people whom it rents out to other firms, where they work as clerks. Rent-a-Clerk charges its customers $10 per hour

---
[8] This is the task of outside *auditors*, accountants who check the work of many firms' own accountants and bookkeepers.

TABLE 7-2. Income Statement of Rent-a-Clerk, Inc., for the Year Ending December 31, 1987

Revenue		$1,000,000
(100,000 hours rented out at $10 per hour)		
Minus expenses (or costs)		
Wages paid to people rented out (100,000 hours at $7 per hour)	$700,000	
Newspaper advertising	50,000	
Office rent	45,000	
Wages for office workers	80,000	
Other office expenses	17,000	
Depreciation on typewriters	3,000	
Interest on bank loan	5,000	
		900,000
Net income (or profit) before tax		$100,000
Minus corporate income tax		20,000
Net income (or profit) after tax		$ 80,000

per clerk and pays the people it hires $7 per hour. During 1987 it rented out 100,000 person-hours of labor. In order to operate the business, it had to rent an office, advertise in newspapers, pay its office workers, and pay for postage and telephone service. In addition, the typewriters it owns *depreciated*, or decreased in value. All its out-of-pocket expenses plus the depreciation on its typewriters came to $200,000. Table 7-2 shows the *income statement*, or *profit and loss statement*, for Rent-a-Clerk for 1987.

● **An *income statement*, or *profit and loss statement*, shows the revenues, expenses, and profit (or net income) for a particular firm for a particular period.**

According to this statement, Rent-a-Clerk had a net income or profit after taxes of $80,000 during 1987. Even though Rent-a-Clerk is a simple business, the accountants who drew up its income statement had to deal with a number of complications.

OUTSTANDING BILLS. Very often, a firm is not paid within the year for all the goods or services it sold that year, nor does it pay within the year for all the goods or services it bought. Rent-a-Clerk rented out 100,000 hours of labor during the year, but its customers still have not paid for services received during December. Similarly, Rent-a-

Clerk probably has not paid its telephone bill for December by the end of the year.

However, accountants (and economists) define revenues as the value of goods or services sold or rented out during the year, regardless of when payment is received. Costs are the value of the goods or services used during the year, regardless of when they are paid for. In order to draw up an income statement, an accountant must thus know what payments a firm expects to receive in the future for sales made during the period. Similarly, bills that must be paid in the future for goods or services used during the period must be included in costs.

CASH FLOW. The difference between revenues and costs, on the one hand, and between payments received and made, on the other hand, raises the important concept of cash flow.

● *A firm's cash flow* **is the net amount of money it actually receives in a given period.**

Cash flow may be low even though profits are high—for instance, if customers haven't yet paid their bills. Of course, a firm that is making profits but has no cash flow may eventually find it difficult to operate, since it can't keep paying for the goods and services it needs without having some cash flowing in.

One of the big problems in starting a new business is that cash flow at the beginning, before the firm has succeeded in finding customers, is bound to be low. This is why firms need financial capital to start up—so that they can continue to pay expenses for a while even with little cash flowing in. Eventually, if the business does well, customers will be found, sales will be made, bills will be paid, and the cash flow will be large enough to cover expenses.

CAPITAL AND DEPRECIATION. Rent-a-Clerk rents its office space, telephones, and desks, but it owns the 10 typewriters used by its office staff. These are the only items of physical capital it owns.

● *Physical capital* **is the durable assets (such as machinery, equipment, and buildings) used in operating a firm.**

Rent-a-Clerk bought its typewriters at the start of the year for $1000 each. Those typewriters will be available for use in 1988 and beyond, so that it would not be sensible to treat their full purchase cost ($10,000) as a cost of operating the firm in 1987.

The cost of *using*, rather than the cost of buying, a piece of physical capital should be treated as part of the firm's costs of producing output within the year. Thus Rent-a-Clerk should figure out how much the market value of its typewriters (that is, the price for which they could be sold) declined during the year and count that as a cost. Rent-a-Clerk found that the wear and tear on its typewriters reduced the market value of each one from $1000 at the beginning of the year to $700 at the end of the year. Thus the cost of using the typewriters during the year was $3000 (10 × $300). This amount is shown in Table 7-2 as the cost labeled "depreciation on typewriters."

● *Depreciation* **is the loss of value resulting from the use of physical capital within a given period.**

Because market values may be difficult to observe reliably, particularly for very specialized pieces of equipment, accountants typically use simple rules to estimate depreciation. For instance, if typewriters generally last 4 years, the depreciation each year might be estimated to be one-fourth of the initial purchase price.

The buying or selling of physical capital creates another difference between profit and cash flow. When a firm buys a building, it has a large cash outflow. However, its costs of using that building during the year will be less than the cash outflow, because buildings last a long time. Thus the firm may be making profits in a year in which it actually pays out much more in cash (paying for the building) than it receives from sales.

INVENTORIES. Since Rent-a-Clerk produces services rather than goods, it has no inventories.

● *Inventories* **are goods held in stock by a firm for use in future production or for future sales.**

Within a given year, the Chrysler Corporation may, for example, make 1 million cars and sell only 950,000. It adds 50,000 cars to its inventories. How does this affect its profit? There is no question that its revenues are the amount earned by selling 950,000 cars. Should it figure its costs on the basis of what it takes to make the 950,000 cars it sold or the 1 million cars it made?

From the basic definition of profit at the start of this section, the answer is that the costs should relate to the 950,000 cars it sold. To see whether Chrysler was profitable, we must know whether revenues from the cars it sold exceeded the cost of producing *those* cars. The other 50,000 cars added to inventory are like capital that the firm has made for itself. These cars are a valuable asset, which Chrysler can sell in the future without paying anything to produce them. Both the revenue from selling those 50,000 cars and the actual costs of producing them affect profit when they are sold, not before.

Chrysler had a cash outflow during the year to pay for making 1 million cars. But part of that cash outflow (the cost of making the 50,000 cars added to inventory) should be thought of as going for the purchase of goods available for future sale. Thus an increase in inventories is an investment, like the purchase of typewriters or other physical capital, not a cost of sales made in the current period.

Similarly, companies usually hold stocks or inventories of raw materials needed for production. A company may increase or decrease these inventories during the year. Its costs include the costs of the materials inventories used up in production of the goods sold during the year, *not* the value of raw materials actually purchased within the year. The latter affects cash flow that year, not profit. The effect on profit occurs when goods made with the raw materials are sold, not when the raw materials are purchased. Because they must increase physical capital and inventories, rapidly growing firms often have net cash outflows even if they are very profitable.

INTEREST EXPENSE. Like many firms, Rent-a-Clerk did not obtain enough cash from its initial shareholders to finance its start-up costs, such as buying typewriters, paying its office staff to set up its record-keeping systems and locate the first customers, paying lawyers' and accountants' fees for the paperwork involved in setting up the firm, and more. It borrowed money from a bank to cover some of these costs. The interest paid on the borrowed money is part of the cost of doing business in the current period and thus shows up on the income statement as a cost.

EARNINGS. As we noted previously, Rent-a-Clerk can do two things with its after-tax profits of $80,000. It can pay some or all of its profits to the shareholders as dividends, or it can keep them in the firm as retained earnings. Rapidly growing firms may be highly profitable but extremely short of cash; they often have to borrow money in order to pay any dividends at all and typically don't pay dividends.

The Balance Sheet

The income, or profit and loss, statement shown in Table 7-2 tells us how well a firm did during a given year, but we also want a picture of where it is at any given time. The balance sheet gives this picture.

● A *balance sheet* **shows the assets, liabilities, and net worth of a particular firm at a particular time. The** *assets* **are what the firm owns, and the** *liabilities* **are what it owes.** *Net worth* **is the difference between assets and liabilities.**

Table 7-3 shows the balance sheet of U.S. Snark, Inc., a more complicated business than Rent-a-Clerk, on December 31, 1987. Snark's assets are shown on the left of its balance sheet. U.S. Snark has some cash in the bank. It is owed money by its customers, entered as "accounts receivable." It has an inventory of 10,000 Snarks in its warehouse, each of which cost $10 to produce. The firm also has a factory building, now estimated to be worth $200,000. Two years ago it cost $240,000, but its value has been reduced by 2 years of depreciation of $20,000 per year. Snark's factory and office equipment is listed together and valued at $180,000. That equipment originally cost $300,000, but its value has been reduced over the years by $120,000 of depreciation. The total value of Snark's assets is $590,000.

Snark's liabilities are shown on the right of its balance sheet. Snark has unpaid bills that it owes, and it also has to pay some salaries for work already done. In addition, it has borrowed through a mortgage to finance the building of its factory, and it has a bank loan for its shorter-term cash needs. The total value of its debts is $350,000.

The total value of Snark's assets is higher by $240,000 than the value of its debts, and it therefore has a net worth (excess of assets over liabilities) of $240,000. Total

TABLE 7-3. Balance Sheet of U.S. Snark, Inc.   December 31, 1987

Assets			Liabilities and net worth	
Cash		$ 40,000	Accounts payable	$ 90,000
Accounts receivable		70,000	Salaries payable	50,000
Inventories		100,000	Mortgage from	
Factory building			insurance company	150,000
Original cost	240,000		Loan from bank	60,000
Minus depreciation	40,000			
		200,000	Total liabilities	350,000
Equipment				
Original cost	300,000		Net worth	240,000
Minus depreciation	120,000			
		180,000	Total liabilities	
Total assets		$590,000	and net worth	$590,000

assets on a balance sheet always equal total liabilities plus net worth, because net worth is *defined* as the difference between assets and liabilities.

The balance sheet reflects some of the complications discussed in examining the income statement. The fact that some of the goods sold have not yet been paid for shows up in the accounts receivable part of the balance sheet. The firm's purchase of physical capital, along with the depreciation of that capital, also appears on the balance sheet. So too does any change in the firm's inventories. The amounts the firm has borrowed appear on the balance sheet under "liabilities."

If profits are kept as retained earnings, they will affect the balance sheet. For instance, if retained earnings are kept as cash, the asset "cash" goes up. If the retained earnings are used to pay off the loan at the bank, this liability is reduced. Perhaps the retained earnings are used to buy more machinery; then the asset "equipment" increases. Whatever is done with the retained earnings, they will either increase the firm's assets or decrease its liabilities and thus increase the firm's net worth—the difference between its assets and its liabilities.

Accounting and Market Values

Suppose now that some other firm wants to buy Snark, Inc. Snark looks like a promising company with a good product, satisfied clients, able management, and good morale among its work force. Will the right amount to offer be $240,000, the net worth shown on the company's balance sheet? In general the answer is no. There are two reasons why the market value of Snark, Inc., is likely to exceed $240,000.

First, accounting depreciation is based on the original price paid for physical capital, and it is usually computed according to some simple, standard rule. This is done because it may be hard for those unfamiliar with the business to check a firm's estimates of the market values of its own assets. The values shown for Snark's factory and equipment thus reflect their initial cost and standard rules for calculating depreciation. These accounting values may not equal the market values of the assets. In particular, since Snark is located in a city with a healthy economy, its factory could be sold for $300,000 today, well above the value shown on its balance sheet.

Second, Snark, Inc., has assets that do not appear on its balance sheet at all because there are no simple rules for estimating their values that can be checked by outsiders. These *intangible* assets ignored by accountants include the skills of Snark's employees and their ability to work well together. In addition, the balance sheet does not show that Snark has proved that it knows how to earn profits and that it has good prospects for future growth. A company that buys Snark is buying not only the factory and premises and the cash in the bank, along with the other assets minus liabilities on its balance sheet, but also the skills and knowledge of its employees and its reputation with customers and suppliers.

For both these reasons, a buyer will probably pay more than $240,000 for Snark. The maximum price it will be willing to pay will depend mainly on how much profit it thinks Snark is going to make in future years. Snark's balance sheet may help a potential buyer compute this maximum price, but other information may be at least as important.

Accounting Cost and Opportunity Cost

Just as the accounting values of the assets on a firm's balance sheet generally understate the firm's real value, the accounting costs that appear on its income statement generally omit important elements of the firm's real economic costs of doing business. Since profit is revenue minus costs, *accounting* profit is thus generally greater than *economic* profit. Since we assume that firms maximize *economic* profit, it is important to understand how this difference arises.

Accountants and economists agree that in principle a firm's costs in any period are equal to the value of the resources it uses to produce the goods or services it sells in this period. (This is the definition given at the start of this section.) Accountants focus on costs that can be easily measured (such as the cost of telephone service) or calculated according to simple rules (such as depreciation). But economists begin with the broader notion of opportunity cost, which was introduced in Chapter 1. The opportunity cost of using any resource, such as labor or capital, in any business is the amount that could have been earned by putting that resource to its best alternative use.

Accountants generally ignore two important components of opportunity cost. The first is the *opportunity cost of an owner's time*. Suppose all the stock in Rent-a-Clerk is owned by one person, who works full-time for the firm. She might conclude on the basis of the income statement in Table 7-2 that she has a good business going. But that statement does not take into account the opportunity cost of her own labor—the amount she could have earned if she had worked elsewhere. Suppose she is a very able executive and could earn an income up to $120,000 doing equally pleasant work elsewhere. Then the opportunity cost of her time is $120,000. Subtracting this cost from the net after-tax income of $80,000 shown in Table 7-2 reveals that Rent-a-Clerk in fact had a loss of $40,000 in 1987. The firm's *economic* profit was negative because revenues did not cover all costs, including the opportunity cost of the owner's time.[9]

The second element of opportunity cost neglected in accounting statements is the *opportunity cost of the owners' financial capital*. Even if they do not devote time to a business, the owners (an individual proprietor, the partners, or the original shareholders) generally had to put up financial capital to get it going. In calculating accounting profits, no cost is attached to the use of owned (as opposed to borrowed) financial capital. But of course this financial capital could have been used elsewhere—invested in the stock market, in another firm, or even in a savings account. The opportunity cost of the financial capital supplied by a firm's owners is included in the firm's economic costs but not in its accounting costs.

Suppose the owner of Rent-a-Clerk put up $200,000 to start the business. Suppose also that she could have used this money to buy 1000 shares of the stock of an established firm, no riskier than Rent-a-Clerk, that pays annual dividends of $20 per share. The opportunity cost of the capital she invested in Rent-a-Clerk is thus at least $20,000 ($20 × 1000) per year—the amount she would have earned on this alternative investment. The opportunity cost is exactly $20,000 if this is the best alternative available to her.

Table 7-4 relates the accounting and economic profits earned by the owner of Rent-a-Clerk by taking into account the opportunity costs of her time and financial capital. Despite what her accountants tell her, the owner of Rent-a-Clerk should not be pleased with the performance of her business, and she might even consider closing it.

---

[9] The owner might argue that it is worth $50,000 a year to her to be her own boss. If running Rent-a-Clerk thus gives her $50,000 of *nonpecuniary* (nonmonetary) income in addition to $80,000 in after-tax profits, the economic profit of the firm for 1987 is $10,000 ($80,000 − $120,000 + $50,000). Another way to put this is that the opportunity cost of her time is really only $70,000 ($120,000 − $50,000), because working elsewhere could not actually be equally pleasant. Many small businesses yield their owners, year after year, less than the owners could earn by working for others. Either the owners of these businesses are irrational not to shut them down or they like being self-employed.

TABLE 7-4. Economic Income Statement of Rent-a-Clerk, Inc., for the Year Ending December 31, 1987

Revenues		$1,000,000
Minus accounting costs		900,000
Accounting profit before tax		100,000
Minus corporate income tax		20,000
Accounting profit after tax		80,000
Minus costs omitted from accounting statements		
Opportunity cost of owner's time	$120,000	
Opportunity cost of owner's capital	20,000	
		140,000
Net economic profit (loss) after tax		($60,000)

There are other reasons why accounting profits and economic profits can differ. For instance, accounting depreciation, which is calculated by formula, may not be a good measure of the actual decline in the market value of an asset. (Recall that Snark's factory rose in value even though the accounting statements showed it declining in value by $20,000 every year.) This problem is particularly serious during periods of inflation, when market values are generally increasing. Inflation also makes it difficult to compute the correct value of a firm's inventories and even of its liabilities. (The dollars a firm repays are worth less than the dollars it borrowed if prices have risen in the meantime.) These and other problems reinforce the message that accounting and economic profits and values should not be assumed to be the same.

■ In the rest of this book, we assume that firms maximize profits. This means that however they are organized, firms are in business to make money, and managers accordingly try to make the firm's owners as wealthy as possible. It also means that managers maximize economic profits, not accounting profits. While only approximately correct, this is a sensible and useful assumption. In the next chapter we use it to show how available methods of production and costs of productive inputs together determine the costs of producing goods and services.

Summary

1. This chapter introduces the supply side by looking at industries and firms in the U.S. economy. Nearly 90 percent of output in the United States is produced by the private sector. Services (wholesale and retail trade; finance, insurance, and real estate; and other services) account for more than half of private-sector output. Their share has increased over time at the expense of agriculture and, more recently, manufacturing.
2. There are three types of firms: individual proprietorships, partnerships, and corporations. There are over 12 million individual proprietorships in the United States, but most of them are very small firms. The important business firms are corporations. All three types of firms have owners whose wealth is increased by increases in the firm's profits.
3. A corporation is an organization set up to conduct a particular type of business. Corporations are owned by their shareholders (or stockholders). Each corporation has a board of directors that is elected by the shareholders to hire and supervise the managers who actually run the firm.
4. Shareholders in corporations have limited liability. That is, no matter what happens, they are liable for no more than they invested in the corporation. Partnerships and individual proprietorships have unlimited liability; all the wealth of their owners may be confiscated to pay the firm's debts.
5. Limited liability is one reason why the corporation is the dominant organizational form for large businesses. The other reason is that stock markets make it possible for owners of corporations (shareholders) to sell stock quickly and easily.
6. Economists assume that all businesses are run to make their owners as wealthy as possible. That is, firms are assumed to maximize economic profit. Competition forces firms to behave as if they were maximizing profit, and shareholders attempt to give managers incentives to make maximum profits their goal. Profit maximization is usually a good approximation to actual business behavior.
7. Revenues are the amounts the firm makes by selling its goods or services during a given period. Costs are the expenses of producing the goods or services sold during the period. Profits are the excess of revenues over costs. A firm's profits may be very different from its cash flow, or the net amount of money it actually receives in a given period.

8 The income statement shows the revenues, expenses, and profit for a particular firm for a particular period. The balance sheet shows a firm's assets (what it owns), liabilities (what it owes), and net worth (assets minus liabilities) at a particular time.
9 Balance sheets produced by accountants use simple rules to calculate depreciation and omit assets that are not easily valued. As a result, the market value of a business often exceeds the net worth shown on its balance sheet.
10 Income statements produced by accountants generally omit the opportunity costs of some resources used by firms. The opportunity cost of any resource is the amount it could have earned in its best alternative use. Because accounting statements omit the opportunity costs of the owners' labor and financial capital, accounting profits generally exceed economic profits.

Key Terms

Profit maximization
Service economy
Individual proprietorship
Partnership
Corporation
Shareholder (stockholder)
Board of directors
Limited liability
Dividends
Capital gains
Retained earnings
Financial capital
Physical capital
Depreciation
Inventories
Income statement
Revenue
Cost
Opportunity cost
Accounting profit
Economic profit
Balance sheet
Assets
Intangible assets
Net worth
Market value

Problems

1 What have the important changes in the composition of U.S. output been over the past 40 years? Which sectors have declined and which have expanded?
2 (a) What are the main advantages of the corporation over a large partnership as a way of doing business? (b) List five corporations whose products you buy. (c) Do you buy goods or services from any partnerships or individual proprietors? (d) Is the college or university you attend a corporation? Is it a firm?
3 What are the important differences between firms in the manufacturing industry and those in the service industry? Discuss the differences with respect to size and ownership.
4 (a) Do you think firms actually attempt to maximize profits? (b) Do you think firms should aim to maximize profits, or should they rather have a social conscience and do things such as support charities, the arts, and political campaigns?
5 How would each of the following affect the income statement for Rent-a-Clerk presented in Table 7-2? (a) Rent-a-Clerk still owes $70,000 to the people it rented out during the year. (b) Instead of renting an office, the company owns its office. (c) During the year Rent-a-Clerk was paid by one of the people who owed it money at the end of 1986.
6 (a) Suppose Rent-a-Clerk is sold for $200,000 to a less able person who could earn only $40,000 per year in a management job in another firm. Suppose also that he could earn 12 percent per year on his financial capital if he had invested it elsewhere. How would Table 7-4 be modified? (b) What is the general principle underlying the adjustments made to accounting costs in that table?
7 (a) Suppose U.S Snark, Inc., borrows another $50,000 from the bank and increases its inventory holdings by $50,000. Show how its balance sheet is affected. (b) Explain how the interest paid on the loan will appear in the income statement of U.S. Snark.

Chapter 8
Production and Costs

Supply and demand together determine the quantity of a good produced and sold and its price. We noted in Chapter 3 that the supply schedule or supply curve of any good depends mainly on the costs of producing it. In Chapters 8 and 9 we go behind the supply curve to show exactly how it is determined by the costs of production.

In this chapter we analyze how a firm's costs of production depend on the quantity it produces and on how long it has to adjust its plant and equipment to changes in its environment. Chapter 9 then shows how firms choose what quantities to supply in order to maximize profit—the difference between revenue and cost.

Also, in order to maximize profit, a firm must choose inputs so as to minimize the cost of producing whatever quantity of output it decides to supply. We begin with this choice—the firm's decisions regarding how to produce any given amount of output at the lowest possible cost. We then explore how costs depend on output in the short run and the long run and present the properties of short-run and long-run cost functions that determine firms' supply decisions.

A warning on terminology is in order here. "Cost" is one of those terms that is used every day without being defined precisely. We have already seen that accounting cost and opportunity cost are different concepts. In this chapter you will encounter a number of new, interrelated concepts based on opportunity cost, each with its own definition. The key to understanding these concepts is to recognize that each one is relevant to a different type of business decision. To an economist or a businesswoman, the question, What does it cost to produce an automobile? has no single answer. Different definitions of "cost" apply when, for instance, one is deciding whether to build a new plant, squeeze out one more car from an existing plant this week, or shut down an existing plant for a week or two. In this chapter we discuss briefly the type of decision to which each cost concept applies; then, in Chapter 9, we show how these different cost concepts determine the supply curve in the short run and the long run.

1. Production and the Firm's Time Horizon

Firms use many different inputs, or *factors of production*, to produce goods and services. Some of these are raw materials, some are goods produced by other firms, some are different types of labor with different skills and abilities, and some are capital goods. (Recall that capital is a produced factor of production, such as a machine or a building.)

There are many different ways of combining factors of production to produce a given level of output. For example, an automobile producer could use a lot of labor on simple assembly lines or could employ very few people and a group of expensive, highly sophisticated robots. In order to maximize profits, a firm must choose its production method to minimize the cost of whatever level of output it has selected. Let us see how it does this.

Technical and Economic Efficiency

Any firm setting out to produce a good or service has to become informed about alternative ways of producing its output. Even if the firm is doing something simple, such as selling groceries, it has to make decisions about how much of its space to devote to check-out counters as opposed to display shelves, how many freezer and non-freezer shelves to stock, how often to buy fresh fruit and vegetables, and whether to use sophisticated machines to read prices off cartons or use more labor to stamp prices on boxes and enter the amounts manually in cash registers. A manufacturing firm has to make many more complicated decisions about the techniques it uses to produce its output.

All firms aim to be *efficient* producers. To achieve this goal, a firm must use production methods that are both technically and economically efficient.

● A method of production is *technically efficient* if there is no other method that uses less of at least one input and no more of any other input to produce a given level of output. Equivalently, a method of production is technically efficient if the output produced is the maximum possible using the specified amounts of inputs.

These two definitions are equivalent because both say that there should be no waste. If method A uses more of at least one factor of production than method B and no less of any other input, then method A simply wastes at least one input. That input has an opportunity cost that should not be incurred. Similarly, if it is possible to

TABLE 8-1. Alternative Production Methods for Potatoes

Method	Input requirements			
	Days of labor	Number of tractors	Acres of land	Tons of fertilizer
A	10	3	5	14
B	20	1	3	19
C	10	3	3	25
D	10	4	5	25

produce more using the same amount of factors of production with method B than it is with method A, it is wasteful not to produce the extra output.

Table 8-1 shows four different ways of producing a given quantity of potatoes. Method D is technically inefficient because it uses more land and more tractors than method C. Only if both land and tractors were free might any firm want to use D—and even then there would be no advantage to doing so. No firm should ever use a production method that is technically inefficient.

Methods A, B, and C are all technically efficient. For example, A uses more land but less fertilizer than C, while B uses more labor than C but fewer tractors and less fertilizer. After the firm has focused its attention on the technically efficient methods of production, it must select the economically efficient method in order to minimize costs, since costs must be as low as possible in order to maximize profit.

● The *economically efficient* method of producing any given level of output is the method that minimizes the opportunity cost of the inputs used in production.

In order to attain economic efficiency, a firm must consider the costs of all the inputs it could use. In the example in Table 8-1, the firm must calculate whether, with given costs of land, labor, fertilizer, and tractors, it is cheapest to produce potatoes using process A, B, or C. For instance, if labor were very expensive, method B would be unlikely to be the cheapest; if fertilizer were very expensive, the farmer would not choose method C. Given the costs of the factor inputs, it requires only a simple calculation to decide which method to use.[1]

---

[1] This decision is explored in more general (and complex) cases in Chapter 15.

The Production Function

Corresponding to the distinction between technical and economic efficiency, the choice of the optimal production process is often described as an *engineering* decision followed by an *economic* decision. The engineer or other technical expert selects the processes that have minimum input requirements, throwing out all those which are technically inefficient. Then the businessperson enters to make the economic decision, that is, to select the technically efficient process that has the lowest cost and is thus economically efficient.

Economists use a firm's production function to summarize the engineering information about the technically efficient methods of production that are available to that firm.

● **A firm's *production function* shows the maximum output it can produce with any given set of inputs.**

Because it gives the *maximum* output that can be produced, the production function shows the results of using alternative technically efficient methods of production.[2]

No firm makes either its engineering or its economic decisions once and for all. Firms are continually trying to find more economically efficient (that is, lower-cost) methods of production. When they do, production methods change and supply curves shift. Similarly, when factor prices change, firms must decide whether to shift to a different method of production.

The Short Run and the Long Run

The possibilities for changing production methods vary, depending on how long a firm has to respond to changes in knowledge or market conditions. The important distinction between the short run and the long run reflects this fact.

● **The *long run* is a period of time long enough for a firm to be able to vary all its factors of production. The *short run* is a period of time during which some of the firm's inputs cannot be varied.**

The production choices of a firm are limited in the short run because some inputs are fixed and cannot be adjusted quickly even if their costs change.

In the short run a firm has fixed plant and equipment. Mom's Muffin Shoppe, for instance, has a given store, counter, cash register, and ovens. These inputs cannot be changed in the shortest run of a day or a week. However, if demand for its muffins increases, Mom's can produce more by hiring more hours of labor and using more raw materials, even in the short run. Workers can be paid to work longer hours, extra workers can be hired to work around the clock, muffins can be packed closer together in the ovens, and the counter can perhaps be moved to let more people help with the baking. But Mom's cannot go on obtaining significant increases in muffin production indefinitely by adding more and more workers to use its ovens. At some stage an extra worker will add almost nothing to output; beyond that an extra worker may only get in the way and reduce rather than increase output.

In the long run, on the other hand, a firm can adjust completely to changes in input prices and output markets. With enough time, a firm can change its production methods and obtain the plant and equipment that are best for its new circumstances. Mom's Muffin Shoppe can respond to an increase in demand by renting more space and buying bigger ovens and more cash registers. However, changes of this sort cannot be made very quickly.

The length of time required to adjust *all* productive inputs differs widely among industries. A muffin shop may be able to move to a larger location and double the capacity of its ovens in as little as 2 months. An airline can buy or rent used planes, hire more pilots, lease extra airport space, and offer more flights in a matter of 3 or 4 months. An automobile producer can build and put into production a new plant in a matter of 2 or 3 years. A mining company can reopen a closed mine in a few months, but it may take years to find and develop a new mine.

---

[2] For the mathematically minded: it is common in economics to use an explicit production function that gives the level of output as a function of the input levels. The most famous example is the Cobb-Douglas production function, which gives output (Y) as the following function of the inputs of capital (K) and labor (L):

$$Y = A K^a L^b$$

where A, a, and b are positive constants.

Corresponding exactly to the distinction between the short run and the long run is the equally important distinction between fixed and variable factors of production.

● **A firm can adjust the input of a *variable factor* at will, even in the short run. The input of a *fixed factor* is given in the short run but adjustable in the long run.**

In the muffin example, the ovens are a fixed factor while flour and other raw materials are variable factors. Labor input can be varied less easily than the amount of flour used, particularly if additional shifts are to be added, but more easily than ovens or floor space. Labor is a fixed factor for short runs of a day or so but a variable factor over periods of a few weeks or more.

In general, the cost of producing any level of output depends on whether the firm has had time to adjust all its inputs so as to produce most efficiently. In the rest of this chapter we look at production and cost first in the short run, when some inputs cannot be adjusted, and then in the long run, when all factors are variable.

2. Production in the Short Run

In this section we examine how a firm's output depends in the short run on the amounts of the variable inputs it employs. We thus work with the *short-run* production function, which describes how the level of output depends on the levels of a firm's variable inputs, holding other inputs constant. For simplicity, we focus on an example in which labor is the only variable factor of production.

Table 8-2 shows the relationship between the Gigantic Globe Company's output of globes and the number of workers it employs in globe production, with all other inputs held fixed at their December 31, 1987, levels.

Total Product

The first column in Table 8-2 shows Gigantic's labor input, measured in full-time workers per week, and the second column shows the corresponding level of output in globes per week. Figure 8-1 shows graphically the

TABLE 8-2. Total, Marginal, and Average Products of Labor in Globe Production

Labor input, workers/wk	Total product (output), globes/wk	Marginal product of labor, globes/worker	Average product of labor, globes/worker
0	0		—
		0.4	
1	0.4		0.40
		0.8	
2	1.2		0.60
		1.0	
3	2.2		0.73
		1.1	
4	3.3		0.82
		1.0	
5	4.3		0.86
		0.9	
6	5.2		0.87
		0.8	
7	6.0		0.86
		0.6	
8	6.6		0.82
		0.4	
9	7.0		0.78
		0.2	
10	7.2		0.72

relationship between labor input and total output. The curve shown there is called the total product curve.

● **The *total product* (*TP*) curve shows the relationship between the input of a variable factor (such as labor) and the resulting level of output produced.**

Table 8-2 and Figure 8-1 show that the more workers Gigantic Globe employs, the more globes it produces.[3]

Marginal Product

The third column of Table 8-2 shows the addition to globe output obtained at each level of labor input by

---

[3] In the case of Mom's Muffin Shoppe, we argued that a point could be reached at which additional labor would become unproductive. It is neither technically nor economically efficient to go beyond the point at which labor becomes unproductive, however, because it would then be possible to produce the same amount of output with less input.

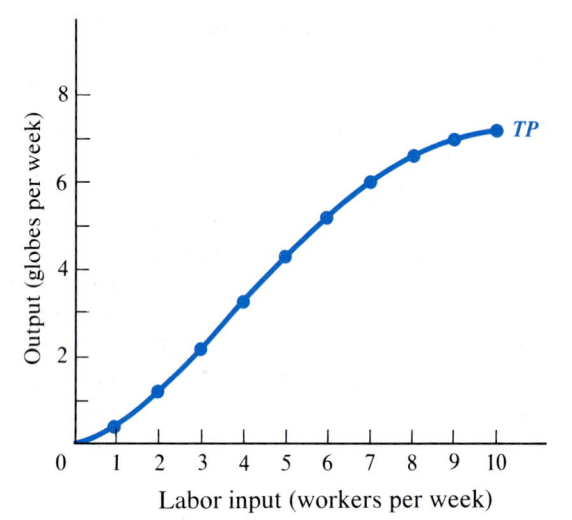

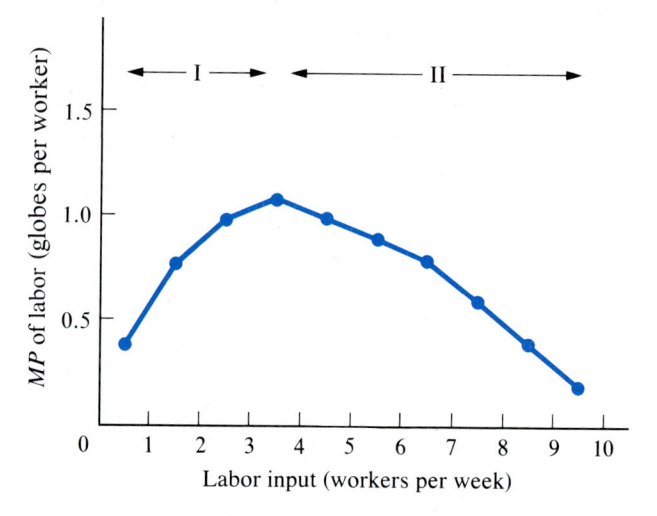

FIGURE 8-1. The Total Product of Labor in Globe Production. The total product (*TP*) of labor curve shows the amount of output produced by different levels of labor input, given the inputs of fixed factors. Each point in the figure corresponds to a row in Table 8-1; these points have simply been connected by straight lines.

adding one more worker. This addition to output is the marginal product of labor.

● The *marginal product* (*MP*) of any variable factor of production (such as labor) is the addition to output obtained by employing an additional unit of that factor.

The marginal product of labor is computed by means of simple subtraction. For example, output increases from 2.2 to 3.3 globes per week when Gigantic's labor input is increased from three to four workers per week. Thus the marginal product (*MP*) of labor when the fourth worker is added is 1.1 (3.3 − 2.2) globes per worker. Figure 8-2 shows the relationship between labor input and the marginal product of labor graphically.

Table 8-2 and Figure 8-2 indicate that the addition to globe output obtained by adding more labor varies with the amount of labor employed. In this example and in general, there are two important stages in the behavior of the marginal product of labor.

In the first stage, at low levels of labor input, the marginal product is positive and increasing. At this stage an extra worker not only adds to output but adds even more than the preceding one. A small work force may not be able to handle all the equipment used in globe production; a larger team may be able to work much more efficiently. Similarly, the first worker in a muffin shop has to do the baking, order raw materials, and attend to the cash register. Output is likely to go up a lot when another worker is added.

In the second stage, at higher levels of labor input, the increase in output obtained by adding one more worker is still positive, but it is decreasing. That is, in this stage the marginal product of adding a worker is lower the more workers Gigantic employs; each additional worker adds less to output than the preceding one. Table 8-3 summarizes these two stages, which are also indicated in Figure 8-2.

DIMINISHING RETURNS. The tendency of the marginal product of labor or any other input to decline if enough is used is so general that it is often referred to as a law.

● The *law of diminishing returns* states that if the quantities of some factors are fixed, the marginal product of any variable factor (such as labor) will, beyond

FIGURE 8-2. The Marginal Product of Labor in Globe Production. The marginal product (*MP*) of labor is the addition to output obtained by adding an extra unit of labor input. The *MP* schedule exhibits first increasing (stage I) and then diminishing (stage II) returns to labor.

TABLE 8-3. The Marginal Product of Labor in Globe Production

Labor input	Stage	Marginal product
0–3	I	Increasing
4–10	II	Decreasing

some level of input, decline as the input of that factor is increased.

In terms of Table 8-3 and Figure 8-2, this law says that stage II is always present in the short run—for any input used in the production of any good or service.

The notion of diminishing returns is part of everyday experience and language. "Too many cooks spoil the broth" not only because each will have his own views as to what to put in but also because they eventually get in one another's way. A student preparing for an examination usually finds study quite productive at first, but after a while each half hour adds less to her knowledge than the previous half hour did. After several hours she may quit and say, probably not accurately, that she did so because diminishing returns had set in.[4] The longer one weeds a garden, the fewer weeds he will find if he devotes another hour to this task. As long as the fixed factors employed by Mom's Muffin Shoppe are given, the marginal products of labor and other variable inputs will eventually decline as more are used.

MARGINAL PRODUCTS AND BUSINESS DECISIONS. As we explore in detail later, the concept of the marginal product of an input is one of the key ideas in the theory of firms' supply behavior. When a firm is deciding whether to increase output in the short run, it must decide whether to hire one more worker. Its decision will depend on whether profits increase as a result of hiring that worker. If the price of output is constant, revenue will go up because the firm has more to sell—and the extra amount it has to sell is exactly equal to the marginal product of labor. It will make sense to hire an additional worker if

---

[4] The statement may not be accurate because people often use "diminishing returns" to mean that the marginal product of effort is low rather than that it is falling. A serious student stops preparing only when the marginal product of additional study has become low, and this usually happens well after diminishing returns have set in.

the extra sales bring in more revenue than the extra cost of hiring that worker.

In analyzing decisions of this sort, it is important to recognize that accounting statements and other descriptions of a firm's history do not directly reveal the values of the marginal products of the firm's inputs. One can see how much labor was used in any period, along with which other inputs and how much output was produced. But historical accounting data on any single period give information about only one point on a graph such as Figure 8-1. The firm nonetheless probably has a good idea from experience of how much more output it can obtain by increasing the labor force by one person.

Average Product

The final column in Table 8-2 shows the average product of labor at each level of labor input.

● The *average product* (AP) of any input (such as labor) is the ratio of output produced to the amount of the input employed.

The average product of labor is often called *labor productivity*. The higher the average product of labor, the more output the firm obtains per unit of labor employed. However, Table 8-2 shows that labor productivity does not depend only on how hard a firm's employees work. Labor productivity in globe production and in general depends on the amount of labor the firm employs. It also depends on the fixed inputs (such as machinery and equipment) used in production. The average product of labor or any other input in any period generally can be obtained directly from historical data.

Figure 8-3 shows graphically the relationship between the average product (AP) and marginal product (MP) of labor in globe production. Both curves are shaped like upside-down U's. Note that *AP is rising where MP is greater than AP and is falling where MP is less than AP*. This important relationship holds between all average and marginal quantities because of simple arithmetic.

For example, suppose a student has taken two exams and gotten grades of 75 on both, so that his average is 75. He then gets a 90 on the third exam. What happens to his average? It rises to 80 [(75 + 75 + 90)/3], since he did better on his most recent exam than he had been doing

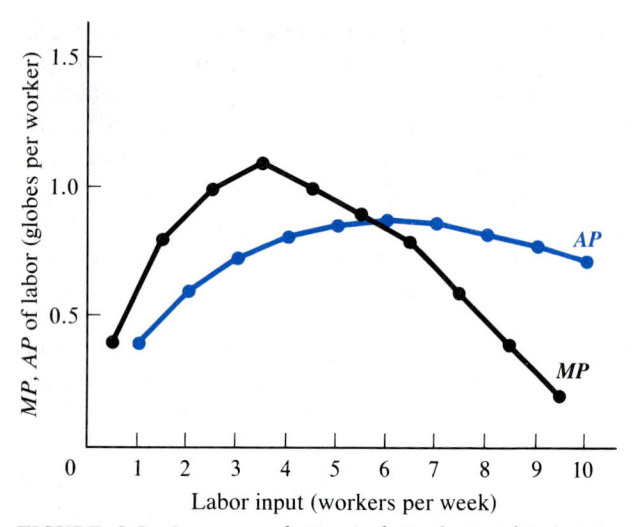

FIGURE 8-3. Average and Marginal Products of Labor in Globe Production. The average product (*AP*) of labor is the ratio of output to labor input. Where marginal product (*MP*) is above average product, the average product curve is rising; where *MP* is below *AP*, the *AP* curve is falling. *AP* is maximized where it intersects the declining *MP* curve.

on average until then. The marginal product of taking the third exam in this example is 90 points, and 75 is the average product of the first two. Because his marginal score is above his average, the average must rise. Similarly, a bad day (a grade below 75 on the third exam) must lower his average.

Thus Figure 8-3 shows that as long as the amount an additional worker adds to output exceeds the average production per worker before he arrived, the average over all workers must go up when he joins the firm. Similarly, when the last worker hired adds less to output than the average, adding that worker must lower the average product of labor.

In Figure 8-3, the *AP* and *MP* schedules intersect at the level of labor input that maximizes *AP*.[5] At points to

the left of the intersection, *MP* exceeds *AP*, and *AP* is therefore rising. At points to the right of the intersection, *MP* is less than *AP*, so that *AP* must be falling. It follows that *AP* is greatest at the point of intersection with the falling *MP* curve.

Now we use the properties of the total, marginal, and average product curves to show how the firm's costs of production change with the level of output.

3. Short-Run Cost Curves

Since labor is Gigantic's only variable factor of production, the firm's short-run cost of producing any level of output must be the cost of the labor required to produce that output plus the cost of the fixed factors the firm employs. We can thus use the relation between labor input and globe output developed in section 2 along with the wage rate and the cost of fixed factors to determine how Gigantic's costs depend on its level of production in the short run.

Fixed and Variable Costs

In discussing production in the short run, we distinguished between fixed and variable inputs. This distinction corresponds exactly to the difference between a firm's fixed and variable costs.

● **Fixed costs (FC) are costs that in the short run do not depend on how much the firm produces. These are the costs of its fixed inputs. *Variable costs* (VC) are costs that depend on the level of the firm's output. These are the costs of its variable inputs. The firm's *total cost* (TC) is the sum of its fixed and variable costs: TC = FC + VC.**

A firm can avoid the costs of its fixed inputs, if at all, only by going out of business entirely. Fixed costs that cannot be avoided even by going out of business are called *sunk costs*. The rent on a firm's office space is a fixed cost that is not sunk, since the firm can avoid this cost by going out of business. On the other hand, the owners of a firm may invest their capital in a specialized machine that can be used only to produce the firm's new product and that has no scrap value. The fixed oppor-

---

[5] This is only approximately true here because we have measured labor input in rather large units—full-time workers. The smaller the units in which the variable input is measured, the closer this statement comes to being exactly true. If we had measured labor input in hours, for instance, Figure 8-3 would appear exactly consistent with this statement even under a magnifying glass.

tunity cost of that capital is a sunk cost, since the investment will be worthless if the new product fails. On the other hand, if a firm temporarily shuts down, it can avoid paying for any of its variable inputs.

The fixed costs of Mom's Muffin Shoppe include the costs of renting, heating, and lighting the store; maintaining the ovens; and having local telephone service. Fixed costs also include the opportunity cost of the financial capital invested in Mom's ovens. This cost is the amount that Mom's owners could earn by selling the ovens and investing the proceeds in the most attractive alternative investment—perhaps the stock market or a savings account.

Variable costs are the costs of using the variable factors of production. Labor and materials generally account for the bulk of variable costs. Because the inputs of the variable factors increase as output rises, variable costs rise with output.

Total and Marginal Costs

Table 8-4 shows fixed (*FC*). variable (*VC*), total (*TC*), and marginal (*MC*) costs at various levels of output for Gigantic Globe. As before, labor is Gigantic's only variable input. The cost of each unit of labor is $200 per week. The level of output is specified in the first column, and the corresponding amount of labor input is shown in the second column.[6] The remaining columns show the different components of cost at each output level.

In this table and in general, as we have seen, *fixed cost* is constant and independent of the level of output. Gigantic's fixed cost of $500 per week represents mainly the opportunity cost of its plant and equipment, which are fixed in the short run. The only way Gigantic could avoid these costs would be to sell off all its assets and thus go out of business.

In the short run, only *variable cost* rises when output is increased. The second column in Table 8-4 shows the labor input required to produce each level of output. These data are consistent with those in Table 8-2 showing the output levels produced by each level of labor input. With workers costing $200 each per week to employ, variable cost per week is simply the number of workers times $200. For example, the seven workers needed to produce 6 units of output cost $1400, and hence variable costs at that level of output are $1400.

In order to see whether it is profitable to produce an additional unit of output, the change in revenue that

---

[6] The data in Table 8-4 are consistent with those in Table 8-2; the only difference is that the two tables consider different levels of labor input.

TABLE 8-4. Output and Costs in Globe Production

Output, globes/wk	Labor input, workers/wk	Fixed cost (*FC*), $/wk	Variable cost (*VC*), $/wk	Total cost (*TC*), $/wk	Marginal cost (*MC*), $/globe
0	0	500	0	500	
1	1.7	500	340	840	340
2	2.8	500	560	1060	220
3	3.6	500	720	1220	160
4	4.5	500	900	1400	180
5	5.6	500	1120	1620	220
6	7.0	500	1400	1900	280
7	8.9	500	1780	2280	380

would result must be compared with the marginal cost of production.[7]

● *Marginal cost (MC) is the cost of producing an additional unit of output. That is, marginal cost is the increase in total cost a firm must incur to produce 1 more unit of output.*

Gigantic's marginal cost at various levels of output is shown in the last column in Table 8-4. *MC* is equal to the increase in *TC* at each level of output. For instance, as output increases from 3 to 4 units, total cost rises from $1220 to $1400. Marginal cost is thus $180 ($1400 − $1220). Note that since only variable cost changes in the short run, short-run marginal cost is equal to the increase in variable cost when more variable factors are used to produce 1 more unit of output. Note also that marginal cost, like the marginal product of labor, cannot be obtained directly from historical accounting data for

---

[7] The idea of *incremental* cost is closely related to the concept of marginal cost. Marginal cost refers to the cost increase produced by a small increase in output, while the change in total cost produced by any particular (large or small) change in a firm's operations is called the incremental cost of that change.

any single period. One must know how costs would change if output changed.

TOTAL AND MARGINAL COST CURVES. Figure 8-4 presents the cost information in Table 8-4 graphically. Figure 8-4a shows total cost (*TC*) and its components, fixed cost and variable cost. The fixed cost (*FC*) schedule is flat, because fixed costs do not change with the level of output. The vertical distance between the *FC* and *TC* schedules represents variable costs, which increase with the level of output.

The relation between output and variable costs follows directly from the total product curve in Figure 8-1.

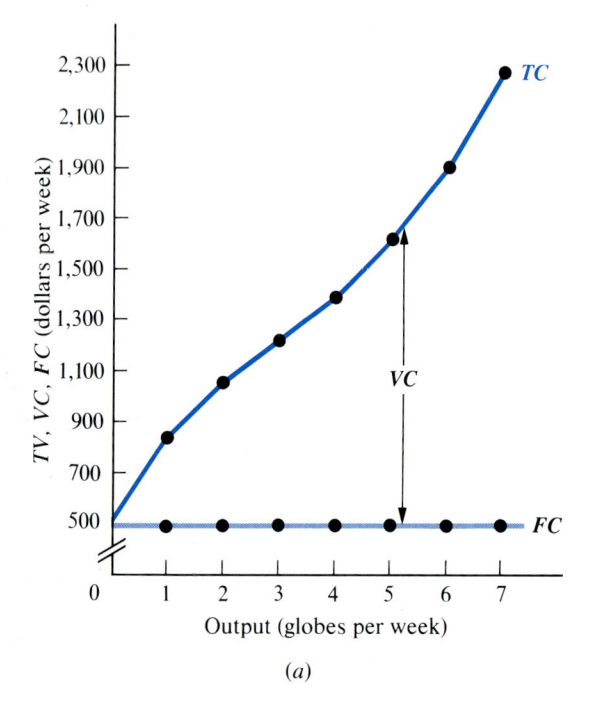

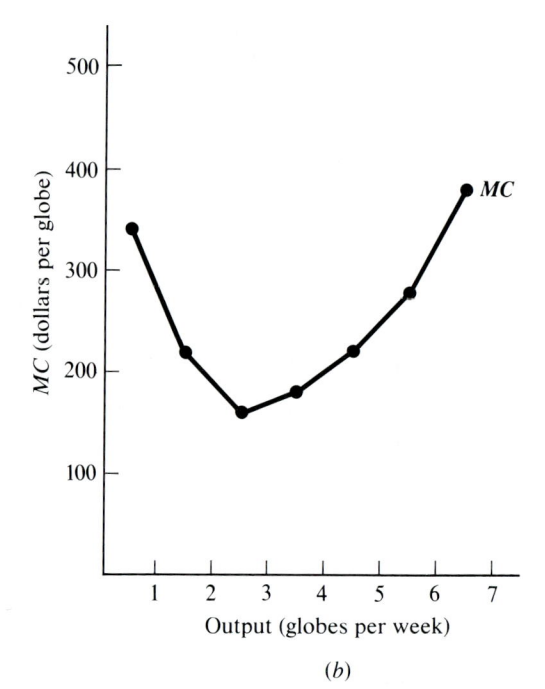

FIGURE 8-4. Costs of Globe Production. Panel (*a*) shows the total cost (*TC*) curve obtained from Table 8-4. The *TC* curve becomes steeper as diminishing returns set in. Total cost is the sum of fixed costs (*FC*), which do not depend on output, and variable costs (*VC*), which rise with output. Panel (*b*) shows the marginal cost of (*MC*) of globe production, that is, the increase in cost required to produce an additional unit of output. The *MC* curve at first declines but ultimately rises because of diminishing returns to labor.

Dividing VC by $200 (the cost per worker) yields the number of workers required to produce each output level. Graphing this relation with workers on the horizontal axis and output on the vertical axis yields the *TP* curve.

Figure 8-4b shows the marginal cost of globe production. This curve is derived from the marginal product of labor (*MP*) curve in Figures 8-2 and 8-3. At low output levels, marginal cost falls as output increases. This occurs because when labor is increased to raise output, each additional worker adds more to output than the preceding worker. In other words, because the marginal product of labor (globes per worker) is increasing, marginal cost [($ per worker) × (workers per globe)] is decreasing at low levels of output. While the first unit of output raises costs by $340, the second unit adds only $220 to costs, and the marginal cost of the third unit is $160.

At higher levels of output, the firm experiences diminishing returns. Each additional worker has less and less capital with which to work, and the marginal product of labor falls. This means that increasing amounts of extra labor are needed to produce 1 more unit of output. Since each extra worker costs $200, the marginal cost of output is rising because the marginal product of labor is falling. By the time output is up to 6 units, it costs $380 to make one more globe.

Thus the law of diminishing returns produces an upward-sloping *MC* curve. At *some* level of output (in this case between two and three globes per week), diminishing returns to labor set in and increasing output levels can be secured only at an increasing marginal cost.

Average Costs

So far we have considered cost concepts that correspond to the total product (*TP*) and marginal product (*MP*) of labor. The last cost concept we need to introduce is average cost, which corresponds to the average product (*AP*) of labor.

● **Average cost is the cost per unit of output. Average variable cost (AVC) is the ratio of variable cost (VC) to output. Average fixed cost (AFC) is the ratio of fixed cost (FC) to output. And *average total cost* (ATC) is the ratio of total cost (TC) to output.**

In equation form, these definitions are as follows:

$$\text{Average variable cost} = AVC = \frac{VC}{\text{output}} \quad (1)$$

$$\text{Average fixed cost} = AFC = \frac{FC}{\text{output}} \quad (2)$$

$$\text{Average total cost} = ATC = \frac{TC}{\text{output}}$$
$$= AVC + AFC \, (3)$$

Equation (3) holds because total cost is equal to the sum of variable cost and fixed cost.

We noted previously that firms use marginal cost to determine whether output should be increased or decreased. Average costs are used to decide whether to produce at all. In particular, if price—which is average revenue per unit of output—is less than average variable cost, the firm will reduce its losses by shutting down in the short run. If price is lower than average total cost, the firm is making negative economic profit and should consider shutting down permanently.

Unlike marginal cost, average total cost can be computed from accounting statements, after adjusting for differences between accounting cost and opportunity cost. In order to compute average variable cost or average fixed cost from accounting data, of course, one must distinguish between fixed and variable inputs.

AVERAGE AND MARGINAL COST CURVES. In Table 8-5 we show *AFC*, *AVC*, *ATC*, and *MC* for Gigantic Globe. These figures are derived from Table 8-4 and the definitions we have just given. Figure 8-5 is a graph of these average and marginal cost schedules.

In Figure 8-5 and in general, the average total cost (*ATC*) schedule is always above the average variable cost (*AVC*) schedule. The gap between the *ATC* and *AVC* schedules is average fixed cost (*AFC*). Average fixed costs decline when output increases, since they are equal to a constant number ($500 in our example) divided by ever larger output levels. Thus as output becomes large, the difference between the *ATC* and *AVC* schedules becomes small; however, at low output levels the difference may be substantial.

Since labor is the only variable factor here, the shape of the *AVC* curve in Figure 8-5 reflects the shape of the

TABLE 8-5. Average and Marginal Costs of Globe Production

Output	FC	AFC	VC	AVC	TC	ATC	MC
0	500	—	0	—	500	—	
							340
1	500	500	340	340	840	840	
							220
2	500	250	560	280	1060	530	
							160
3	500	167	720	240	1220	407	
							180
4	500	125	900	225	1400	350	
							220
5	500	100	1120	224	1620	324	
							280
6	500	83	1400	233	1900	317	
							380
7	500	71	1780	254	2280	326	

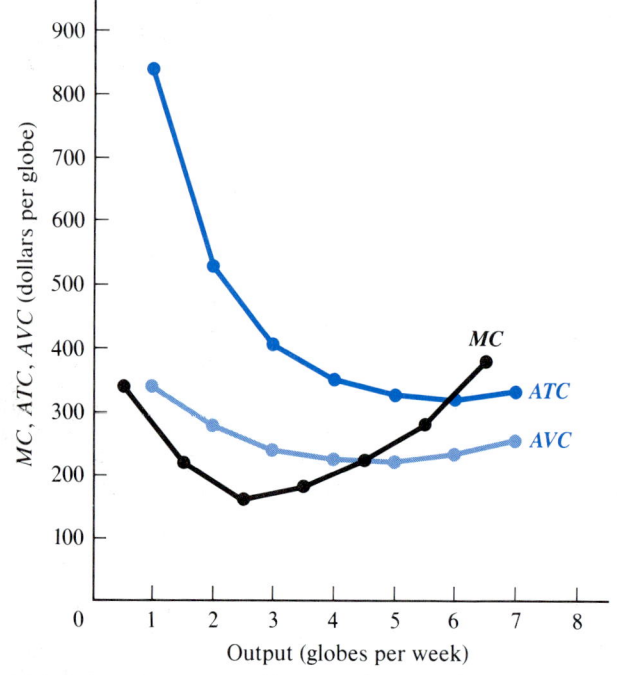

FIGURE 8-5. Average and Marginal Costs of Globe Production. The average variable cost (AVC) schedule is U-shaped, reflecting first increasing and then decreasing returns to labor. Average total cost (ATC) is the sum of average variable cost and average fixed cost (AFC). The marginal cost (MC) schedule cuts both average cost curves at their minimum points.

average product of labor (AP) curve in Figure 8-3. At low levels of output the average product of labor (globes per worker) is rising, so that average variable cost ($200 × workers per globe) must fall when output is increased. At high levels of output the average product of labor is falling, so that average variable cost rises.

The ATC curve has the same basic shape as the AVC schedule, though it has barely begun to turn upward in Figure 8-5. (Because AFC is falling at all levels of output, the ATC curve always reaches its minimum point at a higher level of output than does the AVC curve.) In this example and in general, short-run AVC and ATC curves are described as *U-shaped average cost curves*. Because of the law of diminishing returns, both curves always turn upward at high enough levels of output. As more and more workers are employed to work any given set of fixed inputs, labor productivity eventually falls and average costs accordingly rise.

Finally, the relationship between the MC and AVC curves in Figure 8-5 reflects the general relationship between marginal and average quantities we saw in Figure 8-3. If MC is above AVC, the variable cost of making 1 more unit of output is above the average, so that the average must increase if that unit is produced. If MC is below AVC, then producing an extra unit must lower AVC. Exactly the same logic shows that if MC is above (below) ATC, ATC must be rising (falling).

Figure 8-5 shows the usual pattern: Marginal cost is initially below both average total cost and average variable cost, but because of the law of diminishing returns, it rises above both as output is increased, and it becomes more and more expensive to produce still more by increasing only labor. (Recall the assumption that all other inputs are fixed in the short run.) As the figure shows, the marginal cost curve must intersect the average cost curves (AVC and ATC) at their minimum points.[8] To the left of the intersection, marginal cost is below average cost, so that average cost is falling. To the right of the intersection, marginal cost is above average cost, so that average cost is rising. It follows that the intersection must occur at the lowest value of average cost.

The distinction between average and marginal cost

---

[8] As in the case of the MP and AP curves in Figure 8-3, MC does not intersect either AVC or ATC exactly at their minimum points in the figure because output is measured in large units.

> **Box 8-1. Pricing Electricity at Cost**
>
> Most people agree that regulated private firms that supply electricity should price it "at cost." But how exactly should "cost" be defined in practice? In particular, should price be set equal to average or marginal cost?
>
> If the price that a private firm is allowed to charge for electricity is set equal to the firm's average total cost, the firm will earn zero economic profit. That is, its accounting profits will just cover the opportunity costs of the capital its shareholders have invested. This strikes most people as fair; for a long time this was the standard approach to the pricing of electricity and other public utilities, such as gas supply and telephone service, in the United States.
>
> However, since the 1930s economists have argued that prices should be set equal to marginal, not average, costs. Why? Because only then does the cost a consumer pays for an additional unit of electricity equal the cost of producing that additional unit. If prices are set at average cost, the consumer bears either more or less than the actual costs caused by his decisions to increase or decrease his electricity consumption.
>
> Regulators in the United States resisted this prescription for a long time. Since marginal cost and average cost generally differ, marginal cost pricing generally produces nonzero economic profits. Positive profits seem unfair to consumers; negative profits seem unfair to shareholders. As we have noted, marginal cost is harder to estimate than average cost.
>
> But in recent years regulators in the United States have begun to pay attention to marginal cost. Electricity rates in many states now vary seasonally and by time of day, reflecting similar variations in marginal cost.

also arises in everyday life. The per ounce cost (AC) of cornflakes in a large box is generally less than the per ounce cost in a small box. This means that the marginal cost of buying cornflakes (MC) is below the average cost. The distinction between marginal and average cost is important in the analysis of many government policies as well. Box 8-1 shows that this distinction has been at the center of debates about the prices of electricity set by government regulatory agencies.

Changes in Cost Conditions

Changes in input prices shift the cost curves. An increase in the fixed cost can be visualized in Figure 8-4a as an upward shift of the FC schedule. As a result the TC schedule also shifts upward, and by the same amount. Changes in fixed cost do not shift the marginal cost curve in Figure 8-4b or the average variable cost curve in Figure 8-5, because variable costs are not affected at all by the fixed costs of being in business.

An increase in the price of the variable input—labor—shifts both the TC and MC schedules. The TC schedule shifts because labor costs and thus variable costs are higher at each level of output. But now marginal cost, too, is affected. The cost of an extra unit of output is equal to the wage times the extra amount of labor required to produce another unit of output. With a higher wage at each output level, MC will be higher. Thus the MC schedule in Figure 8-4b also shifts upward when the price of labor rises. Similarly, an increase in the price of labor raises the AVC curve in Figure 8-5.

4. Production and Costs in the Long Run

The long run is distinguished from the short run by the firm's ability to vary *all* factors of production freely in the long run. Whereas a firm's plant and equipment cannot be changed in the short run, the firm can in the long run build or rent more space and install exactly the machinery it needs. In the long run, all factors are variable. In this section we show how long-run average and marginal cost are related to their short-run counterparts.

Long-Run Average Cost

Figure 8-6 shows a series of ATC curves labeled ATC_1, ATC_2, ATC_3. Each of these ATC schedules represents the average total cost of producing different levels of output using plants of different capacity. Larger plants involve more of the inputs that are fixed in the short run, such as floor space and machinery.

ATC_1 corresponds to the smallest plant. Its average cost is below that of the larger plant corresponding to

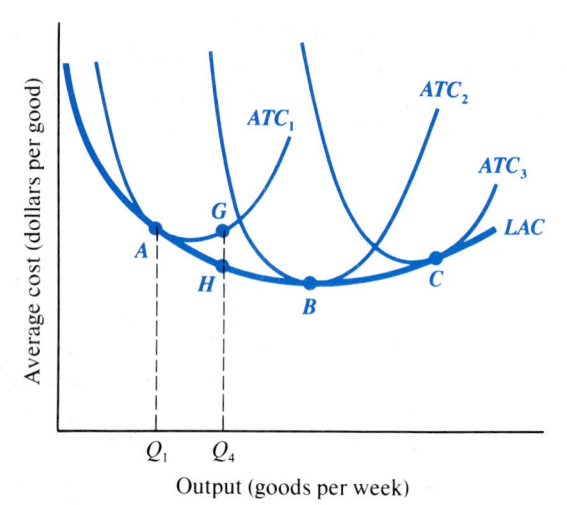

FIGURE 8-6. The Long-Run Average Cost Curve (LAC). The LAC curve shows the lowest long-run average cost of producing each level of output. Corresponding to each point on LAC is an ATC curve for the particular plant (collection of inputs fixed in the short run) that is cheapest to use at that output level.

ATC_2 at low levels of output because its fixed costs are lower. But diminishing returns set in earlier for the smaller plant because there is less machinery and equipment, so that ATC_1 eventually rises above ATC_2. Similarly ATC_3 shows the average costs of a plant larger than that corresponding to ATC_2. Each of these short-run curves is U-shaped for the reasons discussed in the previous section. They differ in the level of output at which they reach their minimum cost levels.

Now suppose a firm's output level has changed and that change persists. The firm's managers will consider making changes in its plant, equipment, and other inputs that are fixed in the short run. If the demand for Mom's muffins increases to the point where the firm must operate its ovens around the clock, for instance, Mom's managers will ask themselves whether costs could be reduced by buying more ovens and employing fewer workers. In the long run, Mom's or any other firm will try to operate with the plant that gives it the lowest possible average cost—since not doing so is just a waste of money.

● The *long-run average cost curve (LAC)* shows the lowest cost of producing any given level of output, allowing all factors of production to vary optimally to minimize cost.

A firm's LAC curve reflects its knowledge as of a given date. Improvements in technology lower costs and thus shift the LAC curve downward.

A firm's long-run average cost curve (LAC) is obtained by finding the plant that yields minimum average total cost at each output level. For example, to produce output Q_1, the best plant is the one described by the ATC_1 schedule in Figure 8-6. The minimum average total cost of producing output level Q_4 is given by point H, which is on an ATC curve (not drawn) that yields lower costs than ATC_1 at point G.

Note that average cost is always at least as low on LAC as it is on any single ATC curve. This occurs because each ATC curve shows the average cost of production for a fixed plant. The plant size on any given ATC curve will not be the right one to produce some levels of output at the lowest cost. Larger plants will be better for larger output levels; smaller plants will be better for smaller output levels. In the long run a firm has complete flexibility to choose the plant that is best for its output level, but in the short run it must live with a single, fixed plant. Since the firm can do more in the long run than in the short run to reduce costs, its long-run average costs can never be higher than its short-run costs.

Corresponding to each point on the LAC schedule is a particular plant with its own particular ATC curve. Figure 8-6 does not show all the ATC curves that underlie the long-run average cost curve shown, but there are many such curves. Each plant's ATC curve touches the LAC curve at the output level where it can produce at lower total cost than any other plant can. Once a firm has built a plant, of course, its costs are determined in the short run by that plant's ATC curve.

Long-Run Marginal Cost

Corresponding to the long-run average cost curve (LAC) there is also a long-run marginal cost curve.

● The *long-run marginal cost curve (LMC)* shows the increase in cost due to an extra unit of output when the firm is free to vary all inputs optimally to minimize costs.

There is a fundamental difference between short-run and long-run marginal cost: In the short run the *MC* schedule reflects only the extra *variable* cost of producing another unit of output. Since plant size is fixed in the short run, short-run marginal cost eventually rises because of the law of diminishing returns. Along the *LMC* schedule, in contrast, marginal cost includes the increase in the opportunity cost of the *optimally chosen* additional plant needed to produce an extra unit of output at the lowest cost. Because everything is variable in the long run, diminishing returns are less important, but the opportunity cost of capital invested to increase plant size must be counted as one of the costs of an extra unit of output.[9]

Figure 8-7 shows a typical pair of *LAC* and *LMC* schedules. These long-run marginal and average cost curves have the same relationship to each other as the short-run marginal and average curves in Figure 8-5 do. That is, if *LMC* is below *LAC*, *LAC* is falling, while if *LMC* is above *LAC*, *LAC* is rising. And the rising *LMC* curve cuts the *LAC* curve at its minimum point, labeled *A* in Figure 8-7.

5. Economies and Diseconomies of Scale

The short-run average total cost curve, *ATC*, is always U-shaped, but the long-run average cost curve is not necessarily U-shaped (although it is in Figure 8-7). The shape of the long-run average cost curve reflects economies and diseconomies of scale, where "scale" refers to the size of the firm as measured by its output

● **There are *economies of scale* (or *increasing returns to scale*) when a firm's long-run average cost falls as output increases. There are *constant returns to scale* when long-run average cost does not depend on the level of output. And there are *diseconomies of scale* (or *decreasing returns to scale*) when long-run average cost rises as output increases.**

When there are economies of scale, bigger is better. When there are diseconomies of scale, on the other hand, small is beautiful—or at least able to produce at lower cost.

Figure 8-8 shows three different cases. There are economies of scale at all levels of output in (*a*). If all firms in an industry have this *LAC* curve, firms with larger plants have a cost advantage over their smaller competitors. There are constant returns to scale in (*b*), so that a firm's average costs do not depend on its size. Finally, there are diseconomies of scale at all output levels in (*c*). If all firms in some industry have this *LAC* schedule, *smaller* firms have a cost advantage over their larger competitors.

Many people seem to think that in most industries there are economies of scale at all levels of output, so that (*a*) depicts the usual case. Are they right? We devote the rest of this section to answering this question.

Economies of Scale

There are three basic reasons why economies of scale arise. The first is *indivisibilities in production*. A firm

---

[9] The short-run *MC* corresponding to any fixed plant will be below *LMC* for low levels of output but *above LMC* for high levels of output at which diminishing returns are important. As this suggests, *LMC* always rises more slowly than any single plant's short-run *MC*, because diminishing returns can be avoided in the long run by increasing both fixed and variable inputs when output is increased.

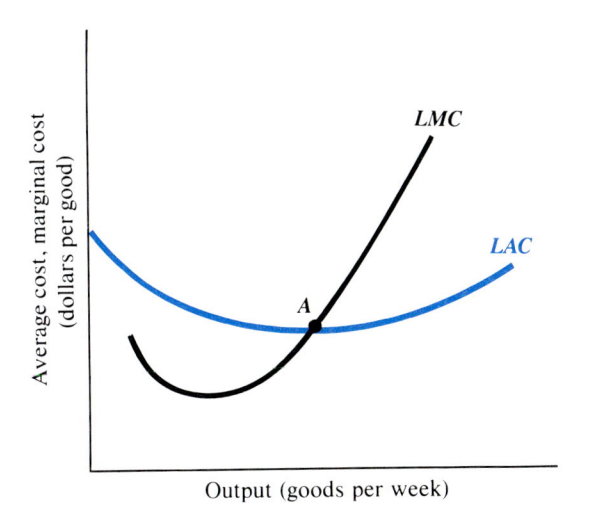

FIGURE 8-7. The Relationship between Long-Run Marginal Cost (*LMC*) and Long-Run Average Cost (*LAC*) Curves. The long-run marginal cost (*LMC*) curve cuts *LAC* at the point of minimum long-run average cost. This relationship holds for *any* pair of average and marginal cost curves, not just for the long-run curves.

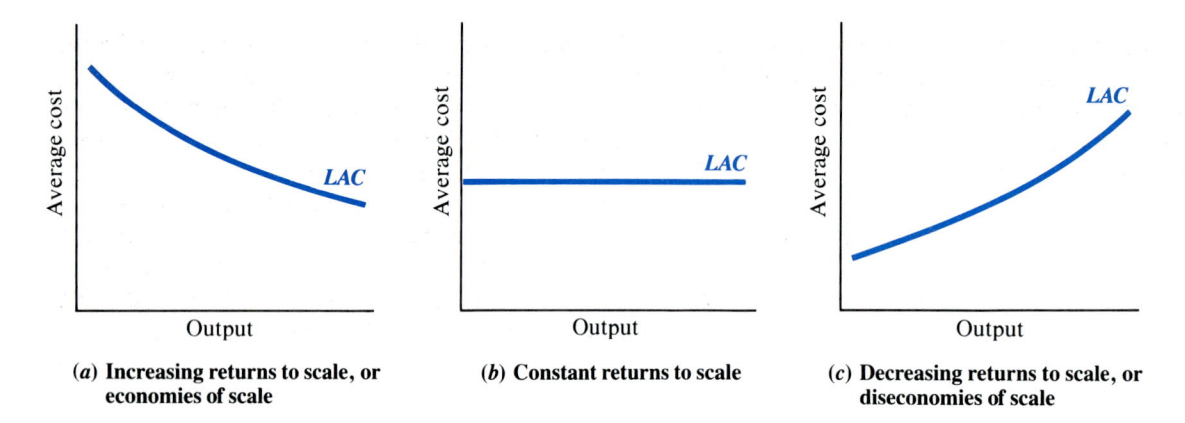

(a) Increasing returns to scale, or economies of scale

(b) Constant returns to scale

(c) Decreasing returns to scale, or diseconomies of scale

FIGURE 8-8. Returns to Scale and the Long-Run Average Cost Curve.

must have minimum amounts of some inputs to be in business at all. For instance, any firm has to be managed, has to keep its accounting records in order, and probably needs a telephone and a desk. These requirements are indivisible in the sense that a firm can't keep only half its books or use half a telephone.

As the firm grows, these inputs do not have to be increased much, and so their costs per unit of output fall. Most managers can manage three workers as well as two, output has to rise a great deal before another phone is needed, and the firm's accounts do not become much harder to handle as it grows. Average cost falls—and thus there are economies of scale—because the same indivisible factors are being spread over more units of output. Eventually, though, this source of economies of scale will disappear as the firm does have to hire more managers, acquire more telephones and desks, and install a more complex accounting system.

The second reason for increasing returns to scale is *specialization*. As a firm gets larger, each worker can concentrate more on one task and handle it more efficiently. Adam Smith, the father of economics,[10] made a strong point about the gains from specialization in his *Wealth of Nations* (1776). His example is, as he calls it, a "very trifling manufacture"—the pin industry. Smith said:

> A workman not educated to this business . . . could scarce . . . make one pin a day, and certainly could not make twenty. But in the way in which this business is now carried on, . . . it is divided into a number of branches. . . . One man draws out a wire, another straights it, a third cuts it, a fourth points it. . . .

Smith went on to describe 18 stages in making a pin. He estimated that the average output per worker (the average product of labor) was 4800 pins per day in 1776. The economies of scale from specialization in this case are impressive. Similar benefits from specialization occur in modern assembly line work, for instance, in the automobile and electronics industries.

The third reason for economies of scale is the existence of *technical economies*. These have to do with capital rather than labor. In many industries, particularly those producing goods rather than services, large scale is needed to take advantage of better physical capital. Engineers have a "rule of two-thirds" that applies to many industries that handle fluids. The rule states that the costs of building a factory or machine rise only two-thirds as fast as its capacity. For instance, oil tankers are essentially cylinders. The amount of oil that can be carried depends on the volume of the cylinder, but the cost of a tanker depends on the surface area that must be enclosed. As the volume of a cylinder increases, the surface area needed to enclose it increases only two-thirds as fast.[11] There are thus large economies of scale in tanker construction.

---

[10] Although Adam Smith is revered as the father of economics, he was not the first economist. Joseph Schumpeter (1883–1950), in his monumental, posthumously published book, *History of Economic Analysis* (Oxford, 1954), traces economics back to the ancient Greeks.

[11] For those who love solid geometry, let X be the ratio of the radius of a cylinder to its height, let V be its volume, and let S be its surface area. Then $S = cX^{-1/3}V^{2/3}$, where c is a constant.

Do these three arguments prove that there are economies of scale in all industries at all output levels? Not really. Note first that the indivisibilities argument applies mainly to small firms; it only suggests that *LAC* curves slope downward at low levels of output. In addition, the second and third arguments for the existence of economies of scale apply mainly to manufacturing firms. Economies of scale are likely to be less significant beyond very low levels of output in service firms such as restaurants and laundries.

Diseconomies of Scale

The main reason there may be diseconomies of scale—so that increases in output raise long-run average cost—is that management becomes more difficult as firms become larger. This phenomenon is described as *managerial diseconomies of scale*. A new, small firm needs only one manager, who is likely to be the owner. As the firm grows, the owner hires vice presidents and other middle-level managers—who must then be supervised. The company becomes bureaucratic, coordination of different departments becomes more complicated, and average costs of production *may* begin to rise.

The argument that lies behind the U-shaped *LAC* curve in Figure 8-7 is that economies of scale dominate at low levels of output, but eventually, as the firm becomes very large, managerial diseconomies of scale outweigh these economies and average costs begin to rise.

But the shape of the average cost curve in any particular industry is not determined by general arguments about what is likely to happen. Rather, it is a matter of *fact* that depends largely on the industry's production function. It is worthwhile looking at some facts.

Returns to Scale in Practice

Figure 8-9 shows some actual average cost data. Figure 8-9a is based on a study of cement plants, and (b) is based

FIGURE 8-9. Long-Run Average Cost Curves in the Real World. The figure shows *LAC* curves for (a) cement and (b) beer brewing. In both cases average cost falls as the level of output rises, but the fall slows as output increases in (b). (*Sources*: Cement: Mark E. McBride, "The Nature and Source of Economies of Scale in Cement Production," *Southern Economic Journal*, July 1981, pp. 105–115; beer: C. F. Pratten, *Economies of Scale in Manufacturing Industry*, Cambridge University Press, Cambridge, 1971, p. 75.)

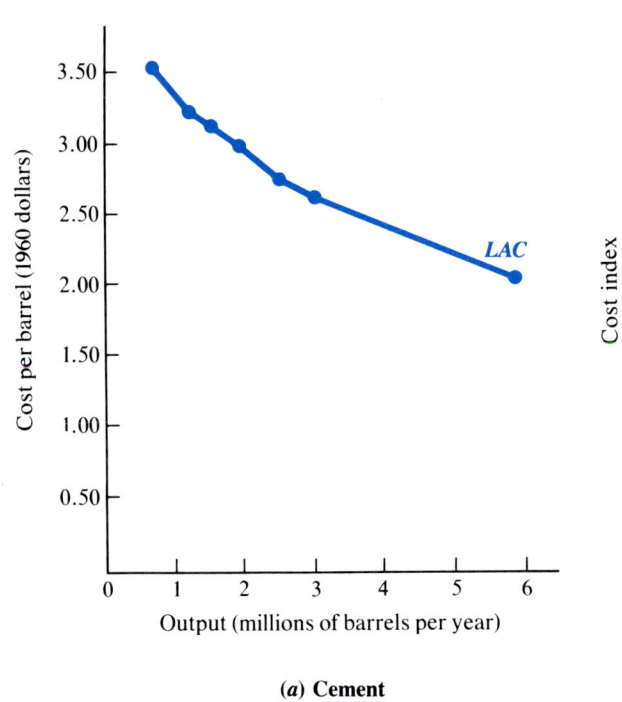

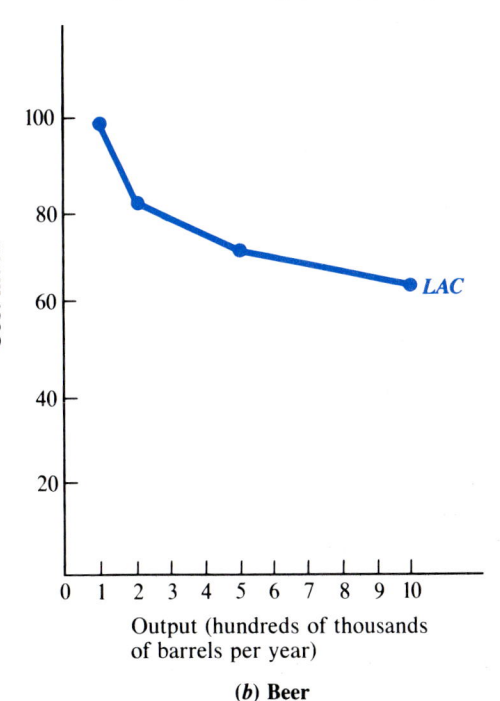

(a) Cement

(b) Beer

on a study of the average costs of producing beer in breweries of different sizes in the United Kingdom. In both industries there are economies of scale (falling *LAC*) at all levels of output, particularly at low levels. There is no evidence of decreasing returns to scale at any level of output.

The *LAC* curve in (*b*) is typical of most of the many such curves that have been estimated for manufacturing industries. Average costs fall rapidly at low levels of output. As output rises, average costs continue to fall, but less rapidly. At high levels of output the *LAC* becomes essentially flat; there are either constant returns to scale or relatively unimportant economies of scale. Diseconomies of scale are very rarely encountered in studies of manufacturing industries.

Economists have attempted, for some industries, to measure the level of output at which economies of scale become relatively unimportant for an individual firm. This *minimum efficient scale* (MES) is usually defined as the smallest scale of production at which doubling output would reduce average cost by less than 5 percent.

Table 8-6 contains estimates of minimum efficient scale for several manufacturing industries. Scale is given both as an output level and as a percentage of total U.S. output. Of the industries shown, only the household refrigerators industry has an MES that is more than 10 percent of total U.S. output. There are a few other such industries, not shown in the table, including automobiles, but most MESs are below 10 percent of total U.S. output.

In summary, there are indeed important economies of scale for many firms, particularly in manufacturing, but these economies generally stop being significant at output levels that are small relative to the size of the entire U.S. industry.[12] The *LAC* curves of these firms become approximately flat at high levels of output, and their average costs become approximately constant. Such curves are often described as *L-shaped LAC curves*. It is as if the upward-sloping part of the *LAC* curve in Figure 8-7 had been cut off and replaced by a horizontal line.

For other firms, especially those in service industries, the U-shaped long-run average cost curve probably gives a good description of cost conditions. From now on we will work mainly with the U-shaped *LAC* curve, but we will also refer at several places to *LAC* curves, like those shown in Figure 8-9, that exhibit increasing returns to scale at all levels of output.

■ There is no simple answer to the question, How much does it cost to produce a good? except, "It depends." Two distinctions introduced here are especially important. The average cost of producing any particular output of cornflakes will differ from the marginal cost of increasing that output. And both average cost and marginal cost will generally be different in the long run from what they are in the short run. We next employ these distinctions to see how firms decide what quantities to supply of the goods and services they produce.

TABLE 8-6. Output Levels at Which Economies of Scale Become Small

Industry	Minimum efficient Scale (MES)	MES as percentage of U.S. output
Cigarettes	36 billion cigarettes per year; 2275 employees	6.6
Paints, varnishes, and lacquers	10 million gallons per year; 450 employees	1.4
Nonrubber shoes	1 million pairs per year; 250 employees	0.2
Household refrigerators	800,000 units per year	14.1

Source: L. W. Weiss, "Optimal Plant Size and the Extent of Suboptimal Capacity," in R. T. Masson and P. D. Qualls (eds.), *Essays in Honor of Joe S. Bain*, Ballinger, Cambridge, Mass., 1976. U.S. output in 1967 was used to compute the last column.

[12] Two notes of caution. First, in some industries, such as electricity supply, economies of scale may be important at all output levels. Such industries, called *natural monopolies*, are considered in Chapters 13 and 14. Second, the U.S. market for most goods is the largest in the world. In smaller markets, such as those in many developing countries, even a single plant that supplies the entire market may be unable to take full advantage of economies of scale. This means that attempts by small countries to become self-sufficient by producing everything they consume are likely to be very expensive relative to the alternative of producing and exporting some goods and importing others.

Summary

1. The production function describes all technically efficient production methods by showing the maximum output that can be produced using given amounts of inputs. Economically efficient production minimizes the opportunity cost of the inputs used to produce any given output.
2. In the short run, the inputs of variable factors can be changed, whereas the inputs of fixed factors are constant. In the long run, the input levels of all factors are variable.
3. Increases in output can be obtained in the short run only by increasing the inputs of variable factors (typically labor and materials). The total product (*TP*) of labor curve shows the amount of output produced by different levels of labor input, given the quantity of fixed factors.
4. The marginal product (*MP*) of labor is the addition to output obtained by increasing labor input by 1 unit. The average product (*AP*) of labor is the ratio of total output to labor input. The marginal product of labor must be considered in hiring decisions; the average product is relevant to the decision to shut down.
5. The marginal product of labor initially increases as labor input increases. But eventually the marginal product begins to decline as diminishing returns to labor set in. Diminishing returns to labor are a result of ever-increasing amounts of labor being put to work with the same constant quantity of capital and other fixed factors.
6. The law of diminishing returns states that the marginal product of a variable factor of production will, beyond some level of input, decline as the input of that factor is increased.
7. Fixed costs are the costs of a firm's fixed factors; they are thus independent of the level of production in the short run. Variable costs, by contrast, depend on the amount of the variable factors and thus on the level of production. Total costs are equal to fixed costs plus variable costs.
8. Marginal cost (*MC*) is the increase in total cost required to produce 1 extra unit of output. Marginal cost must be used in deciding how much to produce.
9. Average costs are costs per unit of output. Average total cost (*ATC*) is total cost divided by output; average variable cost (*AVC*) similarly is variable cost divided by output. Average variable cost must be considered in deciding whether to shut down in the short run. *AVC* and *ATC* curves are U-shaped, mirroring the rising and falling portions of the average product of labor curve.
10. Changes in cost conditions shift the cost curves. An increase in fixed costs does not affect the marginal cost curve, but an increase in the price of a variable factor will affect the *AVC*, *ATC*, and *MC* curves.
11. Average total or variable cost is falling whenever marginal cost is below average and rising whenever marginal cost is above average. Marginal cost is equal to average cost when average cost is at its minimum.
12. The long-run average cost curve (*LAC*) shows the minimum average cost of production when all factors of production are freely variable. Corresponding to every point on an *LAC* curve is a particular scale of plant (collection of inputs that are fixed in the short run) with its own *ATC* curve.
13. The long-run marginal cost curve (*LMC*) shows the extra cost required to produce 1 more unit of output when all factors are freely variable. It has the same relationship to *LAC* that the short-run marginal cost curve has to average total cost.
14. The shape of the long-run average cost curve is described in terms of economies and diseconomies of scale. When there are economies of scale, long-run average cost declines with the level of output; when there are diseconomies of scale, the *LAC* is rising. The *LAC* is flat when there are constant returns to scale.
15. Data suggest that there are economies of scale in many manufacturing industries but that they become relatively unimportant at levels of output that are typically small relative to the size of the U.S. market. The corresponding *LAC* curves are described as L-shaped. For many service industries a U-shaped *LAC* curve is probably a good description of the facts.

Key Terms

Technical efficiency
Economic efficiency
Production function
Short run and long run
Fixed and variable factors
Total product (*TP*) curve
Marginal product (*MP*)
Average product (*AP*)
Law of diminishing returns
Fixed, variable, and total costs
Marginal cost (*MC*)

Average fixed cost (*AFC*)
Average variable cost (*AVC*)
Average total cost (*ATC*)
U-shaped short-run average cost curves
Long-run average cost (*LAC*)
Long-run marginal cost (*LMC*)
Economies of scale, or increasing returns to scale
Constant returns to scale
Diseconomies of scale, or decreasing returns to scale
L-shaped *LAC* curves

Problems

1. (*a*) Explain the notion of technically efficient production. (*b*) Suppose you added a fifth process, *E*, to Table 8-1, using 10 units of labor, two tractors, 3 units of land, and 14 units of fertilizer. Would that process be technically efficient? (*c*) What would you conclude about the technical efficiency of the other processes in Table 8-1 if process *E* were available?
2. (*a*) Suppose the use of 1 unit of labor costs $10, one tractor costs $50, 1 unit of land costs $20, and 1 unit of fertilizer costs $3. Find the economically efficient method of production in Table 8-1 (that is, calculate which method of production costs the least). (*b*) Explain the difference between the engineering and the economic problems in choosing among alternative production processes. Why is the choice of production method not a purely engineering question? [You may want to use your answer to (*a*) in answering (*b*).]
3. Explain the distinction between the short-run and long-run production possibilities open to a firm.
4. In Table 8-2, suppose the entries in the second column read 0, 2, 6, 12, 18, 23, 27, 30, 32, 33, 34. Calculate the marginal and average products of labor (the new third and fourth columns) at each level of labor input.
5. Explain the two stages of production shown in Table 8-3. Do you believe that (*a*) there must always be increasing returns initially and/or that (*b*) diminishing returns must always set in eventually? Why?
6. (*a*) Give an example of a situation in which the marginal product of labor could be negative. (*b*) Would a firm ever hire labor with a negative marginal product?
7. Discuss the items that enter fixed costs and relate your discussion to the notion of opportunity costs presented in Chapter 7.
8. Show the effect in Table 8-4 of (*a*) an increase in fixed costs to $800 and (*b*) an increase in the weekly wage to $250. Use your calculations to produce a new Table 8-4 with the modified data.
9. Use your calculations of the effect of a wage change in problem 8 to draw both the original *MC* curve (when the wage is $200) and the new *MC* curve (when the wage is equal to $250). Discuss how a wage change shifts the *MC* curve.
10. Explain the relationships between the average total cost curve and (*a*) the average variable cost curve and (*b*) the marginal cost curve.
11. Suppose that there are only two possible sizes of plant for a firm and that ATC_1 and ATC_3 in Figure 8-6 are the *ATC* curves for those two plant sizes. What is the *LAC* curve in this case?
12. Explain carefully the difference between (*a*) diminishing returns to labor (or any other variable input) and (*b*) decreasing returns to scale.
13. (*a*) Draw an *LAC* curve that has increasing returns to scale at all levels of output. (*b*) Which of the following statements about the corresponding *LMC* curve is correct: (i) The *LMC* curve is everywhere below the *LAC* curve. (ii) The *LMC* curve must be falling.

Chapter 9
Supply in a Competitive Industry

In everyday language we would describe a market in which two firms are waging a bitter price war as "competitive." However, such a market is not *perfectly competitive* in the terminology of economics. For economists, a perfectly competitive market contains many sellers, none of whom has *any* influence at all on the price at which he sells. Perfect competition thus describes an extreme case by comparison with everyday experience, since in many real markets individual sellers *can* in fact affect price. We will show here why the theory of supply under perfect competition is nonetheless very useful and important in understanding real-world markets.

We draw on the concepts of the preceding two chapters to develop a complete model of the competitive (or perfectly competitive) market. In Chapter 7 we argued that business firms maximize profit (the difference between revenue and cost), and in Chapter 8 we saw how cost depends on the quantity produced. Here we put the pieces together to analyze how perfectly competitive firms choose the quantities they produce and supply in order to maximize profit. We then show how firm and market supply curves are determined by the costs of production.

The economics of competitive markets highlights the decisions firms must make in a market situation where they face given prices at which they can sell their output and buy the factors of production they employ. The key decisions to be made, on the basis of profit maximization, are whether to produce at all and how much to produce. From the behavior of individual firms we can build a theory of industry supply. The theory helps answer questions about the short- and long-run effects of various disturbances in a market on price and on output and employment.

For example, we might want to know the effect of an increase in the price of fertilizer on the price of wheat and wheat production. Perhaps not surprisingly, the price will rise both in the short run and in the long run. But what about the effect of an increase in the price of land on wheat prices? In the short run there is no effect at all; only in the long run will wheat prices rise to reflect the increase in costs. As we will see, there are significant distinctions between the short run and the long run

158 Part Two: Supply, Demand, and Product Markets

which provide quite general guiding principles for economic behavior.

We begin by defining and describing perfectly competitive markets. Then we show how perfectly competitive firms choose the profit-maximizing quantities to supply and how those choices link supply curves to cost curves. We start with the short run and then analyze long-run supply decisions and supply curves.

1. Perfectly Competitive Firms and Markets

In this section we answer three questions: When is a single firm perfectly competitive? When is a whole market perfectly competitive? Why is the extreme case of perfect competition important?

The Perfectly Competitive Firm

An individual farmer is a good example of a perfectly competitive firm. He certainly does not expect *his* sale of an extra bushel of wheat, corn, or potatoes to affect the market price of those goods. A farmer takes prices as given and rightly expects that at the going price (whatever that price may be) he can sell as much as he chooses.

● A *perfectly competitive firm* takes the price of its output as given and unaffected by the amount it sells.

This definition implies that a perfectly competitive firm faces a demand curve like the one shown in Figure 9-1a. A firm facing that demand curve can sell any amount of output it can produce at the going market price, P_0, or at any lower price. But at any price that is above P_0, by even a tiny amount, quantity demanded is zero. A perfectly competitive firm loses all its customers if it tries to raise price. With this demand curve, the firm naturally takes P_0 as given and unaffected by the amount it chooses to sell. A perfectly competitive firm is said to be a *price taker*, since it takes the market price it will get for its output as constant when it selects output to maximize profit. Price-taking behavior is a realistic description of firms in agriculture, fishing, and some other industries in which there are many sellers and output is completely standard. Segments of the textiles industry and some primary metal producers are other examples.

Not all firms are perfectly competitive, of course. Figure 9-1b shows the downward-sloping demand curve that faces monopolists and other *imperfectly competitive* firms (which are studied in Chapters 11 and 12).[1] A firm facing such a demand curve can generally raise its price without losing all its customers, and it may have to lower price a lot to increase the demand for its output substantially. Because imperfectly competitive firms can choose the price at which they sell, they are known as *price*

[1] Recall that a monopolist is the only seller of some good or service. Chapters 11 and 12 discuss other types of imperfectly competitive sellers as well.

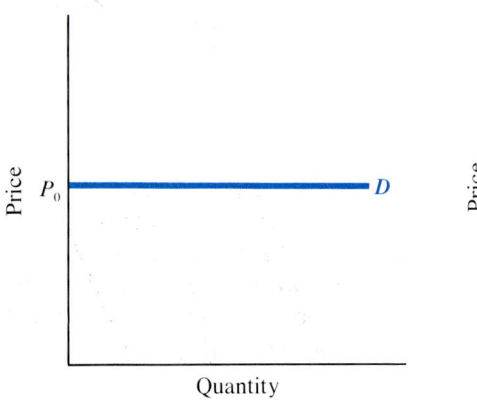

FIGURE 9-1. Demand Curves for Perfect and Imperfect Competitors. A perfectly competitive firm can sell as much as it wants at the market price, P_0. Its demand curve is horizontal, as in (*a*). Imperfect competitors face downward-sloping demand curves, as in (*b*).

(*a*) The competitive firm's demand curve

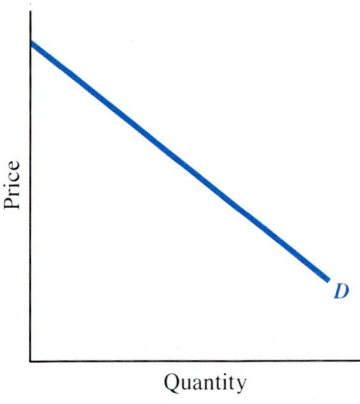

(*b*) The demand curve facing an imperfect competitor

makers, in contrast to perfect competitors, which are price takers. Perfect competitors do not struggle with identifiable rivals (as Coke struggles with Pepsi, for instance). Rather, they do battle with impersonal market forces.

Perfectly Competitive Markets

How do wheat farmers and other perfectly competitive firms come to face demand curves like the one shown in Figure 9-1a? How can firms' demand curves be flat even though the market demand curve slopes downward? After all, the market demand curve for wheat and most other products looks like Figure 9-1b; small increases in price do not suddenly drive the quantity demanded to zero. Five conditions are necessary for perfect competition to occur.

● **All sellers in a market will be perfectly competitive if (1) each is small relative to the market, (2) the product is homogeneous, (3) buyers are well informed about sellers' prices, (4) sellers act independently of each other, and (5) firms can leave and enter the industry freely.**

The first of these conditions ensures that no single firm can have a noticeable impact on the total quantity supplied. It is clearly met in markets for farm products. Even if a small farmer triples her output of wheat, the percentage change in the total U.S. quantity supplied will be completely negligible, and hence so will any effect the individual might have on price. The farmer is therefore right to assume that the price at which she sells is independent of the amount she produces. She thus behaves perfectly competitively.

The second condition, that the product be homogeneous, ensures that consumers are just as happy to buy the good from one producer as from another. Products in many markets are homogeneous; salt is salt, any 1-pound lobster looks much like another, and grades of wheat and other agricultural products are agreed-upon standards, whereas one oil painting is not like another. If products are homogeneous and if the third condition is satisfied, so that buyers are aware of all sellers' prices, any seller raising price will lose all her customers. That is exactly what the demand curve in Figure 9-1a shows. As long as buyers are well informed, no firm can charge more than the others charge.

The fourth condition requires that all firms in the industry act independently. Perfectly competitive sellers do not get together to agree on the price they will all charge or on the total quantity supplied, as, for instance, OPEC was able to in the mid-1970s, when it effectively controlled world oil supply. Rather, each firm goes about its own business, trying to choose the right level of output—the output level that maximizes its profits—on the assumption that it cannot affect price.

The final condition, that firms be able to enter and leave the industry freely, ensures that any firm with a better method of production can come into the industry and that firms that are losing money can exit at will. Free entry and exit helps ensure that existing firms in an industry cannot raise price by agreeing to reduce outputs, since any price rise is likely to provoke the entry of new firms that will increase the quantity supplied.

When these five conditions are met, the supply side of the market is perfectly competitive. A bit more is required for the market as a whole to be competitive.

● **A *market* is perfectly competitive if all sellers in the industry are perfectly competitive and there are many buyers, each well informed about sellers' prices, small relative to the market, and acting independently.**

Like large sellers, large buyers can affect price by their own actions, and groups of buyers acting together can manipulate price, for instance, by agreeing to buy nothing if sellers charge more than some minimum price. When buyers manipulate price rather than behaving as price takers, the market is imperfectly competitive.[2]

An Important but Extreme Case

Some markets satisfy all the conditions for perfect competition. Examples include most markets for agricultural products and the markets for most stocks and bonds traded on the New York Stock Exchange. (One share of IBM stock is just like another, for instance.) However, many markets are clearly not perfectly competitive. In

---

[2] Recall that we assumed price-taking behavior in the analysis of consumer buying behavior presented in Chapter 6.

some, such as those for automobiles and airliners, a few large firms make most of the sales; in others, such as those for restaurant meals and magazines, there are many sellers but no two supply exactly the same product. Why, then, do we devote so much attention to the rather extreme case of perfect competition? There are two main reasons.

First, the supply-demand model presented in Chapter 3 is strictly valid only in perfectly competitive markets, as we show in Chapter 11. But that model still does a good job of explaining many markets that do not exactly meet all the conditions for perfect competition. The concept of perfect competition is thus more widely useful than our discussion so far might suggest, and so is the theory of competitive supply developed in this chapter.

Second, perfectly competitive markets serve as an ideal to which other types of markets can be compared. As Chapter 10 will demonstrate, Adam Smith's invisible hand operates best to allocate resources efficiently when markets are perfectly competitive. And as we will see in Chapters 11 and 12, one can learn a lot about the various forms of imperfect competition by comparing them with the ideal of perfect competition.

2. The Firm's Short-Run Supply Decision

As we argued in Chapter 7, any firm will choose the level of output that maximizes its profit. In this section we present a two-step procedure for selecting the optimal output of a perfectly competitive firm in the short run. The first step is to select the best *positive* output level. This gives the profit-maximizing quantity supplied *if* the firm is going to supply anything at all. The second step is to compare the profits from producing that output to the profits from shutting down and producing nothing and then choose whichever action is better.

Most people apply this two-step procedure in their daily lives. Suppose you are considering buying a new bicycle. Your first step will probably be to shop around for a bike that meets your needs at a reasonable price. That is, you will look for the bicycle that you would prefer to buy *if* you decide to buy one. Your second step will then be to decide whether to buy the bike you found in the first step.

Finding the Optimal Positive Output

The firm finds its *optimal positive output*—the level of output that maximizes profit under the assumption that it is not going to shut down—by applying the same sort of marginal analysis we used in Chapter 6 to study consumer spending behavior. The firm begins by checking whether it can increase profit by producing a bit more or a bit less than it is currently producing.[3] If it can increase profit by increasing output, it should repeat the same check at a slightly higher level of output. Alternatively, if a decrease in output would increase profit, the firm should consider a still slightly lower level of output. When the firm finds that profits cannot be increased by changing output, profits must be at their maximum possible level—given that the firm is not going to shut down. The optimal positive output has then been found.

Since profit is the difference between revenue and cost, a small, 1-unit increase in output will increase profit only if the extra revenue brought in by selling 1 more unit exceeds the cost of producing *that unit of output*. What are these changes in revenue and cost? Because a perfectly competitive firm faces a horizontal demand curve like D in Figure 9-1a, the price it receives for its output does not depend on how much it produces. If 1 more unit is sold, the increase in revenue will thus be equal to the original market price of the good, P_0. On the cost side, the extra cost of producing 1 more unit of output is equal to *marginal* cost, *MC*, as we discussed in Chapter 8.

It follows that if the going price exceeds marginal cost at any particular output level, the firm would earn more profit by producing 1 more unit, since the increase in revenue, P_0, would exceed the increase in cost, *MC*. If price is below marginal cost at some output level, the same argument shows that the firm could increase profits by producing 1 unit less. If no change in output can increase profits, they must be at their maximum level—given that the firm decides to remain in operation. Thus at the best positive output level, price is equal to *marginal* cost.

This analysis is summarized by the *marginal condition* for optimal output choice in the short run.

---
[3] If the firm is not currently producing anything, it can begin by performing this check at any positive output level.

● **A perfectly competitive firm can increase profit by increasing output whenever the going market price exceeds the marginal cost of production ($P > MC$). Whenever price is less than marginal cost ($P < MC$), profit can be increased by reducing output. At the optimal positive output, which maximizes profit given that the firm does not shut down, price must therefore equal marginal cost ($P = MC$).**

This rule is illustrated graphically in Figure 9-2. P_0 is the price at which the firm can sell any amount of its output. It is taken as given by the perfectly competitive firm. The short-run marginal cost curve is labeled MC. As we discussed in Chapter 8, marginal cost rises at high levels of output because of the law of diminishing returns. The optimal positive output level is shown by point E, where $P_0 = MC$, corresponding to output Q^*.

Deciding Whether to Produce

After it has used the marginal condition to see how well it can do if it produces a positive output, the firm must decide whether to produce the optimal positive output or nothing at all. It may be losing money even when price is equal to marginal cost. In that case the firm can avoid or reduce its losses by shutting down operations. A firm might be maximizing its profits (or, equivalently, minimizing its losses), given that it is producing, by losing $1000 per week, if at any other positive level of output it would lose more. But perhaps if it stopped producing altogether, it would lose only $800 per week. If so, it should not produce at all.

If a firm shuts down temporarily and produces nothing in the short run, its revenues and *variable* costs will both be zero, but it can avoid its *fixed* costs only by going out of business altogether. In the short run a firm's fixed costs do not depend on whether it hires any variable factors to produce output. If the owner of a fishing boat decides not to operate it for a few weeks, for instance, she must still pay rent to the owner of the dock to which it is moored. She will generally pay exactly the same rent if the boat is operated, however, since the dock owner must keep the mooring available. Since the cost of dock space is fixed, the boat owner should ignore it when she decides whether to take the boat out. It will be optimal to

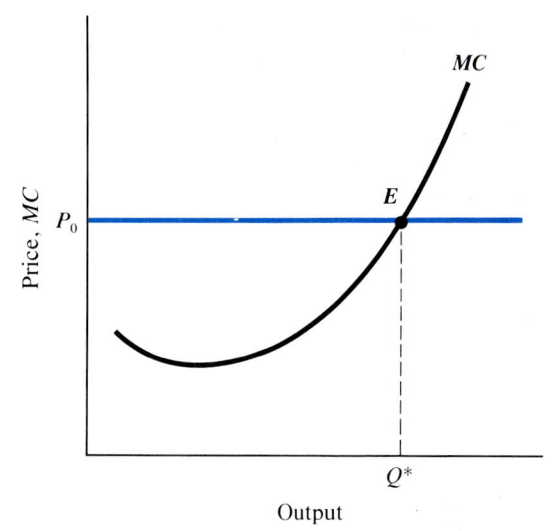

FIGURE 9-2. The First Rule of Profit Maximization: $P = MC$. The firm chooses the output level, Q^*, at which price is equal to marginal cost. At output levels below Q^*, an increase in output yields extra profits since $P > MC$. Beyond Q^*, a contraction in output raises profits since $P < MC$.

operate the boat if, and only if, the revenue from a trip exceeds the variable cost involved.

Suppose, for example, the variable cost of taking the boat out for a week is $1000 and the expected revenue from a 1-week trip is $1200. Let FC be the weekly cost of renting dock space. Putting aside any other fixed costs for the moment, profit is ($1200 − $1000 − FC) if the boat is taken out and ($−FC$)—a loss of FC—if it is not. It is clearly better to take the boat out no matter what it costs to rent dock space. On the other hand, if expected revenue is only $800, the boat should not be operated at any level of FC. Any other costs that are fixed in the short run, such as the interest on the loan taken out to pay for the boat, can similarly be ignored in making this decision.

Thus in general if revenue exceeds *variable* cost at a firm's optimal positive output, the firm should produce the optimal positive output in the short run. Then it is at least covering part of its fixed costs and is making smaller losses than it would if it stopped producing. Since price is equal to revenue per unit of output and

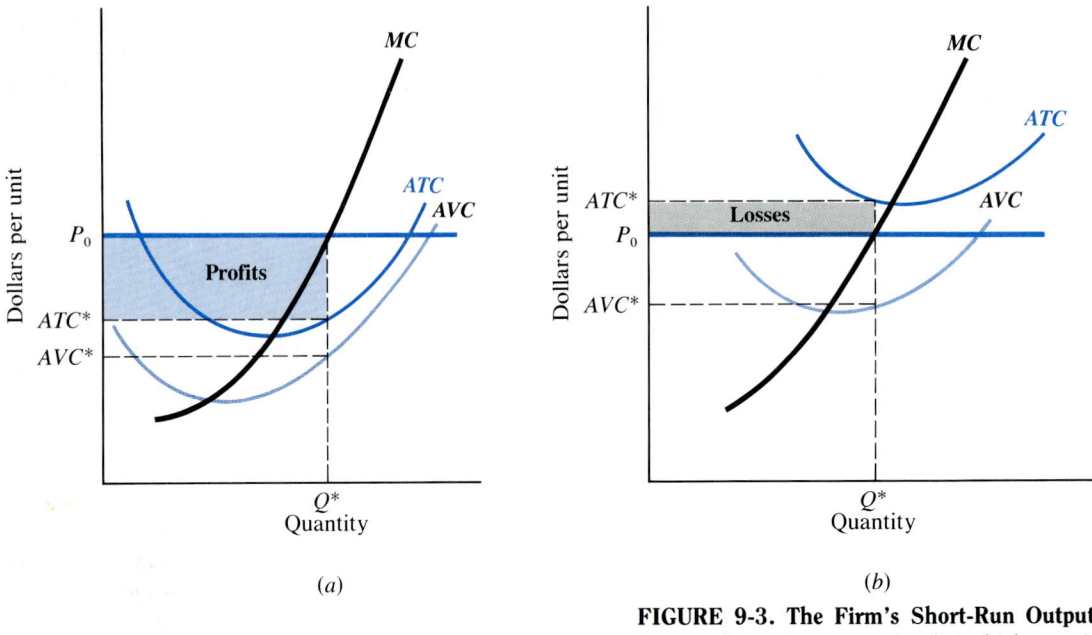

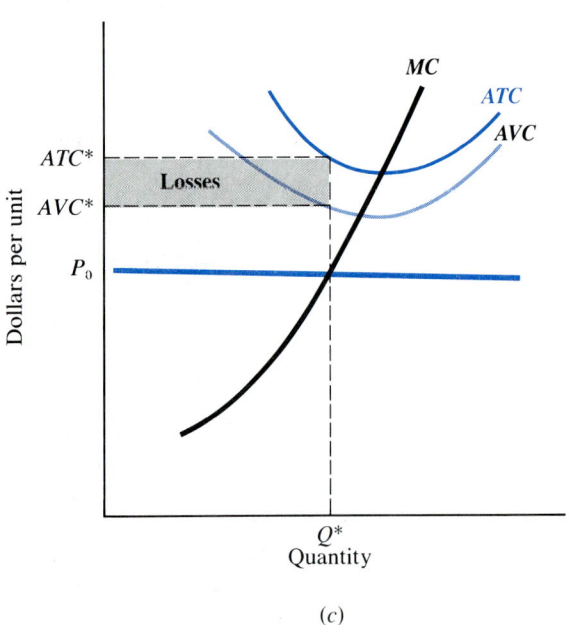

FIGURE 9-3. The Firm's Short-Run Output Decision. The firm produces that output level at which marginal cost is equal to price, so long as price exceeds average variable cost. Thus in (a) and (b), the firm produces Q^*, even though in (b) price is below ATC and the firm is losing money. In (c), the firm does better to produce zero than Q^*, the level at which $MC = P$. In (a), the firm earns profits; in (b) and (c), it loses money in the short run.

average variable cost is equal to variable cost per unit of output, it is equivalent to say that the optimal positive output should be produced if price exceeds average variable cost. If price is below average variable cost, the firm should shut down.

Hence we have the second rule for optimal output choice in the short run, the *total condition*, or *profit check*.

● **The firm should compare price and average variable cost (AVC) at the optimal positive output level, where $P = MC$. If price equals or exceeds average variable cost ($P \geq AVC$), the firm should produce the optimal positive level of output. If not ($P < AVC$), the firm should shut down.**

If price is $6 and average variable cost is $2 at the optimal positive level of output, the firm should produce. If average fixed cost is $3, the firm will make a positive economic profit on each unit of sales and its owners will be happy to continue producing indefinitely. If average fixed cost is $5, it will not cover its total costs. However, it is still better off in the short run producing than shutting down, since it cannot avoid its fixed costs.

The Two-Step Procedure

Putting these two steps together, the perfectly competitive firm's profit-maximizing short-run output decision is made as follows.

- Find the level of output where $P = MC$.
- If $P \geq AVC$, produce that output. If it is not, shut down.

Since fixed costs do not affect either marginal cost or average variable cost in the short run, *changes in the costs of fixed inputs have absolutely no effect on the quantity supplied in the short run*. This principle explains the difference in the short-run effects of changes in the prices of fertilizer and land noted at the start of this chapter.

Figure 9-3 shows three possible results of this two-step procedure. In all three panels, the optimal positive output level is Q^*, and ATC^* and AVC^* are the values of average total cost and average variable cost, respectively, at that output. In (a), price exceeds average total cost at output level Q^*. The firm is making profits equal to $(P_0 - ATC^*)$ per unit on an output of Q^* units, so that its total profit is equal to the shaded area. The optimal positive output level should certainly be produced in this case.

In (b) and (c), average total cost exceeds price at all output levels. There is thus no way to make a positive profit; the question is how to minimize losses. If output Q^* is produced, losses are the per unit loss, $(ATC^* - P_0)$, times Q^*. This is equal to the shaded area in (b). If a firm shuts down, its losses are equal to its total fixed costs. Total fixed cost can be computed as average fixed cost at output level Q^*, $(ATC^* - AVC^*)$, times Q^*. This is equal to the shaded area in (c). In (b), the firm loses less by producing than by shutting down because AVC^* is less than the going price. In (c), where AVC^* is greater than price, the firm minimizes its losses by shutting down.

Box 9-1 shows that the two-step procedure developed in this section applies to a wide range of decisions in economics and in everyday life. The first step teaches us

---

Box 9-1. Marginal Conditions and Sunk Costs

Two principles of economics used in the analysis of supply keep coming up both in economics and in life. The first is the *marginal principle*. In deciding how much to produce, the firm asks itself how producing 1 more or 1 less unit of output will affect its profits. It sets output so that profits cannot be increased by changing the level of output. If profits cannot be increased, they must be as big as they can be, or at a maximum.

The general principle is that in any situation consumers or producers or government officials can find the best position to be in by asking whether the situation can be improved by varying, at the margin, purchases or output or government spending, as the case may be. How much labor should the firm employ? It compares the cost of an extra worker with the value of the output the worker will produce. If the value of the output the extra worker will produce is more than the wage, the firm hires him. How wide should a bridge be built? Should it have four lanes or six? To get the right answer, compare the extra cost of building a six-lane bridge instead of a four-lane bridge with the benefits drivers would get from the extra two lanes. These are marginal conditions, and the question is whether to do or have a little bit more or a little bit less. Following this rule will lead to an optimal situation.

Of course, it is also necessary to look at the big picture. Not only does the firm have to set marginal cost equal to marginal revenue, it also has to be sure it is earning a profit. Should it close down completely, for instance? Should a bridge be built at all? The marginal conditions and the big picture, or *total conditions*, go together.

The second general principle is that *sunk costs are sunk*. If certain costs have been incurred and cannot be affected by your decision, ignore them. They should have no role in your decision. In deciding how much to produce in the short run, the firm pays no attention to its fixed costs. Those costs are there no matter what the firm does. They are therefore irrelevant to the firm's decision. Suppose we are halfway through building a bridge and we are told that completion will cost four times as much as originally budgeted. Should we proceed? The answer is quite independent of the amount that has already been spent to get half the bridge built. We need to compare the benefits of having the bridge with the marginal cost of completing it.

The *sunk cost fallacy* is the view that sunk costs should matter. Whenever issues involving sunk costs arise, it always seems natural to think that it would be a pity to waste all the money that has been spent already. But that natural tendency does not lead to sound decisions. Bygones should be bygones.

the *marginal principle*: Find better outcomes by comparing the costs and benefits of small changes. The second step teaches us to avoid the *sunk cost fallacy*: Avoid allowing decisions to be affected by costs that can't be changed.

3. Firm and Market Short-Run Supply Curves

We have just shown how a perfectly competitive firm decides how much to supply in order to maximize its profits, taking into account its costs at alternative output levels and the given price of its output. In this section we derive the firm's supply curve by focusing on the relation between quantity supplied and output price. We then obtain the market supply curve by addition, just as we obtained the market demand curve in Chapter 6, and show how changes in costs are reflected in shifts in supply curves.

The Firm's Short-Run Supply Curve

A firm's supply curve shows the quantity of output it will supply at all possible values of the market price of output. Using the results of section 2, we can easily compute the quantity a perfectly competitive firm will supply at any given market price. If price is P_1 in Figure 9-4, for instance, the firm's demand curve is the horizontal line labeled D. By seeing where this line intersects the marginal cost curve, labeled MC, we find the optimal positive output, Q_1. Since P_1 is greater than average variable cost, AVC, at this output level, the firm will maximize profit by supplying Q_1 rather than by shutting down. This same two-step graphic procedure can be used to compute the quantity supplied at any other price.

Now recall from Chapter 8 that a firm's marginal cost curve intersects its average variable cost curve at the point at which average variable cost is minimized. At all higher levels of output, marginal cost is greater than average variable cost, and average variable cost is above its minimum level—as Figure 9-4 illustrates. Thus for any price, such as P_1, that is above the minimum level of average variable cost, the firm's horizontal demand curve intersects its marginal cost curve where marginal cost is above average variable cost. It follows that price is above average variable cost at such points, and the firm should produce its optimal positive output. On the other hand, if price is below the lowest level of the firm's average variable cost, the firm should shut down.

• **The short-run supply curve of a competitive firm shows the quantity of output it will supply at each level of price in order to maximize profit. The firm's short-run supply curve coincides with its marginal cost curve for prices above the minimum level of average variable cost (AVC). If price is below the minimum level of AVC—which is called the firm's short-run shutdown price—the firm will shut down and supply zero.**

The firm's short-run supply curve shown in Figure 9-4 is thus the thickened portion of its marginal cost curve that lies above its *shutdown price*—the minimum level of its average variable cost. For prices above the shutdown price, the quantity supplied can be read off the marginal cost curve, as we have demonstrated. If the market price is below the shutdown price, the firm minimizes its losses by shutting down and producing nothing.

Figure 9-4 also shows the *break-even price*, equal to the minimum level of average total cost. If the market

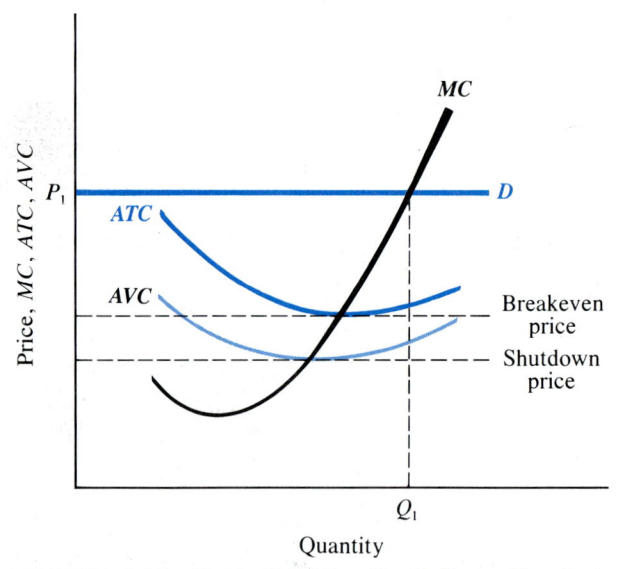

FIGURE 9-4. The Firm's Short-Run Supply Curve. The short-run supply function of the firm is the portion of the marginal cost curve that is above the *AVC* curve. It is shown by the thick portion of the *MC* curve.

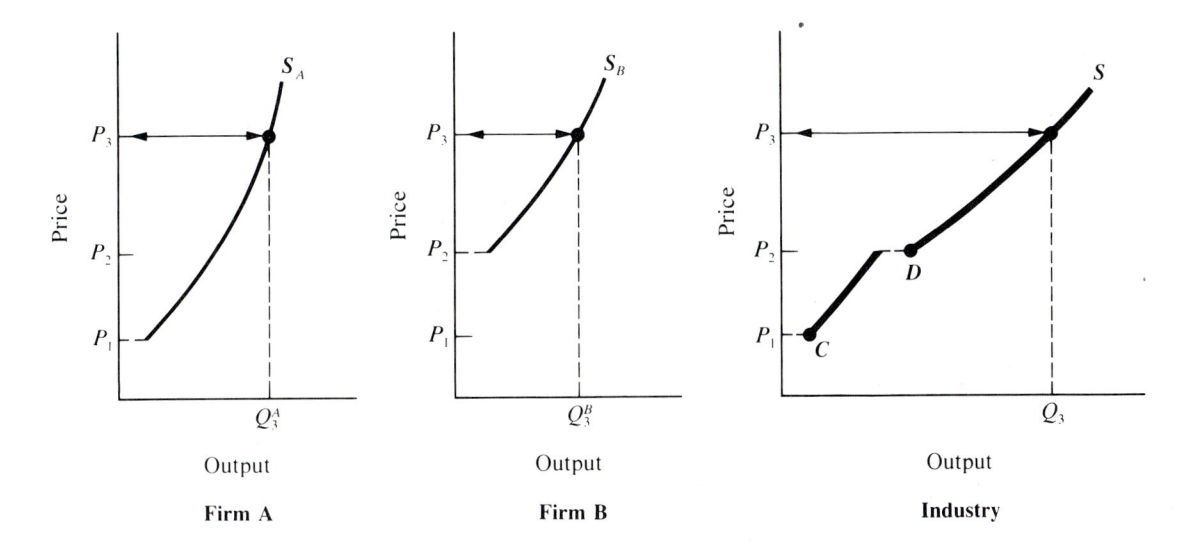

FIGURE 9-5. Adding Firms' Supply Curves to Get the Industry's Supply Curve. The industry supply curve is obtained by adding, horizontally, the supply curves of all the firms in the industry.

price is equal to the break-even price, price is equal to average total cost and the firm is therefore just breaking even, making neither a profit nor a loss in economic terms. At higher prices it is enjoying positive profits; at lower prices it is enduring losses in the short run. Since average total cost is greater than average variable cost at all output levels (because of fixed costs), the break-even price is always above the shutdown price. If the price of output is between the shutdown and break-even prices, the firm will produce its optimal positive output in the short run even though it is not covering all its costs. But in the long run it will have to lower its average total cost or go out of business.

A firm's short-run supply curve slopes upward for exactly the same reason that its marginal cost curve slopes upward, since the two curves coincide. As we discussed in Chapter 8, marginal cost curves slope upward because of diminishing returns. Beyond some level of output, the amount of labor and other variable inputs the firm has to hire to increase output by 1 more unit increases as output rises, because the amount of machinery, equipment, and other fixed inputs used in production cannot be increased in the short run. The more strongly diminishing returns are at work, the steeper the firm's supply curve. Conversely, if diminishing returns are weak, the supply curve will be nearly flat. There are thus tight links between production conditions, costs, and supply decisions.

The Market's Short-Run Supply Curve

The quantity of output supplied to the market at each price is the sum of the output levels of all the firms in the market. In the short run, the number of firms and their fixed factors are constant. New firms do not have time to build factories and organize production, so in the short run all the output must come from firms that are already in operation.

Figure 9-5 shows how the short-run market supply curve is related to the supply curves of individual firms. For simplicity, Figure 9-5 shows a situation in which there are only two firms, A and B. Each is perfectly competitive, taking price as given. Each firm's supply curve is, as in Figure 9-4, the portion of its marginal cost curve that is above the shutdown price. P_1 is the shutdown price for firm A, and P_2 is firm B's (higher) shutdown price. The output supplied by each firm drops to zero when price falls below its shutdown price.

At any price, the total quantity supplied to the market is the sum of the quantities supplied by both firms. For instance, at price P_3, firm A supplies quantity Q_3^A and firm B supplies Q_3^B. The total quantity supplied at price P_3 is thus $Q_3 = Q_3^A + Q_3^B$. The complete market supply curve is obtained by adding up the output supplied by both firms at each possible price.[4] The market supply curve when there are many firms is obtained in exactly the same way.

● The *short-run market supply curve* is obtained by adding the quantities supplied by all firms at each possible price.

Market supply curves are thus obtained by the same process of horizontal addition that we used to obtain market demand curves from individual demand curves in Chapter 6. The market supply and demand curves, in turn, determine the market price. Price is thus affected by all sellers together, though not by any single seller individually.

The quantity supplied in the short run in a perfectly competitive market increases when the market price rises for two reasons. First, the supply curve of each individual firm slopes upward, and hence each firm supplies a larger quantity. Second, as price rises, firms that had been shut down come into production as their shutdown price is reached. The number of firms *in* the market (that is, with the fixed inputs necessary to operate) is fixed in the short run, but the number *operating* generally increases as the output price rises.

Shifts of Short-Run Supply Curves

The effects of changes in costs of production are represented as shifts in market supply curves. We can now be more precise about this.

Short-run firm and market supply curves are drawn for given *amounts* of fixed inputs (such as plant and equipment), for given *prices* of variable inputs (such as

---

[4] The industry supply curve shown in Figure 9-5 has a flat segment at the shutdown price of firm B. The flat segment reflects the fact that a small increase in price, from just below P_2 to just above P_2, brings a new firm into production and therefore produces a noticeable upward jump in the quantity supplied when there are only two firms. When there are many firms, the supply curve becomes smooth because the output of one firm more or less makes very little relative difference in terms of total industry output.

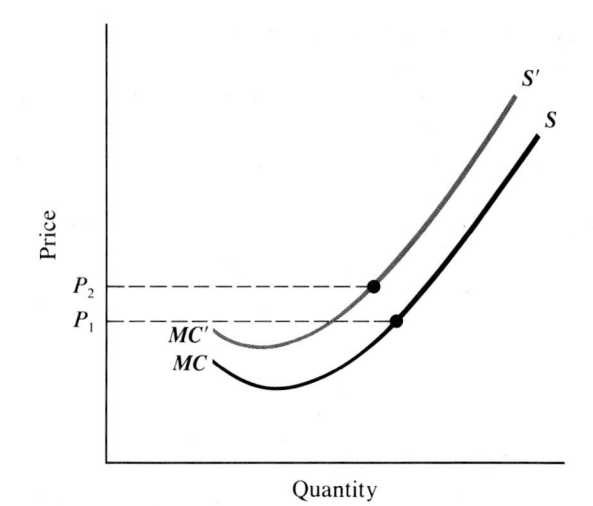

FIGURE 9-6. The Effects of an Increase in the Wage on the Firm's Supply Curve. An increase in the wage raises the marginal cost of production, shifting the supply curve from S to S'. The minimum *AVC* also increases (not shown), thereby increasing the shutdown price from P_1 to P_2.

labor and materials), and for a given *state of technology*. Short-run supply curves are shifted only by changes in these three factors. Changes in the prices of fixed inputs have no effect on supply in the short run.

Consider first a change in the price of a variable factor, such as an increase in the wage of fishermen. An increase in the price of a variable factor raises both marginal cost and average variable cost at all output levels. This is illustrated graphically as an upward shift in the firm's *AVC* and *MC* schedules. In Figure 9-6, a firm's marginal cost shifts from *MC* to *MC'* because of an increase in wages. Because *AVC* also shifts upward, its shutdown price rises from P_1 to P_2. The firm's supply curve thus shifts upward and to the left, from S to S'. Correspondingly, the industry supply curve also shifts upward and to the left when wages rise. All else equal, then, an increase in the wage of fishermen will reduce the quantity of fish supplied at every price and thus lead to an increase in equilibrium price and a reduction in equilibrium quantity.

Changes in the amounts of fixed inputs available change both marginal cost and average variable cost in the short run, as we argued in Chapter 8. If a fishing firm has several boats and one is sunk, for instance, its workers will be less productive because they will have less capital to work with. Its marginal cost and average variable cost will both be higher at all output levels, so that its short-run supply curve will shift in the manner illustrated in Figure 9-6. On the other hand, increases in boats, machinery, and other fixed inputs will have the effect of shifting short-run supply curves downward and to the right (as shown by a shift from S' to S in Figure 9-6), thus tending to lower equilibrium price and raise equilibrium output.

Finally, as firms adopt new technology that makes it possible to obtain more output from a given set of inputs, their short-run supply curves shift downward and to the right. (We discuss this process further subsequently.) As Box 9-2 illustrates, government programs that ignore changes in technology can encounter serious problems as a consequence.

Box 9-2. Dairy Price Supports

The U.S. government has for many years supported the incomes of dairy farmers by guaranteeing a minimum price for dairy products. The support price is calculated to keep milk-price increases in line with the increases in a broad index of the prices of the inputs used by farmers. The support price has been so high in recent years that the government has been accumulating mountains of dairy products at enormous costs to the taxpayer.

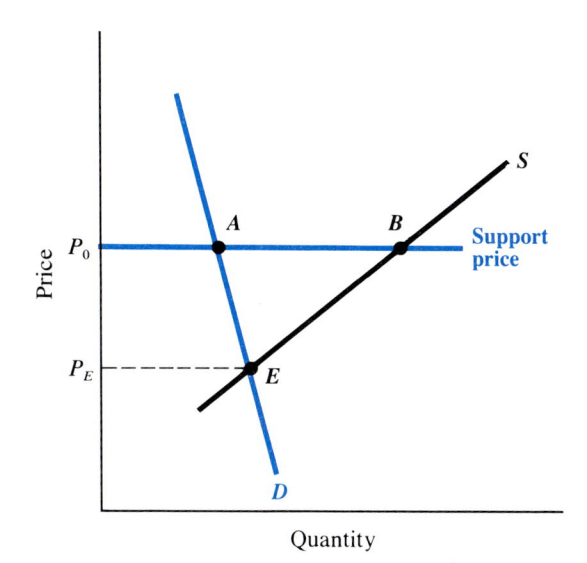

FIGURE 9B-1. The Dairy Price Support Scheme. The government fixes a support price, P_0, for milk so as to protect dairy farmers' incomes. But the support price exceeds the equilibrium price, P_E, and quantity supplied at the support price far exceeds quantity demanded. Excess supply increases over time as productivity increases shift the short-run supply curve downward and to the right.

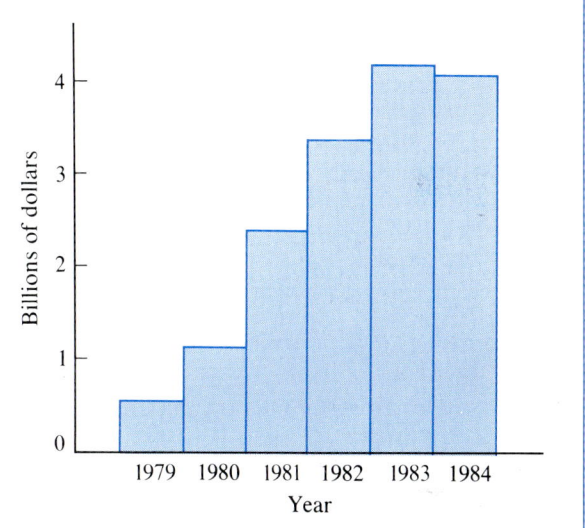

FIGURE 9B-2. The Government Dairy Mountain. The figure shows the value of the dairy products—butter, cheese, and dried milk—owned by the government. (*Source, Statistical Abstract of the United States, 1986*, Table 1152.)

Figure 9B-1 illustrates the problem. The demand curve for dairy products is D, and the short-run supply curve is S. On the supply side the industry is perfectly competitive, meeting the five conditions for competition listed in section 1. The government sets a support price of P_0 and guarantees that if quantity supplied exceeds quantity demanded at this price, it will buy the excess. In Figure 9B-1, the government has to buy amount AB every year because the support price is above the equilibrium price, P_E, at the market's equilibrium point, E.

To maintain the price at the target level, the government in 1984 spent $2 billion on dairy products, about 11 percent of the total value of milk production by farmers. Figure 9B-2 shows how the government's stocks of dairy products have increased. At the end of 1984 the government held over 1.4 *billion* pounds of nonfat dry milk as well as cheese and butter stocks amounting to more than 40 percent of the total production of cheese and butter in that year.

Of course, if the government were to sell its stockpiles, it would drive down the market price. Then it would defeat the purpose of the scheme, which is to keep price high. The government has given some cheese away to low-income households and has tried to sell and give away some dairy products abroad. These efforts, along with a fall in production, account for the slight reduction in government holdings in 1984.

The problem has become worse over time because strong productivity growth has shifted the dairy industry's short-run supply curve rapidly to the right: The amount of milk produced per cow increased by almost 40 percent between 1970 and 1984. On the other side of the market, the demand curve for milk has shifted only slowly to the right, since the quantity of milk demanded does not rise as rapidly as consumers' income. Thus, because of technical change, the equilibrium price, P_E, has risen less rapidly than the support price, P_0, which is based only on changes in input costs. And the excess supply at the support price has accordingly grown rapidly.

The government has tried to reduce the support price from time to time. In early 1985, for instance, the Congressional Budget Office concluded:

> The case for reducing the level of milk price support is based on the belief that the program has increased dairy farmers' incomes at the expense of taxpayers. . . . The level of support in recent years has been so high relative to milk production costs that dairy farmers have produced for the government rather than the market.

But dairy farmers are a well-organized special interest, and they have thus far been able to block significant reductions in dairy supports.

Note: For more on this program, see Congressional Budget Office, *Reducing the Deficit*, February 1985, Part II, pp. 161–162; and Michael T. Belongia, "The Dairy Support Program: A Study of Misdirected Economic Incentives," Federal Reserve Bank of St. Louis, *Review*, February 1984. See also the discussion of concentrated interests in Chapter 4.

4. Long-Run Supply Curves

Long-run supply curves for the firm and the industry are derived in essentially the same way as are short-run supply curves. For the *firm*, the long run differs from the short run because *all inputs are freely variable in the long run*. The distinction between fixed and variable inputs applies only to the short run. For the *industry*, there are two differences between the short run and the long run. Not only can all *existing* firms adjust their inputs freely, but also *the number of firms in the industry can change* because old firms can leave and new ones can start up.

The Firm's Long-Run Supply Decision

Just as in the short run, marginal cost is the prime determinant of the firm's long-run supply decisions. Recall from Chapter 8 that a firm's long-run average cost curve, *LAC*, and the corresponding marginal cost curve, *LMC*, describe its costs when it can vary all its inputs freely, thus achieving the lowest possible cost of producing any given level of output. As we now show, a firm's long-run profit-maximizing output level is obtained by means of a two-step procedure. Just as in the short run, the first step involves marginal cost and the second step depends on average cost.

In the first step, the firm uses the same marginal calculation to find its optimal positive output level in the long run that it used in the short run. The only difference is that the *marginal condition* for optimal output choice in the long run involves long-run, not short-run, marginal cost.

● **In the long run, if a firm decides to operate, it will produce its optimal positive output level, which is the level of output at which price is equal to long-run marginal cost: *P = LMC*.**

In the second step, as in the short run, the firm must decide whether to operate. In the long run, a firm will stay in business only if it covers *all* its costs, including the opportunity cost of the capital invested in plant, equipment, and other inputs that are fixed in the short run. If price is too low to cover all its costs, the firm should leave the industry entirely. This argument translates directly into the long-run *total condition*, or *profit check*, for optimal output choice.

TABLE 9-1. The Perfectly Competitive Firm's Optimal Supply Decision

Period	Marginal condition	Profit check
Short run	Choose the output level where $P = MC$	Produce only if $P \geq AVC$ Shut down if $P < AVC$
Long run	Choose the output level where $P = LMC$	Produce only if $P \geq LAC$ Leave the industry if $P < LAC$

● **The firm should operate in the long run only if price is greater than or equal to long-run average cost: $P \geq LAC$.**

Table 9-1 summarizes the firm's criteria for determining the optimal output level in the short run and in the long run. The criteria are remarkably similar. Indeed, because all costs are variable in the long run, the criteria can be said to be the same in both cases: Choose output so that set price equals the relevant marginal cost, then produce output level if price covers the average variable cost of production.

The Firm's Long-Run Supply Curve

Figure 9-7 illustrates the relationship between a firm's long-run cost curves and its long-run supply curve. This relationship is essentially the same as it is in the short run.

● **The *long-run supply curve of a perfectly competitive firm* is the portion of its *LMC* schedule above the point at which *LAC* is minimized.**

In Figure 9-7 *LAC* is minimized at output level Q_A. The corresponding value of *LAC*, P_A, is the firm's long-run break-even price.

● **A firm's *long-run break-even price* is the lowest price at which it can just break even in the long run. It is the firm's minimum long-run average cost, the lowest point on its *LAC* curve.**

The supply curve of the firm illustrated in Figure 9-7 thus coincides with the thick segment of its long-run marginal cost curve above P_A.

If price is below P_A in Figure 9-7, the firm will not produce in the long run; if price is above P_A, it will operate. The long-run break-even price, P_A, plays a role in the long run similar to the role played by the shutdown price in the short run; both give the lowest price at which the firm will produce. In the long run, though, the break-even price is the price below which the firm leaves the industry permanently rather than temporarily shutting down. The owner of a fishing boat shuts down in the short run by leaving her boat at the dock; she leaves the industry permanently when she sells or scraps the boat and takes up another line of work.

On the other hand, if price is above the long-run break-even price, P_A in Figure 9-7, price will be above average cost at the output level where $P = LMC$. At price P_B in Figure 9-7, for instance, P equals LMC at output Q_B. At this output, price exceeds average cost by the distance EF, and the firm should produce and supply Q_B. Then, because profit per unit of output is equal to price

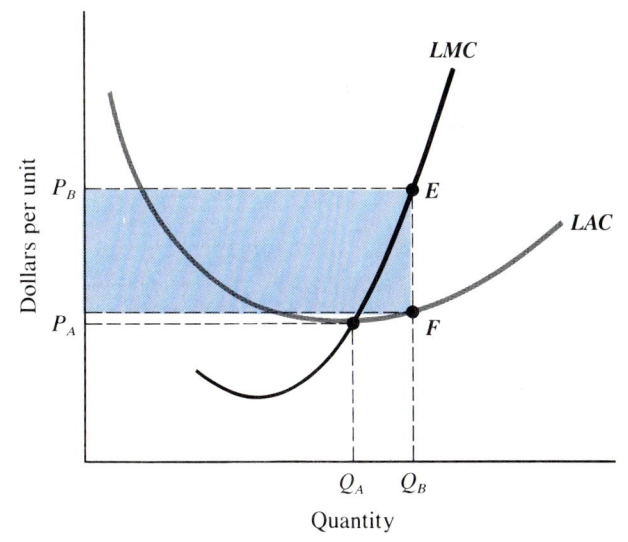

FIGURE 9-7. The Firm's Long-Run Supply Curve. The firm's long-run supply curve is the *LMC* curve above the long-run break-even price, P_A, which is equal to minimum long-run average cost. At any higher price, such as P_B, the firm makes profits. At any price below P_A it would lose money in the long run and would therefore leave the industry.

minus average cost, the shaded area in Figure 9-7 is equal to the firm's economic profit, or profit per unit times output, Q_B. Firms that receive positive economic profits are also described by economists as receiving *above-normal* (or *supranormal* or *supracompetitive*) profits. Such firms are more than happy to remain in business. Moreover, as we shall see, their success is likely to attract others into the same industry.

Because all factors are variable in the long run, diminishing returns are less important than they are in the short run, and any firm's *LMC* curve is flatter than its short-run *MC* curve. Accordingly, the firm's long-run supply curve is flatter, or more elastic, than its short-run supply curve.[5] That is, an increase in price produces a greater increase in quantity supplied in the long run than it does in the short run because the firm has time to adjust factors that are fixed in the short run in order to produce additional output at the lowest possible cost.

The Market's Long-Run Supply Curve

In the long run, as in the short run, the market supply curve is obtained by adding together the quantities supplied by all firms at each level of price, but there is one very important difference. Since firms can enter or leave the market in the long run, we must add together the outputs of all firms *potentially* in the market. In general, different points on the market's long-run supply curve correspond to different numbers of firms in the supplying industry.

Figure 9-8 shows the short-run and long-run supply curves of a perfectly competitive market. The long-run supply curve, *LS*, is flatter than the short-run curve, *S*, for two reasons. First, the long-run supply curve is flatter than the short-run supply curve for *each firm* in the industry, as we discussed previously. Second, in the long run the *number of firms* in the industry rises when price increases. When the price of output rises above average costs, entrepreneurs see profit opportunities and attempt to get into the business. Such entry takes time, however, and it occurs only in the long run, after a price increase has been maintained for a while. Similarly, if the output price falls and stays low for a while, firms will start to leave the industry. Thus output rises more in the long run than it does in the short run in response to a price increase because entry occurs only in the long run, and output falls more in the long run than in the short run in response to a price decrease because exit occurs in the long run.

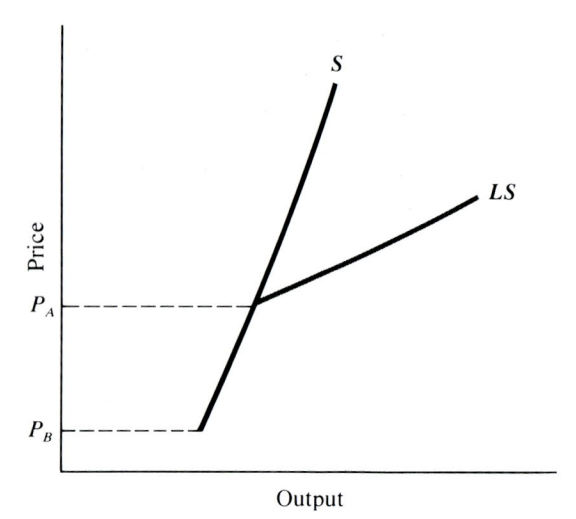

FIGURE 9-8. Short- and Long-Run Industry Supply Curves. The long-run industry supply curve, *LS*, is flatter (more elastic) than the short-run supply curve, *S*. The long-run break-even price, P_A, is above the short-run shutdown price, P_B.

In the long run, the total quantity supplied falls to zero if price remains below the long-run break-even price, P_A in Figure 9-8. In the short run, price must fall to the short-run shutdown price, P_B, before supply vanishes. P_A is greater than P_B because in the short run firms have to cover only their variable costs, whereas in the long run all costs have to be covered.

Shapes of Long-Run Market Supply Curves

So far we have shown the long-run supply curve as upward-sloping, but the long-run supply curve of a perfectly competitive market may be horizontal, or completely flat. Such a supply curve means that in the long run sellers will supply any quantity that buyers demand at a constant price.[6]

---

[5] Recall the discussion of elasticity of supply in Chapter 5.

[6] In Chapter 5 we described a flat supply curve as infinitely elastic, or perfectly elastic.

We now show that this case arises if all the firms actually and potentially in a market have exactly the same long-run average and marginal cost curves and if input prices do not depend on the total level of industry output. The long-run marginal and average cost curves for a typical firm in such a market are shown in Figure 9-9. The cheapest way for such a firm to produce output in the long run is to produce Q^* units per period. This yields a long-run average cost of LAC^*.

To see why the long-run market supply curve is flat, note first that quantity supplied will be zero in the long run at all prices below LAC^*. Now suppose that price settles at a price such as P_2, above LAC^*. At price P_2, every firm in the industry produces Q_2 in the long run and makes a positive economic profit, since price is above long-run average cost. This means that new firms will come into the industry to get some of the profits for themselves. As they enter, they increase the industry's output, thereby causing the price of output to fall. Thus the price cannot in the long run remain at P_2.

The only price at which the industry can be in long-run equilibrium, with no entry or exit of firms changing the quantity supplied, is LAC^*. At this price, no firm in the industry is making positive economic profits and none is suffering a loss. There is thus no incentive for entry or exit.

Supply curves for this market are shown in Figure 9-10. In the short run, the number of firms in the industry is fixed and the industry supply curve, S, is therefore upward-sloping. In the short run, the quantity supplied is zero for prices below P_1, which is the typical firm's shutdown price. In the long run the price in this industry must be P^*, as we just argued. The long-run supply curve for the industry is thus the horizontal line LS. At each point on this curve, each firm in the industry is producing Q^* per period, as shown in Figure 9-9. At higher levels of total output, there are more firms in the market but the long-run output per firm does not change.

Should we expect long-run industry supply curves to be flat in practice? Not necessarily. Long-run supply curves may slope upward for some industries, for two reasons. First, there may be important differences among actual and potential sellers. Cost differences may arise because management in some firms is better than it is in others. Or the factors of production, especially raw

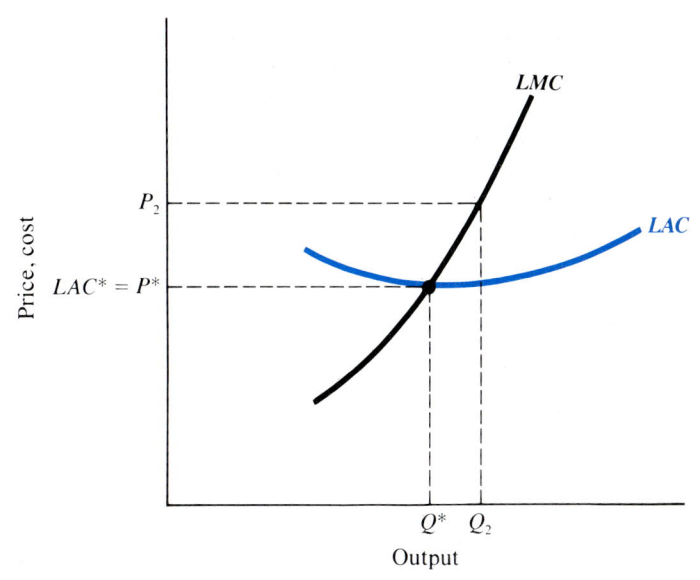

FIGURE 9-9. The Minimum Cost Level of Output. Output is produced most cheaply in the long run at the long-run break-even point, with output level Q^*. The corresponding long-run average cost is LAC^*.

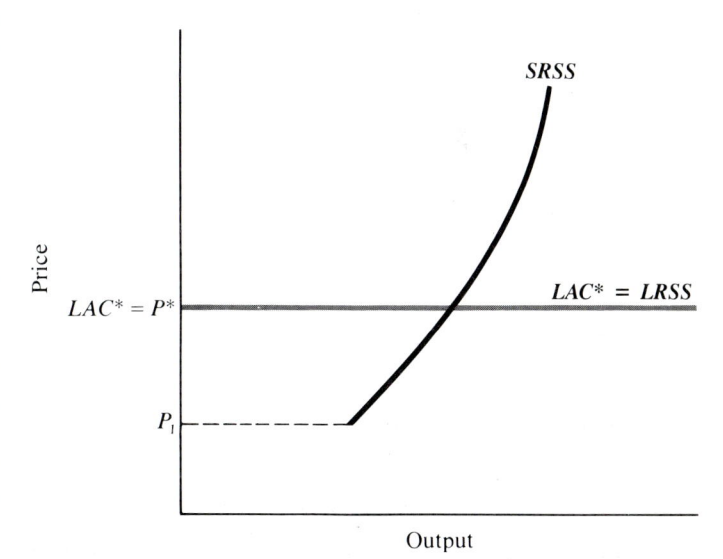

FIGURE 9-10. Upward-Sloping Short-Run and Horizontal Long-Run Industry Supply Curves. When all firms have identical cost conditions and input prices are constant, the long-run supply curve, LS, is horizontal at price P^*. The short-run supply curve S, is upward-sloping because the number of firms is fixed. P_1 is the short-run shutdown price, and P^* is the long-run break-even price.

materials, may differ in quality from one firm to another. If there are many different potential sellers, each with a different long-run break-even price, there will be many different market prices that are consistent with long-run equilibrium. The higher the price, the more firms will be in the market. At very low prices only the most efficient (lowest-cost) producers can cover all their costs. If price rises, those firms will earn above-normal profits and less efficient producers will find it attractive to be in the business. The long-run supply curve thus rises when firms' long-run costs differ because increases in price increase the number of firms operating in the long run.

Second, the prices of the inputs used by sellers may rise as total production increases. Some industries are important buyers of particular specialized inputs. These may be particular types of land, raw materials such as coal and copper, or some specialized kinds of labor. The wine industry is an important user of land suitable for growing grapes; the electric power industry uses most of the coal produced in the United States; and the NBA is an important employer of tall male athletes. As an industry expands and its demand for such specialized inputs grows, the prices or wages of those inputs will rise. This will increase all firms' costs, and the industry supply curve will therefore have a positive slope.

Shifts of Long-Run Supply Curves

Two sorts of changes shift long-run supply curves. First, because there are no fixed inputs in the long run, changes in the price of *any* input affect firms' long-run average and marginal costs and thus shift firm and market long-run supply curves. For example, if the interest rate goes up, so does the opportunity cost of capital tied up in a firm's plant and equipment. Since in the long run the firm will change its plant and equipment as its output changes, its long-run average and marginal costs will rise at all output levels, and its long-run supply curve will shift upward. It will take a higher output price than before to make it optimal to supply any particular quantity of output. Since the market supply curve is determined by adding the quantities supplied by all firms, it too will shift upward.

Second, long-run cost and supply curves are shifted by changes in technology. Over time technology improves as new types of machinery become available and better ways are discovered to produce the same amount of output at a lower cost.

● **Technical progress (or increases in productivity) occurs whenever it becomes possible with given input prices to produce a given level of output at a lower cost.**

As new technology comes into use, firm and market supply curves shift downward. Technical progress is particularly important in the long run because it is generally hard to employ new technology rapidly. In the short run each firm is stuck with its particular machinery and other fixed factors. In the long run, however, firms can adjust their operations completely to react to changes in technology. Technical progress is important in many industries, and a firm's ability to increase its productivity as rapidly as its competitors do is often the main determinant of its long-run profitability and its ability to remain in business, as Box 9-3 illustrates.

Supply Curves and Industry Marginal Cost

In a perfectly competitive market, price is equal to marginal cost for every firm that is producing. Thus at every level of output, the industry supply curve shows the marginal cost of production for all firms that have positive output. The supply curve shows the cost to the industry as a whole of increasing output by 1 unit.

● **The industry supply curve is the industry's marginal cost curve.**

This relationship applies in both the short run and the long run: The short-run supply curve is the short-run marginal cost curve of the industry, and the long-run supply curve is its long-run marginal cost curve. We return to this point in Chapter 10, when we show why perfect competition allocates resources efficiently.

■ This chapter has been concerned with how to maximize profit in perfectly competitive markets and with the implications of profit maximization for the supply of goods and services. Can you use this material to get rich by organizing a firm and maximizing its profits? Probably not. Only the lowest-cost producers in a perfectly

Box 9-3. Long-Run Adjustment to Import Competition

The ability of U.S. firms to increase their productivity is becoming increasingly important as imports rise in many industries. Imports from Japan and from less-developed countries such as Korea, Brazil, and Mexico are posing an increasing threat to U.S. producers. The question for many sectors—steel, automobiles, footwear, textiles—is whether they can make adjustments to cut their costs and stay in business.

The automobile industry provides a particularly clear and much-discussed example.[7] Figure 9B-3 shows the share of imports in total new car registrations. Imports, especially from Japan, jumped dramatically in 1978–1981. Imported cars were smaller and lower-priced than U.S. cars, they were more fuel-efficient, and many consumers felt they were better made.

This sharp increase in import penetration, along with the U.S. recession of 1979–1982, hurt domestic producers so much that employment in the industry declined by more than 20 percent. The accounting profits of U.S. automobile producers were negative. Even though they were clearly not earning normal profits, these firms did not leave the industry.

They claimed that *in the long run* the industry could be profitable. To help the U.S. auto industry, President Carter temporarily limited imports of cars. These curbs were renewed in 1983, and their effects are visible in Figure 9B-3. In 1985 President Reagan declined to renew them for yet another period, but pressure on the Japanese to restrict exports to the United States remained strong.[8]

Even so, the pressure on domestic auto producers to find ways of cutting their costs is now much stronger than it was before 1978. To cut costs, they will have to continue to redesign products and change production methods. If they are unable to reduce costs to compete with the imports, they may stop producing some cars altogether and become merely distributors of foreign cars.

The same issues arise in the steel industry. Eight large producers accounted for more than 80 percent of the U.S. market in 1960. Today their share is less than 60 percent and falling. These firms face increased competition from low-cost foreign producers and from domestic minimills that use a more cost-effective production technique. Unless the price of steel rises, the traditional steel industry must either cut its costs dramatically or go out of business altogether. But if the government raises the price of steel in the United States to protect the domestic steel industry, it will hurt the domestic auto industry, since firms outside the United States will be able to build cars with less expensive steel.

---

[7] The alert reader will have noted that this industry does not satisfy the five conditions for perfect competition presented in section 1 because there are not many small producers of automobiles. But even imperfect competitors must keep pace with their rivals' productivity or risk being driven out of business.

[8] The sources and forms of this pressure are discussed in Chapter 23. Japan voluntarily maintained some quotas through 1987.

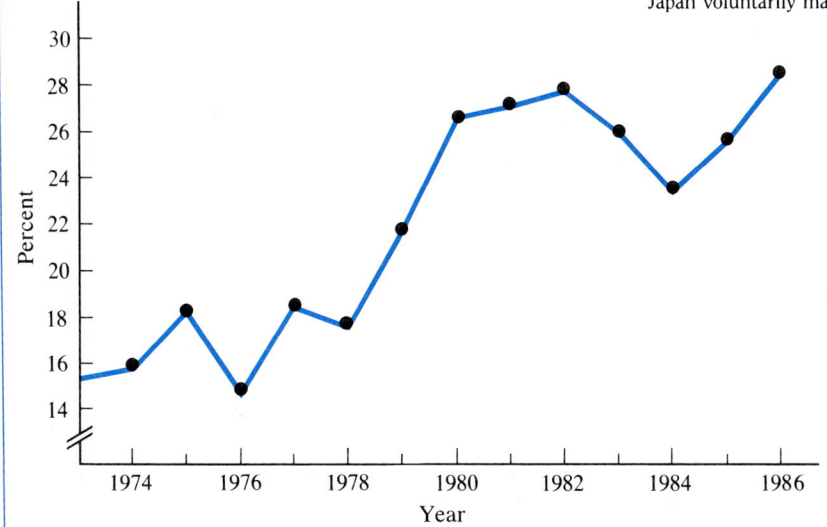

FIGURE 9B-3. The Share of Imported Cars. Since 1978, the share of imported cars (as a percentage of new car sales in the United States) has increased sharply. (*Source: Survey of Current Business*, various issues.)

competitive market make above-normal profits, and we haven't told you how to organize a low-cost firm. High profits are more common in the imperfectly competitive markets we study in Chapters 11 and 12. But carefully following the approach to decision making used in this chapter will save you from costly mistakes both in business and in everyday life. If you remember nothing else, remember to avoid the sunk cost fallacy!

Summary

1. The perfectly competitive firm takes as given the price at which it can sell its output. It acts as a price taker, unlike imperfectly competitive firms, which are price makers.
2. For a market to be perfectly competitive, there must be many sellers, each small relative to the market; product homogeneity; well-informed buyers; free entry and exit by firms; and independent decisions by both suppliers and demanders. Some industries, especially in agriculture, satisfy these conditions, but the competitive model is useful even when these conditions hold only approximately.
3. If it produces at all, a perfectly competitive firm maximizes its profit by producing the optimal positive level of output at which the revenue from an extra unit sold—the market price—is equal to marginal cost. This is true in both the short run ($P = MC$) and the long run ($P = LMC$).
4. In the short run the costs of fixed inputs do not affect the quantity supplied. A competitive firm maximizes profit by producing only if price is at least equal to average variable cost ($P \geq AVC$). Otherwise, the firm can reduce its losses by shutting down temporarily.
5. The short-run supply curve of a perfectly competitive firm coincides with the portion of its marginal cost curve that is above its shutdown price, which is the minimum value of average variable cost.
6. The short-run market supply curve is obtained by adding (horizontally) the supply curves of the firms in the market. At each price the total quantity supplied is the sum of the quantities supplied by each firm.
7. In the long run, all factors of production are variable and all costs must be covered. A perfectly competitive firm produces in the long run only if price is at least equal to long-run average cost ($P \geq LAC$). Otherwise, it leaves the industry.
8. The long-run supply curve of a perfectly competitive firm coincides with the portion of its long-run marginal cost curve that is above its long-run break-even price, which is the minimum value of long-run average cost.
9. The long-run industry supply curve is flatter than the short-run industry supply curve both because each firm's long-run supply curve is flatter than its short-run supply curve and because there is entry and exit of firms in the long run.
10. If all firms have identical technologies and can acquire inputs at prices that are independent of industry output, they will all have the same long-run average and marginal cost schedules. The market's long-run supply curve will be flat in this case; any quantity demanded will be supplied at a constant price equal to the minimum value of long-run average cost.
11. In the short run the industry supply curve is shifted mainly by changes in the prices of variable factors. In the long run changes in all factor costs and technical change shift the supply curve.
12. In both the short run and the long run, the supply curve of a perfectly competitive industry is the industry's marginal cost curve.

Key Terms

Perfectly competitive firm
Perfectly competitive market
Price taker and price maker
Marginal condition
Optimal positive output
Total condition, or profit check
Sunk cost fallacy
Firm's short-run supply curve
Short-run shutdown price
Short-run break-even price
Market's short-run supply curve
Firm's long-run supply curve
Long-run break-even price
Above-normal profits
Technical progress
Industry's marginal cost curve

Problems

1. Explain why a firm in a perfectly competitive market would not cut its price below the market level to attract more customers. Use Figure 9-1 as part of your explanation.
2. (*a*) Can you think of any nonagricultural markets that are perfectly competitive? Explain your choice in terms of the five criteria set out in section 1. (*b*) Which, if any, of the following industries are close to being perfectly competitive? Explain your answer in each case in terms of the five criteria. (i) soft drinks, (ii) fast-food restaurants, (iii) the automobile industry, (iv) the sock industry, (v) the market for apartment rentals in your town or city.
3. When farm prices are low, farmers say they are losing money. Why, then, do they continue in production? Explain, showing what must be the relationship between price, *ATC*, and *AVC* in this case.
4. Show the effect of a large increase in wages on the short-run and long-run quantities of output supplied by a competitive firm.
5. In the short run a firm is doing as well as it can but is making losses because $P < ATC$. Is it possible that the firm should stay in business in the long run even if price remains at the current level? Illustrate your answer by showing the relationship between the *ATC* and *LAC* curves.
6. Consider two competitive firms in the same market that have identical technologies and fixed inputs and face the same factor prices. (*a*) Draw the short-run supply curve for one firm. Now show what the industry supply curve looks like. (*b*) Suppose a third firm is added which has smaller quantities of fixed inputs. What does the industry supply curve look like now?
7. Show a situation where initially an industry is in long-run equilibrium. Now assume price increases. (*a*) Show the short-run adjustment of the industry. (*b*) Show the long-run adjustment and explain how it differs from the short-run response. (*c*) Do the firms initially in the industry make more profit in the short run or in the long run?
8. Suppose there is an increase in factor prices but the market price remains unchanged. What happens to the number of firms in the industry in the short run? In the long run?
9. The U.S. government is considering reducing the support price for milk. (*a*) Show the short-run and long-run adjustment of price, quantity, and profits. (*b*) Do you think the long-run supply curve of the dairy industry is perfectly elastic? Why or why not?
10. Will an increase in the price of fertilizer have a greater effect on the price of wheat in the short run or in the long run?

Chapter 10
The Invisible Hand: Competition and Economic Efficiency

In 1776 Adam Smith, one of the founding fathers of economics, argued that competing individuals acting only for their own gain are led, as if by an invisible hand, also to promote the public interest.[1] Following Smith, many economists have developed the argument that competition is good for society as a whole.

Experience certainly suggests that competition benefits buyers because it implies lower prices or better service. For instance, in 1985, when the Northrop Corporation offered its Tigershark plane to the U.S. Air Force in competition with General Dynamics's F-16, General Dynamics reduced the price of the F-16 by 30 percent, or $6 million. When Japan agreed to limit its car exports to the United States, thus reducing competition for U.S. producers, U.S. producers raised their car prices. For the first 20 years that Eastern Airlines operated its shuttle flights between New York and Boston it served no refreshments on the trip; when Pan Am opened a competing shuttle in 1986, Eastern began serving snacks and drinks during the flight.

But the exact lesson of these examples is not so clear. In each case consumers are made better off by competition, but some producer is being made worse off by lower prices. In some cases more competition even makes *some* consumers worse off. When the Bell System, AT&T, was broken up and competitors entered the long-distance telephone business, long-distance rates fell but local telephone rates went up. The increased competition made callers who used mainly local service worse off.

Adam Smith and later economists have shown that *perfect* competition is good for the economy as a whole because it leads to an *efficient* allocation of resources, one in which there is no waste. We begin in section 1 by defining and discussing the notion of efficiency used in this context. We then show why perfect competition leads to efficiency. The central insight is that well-informed buyers and sellers trade only when both are made better off. Thus voluntary exchange tends to guide resource use in directions that make participants in the economy better off. We use the analysis of consumer demand and business supply developed in earlier chapters to show that exactly the right amount of production

[1] Adam Smith, *The Weath of Nations*, Modern Library Edition, 1937, p. 423.

and exchange occurs in perfectly competitive markets. Sections 2 and 3 focus on a single market, and section 4 considers a whole economy composed of perfectly competitive markets.

The material discussed in this chapter is central to understanding the virtues—and some of the limitations—of the price system. It is thus also central to comparisons between capitalism and alternative economic systems.

1. Efficient Resource Allocation

The benefits of competition have been generally understood since Adam Smith and perhaps even before, but the precise sense in which perfect competition allocates resources efficiently was formally defined by the Italian economist Vilfredo Pareto (1848–1923).[2] Economists use his definition of efficiency, called Pareto efficiency.[3]

● **Resources are allocated *(Pareto) efficiently* when no person can be made better off without some other person being made worse off.**

In a Pareto-efficient situation there is no waste. If after society has decided what, how, and for whom to produce it is still possible to make at least one person better off without making another person worse off, resources are being wasted. The extra output obtained by eliminating that waste can be used to make somebody better off without hurting anyone else. In the rest of this chapter, we demonstrate that perfectly competitive markets produce a Pareto-efficient allocation of resources.

Pareto efficiency offers a criterion for telling whether in a particular situation there is or is not waste. But this criterion does not by itself tell us how resources *should* be allocated because it relates to only two of the three basic economic questions: what to produce and how to produce it. It completely steers clear of the tough issue of *for whom* to produce. Resources may be (Pareto) efficiently allocated even in situations of extreme inequality, where some people are starving and others are living in opulence.

Efficiency and Equity

A simple example will serve to clarify the notion of Pareto efficiency. Consider an economy in which there are only two people, Diane and Marge. The *utility possibility frontier* in Figure 10-1 shows combinations of the utility levels that can be attained by Diane and Marge. Each of them derives utility only from the goods she herself consumes. Given the amount of resources in the economy, the frontier shows for each level of Marge's utility the maximum level of utility that can be attained by Diane.

The utility possibility frontier is negatively sloped because if no resources are wasted, making one person better off necessarily means taking resources from the

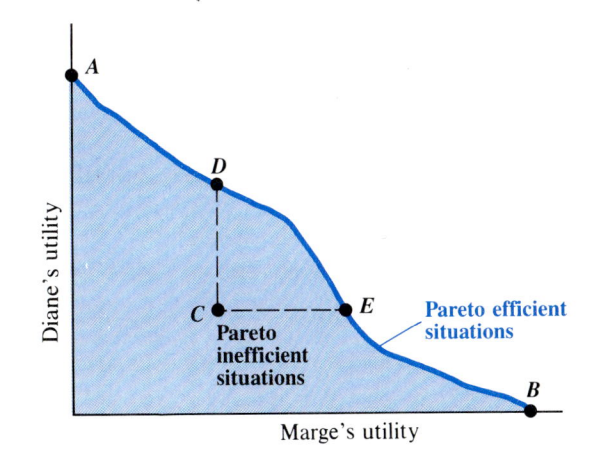

FIGURE 10-1. The Utility Possibility Frontier. The frontier shows for each level of utility attainable by Marge the maximum utility level that can be reached by Diane. From any point within the frontier, such as C, at least one person can be made better off without hurting the other by moving to the frontier. Points inside the frontier are thus not Pareto-efficient. It is not possible to compare points on the frontier using the concept of Pareto efficiency.

---

[2] Pareto's greatest work, published in 1909, is available in translation as *Manual of Political Economy*, Augustus M. Kelley, New York, 1971. Before becoming a professor at the University of Lausanne, Switzerland, Pareto had been an engineer and manager of railroad companies.

[3] Economists use the terms "Pareto efficiency" and "Pareto optimality" interchangeably.

other person and hence making her worse off.[4] The only points that can be attained are those *on* or *inside* the frontier. Points above the frontier cannot be reached because resources are scarce.

At point A, all of society's goods have been given to Diane. Her utility is at the maximum level it can reach given the available goods. (Remember that she derives utility only from her own consumption and thus is not upset by the fact that she has everything and Marge has nothing.) At point B, Marge has all available goods and her utility is similarly at its maximum possible level. Moving from A to B, there is a trade-off as goods are transferred from Diane to Marge, with Diane getting steadily worse off and Marge becoming better off. *Both points A and B are Pareto-efficient, because in neither situation can one person be made better off without the other being made worse off.*

Now consider points C, D, and E. Point C is not Pareto-efficient. From point C it is possible to make Diane better off by moving to point D on the utility possibility frontier. It is also possible to make Marge better off by moving to point E. Indeed, at any point between D and E both people are better off than they are at C. The concept of Pareto efficiency is useful in identifying situations such as C, from which at least one person can be made better off without someone else becoming worse off.

The main limitation of the concept of Pareto efficiency is that it does not give us any way to rank points *on* the utility possibility frontier. Moving from D to E, for example, makes Marge better off, but at the expense of Diane, who becomes worse off. Both D and E are Pareto-efficient points, because it's not possible to make one person better off at D or E without making the other worse off. Points A and B are also Pareto-efficient. In fact, *all* the points *on* the utility possibility frontier are Pareto-efficient. On the other hand, no point *inside* the utility possibility frontier is Pareto-efficient, because by moving to the frontier we can make at least one person better off without reducing the utility of the other person.

The notion of Pareto efficiency rests on the relatively

[4] We are excluding here the possibility of altruism, in which one person's happiness increases another's utility. In such a situation the utility possibility schedule would not necessarily be negatively sloped throughout.

uncontroversial value judgment that waste is a bad thing, since somebody can be made better off if waste can be eliminated. But this value judgment is not enough to tell us completely how resources should be allocated. In order to choose among Pareto-efficient points, we must deal explicitly with the question of fairness or equity. While most people agree that waste is a bad thing, it is much harder to get agreement about these other issues. Most of us think that points A and B in Figure 10-1 are "unfair," for instance, but there is no reason why we (let alone Marge and Diane) would be likely to pick the same Pareto-efficient point as socially best. There is no scientific, value-free way to choose among Pareto-efficient resource allocations.

Efficiency and Value Judgments

The rest of this chapter shows that the allocation of resources is Pareto-efficient when markets are perfectly competitive. In other words, perfectly competitive markets ensure that the economy automatically reaches a point on the utility possibility schedule—a point where no person can be made better off without someone else being made worse off. But does this mean that competitive, Pareto-efficient resource allocations are socially optimal in any sense? Unfortunately not. There is no reason to think that a competitive economy will wind up at the socially best Pareto-efficient point.

Everyone in society may agree that a more equal distribution of income is preferable to a less equal one, for instance. Thus points such as D in Figure 10-1 are generally preferred to those with extreme inequality, such as A and B. But nothing prevents a competitive economy from producing an extremely unequal distribution of income. In that case the allocation of resources would be Pareto-efficient but not necessarily socially optimal, because society would prefer to be at some other point on the utility possibility frontier.

In fact, many of the most controversial issues in economics and politics *are* about policies that would benefit one group (tenants, farmers, automobile producers) at the expense of others. These issues involve social values and the worthiness of different groups of people, and economists' training gives them no special expertise in such matters. They are not especially able to judge the worthiness of farmers, for instance, or to decide whether the family farm is a unique institution, the backbone of the country's values, which deserves taxpayer support to ensure that it continues to survive.

Does this mean that the concept of Pareto efficiency and the conclusion that perfectly competitive markets allocate resources efficiently is valuable only in debates about the merits of capitalism? It does not. The concept of Pareto efficiency is a very useful one, because eliminating waste is always a good idea.

There are many instances where economists equipped with an understanding of the notion of Pareto efficiency can play a major role in identifying *efficient* ways of using scarce resources in implementing policy objectives. For instance, economists can often show that there are cheaper ways than current farm programs of giving farmers the level of income that politicians think they deserve. Or economists can compute the cost to consumers (in higher automobile prices) of each automobile worker's job saved by restricting imports (the figure in 1984 was $165,000 per year) and suggest cheaper ways of helping those people while allowing consumers to benefit from the competition provided by foreign automobile producers. Thus the concept of Pareto efficiency is far from useless in making decisions about public policy.

2. The Price System and Efficiency

In this section we show how individual perfectly competitive markets allocate resources efficiently. We show first that in perfectly competitive equilibrium the valuation of an extra unit of output by consumers exactly equals the marginal cost of producing that extra unit. We then discuss the implications of this equality, first for social optimality and then for the operation of the price system.

Marginal Cost and Marginal Valuation

Chapter 9 showed that the supply curve in a perfectly competitive market is the marginal cost curve of the supplying industry. Thus at each level of output, the supply curve shows the cost to the industry and to the economy as a whole of increasing the industry's output by 1 unit.[5] The marginal cost curve can also be interpreted as showing the value in alternative uses (in other industries, for instance) of the resources now used to produce the last unit of output in this industry.

On the other side of the market, we saw in Chapter 6 that the demand curve measures consumers' marginal valuation of the product. At each level of output, the demand curve shows how much consumers are willing to pay for an extra unit of the good.

Since the market equilibrium point is reached where the supply and demand curves cross, it follows that

● **The equilibrium price in a perfectly competitive market is equal to both the valuation by consumers of an extra unit of the good and the cost to the economy of producing an extra unit of the good.**

Thus the following equality holds at the equilibrium point in a perfectly competitive market:

$$\text{Marginal valuation by consumers} = \text{price} = \text{marginal cost of production} \quad (1)$$

Figure 10-2 illustrates this condition. At outputs below the perfectly competitive equilibrium level, Q_0, consumers are willing to pay more than marginal cost for an additional unit of output. For example, at output level Q_1, consumers are willing to pay $4 for an extra unit of the good. This exceeds the marginal cost to the economy of producing 1 more unit, which is $2 in this case. Thus consumers can be made better off by reducing the use of labor and other productive resources in other industries and reallocating them to this particular market so that output can be increased. In a market economy this happens automatically. As long as consumers are willing to pay more than marginal cost for additional output, firms will expand output to maximize profit and consumers will buy the increased production in order to maximize utility. Both parties gain from further production and exchange whenever output is below the perfectly competitive equilibrium level.

---

[5] Costs to the industry are the same as costs to the economy as a whole only if all other markets in the economy are competitive, including markets for capital, labor, and other productive inputs, and none of the other sources of market failure discussed in Chapter 3 are present. We make these assumptions in this chapter, since our focus is on economies that are perfectly competitive throughout.

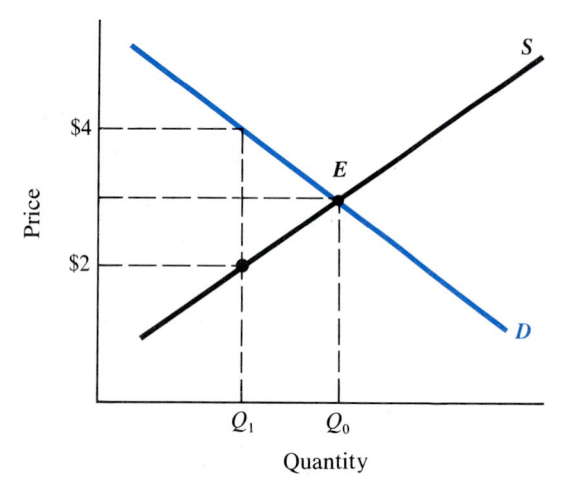

FIGURE 10-2. Supply and Demand in a Competitive Industry. The supply curve in a competitive industry shows the marginal cost of production of each additional unit of the good. The demand curve represents the valuation consumers put on each extra unit of the good. For instance, at quantity Q_1, consumers are willing to pay $4 for an extra unit of the good, and marginal cost is only $2.

On the other hand, if output exceeds that level, the savings in cost from a reduction in output will exceed the loss to consumers. Efficiency thus calls for a reduction in output: Resource use should be cut back in this industry, since the alternative uses are more valuable to consumers. Only at point E is the marginal valuation of consumers exactly equal to the marginal cost of producing an extra unit. There is no way to produce and sell more so as to make both buyers and sellers better off, since no buyer is willing to pay the marginal cost of production.

Social Optimality

At point E each consumer values the last unit of his or her purchases at its marginal cost, or the cost of producing that output. Thus, given each consumer's income, the competitive market allocates resources efficiently: At any point other than E all consumers could be made better off. If less than Q_0 were being produced, all consumers would be willing to pay more than the marginal cost of producing an extra unit of output in order to increase output in this market. If more than Q_0 were being produced, each consumer would value the last unit of the good consumed at less than its marginal cost and would be made better off if the resources used in producing that good were used to produce *other* goods instead.

Thus, *given each consumer's income*, a competitive market makes each consumer as well off as possible. Hence the allocation of resources is Pareto-efficient. But as we have noted, it is not necessarily socially optimal. In saying that markets allocate resources efficiently, we implicitly take the distribution of income in the society as given. To make the leap from Pareto efficiency to social optimality we need to argue that the existing distribution of income in society is optimal.

Markets treat the dollars spent by millionaires exactly the same way they treat dollars spent by the homeless. If, as is sometimes said, people vote with their dollars to decide the allocation of resources in a market economy, the rich have more votes than the poor. For instance, the marginal value placed on food in a competitive market is the same for all individuals. But if income were redistributed toward the poor, the poorest people in society would consume more food, each consumer's marginal valuation of food would change, and the quantity of food produced would change.[6] The distribution of income thus determines both the economy's valuations of particular goods and the particular Pareto-efficient allocation of resources produced by perfect competition.

In what follows we describe market valuations as society's valuations. This is strictly true only if the current distribution of income is socially optimal, and this is necessarily a controversial assumption. Some people contend that there can be nothing close to "optimal" about the distribution of income in a wealthy society like ours in which almost half of all black children live in poverty. However, others reply that if people did not on balance approve of the existing distribution of income, they would ask their elected representatives to use taxes and transfers to change it. In fact, many policies that interfere with the operation of competitive markets do so

[6] Of course, the formerly rich would consume less. But because the income elasticity of food consumption is less than 1, the increase in consumption by the formerly poor would almost certainly outweigh the reduction in consumption by the formerly rich.

to affect the distribution of income. At any rate, with its controversial nature noted, we proceed to employ the assumption that the distribution of income is optimal. In this special case the price system in competitive markets will ensure the socially optimal resource allocation—the right point on the utility possibility frontier.

The Role of Prices

In a competitive market economy, prices guide resources to their optimal uses. For instance, under competition the price at which she can sell a bicycle guides the producer's decision whether to incur the marginal cost of making another one. The price is also the basis on which the consumer decides whether to buy one. He generally cares nothing about the marginal cost of bicycle production; he uses the price to decide whether he'd be better off buying a bicycle or buying something else.

Similarly, the market price of wheat equals the marginal value to consumers of having more wheat available. If a farmer decides to produce more wheat, the marginal value of that production to consumers must at least equal its marginal cost or resources will be wasted. If both buyers and sellers are well informed, wheat and bicycles get produced and bought only when both parties are made better off as a consequence. The market price, by intermediating between the consumer and the producer, makes consumers' valuations of a product equal to the marginal cost of production.

Prices also guide the market system's response to changes in demand and cost conditions. Suppose the demand curve for oranges shifts from D to D' in Figure 10-3. Suppose that in the very short run firms can't adjust their outputs and continue to produce quantity Q_0, the initial equilibrium quantity. Now consumers value an extra orange at P_2, well above the marginal cost of production. Society as a whole can be made better off if more oranges are produced, because consumers are willing to give up P_2 to obtain another orange but it costs only P_0 to increase orange production by 1 unit.

If output remains at Q_0, price will rise to P_2. Because price is above marginal cost, firms can increase their profits by growing more oranges. And they will keep expanding orange output until the industry is in equi-

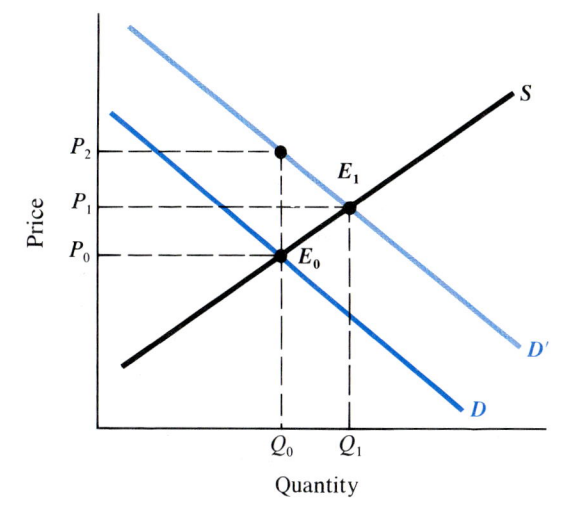

FIGURE 10-3. A Shift in Demand in a Competitive Industry. When demand shifts from D to D', consumers value an extra unit of the good more highly than before. Before the shift, output was Q_0, with consumers valuing an extra unit at P_0. Now they value an extra unit of the good when output is at Q_0 at P_2. Because consumers' valuation of goods has risen, output expands until a new equilibrium is reached at E_1.

librium at point E_1, with equilibrium price and quantity at P_1 and Q_1. At this new equilibrium the level of output is optimal from the point of view of society as a whole.

Throughout this process, consumers and producers focused entirely on price. Consumers didn't have to know anything about the techniques or costs of orange production, and producers didn't have to ask consumers how much they were willing to pay for more oranges. No central direction or planning was necessary. Prices conveyed all the necessary information to all the participants in this market.

3. Consumers' and Producers' Surplus

In this section we reintroduce *consumers' surplus* and introduce the similar concept of *producers' surplus*. These provide another way of seeing why a competitive equilibrium is efficient. They are also used to analyze the effects of monopoly and other distortions.

Consumers' Surplus

In Chapter 6 we defined consumers' surplus as follows:

● **Consumers' surplus** is the difference between the maximum amount consumers would be willing to pay for the quantity of a good they demand and the amount they actually pay. It is measured as the area between the demand curve and a horizontal line at the market price.

Figure 10-4 shows a typical downward-sloping demand curve which indicates the marginal value of each unit of the good consumed in any particular period. The demand curve slopes downward because reductions in the price of any good or service encourage consumers to switch to it and away from substitute products. At lower prices, consumers use more of the good, thus buying units with lower marginal value. The lower the price of hamburgers, the more hamburgers will be eaten each week;

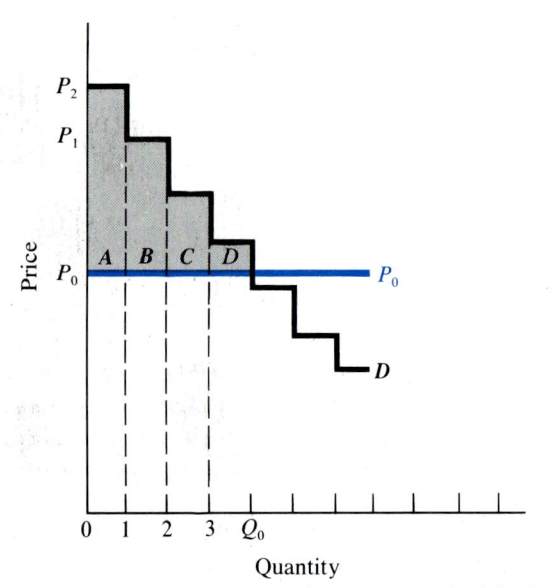

FIGURE 10-4. Consumers' Surplus. The step schedule, D, is the demand curve. Consumers are willing to pay P_2 for the first unit of the good but pay only P_0. Therefore $(P_2 - P_0)$, shown as the shaded area A, is the consumers' surplus on the first unit. They are willing to pay P_1 for the second unit but pay only P_0; thus B is the consumers' surplus on the second unit, and so on. The entire shaded area is the total consumers' surplus when market price is P_0.

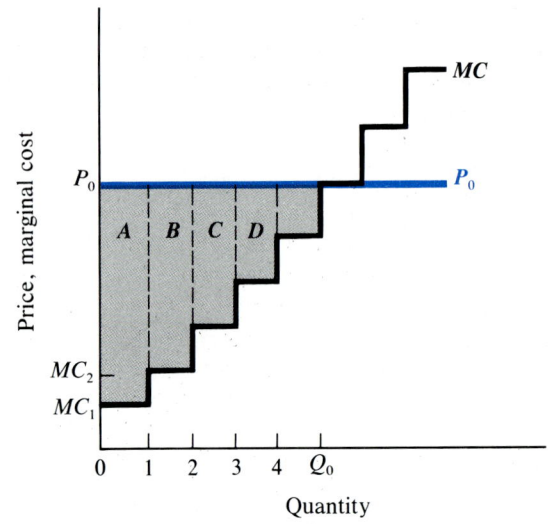

FIGURE 10-5. Producers' Surplus. The marginal cost schedule, MC, is shown with steps. Price is P_0. The firm produces the first unit of output at a cost of MC_1 but sells it at price P_0; it realizes a surplus equal to the shaded area A. The producers' surplus asociated with the second unit of output is B, and so on. If the firm or industry produces amount Q_0, the total producers' surplus is the entire shaded area.

the more hamburgers eaten each week, the less pleasure the last one will bring.

We assume that consumers can in fact purchase any amount of the good at a given price, P_0. We are interested in the amount consumers are willing to pay and the amount they actually pay. Consumers are willing to pay P_2 to obtain the first unit of the good, but they have to pay only P_0. They thus have a surplus of $P_2 - P_0$ on the first unit, equal to area A. They have a surplus equal to area B on the second unit. In total, measured in dollars, consumers' surplus associated with a price P_0 is equal to the shaded area.

The shaded area in Figure 10-4 represents the total benefits consumers receive from being able to buy the good at price P_0. If we are willing to take a further step, we can also interpret it as *society's* valuation of consumers' surplus. This step is to assume that a dollar's worth of benefits to any consumer is also a dollar's worth of benefits to society. This is equivalent to assuming that the distribution of income in society is optimal, an assumption which we have already discussed and which we flag yet again. Without this assumption we cannot meaningfully add surpluses across individuals.

Producers' Surplus

There is also a surplus to be measured on the supply side. Firms derive producers' surplus on every unit of a good that they sell at a price in excess of the marginal cost of producing *that unit*.[7]

Figure 10-5 shows how to calculate producers' surplus. The supply curve shows the marginal cost of producing each unit of output. This is the minimum price at which producers would be willing to sell that unit of output. But if actual price is P_0, then producers' surplus will equal the shaded area in Figure 10-5. The derivation is exactly the same as it was for consumers' surplus in Figure 10-4. Producers are willing to sell the first unit at MC_1, but they can sell it at a higher price, P_0. They therefore enjoy a surplus equal to the shaded bar labeled A. A second unit can be produced at MC_2; with a sales price of P_0, it yields a producers' surplus equal to the area labeled B. Total producers' surplus then consists of the entire shaded area above the MC curve and below the given price.

● ***Producers' surplus* equals the cumulative excess of price over the marginal cost of production. It is measured as the area between the supply curve and a horizontal line at the market price.**

Efficiency of Competitive Equilibrium

We now show that in equilibrium in a perfectly competitive market, producers' plus consumers' surplus is maximized. We combine the analyses in Figures 10-4 and 10-5.

Consider the equilibrium at point E in Figure 10-6. Suppose instead of the equilibrium output, Q_0, output

---

[7] This surplus doesn't necessarily all show up in the form of profit. If wine producers rent their land, those rents will probably increase if the demand for wine rises sharply. In general, some producers' surplus will take the form of economic rents (which are discussed in Chapter 16) received by the suppliers of specialized inputs.

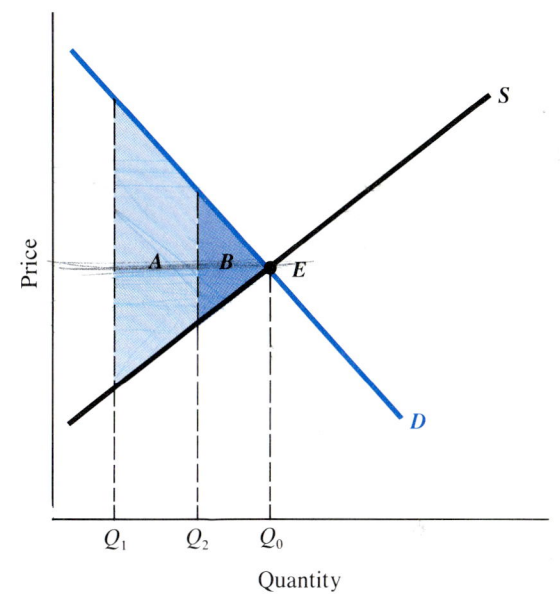

FIGURE 10-6. Consumers' and Producers' Surplus and Efficient Production. In moving from output level Q_1 to Q_2, the gain in consumers' plus producers' surplus is shown by the shaded area labeled A. Output should be expanded as long as there is a surplus (consumers' plus producers') from doing so. By moving from Q_2 to output level Q_0, society gains the extra area of surplus, B. Consumers' plus producers' surplus is maximized at the competitive equilibrium, E.

were only Q_1. How much would society gain from an expansion to Q_2? We saw earlier that increasing output raises social welfare if the marginal valuation by consumers exceeds the social cost of the extra resources required, which is given by marginal cost. Using the surplus concepts just developed, we can now argue that the gain in welfare for society as a whole is the increase in consumers' surplus plus the increase in producers' surplus. That sum is equal to the shaded area between the demand curve and the MC curve. We thus have a ready measure of the value to society of an expansion in output in any industry.

● **The value to society of an expansion in output in any industry is equal to the sum of extra consumers' surplus and extra producers' surplus. This is given by the area between the demand curve and the supply curve between the old and new output levels.**

In Figure 10-6 the shaded area labeled A measures the benefit of increasing output from Q_1 to Q_2. From the diagram it is clear that there is a net gain: At output level Q_1 the marginal valuation by consumers exceeds marginal cost, so that increasing output to Q_2 raises welfare by the entire area labeled A. Hence output should be increased to Q_2. But at Q_2 marginal valuation still exceeds marginal cost, so that output should be increased even further. In fact it should be increased all the way to point Q_0, since an increase from Q_2 to Q_0 will raise total surplus further, by an amount equal to area B. If output is increased beyond Q_0, total surplus falls because consumers value the additional output at less than the marginal cost of producing it. Thus at point Q_0 the sum of consumers' and producers' surplus is maximized.

The analysis of consumers' and producers' surplus shows why the perfectly competitive equilibrium is efficient: Any departure from it makes buyers and sellers together worse off. If output is below the competitive equilibrium level, not enough of the good is being produced: There is a net gain to producers and consumers if more is produced. If output is above the equilibrium level, a reduction in output will increase the sum of consumers' and producers' surplus, thus producing a net gain for society as a whole.

Only under perfect competition do profit-maximizing firms and consumers interact to establish an equilibrium in which marginal valuation equals marginal cost and the sum of producers' and consumers' surplus is maximized. Under monopoly and other forms of imperfect competition, supply is restricted so that consumers' valuation of goods exceeds their marginal cost. Since consumers' plus producers' surplus is maximized only at the competitive output level, it follows that the increase in profits produced by monopolistic output restriction is less than the fall in consumers' surplus. We develop these points in detail in Chapter 11.

Efficiency and Equity

Despite the efficiency of competitive markets and the competitiveness of agricultural markets, the U.S. government spends billions of dollars each year to subsidize farmers by raising the prices of agricultural products. Many other countries have similar policies. Governments defend these and other actions that overrule competitive markets by appealing to notions of equity or fairness.

In terms of Figure 10-1, it is not unreasonable to prefer inefficient point C to efficient points A and B. If competitive markets could yield only either A or B, it would be hard to get excited about the virtues of competition or efficiency. If point C could be obtained only by overruling the results of competition (by imposing price controls, for instance), society would face a trade-off between equity and efficiency. As the discussion of rent control in Box 10-1 indicates, some choices of this sort do arise in practice. In these cases economists can contribute by computing the costs of achieving a "fair" allocation of resources and seeking to reduce that cost.

Whenever Pareto efficiency is sacrificed in the name of fairness or to achieve some other worthy goal, the dollar gains to those who are helped are less than the cost to those who are hurt, since total surplus is not maximized. Economists seek to reduce the net cost of achieving the aims of such policies. After the net cost of achieving fairness or any other noneconomic goal has been made as small as possible, it requires a value judgment to decide whether the cost should be incurred. If it cost at least $1000 in taxes to transfer $1 to the truly needy, for instance, society might well decide that these transfers were too expensive—though they would serve a worthy purpose. This would be a value judgment, and as we noted previously, there is no scientific way to put a price on fairness.

Economists can make another kind of contribution as well. The point on society's utility possibility frontier that is reached by a competitive economy depends on who owns what resources. If Diane owns all the capital in society, competition will yield a point near A on the frontier in Figure 10-1; increasing Marge's share of capital will move the competitive outcome toward B. If there were a way of redistributing resources between individuals that did not affect efficiency, then a competitive economy could reach *any* Pareto-optimal allocation. This result means that it may be possible to find ways of producing fair allocations of resources that are also efficient. Economists involved in policymaking work to find ways of doing this.

Box 10-1. Rent Control in the Short Run and in the Long Run

During World War II, few resources were devoted to building new housing in the United States. At the end of the war, millions of soldiers, sailors, and marines came home, married, and looked for places to live. In most cities the demand curve for apartments shifted sharply to the right. Because the supply of apartments is inelastic in the short run, rents rose dramatically.

This is exactly what should happen under perfect competition. When rents are high, this means that new apartments are valued highly by consumers and that it is profitable to build them. But high rents also make landlords wealthier and tenants poorer. At the end of World War II, it was argued that since many of the new tenants had just fought for their country, while landlords had done nothing to make themselves especially deserving, the sharp increase in rents was simply unfair. Rent controls seemed to be an easy way to restore fairness to the housing market, and many cities adopted rent control programs.

Rent controls are ceilings imposed on the amount of rent a landlord is allowed to charge a tenant. The short-run effects of rent controls are shown in Figure 10B-1a. The short-run supply curve, S_S, and the short-run demand curve, D_S, are both inelastic. The short-run equilibrium rent in this market is P_S; rent controls, however, prohibit landlords from charging more than P_C and as a result restrict supply to Q_{SS}. The controls produce an excess demand equal to $Q_{DS} - Q_{SS}$ because more apartments are demanded at price P_C than are supplied at that price. If the demand and supply curves are steep enough, this gap will not be large enough to produce long lines of people seeking apartments.

Who in the queue will get the apartments? One rule is first come, first served. But often controls lead to a black market where those who cannot get an apartment make under-the-table payments to landlords to be put ahead in the queue. Black markets are common whenever goods are rationed, whether it is food and clothing in the Soviet Union or apartments in New York.

Imposing controls reduces producers' surplus. The *net*

FIGURE 10B-1. The Short-Run and Long-Run Effects of Rent Control. In both the short run (a) and the long run (b), limiting rents to P_C transfers an amount equal to A from landlords to consumers and produces a net loss to society as a whole equal to the sum of areas B and C. In the long run the transfer is smaller and the loss is higher than in the short run.

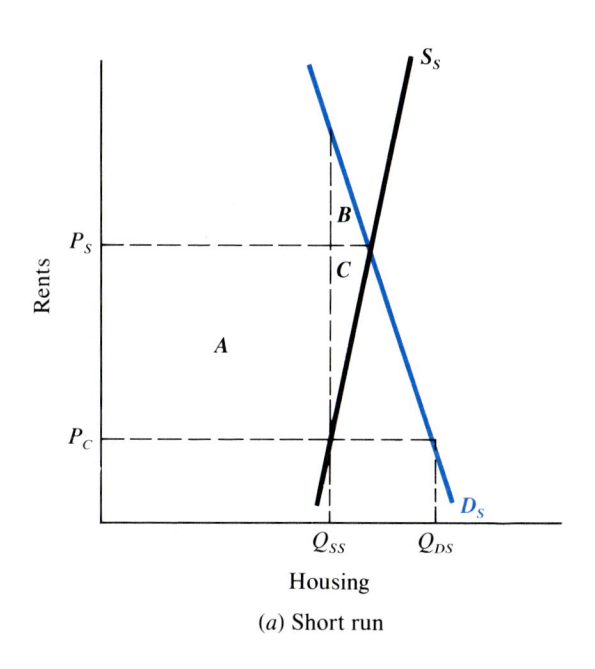

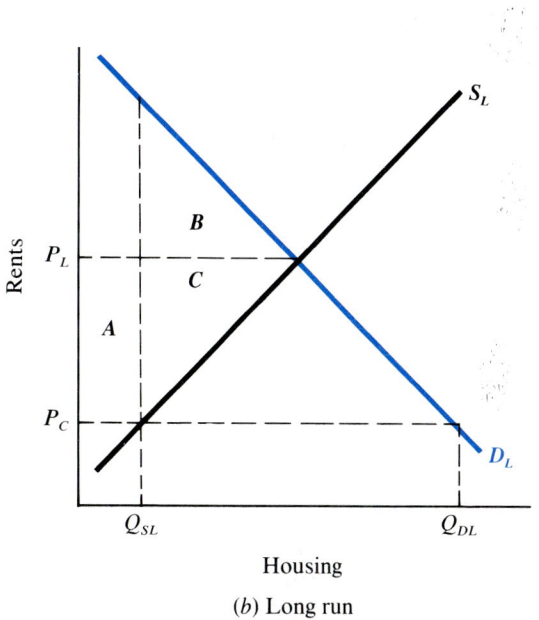

(a) Short run

(b) Long run

reduction in producers' surplus is the sum of areas A and C. Of these, area A represents a transfer from producers to consumers as a result of the reduced rent. Area C represents a loss of producers' surplus resulting from fewer apartments being rented out. The net increase in consumers' surplus is the difference between area A (reduced rents on available apartments) and area B (lost surplus on apartments not supplied because of low rents). To calculate the net cost to society as a whole we look at the sum of changes in consumers' and producers' surplus. This sum is equal to the areas B and C. Thus rent control brings with it a net cost. But at the same time it allows a transfer of area A from landlords to tenants. This is the cost of achieving "fairness." The benefit-cost ratio for rent control is the ratio $A/(B + C)$. By experimenting with the demand and supply schedules we can show that when these are very inelastic, the benefit-cost ratio is relatively favorable.

But saying that the short-run benefit-cost ratio is favorable is not a decisive argument for rent control. It neglects two issues. First, fairness may not really require that rents be reduced. After all, some tenants are rich and many landlords are not. If the real concern is with the welfare of returning veterans, why not simply give them money and let them spend it as they like? Landlords may not be especially deserving, but their profits will be short-lived if high rents caused by increased demand induce others to construct lots of new apartments.

Second, even if fairness does require that rents be reduced, so that society really does face a trade-off between equity and efficiency, the long-run costs of fairness may be much higher than the short-run costs. Figure 10B-1b shows the long-run effects of rent controls. The long-run demand (D_L) and supply (S_L) curves are more elastic than are the short-run curves shown in Figure 10B-1a. Because of this, the excess demand for rental housing, $Q_{DL} - Q_{SL}$, is much larger in the long run. In the long run landlords have much more scope for reducing the supply of housing in response to a reduction in rents by simply not maintaining buildings or closing them down. The amount transferred from landlords to tenants is smaller, because the supply of housing has been reduced, and the cost of that transfer has increased.

Note: For an interesting—and discouraging—discussion of the effects of New York City's long-standing rent control program which confirms the implication that rent controls reduce the long-run supply of housing, see "Urban Decay and Regulatory Sprawl," *Regulation*, September/October 1985.

The discussion of rent control in Box 10-1 offers an application of welfare economics. Another issue on which you may have a view is day care. Should society provide day care facilities for all mothers who are working? Or should working mothers (and fathers) simply receive a tax credit which is sufficient to buy day care? Or should society ignore the special problems of working parents? One easy answer is that society should provide day care facilities for whoever needs them. But what if an extra hour of day care costs $39 but is worth only $13 to working mothers?

We cannot simply make a long list of things government "ought" to provide and not ask who pays. At the least we must ask whether at the margin the various services are worth to their beneficiaries what it costs society to deliver them. Society, through the political process, may decide to provide services for which marginal benefit falls far short of marginal cost. But because resources are limited, it should at least be aware of the costs of the provisions it is making on the grounds of fairness.

4. Economywide Competition and Pareto Efficiency[8]

We turn now from the study of equilibrium in a single competitive market to consider general, economywide equilibrium in an economy in which all markets are perfectly competitive. Our analysis builds on the properties of consumer behavior and competitive supply developed in earlier chapters. We show that when consumers maximize utility, equating ratios of marginal utilities to price ratios, and firms equate marginal costs to the prices they face, economywide resources will be efficiently allocated.

We look first at consumers, then at producers, and finally at markets. We compare the requirements for Pareto efficiency with the implications of utility maximization, then profit maximization, and finally market equilibrium.

---

[8] *Note to instructors*: The material in this section is more difficult than the rest of the chapter and may be omitted without loss of continuity.

Consumer Behavior and Efficiency in Consumption

In Chapter 6 we showed that a consumer allocating his budget optimally equates the ratio of the marginal utilities of any two goods to the ratio of their prices. Thus if we limit our attention to two goods, apples (A) and bananas (B), each individual in the economy sets

$$\frac{MU_A}{MU_B} = \frac{P_A}{P_B} \qquad (2)$$

The left-hand side of equation (2), the ratio of marginal utilities, is equal to the consumer's marginal rate of substitution of apples for bananas.[9]

● The *marginal rate of substitution* of good A for good B (MRS_{AB}) **measures how many extra units of good B the consumer must receive to compensate him for giving up 1 unit of good A—or, equivalently, how many units of good B the consumer would give up to get 1 more unit of good A.**

For example, suppose MU_A/MU_B is 4, with MU_A equal to 20 and MU_B equal to 5. By giving up one apple the consumer loses 20 utils. To make up for that, he has to be given four bananas. In the other direction, he would just be willing to give up four bananas to get one additional apple. Hence the marginal rate of substitution of apples for bananas is 4 (= 20/5) in this case.

Because the ratio of marginal utilities is equal to the price ratio, we can write

$$MRS_{AB} = \frac{P_A}{P_B} \qquad (3)$$

Note the implication of consumer optimization: *Every consumer in the economy equates the marginal rate of substitution of apples for bananas to the ratio of the price of apples to that of bananas.* Since all consumers face the same price ratio, the marginal rate of substitution of apples for bananas will be equal for all consumers. Hence there is no way to reallocate the consumption of these goods among consumers to make anyone better off without making someone else worse off.

To see why, consider a situation where the marginal rate of substitution is not equalized between individuals. We show that in this case reallocating resources can make at least one person better off. Suppose that Marge's MRS_{AB} is 2 and Diane's is 3. This means that Marge would be willing to trade one apple for two or more bananas. Diane, on the other hand, would be willing to give up as many as three bananas to get another apple. Thus if Diane gives Marge three bananas in exchange for one apple, Diane is no worse off and Marge is better off. And if Diane gives Marge 2½ bananas in exchange for 1 apple, both are better off.

Whenever consumers' *MRS*'s differ, there exist trades of this sort that would make both parties better off. Because consumers' *MRS*'s are all the same in a market economy, no such trades exist. This is summarized by the notion of efficiency in consumption.

● An allocation of resources is *efficient in consumption* **if it is impossible to reallocate the total quantities consumed of each good among consumers so as to make at least one better off without making anyone else worse off. Because the *MRS* between any pair of goods is equal for all consumers in a perfectly competitive economy, equilibrium in such an economy is efficient in consumption.**

This is the first step in showing that the price system allocates resources efficiently. The next step is to bring producers into the discussion.

Competitive Supply and Production Efficiency

In Chapter 9 we showed that each firm in a competitive industry chooses that level of output at which marginal cost is equal to price. Thus under competition, for all firms producing apples and bananas,

$$MC_A = P_A \quad \text{and} \quad MC_B = P_B \qquad (4)$$

Because the marginal cost of producing apples is the same for all apple producers, there is no way to reallocate total apple production among firms so as to reduce the apple industry's total cost. If *MC*'s aren't equal for all firms, total industrywide cost is reduced if low-*MC* firms increase output and high-*MC* firms cut back. When mar-

---
[9] This concept is also discussed in the Appendix to Chapter 6.

ginal costs are all equal, no such cost-reducing reallocations exist and we have efficiency in production.

● **An allocation of resources is *efficient in production* if it is impossible to reallocate the total production of any good among firms so as to reduce the total, industrywide cost of producing that good. Because marginal costs are equal for all producers of any good in a perfectly competitive economy, equilibrium in such an economy is efficient in production.**

In order for more apples to be produced, land, labor, and other resources will have to be taken from the production of bananas (or other goods). Another way to think of the marginal cost of producing apples is to focus on the reduction in the output of bananas that would be necessary in order to produce one more apple. This idea is captured by the marginal rate of transformation.

● **The *marginal rate of transformation* of good A for good B (MRT_{AB}) is the increase in the output of good B that can be obtained by reducing the output of good A by 1 unit—or, equivalently, the reduction in the output of B necessary to permit the output of A to increase by 1 unit.**[10]

Suppose one less apple is produced; this frees up resources worth MC_A. How many bananas can society obtain using those resources? To obtain one banana costs society MC_B, so that a dollar's worth of resources can produce $1/MC_B$ bananas. Thus society can obtain MC_A/MC_B more bananas by giving up one apple, and the marginal rate of transformation of apples for bananas is equal to this ratio.

$$MRT_{AB} = \frac{MC_A}{MC_B} \quad (5)$$

The marginal rate of transformation of apples for bananas measures the *opportunity cost* of increasing the output of apples, that is, the number of bananas that must be given up to get one more apple.

---

[10] The marginal rate of transformation of any one good for any other good depends on the quantities of all goods and services produced in the economy. If there are only two goods in the economy, the *MRT* of one for the other is equal to −1 times the (negative) slope of the production possibility frontier discussed in Chapter 1.

Combining equations (4) and (5), we obtain

$$MRT_{AB} = \frac{P_A}{P_B} \quad (6)$$

That is, under competition, the marginal rate of transformation of apples for bananas is equal to the ratio of the price of apples to the price of bananas.

This completes the second building block. We now have seen that under perfect competition the marginal rate of transformation equals the price ratio. The concluding step is to demonstrate that since consumers and producers all face the same price ratio, resources are efficiently allocated in production and in consumption at competitive equilibrium.

Exchange Efficiency and Pareto Optimality

Combining the two building blocks, we obtain a fundamental result about perfect competition.

● **Under perfect competition, the marginal rate of transformation in production of any good A for any other good B is equal to every consumer's marginal rate of substitution of A for B.**

This result implies that there is no way to make consumers better off by changing the mix of goods produced. We thus have demonstrated that the price system in a competitive economy allocates resources efficiently.

To see why this is true, let us consider a specific example in which the marginal rate of transformation of A for B is not equal to the corresponding marginal rate of substitution. Let the marginal rate of transformation be 3, meaning that to produce one more apple, the output of bananas would have to be reduced by three. Suppose that the marginal rate of substitution is 4, so that consumers value an extra apple at four times the value they put on a banana. The first row in Table 10-1 illustrates this situation.

How should the allocation of resources be changed in this case? If society produces one more apple and three fewer bananas, consumers will be better off because they all prefer one apple to three bananas. The second row of Table 10-1 shows the opposite situation. If the marginal rate of transformation of apples for bananas exceeds the corresponding marginal rate of substitution, consumers

TABLE 10-1. Marginal Rates of Substitution and Transformation

MRS_{AB}	MRT_{AB}	Conclusion	Decision
4	3	Consumers' valuation of A relative to B exceeds its opportunity cost in production	Increase output of A and reduce output of B
3	5	Consumers value A relative to B at less than its opportunity cost in production	Reduce output of A and increase output of B
3.5	3.5	Consumers' valuation of A relative to B is equal to its opportunity cost in production	No change in output; the situation is Pareto-efficient

can be made better off by increasing the production of bananas. Since consumers would rather have five bananas than one apple (they would willingly trade an apple for three or more bananas), apple production should be reduced and banana production increased.

We have thus established that a perfectly competitive economy is efficient in exchange.

● **An allocation of resources is *efficient in exchange* if it is impossible to change the total outputs of the goods and services produced so as to make at least one consumer better off without making any consumer worse off. Because all consumers' marginal rates of substitution are equal to the corresponding marginal rates of transformation in a perfectly competitive economy, equilibrium in such an economy is efficient in exchange.**

We have completed the demonstration that equilibrium in a perfectly competitive economy produces a Pareto-optimal allocation of resources.

● **In a perfectly competitive economy, all goods are efficiently produced (production efficiency) and efficiently allocated among consumers (consumption efficiency). In addition, the mix of goods produced cannot be changed to make consumers better off (exchange efficiency). Therefore, the allocation of resources produced by a competitive economy is Pareto-efficient.**

The Role of Prices

Prices play the central role in guiding a competitive economy to a Pareto-optimal allocation of resources. Under competition the ratio of the price of A to that of B is the marginal opportunity cost of producing A in terms of the amount by which the output of B must be reduced (MRT_{AB}). Thus prices tell consumers to buy relatively little of A when its opportunity cost in terms of B is high.

Similarly, the ratio of the price of A to the price of B is exactly equal to the ratio of consumers' marginal valuation of A to their marginal valuation of B (MRS_{AB}). Prices thus tell businesses to produce a lot of A and relatively little B when consumers place a high value on A relative to B.

Real economies produce thousands of different goods and services. But as long as all markets are competitive, all price ratios will equal the opportunity cost of one good in terms of another. Those price ratios in turn will guide consumers to make spending decisions that fully take into account the costs to society of meeting their demands. If the cost of oil rises, so will the prices of gasoline, heating oil, airline travel, and plastics produced from petroleum. Consumers will be led, "as if by an invisible hand," to change their behavior so as to reduce the demand for these products and thus conserve oil.

Similarly, if consumers' tastes change, market prices will change and producers will be led, with no central planning or direction, to change the pattern of production so as to respond to the new pattern of tastes.

The Distribution of Income

It bears repeating yet again that the notion of Pareto efficiency is quite limited. In terms of the utility possibility frontier in Figure 10-1, a perfectly competitive economy could be at *any* point on the frontier. It is quite possible for an economy to be at a Pareto-efficient equilibrium in which some people are starving and others are homeless.

■ What use is the demonstration that perfectly competitive markets allocate resources efficiently? To say that competition allocates resources efficiently is to say that competition avoids waste. This part of the demonstration of the merits of competition is broadly accepted. But to say that competition yields the *best* allocation of resources is to accept the market-determined distribution of income, and this is necessarily a value judgment. Still, economists, even those who think the existing distribution of income is unfair, typically stand up for competitive markets. The main reason is that competitive markets work well whatever the distribution of income. Even if income is redistributed through the tax system or in any other way, competition will produce an efficient allocation of resources with the new distribution of income. On the other hand, the costs of preventing competitive markets from working, for instance by imposing rent controls, can be quite high for society as a whole—and sometimes even for those who are intended to benefit from overruling the price system.

Summary[11]

1. Economists use a very specific definition of economic efficiency. A situation is Pareto-efficient when no person can be made better off without some other person being made worse off.
2. The concept of Pareto efficiency is restrictive because it cannot be used to compare many real-world situations in which a policy makes some people better off only by making others worse off.
3. At a perfectly competitive equilibrium the marginal cost of producing a good is equal to the marginal value consumers place on that good. They are equal because firms equate marginal cost to price and households equate marginal valuation to price. Since everybody faces the same prices, the competitive equilibrium implies equality of marginal cost and marginal valuation.
4. Levels of output lower than indicated by the competitive equilibrium are inefficient because consumers are willing to pay more than marginal cost for increases in production. At outputs above the competitive equilibrium level, the costs producers save exceed the losses to consumers from reducing consumption.
5. Consumers' surplus—the excess of the amount consumers are willing to pay for a good over the amount they actually pay—is measured by the area between the demand curve and the price being paid.
6. Producers' surplus—the cumulative excess of the price over the amount at which producers would be willing to supply a good—is measured by the area between the supply curve and the price line.
7. So long as we are willing to treat a dollar's worth of benefit to any individual as being equal to a dollar's worth of benefit to society, consumers' and producers' surpluses also measure benefits to society.
8. Away from the competitive equilibrium point, the sum of consumers' and producers' surplus can be increased by moving production toward the competitive equilibrium. This is another way of showing that competitive equilibrium in a single industry is efficient.
*9. The marginal rate of substitution of good A for good B is the number of units of good B the consumer requires in compensation for giving up 1 unit of good A. It is equal to the ratio of the marginal utility of good A to that of good B.
*10. Because marginal rates of substitution are equal to the same price ratios for all consumers under competition, competitive equilibriums are efficient in consumption: There is no way to reallocate available supplies of goods among consumers so as to make anyone better off without making someone else worse off.
*11. Under competition, all producers of any good equate marginal cost to price. This implies efficiency in production: It is impossible to reallocate total output among firms so as to reduce the industry's total cost of production.
*12. The marginal rate of transformation of good A for good B is the number of units of good B that have to be given up in production in order to produce 1 more unit of good A. If markets are competitive, it is equal to the ratio of the marginal cost of producing good A to the marginal cost of producing good B—and thus to the ratio of the price of A to the price of B.
*13. Under competition, the marginal rate of substitution between any pair of goods is equal to the marginal rate of transformation between them. This ensures efficiency in exchange: It is impossible to make consumers better off by changing the production levels of any goods.
*14. Because equilibriums in competitive economies are efficient in consumption, production, and exchange, they produce Pareto-optimal allocations of resources.

---

[11] The starred items in the summary, key terms, and problems relate to material in section 4.

Key Terms

Utility possibility frontier
Pareto efficiency
Consumers' surplus
Producers' surplus
Marginal rate of substitution*
Marginal rate of transformation*
Efficiency in consumption*
Efficiency in production*
Efficiency in exchange*
The role of the price system
Efficiency and income distribution

Problems

1. Define the concept of Pareto optimality and state whether it would be useful in considering the following problems: (*a*) increasing taxes on the old to help unemployed young workers and (*b*) improving the system by which the Pentagon contracts for weapons so that costly mistakes in producing weapons become less frequent.
2. Draw a utility possibility frontier and explain why many allocations that are Pareto-optimal might be thought to be unfair or unjust.
3. Use the concept of consumers' surplus to show why consumers benefit when the price of a good is reduced. Is there any relationship between the amount they gain and the change in the amount they spend on the good? (*Hint*: Assume that the demand for the good is inelastic and ask what happens to total spending on the good when its price falls.)
4. Using the concepts of consumers' and producers' surpluses, show why the allocation of resources in a competitive industry is optimal.
*5. (*a*) The marginal utility of good A is 3, and that of good B is 4. What is the marginal rate of substitution between B and A, and what does that mean? (*b*) The marginal cost of producing good A is $3. The marginal cost of producing good B is $2. What is the marginal rate of transformation of B into A?
*6. In Problem 5, explain how the allocation of resources in the economy can be improved.
*7. Again using Problem 5, explain how competition would bring about the optimal allocation of resources. In particular explain the role of prices in signaling how resources should be reallocated.
*8. Suppose there are many goods in the economy. Using the concepts of efficiency in consumption, efficiency in production, and efficiency in exchange, explain why competition in all markets will bring about an allocation that is Pareto-optimal.

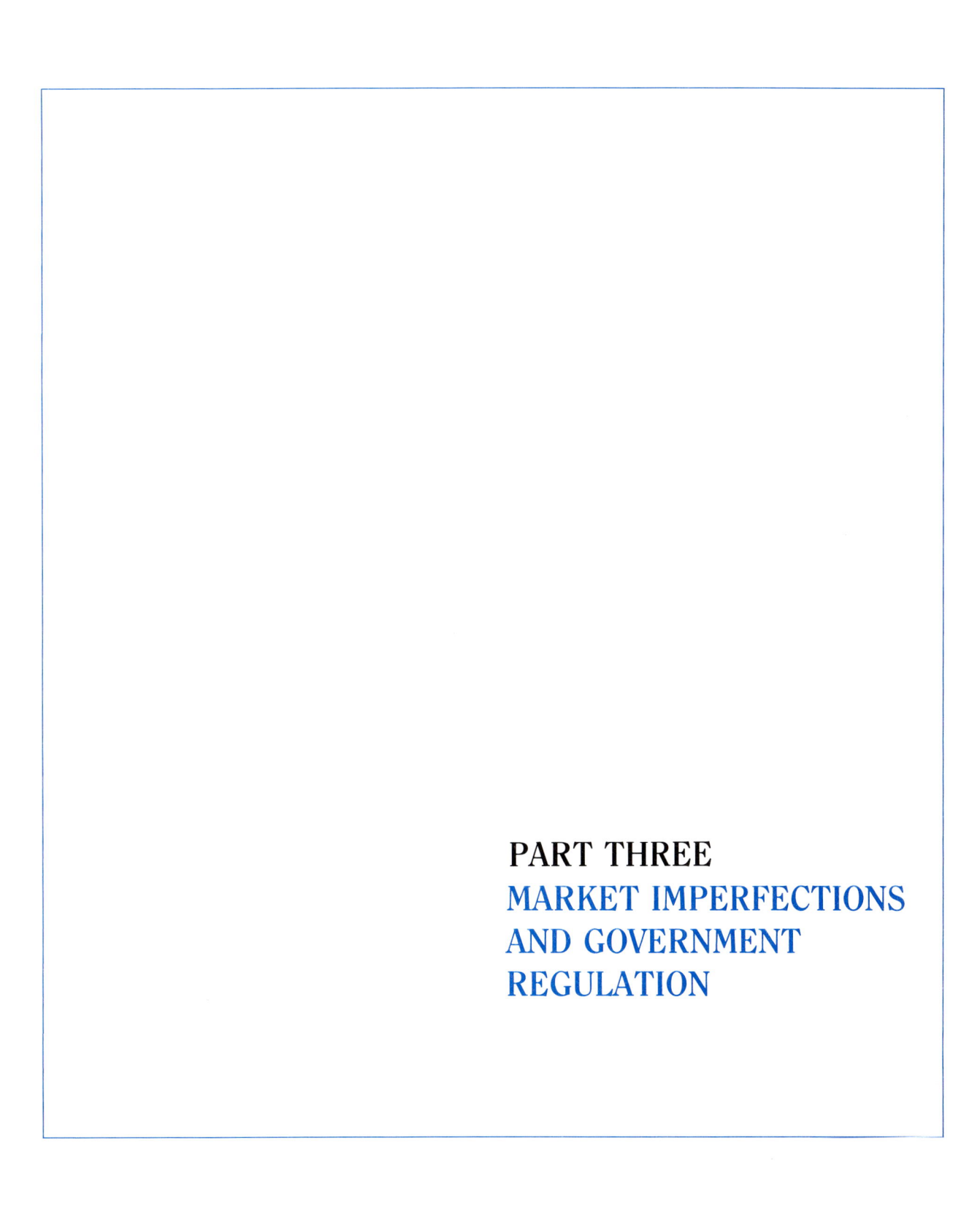

PART THREE
MARKET IMPERFECTIONS AND GOVERNMENT REGULATION

Chapter 11
Imperfect Competition: Monopoly

In Chapter 10 we learned that perfectly competitive markets allocate resources efficiently without government intervention, but this does not prove that *real* market economies are automatically efficient. In Chapter 4 we briefly discussed three important reasons why real markets may fail to work well: monopoly power, externalities, and imperfect information. In Part 3 we study these market failures and the ways in which government policy deals with them. This chapter and Chapter 12 analyze the workings of *imperfectly competitive* markets, in which sellers have monopoly power. Chapter 13 provides a general overview of government regulation of economic activity, and Chapter 14 concentrates on antitrust and regulatory responses to the problem of monopoly power.

In many industries leading firms know they are such a big part of the market that they can affect the market price by their own actions. Such firms would be foolish to ignore this power by pretending that price is beyond their control and behaving like perfect competitors. Firms large enough to affect price are likely to pay careful attention to what other leading firms in the industry are doing: Ford worries about General Motors' new models and prices; the Kellogg Company worries about General Mills; and one supermarket chain worries about the others' specials for the week. All these firms advertise, as do some businesses, such as restaurants and drugstores, that have many competitors that provide similar—but not identical—goods and services. Even restaurants and drugstores have some ability to affect the prices they receive.

None of these cases meets all the requirements for perfect competition discussed in Chapter 9.

● **Markets where either buyers or sellers take into account their ability to affect market price are *imperfectly competitive*.**

Many markets are imperfectly competitive, such as the markets for automobiles, breakfast cereals, and restaurant meals. In this chapter and Chapter 12 we analyze how real markets can differ from the ideal of perfect competition and why these differences arise. We examine how the differences affect firms' behavior and the allocation of resources.

We begin in section 1 by describing the main types of imperfectly competitive markets, including *monopolies*, to which we devote the rest of this chapter.

● A *monopoly* is the only seller of a particular good or service in a market.

In terms of the number of sellers and in other important respects as well, monopoly is the most extreme form of imperfect competition. Like perfect competition, it thus serves as a useful benchmark to which other market structures can be compared.

1. Imperfectly Competitive Markets

There are many buyers and sellers in a perfectly competitive market, none of which is large enough to affect the market price. As a consequence, competitive buyers and sellers treat price as being fixed and beyond their control. In order to maximize profits, sellers then choose the output level at which marginal cost equals price. However, in imperfectly competitive markets, individual sellers *can* affect the price they receive for their outputs. They naturally take this ability into account in figuring out how to maximize profits. Thus, as we shall see, the rule for competitive output choice, $P = MC$, is not profit-maximizing under imperfect competition.

Table 11-1 summarizes the main features of the three broad types of imperfectly competitive markets—*monopolistic competition*, *oligopoly*, and *monopoly*—that are most important in practice. We look at each in more detail subsequently. In markets of all three types, as in perfect competition, there are many buyers, each too small to affect market price noticeably by his own actions. Buyers are thus price takers, and their behavior is described by market demand curves.

Monopoly and Monopoly Power

The most extreme case of imperfect competition is a monopoly, a market with a single seller and no possibility of entry by others. In the case of diamonds, for instance, de Beers Consolidated Mines until the early 1980s had virtual control over *all* sources of supply in the non-Communist world. Other examples include Polaroid's monopoly of instant photography, the only grocery store in an isolated small town, and most local cable television operators. In most cities local telephone service and electricity are also provided by monopolies, but the prices charged by these sellers are regulated by government agencies, as we discuss in Chapter 14.

In the real world, monopoly is always a matter of degree. One might argue that every grocery store is a monopolist, since no two carry exactly the same brands of all items. However, this is not generally a useful way to look at the grocery business, since the prices charged by one store affect the demands faced by others nearby. A true monopolist has no such identifiable rivals.

Because a monopolist is the only supplier of some good or service, the price it receives for its output is determined by the *market* demand curve for its product. Because the market demand curve for diamonds slopes downward, de Beers knows that the more diamonds it produces, the lower the price it will receive for each. It can thus raise the market price by cutting back on the amount it sells; de Beers has monopoly power.

TABLE 11-1. Principal Market Types

Structural characteristic	Perfect competition	Imperfect competition		
		Monopolistic competition	Oligopoly	Monopoly
Number of sellers	Many	Many	Few	One
Barriers to entry	No	No	Usually	Yes (no entry)
Product differentiation	No	Yes	Perhaps	No (one product)
Examples	Agriculture, individual stocks	Restaurants, drugstores	Automobiles, breakfast cereals	Diamonds, instant photos

● A seller has *monopoly power* (or *market power*) if it can raise the price of its product by restricting its own output.

A firm doesn't have to be a monopolist to have some monopoly power; even small grocery stores in large cities have some control over the prices they charge. The difference between such firms and, say, the de Beers diamond monopoly is one of degree; de Beers has more control over the price of its output.

Table 11-1 points to another important difference between perfect competition and monopoly. In perfect competition there are no impediments or barriers to the entry of new producers. Thus if the market price of wheat rises above the long-run average cost of producing it, farmers switch from other crops to wheat. This process tends to eliminate economic profits in perfectly competitive industries.[1] In monopoly markets, on the other hand, there are *barriers to entry* that make it impossible for any new seller to enter. Because of this, a monopoly may enjoy a substantial flow of profits more or less indefinitely.

Monopolistic Competition

As the name suggests, monopolistic competition has features of both monopoly and perfect competition.[2] As in monopoly, each firm produces a product that buyers consider different from the products of all other sellers. There is competition, however, because many other sellers offer products that are close but not perfect substitutes for each other. Essentially, monopolistic competition is perfect competition plus product differentiation.

● A market is characterized by *product differentiation* when buyers consider the products of competing sellers to be close but imperfect substitutes.

Product differentiation gives each monopolistic competitor some market power, since each competitor can raise price slightly without losing all its customers. There are many wheat farmers in Kansas and many restaurants in Kansas City, for instance, but wheat is not differentiated and restaurants are. Thus a wheat farmer will sell nothing at all if she tries to charge a penny more than the going market price, while a restaurant owner can vary the prices on the menu slightly without producing huge changes in the demand for his food. However, he doesn't have much monopoly power if there are many other similar places to eat in town.

Where product differentiation is possible, sellers must decide exactly which products to produce, and they may find it profitable to advertise. The possibility of product differentiation also raises new and difficult efficiency questions. Is the optimal set of products produced under monopolistic competition? Do sellers spend the socially optimal amount on advertising? We address these questions in Chapter 12.

In monopolistic competition, as in perfect competition, there are no barriers to the entry of new firms. It is not hard to open a new restaurant, gas station, or drugstore in most large cities. Because there are no barriers to entry, firms in monopolistically competitive industries tend not to be especially profitable in the long run.

Oligopoly

Oligopoly means few sellers. An oligopolistic market is one in which most of the output is produced by a handful of large firms, each large enough to affect the whole market by its own actions. The automobile, steel, and breakfast cereal industries are oligopolies. Individual oligopolists can *affect* price by themselves, as in monopoly, but price is *determined* by the actions taken by all sellers, as in perfect competition. This makes oligopolists' decisions more complex than those of firms in other types of markets. Each firm has to work out not only how buyers will react to what it does but also how other firms in the industry will respond, since those responses will affect its profits. If General Motors is considering a price

---

[1] As we noted in Chapter 9, however, if firms have different long-run average cost curves, the most efficient firms in a competitive industry can earn positive economic profits in the long run.

[2] The study of monopolistic competition was begun by Harvard's Edward H. Chamberlin. His 1933 book, *Monopolistic Competition*, argued that almost all markets in modern economies are imperfectly competitive. Also in 1933 and independently, Joan Robinson of Cambridge University published *The Economies of Imperfect Competition*, which stressed the same point and developed the modern theory of monopoly behavior.

increase, for instance, it must predict the responses of Ford, Chrysler, and its other rivals in order to calculate the resulting change in its sales.

In oligopolistic markets, products may be differentiated, as in the case of automobiles and breakfast cereals, or approximately identical, as in the case of steel and aluminum. When product differentiation is possible, firms must make decisions about product design and advertising. In order to calculate the effects of changes in these variables, as well as the affects of changes in price, oligopolists must predict the likely reactions of their rivals.

Oligopoly is intermediate between monopoly and competition in another sense. There are no barriers to entry when competition is perfect, and there is no possibility of entry under monopoly. In oligopolistic markets there are usually some barriers to entry, but they are not so high as to make entry utterly impossible. The lower the barriers to entry, the more likely that new firms will be attracted if established sellers are making high profits, and thus the lower the industry's profits in the long run.

Markets with Large Buyers

In all the market types described in Table 11-1 there are many buyers. Since each is small relative to the market as a whole, they all take price as given in making decisions. Most markets in real life, particularly those in which buyers are consumers, satisfy this condition, but there are a few exceptions.

Corresponding to monopoly and oligopoly on the selling side of a market are *monopsony* and *oligopsony*, respectively, on the buying side. A monopsonist is the only buyer in a market. For instance, the U.S. government is frequently a monopsonist in markets for sophisticated, expensive weapons such as aircraft carriers and nuclear warheads. An oligopsony is a market in which most sales are made to a few large buyers. As buyers, the automobile producers are oligopsonists in the market for automobile tires. Because monopsony and oligopsony are relatively uncommon, we do not analyze them explicitly in this text.[3]

---
[3] In more advanced texts it is shown that the basic ideas developed in the analysis of monopoly and oligopoly in this chapter and Chapter 12 also apply, with some modification, to these other, less common market types.

2. Marginal Revenue and Monopoly Output

We now turn to the study of monopoly markets. In this section we show how monopolies select output in order to maximize profit. Section 3 then compares monopoly with perfect competition and demonstrates why monopoly generally leads to an inefficient allocation of resources. In the remainder of the chapter we ask why some markets become monopolies and then consider extensions of the basic monopoly model developed in this section.

Because a monopolist determines the market price, he cannot sensibly behave as a perfect competitor and take price as fixed. He instead takes the whole downward-sloping market demand curve as fixed. We thus begin our analysis of monopolistic profit maximization by looking at changes in revenue along such curves.

Marginal Revenue

The Acme Corporation has a patent that makes it the only firm in the world allowed to produce widgets. In order to find the level of output that maximizes its profits, Acme must go through the same sort of marginal analysis that a competitive firm uses in order to determine its optimal positive output. If producing one more widget per week would add more to revenue than to cost, output should be increased. If reducing output would lower costs more than revenues, output should be reduced. That is, Acme must compare marginal cost, MC, with marginal revenue.

● *Marginal revenue*, MR, is the change in revenue obtained by selling 1 more unit of a good.

For a perfectly competitive firm, marginal revenue is always equal to price, because such a firm can sell as much as it wants at the current price. This is true *only* under perfect competition, where the firm faces a horizontal demand curve. We now show that for a monopolist or any other imperfect competitor facing a downward-sloping demand curve, marginal revenue is *less* than price. The basic reason is that if the demand curve slopes downward, sales can be increased only by lowering price.

The first two columns in Table 11-2 show the market demand schedule for widgets. At a price of $2, seven

TABLE 11-2. Demand, Total Revenue, and Marginal Revenue

Quantity demanded, units/week	Price, $/unit	Total revenue quantity × price, $/week	Marginal revenue, $/unit
0	16	0	
			14
1	14	14	
			10
2	12	24	
			6
3	10	30	
			2
4	8	32	
			−2
5	6	30	
			−6
6	4	24	
			−10
7	2	14	
			−14
8	0	0	

widgets are demanded per week; at higher prices, the quantity of Acme's output demanded is lower. The third column shows Acme's total revenue, which is just price times quantity, at different levels of price. Total revenue first increases as the price is cut and then decreases when the price gets low.

The data in the first three columns of Table 11-2 are shown graphically in Figure 11-1. Acme's demand curve, D, is shown in the upper panel, and the corresponding total revenue schedule is shown in the lower panel. For instance, when price is $12 ($P_0$), quantity demanded is two widgets per week and total revenue is $24. Total revenue at this output level is shown by the shaded area $B + C$ in the upper panel. When price is lowered to $8, total revenue is equal to area $A + C$. Since that area is larger than $B + C$, we can see from the diagram that total revenue must increase as output rises from 2 to 4 units. This is confirmed in the lower panel, where total revenue is shown to be $32 when output is 4 units.

The last column of Table 11-2 shows Acme's marginal revenue. At each level of output in Table 11-2, except for the first unit, marginal revenue is less than price. This occurs because Acme can increase its weekly widget sales only by cutting price—and price cuts apply to all widgets sold in any week. Thus if Acme decides to sell one more widget a week, it will gain the price of that widget, but it will lose from having to sell the original weekly level of output at a lower price.

A specific example from Table 11-2 illustrates these effects. The demand schedule shows that two widgets can be sold for $12 each, but to sell three widgets a week,

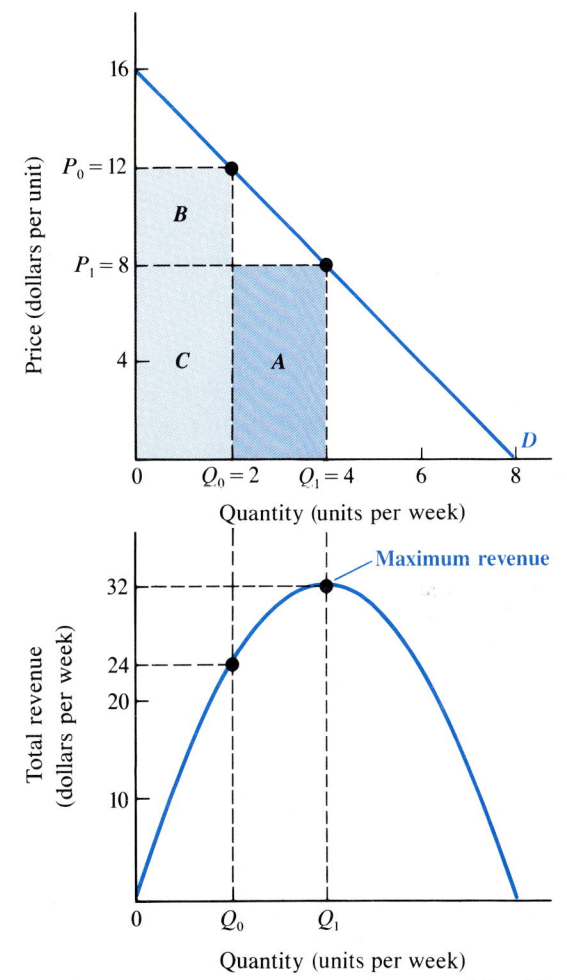

FIGURE 11-1. A Monopolist's Demand Curve and Total Revenue. The demand curve facing the monopolist is D in the upper panel. As price is cut from P_0 ($12) to P_1 ($8), the monopolist's total revenue changes from area $B + C$ to area $A + C$. Because area A is bigger than area B, total revenue increases. This is also shown in the lower panel, which depicts total revenue (price times quantity) for every level of output. Total revenue is in fact maximized at price P_1.

Acme must reduce the price to $10 each. The increase in total revenue when sales increase from 2 to 3 units is $6 ($30 − $24). There are two components to this change. The first is the $10 Acme receives from a buyer when it actually sells the third widget. The second component is a loss of $4 that arises because each of the first two widgets sold now brings in $10 instead of $12; price had to be cut in order to sell the third unit. Thus Acme gains $10 on the third unit but loses $4 from the lower price at which the original output of 2 units is sold, giving a net marginal revenue of $6.

The following equation describes the general relation between price and marginal revenue:

$$\begin{aligned}\text{Marginal revenue} &= \text{increase in total revenue from} \\ &\quad \text{selling 1 more unit of output} \\ &= \text{price at which the extra unit of} \\ &\quad \text{output is sold} \\ &\quad \textit{minus} \\ &\quad \text{the loss in revenue because the} \\ &\quad \text{original output is now sold at a} \\ &\quad \text{lower price}\end{aligned} \quad (1)$$

Since a perfectly competitive firm can sell as much or as little as it wants without affecting the price it receives, marginal revenue is equal to price under perfect competition.

In the upper panel of Figure 11-2 we add the marginal revenue (MR) curve from Table 11-2 to the demand curve from Figure 11-1. For example, the marginal revenue from increasing output from 1 to 2 units is $10. This is shown by point G on the MR curve.[4] Note that the MR curve starts out at the same point on the vertical axis as does the demand curve. Equation (1) indicates that marginal revenue on the first unit of output always equals the price of that unit, since there is no "original output" that yields less revenue because price must be cut to increase demand. After the first unit is sold, however, MR is less than price, because both effects described in equation (1) are then present.

The MR curve in Figure 11-2 intersects the horizontal

[4] Point G is shown at an output level of 1½, between 1 and 2, just as in Table 11-2, since it shows the response of revenue to an increase in output from one to two widgets per week.

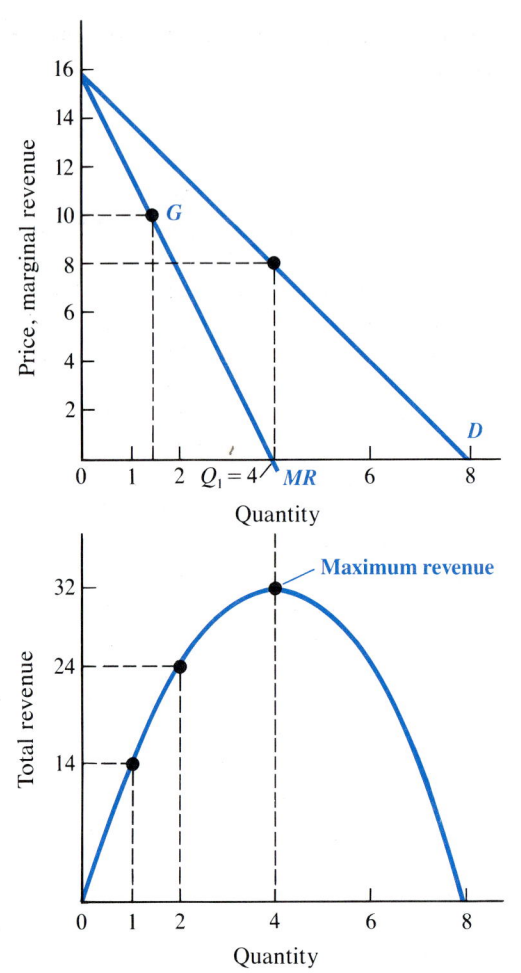

FIGURE 11-2. Price, Total Revenue, and Marginal Revenue. If output is increased from 1 unit to 2 units, total revenue increases by $10 ($24 − $14). This can be read off the total revenue curve in the lower panel or the marginal revenue curve, MR, in the upper panel. For outputs below the revenue-maximizing level, MR is positive; beyond the revenue-maximizing output, MR is negative.

axis at the point where total revenue is at a maximum. Whenever marginal revenue is positive, total revenue can be increased by increasing sales, and thus total revenue cannot be at its maximum level. Whenever marginal revenue is negative, the same logic says that total revenue can be increased by reducing sales. Only when marginal revenue is equal to zero can total revenue be at its maximum.

Optimal Monopoly Output

In order to maximize profit, a monopolist follows the same sort of two-step procedure that a perfectly competitive firm follows. In the first step, both types of firms calculate the *optimal positive output*, which is the output that maximizes profits given that the firm produces anything at all. Whereas a perfect competitor uses market price in these calculations, as we saw in Chapter 9, a monopolist uses marginal revenue. In the second step, both types of firms decide whether to produce the optimal positive output or to shut down and produce nothing at all. The second step for a monopolist is even closer to that for a perfect competitor.

Figure 11-3 shows the demand curve, D, and the marginal revenue curve, MR, from Figure 11-2. It also includes the firm's marginal cost curve, MC. MC for a monopolist, as for any firm, shows the increase in the firm's total cost when it increases output by 1 unit.

When a monopolist increases output by 1 unit, the increase in revenue is equal to marginal revenue. The increase in cost is equal to marginal cost. If marginal revenue exceeds marginal cost, total revenue goes up more than total cost, and profits therefore increase. Thus output should be increased. But if the last unit of output adds more to costs than to revenue, output should be reduced. Thus if the firm produces anything, it maximizes profits by producing the output level at which marginal revenue equals marginal cost.

- **At the optimal positive output for a monopoly, which maximizes profit given that the firm does not shut down, marginal revenue must equal marginal cost ($MR = MC$).**

As we saw in Chapter 9, a perfectly competitive firm maximizes profit by selecting the output level at which price is equal to marginal cost. Since price is equal to marginal revenue under perfect competition, one can say that a competitive firm also selects output so that marginal cost equals marginal revenue.

If a monopolist decides to produce at all, she will set price so that the quantity demanded equals her optimal positive output. Because marginal cost is equal to marginal revenue at the optimal positive output, and marginal revenue is less than price, it follows that this price will be greater than marginal cost. Thus if she decides to produce at all, *the monopolist maximizes profit by charging a price above marginal cost*.

Suppose, for instance, that Acme's marginal cost is constant at $8 per widget and that it is currently producing one widget per week. Table 11-2 shows that it could increase its profits by $2 per week, the difference between MR ($10) and MC ($8), by increasing its output by one widget per week. A further increase to three widgets per week would lower profit by $2, since marginal cost

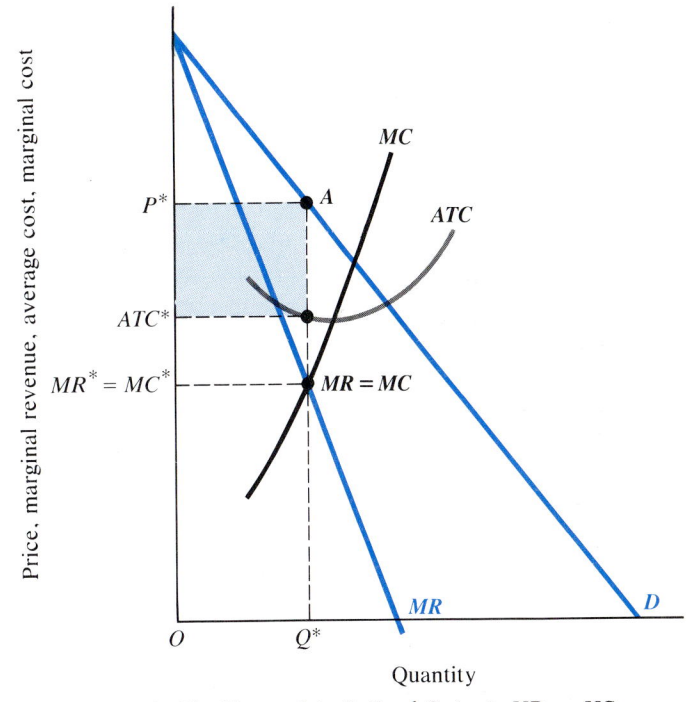

FIGURE 11-3. The Monopoly's Optimal Output: $MR = MC$. The monopolist's marginal cost schedule is MC, and its marginal revenue schedule is MR. For outputs less than Q^*, MR is greater than MC, so that increases in output raise profits. Above Q^*, decreases in output raise profits. The monopoly's optimal output is therefore Q^*, where $MR = MC$. At this output level price, P^* exceeds average total cost, ATC^*. Total monopoly profits equal the shaded area, $(P^* - ATC^*) \times Q^*$.

TABLE 11-3. The Monopolist's Optimal Supply Decision

Period	Marginal condition	Profit check
Short run	Choose the output level where $MR = MC$	Produce only if $P^* \geq AVC$ Shut down if $P^* < AVC$
Long run	Choose the output level where $MR = LMC$	Produce only if $P^* \geq LAC$ Leave the industry if $P^* < LAC$

Note: P^* is the price at which the quantity demanded is equal to the optimal positive output, where $MR = MC$ in the short run or $MR = LMC$ in the long run.

($8) would exceed marginal revenue ($6). Acme's optimal positive output is thus two widgets per week. The second column of Table 11-2 shows that in order to sell two widgets per week, Acme must set the price at $12—well above its marginal cost of $8.

As under perfect competition, the only difference between the short-run and long-run computations of the optimal positive output is that the latter involve long-run marginal cost. In the short run a monopolist, like a perfect competitor, continues production as long as variable costs are covered, while in the long run total cost must be covered. Table 11-3 summarizes the rules for profit-maximizing monopoly behavior. It differs in two ways from Table 9-1, which deals with the perfectly competitive case. First, marginal revenue replaces price in the marginal condition used to compute optimal positive output. Second, in the profit check the monopolist uses the price at which quantity demanded is equal to the optimal positive output level, while the perfect competitor uses the going market price, which he cannot affect.

PRICE MAKERS VERSUS PRICE TAKERS. Perfect competitors are described as *price takers*, since they take the market price as given and beyond their control. We have seen that a competitive firm's output decisions can be summarized by a supply curve, which shows how much the firm would produce at each given price. Monopolists do not take price as given. They are described as *price makers* since they take the market demand curve as given and choose both price and output. Since there is no general relation between the monopolist's price and output, there is no supply curve for a monopolist.

We thus cannot say that monopoly price and output are determined by supply and demand. But in monopoly, as in perfect competition, price and output are determined by both demand and cost conditions. Marginal cost is the key element on the cost side in both cases.

Monopoly Profits

Figure 11-3 shows Acme's actual short-run average total cost schedule, ATC, with its usual U shape. At the optimal positive output level, Q^*, Acme's average total cost is ATC^*. The firm's profit per unit will be equal to the price, P^*, minus the cost per unit, or average cost, ATC^*. In the case shown, Acme will therefore more than cover its costs, and it will elect to produce output Q^*. In fact, its total profit is equal to the shaded area: profits per unit ($P^* - ATC^*$) times total output (Q^*).

It is important to recall that average cost already includes the opportunity costs of *all* resources involved in producing output, including the opportunity cost of the capital supplied by the firm's owners. Thus the shaded area shows Acme's economic profit, not its accounting profit. Here, since Acme is a monopoly, its economic profit would be called *monopoly profit*, since it reflects Acme's ability to raise price above marginal cost without attracting competition.

Do all monopolies make monopoly profits? Not at all. If nobody wants to buy widgets, Acme won't even make any accounting profits. Monopoly newspapers in many isolated small towns have failed over the years in the face of competition from radio and television. The products described in many patents, which only the patent owner is allowed to produce, are never in fact produced. A monopoly can earn monopoly profits only if the demand curve for its product lies above its average cost curve, as the demand curve in Figure 11-3 does for outputs near Q^*. In this case it can earn monopoly profit indefinitely, as long as no other sellers can enter the market.

Demand Elasticity

In Chapter 5 we introduced the price elasticity of demand, E, as a measure of the responsiveness of the quantity demanded to changes in price. Recall that if E is greater than 1, so that the demand schedule is *elastic*, a price cut increases the quantity demanded so much that total revenue increases. That is, an increase in quantity sold requires only a small price reduction, so that revenue increases when output is increased. On the other hand, if E is less than 1, so that the demand schedule is *inelastic*, a price cut increases total demand so little that total revenue decreases. This just means that an increase in quantity sold requires a large price reduction, so that revenue decreases when output is increased. Since marginal revenue measures the change in total revenue when output is increased, these results imply the following:

- **If demand is elastic ($E > 1$), marginal revenue is positive. If demand is inelastic ($E < 1$), marginal revenue is negative. Marginal revenue is zero at the output level at which $E = 1$; this is the point at which total revenue is maximized.**

This relationship between elasticity and marginal revenue has an interesting implication.

- **A profit-maximizing monopolist always selects an output level at which demand is elastic.**

There are two ways to see that this must be true. First, since marginal cost equals marginal revenue for a producing monopolist and since marginal cost is positive, marginal revenue must also be positive at the profit-maximizing output. It then follows from the previous discussion that demand is elastic at this point. Second, at any output level at which demand is inelastic, marginal revenue is negative so that a reduction in output would increase revenue. Since a reduction in output would also reduce costs, it must always increase profit when demand is inelastic. But if profit can be increased, it must not have been at a maximum to start with.

This result means that there are generally good substitutes for a monopolist's output *at the profit-maximizing price*. Suppose that only one firm, Disko, produced compact disk players and that its marginal cost was $20. If Disko charged $20 for its players, few people would even consider old-fashioned record players. Disko's demand would be inelastic at this price: If it raised the price, it would lose few sales to record players, and thus it could increase profits by raising price. If Disko raised its price to $500 or so, however, record players would be an attractive alternative for many buyers. Demand would probably be elastic at this higher price; a price cut would probably increase sales substantially.

We noted in Chapter 5 that the elasticity of demand for any product is likely to be larger the better are the available substitutes. And the higher the price of any product relative to the prices of possible substitutes, the more attractive those substitutes become. Box 11-1 provides an illustration of this principle.

3. Monopoly Versus Competition

We now use the model of monopoly output choice we have developed to show why monopoly power leads to an inefficient allocation of resources. To do this, we use Figure 11-4 to see what happens if a competitive industry becomes a monopoly. We assume that the demand curve, D, is the same whether the market is monopolized or competitive. We also assume that costs are the same for the monopolist as they are for the competitive industry. Here a word of explanation about the supply curve is necessary. We saw in Chapter 9 that the supply curve of a perfectly competitive industry is that industry's marginal cost (MC) curve. That is, the industry supply curve shows, at every level of output, the increase in costs resulting from increasing industry output by 1 unit. Likewise, the monopoly's MC schedule shows the increase in costs from producing 1 more unit of output. Thus if a competitive industry is monopolized and input prices and production techniques do not change, the competitive industry's supply (and MC) curve becomes the monopolist's marginal cost curve.

Price and Output

When the industry depicted in Figure 11-4 is competitive, equilibrium output is given by Q_c and equilibrium price is P_c. This is the point at which quantity supplied is equal to quantity demanded. After the industry is monopolized, output is chosen so that marginal cost (MC) and marginal revenue (MR) are equal in order to maximize profit. The monopoly thus selects output

Box 11-1. The Cellophane Monopoly?

In an important antitrust case decided in 1956, the U.S. Supreme Court found that even though Du Pont controlled almost all cellophane production in the United States, it was not a monopolist. The Court held that the market was not "cellophane," as the government had charged, but rather "flexible packaging materials," including waxed paper, greaseproof paper, various foils, and films of Pliofilm, glassine, polyethylene, Saran, and other substances. Cellophane accounted for only 18 percent of this broader market, hardly enough to make Du Pont a monopolist.

The Court noted that "despite cellophane's advantages it has to meet competition from other materials in every one of its uses." It argued that because of this, buyers were sensitive to price, and the quantity of cellophane demanded would thus fall sharply if Du Pont attempted to increase its price. Critics of this decision have made three arguments in favor of the proposition that Du Pont was a monopoly.

First, many have pointed out that Du Pont earned very high profits on its cellophane business. But this doesn't show that the Court was wrong. If all flexible wrapping materials provided basically the same services to buyers, one could think of Du Pont's patents on cellophane as simply having given it a cheaper way of providing those services. Even under perfect competition, firms that have lower costs of producing the final product can earn very high profits. One would like to know whether Du Pont's price was above its marginal cost, but it seems that no evidence was gathered on this point.

Second, the price of cellophane did not always change when the prices of other flexible wrapping materials changed, as it would have if Du Pont had been a price taker and all these materials had been essentially identical. In fact, cellophane was generally much more expensive per square foot than other materials, and the Court noted its "advantages" over other materials in many uses.

Finally, the evidence that buyers of cellophane were willing and able to switch to other products if prices changed slightly might have been a symptom of monopoly, not of competition. If, *at the going price*, buyers are not sensitive to price, so that demand is inelastic, the market cannot be a monopoly—since a monopolist would raise price in order to increase profits. If Du Pont had been a monopolist, it would have raised the price of cellophane until its demand became price-elastic because the high price of cellophane made it sensible to consider using other wrapping materials—exactly the situation the Court found.

Note: For discussions of this case, see George Stocking and Willard Mueller, "The Cellophane Case and the New Competition," *American Economic Review*, March 1955; and Richard Posner, *Antitrust Law: An Economic Perspective*, University of Chicago Press, 1976.

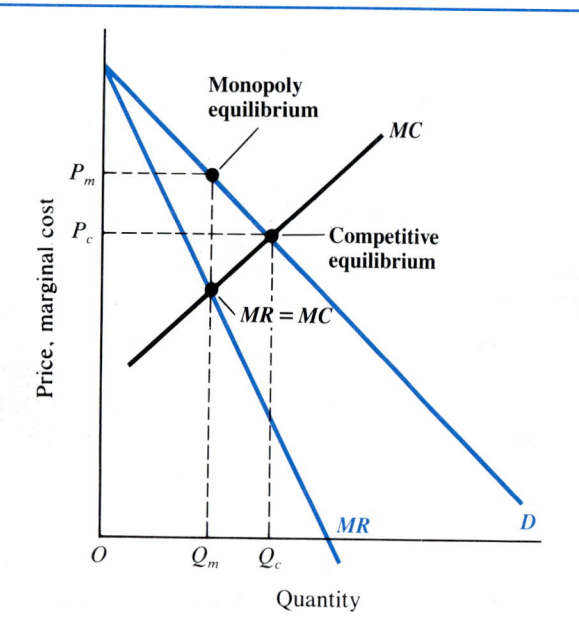

Q_m and charges price P_m so that this quantity is demanded by buyers.

As Figure 11-4 shows, when both a monopoly and a competitive industry face identical demand and cost conditions, output is lower and price is higher under monopoly than under competition. This is the basic charge against monopoly.

FIGURE 11-4. Price and Output under Competition and Monopoly. The industry demand curve is D. The curve MC is the supply curve under competition and the marginal cost curve under monopoly. Under competition, price (P_c) and output (Q_c) are determined by the intersection of supply and demand curves. Under monopoly, output (Q_m) is chosen at the level where $MR = MC$, and price (P_m) is read off the demand curve at that output level. Replacing competition by monopoly raises price and lowers output.

● **Compared to perfect competition, monopoly restricts output and raises price.**

Why doesn't the monopolist expand output beyond Q_m? After all, buyers are willing to pay more than marginal cost for additional units of the good, at least until total output reaches Q_c. The monopolist cannot increase his profits by satisfying these demands, however, since he would have to cut the price to *all* buyers in order to increase sales. If he cut price in order to increase output 1 unit above Q_m, his revenue on the extra unit would exceed the marginal cost of producing it, since price exceeds marginal cost. However, since marginal revenue is less than marginal cost for outputs above Q_m, this gain would be outweighed by the loss in revenue on the original level of output, Q_m, caused by the price cut. The difference between monopoly and perfect competition thus arises because marginal revenue is below price.

Social Cost of Monopoly

Is restricting output and raising price a bad thing for society as a whole? That is, is monopoly incompatible with Pareto efficiency? To answer this question, Figure 11-5 shows the market demand curve and the marginal cost curve for a particular monopolized good, say, diamonds. Point E would correspond to the competitive equilibrium, where the industry supply curve, which is the MC curve, intersects the demand curve, D.

As Chapter 10 noted, at each quantity level the demand curve tells us the price that consumers are willing to pay for an additional unit of the good. Thus at quantity Q_m consumers are willing to pay P_m for an additional unit of output, so that price, P_m, measures the value to consumers of 1 more unit of the good. On the supply side, the cost of producing an additional unit of the good is given by the MC schedule. At quantity Q_m the marginal cost of producing an extra unit of output is MC_m.

In a situation like the one shown in Figure 11-5, an expansion in output would benefit *society*, since the value to consumers of an additional unit of output exceeds the (marginal) cost of producing it. But if Q_m is the monopoly output, an expansion in output would not benefit the *monopolist*. The reduction in the price of existing output would outweigh the increased revenue from additional sales. This is why monopolists restrict output, thus giving rise to the social cost of monopoly.

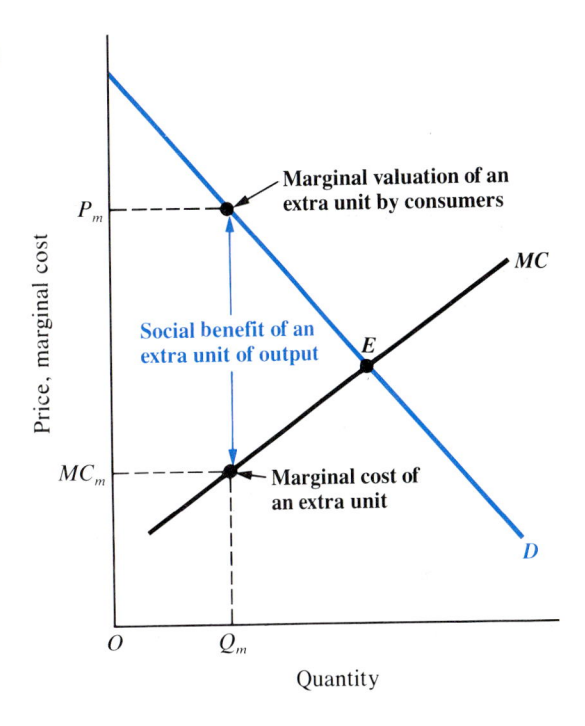

FIGURE 11-5. The Social Cost of Monopoly: $P > MC$. The demand curve, D, shows that at output level Q_m, the value to consumers of an extra unit of output is P_m. The marginal cost schedule, MC, indicates that at this output level, the cost of producing an extra unit is MC_m. Thus at output level Q_m, as at all outputs where price exceeds marginal cost, society as a whole would benefit from increasing output. But the monopolist, realizing that output increases would lower price, finds it in his interest to operate to the left of the socially optimal point E.

The idea that a monopoly creates a social cost by restricting output is particularly obvious if we consider a monopolist who controls the supply of a commodity that is costless to produce. For instance, the commodity may be access to a beautiful mountain view. Because the view can be made available at no cost, the public should enjoy as much of it as it wants, taking enough glimpses so that the marginal valuation is exactly zero. In other words, we should be at a consumption point where consumers are willing to pay precisely zero, no more and no less, for an additional peek. Of course, the monopolist would charge people to see the views, and that would restrict output to a lower level. Social cost arises because access to the mountain view that would have given satisfaction at no cost is restricted by the profit-maximizing monopolist.

Let us see now how this social cost can be measured. In Figure 11-6 we show again the competitive equilibrium, E, and we also show the monopoly equilibrium at point A. At the competitive equilibrium, price equals marginal cost so that the value to consumers of an extra unit of output just equals the marginal cost of producing it. No gain to society would come from raising output beyond the competitive equilibrium or from cutting it below that level. As we showed in Chapter 10, the competitive equilibrium is Pareto-efficient.

Monopoly equilibrium is not Pareto-efficient. The price faced by consumers, P_m, exceeds the marginal cost of increasing output, MC_m. Thus consumers would be willing to pay more for an additional unit of output than it would cost the monopolist to produce it.

Beginning at the monopoly output, Q_m, suppose output were somehow increased by 1 unit. The corresponding social gain would be the difference between the marginal value of that extra unit to buyers and the marginal cost of providing it, or $(P_m - MC_m)$. Similarly, if a second additional unit were then produced, the additional gain to society would be the difference between marginal value (P) and marginal cost (MC) at that output level. Proceeding in this fashion until output reaches the competitive level, Q_c, we see that the vertical gap between price and marginal cost at each output level measures the net benefit of increasing production by 1 more unit. Adding these vertical gaps, we obtain the shaded triangle ABE as the total social gain that would be produced by an increase in output from the monopoly level to the competitive level.[5]

We can now see that the social cost of monopoly is an opportunity cost. It is the total benefit (valuation minus cost) that society gives up by allowing production to be restricted to the monopoly level rather than expanded to the competitive level.

---

[5] In terms of the concepts defined and explained in Chapter 10, area ABE in Figure 11-6 is the amount by which the sum of consumer's and producer's surplus would be increased by moving from the monopoly output level to the competitive output level.

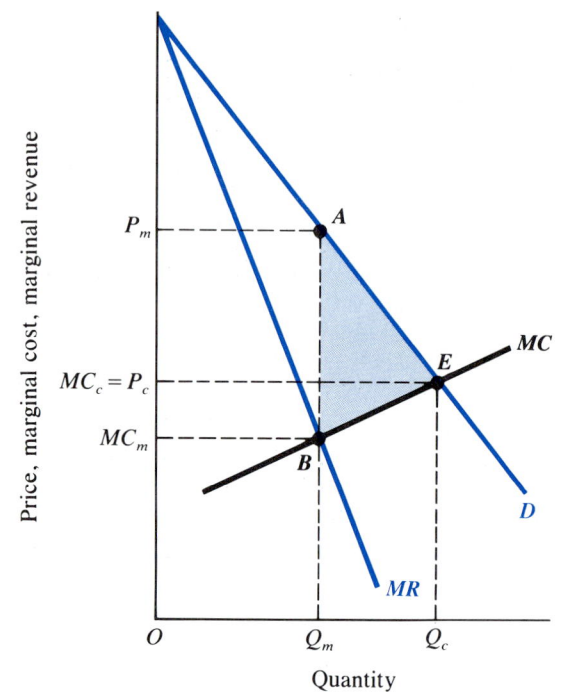

FIGURE 11-6. Measuring the Total Social Cost of Monopoly. A competitive industry would produce at point E, where marginal cost exactly equals price—and thus the marginal valuation of an extra unit of output by consumers. The monopolist, by contrast, restricts output from Q_c to Q_m, where price (P_m) exceeds marginal cost. The total cost to society of monopoly is the cumulative excess of price over marginal cost, which is the shaded area ABE.

● **The social cost of monopoly output restriction is equal to the cumulative excess of marginal valuation over marginal cost, from the monopoly output level to the competitive level.**

4. Why Do Monopolies Exist?

A successful monopoly earns profits that are attractive to other firms too. How, then, do monopolists keep other firms out? What are the reasons for the existence of monopolies? There are three chief reasons, which we discuss briefly in this section.

Natural Monopoly

One of the examples of monopoly given at the beginning of this chapter—local telephone service—points to the main reason for the existence of monopolies: *economies of scale*. Because of scale economies, some industries are natural monopolies.

● An industry is said to be a ***natural monopoly*** if any level of output is more cheaply produced by one firm than by two or more.

To examine this case, we show in Figure 11-7 the demand and cost curves for a monopoly in an industry in which there are economies of scale at all output levels. The higher the level of output, the lower the average cost, and therefore, as was shown in Chapter 8, marginal cost is below average cost at all points.

Monopoly price and output are at point A, at the output level where $MR = MC$. At point A the monopoly is earning profits equal to the shaded area, $(P_m - AC_m) \times Q_m$. What would the equilibrium be if this were a competitive industry? Our first instinct might be to take the MC curve as the competitive industry's supply curve and look for the point where the supply and demand curves cross. This is point C in Figure 11-7. But that point cannot be a long-run competitive equilibrium. Because there are economies of scale, marginal cost is always below average cost. Thus if price were equal to marginal cost, as at point C, average cost would be higher than price, and there would be a loss equal to the distance CG on every unit of the good sold. Because there are economies of scale at all output levels, this industry could not have a competitive equilibrium.

Monopoly is "natural" here in the sense that it is the cost-minimizing market structure. To see this, suppose we had two firms in the industry, each producing half the industry's total output. How would the average cost with two firms compare with the average cost if the same level of output were produced by a single firm? Because average cost rises as output falls, we would always have the two firms each producing at a point where average costs are higher than they would be if one firm alone produced all the output. Because a single seller can produce more cheaply—owing to economies of scale—it would be difficult for this industry to avoid becoming a monopoly. If there were more than one firm in the industry, one of them could cut price and expand output sharply and thus make it difficult for its smaller rivals to make a profit. Monopoly is thus also "natural" in that it is likely to result from the free operation of market forces.

Essential Resources and Government Policy

The second reason for the existence of monopoly is that a single firm may have control over some scarce and essential resource in the form of either raw materials or knowledge covered by a patent or a kept secret. The de Beers diamond monopoly mentioned above rests on control over raw materials. For many years Xerox had control over the copying process called xerography simply because it had superior technical knowledge, some of which was covered by patents. In both cases it was essentially impossible for competitors to enter the business.

The third reason for the existence of monopoly is

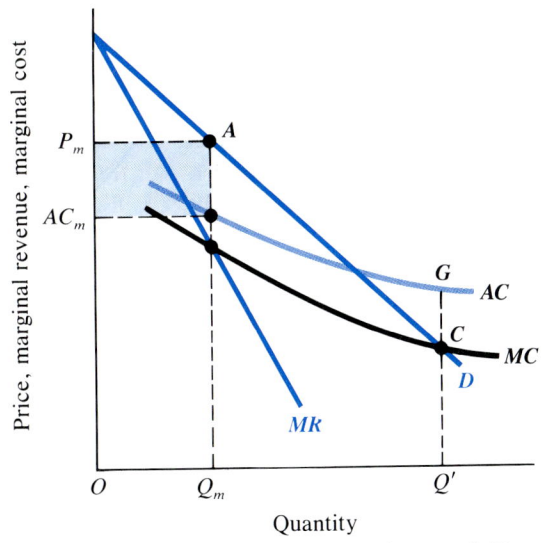

FIGURE 11-7. Economies of Scale and Natural Monopoly. The diagram shows an industry where average cost, AC, is declining and where, accordingly, marginal cost, MC, is below AC. The monopoly would produce output Q_m and make profits equal to the shaded area. Point C, where $P = MC$, cannot be a competitive equilibrium, because price is below average cost.

government restrictions on the entry of new firms. Monopolies may exist because they buy or are given the right to be the single sellers of a good. Thus by law only the local electric company can sell you electricity, and—because it holds the necessary patents—only Polaroid can sell certain types of film and cameras. In some cases the government itself takes the right to be a monopoly; in some countries tobacco can be sold only by government-run monopolies. Some governments have granted the right to import particular goods to a single company. Why would the government create a monopoly in an imported commodity? This could be a matter of politics or payoffs from an importer to government officials or both.

These three reasons are not necessarily independent. The government may give a company the right to be a monopoly if there are economies of scale, for instance. Competition in such cases would be socially wasteful. But in return the government may at the same time seek to regulate the behavior of the company so that the major inefficiencies of monopolization—the social loss from the restriction of output—are reduced. Through the patent system, governments grant inventors temporary monopolies in order to encourage technical progress, as we discuss in section 6.

5. Extensions of the Basic Monopoly Model

In this section we indicate how the basic monopoly model developed in section 2 can be extended to deal with two important phenomena. First, we consider behavior involving *price discrimination*, in which monopolies or other firms with market power charge different prices to different customers. Second, we consider markets in which a single *dominant firm* shares a market with a large number of small price-taking competitors. Both are more common than the pure single-price monopolies discussed thus far, but both can be analyzed by means of simple modifications of the basic monopoly model we have presented.

Price Discrimination

Sometimes firms with market power have two or more groups of customers with different demand curves. For instance, suppose the Happy Skies airline serves both business travelers and vacationers. The demand for vacation travel is elastic, while the demand for business travel is inelastic.

Suppose that Happy Skies is charging the same price to all its customers but that its planes fly half empty. It is making profits but would like to increase its revenues by filling its empty seats. It could fill these seats by cutting the prices it charges to all travelers. However, a reduction in the price charged to business travelers would decrease the revenue from these customers, while a reduction in the price of vacation travel would increase revenue from vacationers. Happy Skies would thus like to cut the price for vacationers only.

In order to charge different prices to the two groups, Happy Skies must be able to decide to which class each customer belongs and also be able to prevent vacationers from buying at low prices and reselling to business travelers. Airlines frequently accomplish both tasks by charging a lower fare to travelers whose trip includes a Saturday. Business travelers usually want to get home for the weekend, while vacationers don't. Vacationers accordingly identify themselves by scheduling their trips to take advantage of the discount. This policy is an example of price discrimination.

● **A firm with monopoly power practices *price discrimination* if it charges different prices to different consumers on the basis of differences in demand elasticities.**[6]

Happy Skies will consider cutting the price for *any* group only if the demand of that group is elastic, since only if the group's demand is elastic does a price cut increase the airline's revenue. On the other hand, if any group of customers has an inelastic demand, Happy Skies can increase its profits by raising the price it charges to that group.

Price discrimination is common. For example, think of subscriptions to specialized journals and magazines. There is typically a high rate for businesses and libraries, which generally have a low elasticity of demand, a rela-

---

[6] It is worth noting that this is only one type of price discrimination, though probably the most common. Price discrimination can also be carried out through *nonlinear pricing*, in which the amount a customer pays is not directly proportional to the amount he buys. Quantity discounts are the most common examples of nonlinear pricing.

tively low rate for individuals, and an even lower rate for students. In setting different prices for different groups, the publisher attempts to extract as much profit as possible from each individual group. Say, for example, that a journal called *New Energy Review* is published. To firms in the energy business a $200 subscription is nothing, provided the *Review* offers first-rate information. Students can easily read the *Review* in the library and would be unlikely to pay more than $10 for the convenience of having their own copies. Thus price discrimination is a perfectly sensible policy to exploit the low price elasticity of firms while still having sales and profits in the student market.

Here is another example. Most museums offer a special low entry fee for students and a higher fee for other visitors. Once again we see price discrimination. Is this an attempt by the museum to bring culture to the young, or is it an attempt to maximize museum revenues? Fortunately, there is no conflict between these two aims, and we do not have to answer the question, but the fact is that students have a much higher elasticity of demand for museum visits than do most adults. Cutting the entry fees for them (and for families) brings in more of them without impairing the revenue from higher prices charged to the less price-sensitive. Since even sellers with little market power can practice price discrimination, pricing of this sort is very common.

If a firm has market power and can practice price discrimination, it increases its own profits and transfers benefits from the group with inelastic demand to the group with elastic demand. The group with elastic demand will be able to buy more at a lower price but leave the seller with increased profits. Someone must pay. That someone is the group with a demand that is relatively unresponsive to price, which therefore can be squeezed. Society as a whole may gain or lose; it all depends on the sizes of the groups and the relations between their demand curves.

Dominant Firms

At the start of this century the U.S. steel industry contained many small sellers. The U.S. Steel corporation was created in a massive merger in 1901. At that time it had about 65 percent of total U.S. steel-making capacity. Strictly speaking, U.S. Steel wasn't a monopolist, since many other firms produced steel, but its behavior can be analyzed using a simple extension of the monopoly model developed in section 2.

Because each of U.S. Steel's rivals was too small relative to the steel market to affect price by its own actions, they behaved as competitive price takers. The behavior of the firms in this *competitive fringe* can thus be summarized by a supply curve. U.S. Steel, in contrast, was able to affect price by its own actions. Such a *dominant firm* must take into account both the relationship between price and quantity along the market demand curve *and* the effects of its actions on the behavior of the competitive fringe.

Figure 11-8a shows the market demand curve, D, for an industry with a dominant firm and a competitive fringe, along with the supply curve of the competitive fringe, S. Suppose the fringe firms take as given the price set by the dominant firm. They will sell as much as they want to supply at that price. Thus the amount the dominant firm can sell at any level of price is the *difference* between total market demand and the quantity supplied by the competitive fringe.

This difference is the excess demand curve, ED, in Figure 11-8b, which corresponds to the difference between the D and S curves. (Distance AB is the same in both parts of the figure, for instance.) Since the dominant firm faces demand curve ED, it maximizes its profits by choosing the output level, Q_{df}, at which the corresponding marginal revenue curve, MR, intersects its marginal cost curve, MC.[7] In order to sell Q_{df} units of output per period, it will set price equal to P_{df}, which is read off from its own demand curve, ED. At this price market demand is equal to Q_d, and the competitive fringe supplies Q_{cf}.

Note that ED is flatter than D, because price increases now reduce the dominant firm's demand in two ways: by reducing total market demand and by increasing the quantity supplied by the competitive fringe. The more elastic the competitive fringe's supply curve, the more elastic the dominant firm's demand curve. Since the fringe's supply curve will be more elastic in the long run

---

[7] Of course, as we discussed in section 2, it will produce at this level in the short run only if the corresponding market price, P_m, exceeds its average variable cost. And if P_m is less than long-run average cost, it will leave the industry entirely in the long run.

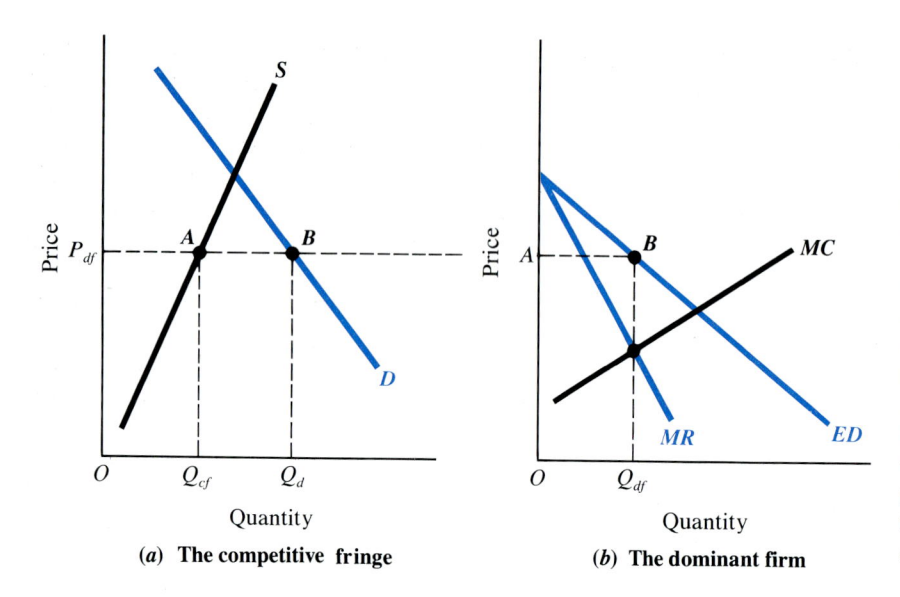

FIGURE 11-8. (*a*) **The Competitive Fringe and** (*b*) **the Dominant Firm.** The industry depicted includes a dominant firm and a competitive fringe of small firms that behave competitively. The supply curve of the competitive fringe is S, and the *market* demand curve is D. The dominant firm faces the *excess* demand schedule ED, the difference at each price between the quantity demanded and the quantity supplied by the competitive fringe. The dominant firm chooses output level Q_{df}, at which MR = MC. The total quantity demanded at the corresponding price, P_{df}, is Q_d, of which Q_{cf} is produced by the competitive fringe and the rest by the dominant firm.

than in the short run, the dominant firm's demand curve will also be more elastic in the long run.

To see what this implies, suppose the dominant firm and all competitive fringe firms face the same constant input prices and have the same L-shaped long-run average cost curves,[8] with a minimum average total cost of $10 per unit. This means that the long-run supply curve of the competitive fringe is perfectly flat at a price of $10. Then in the long run the dominant firm will be unable to keep the market price above $10. It will thus be unable to earn excess profits in the long run. If it restricts its own output to hold price above this level in the short run, it will encourage the entry of new fringe firms and the expansion of its existing competitors. Unless such entry and expansion can somehow be discouraged, the dominant firm will lose its dominant position in the long run. (By 1925 U.S. Steel's share of industry capacity had declined to 42 percent, other firms had expanded, and the industry had become an oligopoly.) On the other hand, if the dominant firm has a cost advantage over other producers, it may be happy with a price below $10 that will permit it to remain dominant indefinitely.

---

[8] See Chapter 8 for a discussion of *LAC* curves of this sort, which decline as output increases at low levels and then flatten out, with no tendency for average cost to rise at high levels of output.

6. Monopoly and Progress

So far we have concentrated on a monopoly operating with fixed, unchanging technology. Under these conditions there is not much to be said for monopoly beyond the fact that economies of scales make it efficient to have only one producer in some industries.

But the picture changes when we think about innovation and technical progress. Monopoly is bad, but a stagnant technology is worse. Most people would rather have automobiles produced by a monopoly than buggies produced by a perfectly competitive industry. Recognizing this, most governments grant temporary monopolies to inventors in order to promote technical progress. In the United States, patents provide 17-year monopolies. Many large firms, such as Gillette, AT&T, Xerox, and Polaroid, began as patent monopolies. Laws protecting trade secrets sometimes give rise to even longer-lived monopolies.

In principle, a system in which inventors received cash prizes but could not restrict anyone from using their inventions could be better for society as a whole than a patent system, since it would avoid the output restriction that accompanies patent monopolies. But the problem in practice is that the economically right prize for any invention depends not on its technical brilliance but on its value to society. And nobody has figured out how to determine the social value of an invention accurately without actually putting it on the market and seeing what buyers are willing to pay for it. A system of rewards based on temporary monopolies does just this and accordingly seems the best available way to encourage technical progress in practice.

There may be another link between monopoly and technical progress. Joseph Schumpeter and others have argued that large firms with significant monopoly power are desirable because they speed technical change.[9] Schumpeter argued that firms with monopoly power can spend their monopoly profits on research and are likely to do this to protect or enhance their monopoly power. By doing research they benefit both themselves and society as a whole. Perfectly competitive firms, in contrast, have no excess profits to invest or protect. Schumpeter further argued that there may be economies of scale in research and development; putting two small laboratories together may increase the total research output.

The first part of Schumpeter's argument has to do with the *effort* devoted to technical progress. This argument implies that large firms with monopoly power will spend more, as a percentage of sales revenue, on research and development than will small competitive firms. This implication appears to be supported by the fact that very small firms do not engage in much, if any, research and development. But in most sectors of the economy, once a certain size of firm is reached, there appears to be little relationship between the size of a firm and the fraction of its sales revenue devoted to research and development. While industries with structures approaching the competitive ideal tend to do little research (consider farmers), those which are close to monopoly are generally not much better. A small amount of market power may increase inventive effort, but overwhelming market power may reduce it.

The second part of Schumpeter's argument has to do with the *results* of spending on research and development. If firm A spends twice as much as firm B, is it likely to produce more or less than twice as much technical progress? It is, of course, difficult to decide how to measure the output of research and development activities, but the evidence suggests that in most sectors B is unlikely to produce much more than twice as much as A. Additionally, studies of important inventions often find that middle-sized firms outperform industry leaders.

The conclusion, then, is that firms have to be of a reasonable size to undertake research and development efforts, and some market power may help. But technical progress in most areas does not seem to depend on giant firms that have great monopoly power. Because of the patent laws, monopoly is more likely to be the result of technical progress than its cause.

■ Monopoly is both the most extreme form of imperfect competition and the easiest to analyze. As we see in Chapter 12, most real markets are intermediate between monopoly and competition in important respects. Moreover, while the choice for society as a whole between monopoly and competition appears easy, natural monopolies and the more common intermediate market types pose more difficult policy choices, which we explore in Chapter 14.

---

[9] Schumpeter, an Austrian economist who taught at Harvard, made these arguments in his wide-ranging book *Capitalism, Socialism, and Democracy*, published in 1943. Schumpeter's discussion of technical progress is stimulating but somewhat unclear, and there have been many debates about what he really meant to say.

Summary

1 In imperfectly competitive markets, in contrast to perfectly competitive markets, buyers and sellers can raise the price of their product by restricting their own output. The extreme case of imperfect competition is monopoly, where there is only one seller and no possibility of entry by others. Other important types of imperfectly competitive markets are monopolistic competition (many sellers, easy entry, and product differentiation) and oligopoly (few sellers, possibly product differentiation, and barriers to entry).

2 Marginal revenue is the change in revenue which is obtained by selling 1 more unit of output. Marginal revenue is less than price for a monopolist producing a positive level of output.

3 The optimal positive output for a monopolist is the level at

which marginal revenue equals marginal cost. Demand is always price-elastic at this point. The monopolist produces his optimal positive output if the corresponding price at least equals average variable cost in the short run and average total cost in the long run.
4. The monopolist does not have a supply curve, because she takes the whole demand schedule, not any single price, as given in making her price and output decision.
5. A monopolist always charges a price above marginal cost. Moreover, output in a monopoly industry is smaller than output in a competitive industry with the same demand and cost conditions, and the monopoly price is higher than the competitive price.
6. The monopolist's restriction of output is not socially desirable because the value consumers place on increased production exceeds the cost of increasing production—but production is held down by the monopolist to avoid the need to cut price for all buyers in order to increase sales.
7. There are three main reasons for the existence of monopoly. First, there are some natural monopolies, in which costs are minimized when only one firm is producing. Second, the monopolist may have control over a source of raw materials or some special technical knowledge. Third, the government may have given monopoly rights to a single firm.
8. Firms with market power commonly practice price discrimination by charging different prices to different types of buyers on the basis of differences in demand elasticities. Buyers with more elastic demand tend to pay lower prices.
9. If a single large firm faces a number of small price-taking rivals, the quantity of its output demanded at any price is given by the difference between the total quantity demanded and the quantity supplied by the competitive fringe. The large firm behaves as a monopolist, taking as given the demand schedule thus determined. In the long run, expansion by competitors may erode its market power.
10. Monopoly can result from technical progress, via the patent system, but there is no strong evidence that large firms with great monopoly power are especially important in promoting technical progress.

Key Terms

Imperfect competition
Monopoly
Monopoly (or market) power
Product differentiation
Monopolistic competition
Oligopoly
Marginal revenue
Monopoly profit
Price makers versus price takers
Natural monopoly
Price discrimination
Dominant firm
Competitive fringe

Problems

1. In the last month, what goods or services have you bought in a market best described by (a) perfect competition, (b) monopoly, (c) monopolistic competition, (d) oligopoly?
2. Recall the stadium manager in Chapter 5 on pages 80–83. At what level of marginal revenue would he maximize total revenue?
3. The accompanying table below shows the demand schedule facing a monopolist who produces at a constant marginal cost of $5.

Demand Schedule Facing a Monopolist

Price, $	Quantity demanded
9	0
8	1
7	2
6	3
5	4
4	5
3	6
2	7
1	8
0	9

(a) Calculate the firm's marginal revenue schedule. (b) What is the profit-maximizing output for the monopolist? (c) What is the optimal price for the monopolist? (d) What would the equilibrium price and output be for a competitive industry? (e) Explain in words why the monopolist produces less and charges a higher price than does a competitive industry.

4. Suppose now that in addition to the constant marginal cost of $5, the monopoly incurs a fixed cost of $2 just to be in business. (a) What is the monopolist's optimal level of output? (b) What is the monopolist's profit-maximizing

price? (c) What effects do fixed costs have on the monopolist's profits, and why?

5. Under the demand assumptions in Problem 3, assume now that the monopolist's total costs are as given in the accompanying table. (a) Calculate the marginal cost schedule. (b) What are the optimal price and quantity for the monopolist? (c) How much profit does the monopolist make?

A Monopolist's Total Costs

Quantity Supplied	Total Cost, $
0	4
1	9
2	13
3	16
4	20
5	25
6	31
7	37
8	44

6. (a) What is the social gain in Problem 3 from moving from the monopoly equilibrium to the competitive equilibrium? (b) In what sense exactly is this a gain, and to whom? (c) How much does the monopolist lose as a result of the move to the competitive equilibrium?

7. Suppose now that the marginal cost decreases to $3 in Problem 3. (a) What is the effect on the equilibrium price and quantity? (b) Does the price change by more or less than the change in cost? (c) How does that compare with the effects of a change in marginal cost on price in a competitive industry?

8. Explain why a monopolist always sets a price high enough so that the demand for his product is elastic. Explain why a monopolist with positive marginal costs never maximizes her revenue.

9. Producers of instant coffee and other products sold in supermarkets often include in their products coupons that entitle consumers to discounts on future purchases. Most of these coupons are not used. Explain why the use of coupons may be a form of price discrimination.

10. Pick any three products with which you are familiar that did not exist 20 years ago. Describe the industry currently producing each one. Did these products originate with large or small companies or with individual inventors?

11. The US patent system grants 17-year monopolies to inventors. Is it clear that society would be better off if the patent life were shortened to 10 years? Discuss the costs and benefits of this change.

12. In Figure 11-3 you can see that in the monopoly equilibrium we have drawn, ATC^* is above the minimum value of average total cost. Why does the monopoly not expand production to reach a lower level of average costs? Would the reduction in average costs raise profits? Explain.

Chapter 12
Oligopoly and Monopolistic Competition

This chapter completes the discussion of imperfect competition that began in Chapter 11. We focused there on the most extreme form of imperfect competition: monopoly. Here we consider the two main types of market structures intermediate between perfect competition and monopoly: oligopoly and monopolistic competition.

Oligopoly and monopolistic competition are more common in practice than either perfect competition or monopoly. These intermediate cases are also more complicated than either of the extreme cases. Nonetheless, a few general principles enable us to understand quite a bit about the oligopolistic and monopolistically competitive markets we encounter every day.

The distinguishing feature of oligopoly is *fewness*. As Chapter 11 stated,

● An *oligopoly* is an industry in which most sales are made by a few firms, each able to affect the market price by its own actions.

Automobile manufacturing, the production of breakfast cereals, television broadcasting, and many other industries are dominated by a few large firms whose names are household words (General Motors, Ford, Kellogg's, General Mills, NBC, CBS, etc.). Because each oligopolist faces only a small number of rivals, his actions will generally affect each of them noticeably. In maximizing profits he must take into account his interaction with these rivals. He must therefore try to predict their actions and reactions to his own actions, recognizing that his rivals are also trying to predict *his* own actions and reactions. These interactions make the problem of profit maximization in oligopoly very difficult and consequently make oligopoly behavior hard to predict.

The distinguishing feature of monopolistic competition, on the other hand, is product differentiation.

● Under *monopolistic competition*, a large number of firms produce *differentiated products*. Their products are close but imperfect substitutes for each other.

Monopolistic competition is especially common in the retail trade and service sectors of the economy. There are many restaurants, gas stations, real estate offices, and hairstylists in most cities. Each has some control over the price at which she sells. But because there are many sellers in these markets, the actions taken by any one seller are unlikely to be noticed by any other seller, and there is thus no need to worry about their reactions. As with perfect competitors, each monopolistic competitor sensibly believes that she is too small to affect the way other firms behave. However, monopolistic competitors, unlike perfect competitors, have some freedom to set their own prices.

We begin by discussing the importance of fewness and product differentiation in the U.S. economy and then explain why these structural features arise. Sections 2 and 3 consider the determinants of oligopoly behavior. When do oligopolists behave like perfect competitors, like monopolists, or like neither? Section 4 discusses monopolistic competition. In both oligopoly and monopolistic competition, products may be differentiated and advertising, product design, and other forms of nonprice competition may be important. Section 5 considers these aspects of business behavior and their implications for economic efficiency. Are too many brands of toothpaste produced or too few? Is there too much advertising or too little?

1. Concentration and Differentiation in the U.S. Economy

Markets with only one seller—monopolies—are relatively rare, as are perfectly competitive markets in which no seller has an appreciable share of total output and all products are identical. In many markets the largest sellers are much larger than the smallest, and product differentiation is common.

Seller Concentration

A market looks more like a monopoly the greater the *seller concentration*, that is, the greater the share of sales accounted for by a few leading sellers. A monopoly has the maximum possible seller concentration; perfect competition is at the opposite extreme. A common measure of seller concentration is the *four-firm concentration ratio*, which is the percentage of sales in an industry made by the four largest firms. Table 12-1 presents four-

TABLE 12-1. Four-Firm Concentration Ratios for Concentrated U.S. Manufacturing Industries

Industry	Four-firm concentration ratio*
Spark plugs	97
Milk and beverage cartons	96
Chewing gum	95
Nylon fibers	94
Home washing machines and dryers	93
Electric light bulbs	90
Cigarettes	90
Home refrigerators and freezers	90
Home woodworking machinery	87
Breakfast cereals	86
Flat glass	85
Cat food	84
Corn oil	83
Greeting cards	80

* Shipments by the four largest U.S. suppliers as a percentage of total U.S. shipments.

   Source: U.S. Bureau of the Census, *1982 Census of Manufacturers*: "Concentration Ratios in Manufacturing," 1986, Tables 5 and 6.

firm concentration ratios for some highly concentrated U.S. manufacturing industries.[1]

Table 12-1 shows that we use the products of highly concentrated oligopolies every day. However, most U.S. manufacturing industries are not so near the monopoly end of the competition spectrum. Table 12-2 shows the shares of total manufacturing shipments (roughly equal to dollar sales) accounted for by industries with differing degrees of concentration. Only 6.4 percent of sales are made by industries in which the four largest firms account for more than 80 percent of sales. In contrast, nearly 20 percent of total output comes from industries where the four largest firms account for less than 20 percent of sales. Table 12-2 shows that the industries with high concentration do *not* account for the lion's share of economic activity in manufacturing. Most (60.7

[1] The concentration ratios used in this section refer to domestic producers only and thus overstate concentration when there is competition from foreign suppliers, as in the automobile industry. On the other hand, the published concentration ratios understate concentration in some industries, such as cement, where markets are local or regional rather than national.

TABLE 12-2. Share of Industrial Sales Classified by Concentration

	Four-firm concentration ratio*				
	0–19	20–39	40–59	60–79	80–100
Share of total manufacturing shipments, %	19.3	43.0	17.7	13.8	6.4

*Shipments by the four largest U.S. suppliers as a percentage of total U.S. shipments.
Source: U.S Bureau of the Census, *1982 Census of Manufacturers*: "Concentration Ratios in Manufacturing," 1986, Table 5.

percent) of manufacturing output is produced in industries where the four-firm concentration ratio is 20 to 59 percent. Although data on seller concentration in non-manufacturing markets are less complete, the available evidence suggests that seller concentration tends to be even lower than it is in manufacturing.[2]

Why Are Markets Concentrated?

ECONOMIES OF SCALE. In some industries large firms may be able to produce more cheaply than small firms can. If there are economies of scale at all levels of output, the industry is a natural monopoly, as we discussed in Chapter 11. In less extreme cases, long-run average cost may decline with increases in output up to some level of output, called the *minimum efficient scale* (MES), and be approximately constant as output increases beyond that level.[3] If the MES is large enough relative to the total quantity demanded, there may be room for only a few firms large enough to produce efficiently. Such industries are described as *natural oligopolies*.

Scale economies of this sort also create barriers to entry that keep out potential competitors and thus preserve profitable oligopoly market structures.

● *Barriers to entry* keep potential competitors from entering industries in which established sellers are earning excess profits.

[2] The large public utility industries (water supply, electricity, local telephone service, gas distribution) are generally monopolies, but they are also either regulated or government-run.
[3] We referred to such long-run average cost curves as L-shaped in Chapter 8.

To be able to offer its output at the market price, an entrant into a natural oligopoly would have to produce on a large scale, but that is difficult for a firm to start doing from the outset. Moreover, entry of a new firm operating at a large scale, by adding a lot to supply, may depress price below even the long-run average cost of an efficient firm. Thus even if established oligopolists are earning excess profits, an outsider may find it unattractive to enter the business.

The importance of economies of scale varies considerably among industries. Table 12-3 shows estimates of the MES of a plant (defined as a factory or other place where production occurs) as a fraction of the total U.S. market for a number of industries. Plant MES as a percentage of total U.S. demand is largest for the diesel motor industry, where four fully efficient plants could more than meet the total market demand. The automobile industry could accommodate nine plants of efficient scale (nine plants, each producing 11 percent of total demand, would account for 99 percent of demand), while the bicycle industry has room for 47 and the machine tool industry could accommodate over 300.

Despite some qualifications,[4] Table 12-3 makes its point well: There are industries in which output can be produced most cheaply when there are only a few plants in the industry. These industries are natural oligopolies; they tend to be highly concentrated in all modern economies. As Box 12-1 illustrates, innovations that change an industry's long-run average cost curve generally produce corresponding changes in seller concentration.

MERGERS, EFFICIENCY, AND LUCK. Many U.S. industries are more concentrated than is required by scale econo-

[4] The figures in Table 12-3 understate the minimum efficient *firm* size if there are economies of scale in the management of multiple plants. Such economies do not seem to be important in most cases, but they are difficult to measure. Scale economies are also understated if transportation costs are high, because the market relevant to a particular plant is then smaller than the entire United States. A cement plant of minimum efficient scale would account for about 40 percent of an average regional market in that industry, for instance. On the other hand, if goods are cheap to transport and are actively traded internationally, the relevant market is generally not the United States but the world. U.S. automobile manufacturers, for instance, are effectively competing in a world market, which can sustain many more firms producing at efficient scales than could the U.S. market alone.

mies in production, because the largest firms are larger than appears to be necessary to minimize production costs.[5] For instance, if the top four cigarette producers had operated at MES, they would have accounted for 26 percent of sales, but they in fact accounted for over 80 percent. Despite relatively unimportant scale economies in production, some industries, such as cigarettes, remain concentrated for long periods. This indicates that economies of scale in the production of goods and services are not the only source of concentration and the barriers to entry that preserve it.

In some countries mergers among competitors are an important source of concentration, but in recent years the U.S. antitrust laws have prevented most mergers that would increase concentration markedly (as Chapter 14 discusses). Concentration may arise because some firms are more efficient than others and grow at the expense of their rivals. Even if all firms are equally efficient on average, some may grow larger than others simply because they experience a long run of good luck.

TABLE 12-3. Minimum Efficient Plant Scales

Industry	Minimum efficient plant size as % of 1967 U.S. industry demand
Small diesel engines	25.5
Turbogenerators	23.0
Electric motors	15.0
Refrigerators	14.1
Cellulosic synthetic fiber	11.1
Passenger auto production	11.0
Commercial aircraft	10.0
Cigarettes	6.6
Passenger auto tires	3.8
Detergents	2.4
Bicycles	2.1
Portland cement	1.7
Flour mills	0.7
Machine tools	0.3

Source: F. M. Scherer, *Industrial Market Structure and Economic Performance*, 2d ed., Rand McNally, Chicago, 1980, pp. 96–97.

[5] This is less true outside the United States, where smaller national markets make higher levels of concentration necessary for efficiency.

Box 12-1. Rising Concentration in the Beer Industry

In 1935, shortly after the repeal of Prohibition, 750 breweries were operating in the United States. By 1947 there were 465 breweries, representing 404 independent companies. Between 1947 and 1980 beer consumption in the United States roughly doubled, but in 1980 there were only 82 breweries and 41 independent companies in the industry. In 1947, the five largest brewers accounted for 19 percent of industry sales and the 10 largest accounted for 28 percent. In 1980 the corresponding figures were 75 percent and 94 percent, respectively. What caused this rapid decline in numbers and dramatic increase in concentration? Why did most firms have a single plant in 1947, while there were an average of two plants per firm in 1980?

Most observers point to three related developments that increased the importance of scale economies in this industry. First, advances in brewing technology increased the MES of a brewery. The U.S. beer market in 1980 was large enough for only about 38 fully efficient breweries. Second, advances in transportation technology made it economical for breweries to serve larger geographic areas. This made it easier to take advantage of scale economies by building large breweries and selling in distant cities, many of which had been served only by small local firms. In the face of increased competitive pressure in many areas, large numbers of old, small, inefficient breweries closed, while the number of very large breweries actually increased.

Neither of these developments explains the rise of firms operating several breweries. This can be ascribed at least in part to the growth of network television in the 1950s and the sharp reduction in the cost of television advertising. Ads on network television cost more than ads in newspapers, but they reach many households and the per household cost is relatively low. These ads seem to be a good way to sell beer, but they can be used efficiently only by large firms that sell nationwide. Because of transportation costs, the most efficient way to sell beer everywhere in the United States is to operate several large breweries in different regions. Thus the dramatic changes in the structure of the beer industry have been driven by changes in technology that have given rise to greater economies of scale in producing and marketing beer.

Note: For more on this industry, see "The Battle of the Beers," *Newsweek*, Sept. 4, 1978; and Kenneth G. Elzinga, "The Beer Industry," in Walter Adams (ed.), *The Structure of American Industry*, 6th ed., Macmillan, New York, 1982.

OTHER BARRIERS TO ENTRY. In many countries companies with political influence succeed in establishing legal monopolies or cartels to produce or import goods. In most U.S. oligopolies government restrictions on entry are not important. Barriers to entry are more likely to arise from control over key raw materials or (through patents or trade secrets) technology or from consumer's reluctance to experiment with new and untried products when existing brands perform well.

Product Differentiation

The importance of product differentiation in any market depends on the extent to which buyers *perceive* competing products to be different. There is thus no easy way to gather data on the importance of product differentiation across markets. However, it is clear that there are many markets—automobiles, stereos, toothpaste, and clothing, among others—in which product differentiation is important.

Most product differentiation was created by profit-maximizing sellers who responded to consumers' different tastes and desires for variety. If all the restaurants in town serve only hamburgers, it will be profitable for a new entrant to differentiate his product by serving fried chicken or steak. Automobile manufacturers are constantly on the lookout for features that might distinguish their products from those of their rivals. Some products lend themselves to differentiation more than others, of course: Wheat is wheat, and for most purposes pencils are pencils.

If a firm wants to sell a differentiated product, it must spend money to describe it to buyers and persuade them to try it. On the other hand, firms selling standardized products need at most to let buyers know they exist. Thus one way to get a feeling for the importance of product differentiation in the U.S. economy is to look at advertising and other *selling costs* as a percentage of sales revenue. The composition and level of selling costs vary markedly among industries, as Table 12-4 illustrates.[6] Even pulp mills must spend some money to

---

[6] These data probably overstate somewhat the importance of "other" selling costs. Some firms seem to have included the cost of price cuts made to get the business of large buyers.

TABLE 12-4. Selling Costs as a Percentage of Sales Revenue, 1976

Industry	Advertising	Other costs	Total
Proprietary drugs	19.1	14.6	33.7
Bread, cake, and related products	2.3	28.6	30.9
Hosiery	10.9	14.7	25.6
Typewriters and office machines	1.1	24.4	25.5
Distilled liquor	11.3	12.9	24.2
Cookies and crackers	2.3	18.9	21.2
Cigarettes	8.1	6.9	15.0
Household furniture	1.5	7.6	9.1
Newspapers	0.7	6.0	6.7
Ready-mixed concrete	0.1	2.1	2.2
Metal cans	0.0	1.5	1.5
Pulp mills	0.0	0.9	0.9

Source: U.S. Federal Trade Commission, Bureau of Economics, *Statistical Report: Annual Line of Business Report, 1976,* Washington, May 1982, Tabel 2–7.

contact customers. In many industries more is spent on salespeople than on advertising. Overall, the large fraction of revenues spent on selling costs in many industries certainly shows the importance of product differentiation in the U.S. economy.

2. Collusion and Rivalry in Oligopoly

There are always two forces at work pushing oligopoly behavior in opposite directions. The first force is the firms' common interest in maximizing total industry profits by colluding and acting together as if they were a single profit-maximizing monopolist.

● **Collusion is an explicit or tacit agreement among firms in an industry to fix prices and outputs or otherwise limit rivalry among themselves.**

Explicit collusion involves an actual agreement among the firms, while *tacit* collusion rests on an unspoken understanding. Oligopolists engage in *rivalry* when they attempt to take business from each other.[7] Collusion doesn't always cover all forms of rivalry. Colluding firms may agree on the price they will all charge, for instance, but not limit advertising spending or restrict the introduction of new products. In the United States, explicit collusion is almost always illegal while tacit collusion is generally legal.[8]

The second force affecting oligopoly behavior is each seller's selfish interest in maximizing her own profits, even if the industry's total profits are reduced as a consequence. A large piece of a small pie may be better than a small piece of a large pie. Colluding oligopolists will behave like a monopolist and thus, as we saw in Chapter 11, set a monopoly price above marginal cost. But then each individual firm would increase its profits a lot if it could *cheat* on the agreement by cutting price just a bit and taking substantial business from its rivals. If all firms engage in price-cutting rivalry, however, the market price will fall and all sellers will be worse off than they were under collusion—though both buyers and society as a whole will benefit, as Chapter 11 demonstrated.

Thus the possibility of getting together to maximize total industry profits leads oligopolists to attempt collusion. If they succeed, the industry will resemble a monopoly. However, the possibility of each seller's increasing his share of industry profits by engaging in rivalrous, noncollusive behavior may lead some firms to reject collusion or tempt them to break collusive agreements. If all behave noncollusively, all will earn lower profits, and the market price will fall toward the competitive level.

The Oligopolists' Dilemma

Figure 12-1 helps us understand why collusion is difficult. It describes the following situation. Two firms, Alpha and Beta, are the only sellers in a market. Each can set either a high price or a low price. If both set a high, monopoly price, each will make excess profits of $20

---

[7] This sort of behavior is often called "competition" in everyday language. But since it is *not* the same thing as the behavior of a perfectly competitive seller, it is clearer to use a label that does not suggest perfect competition.

[8] The law against explicit collusion is part of the so-called antitrust laws, which are discussed in detail in Chapter 14.

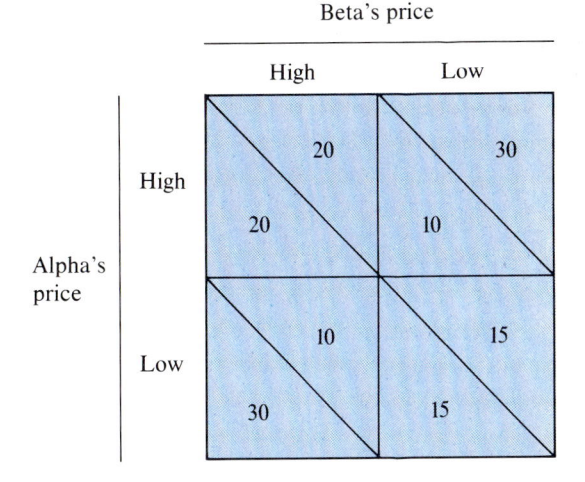

FIGURE 12-1. The Oligoplists' Dilemma. By deciding whether to charge a high or a low price, Alpha and Beta together determine how much profit each will receive. If they can cooperate, both will charge a high price and both will earn $20 million. If each maximizes his own profit, however, both will charge a low price and both will earn only $15 million.

million, while if both set low prices, profits will be only $15 million each. The incentive to collude is thus present, but so is the incentive to cheat: If one firm sets a high price and the other sets a low price, the low-price firm makes $30 million and the high-price firm makes only $10 million.

In each cell in Figure 12-1, Alpha's profit is shown below the diagonal and Beta's is shown above the diagonal. Like all oligopolists, Alpha and Beta jointly determine both their profits: Alpha chooses a row, and Beta chooses a column. The actions of each have a strong effect on the other.

If Alpha and Beta can act together, it is clear that both will charge a high price. But what if each acts independently to maximize its own profit? If Beta charges a high price, Alpha maximizes profits by undercutting and charging a low price. If Beta charges a low price, Alpha makes more by avoiding being undercut and also charging a low price. That is, Alpha maximizes its profits by charging a low price no matter what it thinks Beta will do. Beta's calculation is exactly the same, so Beta also always charges a low price. Both are thus worse off than they would be if they had been able to act together—and buyers are better off.

Suppose Alpha and Beta attempt collusion. Their top executives meet secretly (and illegally) and agree to charge a high price. Does this solve the problem? Not at all, since, in accordance with the arguments just mentioned, each has an incentive to violate the agreement and charge a low price whether or not she thinks her rival will also cheat. Effective collusion requires both agreement and some means of preventing cheating.

The basic situation analyzed here is often called the prisoners' dilemma and is illustrated by the problem facing two thieves held in separate cells who can either confess or not confess to a robbery they committed together. If the payoffs (reductions in jail sentence) follow the pattern in Figure 12-1, both prisoners find it in their individual interest to confess, even though both would be better off if both kept quiet. In this case threats of revenge might prevent cheating on an agreement, made in advance, not to confess if caught.

The prisoners' dilemma is applicable not only to felons and oligopolists. The public goods problem discussed in Chapter 4 is at heart a prisoners' dilemma. Even if you would like a larger defense budget, it is not in your own individual interest to write a check to the Department of Defense. The problem of slum neighborhoods has the same structure: All building owners might be better off if all spent money to renovate, but it rarely makes sense to go it alone and invest a lot in a slum. The list of similar situations is long and includes such diverse problems as air pollution and the arms race.

When Does Collusion Occur?

The central problem in analyzing oligopolies is predicting when collusion will occur. This requires predicting when firms will be able both to agree to restrict rivalry and to prevent violations of that agreement. Economists have not solved this problem fully, but they have identified a number of factors that make collusion more or less likely.

1. Collusion is more likely the more favorable the legal system is to explicit agreements to raise price and restrict output. At one historically rare extreme, collusion is relatively easy if the courts will enforce contracts among rival sellers that specify prices and outputs. In this case the threat of lawsuits can deter cheating. If there are no legal obstacles to agreeing on prices and outputs but courts won't enforce collusive agreements, firms that attempt to collude must find some other threat to deter cheating. International cartels, such as OPEC (which is discussed subsequently), operate under these conditions. Finally, if explicit collusion is illegal, as in the United States, it is riskier and more difficult to negotiate a collusive agreement in the first place.

2. Collusion is more likely the fewer firms that must be involved. It is harder to negotiate anything when there are many people involved, and it is harder to detect violations of a collusive agreement when there are many sellers. U.S. farmers sometimes attempt to restrict the output of particular commodities, for instance, but without government help these attempts at collusion invariably fail because every individual farmer knows that he can sell more than his allotted quota without affecting market price—and thus cheat without being caught. If there are only a few sellers, however, they can watch each other very closely, and cheating is then more likely to be detected. High seller concentration thus makes collusion more likely, but it does not by any means make it certain.

3. Collusion is more likely when it is easy to agree on the best cooperative actions and when such an agreement must be reached infrequently. Cost differences make it hard to agree on the best price, for instance, since high-cost firms want higher market prices than do low-cost firms. Differences in products may require agreement on a large set of prices. Rapid changes in costs or demands require frequent changes in collusive agreements.

4. Collusive agreements are more likely to last the easier it is to detect violations of the agreement. Detection is hard if firms can't find out the prices their rivals charge or the quantities they sell. Firms rarely manage to agree not to compete by spending on advertising or research, in large part because such spending is hard to observe. On the other hand, if customers can be assigned to firms, perhaps by giving each firm a monopoly in some geographic area, cheating is relatively easy to detect. For example, the large international chemical companies be-

tween the world wars divided up the world, and each sold in different countries.

5 Collusion increases prices and profits and thus attracts new firms. In order for collusion to be profitable in the long run, the entry of new sellers must be prevented. Sometimes there are barriers to entry that accomplish this automatically; sometimes the colluding sellers can take actions to discourage or eliminate new entrants. But sometimes entry occurs and drives price down toward the competitive level, eliminating the monopoly power of the colluding firms.[9]

---

[9] Markets in which entry is so easy that price cannot rise above the competitive level without quickly attracting new entrants are said to be *perfectly contestable*. In this extreme case, collusion cannot raise profits at all.

3. Varieties of Oligopoly Behavior

As the preceding discussion suggests, oligopolists in practice behave in many diverse ways. In this section we discuss some of the types of behavior that can occur, beginning with the clearest kind of collusion.

Explicit Collusion: Cartels

When the firms in an industry meet and explicitly agree on prices and outputs, they are said to form a *cartel*. As we have noted, explicit collusion is illegal in the United States today, and cartels are thus relatively rare. But they do sometimes form, and we occasionally read stories about corporate executives going to jail for price-fixing. Box 12-2 describes a particularly important case of illegal price-fixing.

Box 12-2. The Great Electrical Conspiracy

Beginning in the 1930s, executives of General Electric, Westinghouse, and the other major U.S. producers of heavy electrical equipment participated in secret cartels aimed at eliminating rivalry in each of their main product lines, which included generators, transformers, circuit breakers, and insulators. This equipment is purchased by enterprises that generate, transmit, and distribute electricity. Some of these enterprises are government-owned; for instance, the city of Los Angeles sells electricity to its residents. Some are privately owned but are regulated by the government (as we discuss in Chapter 14); for instance, New Yorkers buy their electricity from a private firm, Consolidated Edison.

The government enterprises that bought equipment from cartel members required interested suppliers to submit secret bids. The lowest bid was selected and the winner announced, but the amounts of all bids were kept secret. The cartels handled this sealed-bid business by first agreeing on each member's share of the business and then drawing up code sheets that indicated which firm was entitled to be the low bidder in each future 2-week period. The code sheets also specified how much the other bidders in this "phases of the moon" system would inflate their bids. Thus no two firms ever submitted identical bids, which might have aroused suspicion, but cheating was nonetheless immediately visible to all cartel members.

Privately owned enterprises usually did not conduct sealed-bid auctions. The participants in the cartel simply agreed to stick to their announced prices in dealing with these customers. They did not assign customers to particular firms. This made cheating difficult to detect. There was no way for General Electric to tell whether it had lost an order to Westinghouse because the buyer liked the Westinghouse salesperson better or because Westinghouse had cheated on the agreement and cut its price.

In fact, there was a good deal of cheating during the operation of these cartels. Sometimes other firms decided to punish the cheaters, and major price wars broke out. (These were called "white sales" by both buyers and sellers.) At other times some firms simply refused to participate in one or more of the cartels, feeling they could do better by competing vigorously to increase their share of the market than by colluding.

These illegal arrangements ended in 1960, when the firms and executives involved were indicted for price-fixing by a federal grand jury. Twenty-nine companies were fined nearly $2 million and were required to pay many times that amount in damages to overcharged customers. Seven executives were sent to jail, and 23 others received suspended sentences and 5 years of probation.

Note: For an interesting discussion of these cartels, see Richard Austin Smith, "The Incredible Electrical Conspiracy," *Fortune*, April/May 1961.

The legal status of cartels has changed over time and differs among countries. Professional baseball, for instance, enjoys a special legal exemption from the U.S. law against cartels, though basketball, football, and hockey do not. Attitudes to cartels and other agreements among firms abroad are generally more lenient, though the trend in Europe has been increasingly to make such agreements illegal. Cartel behavior is more common in Japan.

In the nineteenth century, cartels were legal in the United States and existed in many industries. These cartels differed considerably in their organization, operation, and success. The railroads in particular organized a number of cartels. These were plagued by frequent price wars, which usually began as attempts to punish firms that were thought to have given secret price cuts to win business.

The most famous, and for a decade the most successful, modern cartel has certainly been OPEC, the Organization of Petroleum Exporting Countries. OPEC was set up in 1960 but became active only in 1973.

Thereafter OPEC operated as a cartel, with its 12 member countries (including the large producing nations of the middle east along with Indonesia, Nigeria, and Venezuela) getting together regularly to decide on prices to charge. For some time world oil prices stayed close to the agreed-upon OPEC prices. But prices began to fall in early 1980s, and in early 1986 OPEC's pricing agreements collapsed. What happened?

Figure 12-2 shows that OPEC prices increased sharply twice after 1973. The first occasion was in 1973–1974, when the cartel exercised its muscle for the first time, reducing its output during and after the Yom Kippur war between Israel and its neighbors in October 1973. Because the short-run demand for oil is inelastic, oil prices quadrupled. In 1979–1980, when the Iranian revolution disrupted oil supplies, the price doubled again. OPEC's total oil revenues increased by 340 percent from 1973 to 1980, even after adjusting for the general increase in prices over that period. The cartel was hugely successful in restricting output and increasing its members' profit.

The OPEC nations are of course not the only producers of oil in the world; in 1973 non-OPEC nations (including the United States, the Soviet Union, Norway, Mexico, and Britain) accounted for 44 percent of world production. But as the discussion of the dominant firm

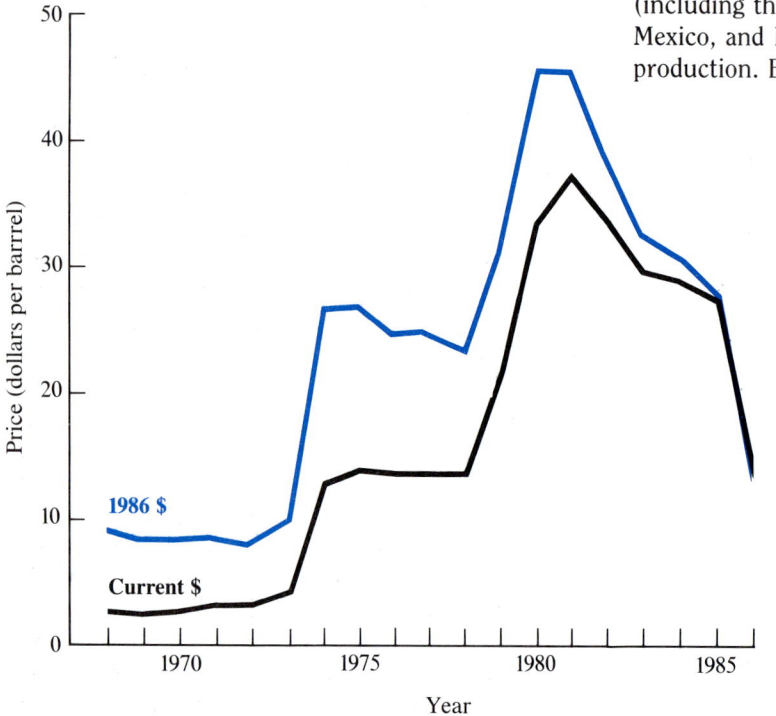

FIGURE 12-2. The Price of Imported Crude Oil, 1968–1986. The nominal (current dollar) and real (1986 dollar) acquisition cost of crude oil imported by U.S. refiners. (*Source:* Data compiled by the U.S. Department of Energy and reported in various publications.)

model in Chapter 11 showed, a cartel need not control all output in order to have considerable monopoly power. Thus OPEC, acting like a single dominant firm facing a large number of relatively small competitors, could still control the market price by setting its own output.

When OPEC first succeeded in raising prices in 1973, many economists predicted that the cartel would soon collapse because of the oligopolists' dilemma we have discussed. These observers felt that some cartel members would make secret price cuts in order to increase their own outputs. A general price drop would then occur when the others figured out what was going on. No such breakdown occured in the 1970s, even though OPEC took no steps to limit its members' outputs or punish price-cutting.

Most observers now think that OPEC's stability resulted mainly from the dominant role of Saudi Arabia, the biggest producer. Saudi Arabia essentially acted as a dominant firm *within* the cartel. The OPEC price was enforced mainly by Saudi Arabia's willingness to maintain the cartel agreement. Once price had been agreed upon, the other countries acted as price takers and sold as much as they wanted.[10] So long as Saudi Arabia was willing to adjust its own output so that the total quantity supplied equaled quantity demanded at the cartel price, other OPEC members could sell as much as they wanted at that price.

But OPEC ran into trouble in the 1980s. Because of higher prices, the world as a whole used almost 4 percent less oil in 1984 than it had in 1973, despite an increase of nearly 30 percent in the real GNP of the industrialized countries. Higher prices also induced non-OPEC countries to increase oil production by almost 50 percent over this period. In order to maintain high prices in the face of these developments, OPEC had to decrease its own production by about 45 percent, and Saudi Arabia cut production by 80 percent. Even so, as Figure 12-2 shows, price nonetheless fell in both nominal and real terms after 1981, and the dollar value of OPEC exports has decreased every year since 1980. OPEC accounted for only 32 percent of the world oil production in 1984.

Eventually, in early 1986, Saudi Arabia recognized that the dominant firm cartel, in which it had absorbed large losses in production to support the world price, was not serving its interest. It began to produce more oil, driving the world price down from nearly $30 a barrel to below $10 in a few months. In December 1986 the OPEC nations all agreed to abide by limits on oil production, and some nonmembers (Mexico, Norway, and the Soviet Union) also announced that they would reduce production. Oil prices quickly recovered to around $18 a barrel—still well below the real prices that had prevailed during the 1974–1985 period. But prices began to slip again in February 1987. It remains to be seen if the cartel can maintain monopoly prices now that Saudi Arabia is unwilling to bear all the rising costs of restricting output.

Tacit Collusion: Leadership and Stability

Because explicit agreements about price among private corporations are frequently illegal, oligopolists often seek ways to cooperate tacitly, without explicitly reaching agreements. Firms can send messages to each other in a variety of public, legal ways, and they can employ a variety of devices to make cheating easier to detect.

In the early 1950s, for instance, breakfast cereal firms competed by including expensive toys in most cereal boxes. After one executive made a speech announcing that his firm would sharply reduce its use of these premiums, the other major producers adopted the same policy, and all became more profitable. Price changes for some products, such as sandpaper, are often announced months in advance. This gives other firms a chance to comment on the proposed prices, by their own responses, before they go into effect. The first firm to announce a price change often revises its announcement if its rivals don't announce the same changes. Oligopolists sometimes sign long-term contracts with their customers obligating them to meet any lower price offered by another seller or to charge all of their customers the same price. These practices make it more difficult for secret price-cutting to undermine collusion.

From the early 1920s until World War II, the three major cigarette producers—Reynolds (Camels), American Tobacco (Lucky Stikes), and Liggett & Myers

---

[10] Actually, Saudi Arabia was not the only country in OPEC that did not take price as given. Kuwait and some other Arab nations frequently coordinated their actions with Saudi Arabia.

(Chesterfields)—charged identical prices and managed to avoid price wars entirely. The device used by the cigarette producers to accomplish this was price leadership.

● In oligopolistic *price leadership*, a single firm (the *price leader*) is tacitly assigned the role of determining industry prices. The other firms keep their prices constant until the leader announces a change in its prices, and they generally follow by announcing the same change.

The price leader judges when to change price. If it is right, the other firms follow and the leader effectively changes the industry's price without having explicitly colluded with the other firms. If the other firms do not follow suit, the price change is vetoed, and the leader will get back into the pack by withdrawing the increase. The leader is usually the largest firm, but if its announcements are vetoed by the others too often, another leader may emerge.[11] Price leadership has been observed in many oligopolistic industries, including steel and automobiles in the post–World War II period.

In industries with price leaders, prices tend to remain constant over relatively long periods. The leader is reluctant to rock the boat and risk losing its position by announcing changes that may be vetoed. But why don't the other firms change their prices when cost or demand conditions change?

THE KINKED OLIGOPOLY DEMAND CURVE. The kinked demand curve model provides an explanation.[12] A firm that is not the price leader might reasonably assume that if it cut price all its rivals would match the cut, while if it raised price none would follow its lead.

The implications of this assumption are shown in Figure 12-3. The current price is P_0. If the nonleader firm raised price above this level, it would lose sales rapidly because its rivals would keep their prices at P_0. For prices above the going price, the firm's demand curve is therefore very elastic. If it lowered price, on the other hand, the firm would not gain much business, because its rivals would match its price cuts. The demand curve implied by this reasoning is labeled D in Figure 12-3; it is more elastic at prices above the current price, P_0, than it is at lower prices. Because the demand curve is flatter for prices above P_0 than it is for lower prices, its slope changes at P_0, producing a kink in the curve.

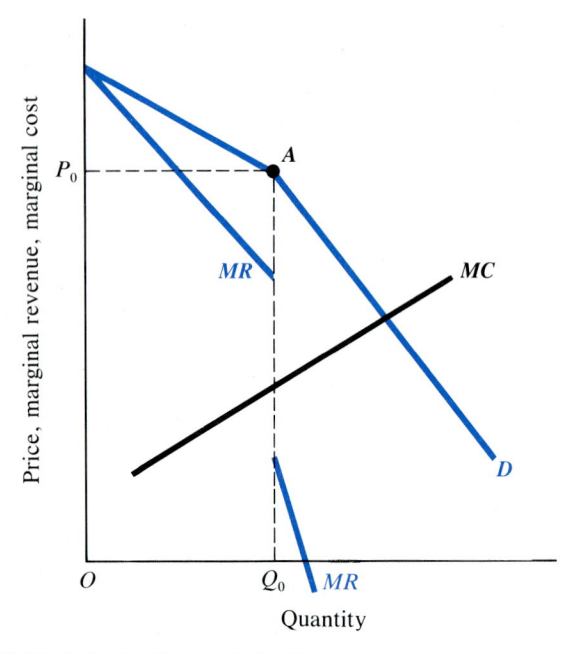

FIGURE 12-3. The Kinked Oligopoly Demand Curve. In an industry with a price leader, each follower assumes that rivals will match his price cuts but not his price hikes. Followers thus face a demand curve with a kink at the going price, P_0, and a discontinuous marginal revenue schedule, MR. Because of the gap in the MR schedule, the follower will not change price even if the marginal cost schedule, MC, shifts by a small amount.

---

[11] Even in industries without a clear price leader, somebody has to be first to announce a price change. In true price leadership the *same* firm tends to be first over a relatively long period, and, as discussed in the next paragraph, price changes are relatively rare even when costs and demands are changing.

[12] This model, which was invented almost simultaneously in 1939 by Paul Sweezy in the United States and by R. L. Hall and C. J. Hitch in England, is sometimes presented as a complete theory of oligopoly pricing. But since it says nothing at all about the level of price, it is not a complete theory. If it described all sellers in an oligopoly, it would predict that prices would change less often in oligopoly than they do in monopoly. But many studies have shown that this prediction is not consistent with actual market behavior.

Figure 12-3 also shows the firm's marginal cost curve, *MC*, and its marginal revenue curve, *MR*. Because the demand curve is kinked at price P_0, the *MR* curve is discontinuous at the corresponding output, Q_0. At outputs below Q_0, marginal revenue is close to price because only small price cuts are required to increase the quantity demanded when rivals' prices are fixed. At outputs above Q_0, marginal revenue is much lower than price because price must be cut sharply to increase the firm's demand when rivals match price cuts. The *MC* curve goes through the gap in the *MR* curve. At any price above P_0, marginal revenue exceeds marginal cost and the firm should reduce price and increase quantity. At any price below P_0, marginal revenue is less than marginal cost and the firm should therefore increase price and reduce quantity. As long as there is a kink at P_0, the *MC* curve will pass through the gap in the *MR* curve even if costs change slightly, and the optimal price will remain P_0. The conclusion is that a follower in an oligopoly with a price leader generally maximizes its profits by keeping price at the current level until the leader announces a change.

Noncollusive Oligopoly Behavior

How do oligopolists behave when there is neither explicit nor tacit collusion? Even if collusion is effective for a time, it often breaks down because one or more firms feel they have more to gain by breaking the rules than by obeying them. When firms cannot collude, the essential problem of oligopoly becomes one of strategies: Each firm makes an assumption about the demand it faces and about its rivals' reactions to its own actions. Each firm than acts to maximize its own profits on the basis of its beliefs about how its rivals will respond. It decides how to react to its rivals' actions in exactly the same way.

There are no firm, general predictions about the outcomes of such interactions among noncooperating oligopolists. Price may be almost anywhere between the competitive and monopoly levels, and it may vary sharply over time. What happens depends critically on how each oligopolist assumes the others will react to what it does. If each thinks its rivals will not respond to its price cuts, for instance, and all try to be the low-price firm, prices may fall to competitive levels. If such a price war occurs, however, all firms will probably change their views of their competitors' behavior. Price may then rise, perhaps even high enough to set off another round of price-cutting.

Even when collusion is not effective, most economists expect oligopoly prices to be above competitive levels much of the time. But how far above that level they rise depends both on what oligopolists know and believe about their rivals' behavior and, as we now discuss, on the ability of new sellers to enter the industry.

Entry Deterrence and Predation

Thus far in this section we have ignored the possibility of entry by new sellers. This possibility adds two new features. First, as we mentioned previously, if there are no barriers to entry, there is no way for price to remain above the competitive level in the long run. Above-normal profits will attract new entrants, and their additions to total output will drive price down to competitive levels. Without barriers to entry, collusion cannot raise profits in the long run.

Second, as we now discuss, the possibility of entry may affect the behavior of established oligopolists. They may take actions designed either to prevent new entrants from appearing or to drive them from the market before they can become established.

In order to deter entry, colluding sellers may set output above the monopoly level. If there are economies of scale, this may deter entry by forcing an entrant either to build a small plant with high average cost or to build a large, expensive plant and risk driving price below cost by adding a lot to total industry output. The practice of charging the highest price that just prevents entry is called *limit pricing*.

Alternatively, established firms may maintain excess capacity in order to make believable a threat to increase output sharply if entry occurs. This is a threat to engage in predatory pricing.

● **Firms engage in *predatory pricing* when they cut price in order to drive other firms from the industry.**

Typically the predator cuts prices very sharply, to a level where she is losing money but where she hopes the competition is suffering more and cannot long survive in the industry. In order for predation to be profitable, entry must generally be difficult. If not, the predator's losses will just make it less able to deal with the next entrant and the one after that.

Small firms that are unable to match the prices of larger rivals often accuse the latter of predatory pricing. But in most cases of this sort, entry is easy and predation would not be sensible. Usually the larger firms simply have lower costs and are not engaging in predation.

But while predatory pricing is relatively rare, it does occur. A particularly clear example is provided by the Hankow Shipping Conference of the late nineteenth century. This was a cartel of ship owners who had fixed freight rates in shipping between China and the United Kingdom and also had a clear policy toward new entrants:[13]

> In 1885 the Conference decided that "if any non-Conference steamer should proceed to Hankow to load independently, any necessary number of Conference steamers should be sent at the same time to Hankow to underbid the freight which the independent shipowners might offer, *without any regard to whether the freight they should bid would be remunerative or not.*"

Thus if any other ships tried to enter the business, members of the conference would undercut them, no matter how much the members might lose in the process. The members of the conference were willing to take losses in the short run to keep out other entrants and thereby make excess profits from their monopoly position in the long run.

4. Monopolistic Competition

We now turn our attention from fewness to product differentiation. The theory of monopolistic competition[14] describes a situation in which there are a variety of goods, with each firm producing a good that is a close substitute for the others. For examples, think of firms that compete by choosing to sell at nearby locations, offering slightly different services or menus, or producing closely related varieties of toothpaste or ice cream. Everyone knows that ice cream is good, but not everyone agrees which kind is best. Each ice cream parlor thus faces a downward-sloping demand curve.

Downward-sloping demand curves, reflecting product differentiation, distinguish monopolistic competition from perfect competition. If a monopolistic competitor cuts its price, the quantity of its product demanded increases because some buyers will switch to it from other sellers. Because products differ, not all buyers switch, as they would in perfect competition. Because its demand curve slopes downward, a monopolistic competitor can choose the price that maximizes its profits. But because it is too small to affect the market as a whole very much, it assumes that competitors do not react to its pricing decision.

Short-Run Equilibrium

In the short run there are a fixed number of firms in the industry. As in monopoly, each takes its downward-sloping demand curve as fixed and chooses price to maximize profit. As in perfect competition, all sellers may be making profits in the short run.

In Figure 12-4 we show the average and marginal cost curves for a single ice cream parlor, firm K, which faces a downward-sloping demand curve. The average cost curve has the U shape familiar from earlier chapters. The firm selects output Q_0, where marginal revenue is equal to marginal cost, and charges price P_0. Initially firm K is making economic profits at this point, equal to the shaded area $(P_0 - AC_0) \times Q_0$. In the short run a monopolistic competitor thus looks like a monopolist.

Long-Run Equilibrium

Things look very different in the long run because entry can occur. The demand curve facing each monopolistic

---

[13] Quoted from B.S. Yamey, "Predatory Price Cutting: Notes and Comments," *Journal of Law and Economics*, April 1972, p. 139 (italics added). Copyright © by the University of Chicago. You may be struck by the fact that this is a very old example. The problem with finding good recent examples is that predatory pricing is now generally illegal, and documents like the one quoted in the text constitute damning evidence. Firms are thus very careful about committing predatory strategies to paper.

[14] This is the title of a famous book published by Harvard's Edward H. Chamberlin in 1933 that develops the analysis that follows.

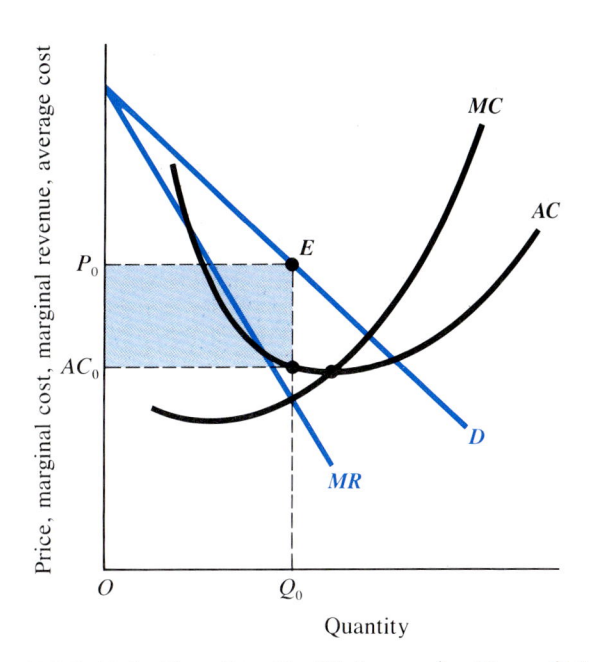

FIGURE 12-4. Short-Run Equilibrium under Monopolistic Competition. Each monopolistic competitor faces a downward-sloping demand curve; price cuts are necessary to increase output. Monopolistic competitors take this into account just as monopolists do, choosing output level Q_0, where $MR = MC$. Profits, here equal to $(P_0 - AC_0) \times Q_0$, invite entry.

competitor depends on the prices and number of close substitutes for its product. The more competing substitute brands and the lower their prices, the smaller the demand for any firm's output.

If monopolistic competitors are making profits in the short run, other firms will come into the industry. Even with product differentiation, new firms—producing close but not perfect substitutes for existing goods—will be attracted into the industry as long as existing firms make profits. As entrants move in and increase the number of available substitutes, the demand curves of existing firms shift to the left. Entry continues until all firms have been driven to the point of zero profits.[15]

The high profits shown in Figure 12-4 will thus attract other firms into the ice cream parlor business. As they

[15] As under perfect competition, if firms differ in efficiency, some may earn positive economic profits even in the long run.

enter, the demand curve for firm K is shifted to the left because some of its customers move to the new firms. New competitors continue to enter so long as firm K and similar firms are earning economic profits. Entry stops when firm K and other firms in the industry are earning zero profits or, in other words, when price is equal to average cost.

The long-run equilibrium position of firm K is shown in Figure 12-5. In order to maximize profit given its new demand curve, D', firm K produces output Q', at which marginal cost is equal to marginal revenue. It thus sets a price, P', above marginal cost. But it earns zero economic profit because the demand curve is tangent to (just touches) the average cost curve, AC, at this price and output. At this *tangency equilibrium*, profits are zero ($AC' = P'$) and there is therefore no entry into the industry.

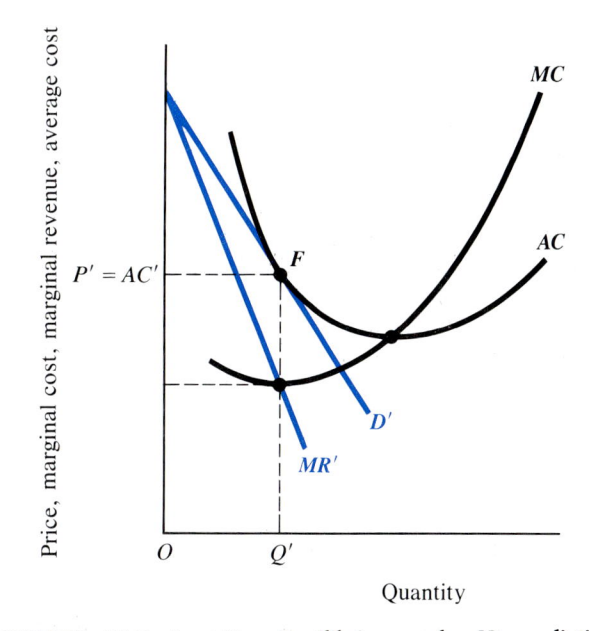

FIGURE 12-5. Long-Run Equilibrium under Monopolistic Competition. Under monopolistic competition, profits attract new entry. In long-run equilibrium, profits are therefore zero. As in the short run, marginal cost equals marginal revenue for each firm; price is above marginal cost and equal to average cost. Equilibrium occurs at point F, where the demand curve is tangent to the average cost curve. Because of entry, the firm's demand curve has shifted from D in Figure 12-4 to D' here.

Monopolistic versus Perfect Competition

Both perfect competition and monopolistic competition involve large numbers of sellers, each one correctly assuming that the others will not notice her actions. Competitive firms take a common market price as given while a monopolistic competitor only assumes given the price charged by their competitors. Because products are differentiated under monopolistic competition, while under perfect competition, they are homogeneous, the long-run equilibria in these two types of markets differ in three important ways.

First, monopolistic competitors do not produce at the point of minimum average cost. As Figure 12-5 indicates, each firm could lower its average cost by producing more. But, like monopolists, monopolistic competitors do not produce more because they would have to cut price to all buyers to increase the quantity of their output demanded.

Second, price exceeds marginal cost, so that there is a gap between the value consumers place on each good and its cost of production. Thus monopolistic competition, like monopoly, does not lead to a perfectly efficient allocation of resources.

Third, because price exceeds marginal cost, each firm would willingly sell more than it does at the existing price. Like a monopolist, it will not cut price to raise the quantity demanded beyond the point where marginal revenue equals marginal cost. But if new customers showed up wanting to buy at the existing price, any monopolistic competitor would profit from selling to them. Sellers may thus advertise in order to attract the attention of potential buyers. In contrast, firms in a perfectly competitive industry always sell just as much as they want at the going price. If another customer shows up and asks to buy more at the going price, a perfect competitor replies that he is not interested in selling more, because an increase in output would raise marginal cost above price.

The theory of monopolistic competition is of considerable value for focusing attention on situations where there are many firms selling slightly different products and for bringing product variety squarely into the picture. As we have just discussed, its predictions depart in important ways from the model of perfect competition.

5. Nonprice Competition: Variety and Advertising

In both oligopoly and monopolistic competition, sellers in the same market often provide a variety of similar products and advertise those products heavily. This observation raises two important questions on which this section focuses. First, do these markets provide the right amount of variety, or do firms try too hard to distinguish their goods from their competitors' goods, creating wasteful excesses of variety? Second, when firms advertise to differentiate their products and increase the demand for them, do they waste society's resources? Or is advertising an efficient way to provide information?

Variety

Because it is generally expensive to provide variety, society must choose to produce only some of the enormous number of conceivable goods and services. Consider a set of possible goods that are close substitutes and suppose that there are increasing returns to scale at low levels of output, as on U-shaped average cost curves. Then if we tried to produce all imaginable goods, they would all be produced at high cost—like customized cars or vans—because we would make just a few of each and get no benefit from economies of scale. In most markets it is likely to be better to restrict the number of goods produced, compensating by exploiting economies of scale to produce more of each at lower unit costs.

The theory of monopolistic competition illustrates the trade-off between variety and low cost. Under monopolistic competition the long-run industry equilibrium is one in which each firm has price equal to average cost. But average cost is above its minimum level (see Figure 12-5), and price exceeds marginal cost. If fewer firms produced more output each and set price equal to average cost, prices and unit costs would be lower. But there would be less variety than in the monopolistic competition equilibrium, and consumers value both variety and low prices.

Do market economies generally make the right choice between greater variety and lower unit costs? Looking around in the shops, we often have the feeling that there is too much variety, with manufacturers wasting resources to produce many nearly identical brands of some products. However, economists have not been able to make a strong case that we have too much, just enough, or too little variety.

The larger the total market, the less expensive it is to provide any given level of variety. As the economy grows and people in it become richer, it is efficient to increase variety because demand for all goods is rising. In a very poor country, there may be enough demand to buy the output of only one (monopoly) firm in many markets. As the economy grows and consumers' demand therefore expands, there is room for entry by more firms and market structures evolve toward monopolistic competition, giving consumers the benefits of variety.

The same gain can be achieved by taking advantage of international trade between countries. Much of the trade between the advanced industrialized countries takes place in the same industry. Germany and France sell each other cars, for instance. This trade in differentiated products makes people in both countries better off by giving them access to a broader range of products, each of which is produced for the world market and can therefore be produced on a reasonably large scale.

Advertising

In 1985, $95 billion was spent on advertising in the United States. This was more than half the world's total and amounted to 2.4 percent of U.S. GNP. Advertising is divided among the major media as shown in Table 12-5. Local advertising is done mainly by retailers, and national advertising by manufacturers and service firms that sell nationwide. It may be somewhat surprising that a good deal more is spent on local newspaper advertising than on national television advertising.

It is hard to generalize about advertising because it comes in such different forms. Much of the advertising we see on television appears to be pure waste, containing no useful information. Does anybody really learn anything from hearing "Coke is it!" for the ninety-ninth time? And a good deal of advertising by rival firms seems to cancel out. Would people really change their behavior noticeably if Coca-Cola, Pepsi-Cola, and the others all cut their advertising spending in half?

On the other hand, a lot of advertising provides information about the availability and prices of goods and services that consumers otherwise would have to spend resources to obtain in some other way. Think of the Yellow Pages and your walking fingers saving shoe leather and gasoline. After newspaper strikes, consumers often report that they missed the ads at least as much as anything else, and newspaper advertising makes up more than a quarter of all advertising. It is perhaps not surprising that economists have been no more successful in demonstrating that there is too much advertising than in showing that there is too much variety. And nobody has come up with a better way of providing information about available goods and services.

TABLE 12-5. Percentage Breakdown of U.S. Advertising Expenditures in 1985

	Percentage of total advertising spending		
Medium	National	Local	Total
Newspapers	3.5	23.3	26.8
Television	16.0	6.0	22.0
Radio	1.8	5.0	6.8
Magazines	5.5	0.0	5.5
Direct mail and other	29.4	9.6	39.0
All media	56.0	44.0	100.0

Source: *Advertising Age*, December 16, 1985, p. 10.

In some markets advertising seems to raise prices. Unadvertised liquid bleaches sell for substantially less than chemically identical but heavily advertised brands, for instance. But in other cases advertising makes it easier for consumers to identify and evaluate competitors, and thus it tends to lower prices. One study found the price of eyeglasses to be about 25 to 30 percent lower in states that permitted advertising than in states that did not, for example. Some economists argue that heavy advertising by established firms can build customer loyalty and thus create barriers to entry. Others reply that new brands are generally the most heavily advertised, so that advertising is an important means of entry.

A difficult and important issue is whether advertising manipulates consumers' tastes. Are we, as many feel, the greedy consumers we are despite human nature and because of advertising? Or is it merely human nature that ensures that we are serious consumers of even frivolous goods? Does advertising follow changes in society or cause those changes? These are important questions because we usually judge the economic system by its ability to satisfy our desires. But if part of the system is creating our wants, it is not too comforting to know that those wants are efficiently satisfied. If we want the latest in electronic watches with twelve-tone alarms only because a clever advertising agency has persuaded us that everyone should have one, it is difficult to be impressed by the economy's success in providing us with such a watch.

Unfortunately economics provides no clear-cut answers to these questions. Most of our wants are learned; nobody but a mink is born wanting a mink coat. And advertising is all around us. However, we should be on guard against the simpleminded notion that all our wants are the creation of manipulative advertising. Mink coats aren't heavily advertised, and many new and heavily advertised products do indeed make life appreciably easier and more interesting.

■ Like monopoly, and unlike perfect competition, oligopoly and monopolistic competition do not generally produce a perfectly efficient allocation of resources. Unlike either of the extreme cases, oligopoly and monopolistic competition are very common. In the next two chapters we will see how government regulatory policy responds to monopoly power and other sources of market failure. One thing should be clear in advance, however: Government regulation does not seriously attempt to make all markets perfectly competitive. That would be an impossible job. As a practical matter, the government can at best deal with unusually serious market failures. This is not as bad as it may sound, however. While few markets operate exactly as if they were perfectly competitive, many come close.

Summary

1. Oligopolies—industries in which most sales are made by a few firms—exist in part because economies of scale make it efficient for there to be only a small number of sellers. But seller concentration is often higher than required by scale economies in production.
2. Economies of scale also give rise to barriers to entry, which enable oligopolists to earn profits without attracting new entrants.
3. Product differentiation, which is important in many markets, arises because sellers find it profitable to respond to buyers' different tastes and desires for variety. Product differentiation is usually associated with advertising and other selling costs.
4. There are two basic forces at work in determining the behavior of oligopolists. By colluding, firms can keep price above the competitive level and make profits. By violating a collusive agreement, individual firms can do better for themselves so long as the other firms do not respond. The oligopolists' dilemma illustrates the tension between these two forces.
5. Collusion is most likely to occur when it is legal and when there are a small number of sellers. Differences among firms or products, changes in costs and demands, and the ability to make secret price cuts tend to make collusion more difficult.
6. When collusion is legal, oligopolists often set up cartels to fix price and restrict output. Cartels often break down because firms cheat on the agreement. The OPEC cartel was successful for a long time in large part because of Saudi Arabia's willingness to restrict its output and allow the other suppliers to sell as much as they wanted at the cartel price.
7. When explicit collusion is illegal, firms sometimes find ways of cooperating tacitly. This is often done by tacit agreement that one firm will act as the price leader and others will match its price changes. The kinked demand curve model shows why nonleader firms in such an industry don't change prices even when costs change.
8. If firms cannot collude, their behavior depends on how each expects the others to react to what it does. Prices may vary between the monopolistic and competitive levels.
9. In order to discourage the entry of new firms, colluding oligopolists may set price below the monopoly level. Predatory pricing is sometimes used to drive out new entrants, but this is not a common practice.
10. Monopolistic competition exists when there are many firms

selling similar products, with each firm facing a downward-sloping demand curve. The entry of new firms selling close substitute products drives down price and profits. The long-run equilibrium occurs where firms have zero profits, as in perfect competition, but price exceeds marginal cost.

11 Because of economies of scale, it is not economical to produce all possible goods. It is not clear whether monopolistic competition yields too much or too little variety.

12 Over 2 percent of GNP is spent on advertising of various sorts. The effects of advertising seem to vary considerably, and there is no good argument that there is too much or too little advertising.

Key Terms

Seller concentration
Concentration ratio
Minimum efficient scale
Natural oligopoly
Explicit collusion
Tacit collusion
Oligopolists' (or prisoners') dilemma
Cartel
Price leader
Kinked demand curve
Limit pricing
Predatory pricing
Tangency equilibrium

Problems

1 The demand curve facing an industry is as follows:

Price	Quantity	Price	Quantity
10	1	5	6
9	2	4	7
8	3	3	8
7	4	2	9
6	5	1	10

(a) Suppose that the industry is a monopoly and that the monopolist has constant marginal costs of production equal to 3 (also equal to average cost). Using the analysis in Chapter 11, find the price and output that the monopolist will choose. (b) Now suppose there are two firms in the industry, which is therefore a duopoly. Assume that each can produce at a constant average and marginal cost of 3. What price and output level will maximize their joint profits if they collude effectively? (c) Why do the two firms have to agree on the level of output each will produce? (d) Why may each firm be tempted to cheat if it can avoid retaliation by the other? What does this tell you about the behavior of oligopolists?

2 Suppose one of the firms in the industry (call it firm Z) decides to cheat on the agreement and believes that the other firm (firm A) will continue to keep its price fixed. (a) What will firm Z do? (b) How do you expect firm A to react? (c) Where might a process like this end?

3 Name five oligopolists from which you bought some good or service in the last year. (a) For which of these do you think economies of scale are the main reason why seller concentration is high? Why? (b) What other forces increased seller concentration in these industries? (c) Can you identify any reasons why it would be difficult for a new firm to enter any of these industries? Has there been any recent entry in any of these cases?

4 In many countries there are dairy or fruit marketing boards. These are organizations to which the farmers who grow a particular type of fruit or who produce dairy products belong and through which they sell their output. In some cases the marketing board tells its members how much of the product they will be able to sell to the board in that year. In other cases the board merely buys as much as the farmers wish to sell and pays the farmers the amount the board obtains by selling the product, adjusted for the board's costs. (a) Under one of these arrangements, the board is likely to be acting as a cartel. Which? (b) Why might the cartel-like arrangement be unstable unless it had legal powers to require all farmers to sell their products only to it?

5 This question is about the importance of entry. Go back to Problem 1. Assume that one firm can produce more cheaply than any other, at a constant marginal and average cost of 3. Suppose all other firms that potentially could enter the industry can produce at a constant average and marginal cost of 5. (a) What price will the single firm in the industry charge? (b) What price would it charge if there were no possibility of entry? (c) What, therefore, has the threat of entry done to price?

6 Service station and automobile repair dealers have sometimes suggested that mechanics should be licensed to ensure that repairs are done by qualified people. Some economists have argued that there is no need for licensing. So long as the mechanics are trained at a reputable institution (fre-

quently automobile manufacturers provide training courses), any customer who cares will be able to find a qualified mechanic by asking about his training. (a) Why should these economists argue against licensing? (b) Evaluate the arguments for and against licensing of auto mechanics. (c) Are the arguments different in the case of doctors? Why or why not?

7 Table 12-5 gives the percentage of total advertising expenditure accounted for in different media in 1985. (a) Having been exposed to much of this advertising, can you classify any of these expenditures as informative versus persuasive? (b) Why does the distinction between informative and persuasive advertising matter? (c) Do you think the distinction is a useful one? (d) Is there a case to be made on economic grounds for banning certain types of advertising?

8 Are all possible colors of towels produced? Why or why not? If you were given the power to do so, how would you decide how many different colors should be on the market?

9 The accompanying table describes the demand curve an oligopolist thinks he faces. His marginal cost of production is constant and equal to 3.

A Kinked Demand Curve

Price	Quantity	Price	Quantity
10	0	5	13
9	3	4	14
8	6	3	15
7	9	2	16
6	12	1	17

(a) What is the firm's optimal price and level of output? (b) To what level would his cost of production have to rise before he would increase price?

Chapter 13
Regulation of Economic Activity

The term "regulated industry" usually suggests public utilities such as electric and telephone companies. These and other industries are subject to *economic regulation*, in which government agencies set prices and often determine who can sell what. But even though most industries are not regulated in this way, it is no exaggeration to say that all industries in the United States (and in most other developed market economies) are regulated.

Consider, for instance, the automobile industry, which is not subject to economic regulation. However, the U.S. Federal Trade Commission (FTC) determines whether automobile advertising is false or misleading, the U.S. Environmental Protection Agency (EPA) regulates pollution from plants that produce automobiles and parts, and the U.S. Occupational Safety and Health Administration (OSHA) enforces rules designed to protect auto workers from job-related risks. In addition, the gasoline consumption of new cars is regulated by the secretary of transportation, pollution from automobiles is regulated by the EPA, and auto safety is regulated by the U.S. National Highway Traffic Safety Administration (NHTSA). It has been estimated that the costs of the latter two programs alone amount to about $2600 per car.[1] All these programs are examples of *social regulation*, which is concerned with such issues as health, safety, discrimination, and protection of consumers and the environment.

While the automobile industry is an extreme case, it is not unique. "Commercial banks and other depository institutions . . . may be the most heavily regulated institutions in the American economy after electric utilities."[2] Lawyers and hairstylists must pass examinations before they are allowed to go into business. Even corner grocery stores cannot open on just any corner, since zoning boards regulate land use in most cities and towns. Essentially all firms in the economy are subject to antitrust laws, under which the government bans cartels,

---

[1] Robert W. Crandall, Howard K. Gruenspecht, Theodore E. Keeler, and Lester B. Lave, *Regulating the Automobile*, Brookings Institution, Washington, 1986. The figure in the text is in 1985 dollars.

[2] Lawerence J. White, "The Partial Deregulation of Banks and Other Depository Institutions," in Leonard W. Weiss and Michael W. Klass (eds.), *Regulatory Reform: What Actually Happened*, Little, Brown, Boston, 1986, p. 169.

stops some mergers, and prohibits business practices it finds to be anticompetitive.

We begin this chapter with a general overview of government regulation of economic activity. Section 1 reviews economic arguments for regulation, which are based on the shortcomings of the market system, or *market failures*, that were introduced in Chapter 4. But regulatory decisions are political, and much government regulation takes place where there is no obvious market failure. Regulators are also political, and regulation may work poorly even when government intervention is in principle justified. We discuss the actual scope of regulation and the behavior of regulatory agencies in section 2.

The rest of this chapter concentrates on regulation that is *not* a response to the problem of monopoly power. Section 3 deals with the economic rationale and actual effects of one of the most important programs of social regulation: environmental protection. Section 4 considers social regulation aimed at protecting workers and consumers from health, safety, and other risks. Finally, section 5 describes the recent *deregulation* movement and its effects, concentrating on the airline industry. In Chapter 14 we complete the picture by studying antitrust and economic regulation of natural monopolies.

1. Market Failure, Politics, and Regulation

Politicians, not economists, decide which regulatory agencies are established and what they are supposed to do. Economic analysis affects decisions to regulate and deregulate, but only in an indirect fashion. "There is a saying that economists make bullets that lawyers fire at one another."[3] Lawyers, serving as legislators or regulators, may overlook or decide not to use the ammunition provided by economists, and those who do use it may find themselves politically outgunned. We first examine what economics has to say about the desirable scope of regulation and then consider the creation and behavior of regulatory agencies in practice.

---

[3] Merton J. Peck, quoted in *Unsettled Questions on Regulatory Reform*, American Enterprise Institute, Washington, 1978, p. 13.

Market Failure

Prices are the central allocative mechanism in a market economy. Prices guide consumers' choices among alternative goods, and they guide the allocation of resources among various industries. On the demand side, competitive prices reflect the valuation of an extra unit of the good by consumers. On the production side, they reflect the marginal cost of an extra unit of the good to producers and to society as a whole. When competitive markets clear, the equilibrium price that equates the quantity demanded with the quantity supplied also equates the marginal valuation of a good with the marginal cost of supplying it. As Chapter 10 demonstrated, perfect competition produces an optimal resource allocation, because in each market costs and benefits are equated at the margin.

But as Chapter 4 discussed, it is certainly possible that although prices clear a market, they do not reflect the marginal valuation of consumers or the marginal cost to society of an extra unit of output. If not, there is a market failure that leads to an inefficient allocation of resources. Economic arguments for regulation generally involve one or more of the following sources of market failure discussed in Chapter 4.

MONOPOLY POWER. As we saw in Chapter 10, the exercise of monopoly power leads to output restrictions, as sellers increase their profits by raising prices above competitive levels. Antitrust policy deals with the monopoly problem in most sectors. Where economies of scale make monopoly necessary for efficiency (and thus "natural"), economic regulation or government ownership is called for. These responses to monopoly power are the focus of Chapter 14.

EXTERNALITIES. Some production or consumption activities directly impose costs or benefits on consumers or firms that are not directly involved. Even when we drive our new, small, fuel-efficient cars, we make the air dirtier for everyone. If we drove older or larger or noisier cars, the spillover effects of our actions would be more serious. When a new supermarket opens in a residential area, nearby homeowners find they live on busier streets.

Externalities provide an economic rationale for regulation of pollution, restrictions on land use, control of radio and television broadcasting, and other programs.

IMPERFECT INFORMATION. One of the assumptions of the model of perfect competition is that buyers and sellers know everything they need to know in order to pursue their self-interest. Unfortunately, this assumption is often wrong. Buyers may be unaware of the risks associated with certain products, and sellers have little incentive to inform them about these risks. Sellers of labor may be unaware of job-related risks, particularly those involving long-term health hazards. Their employers may be no better informed on this score.

■ Were all regulatory agencies in fact created to deal with one or more of these problems? Once established, do they focus on eliminating market failures? To answer these general questions, we must look at U.S. regulatory agencies and their behavior in practice.

2. Regulation in Practice

Table 13-1 lists the major federal regulatory agencies in 1980, along with their main areas of responsibility and their 1980 and 1985 budgets (both measured in 1985 dollars) for regulatory activities. These agencies are usually referred to by their initials—ICC, FCC, FERC, CAB, etc.—and are thus often called an "alphabet soup" as a group.

Economic regulation in its modern form began in 1887, when the Interstate Commerce Commission (ICC) was established. The ICC, like most agencies engaged in economic regulation, has several members and makes decisions by majority vote. The first federal antitrust law was passed in 1890. Between 1907 and 1920, most states set up commissions to regulate the prices charged by public utilities. The coverage of economic regulation at the federal level was expanded in the Great Depression of the 1930s and once more in the early 1970s, when the prices of oil, gasoline, and related products were regulated.

Social regulation in the United States dates from 1906, when the Food and Drug Administration (FDA) was established. The scope of social regulation was sharply expanded in the 1960s and especially in the early 1970s under the Nixon administration. Many of these newer agencies are headed by one person rather than a group.

Beginning in the mid-1970s, many critics charged that regulation—both social and economic—had gone too far and was a burden on the economy. The argument was not that the agencies were too expensive to run; the budget numbers in Table 13-1 are small by Washington standards. Rather, it was claimed that regulators imposed excessive costs on the economy as a whole. Instead of eliminating market failures, they were creating new sources of inefficiency.

A good deal of economic *de*regulation has occurred since the mid-1970s: The federal government has stopped setting the prices of oil, most natural gas, and gasoline, and the rates charged by airlines and truckers. Even banks, railroads, and the telephone business have been partially deregulated. Some of these changes are visible in the budget figures in Table 13-1.[4] There has been much less social deregulation, despite efforts by the Ford, Carter, and Reagan administrations. Table 13-1 shows that some of these agencies have experienced serious budget cuts under Reagan, but no legislation that would significantly limit the scope of social regulation has been passed.

The different histories of economic and social regulation reflect the fact that the two sets of agencies have different reasons for existing and react to different kinds of political forces, as we now discuss.

Economic Regulation

The first group of agencies listed in Table 13-1—those concerned with economic regulation—generally limit entry into a particular industry and commonly control both price and service quality. The main economic ra-

---

[4] The Civil Aeronautics Board (CAB) was in fact abolished on January 1, 1985; the 1985 budget figure in the table reflects mainly shutdown costs and the activities of the Department of Transportation in international airline markets.

TABLE 13-1. Major Federal Regulatory Agencies, 1980 and 1985

Agency	Main 1980 responsibilities (date regulated)	Budget* 1980	Budget* 1985
Economic regulation			
Interstate Commerce Commission	Railroads (1887)	100	49
	Trucking (1934)		
	Barge lines (1940)		
Federal Communications Commission	Telephones (1934)	96	95
	Broadcasting (1934)		
	Cable TV (1968)		
Federal Energy Regulatory Commission	Electricity (1935)	90	97
	Pipelines (1938, 1977)		
	Natural gas (1954)		
Civil Aeronautics Board	Airlines (1938)	37	6
Federal Maritime Commission	Ocean Shipping (1936)	15	12
Economic Regulatory Administration	Petroleum (1973)	194	—
Comptroller of the Currency	National banks (1864)	140†	179
Federal Reserve Board	Member Banks (1913)	16	17
Federal Deposit Insurance Corporation	Insured Banks (1933)	163	143
Federal Home Loan Bank Board	Savings and loans (1933)	43	26
Federal Savings and Loan Insurance Corporation	Insured savings and loans (1934)	27	26
Social regulation			
Food and Drug Administration	Safety of food and drugs (1906), cosmetics (1938)	405	410
	Efficacy of drugs (1962)		
Animal and Plant Health Inspection Service	Packing plants (1907)	323	242
Federal Trade Commission	Advertising (1914, 1938)	39	32
Securities and Exchange Commission	Security issues and exchanges (1934)	91	106
Federal Aviation Administration	Airlines safety (1934)	285	264
Nuclear Regulatory Commission	Nuclear plants (1947)	460	448
National Highway Traffic Safety Administration	Auto safety (1970)	74	58
	Fuel economy (1975)		
Environmental Protection Agency	Air, water, and noise pollution (1963–1972)	525	662
	Toxic substances (1976)		
Occupational Safety and Health Administration	Workplace safety and health (1971)	234	221
Mine Safety and Health Administration	Mine safety and health (1973)	180	152
Consumer Product Safety Commission	Consumer products (1972)	50	36

* Regulatory functions only, excluding antitrust, in millions of 1985 dollars.
† For 1982; 1980 not available.

Source: Leonard W. Weiss, "The Regulatory Reform Movement," in L. W. Weiss and M. W. Klass (eds.), *Regulatory Reform: What Actually Happened*, Little, Brown, Boston, 1986, Table 1.

tionale for this sort of regulation is the natural monopoly problem that was introduced in Chapter 11 and analyzed in detail in Chapter 14. But a glance down the second column of Table 13-1 shows that economic regulation has been applied to a large number of industries that nobody claims are natural monopolies. Why?

Several studies of the creation of the Interstate Commerce Commission in 1887 have supported what has come to be known as the capture hypothesis.[5]

[5] See Paul W. MacAvoy, *The Economic Effects of Regulation*, MIT Press, Cambridge, 1965, on the ICC; and George J. Stigler, "The Theory of Economic Regulation," *Bell Journal of Economics and Management Science*, Spring 1971, on the capture hypothesis in general.

- **The *capture hypothesis* assumes that regulatory agencies are set up in the interests of the firms to be regulated and that regulators serve the interests of regulated firms (who have "captured" them through the political process), not consumers.**

These studies argued that the railroads supported their own regulation because regulation would serve to stabilize railroad cartels. Until 1906 the ICC did not set railroads' rates, but it did require them to stick to the rates they announced. By making secret price-cutting illegal, regulation thus made it more difficult for railroads to cheat on collusive agreements.

How can a small group of firms prevail politically against the interests of many consumers? The argument here was discussed in Chapter 4. It is harder to organize a large number of people who care only a little about an issue than a small, wealthy group that cares a lot. If regulation can be used to create monopoly power, a few will gain a lot and many will lose a little. The few may well triumph.

The capture hypothesis turns on its head the idea that economic regulation is designed to protect the public interest from monopoly. Is this hypothesis right? It is easy to point to examples of industries that like being regulated: The airlines and telephone companies welcomed it, and both airline and trucking firms strongly opposed deregulation. But a closer look reveals a more complex pattern.[6] Farmers strongly supported railroad regulation in the 1880s, and they benefitted from restrictions on the pattern of rail rates. Truckers fought regulation in the 1930s; they were regulated mainly because the railroads wanted trucking prices to be *increased* in order to reduce competition from trucks. Similarly, the fact that airlines and trucking were deregulated suggests that a large number of people (air travelers and shippers, for instance) can sometimes be organized into a politically effective force.

Similarly, the capture hypothesis is too simple to explain the behavior of economic regulators well. The laws establishing economic regulation are usually vague and give regulators a lot of freedom to pursue their own goals, and those goals vary over time and among agencies. During the 1960s state commissions regulating electric utilities attracted little attention, and the utilities earned high profits. The commissions may well have been serving the interests of the utilities, as the capture hypothesis predicts. But during the 1970s many state regulators tried to gain political visibility by holding down electricity prices, and the utilities suffered as a consequence.

At the federal level, for a long time the Federal Communications Commission (FCC) taxed long-distance phone calls (by pricing them above cost) to subsidize residential service, the Civil Aeronautics Board (CAB) maintained the profitability of the airlines by preventing all new entry, and the ICC tried to force railroads to continue unprofitable service to small towns. But in the Carter and Reagan years, members of all these agencies pushed vigorously for deregulation. Regulators *are* political, like legislators, but they do not react only to the political power of regulated firms. The capture hypothesis contains a grain of truth, but it does not tell the whole story.

Social Regulation

There is a clear economic rationale for the existence of most of the social regulatory agencies shown in Table 13-1. Most deal with important externalities (such as air pollution) or situations in which decision makers are often not well informed (such as health hazards). Accordingly, few economists have suggested eliminating social regulation, but many have been critical of the existing laws and agencies.

The capture hypothesis is not very helpful in explaining the establishment of social regulation. The Occupational Safety and Health Administration (OSHA), for instance, has jurisdiction over most workplaces in the United States. The firms it regulates are thus not a small, easily organized group. Moreover, they have nothing to gain from being regulated, especially since the law setting up OSHA, like most social regulatory legislation, gives the agency little discretion. It is instructed "to assure so far as possible [to] every working man and woman in the nation safe and healthful working conditions," not just to eliminate unreasonable risks or pro-

---

[6] For a sophisticated discussion of the issues and evidence, see James Q. Wilson, "The Politics of Regulation," in J. Q. Wilson (ed.), *The Politics of Regulation*, Basic Books, New York, 1980.

vide information to workers. The politics of social regulation generally involves large groups: workers, environmentalists, consumers, and large numbers of firms.

Similarly, social regulators are rarely accused of being captured by those they regulate. Social regulators are often professionals in health, safety, and related areas. They are likely to cater to the groups that support their agencies, and they are bound by laws that, like OSHA's, instruct them to eliminate, not to optimize. Thus social regulators are more often accused of being overzealous than of being captives of those they regulate.[7]

3. Externalities and the EPA

We now turn to an important example of social regulation: pollution control to protect the environment. We begin by developing the economic rationale for government regulation of pollution. We then discuss how the EPA has approached its task and conclude the section with a discussion of the potential for regulatory reform.

Externalities and Optimal Regulation

● An *externality* arises whenever the actions of some household or firm directly impose costs or benefits on some other household or firm and these spillover effects are not fully reflected in market prices.

Pollution is the most obvious and important example of an externality. Consider a chemical firm that dumps wastes into a river. These discharges pollute the local water supply, harm fish and birds, and create an offensive smell. The company directly harms area residents. Put another way, it is using the river for waste disposal and not paying the costs involved. The chemical company's private cost of operation is less than the social cost, since it does not pay for the damage it does to the environment. The market prices of the chemicals it produces are thus likely to be less than the true *social* cost of production—which includes the full costs of waste disposal. This in turn leads to an inefficient allocation of resources because too much of these chemicals is consumed: The marginal value of the last unit of output produced is less than the marginal *social* cost of production, so that production should be reduced.

Externalities are not all unfavorable. The homeowner who repaints her house provides benefits to her neighbors since the views out their windows are made more attractive. But since homeowners are not paid for these spillovers, the social benefits from repainting exceed the private benefits. This makes the supply of newly painted houses too small—society as a whole would gain if more were painted, but painting occurs only when the private benefits of painting exceed the costs.

As these examples suggest, externalities involve missing markets. Firms or households consume (waste disposal in the river) or produce (attractive views of newly painted houses) valuable products for which there are no prices. Even if all markets that do exist are perfectly competitive, the economy as a whole will not allocate resources efficiently if some markets are missing. Marginal costs will not equal marginal values for the corresponding goods. Too much will be produced of goods that generate unfavorable or negative externalities, and goods that generate positive externalities will be underproduced.

Why are there missing markets in the first place? Generally because pollution and other important externalities are public goods (or public "bads") in important respects. If you paint your house, all your neighbors have a better view; it is impossible to deny the benefits to any one of them. Everyone living in a city breathes the same air; it is impossible to deny anyone the benefits of a reduction in air pollution. As Chapter 4 discussed, because nonpayers cannot be excluded from consumption, ordinary markets do not work well for public goods. There is thus an argument for government intervention when externalities affect many people.

OPTIMAL INTERVENTION. Should the government step in whenever such an externality is identified? As a practical matter, the answer must be no, because government

---

[7] Although we postpone a detailed discussion of antitrust policy until the next chapter, it is worth noting here that the origins of antitrust laws and the behavior of antitrust agencies are not well explained by the capture hypothesis either. The antitrust laws, like much social regulation, apply to essentially all firms in the economy. And the antitrust agencies, like social regulatory commissions, are mainly staffed by professionals: lawyers and economists.

regulation is not costless. Students may be offended by their professors' taste in ties, for instance, but it is hard to imagine a tie regulation agency that would create benefits equal to its operating costs. In most countries, regulation concentrates on externalities involving land use (power plants are not allowed in residential areas, for instance) and pollution.

Suppose the government has decided to do something about a polluted river. What should its goal be? Since competitive markets allocate resources efficiently, if the government is concerned with efficiency, it should try to mimic the workings of a competitive market. That is, it should seek to replace the missing market.

Figure 13-1 illustrates the principles involved. The horizontal axis shows the extent of pollution reduction in a particular river compared to the situation before government intervention.[8] The curve labeled MC is the marginal cost of reducing pollution by cutting back discharges into the river at the minimum possible total cost. It corresponds to the supply curve in an ordinary competitive market. Recall that in such a market, total output is produced as cheaply as possible because the marginal cost of production is the same for all firms, so that cost can't be lowered by reallocating total output among them. The cost saving from cutting back any one firm's output by 1 unit exactly equals the increase in cost when another firm produces an extra unit. Similarly, the total cost of pollution reduction is minimized when the marginal cost of reducing discharges is the same for all polluters.

There is an important difference, however. The firms that pollute a particular river may be producing very different products using quite dissimilar processes. For some, the cheapest way to reduce discharges may be to treat their wastes before dumping them into the river. Other firms may change the processes they use or change the mix of products they produce. Still others may have no choice but to reduce output or go out of business altogether. The marginal cost of reducing discharges may be very high for some firms and very low for

---

[8] We describe the market as involving "pollution reduction" rather than "pollution" or "waste disposal in the river" so that the horizontal axis measures a good, rather than a bad, as in the usual supply-demand analysis. This does not affect the results.

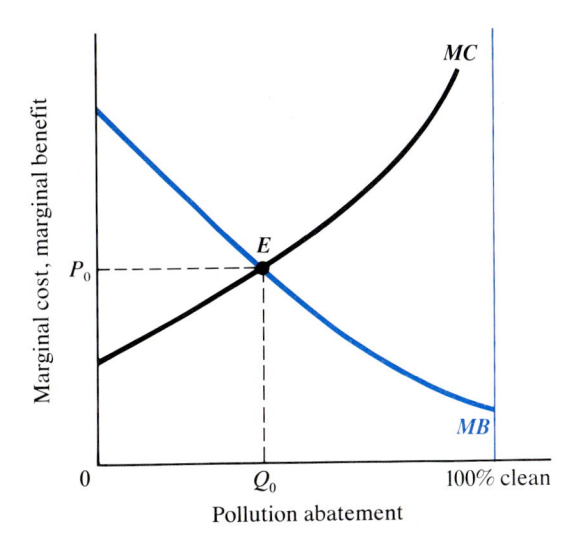

FIGURE 13-1. The Optimal Level of Pollution Abatement. The marginal costs of reducing water pollution increase with the level of abatement. The marginal benefits from further reductions decline as the water becomes cleaner. The optimal level of pollution reduction is Q_0. At this level of pollution, the marginal benefit of a slightly cleaner environment exactly equals the marginal cost of additional reductions in pollution.

others. The MC curve here thus summarizes a more diverse mix of decisions and behavior than do most ordinary supply curves.

We show the MC curve as rising rapidly in Figure 13-1 to reflect the fact that drastic and expensive measures are usually required to produce dramatic reductions in discharges. Figure 13-2 shows the marginal cost of reducing one form of pollution during petroleum refining. Up to 70 percent of the pollution can be eliminated quite cheaply, but getting rid of the last 30 percent is much more expensive.

The MB curve in Figure 13-1 shows the marginal social benefit from pollution reduction, just as an ordinary demand curve shows the marginal social value of increased output. The main difference is that since the river is a public good, it is not possible to exclude consumers from enjoying it. Thus we can't estimate the MB curve by noting the quantity of pollution abatement demanded at different prices. In practice, marginal benefits are estimated in a variety of ways. The value of making a river safe for swimming, for instance, might be

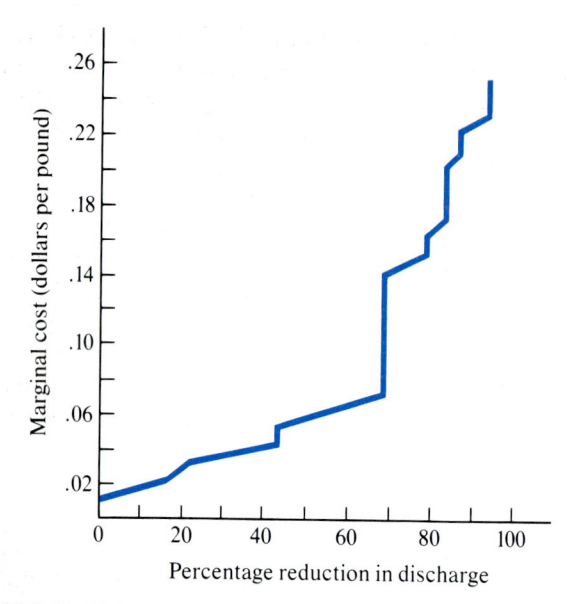

FIGURE 13-2. Marginal Cost of Reducing Pollution from Petroleum Refining. (*Source:* William J. Baumol and Wallace E. Oates, *Economics, Environmental Policy, and the Quality of Life*, Prentice-Hall, Englewood Cliffs, N.J., 1979, p. 213.)

obtained by estimating how many people would swim and placing a dollar value, based on the cost of swimming elsewhere, on each visit. *MB* curves typically decline rapidly, since after a smelly river in which fish can't live has been made clean enough to drink, further increases in water quality have very little effect on anyone.

Once the government knows the *MB* and *MC* curves, its optimal policy is clear. The optimum occurs at point *E* in Figure 13-1, where the marginal cost of reducing pollution is just equal to the marginal benefit from further reductions. If the river is dirtier than at *E*, the benefits from reducing pollution a little exceed the costs; if it is cleaner, society as a whole benefits from allowing firms to lower their costs by increasing emissions.

The idea that there can be too little pollution may seem strange. When people think about pollution, the natural reaction is to say that the less there is, the better. But this looks only at the benefit side of the equation. Since reducing pollution means spending more on pollution-control equipment and less on other good things, it is not necessarily optimal to try to get rid of pollution entirely. Eliminating all air pollution, for instance, would require huge investments in nuclear power and dramatically increase the cost of electricity. How much pollution is economically efficient depends on both the benefits and the costs of a cleanup.

A POLLUTION TAX. In the situation depicted in Figure 13-1, we have shown that the government's task is to reduce pollution by the amount Q_0 as cheaply as possible. How might it do this? If it had enough information, it could compute the cheapest way of reducing discharges and simply tell each polluter what to do. Or it might save on paper by just giving each firm its optimal target and letting the firm figure out how to meet it as cheaply as it could.

But given the many different things that can be done to reduce discharges, no government agency is likely to be able to carry out such a computation in practice, especially since firms have an incentive to overstate how much it would cost them to clean up. There is a simpler solution, however. The government can charge a pollution tax equal to P_0 per unit of pollution discharged into the river. Each firm then increases its profits by reducing its discharges whenever the marginal cost of a 1-unit reduction in pollution is less than the corresponding tax savings, P_0. When each firm has chosen its abatement level to maximize its own profits, the marginal cost of further reductions will then be equal to P_0 for all firms.

Since the marginal cost of reducing pollution is equal for all firms, it follows that a total reduction of Q_0 will automatically be produced at the lowest possible total cost—just as a perfectly competitive market automatically minimizes the cost of producing output. At this point all firms have an incentive to develop and use new ways of reducing pollution even more in order to lower their tax payments. Firms that cannot reduce pollution per unit of output will pay relatively high taxes. Their costs will accordingly rise, leading to price increases that will reduce the consumption of pollution-intensive products.

Is pollution in fact controlled by taxation? Not in the United States. But in the Ruhr River basin of West Germany, pollution taxes have been used since early in this century to control water pollution. Although the total flow of water in this area is less than it is on the Potomac

River and although about 40 percent of German industry is located there, the rivers are generally quite clean by U.S. standards.[9]

Pollution Control by the EPA

In the late 1960s concern over the destruction of the environment through pollution was becoming an important social issue. Figure 13-3 shows the gradual deterioration of Lake Erie and Lake Ontario from 1900 to 1970 in terms of dissolved solids. Similar pictures can be shown for other lakes and for rivers, the high seas, the air in the city, and even the air in the country.[10]

The EPA was set up in 1970 in response to a widespread feeling that pollution was out of hand and needed to be controlled. It administers a variety of programs dealing with air, water, and noise pollution; solid waste; toxic substances; and radiation. The EPA has been instructed to clean up the environment, not to equate marginal costs with marginal benefits. For instance, it is charged with enforcing a 1972 law that sets as a goal "that the discharge of pollutants into the navigable waters be eliminated by 1985." That goal has not been met, and our earlier analysis suggests that this is not on balance a bad thing.

The EPA has never used taxes to control pollution. Instead, it has relied upon two types of standards. *Engineering standards* tell a firm exactly what it must do in order to obey the law. All new coal-burning power plants, for instance, must install devices called scrubbers to reduce the sulfur dioxide emissions that cause acid rain. *Performance standards*, on the other hand, simply limit how much pollution is permitted, leaving it to the firms involved to meet the standard at the lowest cost. Pollution from new automobiles is governed by performance standards that have been set by Congress.

---

[9] For a discussion of this experience, see Allen V. Kneese and Blair T. Bower, *Managing Water Quality*, John Hopkins University Press, Baltimore, 1968.

[10] Data for many types of pollution are summarized in Chapter 2 of William J. Baumol and Wallace E. Oates, *Economics, Environmental Policy, and the Quality of Life*, Prentice-Hall, Englewood Cliffs, N.J., 1979. The authors remind us that pollution has been a serious problem for a long time—in 1700 London had worse air pollution than Los Angeles had 15 years ago.

Economists tend to be critical of the standards approach for several reasons. First, engineering standards may prevent firms from using cheaper ways of cutting pollution. Second, when a firm has satisfied either kind of standard, it has no incentive to reduce pollution further, as it would under a tax system. Third, standards tend to be applied across broad classes of firms, even though the marginal costs involved may differ dramatically. Because the coal used in the west and southwest contains little sulfur, the scrubber standard imposes much higher costs per unit of pollution reduction than it does in the east, where the coal contains more sulfur and the air is dirtier. Fourth, standards often have undesirable side effects. The automobile standards apply only to new cars and make them more expensive. The incentive to replace older cars, which pollute much more, is accordingly reduced. The scrubber standards, which apply only to new power plants, have exactly the same effect.

The EPA argues that standards are easier to enforce than taxes in practice. It is easier to see whether a required device is hooked up or to test periodically to see whether a performance standard is being met than it is to monitor discharges continuously for tax purposes. A pollution tax on automobiles is just not practical. Moreover,

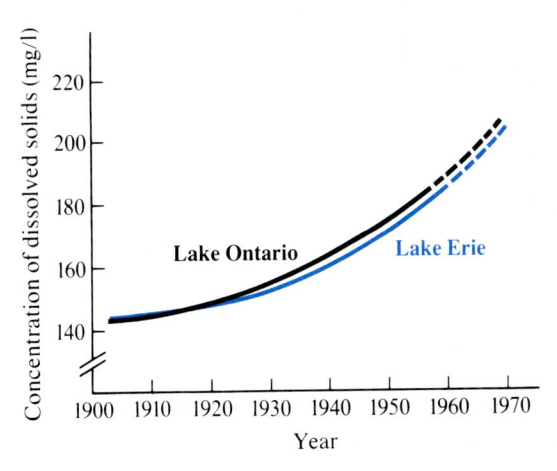

FIGURE 13-3. Changes in the Concentrations of Dissolved Solids in Lake Erie and Lake Ontario, 1900–1970. (*Source:* William J. Baumol and Wallace E. Oates, *Economics, Environmental Policy, and the Quality of Life,* Prentice-Hall, Englewood Cliffs, N.J., 1979, p. 16.)

the law calls for the elimination of pollution, and the effects of a pollution tax on the level of pollution are hard to predict because *MC* curves are hard to estimate. The EPA argues that standards have more certain effects, but our previous discussion of automobile standards shows that the effects of standards are not always easy to predict either.

HAS THE EPA SUCCEEDED? Have the EPA's regulations reduced pollution? Measurements of air quality generally show improvements since 1970, but they also show comparable improvements during the 1960s, before the EPA was established.[11] In both periods, the economy moved away from producing goods and toward services, and improvements in the efficiency of automobile engines and power plants also reduced pollution. Table 13-2 presents data on air pollution emissions since 1970. Pollution is down in all but one category: nitrogen oxides. Since economic activity as measured by real GNP grew by 36 percent over the period covered, there has clearly been a sizable reduction in the ratio of pollution to production. The dramatic decline in lead emissions is mainly due to the elimination of lead from gasoline. The EPA is inclined to take all the credit for the other improvements. Its critics say that most of these gains would have occurred without the EPA.

The record on water pollution is even harder to sort out. The Charles River in Boston no longer smells, and fish have returned to Lake Erie. But 34 percent of the nation's waterways failed to meet EPA standards for bacteria in 1983, compared with 36 percent in 1975. On the whole, water quality seems to have improved less rapidly than air quality, and EPA's share of the credit is equally unclear.

While the benefits of the EPA's programs are controversial, there is no doubt that the costs have been high. Table 13-3 shows some data on expenditures for pollution abatement and control in the United States. Total expenditure for pollution avoidance in 1983 was about 2 percent of GNP. This is about 30 percent of spending on national defense and slightly exceeds both outlays for industrial research and development and total investment in new housing.

TABLE 13-3. Pollution Control and Abatement Expenditures (Billions of 1985 Dollars)

Type of expenditure	1975	1983
Pollution abatement	52.0	57.5
Regulation and federal monitoring	1.2	1.3
Research and development	2.0	1.6
Total	55.3	60.5

Source: *Statistical Abstract of the United States, 1986*, Table 360.

Is There a Better Way?

Many studies have found that the EPA's policies make it much more expensive than necessary to clean up the environment. Table 13-4 presents estimates of the costs of reducing sulfur dioxide emissions from electric generating plants. The current regulations will reduce emissions by about 24 million tons, at a total cost of about $7 billion per year. Since the electric power industry is regulated, as we discuss in Chapter 14, these costs will be paid by consumers in the form of higher electricity prices. As we have noted, the current EPA regulations apply only to new power plants, and they prescribe the methods that must be used to reduce pollution.

Suppose we were to continue to regulate only new plants and to insist on the same level of pollution reduction but were to allow each plant to reduce pollution in the cheapest way. The second row of the table shows that this would save about $700 million per year. Thus costs

---

[11] See Robert W. Crandall, *Controlling Industrial Pollution*, Brookings Institution, Washington, 1983, for an assessment of the evidence on air pollution.

TABLE 13-2. Emissions of Air Pollutants in the United States (Millions of Tons)

Pollutant	1970	1977	1983
Particulates*	19.8	9.9	7.6
Sulfur oxides	31.1	29.0	22.9
Nitrogen oxides	20.0	23.0	21.4
Hydrocarbons	29.8	26.0	21.9
Carbon monoxide	108.3	89.4	74.5
Lead (thousands of tons)	224.6	155.6	51.7

* Smoke, dust, and fumes.

Source: *Statistical Abstract of the United States, 1986*, Table 352.

TABLE 13-4. Alternative Strategies for Controlling Sulfur Dioxide Pollution from Electric Generating Plants, 1990

Control strategy	Emission reductions*	Total cost†	Cost per ton‡
Current requirements			
Current policy	23.91	7.05	295
Performance standards	23.91	6.35	266
Regional limits	23.91	4.47	187
Optimal pollution tax			
Low benefits	19.12	2.67	140
Medium benefits	24.12	4.26	177
High benefits	29.84	6.44	216

* Millions of tons reduction versus no controls.
† Billions of 1980 dollars per year.
‡ 1980 dollars per ton per year.
    Source: Lewis J. Perl and Frederick C. Dunbar, "Cost Effectiveness and Cost-Benefit Analysis of Air Quality Regulation," *American Economic Review*, May 1982, Tables 1 and 2.

could be reduced by about 10 percent by moving from engineering standards to performance standards.

The third row in Table 13-4 describes the effect of keeping the same emission reduction in each region of the country but making those reductions from both new and old plants in order to minimize cost. This change would reduce costs by another $1.9 billion. Table 13-4 thus shows that the current policies cost about $2.5 billion (0.7 + 1.9), or almost 60 percent, more than the minimum possible cost for the same air quality.

This suggests that a great deal of money could be saved by moving from engineering standards to pollution taxes. But as we have noted, it is not simple to come up with the tax rate. Neither the marginal costs nor the marginal benefits of pollution reduction are likely to be known precisely in practice. The last three rows in Table 13-4 show that the optimal level of pollution reduction from electric power plants is quite sensitive to which of three alternative estimates of marginal benefits is adopted. Uncertainties about marginal cost, which are not considered here, may also be important in practice.

Economists have suggested an alternative to pollution taxes that avoids some of these problems. Suppose the EPA were to decide, much as it does now, how much pollution is permissible in each region and then issue permits to firms, with each permit specifying how much the firm is allowed to pollute. So far this is essentially a system of performance standards. The key difference is that the EPA could allow firms to buy and sell these permits. Firms that could cut pollution way down could make money by selling the permits they didn't need. Firms that found pollution reduction expensive would have to buy more permits than they were issued. This *tradeable permits* approach also serves to minimize cost, but it guarantees that desired levels of air quality will be achieved. In recent years the EPA has been moving, though slowly, toward a system of tradeable permits. Firms are allowed to build new factories in areas with dirty air if they can show that total pollution in the area will be reduced. They can do this by paying other firms to reduce their pollution.[12]

4. Information and Protection

Let us now consider another set of social regulatory programs. The second type of market failure that provides an economic rationale for social regulation occurs when households or firms cannot fully judge the attributes of the products they are buying or the working conditions in which they operate. There is less than full information because gathering information is costly, but this implies that relatively risky goods or activities might not be known as such and would therefore be overconsumed.

A worker who does not know that exposure to high levels of benzene, which are found in some chemical plants, may cause cancer will be willing to work for a lower wage than he would if he were aware of all the risks. The private cost of producing the chemicals involved will therefore be lower than the true social cost, since the firm is not paying for the risks it imposes on its workers. The chemicals will be overproduced, firms will have no incentive to reduce workers' risks, and workers will die of cancer.

Stories of unsanitary conditions in the food-processing industry led to the establishment of the Food and Drug

[12] See Thomas H. Tietenberg, "Uncommon Sense: The Program to Reform Pollution Control Policy," in Leonard W. Weiss and Michael W. Klass (eds.), *Regulatory Reform: What Actually Happened*, Little, Brown, Boston, 1986.

Administration (FDA) and the Animal and Plant Health Inspection Service. The FDA's jurisdiction has been expanded over the years. It now inspects the purity of food entering interstate commerce; governs the labeling of food, drugs, and cosmetics; and sets standards for testing the safety and efficacy of drugs. The rationale for all these programs is buyers' lack of good information; one can't tell by looking whether food is contaminated, for instance.

Information failures also rationalize the existence of three important and controversial agencies that were established in the early 1970s. The Consumer Product Safety Commission (CPSC) regulates the design and safety of consumer products. The National Highway and Traffic Safety Adminstration (NHTSA) regulates the design of automobiles in the interest of safety. Finally, OSHA regulates accident and health risks in the workplace. Many of the other agencies listed in Table 13-1 also act to protect workers and consumers from risks and misinformation.

We first discuss the basic issues in this general area. We then consider current regulatory programs and proposals for reform.

Information, Standards, and Paternalism

It is important to understand at the outset that the existence of risk does *not* constitute evidence of market failure or grounds for government intervention. Well-informed people often take health and accident risks for a variety of reasons. Driving long distances is more dangerous than flying but it may be cheaper and more interesting. Using a sharp knife instead of a dull one increases the risk of injury but makes it easier to cut things. Divers are well paid, in large part because everyone knows their work is dangerous.

There is market failure only when individuals are not well informed about the risks they are bearing. This might suggest that the government should intervene only to obtain and distribute information. Obtaining information may require basic research. This is particularly likely in the case of long-term health risks. Suppose that both mill owners and workers suspect that exposure to cotton dust causes lung disease. Who will do the research required to see if this is the case? The firms have every incentive not to do it, since workers will demand higher wages if they know their jobs are dangerous. The workers are unlikely to be able to pay for basic research. There is a clear argument for government-financed research to evaluate poorly understood health risks.

Once the government learns about risks that firms and consumers should be aware of, why not just give out the information and stop there? After all, competitive markets will allocate resources efficiently if buyers and sellers are well informed, even if risk is present. But information about many of the risks we face every day in our complex environment is not easy to understand or evaluate. For instance, debate raged for many years about whether cigarettes cause cancer or simply attract people who are likely to develop cancer for other reasons. Doctors, biochemists, engineers, and safety specialists can debate the severity of particular hazards for years. Nonspecialists are often incapable of understanding what is said in these debates, let alone evaluating the arguments. Information provision is just not a sensible strategy in many cases.

What else can be done? There are two alternatives. The first is to rely on *incentives* such as the pollution tax. In fact, the market automatically provides some incentives for risk reduction. Workers demand higher wages for jobs known to be hazardous, and employers can cut their costs if they can reduce risks. If a worker falls from an unsafe ladder and breaks her leg, her employer can be made responsible for the costs and perhaps be required to pay a premium for pain and suffering. But it is not always easy to tell who is at fault. Suppose the same worker develops cancer after many years of smoking and working for several chemical companies. Who should pay? Or if a child falls from a bicycle and breaks her leg, should the bicycle manufacturer be held liable?

The second alternative is to require that risks be reduced. Regulation in the area of protection and risk reduction has concentrated on *setting standards*, mainly engineering standards. The idea here is that well-informed regulators can make for us the decisions we would make if we were well informed ourselves. Thus NHTSA focuses on the design of new cars, the CPSC on the design of consumer products, OSHA on the design of the workplace, and the FDA on prescribing testing procedures for new drugs.

There is a clear bias in this system. Agencies concerned with protection from risk are staffed by specialists in the hazards they regulate. Just as economists think that people should be more aware of economics, safety specialists think that people should worry more about the risks they face. Regulators thus tend toward *paternalism*, toward making the decisions they think we *should* make, not the decisions we *would* make if we were well informed.

The controversy over seat belts and air bags illustrates this tendency nicely.[13] It is well known that those who wear lap and shoulder belts are much less likely to be injured or killed in auto accidents than are those who don't. Despite decades of publicity on this point, however, only 10 to 15 percent of drivers use seat belts. One reaction to this statistic might be that drivers are as well informed about these risks as about most others and that their judgment should be respected. But the government has reacted differently. In the late 1970s NHTSA proposed that all new cars be required to be equipped with air bags, which protect occupants by inflating on impact. Air bags are considerably more expensive than seat belts and are noticeably less effective, but drivers cannot decide not to use them. The Reagan administration has moved away from air bags and instead has pressured the states to require drivers to use seat belts. The only reason for requiring air bags or for compulsory seat belt laws is the conviction that drivers are not making the decisions they *should* be making.

Regulatory Failures

Most public discussion of the FDA, the CPSC, OSHA, and NHTSA consists of critiques of apparently irrational decisions they have made. But the agencies are not entirely to blame; sometimes Congress forces irrationality upon them.

The *Delaney amendment* requires the FDA to ban any food ingredient that causes cancer in people or animals. The FDA had no choice but to ban saccharin in 1977, after experiments showed that rats fed with enormous amounts of saccharin got cancer. This ban generated strong opposition. Some argued that more people would die because of the increased risk of heart attack associated with being overweight (as a result of eating sugar instead of saccharin) than would be saved from cancer. The political outcry from saccharin users (including producers and drinkers of diet soda) was so strong that Congress granted a special exemption. Saccharin is thus still available, even though it does cause cancer in rats. Similarly, when the FDA discovered that red dye #2, which is used for making foods red, causes cancer, it had to ban the dye. However, there were alternative dyes, producers and consumers of hot dogs did not suffer too much from this ban, and the ban remains in force.

Many criticisms are directed at the agencies themselves. Critics of the FDA allege that it has been far too concerned with keeping harmful drugs off the market.[14] We can be almost sure that any new drug that is certified is safe and effective, but we can also be sure that some good drugs have failed the FDA's tests. Besides, the critics say, by requiring very time-consuming tests, the FDA deprives consumers of help they could be getting from drugs during at least 3 or 4 years of unnecessary delay.[15] Moreover, because passing the FDA's tests is expensive, research on cures for diseases that affect small numbers of people has been made unprofitable. Indeed, some drugs in common use abroad are not available in the United States because the market for them is too small to justify the costly testing required by the FDA. The FDA responds to all this by noting that Congress told it to keep unsafe drugs off the market, not to balance costs and benefits.

OSHA has been perhaps the most controversial U.S. regulatory agency.[16] Shortly after it was established, OSHA took over 4000 voluntary standards that had been adopted by industry groups at one time or another and made them into government rules. Many of these were absurd—split toilet seats were required, for instance—and some of the worst have been withdrawn under fire, but OSHA has continued to concentrate mainly on safety

---

[13] Chapter 4 in Crandall, Gruenspecht, Keeler, and Lave (see footnote 1) discusses this issue.

[14] For a general discussion, see Henry G. Grabowski and John M. Vernon, *The Regulation of Pharmaceuticals*, American Enterprise Institute, Washington, 1983.

[15] The FDA has speeded its procedures in the last few years.

[16] For a general discussion of OSHA, see W. Kip Viscusi, *Risk By Choice*, Harvard University Press, Cambridge, 1983.

risks. Since it is much harder for workers to understand health risks than to understand the likely causes of accidents, many critics have suggested that OSHA should concentrate on health risks instead.

OSHA mainly issues engineering standards governing the workplace, even though changes in worker behavior would often be much more effective in reducing risk. For instance, it set maximum noise levels for all factories so that the hearing of workers would not be damaged. These standards, which imposed costs of about $20 billion on the private sector, did not take into account huge differences in the cost of noise abatement across industries. Thus the cost per worker protected ranged from $20,000 to over $200,000. Nor did OSHA seriously consider requiring employers to provide employees with hearing protectors of the sort worn by airport workers near jet engines and setting a performance standard for hearing loss, even though comparable benefits could have been obtained with this approach at about a tenth the cost. OSHA argued that workers wouldn't wear the hearing protectors and that therefore factories had to be redesigned. Critics have argued that OSHA should generally place more emphasis on training and education of workers and rely on performance standards.

Despite OSHA's focus on safety, many studies have found that it has had no effect on industrial accidents, even though businesses complain loudly about the standards it sets. Part of the answer may lie in its enforcement budget. OSHA inspects about 70,000 workplaces annually; this means that an average firm has less than 1 chance in 200 of being inspected in any year. Since the average fine per violation detected is only about $57, it is not surprising that about a third of all inspections find serious violations.[17]

Regulatory Reform

Few observers doubt that important market failures occur because information is imperfect, but fewer still think that current regulatory programs work well. What alternatives are available? In some areas, private agencies set and enforce standards. Underwriters Laboratories tests electrical equipment, Sotheby's certifies the quality of Rembrandts, rabbis certify kosher food, and Moody's rates the credit standing of firms. Box 13-1 provides a particularly striking example of successful private regulation of risks.

Most examples of successful private regulation involve situations in which cause and effect are well understood. But the public's interest, and therefore its insistence on standards, is particularly important when very little is known about the products to be placed in the market and when the consequences for society of any error may be catastrophic. It is thus entirely reasonable for society to impose its evaluation of risk on the builders of high rises,

---

[17] Similar complaints have been voiced about the CPSC, which the Reagan administration once tried to abolish.

Box 13-1. Private Regulation of Risk

The *Sultana* pushed out of the Memphis dock early that morning of April 27, 1865; its paddle-wheels spinning smoothly through the Mississippi water, plumes of black coal smoke pouring out of its twin funnels. On board were 2,400 Union soldiers being exchanged for Confederate prisoners. Weak from months of prison camp, the men clogged every cranny of the *Sultana*—built to carry only 400 passengers.

Then, without warning, a huge explosion, estimated to have had the force of a thousand pounds of dynamite. The blast ignited an uncontrolled bonfire. At least 1,200 Union men burned to death or drowned. The steam boiler had exploded.

After 100 years of steam technology, boilers continued to explode with alarming regularity in mines, locomotives, and factories. Hundreds of people died each year.

The news of the *Sultana's* black day galvanized Jeremiah Allen and three of his friends. They formed the Hartford (Conn.) Steam Boiler Inspection and Insurance Co. (it still exists). They offered to insure any boiler that they inspected for safety. They put their own money on the line. Within a few decades, the idea of private boiler inspection took hold. Boiler-explosion rates plummeted.

Note: Excerpted from Earl Ubell, "The Privatizing of Regulation," *Newsweek*, Nov. 23, 1981, p. 35.

the producers of toxic substances, the developers of new drugs, and the owners of nuclear plants rather than rely on the assumption that the private sector will set and enforce reasonable standards.

On the other hand, most federal regulation of risks has taken as its ultimate goal perfect safety, not correction of market failure. Politicians and safety regulators often proclaim that human life is undebatably beyond economic calculation and that wherever the issue arises, absolute priority must be given to preserving human life and health, whatever the cost. Economists reply with two points. First, society cannot in fact afford to implement such a policy in all activities. Even if we could build perfectly safe cars, which we can't, they would be outrageously expensive and some of them would kill pedestrians. Second, people voluntarily and knowingly take risks every day in order to make more money (professional divers), save time (jaywalkers), or have fun (sky divers). Why should politicians or regulators be much more averse to risk than are the people they serve?

The uncomfortable task of the economist in this area is to point out that even when human life and health are at stake, we do need to use economic analysis to evaluate alternative approaches to achieving maximum welfare. The goal of a riskless society is not a sensible one, as even regulators are forced to recognize in practice. Moreover, resources ought not to be wasted in the course of achieving risk reduction any more than in accomplishing other worthy goals. If we decide for some reason that industrial accidents should be reduced 20 percent, society as a whole gains if we do this as cheaply as possible. But this requires that the marginal benefit in terms of accident reduction from spending a dollar to reduce any one cause of accidents must be equal to the marginal benefit from spending it on accident reduction elsewhere. Current regulations bear no relation to this efficient pattern; marginal costs per death avoided vary all over the lot.

Economists have long called for regulatory activity to be subjected to cost-benefit analysis. The Ford, Carter, and Reagan administrations have agreed, but regulators have generally resisted this prescription. At the very least, even if society does decide that certain rights (health, life) are to be set beyond economic calculation, we should still try to guarantee these rights at minimum cost. As economists become more experienced with cost-benefit analysis and acquire more information about the prices people place on risk in their day-to-day informed choices, there will be increasing conflict over the value of regulation between those who argue for cost-effective regulation and those who argue that certain values are beyond economic calculation. There is no doubt that the latter case can be very persuasively stated.[18]

5. Airlines and the Deregulation Movement

As section 1 noted, a great deal of economic deregulation occurred in the late 1970s and early 1980s. Economists can claim some credit for this.[19] They had long noted that economic regulation had been applied to industries that were plainly not natural monopolies—trucking and airlines were the prime examples. Beginning in the early 1960s, careful studies of the behavior of economic regulators made it increasingly clear that regulation did not generally serve the public interest by correcting market failure.[20] Regulators pursued a variety of goals, which usually included keeping regulated firms in business but rarely included efficiency. Because of the shortcomings of economic regulation in practice, economists began to argue that only industries in which competition was clearly impossible should be regulated. Thus many supported the introduction of competition into the long-distance telephone business, even though some engineers argued that it was a natural monopoly.

During the 1970s, politicians began to find it useful to fire these bullets supplied by economists. Legislation deregulating the airlines and most natural gas producers was passed in 1978. Competition in long-distance telephone service began in earnest the same year. President Carter began gradual decontrol of oil prices in 1979;

---

[18] See the very forceful statement by Steven Kelman in "Cost Benefit Analysis: An Ethical Critique," *Regulation*, January–February 1981.

[19] For an account of the deregulation movement that stresses the role of economic analysis, see Martha Derthick and Paul J. Quirk, *The Politics of Deregulation*, Brookings Institution, Washington, 1985. Economic effects are assessed in Leonard W. Weiss and Michael W. Klass (eds.), *Regulatory Reform: What Actually Happened*, Little, Brown, Boston, 1986.

[20] Recall the discussions of the capture hypothesis in section 1; in Chapter 14 we will see that similar conclusions apply to public utility regulation.

President Reagan wiped out the remaining controls just after he took office in 1980. In the same year legislation introduced by the Carter administration was passed that deregulated trucking and most railroad rates, and the sale of telephones and related equipment was deregulated by the FCC. Laws passed in 1980 and 1982 reduced the regulation of banks and other depository institutions.

Airline Deregulation

Airline deregulation is important not only in its own right but because its perceived success strengthened advocates of deregulation in other sectors.[21] Airline regulation began in earnest in 1938 with the establishment of the Civil Aeronautics Board (CAB). This agency set fares for all interstate flights, told each airline which routes it was allowed to serve, and until 1978 barred new entrants into the business from serving major routes.

The airlines, because of restricted entry and regulated fares, shifted from price competition to nonprice competition. Instead of cutting prices to increase business and profits, the airlines competed through the quality of the meals they offered and the number of flights they scheduled. While passengers appreciate good meals and frequent flights, they also appreciate lower prices. But because the CAB controlled prices, competition took place only on other dimensions. Competition went too far on the service front and not far enough on prices.

In 1975 the Senate held well-publicized hearings on the effects of CAB regulation. Economists testified that regulation was not necessary in this industry and imposed significant costs on society. They pointed out that the essentially unregulated airlines operating within California and Texas charged fares much lower than those of regulated interstate airlines serving comparable routes. In this same period the CAB itself published a study suggesting that airline regulation be abolished.

Soon after his inauguration, President Carter appointed two economists, Alfred Kahn and Elizabeth Bailey, to the CAB.[22] Kahn was named its chairman.

Under their leadership, the CAB moved rapidly to give airlines increasing freedom to choose both prices and routes. The results were generally conceded to be favorable. Despite opposition from airlines, which feared that competition would reduce their profits, and airline workers' unions, which feared that the entry of nonunion airlines would put downward pressure on their wages, Congress passed legislation in 1978 that removed most airline regulation and even abolished the CAB effective January 1, 1985.

Effects of Deregulation

Economists expected airline deregulation to lower prices, thus increasing the demand for air travel, and to promote the entry of new carriers. As Table 13-5 shows, these expectations have been realized. Adjusted for changes in costs, the airlines' receipts per passenger mile have dropped sharply. Passenger miles flown have more than doubled since 1970, even adjusting for changes in the population. (Of course, much of this growth would have occurred anyway, since the income elasticity of the demand for air travel is high.) The number of airlines has increased dramatically, and there is no evidence in the table to support the charge that deregulation has made air travel less safe.

The data in Table 13-5 do suggest a puzzle. There have been no dramatic innovations in aircraft design since 1978, fares have risen much less than have the costs of fuel and labor, yet the industry is generally earning adequate profits. Either it was earning monopoly profits before deregulation—and this does not seem to have

TABLE 13-5. The Airline Industry Before and After Deregulation

	1970	1975	1980	1984
Cost-adjusted fares*	100	80	43	41
Per capita miles flown	510	611	884	1030
Load factor†	49.7	53.7	59.0	59.2
Air carriers	41	35	63	95
Total accidents	39	28	19	12
Fatal accidents	2	2	1	1

* Index: 1970 = 100, adjusted for changes in input prices.
† Approximately equal to the percentage of airline seats filled.
   Source: *Statistical Abstract of the United States, 1986*, Tables 1081 and 1082.

---

[21] A good general reference is Elizabeth E. Bailey, David R. Graham, and Daniel P. Kaplan, *Deregulating the Airlines*, MIT Press, Cambridge, 1985.

[22] Alfred Kahn is a onetime dean at Cornell University who is famous for his wit. An example is the comment he made on *Meet the Press*: "A dean is to the faculty what a lamppost is to a dog." Elizabeth Bailey is currently a dean at Carnegie-Mellon University.

been the case—or costs per passenger mile have fallen substantially even though the same planes are being used.

One reason costs per passenger mile have fallen is that, as Table 13-5 shows, the load factor, or roughly the percentage of airline seats that are filled, has risen slightly. But the main reason for lower costs seems to be changes in airlines' route structures. By 1984, most airlines had become "hub and spoke" systems. Many American Airlines flights go to or leave from Dallas, for instance, so that a map of American's routes shows many spokes emerging from a hub at Dallas. A long trip on American usually involves a change of planes in Dallas. Atlanta is also a major hub, and some Florida residents assert that, "You may go to heaven or hell when you die, but you'll certainly stop in Atlanta on the way." A major cost of CAB regulation, which was not at all obvious at the time, is that the way the board allocated routes to airlines prevented the emergence of efficient hub and spoke route structures.

On the other hand, the changes in route structures that followed deregulation have produced changes in the pattern of service. Some cities have lost jet service, and some travelers find that what used to be nonstop flights now involve changing planes at crowded hub airports. Have reductions in the quality of airline service outweighed price cuts, so that travelers are in fact worse off than they were? A recent study which looked carefully at both service quality and fares on a wide variety of routes and examined the effects of deregulation on both business and pleasure travelers came to just the opposite conclusion.[23] The estimated annual benefits of deregulation to all travelers were about $10 billion (in 1985 dollars), carriers' profits were higher than they would have been under regulation, and no substantial group of travelers was noticeably worse off. Airline deregulation seems to have been a very good idea indeed.

■ Economists like to talk about airline deregulation not only because their advice was followed but also because it proved to be basically correct. Economists also enjoy talking about deregulation of other industries that should never have been regulated in the first place and about more efficient ways of controlling externalities such as pollution. But social regulation concerned with information failures produces less cheerful conversations. These programs generally address serious problems with no simple solutions. While the past three administrations have accepted the value of careful cost-benefit analysis of social regulation, Congress and most regulators have not. The great days of economic deregulation are behind us; the future holds difficult and painful debates on the reform of social regulation—and, as the next chapter indicates, on antitrust activities and the regulation of natural monopolies as well.

[23] Steven Morrison and Clifford Winston, *The Economic Effects of Airline Deregulation*, Brookings Institution, Washington, 1986.

Summary

1 Three main market failures provide economic justification for government regulation: monopoly power, externalities, and imperfect information.
2 In the United States, economic regulation, which involves control over price, entry, and service quality in particular industries, began in earnest with the establishment of the Interstate Commerce Commission in 1887. It was extended to public utilities just before World War I and to other industries in the 1930s and early 1970s.
3 Social regulation, which addresses externalities and problems of imperfect information, began with the establishment of the Food and Drug Administration in 1906. The scope of social regulation expanded dramatically in the 1960s and early 1970s.
4 Economic regulators, who often control industries that are not natural monopolies, are sometimes accused of serving mainly the interests of those they regulate, though the evidence suggests that they respond to other political pressures as well. Social regulators are more often accused of being overzealous, of pursuing the agency's goals without regard to the costs involved.
5 Externalities exist when the production or consumption of a good has spillover effects on other individuals and the spillover effects are not fully reflected in prices. Externalities exist when a market is missing.
6 Economically efficient pollution control requires equating the marginal social cost of additional cleanup to the marginal social benefit it would produce.

7. The optimal level of pollution, which is generally not zero, can be achieved at the lowest possible cost, at least in principle, by putting a tax on pollution, thus mimicking the operation of the missing competitive market. A system of tradeable permits can accomplish the same goal.
8. In the United States, the Environmental Protection Agency (EPA) controls pollution by setting engineering standards (which prescribe actions) and performance standards (which prescribe results). While the environment is cleaner than it was in 1970, it is not clear how much of this is due to EPA regulations, which have imposed high costs on society.
9. Regulatory agencies concerned with information failures have been criticized for neglecting the costs of their actions (although sometimes Congress has given them no choice), not concentrating their efforts on risks about which the public is poorly informed (particularly long-term health risks), and paternalistically overprotecting the public.
10. Around 1980, the deregulation movement reduced the scope of economic regulation dramatically. Airline deregulation seems to have benefitted most travelers and the airline industry as a whole, and it has led to a radical and efficiency-enhancing change in airline route structures.

Key Terms

Economic regulation
Social regulation
Market failure
Externality
Information failure
Capture hypothesis

Pollution tax
Engineering standards
Performance standards
Tradeable permits
Paternalism
Deregulation

Problems

1. (*a*) Define the term "externality." (*b*) Show why, when there is an unfavorable externality, the output of the good generating that externality is excessive.
2. Why is it more efficient to charge prices for polluting than to tell each polluting firm to reduce its discharges by the same percentage?
3. (*a*) Why are there regulations for the safety of the workplace? (*b*) Should the aim be to prevent all workplace accidents?
4. Some people argue that if someone knows exactly what risk she is taking in her current job, there is no reason to try to control working conditions in any way. Others argue that society should not permit people to take extremely dangerous jobs whether they want to or not. Which side do you support, and why? (You do not have to stick to purely economic arguments, but you should bring in the relevant economic arguments.)
5. The EPA has regulated auto emissions by requiring cars to meet certain standards. Suppose a meter is invented that can be put on each car to measure the amount of pollutants emitted each year. (*a*) How might the EPA go about reducing the amount of pollutants in this case? (*b*) What are the benefits of the approach outlined in your answer to (*a*) compared with the benefits of the current approach, in which the pollution levels of new cars are specified by the EPA?
6. The text states that scrubber standards for cleaning coal impose higher per unit costs of pollution reduction in the west and southwest than in the east. Explain.
7. What are the economic arguments for and against (*a*) compulsory use of air bags, (*b*) stiff fines for people who don't use seat belts and the requirement that all cars must have seat belts, and (*c*) a requirement that car manufacturers must give customers the choice of having seat belts or air bags or no safety equipment in their cars.
8. (*a*) Is there any reason why society should want to keep off the market drugs that cause no harm, assuming that they do not cure the diseases they are said to cure? (*b*) It is sometimes argued that a regulatory agency will always tend to overregulate because it is blamed for the bad things that happen despite its regulations (e.g., a plane crash) but not blamed so much for the good things it prevents that no one knows about (e.g., a useful drug may be kept off the market for a long time). Does this argument make sense?
9. A newspaper article claims that there are 310 regulations that apply to pizza. For example, mozzarella cheese must contain between 30 and 45 percent fat and come from pasteurized cow's milk. The tomato sauce must be of the "red or reddish" variety and contain at least 24 percent "natural tomato soluble solids." Can you see any justification for such regulations? Explain.
10. Why did the Teamsters' Union, which does not own trucking firms, oppose the deregulation of interstate trucking? (Note that the Teamsters were essentially a monopoly supplier of labor to the regulated trucking industry, which charged rates based on cost.)
11. Box 13-1 describes a company which both certifies and insures boilers. (*a*) How well would the company have done if it had only certified boilers? (*b*) Do you think such certification could work for drugs? Explain.

Chapter 14
Government and the Monopoly Problem

On January 9, 1982, the front page of *The New York Times* reported:

> U.S. SETTLES PHONE SUIT, DROPS I.B.M. CASE;
> A.T. & T. TO SPLIT UP, TRANSFORMING INDUSTRY
>
> The American Telephone and Telegraph Company settled the Justice Department's antitrust law suit today by agreeing to give up the 22 Bell System companies that provide most of the nation's telephone service.
>
> On a landmark antitrust day, the Justice Department also dropped its marathon case against the International Business Machines Corporation, a suit that had sought to break up the company that has dominated the computer industry.
>
> The A.T. & T. agreement, if finally approved by a Federal Court, would be the largest antitrust settlement in decades and is likely to be compared in history with the 1911 settlement that divided the Rockefeller family's Standard Oil Company into 33 subsidiaries . . . .[1]

The antitrust laws applied in these two historic cases also apply to almost all businesses, small as well as large, that operate in the United States.

As Chapter 13 discussed, business firms' actions are also restricted by regulation of two basic types. In *economic regulation*, government agencies set prices and often determine who can sell what. Both before and after the AT&T antitrust case, for instance, prices for local telephone service were set by state agencies. In *social regulation*, on which Chapter 13 concentrated, government agencies deal with such issues as health, safety, discrimination, and protection of consumers and the environment.

This chapter is concerned with antitrust activities and economic regulation as government responses to market failures caused by *monopoly power*—the ability of a seller or group of sellers to restrict output and raise prices above competitive levels. We begin with a general discussion of the problem of monopoly power and show why antitrust is designed to *supplement* market forces, while economic regulation is designed to *replace* those forces. Section 2 then deals with antitrust policy as it has been shaped over the years by politicians, lawyers, judges, and, to some extent in recent years, economists.

[1] Ernest Holsendolph, *New York Times*, Jan. 9, 1982, p. 1. Copyright © 1982 by the New York Times Company. Reprinted by permission. The AT&T agreement, after some modifications, was approved.

While both major political parties often call for vigorous enforcement of the antitrust laws, they almost as often have different things in mind. Finally, section 3 takes up the application of economic regulation in industries in which competition is neither possible nor desirable. We explore the task of regulating a natural monopoly in principle and the performance of regulators in practice.

1. The Monopoly Problem

In Chapters 11 and 12 we saw that monopolies—and some oligopolies for that matter—tend to restrict output to levels below the competitive level. Such exercises of monopoly power yield the firms involved abnormally high profits. However, as we saw in Chapter 11, they also produce a social loss by creating a difference between the marginal cost of output and the value of an additional unit of output to the consumer. In this section we first show that the economically efficient response to the actual or potential existence of monopoly power depends on the importance of economies of scale in the industry involved. We then discuss the importance of the monopoly problem in the United States today.

Monopoly Losses and Antitrust

Figure 14-1 shows the cost to society of monopolistic output restriction. In the industry depicted, long-run average and marginal cost are both constant and equal to *LMC* at all levels of firm and industry output. There are thus constant returns to scale. Under perfect competition, the industry equilibrium would be at point *B*, where the long-run supply curve, *LMC*, intersects the market demand schedule, *D*. But under monopoly, output is restricted to the level at which $MR = LMC$. Monopoly output therefore is only Q_M and monopoly price is P_M, which is higher than the competitive price, P_C. The restriction of output implies that the value of an extra unit of the good to consumers exceeds the cost to society of producing it. As in Chapter 11, the triangle *ABC* measures the welfare cost of output restriction as the sum of the differences between value and marginal cost for each unit of output that would be produced under competition but not under monopoly.

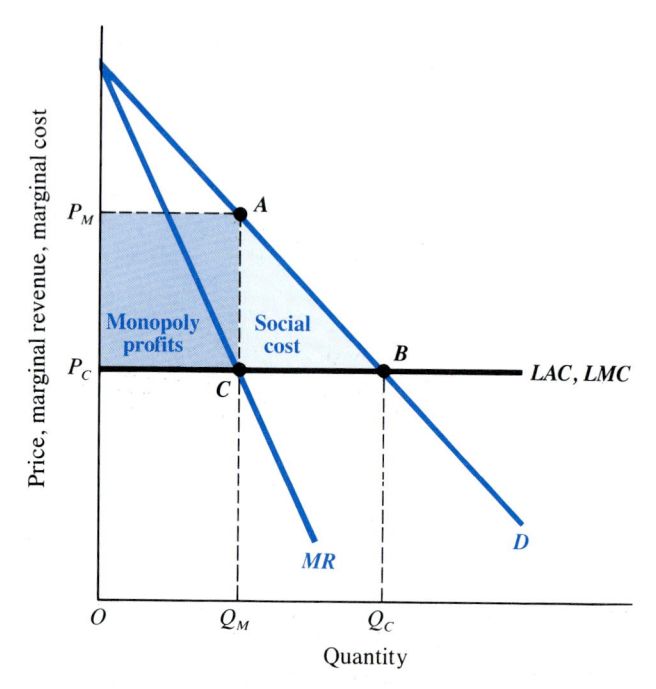

FIGURE 14-1. The Social Cost of Unnatural Monopoly. The industry shown has constant long-run average and marginal cost. Under perfect competition, which is feasible because there are constant returns to scale, equilibrium would be at *B*. Under monopoly, output is restricted to the point where $MR = LMC$, and thus only Q_M is produced. The monopolist earns excess profits equal to the rectangle $P_M P_C CA$, but society suffers a net welfare loss equal to the triangle *ABC*.

Figure 14-1 depicts a situation in which competition is both feasible and desirable because there are constant returns to scale. Since small firms have the same flat long-run average cost that large firms have, they run no risk of being driven out of business by larger rivals, and many small sellers would have no higher costs than would a monopoly. With many small sellers, each taking price as fixed, price will be driven to P_C by competition. As Chapter 10 discussed, no form of government price regulation can do better.

● **Antitrust policy attempts to protect and enhance competition by making it harder to create, exercise, or protect monopoly power.**

Antitrust policy is ideally suited for dealing with markets

of the type shown in Figure 14-1, where competition would allocate resources well if the monopoly were broken up.

Natural Monopoly and Regulation

As we also discussed in Chapter 11, there are markets in which competition is not desirable or even feasible. If production involves important economies of scale, so that long-run average cost always declines as output increases, it is more efficient to have a single producer than to have a multifirm industry. In such *natural monopolies* competition is not generally desirable because having more than one seller would raise costs. Competition is also not generally feasible because the largest firm always has a cost advantage over its rivals, and firms that are small relative to others are unlikely to survive. But this raises a clear problem: If the industry is left in the hands of a monopolist, how can we be sure that consumers will receive the benefits of economies of scale?

Figure 14-2 depicts a natural monopoly with a decreasing long-run average cost curve, *LAC*. If the industry were operated by a monopoly, output would be set at Q_M and price at P_M. The monopoly would earn profits equal to the area $P_M EBC$. Socially optimal operation of the industry is described by point E', where *LMC* is equal to price—and thus to the value to consumers of an extra unit of output. Output levels below Q' are inefficient because consumers would be more than willing to pay the marginal cost of producing more (the *LMC* schedule is below the demand curve). Similarly, if output is above Q', the cost savings from reducing production exceed the value of that production to consumers (the *LMC* schedule is above the demand curve). Thus output Q' is optimal for society as a whole.

But how is that output level to be achieved? We cannot get there through competition, because with many firms we would fail to take advantage of the available scale economies. Price and output would be set competitively, but each firm would operate at lower volume and thus with higher average costs than could be achieved by a single monopoly producer. We need monopoly production to minimize costs by exploiting scale economies. Antitrust action to prevent the establishment of a natural monopoly would thus be counterproductive. On the other hand, an unregulated monopoly would restrict output to Q_M and thus impose costs on society equal to the shaded area in Figure 14-2. Efficiency thus requires that market forces be replaced; the monopoly producer must be forced to produce more than Q_M (and to charge a price below P_M) either by regulation or by government ownership and operation.

The Costs of Monopoly Power

Is monopoly power a real problem in the United States? How large are the costs it imposes on society? Adding estimates of triangles like *ABC* in Figure 14-1 across

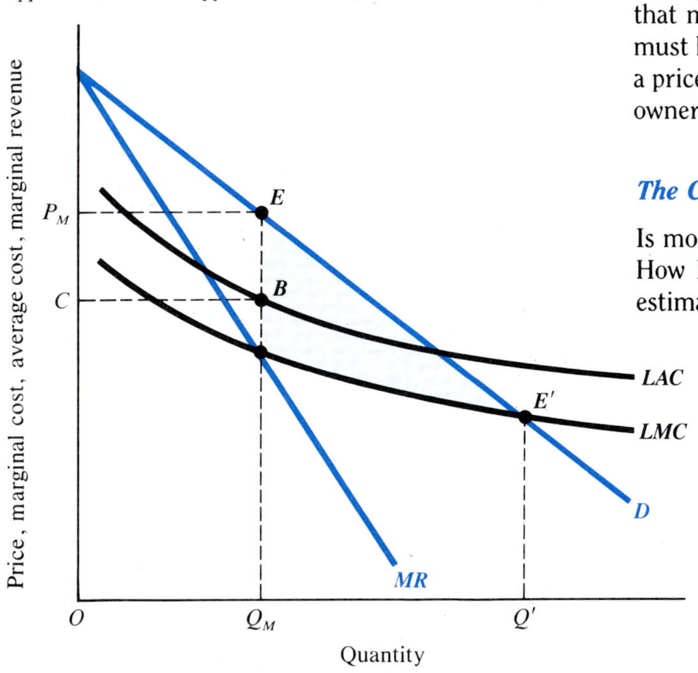

FIGURE 14-2. The Problem of Natural Monopoly.
The diagram shows an industry with economies of scale, reflected in the falling long-run average cost curves, *LAC*. It is socially optimal to have a single seller producing output Q'. But market forces are likely to produce monopoly. And an unregulated monopoly would set $MR = LMC$ and thus produce output Q_M, earning excess profit equal to the rectangle $P_M EBC$ and causing a welfare loss equal to the shaded area.

markets generally leads to estimated monopoly losses below 1 percent of GNP. First, why are estimates of this sort so low? Second, do these estimates imply that monopoly is not a serious problem in the United States and that there is no reason to spend money on antitrust enforcement and economic regulation?

The first question is easily answered: Relatively low estimates of monopoly losses reflect the fact that very few firms report huge rates of profit. Because there are no data on marginal cost, estimates of the welfare cost of monopoly usually rest on the assumption that long-run marginal costs are constant, as in Figure 14-1, so that marginal cost equals average cost, and accounting data are used to compute average cost. Given this assumption, the costs of monopoly will be estimated only for those firms for which price is above average cost (including the allowance for normal profits). In Figure 14-1 the costs of monopoly will be high only if the distance AC, equal to $P_M - LAC$, is large. Thus only if there are large differences between price and average cost, or high profit rates, will we get large estimates of the social costs of monopoly. And few firms or industries report extremely high rates of profit over extended periods of time.

The second question is whether small estimates of the costs of monopoly, reflecting relatively small differences in reported profit rates, mean that the monopoly problem is too small to worry about. There are two reasons why this conclusion does not follow. First, the costs of monopoly may be small precisely because we have antitrust laws and economic regulation, preventing firms from acquiring or exercising monopoly power. Imagine the prices that might be charged by a monopoly manufacturer of telephones or an unregulated local phone company, for instance. Second, four costs of monopoly are not reflected in differences in reported profit rates, and these costs may be important.

First, monopolies may not minimize costs as carefully as other firms do. Without the threat of competition, monopolies can lead an easy life. For instance, top managers may have plush offices in buildings designed by top architects and travel first class or in corporate jets. They may hire more employees than necessary because they enjoy having many subordinates. All these expenditures are treated as costs, though they should really count as profits.

Second, firms may waste resources (from society's point of view, not their own) in attempting to obtain or defend monopoly positions. To this end, firms may incur costs of lobbying and bringing lawsuits to protect patents or harass competitors. They may maintain excess capacity, so that any potential competitor knows that the existing firm can wage a price war if he enters the industry. Costs of this sort also reduce reported profit rates.

Third, some argue that monopoly creates excessive concentration of political power. In the early days of antitrust enforcement, President Theodore Roosevelt brought a case against the giant Northern Securities Company of J. Pierpont Morgan. Morgan reacted by telling the President of the United States, "If we have done anything wrong, send your man to my man, and they can fix it up."[2] Clearly Morgan felt that he and the President were on the same level. Many feel that such power is incompatible with real democracy.

Finally, the exercise of monopoly power may unfairly redistribute income. In Figure 14-1 the rectangle $P_M P_C CA$ represents the monopoly profits that arise from restricting output. These profits exceed the normal return to capital that is already embodied in the LAC schedule. These excess returns represent a transfer from consumers to the owners of the firm or firms involved, a redistribution of income that has been called a privately collected tax. Such transfers may or may not be a bad thing—the stockholders receiving them may be either wealthy racists or widows, orphanages, and workers' pension funds.

2. Antitrust and Unnatural Monopoly

An economist's ideal antitrust policy would be concerned only with promoting consumer welfare by protecting and enhancing competition, but no economist would argue that it would be realistic to seek to make all markets perfectly competitive. Real antitrust laws, like all other laws, are written by politicians, enforced by lawyers, and interpreted by judges. In this section we discuss the provisions of the U.S. antitrust laws, their enforcement

[2] Quoted in Andrew Sinclair, *Corsair: The Life of J. Pierpont Morgan*, Little, Brown, Boston, 1981, p. 141.

and interpretation by the courts, and ongoing debates about antitrust policy and its effects.

Antitrust Laws and Their Enforcement

The first U.S. antitrust law, the *Sherman Act*, was passed in 1890, not because economists had persuaded Congress that monopoly imposes costs on society as a whole but as a response to changes that had occurred in the U.S. economy.

After the Civil War, the railroads linked the country together and created national markets. In response to this expansion of markets and in order to restrict output, corporations larger than had ever existed were created, many by mergers among competitors. For instance, the Standard Oil Trust, formed in 1882, controlled close to 90 percent of the nation's refining capacity.[3] The American Tobacco Company, formed in 1890, produced close to 100 percent of cigarettes in the United States. Farmers and small businesspersons felt threatened by these new giants, and the Sherman Act was passed mainly in response to antibigness sentiments. It attracted little attention or debate at the time.

The two main sections of the Sherman Act are as vague as many parts of the U.S. Constitution. Section 1 makes illegal "every contract, combination . . . or conspiracy in restraint of trade or commerce." Section 2 makes it illegal to "monopolize, or attempt to monopolize, or combine or conspire . . . to monopolize." Congress left it to the courts to decide what sort of actions were "in restraint of trade" and what it might mean to "monopolize" a market. Judges' interpretations of the Sherman Act, as of the U.S. Constitution, have changed over time.

The courts didn't say that price-fixing generally restrains trade until 1897, and a merger between competitors to form a monopoly wasn't labeled monopolization until 1904. Since then the courts have decided that price-fixing is almost always illegal, while "monopolization" has been declared to be the creation or defense of monopoly by "unreasonable" practices. Monopoly by itself is *not* illegal in the United States; "monopolization" relates to actions, not to market structure. If you are the inventor of a patented new product and yours is thus the only firm in the market, you have broken no law.

Between 1897 and 1904, when cartels were probably illegal but mergers that produced monopoly appeared to be legal, the U.S. economy was transformed by many large mergers. In 1901, for instance, a set of mergers created the United States Steel Corporation, which controlled about 60 percent of U.S. steel-making capacity. One estimate is that this merger wave turned 71 substantial industries that had previously been reasonably competitive or at least oligopolistic into near monopolies.[4]

The other two major U.S. antitrust laws were passed in 1914, in the same session of Congress that gave us income taxes and the Federal Reserve System. The *Clayton Act* prohibited specific anticompetitive practices, and the *Federal Trade Commission Act* set up the Federal Trade Commission (FTC) as an expert body to assist the Department of Justice in enforcing the antitrust laws. The Clayton Act had three main sections.

Section 2, which was strengthened by the Robinson-Patman Act of 1936, addresses *price discrimination*, as follows:

> . . . it shall be unlawful . . . to discriminate in price between different purchasers of commodities of like grade and quality . . . where the effect of such discrimination may be substantially to lessen competition or to create a monopoly in any line of commerce, or to injure, destroy, or prevent competition . . . .

The Robinson-Patman Act was passed in part because of pressure from owners of small grocery stores who felt that the emerging chains (in particular A&P) were able to pressure suppliers to grant them "unfair" discounts.

---

[3] Trusts were entities that functioned like holding companies, a company which holds the stock or ownership in (perhaps many) other companies. This legal device was generally abandoned around the turn of the century, but it lives on in the term "antitrust."

[4] See Ralph L. Nelson, *Merger Movements in American Industry, 1895–1956*, Princeton University Press, Princeton, N.J., 1959; and Jesse W. Markham, "Survey of the Evidence and Findings on Mergers," in *Business Concentration and Price Policy*, Universities–National Bureau Committee for Economic Research, Princeton University Press, Princeton, N.J., 1955. Subsequent merger waves took place during the late 1920s, the late 1960s, and the early 1980s. These mergers rarely produced monopolies, however.

The owners of small stores sought and received protection from Congress.

Section 3 makes it unlawful to sell (or lease) on the condition that the purchaser not buy from a competitor of the seller, where the effect "may be to substantially lessen competition or tend to create a monopoly." This provision has been applied to prevent makers of copiers from requiring users to buy paper only from them (a tying contract) and to prevent a gasoline company from requiring stations selling its gasoline also to sell its tires and batteries (an exclusive dealing arrangement).

Section 7 of the Clayton Act prohibits mergers or purchases of firms "where in any line of commerce in any section of the country, the effect may be substantially to lessen competition or to tend to create a monopoly." This section had no effect on mergers until a technical loophole was closed in 1950 by the Celler-Kefauver Act.

While the Clayton Act is more definite in terms of practices than is the Sherman Act, it still leaves it to the courts to decide when the practices mentioned are likely to lessen competition. As with the Sherman Act, the standards for illegal behavior under the Clayton Act have varied over time.

ANTITRUST ENFORCEMENT. Three types of penalties are applied to those who violate the antitrust laws. First, it is a felony to violate the Sherman Act. The maximum fines under the Sherman Act were raised in 1974 to $100,000 for an individual and $1 million for a corporation. The maximum prison sentence is 3 years. In practice, only price-fixing and other flagrant violations of the Sherman Act are treated as criminal offenses and punished by fines and prison sentences.

Second, many cases result in orders by a federal court or the FTC that require the offending firm to cease certain practices or to take particular actions, such as dissolving a merger or otherwise splitting a firm in order to enhance competition. Third, and very important, firms or consumers who have been injured by violations of the antitrust laws are entitled to treble damages, that is, three times the damages they have suffered. Thus a firm that suffers losses as a consequence of its suppliers' price-fixing can sue the price fixers for three times the amount of its losses.

The antitrust laws are enforced by the U.S. Department of Justice, which alone can bring criminal charges under the Sherman Act, and by the FTC. These agencies have generally been dominated by professionals—lawyers and, in recent years, economists. Their enforcement policy is not well explained by the capture hypothesis introduced in Chapter 13, since the antitrust laws apply to all businesses, not to a small, easily organized group. But changes in the political climate do influence both the vigor with which the antitrust laws are enforced and the kinds of violations on which the enforcement agencies concentrate. In addition to government enforcement, private suits that seek court orders or damages serve to enforce the law.

In the early years of antitrust activity, private suits were rare and government enforcement was not vigorous. The Department of Justice brought only 15 antitrust cases before 1900. Despite Theodore Roosevelt's image as a "trustbuster," only 42 cases were filed between 1900 and 1909. Many early antitrust cases were brought (and won) against labor unions on the grounds that strikes restrain trade.[5] In recent years, both government and private enforcement of the antitrust laws has been much more vigorous, as Table 14-1 reveals.

The table shows that both government and private antitrust enforcement have increased sharply since the early 1940s. The recent increase in government cases

[5] Labor unions were fully exempted from the antitrust laws only in the 1930s.

TABLE 14-1. Antitrust Activity in the Courts

| Period | Antitrust cases filed per year ||
	Government	Private
1941–1945	36	59
1946–1950	51	106
1951–1955	39	209
1956–1960	63	233
1961–1965	69	720
1966–1970	55	654
1971–1975	78	1295
1976–1980	75	1448
1981–1984	112	1155

Source: S. C. Salop and L. J. White, "An Economic Analysis of Private Antitrust Litigation," *Georgetown Law Journal*, April 1986, Table 1.

reflects mainly the Reagan administration's decision to emphasize prosecution of price-fixing. Price-fixing cases tend to be simpler than others, thus making it possible for government lawyers to handle more of them. While most economists applaud vigorous enforcement of the law against cartels, some compain that other anticompetitive practices are being allowed to flourish.

Table 14-1 also shows that private antitrust activity has risen much faster than government enforcement has. The sharp increase in private antitrust activity in the early 1960s reflects the fact that about 2200 private suits for damages were filed against General Electric and the other firms convicted of fixing the prices of electrical equipment during the 1950s. (We discussed this case in Chapter 12.) About $400 million (well over $1 billion in today's dollars) was awarded in these cases. Recent private cases have involved both suits for damages and attempts to force other firms to change policies.

Government Policy and Judicial Interpretation

The antitrust laws have not changed significantly since 1950, but the standards actually applied under those laws have changed substantially. Even though private enforcement is important, private firms do not often bring big, expensive cases. Thus changes in government enforcement policies are more important than Table 14-1 might suggest. Many cities have laws against spitting on the sidewalk that are rarely enforced in practice, for example, and the government has treated the Robinson-Patman Act similarly for over a decade. In addition, the courts ultimately decide what practices are unreasonable under the Sherman Act and when business behavior is likely to lessen competition under the Clayton Act, and they have applied different standards over the years. Recent court decisions have made it harder for private firms to enforce the Robinson-Patman Act, for instance, by making it harder for them to prove that a violation has occurred.

PRICE-FIXING. Since 1940, the courts have made it clear that it is illegal under section 1 of the Sherman Act for competitors to fix prices, and the Reagan administration has made prosecution of price-fixing a top priority. But price-fixing, like murder, occurs with some regularity despite active enforcement and strong penalties. As we have discussed, General Electric and other producers of electrical equipment fixed prices during the 1950s. However, price-fixing does not always involve major corporations. Bakeries and producers of cardboard and paper have often been convicted of conspiring to fix prices and restrict output. In recent years several firms have been convicted of rigging bids on contracts to pave roads and highways.

An interesting recent case involved a 1982 telephone conversation between the president of American Airlines, Robert L. Crandall, and the president of Braniff International, Howard Putnam. Between them, the two airlines accounted for a large fraction of air traffic in the Dallas area. The critical part of the conversation was as follows:[6]

CRANDALL: I think it's dumb as hell . . . to sit here and pound the (deleted) out of each other and neither one of us making a (deleted) dime . . . . We can both live here and there ain't no room for Delta. But there's, ah, no reason that I can see, all right, to put both companies out of business.

PUTNAM: Do you have a suggestion for me?

CRANDALL: Yes, I have a suggestion for you. Raise your (deleted) fares 20%. I'll raise mine the next morning . . . . You'll make more money and I will too.

PUTNAM: We can't talk about pricing.

CRANDALL: Oh (deleted), Howard. We can talk about any (deleted) thing we want to talk about.

However, Putnam was right.

While explicit collusion is clearly illegal, we saw in Chapter 12 that oligopolies may manage to collude tacitly, without explicit agreement. From an economic point of view, it doesn't matter how output is restricted; the effect is the same whether collusion is tacit or explicit. In 1946 the leading cigarette producers were found to have violated the antitrust laws by engaging in "conscious parallelism." This meant that each firm, without any agreement, had adopted policies to restrict output that made sense only because each knew the

---

[6] "American Air Accused of Bid to Fix Prices," *Wall Street Journal*, Feb. 24, 1983, p. 2.

others would do the same. However, no cases of this sort have been won in recent years.

The antitrust laws are thus currently unable to deal directly with tacit collusion in concentrated industries. This is a weakness from an economic point of view. But lawyers argue that a law that cannot be obeyed is unfair and that legislation telling an oligopolist not to make rational decisions would be such a law.

MONOPOLIZATION. Many of the most famous antitrust cases, including the 1911 decisions that dissolved American Tobacco and Standard Oil and the IBM and AT&T cases mentioned at the start of this chapter, have involved charges of monopolization. Many business policies have been found illegal when adopted by firms that dominate their industries, even though smaller firms could legally do the same things.

Attempts to monopolize a market may take the form of *predatory pricing*. Most observers would conclude that predatory pricing is occurring if a firm is charging prices so low that they make sense only because they are likely to drive competitors from the market. Small firms with high costs often accuse larger rivals of predatory pricing. In recent years, the courts have rejected such accusations when the prices in question exceed the average variable cost of the firm charging them.

In the government's case against IBM, which was dropped in 1982, one of the charges was predatory pricing. The government charged that IBM had introduced a new computer model that it planned to sell below cost and had announced a product before it was finished in an effort to prevent Control Data from becoming a viable competitor.

One of the important issues in this case was whether IBM did or did not have a monopoly in the relevant market. The government, arguing that a monopoly did exist, defined the market narrowly as including mainframe computers only, thus giving a large market share to IBM. IBM, in contrast, argued that the relevant market included software and peripheral equipment, since IBM's share in that broader market was significantly smaller and its monopoly power was thus harder to prove. The problem of market definition is an important issue in many cases brought under section 2 of the Sherman Act. (See Box 11-1 for another example.) Reasonable economists often disagree on the best market definition when a large array of goods may be substitutes under some conditions. It is true, for instance, that people sometimes choose to do arithmetic with a pencil rather than a mainframe computer—but are pencils and large computers really in the same market? How about mainframe and personal computers?

In the AT&T case mentioned in the quotation at the beginning of this chapter, the government charged that AT&T had monopolized the telecommunications business by pricing some services below cost, denying other long-distance phone companies access to AT&T local networks, and exploiting its monopoly of the telephone industry to create demand for the equipment produced by Western Electric, a company it owned.

The agreement between AT&T and the Justice Department, which was only slightly modified by the court, was generally viewed as a victory for the government. It required AT&T to divest (sell off) the Bell operating companies that provide local telephone service. This led to a divestiture of over $87 billion in assets in January 1984, by far the largest divestiture in antitrust history. The now-independent local companies have no incentive to treat AT&T more favorably than they treat its long-distance competitors (such as MCI and US Sprint) or other manufacturers of telecommunications equipment. As Box 14-1 describes, the telephone business has experienced dramatic and controversial changes in the last decade, and the end is not in sight

MERGERS. In the 1950s and 1960s, after the Celler-Kefauver Act had made section 7 of the Clayton Act effective, mergers of all sorts were attacked by the government, and almost all challenged mergers were blocked by the courts. During the 1970s, however, many observers argued that merger policy had become too strict. In particular, many *vertical mergers* (between buyers and sellers, such as steelmakers and auto producers) and *conglomerate mergers* (between firms that neither compete with each other nor face each other as buyer and seller, such as steelmakers and bakeries) had been barred, even though they were very unlikely to harm competition. Many *horizontal mergers* (between competitors) involving small firms in markets with low concentration had also been attacked.

Box 14-1. The Telephone Revolution

In the early 1960s, the telephone industry was dominated by a single firm, AT&T, which provided most local service and almost all long-distance service. Telephone service, whether provided by AT&T or by one of several smaller companies, was treated as a natural monopoly. No entry was allowed, and rates were set so as to give AT&T a "fair" rate of return on its invested capital. Because regulators were very concerned to hold down the price of local residential service, many observers argued that long-distance and business services were priced well above cost in order to give AT&T a competitive rate of profit overall. AT&T manufactured almost all the transmission and switching equipment used in the telephone network, and customers could use only telephones leased from AT&T.

Things began to change in the late 1960s. The U.S. Federal Communications Commission began to realize that the manufacture of telephones was not a natural monopoly. It started to move toward full deregulation of this area in 1972; it arrived there in 1980. Consumers and businesses can now choose from a wide range of products provided by a large number of suppliers.

Beginning in the late 1960s, the FCC also began losing faith in the proposition that long-distance telephone service is a natural monopoly. It began allowing limited entry in 1969. In 1977, a court decision forced the FCC to allow essentially unlimited entry into the long-distance telephone business.

The 1984 divestiture discussed in the text continued this revolution. Economists expected it to lead to phone rates closer to costs, but there has been great political resistance to increasing local residential phone rates so that businesses' long-distance bills could be cut. Many expected long-distance rates to be deregulated rapidly, but while AT&T's competitors are not regulated, AT&T still is—in large part because it retains over 80 percent of the long-distance business. Still, long-distance rates have declined sharply. The general impression was that the local operating companies shed by AT&T would become boring enterprises, like water companies. Instead, they have entered many new businesses, some of them at the leading edge of technology, and would enter many more but for limitations placed on them by the federal judge who heard the AT&T case.

What will happen to residential and business phone rates? Will AT&T continue to dominate long-distance service and remain regulated, or will it become a deregulated firm with strong rivals? What will the local telephone companies be allowed to do? What will they try? Will Congress act to sort all this out, or will it continue to let regulators and the courts make all the key decisions? New developments in this industry occur almost daily, but the final answers to these and other questions may not become clear for several years.

Note: For a discussion of the early postdivestiture telephone business, see Paul W. MacAvoy and Kenneth Robinson, "Losing by Judicial Policymaking: The First Year of the AT&T Divestiture," *Yale Journal on Regulation*, 1985.

In 1982 the Reagan administration issued a new set of merger guidelines that described the rules the Justice Department and the FTC would use in deciding which mergers to challenge. Since most merger cases are brought by the government, these rules are quite important. The guidelines (which were slightly revised in 1984) indicated that the government would only rarely attack vertical or conglomerate mergers. Horizontal mergers in unconcentrated markets were also declared legal. Horizontal mergers in concentrated industries would be attacked only if they increased concentration significantly, and a detailed set of numerical standards was announced. Box 14-2 describes these standards and their application to an important recent case. The guidelines also indicated that other factors, such as likely efficiency gains from the merger, barriers to entry, and the extent of foreign competition, would be considered.

The Reagan merger policies have been controversial. Some argue that they represent a return to reason; others contend that the government has promised not to enforce the law. Not surprisingly, the Reagan years have been marked by a sizable merger wave.

Should Antitrust Policy Change?

In considering possible changes in antitrust policy, it is natural to begin with the economic effects of the actual policies we have had. To evaluate these effects, it is necessary to ask what would be different in the U.S. economy without antitrust. That is a hard question to

Box 14-2. The Merger Guidelines, Market Concentration, and Soft Drinks

In 1986 the FTC challenged proposed mergers between Coca-Cola and Dr. Pepper and between Pepsi-Cola and 7-Up on the grounds that either merger would probably reduce competition in the soft drink market. This decision was consistent with the rules laid down in the merger guidelines for horizontal mergers.

The guidelines specify that the Hirschman-Herfindahl index (HHI) will be used to measure concentration. The HHI is calculated by summing the market shares, each squared, of all the firms in the industry. Thus if there are only two firms in the industry, each with a 50 percent share, the index is $50^2 + 50^2 = 5000$. But if one firm has a share of 80 percent and the other firm only 20 percent, the index is $80^2 + 20^2 = 6800$. Thus the index yields larger values when the industry has an uneven distribution of firm sizes. It yields lower values when there are many firms. For example, if there are three firms, each with a 33 percent share, the index is $33^2 + 33^2 + 33^2 = 3267$; if there are 10 firms, each with a 10 percent share, the index is only $10 \times 10^2 = 1000$. Thus the fewer firms there are in an industry and the more the industry is dominated by a small number of them, the higher the HHI measure of concentration.

The merger guidelines establish the criteria shown in Table 14B-1. As the table indicates, mergers are more likely to be challenged the higher the HHI and the greater the increase in the HHI the merger would produce.

Let us see how these standards applied to the proposed soft drink mergers. The premerger HHI in this industry was 2510, so that it was highly concentrated to begin with. Coca-Cola had a market share of 40 percent, and Dr. Pepper's share was 6.5 percent. These two companies thus contributed $40^2 + 6.5^2 = 1642$ points to the premerger HHI. If they were merged, their market share would be 46.5 percent, so they would contribute $46.5^2 = 2162$ points to the postmerger HHI. The merger between Coca-Cola and Dr. Pepper would thus raise the HHI by 520 ($= 2162 - 1642$) points, from 2510 to 3030. This proposed merger clearly violated the guideline standards.

Similarly, you should be able to show that the proposed merger between Pepsi-Cola, with a 28 percent share, and 7-Up, with a 7 percent share, would increase the HHI by 392 points. Both mergers thus clearly violated the standards set down in the guidelines. Why did Coke and Pepsi, knowing this, attempt these mergers in the first place? Because the Reagan administration had previously failed to challenge a number of other mergers that had also clearly violated the guideline standards.

TABLE 14B-1. Postmerger Value of HHI

Less than 1000	1000–1800	Greater than 1800
Market is unconcentrated Challenge no mergers	Market is moderately concentrated Challenge only mergers that raise HHI by at least 100 points	Market is highly concentrated Challenge only mergers that raise HHI by at least 50 points

Note: For more information on the proposed soft drink mergers and for the figures used here to calculate HHIs, see "It's Still a Free-for-All on the Soda Shelf," *Business Week*, July 7, 1986, p. 37.

---

answer in detail, but it is highly probable that without the antitrust laws, firms would have engaged far more frequently in price-fixing agreements, and there would have been more mergers between competitors that led to monopoly or near monopoly. As we have seen in earlier chapters, it is in the interest of firms in an industry to get together, one way or another, to restrict output and raise prices above costs. The many cartels in the U.S. economy in the last century and the massive mergers that followed them support this prediction of theory.

Foreign comparisons also generally support this prediction. Until recently, antitrust was relatively unimportant outside the United States. Governments in other countries have tended to take a more generous view of mergers and cartel arrangements. The European Common Market now has formal antitrust laws, and antitrust has become more important in Canada, Great Britain, West Germany, and some other nations, but enforcement is not vigorous by U.S. standards, in part because private cases are not allowed. Also, governments in some countries still work hand in glove with their local manufacturers to keep out foreign competition and enable the local firms to act more like monopolies. It is thus not surprising that foreign firms often engage in price-fixing and other practices that would be illegal under the U.S. antitrust laws. Nor is it surprising that mergers have been a more important cause of increased concentration outside the United States.

There is little doubt among economists that laws against price-fixing have had a beneficial effect. But some have argued that antitrust policy, even under the Reagan administration, has been too concerned with preventing concentration among U.S. firms. There are two main strands to this argument.

First, antitrust enforcement has often ignored foreign competition. Only three major U.S. firms produce automobiles, for example, but they face a sizable number of foreign competitors. Taking foreign competition into account gives an altogether different picture of the market; it makes increased domestic concentration look much less serious. The merger guidelines do stress that foreign concentration will be considered by the Department of Justice and the FTC, but some argue that it is not given enough weight by these agencies or by the courts.

Second, even if increased concentration implies a move toward monopoly pricing, it may be socially beneficial if it lowers costs. Figure 14-3 shows the long-run marginal cost schedule, LMC, for a competitive industry. Equilibrium under competition is at point E, with output Q_C and price P_C. Now suppose a merger converts the industry into a monopoly, and the merged firm operates more efficiently. We show this by a downward shift of the long-run marginal cost schedule to LMC'. Because the industry is now a monopoly, the merged firm maximizes its profit by reducing output to Q_M, where $MR = LMC'$. Buyers experience a price increase, from P_C to P_M, and they are clearly worse off. The net loss of consumers' surplus is given by the triangle labeled A.[7]

That is not the end of the story, however: Buyers' losses are offset by cost savings. The average cost per unit of output has fallen from LMC to LMC', so that the total cost reduction on output Q_M is equal to the area labeled B. This cost reduction, which is collected as monopoly profit, is also a social saving, since it takes fewer resources to produce the output, Q_M. Since area B is larger than area A in Figure 14-3, the monopolization depicted there, because and only because of the accompanying cost reduction, actually involves a potential net gain in welfare for society as a whole.[8]

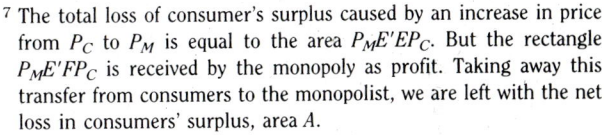

---

[7] The total loss of consumer's surplus caused by an increase in price from P_C to P_M is equal to the area $P_M E'EP_C$. But the rectangle $P_M E'FP_C$ is received by the monopoly as profit. Taking away this transfer from consumers to the monopolist, we are left with the net loss in consumers' surplus, area A.

[8] Whether society regards the change as an actual gain depends on its comparison of the loss by consumers relative to the gain by the monopolist.

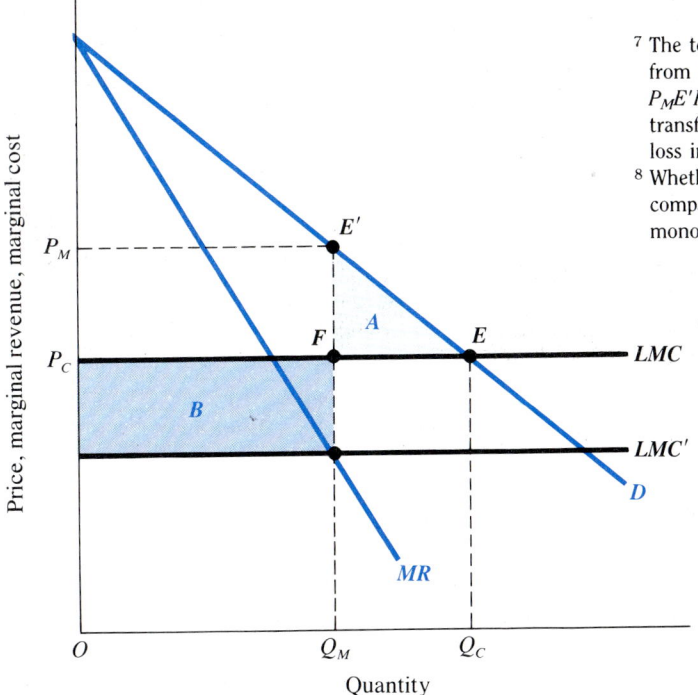

FIGURE 14-3. Monopolization with Cost Reduction. The industry shown is initially competitive, with constant costs per unit of output. Its initial equilibrium is at point E, where the supply (LMC) and demand (D) curves intersect. The industry is then monopolized. This lowers long-run average and marginal cost to LMC' and results in operation at point E'. The net social loss from the increase in price from P_C to P_M is equal to area A, but there is a net gain equal to area B because output Q_M is now produced at a lower cost. In this case society as a whole gains from monopolization, since B is larger than A.

Thus if in some particular case monopolization would lead to substantial cost savings, the antitrust laws could prevent a socially desirable change. The Department of Justice and the FTC do consider evidence of likely cost reduction in deciding whether to challenge proposed mergers, but the courts have consistently refused to do this, holding that the antitrust laws talk about competition, not social welfare.

On the other hand, some observers have argued that antitrust policy in recent years has become too concerned with narrowly economic values. By comparison, in 1962, in a merger case involving two firms that owned chains of shoe stores, the U.S. Supreme Court stated:[9]

> Of course, some of the results of large integrated chain operations are beneficial to consumers. Their expansion is not rendered unlawful by the mere fact that small independent stores may be adversely affected. It is competition, not competitors that the [Clayton] Act protects. But we cannot fail to recognize Congress' desire to promote competition through the *protection of viable, small, locally owned businesses*. Congress appreciated that occasional higher costs and prices might result from the maintenance of fragmented industries and markets. It resolved these competing considerations in favor of decentralization. We must give effect to that decision.

Whatever Congress did or did not intend, merger policy, and antitrust policy in general, has moved far away from the sentiments expressed in this decision. Those who feel that "small is beautiful" for social and political reasons deplore this movement.

3. Natural Monopoly and Economic Regulation

The leading examples of natural monopolies are water, gas, and electricity supply and local telephone and sewer services. These products stand out because of the importance of scale economies in the distribution of services. Installing larger sewer pipes to accommodate twice as many homes raises costs less than double. Running one system of wires for electricity or phone service is less expensive than having two overlapping systems. Similar arguments have been applied to cable television, local bus service, and trash collection. The existence of economies of scale in these public utility industries makes it desirable to have a monopoly supplier, but government intervention is then necessary in order to prevent the exercise of monopoly power. Accordingly, public utilities in the United States and most other nations are either regulated or owned and operated by the government. In both cases, prices are determined by the government, not by the monopoly producer.

Economic regulation as we know it developed in the United States, beginning in the last century. State commissions began to take over the regulatory work of local governments just before World War I, and the federal government's role expanded in the 1930s. The federal government regulates some sales of electricity and long-distance telephone services, among other things, while state commissions set the prices paid by consumers for gas, electricity, and local telephone service in most areas. Regulators are appointed at the federal level and in some states and are elected in others. All operate under vague laws that instruct them to set "fair" or "reasonable" prices and to serve "the public interest."

Natural monopoly services are sometimes provided by the government itself rather than by a regulated private firm. Thus water and sewer services are usually provided by local governments today.[10] Government agencies and nonprofit cooperatives account for about 20 percent of electricity sales in the United States and for a smaller share of local telephone service. A government corporation, the U.S. Postal Service, has a legal monopoly over first-class mail. Except in Great Britain, which has recently switched to private provision of gas and telephone services, natural monopolies are generally operated by the government outside the United States.

Whether the government acts as regulator or producer, it must determine the price to be charged for natural monopoly services. In this section we first describe the task of setting economically efficient prices and then briefly discuss the behavior and performance of economic regulatory agencies in practice.

---

[9] *Brown Shoe Co., Inc. v. United States*, 370 U.S. 294 (1962), emphasis added.

[10] This has not always been the case; in 1896 almost half of U.S. cities were served by private water companies. More recently, local governments have taken over the operations of many private bus companies. In the opposite direction, many cities have recently contracted for garbage collection to be provided by private companies.

The Regulatory Task

The argument that competitive markets allocate resources efficiently (which was developed in Chapter 10) suggests that regulators should try to mimic the operation of competition in natural monopoly sectors. As in competitive markets, costs should be minimized and price should be based on marginal cost. In addition, a regulatory authority must strike a balance between the interests of consumers—who want low prices—and the economic viability of the producer. A program that favors consumers by setting prices far below cost will rapidly bankrupt a regulated firm or require a large tax increase to cover the losses of a government operation. These observations suggest the following basic rules for natural monopoly regulation.

Prices should be as close to marginal cost as possible.
Profits should provide only a normal rate of return.
Production should be efficient.

Let us discuss each of these in turn.

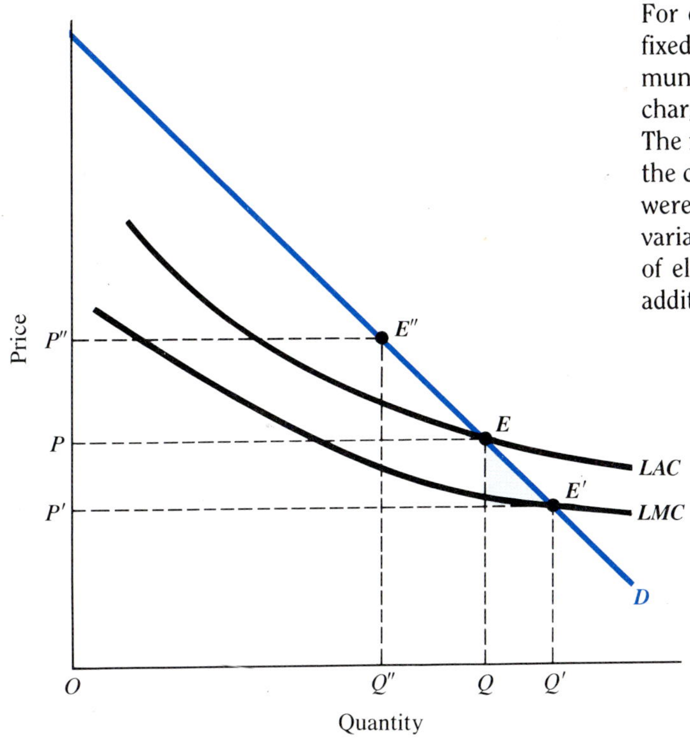

PRICE. Marginal cost pricing ensures that consumers' valuation of additional output is equal to the cost of producing more. Large deviations from marginal cost pricing involve waste. If marginal cost is below price, not enough of the good is being produced; if it is above price, too much is being produced. But average cost declines with output in natural monopolies because of economies of scale. And, as Figure 14-4 illustrates, this means that marginal cost is below average cost. Full marginal cost pricing, which would involve producing output Q', would require charging price P', which is below long-run average cost. The utility would incur losses; its accounting profits, if any, would not provide a normal return on its invested capital. Regulators must thus try to approximate marginal cost pricing and still generate enough revenue to cover costs.

One way this might be done is through a two-part tariff.

● A *two-part tariff* is a price system in which users pay a fixed sum for access to a service and then pay a variable charge for each unit of the service they consume.

For example, in the case of electricity there would be a fixed fee, say, $4 per month, for being connected to the municipal electricity system and then a separate metered charge for each kilowatt-hour of electricity consumed. The revenue from the fixed fee would make it possible for the company to cover its costs even if the variable charge were set equal to marginal cost. Some utilities use a variation of this scheme in which the first few kilowatts of electricity are sold at a high price, with the price of additional units set closer to marginal cost.

FIGURE 14-4. A Regulated Natural Monopoly. At the social optimum at point E', where price equals marginal cost, the firm would not cover its costs, since *LAC* exceeds *LMC* at all output levels. One solution is to set price equal to average cost and operate at point E. Too little output is produced at this point, since P exceeds *LMC*, and the resulting social cost is shown by the shaded area. Still, point E is better for society as a whole than is the unregulated monopoly equilibrium, E''.

A more common but less satisfactory approach is to set price equal to average cost. This approach is illustrated in Figure 14-4. At the socially optimal point, E', price is below long-run average cost. If two-part pricing is ruled out, regulators may elect to set price equal to P. At this point revenues just cover the cost of meeting consumers' demand for output Q.

There are two problems with such average cost pricing. First, at output Q there is underproduction of the good, since price exceeds LMC. The social loss is shown by the shaded area. Second, the marginal cost of providing utility services tends to vary over time. It is usually much less expensive to increase electricity production at midnight, when only the most efficient plants are operating, than at noon, when a utility must often operate all of its generating capacity to meet demand. Prices should reflect changes in marginal cost over time; prices based on average cost generally won't do this properly.

PROFIT. We argued previously that all costs must be covered, so that profits must provide at least a normal rate of return on capital, in order for a public utility to survive. Figure 14-4 shows why profits should not be more generous than this. Suppose the regulated price were P'' and the utility thus operated at point E''. In this case the utility would make substantial excess profits, and we would be far from the social optimum at E', much farther than is required for the utility to earn normal profits. At point E'' consumers pay more for the service than they do even at the average-cost-pricing point, E, they obtain less output, and the output is produced at a higher average cost. The equilibrium at E'' is in no one's interest except the utility company's—since the company is making excess profits. Preventing excess profits protects consumers from needlessly high prices.

PRODUCTION. But if prices always exactly cover costs, so that the utility always earns exactly a normal rate of profit, what incentive does it have to minimize cost? None at all. Under these conditions one would expect costs, and thus prices, to be higher than necessary. It requires hard, often unpleasant work to hold down costs. And some cost increases—large salaries and plush offices for executives, swimming pools for the staff, a cafeteria with subsidized lunches—are positively pleasant. Cost inflation is ultimately borne by the utility's customers.

It is therefore essential that regulators take an active interest in the efficiency of regulated or government-owned firms.[11] They should monitor efficiency by reviewing important management decisions and by making comparisons with utilities providing the same service elsewhere. It may be necessary to provide above-normal or below-normal profits temporarily in order to reward good performance or punish inefficiency.

Regulatory Performance

How well do regulated or government-owned natural monopolies in the United States perform relative to the three standards just presented? The short answer is, "Not very well." A more complete answer would add, "—but no worse on average than natural monopolies elsewhere." In part this mixed record reflects the political aspects of all regulation, which we stressed in Chapter 13; in part it reflects the inherent difficulty of producing good performance without the rewards and penalties provided automatically by competition.

PRICES. Until quite recently, regulators in the United States paid virtually no attention to marginal cost in setting prices; utility rates were based mainly on average costs. Government enterprises in this country were no better, even though some public utilities run by foreign governments (notably the British and French electricity systems) were pioneers in the use of marginal cost pricing.

Because regulators are sensitive to political pressures and have some freedom to pursue their own social and political goals, prices in U.S. public utilities were often used to tax some groups and subsidize others. Rural areas were often subsidized by requiring that prices be the same everywhere in a given state, regardless of costs. Business telephone service and long-distance calling

---

[11] In many situations, regulators must also be concerned with the quality and reliability of service provided. In contrast to production efficiency, however, quality and reliability are relatively easy to measure. The hard problem is deciding on the socially optimal levels of quality and reliability. The likelihood of power outages can always be reduced, for instance, but only at a cost.

were taxed (priced above average cost) in order to subsidize residential service and local calls.

Regulatory performance in this area has improved in recent years, but some regulators still pay very little attention to marginal cost in setting prices.

PROFITS. Even though regulators devote much of their attention to computing normal (or "fair") rates of return on capital, regulated companies sometimes earn high rates of profit. This happened to electric utilities in the 1950s and 1960s as technical progress reduced costs more rapidly than regulators reduced prices. While this experience seems to support the capture hypothesis discussed in Chapter 13, regulators do not always provide regulated firms with high profits. In the 1970s, for instance, rapid inflation and increases in fuel prices raised the cost of electricity dramatically. Utility prices became a hot political issue, and regulators did not raise rates enough to cover costs. As a result, many electric utilities were not allowed to cover their total costs. This led them to cut back on investment and maintenance, raising costs and lowering the quality of service. Similarly, some government utilities show persistent losses (until the 1980s, the U.S. Postal Service), while others appear to earn excess returns (some municipal electric companies).

PRODUCTION. Very few utility regulators and almost no supervisors of government enterprises pay systematic attention to cost minimization. In part this occurs because utility managers generally have much better information than do regulators about the firm's options and their likely consequences. Utilities are sometimes punished for decisions that turn out badly—nuclear plants that are expensive and unnecessary, for instance. But such punishments usually come as a surprise, too late to affect decisions, and utilities are rarely rewarded by commissions when they perform especially well.

This does not mean that there are no incentives to hold down costs, however. Once set, public utility prices are fixed until the regulators act again. While prices are fixed, cost reductions increase profits dollar for dollar. Because the process of regulation takes time, requiring judgments on the cost increases claimed by utilities and listening to the testimony of expert witnesses and consumer groups, regulated prices tend to lag behind changes in costs. Perhaps because of this *regulatory lag*, or because obvious cost inflation can be detected, or because utility managers often take the goal of public service seriously, the efficiency of regulated public utilities in the United States has certainly not been disastrous. But there are many reasons for thinking that it could have been better.

■ Antitrust policy and economic regulation of natural monopolies are distinctly American responses to the problem of monopoly power. We have seen that neither is perfect. Debates about antitrust policy always draw some who want to tighten the rules to make it harder to exercise monopoly power, whatever the current rules happen to be, as well as others who feel that the existing rules prevent businesses from operating efficiently. No approach to regulation or government operation of natural monopolies has escaped serious, well-deserved criticism. The problems of natural and unnatural monopoly power are hard enough in the classroom, where all cost and demand curves are known and the goal is efficiency; they are much harder in the real world, where much is uncertain and goals are politically determined.

Summary

1 The welfare costs of monopoly arise from the monopolist's restriction of output. The social cost of monopoly is measured by the total of the differences between the value consumers place on each unit of lost output and its marginal cost of production.

2 In natural monopolies, where costs fall with increases in output, competition cannot produce efficiency. Such industries are generally either regulated or government-owned; the government, not market forces, sets prices. In other industries, antitrust enforcement can enhance efficiency by promoting and protecting competition.

3 Estimates of the social costs of monopoly output restriction tend to be small, typically less than 1 percent of the economy's total output. This may reflect the effects of antitrust

policy and regulation, and it does not take into account the fact that monopoly may lead to excessive costs of production, create unacceptable political power, and redistribute income unfairly.

4 The first major antitrust law was the Sherman Act of 1890, passed at a time of extensive mergers. The act prohibits agreements that restrain trade (including price-fixing) and monopolization (using "unreasonable" behavior to obtain or preserve a monopoly).

5 The Clayton Act of 1914 prohibits price discrimination, requirements that buyers not deal with a seller's competitors, and mergers, but only when these practices are likely to lessen competition.

6 Price-fixing is often punished by fines or jail sentences. Other antitrust violations usually result in court orders requiring specific actions (such as dissolving a firm) or policy changes. In addition, those who have been injured by antitrust violations are entitled to three times the damages they have suffered. In recent years, private cases seeking treble damages or court orders have been much more numerous than government cases.

7 Reagan administration antitrust enforcement has concentrated on price-fixing and mergers among competitors in concentrated industries. Tacit collusion, price discrimination, and mergers among firms that do not compete have generally been safe from antitrust attack.

8 Since it is in the interest of existing companies in an industry to restrict output, the laws against price-fixing and merging to form a monopoly have probably reduced the exercise of monopoly power in the U.S. economy. Some feel that antitrust policy has not paid enough attention to foreign competition and efficiency gains from mergers, while others argue that it should be used to protect small businesses for social and political reasons.

9 The leading examples of natural monopoly are the public utilities: water, gas, and electricity supply and local telephone and sewer services. In the United States and most other nations, public utilities are either regulated or owned and operated by the government in order to prevent the exercise of market power.

10 In order to produce an efficient allocation of resources, a natural monopoly's prices should be as close to marginal cost as possible. But average cost is declining in a natural monopoly, so that marginal cost is below average cost. Therefore, when marginal cost equals price, price is below average cost and the firm is losing money.

11 Two-part tariffs, in which there is a charge for access to the service and also a charge for each unit of service used, provide one good way out of this problem. Another solution, which has been more common in the United States, is to set price equal to average cost. Under average cost pricing, output is not at its socially optimal level, but the social loss is smaller than it would be if the monopoly were not regulated.

12 Regulators generally try, with varying success, to give public utilities exactly a normal rate of profit. If they always succeeded completely, utilities would have no incentive to minimize cost. It is thus important for regulators to monitor and encourage utility efficiency, but this has proved to be a difficult task.

Key Terms

Antitrust policy
Social cost of monopoly
Natural monopoly
Sherman Act
Clayton Act
Robinson-Patman Act
Federal Trade Commission
Private enforcement of antitrust
Vertical mergers
Conglomerate mergers
Horizontal mergers
Marginal cost pricing
Average cost pricing
Two-part tariff
Regulatory lag

Problems

1 Describe a natural monopoly in words and give some examples. Why will competition not produce an optimal allocation of resources in a natural monopoly industry?

2 (a) When it had a monopoly over long-distance telephone calls, AT&T argued that long-distance telephone service was a natural monopoly. What evidence would have convinced you that they were right? (b) AT&T now has several competitors in the long-distance telephone business. If that business is in fact a natural monopoly, what do you expect to happen to AT&T's smaller competitors?

3 Give four examples that show why accounting costs might be excessive (and thus accounting profit rates understated) in industries with monopoly power.

4 Suppose that an industry is competitive and that average

and marginal costs of production are constant and equal to $5, which is also the price. One million units of output are sold each year. Now the industry is monopolized, and we know that price rises to $8 and output falls to 800,000 units. Given only these facts, how would you estimate the social costs of monopoly in this industry, and what is the number you get as the answer?

5 Consider a competitive industry with constant long-run average and marginal cost. Suppose that all the firms in the industry merge to form a monopoly and that, as a consequence, a major cost reduction takes place. Draw a diagram comparing the competitive equilibrium and the monopoly equilibrium. Is it possible for the move to monopoly to lower price and raise output?

6 (*a*) Alpha and Beta are the only two U.S. manufacturers of glass slippers. The public learns that Beta's slippers break easily during dancing; as a consequence, Beta goes out of business. Alpha thus has a monopoly. Has it monopolized? (*b*) Gamma is thinking about entering the glass slipper business. What might Alpha do to prevent Gamma from becoming a strong competitor? Which of these actions do you think should be described as monopolization and thus be illegal?

7 Many observers feel that the Robinson-Patman Act mainly serves to protect small firms from larger and more efficient rivals. In your mind, is this an argument for or against enforcing the act?

8 It has been argued that antitrust is unnecessary because as soon as a monopoly is formed, other firms will come into the industry and undercut it. Others argue that as soon as a monopoly is formed, it becomes financially powerful enough to sell for a time at so low a price that competitors can never get started. Relate this argument to the notion of predatory pricing and explain why you think predatory pricing may sometimes happen or why it is very unlikely to happen.

9 Describe the main economic conflicts among the three basic rules for regulation of natural monopolies.

10 If a public utility is operated in the public interest, does this mean that the interest of the consumer should be protected in the following ways: (*a*) Charging rural consumers the same prices for gas and electricity as city dwellers, even though it costs more to serve them? (*b*) Having special rates for students and families with many children? (*c*) Arranging for needy people to receive supplies of essential services even if they cannot pay? Explain your answers.

11 After the Three Mile Island nuclear plant broke down in 1979, the Pennsylvania regulatory commission had to decide who was to pay for the cleanup of the radiation damage. (*a*) Who do you think should pay, the customers or the shareholders (the owners of the utility)? (*b*) What are the economic arguments that suggest that either the customers or the shareholders should pay?

PART FOUR
FACTOR MARKETS AND INCOME DISTRIBUTION

Chapter 15
Production and Derived Demand

So far we have concentrated on markets in which consumers are buyers and firms are sellers. In Part 4 we focus on markets for inputs used in production, in which firms are buyers and both firms and households are sellers.

Some goods and services, such as steel, sulfuric acid, marketing research, and office space, are sold only by businesses to other businesses. Goods or services of this sort are called *intermediate products*, in contrast to the *final products* sold to consumers. Businesses also obtain the services of the *primary factors of production*—labor, capital, and land—from households. Individual workers sell labor directly to their employers. Since all businesses are ultimately owned by households, business stocks of capital and land are indirectly supplied by households.

All firms consider the prices of the inputs they buy in deciding both *what* to produce and *how* to produce it. The prices of the factors of production supplied by households determine consumers' incomes and thus determine *for whom* the economy ultimately operates. Thus input markets are an essential part of the circular flow of goods and services between firms and households in market economies that we discussed in Chapter 2.[1]

At the most basic level, markets for productive inputs are just like markets for the final goods and services bought by consumers. Supply and demand is the basic method of analysis in both cases. But a closer look at the determinants of demand and supply in input markets reveals some interesting and important differences.

On the demand side, firms' demands for productive inputs ultimately depend on—are derived from—the demands for final goods and services. Nobody wants sulfuric acid for its own sake; firms buy sulfuric acid because it can be used to make a variety of final goods that consumers want. For this reason, firms' demands for productive inputs are called *derived demands*, and this is a key characteristic of the demand for factors of production. In this chapter we set out the general principles of the demand for inputs by firms.[2]

On the supply side, factors of production are ultimately supplied by households, not by firms. And be-

[1] See Figure 2-1 in particular.
[2] We can also think of the demand for some consumer goods as a derived demand. For instance, the demand for cars is derived from the demand for transportation.

cause consumers' incomes are determined by demand and supply conditions in factor markets, analysis of factor markets is the key to understanding the distribution of income. Chapters 16 through 19 consider important features of the factor markets, paying particular attention to conditions of supply. Chapter 20 analyzes the distribution of income—and the incidence of poverty—that results from the operation of factor markets and government policies.

We begin this chapter by looking in section 1 at a single firm's short-run decision about how much to employ of a single variable input: labor. We analyzed this decision in Chapter 8 in order to understand firms' costs of production; here our focus is on input demand rather than output cost. Section 2 considers the case of several variable inputs and asks how and why firms choose the combinations of factors they use. It explains, among other things, why so much more labor is used in relation to capital in developing countries than in rich countries; for example, there is usually a ticket collector on buses in poor countries but not in rich countries.

In section 3 we show how changes in the prices of both inputs and a firm's output affect the quantities of inputs employed. Section 4 relates the input demands of a competitive industry to those of its member firms.

1. Firm Demand for a Single Variable Input

In the short run a firm's capital stock is fixed. Let us suppose for simplicity that the firm has only a single variable input: labor. In Chapter 8 we saw how a firm that behaves as a perfect competitor—by taking the price of its output as fixed—determines how much labor to hire and thus how much output to produce. But not all firms are perfect competitors. How does a monopolist, for instance, decide how much labor to hire? In this section we will see how the basic principles developed in Chapter 8, along with the notion of marginal revenue introduced in Chapter 10, enable us to understand the short-run demand for labor by *any* firm.

The production function introduced in Chapter 8 shows all the *technically* efficient ways of producing output. As we saw there, the firm's problem is to find the *economically* best way of producing, that is, to find the method and level of production that maximize its profits. In deciding how much to produce, any firm must think marginally. It must decide whether the cost of using 1 more unit of labor is higher or lower than the benefit it would obtain. The cost of using 1 more unit of labor is just the wage.[3] The benefit of using 1 more unit of labor is the increase in the firm's revenue that would result from having more output to sell.

Marginal Revenue Product

Table 15-1 shows the short-run production function of the Ponderous Printer Corporation, given the firm's fixed input of capital and other factors. Output increases as the firm hires more labor. The third column shows the *marginal product of labor*, the amount by which output increases when 1 more unit of labor (in this case, one more worker) is employed. As we saw in Chapter 8, when the work force is small, the marginal product of labor rises as more workers are hired. But here the marginal product of labor declines if more than three workers are employed; the law of diminishing returns comes into play.

To decide whether to employ another worker, Ponderous must compare the *value* of the output the worker would produce with the cost of hiring her. The fourth column of Table 15-1 shows the marginal revenue product of labor, which provides the information the firm needs to decide whether to hire another worker.

● The *marginal revenue product* of any input is the increase in the firm's revenue resulting from using 1 extra unit of that input. Thus the *marginal revenue product of labor* (*MRPL*) is equal to marginal revenue (*MR*) times the marginal product of labor.

As Chapter 11 discussed, a firm's marginal revenue gives the increase in revenue produced by a 1-unit increase in output. The marginal product of labor gives the increase in output produced by a 1-unit increase in labor input. Thus if marginal revenue is $5 per unit of output and the

---

[3] As we will see in Chapter 17, however, if a firm is such a large employer that it can affect the wage rate by its own actions, its cost of using more labor exceeds the wage rate. Since this is a rather special case, we assume throughout this chapter that firms take input prices as given.

TABLE 15-1. Employment and Output in the Short Run

Labor input, no. of workers	Output, goods/wk	Marginal product of labor (MPL), goods/wk/worker	Marginal revenue product, (MPL × $500)	Wage rate, $/wk	Increase in profits, $/wk
0	0				
		0.8	400	300	100
1	0.8				
		1.0	500	300	200
2	1.8				
		1.3	650	300	350
3	3.1				
		1.2	600	300	300
4	4.3				
		1.1	550	300	250
5	5.4				
		0.9	450	300	150
6	6.3				
		0.7	350	300	50
7	7.0				
		0.5	250	300	−50
8	7.5				
		0.3	150	300	−150
9	7.8				

marginal product of labor is 2 units of output per unit of labor input, the marginal revenue product of labor is $10 (= $5 × 2) per unit of labor input.

The example in Table 15-1 assumes that the market for printers is perfectly competitive and that the market price, at which Ponderous can sell as many printers as it chooses to produce, is $500. Because each extra unit of output sold adds $500 to the value of the firm's output, the marginal revenue product of labor is $500 times the marginal product of labor. When the output market is perfectly competitive, so that marginal revenue is a constant equal to the price of output, the marginal revenue product of labor is generally called the marginal *value* product of labor (*MVPL*).

As the work force increases, the marginal revenue product of labor eventually declines for two reasons. First, as we saw in Chapter 11, marginal revenue declines as output increases. Second, the marginal product of labor eventually declines because of diminishing returns.

Optimal Labor Demand

The marginal revenue product of labor shows how much hiring one more worker adds to revenues. But hiring a worker also adds that worker's wage to costs. Thus the net effect on the firm's profits of hiring one more worker is equal to the marginal revenue product minus the wage. This amount is shown in the last column of Table 15-1.

How many workers will Ponderous hire? It will keep adding workers so long as the marginal revenue product exceeds the wage, and it will reduce employment if the marginal revenue product is less than the wage. This means that Ponderous will hire seven workers in order to maximize its profits. The seventh worker has a marginal revenue product of $350 and is paid only $300 per week; hiring the seventh worker thus increases profits by $50 per week. But hiring an eighth worker adds only $250 to revenue, while the addition to cost is $300. Profits therefore fall by $50, and the firm would not want to hire the eighth worker.

Note that the firm's decision about how much labor to hire is the same as the decision about how much output to produce. In deciding to hire seven workers, Ponderous is also deciding to produce the amount of output—7.0 units—that is produced by seven workers, given the fixed capital input available for them to use.

We can state the firm's optimal employment rule as

follows: *Expand employment as long as the marginal revenue product exceeds the wage, and contract employment whenever the marginal revenue product falls short of the wage.* The level of employment is thus optimal when the following condition is satisfied:

$$\text{Wage} = \text{marginal revenue product of labor} \quad (1)$$

A perfectly competitive firm maximizes profit by choosing the employment level at which the wage equals the marginal value product of labor, as we saw in Chapter 8.

Figure 15-1 illustrates this discussion graphically. It depicts a firm that can vary smoothly the amount of labor it uses, by varying the hours per week that its employees work, for instance. The marginal revenue product curve, labeled *MRPL*, is downward-sloping because of diminishing returns to labor and decreasing marginal revenue. The firm faces wage rate W_0.

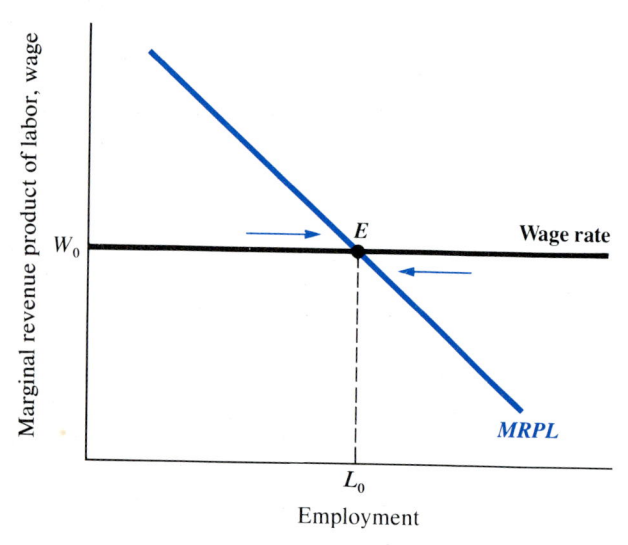

FIGURE 15-1. The Firm's Choice of Employment Level. The marginal revenue product of labor, *MRPL*, declines as the level of employment rises. The firm can hire any amount of labor at the given wage rate, W_0. If *MRPL* exceeds W_0, increasing employment raises revenue by more than costs and thus increases profits. If *MRPL* is less than W_0, reductions in employment increase profits. The firm should thus adjust its employment as indicated by the arrows. It should select employment level L_0, at which the marginal revenue product of labor equals the wage rate.

To select the profit-maximizing level of employment, the firm compares the increase in costs from hiring one more worker with the increase in revenue. That is, it compares the wage with the *MRPL*. So long as the marginal revenue product of labor exceeds the wage, the firm should increase its employment level. If the marginal revenue product of labor is less than the wage, the firm should reduce employment. Thus in Figure 15-1 the firm should hire the amount of labor represented by L_0, the amount of labor at which the marginal revenue product is equal to the wage. The arrows show how the firm adjusts its employment level if that level is different from L_0.

We thus see that *the MRPL curve is the firm's labor demand curve.* At any given wage, the firm will want to hire the amount of labor shown by the *MRPL* curve.

Real Input Price

Suppose that the price at which Ponderous can sell its printers doubles, from $500 to $1000, and the wage rate also doubles, from $300 to $600. How does optimal employment change? You should be able to see that all the numbers in the last three columns in Table 15-1 double but that it is still optimal for Ponderous to employ seven workers.

This illustrates a general principle of input demand under perfect competition. In this case the marginal revenue product of labor is equal to the marginal product of labor, *MPL*, times the price of output. We can then divide both sides of equation (1) by the price of output to obtain

$$\frac{\text{Wage}}{\text{Price of output}} = MPL \quad (1a)$$

In words, equation (1a) says that *under perfect competition,* a firm maximizes profit when it chooses the level of employment such that the marginal product of labor equals the *real wage*—which is the nominal, dollar wage divided by the price of output. Changes in the nominal wage and the output price that leave the real wage unchanged do not affect the quantity of labor demanded. The optimal level of employment rises when the real wage falls and falls when the real wage rises.

2. Firm Demand for Multiple Inputs

Even in the short run, a firm may have several variable inputs: labor, materials, fuel, and so on. And in the long run, a firm is free to vary all inputs. How does a firm determine the quantities of productive inputs it demands in the long run?

In the long run, as a firm changes its capital stock, the quantity of labor it wants to employ will change. The more machinery and other physical capital the firm has in place, the more capital each worker has available to use and the higher is the marginal product of labor at any given level of employment. This increase in labor productivity will increase the demand for labor at all wage rates. Thus the effect of an increase in the firm's capital stock can be depicted as a shift in the demand curve for labor upward and to the right, from *MRPL* to *MRPL'* in Figure 15-2.

The Fundamental Rule for Input Demands

Of course, in the long run the firm also gets to decide how much capital to employ. It makes that decision *exactly* the same way it decides how much labor to employ: by comparing the marginal revenue product of capital with the cost of using an extra unit of capital. The marginal revenue product of capital is just equal to the marginal product of capital—the amount by which using 1 more unit of capital would increase output—times the firm's marginal revenue—the increase in revenue per unit of increase in output. And the cost of using 1 more unit of capital is the rental rate of capital. (Think of the cost of renting a truck for a day as a typical rental rate.[4])

In the long run, the firm will adjust its capital stock so that the marginal revenue product of capital is equal to the rental rate of capital. The lower the rental rate of capital, the more capital the firm will use, just as lower wages increase the quantity of labor the firm demands. If there are other productive inputs—for instance, land, energy, and various raw materials—the firm decides how much of each to employ using exactly the same rule.

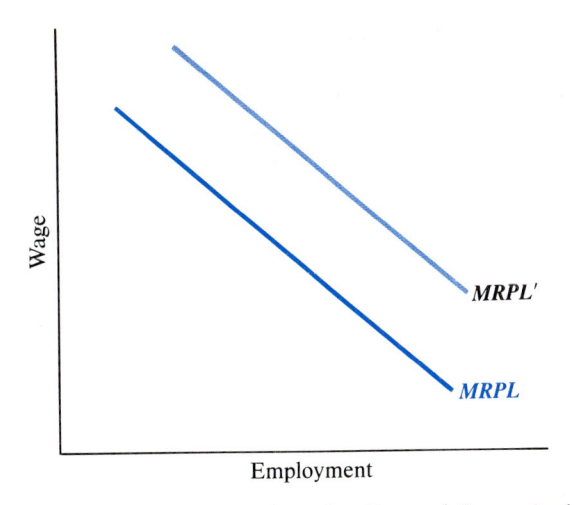

FIGURE 15-2. A Shift in the Labor Demand Curve. An increase in the firm's capital stock raises the marginal product of labor at each level of employment and therefore shifts the firm's labor demand curve (which is just its marginal revenue product of labor curve) upward from *MRPL* to *MRPL'*.

● **To maximize profits, the quantity of each input used should be adjusted so that its marginal revenue product is equal to the cost of using an additional unit.**

[Of course, as we stressed in Chapter 9, a firm must also decide whether it should shut down (in the short run) or leave the industry (in the long run). We omit further discussion of this second step in the output supply and input demand decisions here for the sake of simplicity.]

To explore the implications of this rule, suppose there are three factors: labor, capital, and land. The firm maximizes profits by hiring each to the point where the marginal revenue product is equal to the cost of hiring that factor. Denote by w the wage rate, by r_K the rental rate of capital, and by r_T the rental rate of land.[5] If the firm is maximizing profit, we have just shown that the following three equations must be satisfied:

$$MPL \times MR = w \qquad (2)$$

$$MPK \times MR = r_K \qquad (3)$$

$$MPT \times MR = r_T \qquad (4)$$

---

[4] In Chapter 18 we discuss in detail the relation between the cost of *buying* a unit of capital and the cost of *using* it.

[5] Because land and labor both begin with "L," it is customary to use "t" (for "terra") to denote land.

where *MPL*, *MPK*, and *MPT* are the marginal products of labor, capital, and land, respectively. If the output market is competitive, *MR* equals the price of output, and the quantities on the left in these equations are the marginal *value* products of each of the three factors.

If we divide both sides of equation (2) by *MR* and then by w, we obtain

$$\frac{MPL}{w} = \frac{1}{MR} \qquad (5)$$

Rearranging equations (3) and (4) similarly, we see that all three can be combined to yield

$$\frac{MPL}{w} = \frac{MPK}{r_K} = \frac{MPT}{r_T} = \frac{1}{MR} \qquad (6)$$

Equation (6) is the fundamental rule for a firm to follow in choosing its inputs. The rule applies to *all* inputs that can be varied. Thus it applies in the long run to labor, materials, energy, land, and capital. In the short run it applies to all variable inputs.

In order to interpret equation (6), imagine that the firm is planning to spend one extra dollar hiring inputs.[6] If it hires a dollar's worth of labor, it gets $1/w$ units of labor. (If the wage rate is $2 per hour, for instance, a dollar buys one-half hour of labor.) Each extra unit of labor increases output by *MPL*. Thus *MPL*/w is the amount of extra output obtained by spending one more dollar on labor. Similarly, *MPK*/r_K is the extra output obtained by spending one more dollar hiring capital.

Here is a numerical example illustrating why the basic rule of equation (6) has to be satisfied. Suppose, for example, that *MPL*/w = 2 and *MPK*/r_K = 1. Then an additional dollar spent on labor would increase output by 2 units, while an additional dollar spent on capital would increase output by only 1 unit. If the firm then spent $1 more on labor and cut back spending on capital by $1, its output would increase by 1 unit. Since it could raise output without raising cost, it must not have been minimizing the cost of producing its original level of output. It could lower the cost of producing *that* output level by spending an additional $1 on labor (thus raising output by 2 units) and reducing its spending on capital by $2 (thus lowering output by 2 units), for a net saving of $1. Only when *MPL*/$w$ = *MPK*/r_K is it impossible to reduce the cost of a given output by reallocating spending between capital and labor.

When more than two inputs are variable, we have the general rule expressed algebraically in equation (6): In order to minimize costs, the ratios of marginal product to cost must be the same for all inputs. But how are we to interpret the *MR* term in equation (6)? To answer this question, we begin by noting that a 1-unit increase in output requires 1/*MPL* additional units of labor. (If *MPL* is 2, ½ unit of additional labor adds 1 unit to output, for instance.) The cost of the labor required for a 1-unit increase in output is then w/*MPL*. Similarly, r_K/*MPK* and r_T/*MPT* are the costs of increasing output by 1 unit by spending more on capital and land, respectively.

Since we have seen that these three ratios must be set equal in order to minimize cost, we have the result that if a firm is minimizing cost, the cost of a 1-unit increase in output must be the same no matter which input is increased to produce it. But the cost of a 1-unit increase in output is, by definition, the firm's marginal cost, *MC*. Equating the reciprocals of the ratios in equation (6) and incorporating this result, we have the fundamental rule for choosing the levels of all inputs.

$$\frac{w}{MPL} = \frac{r_K}{MPK} = \frac{r_T}{MPT} = MC = MR \qquad (7)$$

The *MR* term in equation (6) thus reflects the fact that the firm must produce the level of output at which marginal cost is equal to marginal revenue in order to maximize profits, as we discussed in Chapter 11.[7]

We can summarize the results of this analysis as follows:

● **In order to minimize the cost of producing any level of output, the ratios of the cost of using each factor to its marginal product must all be equal. This ratio then equals the firm's marginal cost, which must be set equal to marginal revenue in order to maximize profit.**

---

[6] The reasoning that follows exactly parallels that used in Chapter 6 to show that (marginal utility/price) must be equal for all goods consumed in order to maximize utility.

[7] We derived this same rule in Chapter 9 for the case of perfect competition, in which marginal revenue is equal to the going market price.

Capital-Labor Substitution

The preceding analysis of optimal input demands helps us understand how capital per worker—the capital-labor ratio—is determined. Table 15-2 shows capital-labor ratios for a number of U.S. industries. There is a great deal of variation. Electricity suppliers and other public utilities use a lot of capital per worker, while clothing manufacturing and contract construction are much less capital-intensive. Notice that the service sectors do not have the lowest capital-labor ratios. Banks and insurance companies have expensive buildings designed to inspire confidence and many dollars of capital invested per employee, and even management consultants must buy or rent word processing equipment, reference libraries, and expensive office furniture. Because of capital held in the form of inventories of goods ready for sale, the capital-labor ratio in retail trade exceeds that in furniture manufacturing, where most of the investment is in tools and inventories of raw materials. Data for less-developed nations would generally show lower capital-labor ratios, as we suggested at the beginning of the chapter.

In deciding how much capital to use in the long run, a firm has to compare alternative methods of producing any given level of output. It can typically choose to use relatively much capital and little labor or relatively little capital and much labor. The firm's production function describes the alternative methods of producing each given level of output.[8]

Although we tend to think there is only one right way to do something, that is rarely true of production methods. Typically capital can be substituted for labor all through a production process. A supermarket can use highly sophisticated cash registers and relatively few employees to take the cash, or it can use old-fashioned machines and more people. An airline can use larger planes to fly a given route fewer times per day, thereby using less pilot labor per flight and relatively more capital. An enterprising dentist invests in several chairs, has technicians prepare the patients, and then makes a flying

---

[8] The appendix to this chapter introduces *isoquants*, which show alternative methods of producing each level of output, and demonstrates how the firm chooses its production methods. The analysis there bears a close resemblance to the analysis of indifference curve in the appendix to Chapter 6.

TABLE 15-2. Capital per Worker in U.S. Industries, 1983 (Thousands of 1986 Dollars per Full-Time Worker)

Public utilities	$748.5
Petroleum	451.6
Mining	292.6
Communications	269.6
Transportation	140.9
Other services	100.8
Finance and insurance	85.5
Food	66.6
Textiles	56.9
Wholesale and retail trade	41.3
Printing and publishing	38.7
Furniture and fixtures	27.6
Leather goods	21.3
Construction	18.8
Clothing	17.5

Source: Computed from *Statistical Abstract of the United States, 1986*, Table 900.

visit to repair teeth using very little of his own time.

The lower the ratio of the wage rate, w, to the cost of using capital, r_K, the lower the cost of using labor relative to the cost of using capital. The lower this ratio is, the more attractive labor is relative to capital, and thus the more labor the firm will use relative to capital. In short, the lower w/r_K is, the lower the capital-labor ratio will be.

We now show that this conclusion follows rigorously from our earlier analysis of optimal input demand. Equation (7) can be rearranged to obtain

$$\frac{w}{r_K} = \frac{MPL}{MPK} \qquad (8)$$

Equation (8) says that the lower is w/r_K, the lower is the optimal ratio of the marginal product of capital to that of labor. Now for any level of capital employed, diminishing returns to labor imply that the ratio MPL/MPK falls as more labor is hired. That is, increases in the labor-capital ratio *reduce* the MPL/MPK ratio. Equation (8) therefore shows that the lower the relative cost of using labor, the more labor the firm will use relative to capital.

Thus in countries where labor is cheap—where the wage is low relative to the cost of capital goods—we find firms using much labor and little capital to produce a given level of output; the same level of output would be produced using more capital and less labor in a country where the wage is high. This is why, for instance, ditches are dug using shovels and lots of labor in low-income countries and using machines and little labor in high-income countries.

Equation (8) makes explicit an important point: From the viewpoint of the firm, it is the *relative* costs of using labor and capital that primarily determine the types of production methods it chooses in the long run. A firm chooses its production method by deciding what amount of capital to use: what size factory to build and what equipment to put in it. The marginal product of labor at each level of employment then depends on the amount of capital the firm has put in place.[9]

3. Changes in Firms' Input Demands

Now that we understand how firms choose the quantities of the various productive inputs they demand, we can examine how their choices change when economic conditions change. In this section we show how a firm's input demands respond to changes in input prices, output prices, and productivity. We concentrate on labor for concreteness.

Input Price Changes

We argued previously that the firm's demand curve for labor, its *MRPL* curve, slopes downward because of diminishing returns and decreasing marginal revenue. Thus increases in the wage rate lead the firm to reduce the quantity of labor it demands. What determines the size of these reductions for any given wage increase? Or, more precisely, what determines the elasticity of the quantity of labor demanded by a firm with respect to the wage? The higher this elasticity, the greater the percentage decrease in employment for any given percentage increase in wages.

The key principle here is the following:

● **The better the available substitutes for any particular input, the more elastic will be the firm's demand for that input.**

The ease with which capital and labor can be substituted for each other, which varies considerably among industries, is an important determinant of the long-run elasticity of demand for labor. If labor and capital are very good substitutes, the elasticity of a firm's demand for labor will be high, and a small wage increase will cause a relatively large decrease in the employment of labor in the long run.

What happens to the firm's demand for some other input, say, capital, when the wage rate increases? We argued previously that an increase in the wage rate will reduce the firm's optimal capital-labor ratio, since the cost of hiring labor has risen relative to the cost of using capital. This *substitution* effect increases the demand for capital when the wage rate rises. But there is an offsetting effect. An increase in the wage rate increases the firm's marginal cost at every level of output. And the higher a firm's marginal cost, the lower its optimal output—under perfect or imperfect competition. This *output* effect reduces the demand for capital when the wage rises. Either effect can dominate in any particular case, so that an increase in the wage rate may raise or lower the quantity of capital (or any other input) demanded by a firm.

Output Price Changes

Consider next the effects of a change in the price of output, P, in a perfectly competitive market. Suppose the output price increases. What is the effect on each firm's optimal employment at the given wage rate? Labor is just as productive in physical terms as it was before, but the increase in output associated with increased employment is now worth more. The marginal revenue product of labor is therefore higher at every level of employment. This is shown in Figure 15-3 as a shift in the marginal revenue product schedule upward from $MRPL_0$ to $MRPL_1$.

---

[9] Of course, we have still to ask what determines the relative costs of using capital and labor in the economy. The answer, which is presented in more detail in Chapter 18, is supply and demand. At any point in time, the economy has fixed amounts of capital and labor. The more capital relative to labor, the lower the relative cost of using capital and the higher the relative cost of using labor. This is why workers with the same skills earn more in capital-rich industrialized economies than they do in capital-poor developing economies.

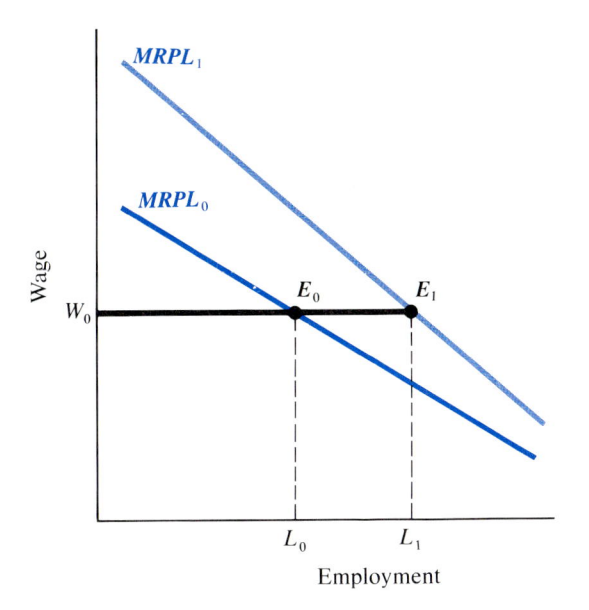

FIGURE 15-3. The Effect on Employment of a Rise in Output Price. In a perfectly competitive market, an increase in the price of output raises the marginal revenue product of labor at all levels of employment. The *MRPL* curve thus shifts upward from $MRPL_0$ to $MRPL_1$. As a result of this shift, the firm's optimal employment level rises from L_0 to L_1. An increase in the demand for the output of an imperfectly competitive firm also generally shifts the firm's *MRPL* curve upward and thus increases its profit-maximizing level of employment.

At the initial level of employment, at point E_0, the new marginal value product exceeds the wage, W_0, since the $MRPL_1$ curve lies above this point. Hence the firm finds it profitable to expand employment. Profits rise as employment increases until point E_1 is reached, where the cost of increasing employment, the wage, is again equal to the increase in revenue obtained by hiring 1 more unit of labor, the marginal revenue product of labor. Employment rises from L_0 to L_1.

The same basic mechanism operates under imperfect competition as well, even though imperfect competitors do not take the output price as given when making employment decisions. An increase in the demand for an imperfectly competitive firm's output will generally raise the firm's marginal revenue at all output levels. An increase in marginal revenue in turn raises the marginal revenue product of labor at all output levels. Thus the firm's demand curve for labor shifts upward, exactly as shown in Figure 15-3, and the quantity of labor it demands at any given wage rate increases.

REAL INPUT PRICES. Under perfect competition, what happens to input demand if the dollar price of output and the dollar cost of all inputs double? Exactly nothing. To show this, note first that under perfect competition, marginal revenue equals the given market price, P. Replacing *MR* by P in equations (2), (3), and (4) and dividing both sides of those equations by P, we obtain equations of the following form for all inputs:

$$\frac{\text{Real}}{\text{input price}} = \frac{\text{dollar input price}}{\text{dollar output price}} = \frac{\text{marginal}}{\text{product}} \quad (9)$$

In words, a perfectly competitive firm maximizes profits by choosing input levels such that the *real price* of every input—which is its nominal, dollar price divided by the dollar price of output—just equals its marginal product. Doubling all input and output prices leaves all real input demands unchanged and thus does not change the quantity demanded of any input.[10] In short, *under perfect competition, the firm's demand for inputs depends on real input prices, which equal the dollar prices of inputs divided by the dollar price of output.*

Productivity Changes

Suppose a firm learns a new way of organizing its production that makes the marginal product of labor higher at all employment levels. Such technical progress would be represented as an upward shift of the *MRPL* curve in Figure 15-3, and it would lead to an increase in the quantity of labor demanded. The effect would be just like that of an increase in the firm's stock of capital, as depicted in Figure 15-2.

4. The Industry's Demand for Inputs

So far our analysis has focused on input demands by an individual firm. If that firm is a monopoly, its input

---

[10] This is essentially the same point we encountered in Chapter 6 when we noted that doubling a consumer's income and all prices would leave the consumer's demands unchanged.

demands are also those of the industry, since it is the only firm in its industry.

In the case of a perfectly competitive industry, which we consider in the rest of this section, the industry demand curve for an input is *not* just the sum of the demand curves of individual firms.[11] The reason for this is that if all sellers in a competitive market respond to a wage change, for instance, by changing their employment, they will generally affect total output. This in turn will affect the price of output, which each firm takes as fixed in making its hiring decisions. We thus go from the labor demand curve of a competitive firm to that of a competitive industry in two steps.

The Industry Demand Curve

The first step in deriving the industry demand curve for labor is to add the firms' demand curves horizontally, as in Chapter 6. At the current price of output, P_0, each competitive firm's demand curve for labor is its *MRPL* curve, as in Figure 15-2. To emphasize the fact that we are dealing with the case of perfect competition, in which marginal revenue equals price, we will refer to these as *MVPL* curves. We add these curves horizontally by adding, at each wage rate, the quantities of labor demanded by each firm in the industry. The result is the industry-level *MVPL* curve, labeled $MVPL_0$ in Figure 15-4.

It would be natural to think of $MVPL_0$ as the industry demand curve for labor, but it would be wrong to do so. The reason for this is that when the industry changes employment, the quantity of output it produces is thereby changed, and the price of its output must change as well. The curve $MVPL_0$, which was drawn on the assumption of a fixed output price, does not reflect the effects of these changes in output price on the demand for labor.

Suppose that the industry is initially in equilibrium at point E_0, with wage W_0 and output price P_0. The curve $MVPL_0$ expresses the demand for labor when the price of output is given at P_0. Now suppose the wage falls to W_1.

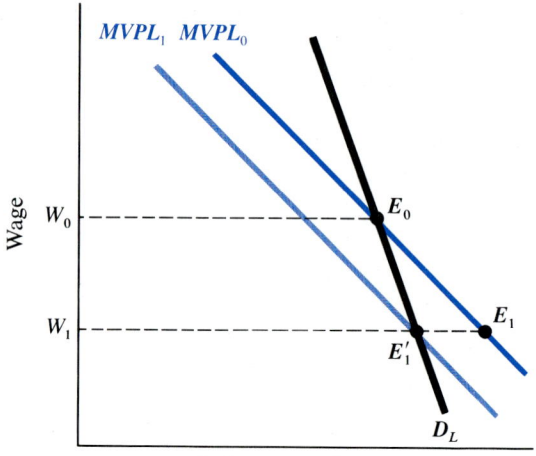

---

[11] The contrast is with the demand curve for a good sold to consumers, derived in Chapter 6, which *is* just the sum of the demand curves of individual consumers.

FIGURE 15-4. A Competitive Industry's Demand for Labor. When the wage is W_0 and the output price is P_0, a perfectly competitive industry is in equilibrium at point E_0. The curve $MVPL_0$ shows how the total labor demand of all firms in the industry increases when the wage rate changes, assuming that the price of output remains at P_0. Thus if the wage falls to W_1, the new equilibrium would be at point E_1 if the price of output did not fall. But as firms expand employment and output, the price of output falls, thus reducing the quantity of labor demanded. The new equilibrium is at point E'_1, with output price P_1 less than P_0. The curve $MVPL_1$ shows how industry employment depends on the wage rate when the output price is P_1. To obtain the industry demand curve for labor, D_L, we join together points such as E_0 and E'_1.

If the output price remained at P_0, the $MVPL_0$ curve shows that the industry would increase employment until it reached the new equilibrium point, E_1. But the output price won't stay at P_0 when sellers hire more workers, since total output will increase and the market price of output will consequently fall below P_0.

The second step in deriving the industry's demand curve for labor is thus to allow for the impact of changes in the price of output. As each price-taking firm increases employment in response to a fall in wages, total output rises, and the price of output falls. And as the price of output falls, every firm will find further hiring less attractive, because the marginal value product of labor has fallen. The actual new equilibrium occurs at point E'_1, with output price P_1 less than the initial price,

P_0. Adding the firm's *MVPL* schedules corresponding to ouput price P_1 yields the new industry-level *MVPL* schedule $MVPL_1$ in Figure 15-4.

By connecting points such as E_0 and E'_1, we get the *industry demand for labor schedule*, D_L, which takes into account the effect of increased employment in reducing the price of output. Whereas the individual firm takes the output price as given and plans a relatively large increase in employment when the wage drops, as all firms together increase employment, they depress the output price and consequently find it optimal to increase employment less than originally planned. Thus the D_L curve is always steeper (less elastic) than the industry *MVPL* curve corresponding to any particular fixed output price.

Industry-Level Input Demand Elasticities

What factors determine the elasticity of a perfectly competitive industry's demand for labor and other productive inputs? As we have seen, the industry labor demand schedule reflects the underlying firms' *MVPL* schedules. Thus the easier it is to substitute between capital and labor in production, the more responsive employment is to wage changes and the more elastic is the industry demand curve for labor.

But the second step in our derivation of the industry-level demand curve points to two additional factors affecting input demand elasticity through induced changes in the price of output. First, if the demand for final goods is very elastic, changes in the quantity supplied will have relatively small effects on the price of output. In this case, firms will not be far off the mark if they assume that the price of output is fixed when they react to a change in wages. That is, D_L in Figure 15-4 will be almost the same as the $MVPL_0$ schedule, which assumed a constant output price.

On the other hand, if the demand for final goods is very inelastic, a rightward shift of the supply curve will lead to a large fall in price, P_1 will be much lower than P_0, and the D_L curve will be much steeper than the $MVPL_0$ curve. Thus, all else equal, *the less elastic is the demand for its output, the less elastic is an industry's demand for all of its inputs*.

The second factor reflects differences in the relative importance of inputs used by a single industry. Corn farmers buy both seed and motor oil. If the price of seed rises sharply, farmers' costs will rise sharply even if they change their methods of production to economize on seed. This in turn means that the price of corn will rise significantly and the quantity of corn demanded by consumers will fall substantially. This output effect will further reduce the quantity of seed demanded. On the other hand, since motor oil is a much less important input in corn production, the output effect would not be noticeable in the case of motor oil. That is, a doubling of the price of motor oil will have a much smaller effect on the price of corn and thus on the quantity of corn demanded than will a doubling of the price of seed. This comparison illustrates a second general principle: *The larger the proportion of total costs accounted for by any input, the more elastic will be the demand for that input*.

■ The relationship between the elasticity of demand for any good and the elasticity of demand for the inputs used to produce it nicely illustrates the principle with which we started this chapter: The demand for productive inputs is a *derived* demand. Inputs are demanded only because there is a demand for the goods they can be used to produce, and it is therefore not surprising that the elasticity of demand for labor by any industry should reflect the elasticity of demand for the good which that industry produces. We have already shown that consumer behavior links markets for complements and substitutes, and the discussion in section 2 shows that business behavior similarly links markets for productive inputs. We now see that markets for inputs and outputs are linked, as we first discussed in Chapter 2. In order to complete our analysis of markets and their operation, we next turn to the supply of the primary factors of production and the determination of consumers' incomes.

Summary

1. Demands by firms for intermediate products and primary factors of production are *derived* from consumers' demands for the final goods and services firms produce. Consumers' incomes are primarily determined in the markets for the primary factors of production (land, labor, and capital) they supply.
2. In order to select the optimal level of employment, a firm must compare the addition to revenue produced by hiring one more worker with the cost of hiring that worker. The same comparison must be made for all other productive inputs.
3. The addition to revenue produced by hiring an additional worker is the marginal revenue product of labor, which is equal to the marginal product of labor times marginal revenue. If the firm is a perfect competitor, the marginal revenue product is called the marginal value product and is equal to marginal product times the price of the firm's output. The condition for the optimal level of employment is that the marginal revenue product of labor must equal the wage rate.
4. In order to select the quantities of all inputs that minimize cost, the ratio of input price to marginal product must be the same for all inputs. This ratio is equal to the firm's marginal cost, which must be equal to marginal revenue in order to maximize profits.
5. Given the price of output, an increase in the price of any input reduces the quantity of that input which the firm demands. The firm's demand for any input is a function of its real cost, or its dollar cost divided by the price of output. The better the available substitutes for any input, the more elastic will be a firm's demand for that input.
6. Each competitive firm assumes that the price of its output is fixed. But when all the firms in an industry change the amount of any input they demand, they change the quantity supplied and thus the price of output. Thus the industry-level demand elasticity for any productive input reflects the quality of substitutes for that input, the elasticity of demand for output, and the importance of that input as a proportion of total costs.

Key Terms

Derived demand
Intermediate products
Final products
Primary factors of production
Marginal revenue product
Marginal value product
Firm's real wage
Firm's input demand curve
Industry's input demand curve

Problems

1. In what sense is it true that a firm's demand for inputs and its decision on how much to produce are the same?
2. Define the marginal revenue product of labor and the marginal value product of labor. Explain why both eventually decline.
3. Suppose a firm must pay a tax of 5 percent of the wage paid to labor. (Think, for instance, of an employer who must pay a share of an employee's contributions to Social Security.) In view of the analysis in section 1, how does the imposition of such a tax affect the firm's demand for labor? Use a diagram to illustrate your answer.
4. Amalgamated Frisbee has just increased its capital stock. (*a*) What is the effect on Amalgamated's demand curve for labor? (*b*) What is the impact on the firm's employment?
5. Suppose that the demand curve for a final good produced by a perfectly competitive industry is completely inelastic. (*a*) Use a diagram to show the effect of a decline in wages on the production and price of the final product. (Recall that a change in wages has the effect of shifting the industry's supply curve.) (*b*) If the industry's capital stock is fixed in the short run, what does its demand curve for labor look like?
6. The fast-food industry uses both labor and paper cups to produce its output. Would you expect the industry's demand curve for labor to be more or less elastic than its demand curve for paper cups? Why?

Appendix: Isoquants and the Firm's Choice of Production Technique

The production function introduced in Chapter 8 describes technically efficient methods of production. In order to maximize its profits, a firm must choose the least-cost or economically most efficient method of production from those technically efficient alternatives.

In this appendix we introduce *isoquants* that describe

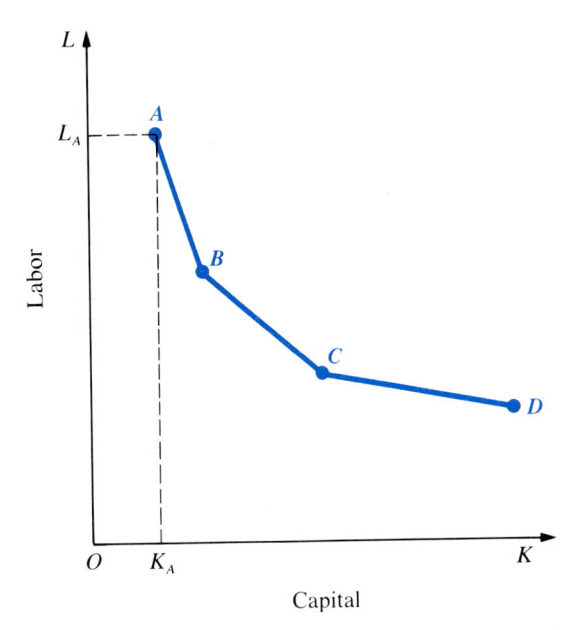

FIGURE 15A-1. An Isoquant. Points A, B, C, and D show the four different combinations of capital and labor inputs that can be used to produce 1 unit of output. By connecting them, we obtain an *isoquant*, which shows the combinations of inputs that can be used to produce a particular level of output.

the technical possibilities open to the firm, and we show the firm's choice of production technique. Figure 15A-1 shows the four available methods of producing a given level of output. Technique A uses amount K_A of capital and L_A of labor. It uses more labor and less capital than any of the other three possible techniques, B, C, and D. Technique A is thus the most labor-intensive technique, and technique D is the most capital-intensive.

Connecting points A, B, C, and D yields an *isoquant* ("iso" = the same, "quant" = quantity), showing the different combinations of capital and labor, all representing different technically efficient production methods, that produce the same level of output. For instance, if the activity is digging a ditch, A is the technique that uses lots of workers with shovels and D is the technique that uses a backhoe with one operator.

In the usual case, where there are many ways of producing any given level of output, this process yields smooth isoquants such as curves I, I', and I'' in Figure 15A-2. Each of these isoquants shows all combinations of capital and labor that can be used to produce a single given level of ouput. Starting at any point on I, we can move to I' by adding more labor. Since this increases output, output is higher on isoquant I' than it is on I and, similarly, higher yet on I'' than on I'. All the possible isoquants make up an *isoquant map*, which provides a full description of the possible methods of production. Isoquants look very much like the indifference curves discussed in the appendix to Chapter 6, and the analysis here is closely related to the analysis there.

Properties of Isoquants

The *slope* of an isoquant is equal to the ratio of the marginal product of capital to that of labor.[12] Why? Start at any point on isoquant I in Figure 15A-2 and move down by reducing labor input by 1 unit. How far to the right must you move to get back on I? That is, if labor input has been reduced by 1 unit, how much capital must the firm add to bring output back to its original level? The output lost through the reduction of labor input by 1 unit is equal to the marginal product of labor, MPL. Each extra unit of capital increases output by MPK, so that each unit of output increase requires $1/MPK$ extra units of capital. Since output must be increased by MPL units, MPL/MPK units of capital have to be added. The slope of the isoquant is equal to the ratio of the change in labor (1) to the change in capital (MPL/MPK) as we move along the curve, and this ratio is equal to MPK/MPL.

The *spacing* of isoquants reflects *returns to scale*. If there are constant returns to scale, doubling both inputs will double output, tripling both inputs will triple output, and so on.[13] At point B'' in Figure 15A-2, the levels of both inputs are double those at B. Then, with constant returns to scale, output on I'' will be double output on I. If there are decreasing returns to scale, output on I'' is less than twice that on I; if there are increasing returns to scale, output on I'' is more than double that on I.

The isoquants in Figure 15A-2 are *curved away from the origin of the figure*. They become flatter as more capital is used to produce any given level of output.

---

[12] As in the case of indifference curves, we avoid confusion by ignoring the fact that isoquant slopes are negative.
[13] With constant input prices, this is exactly equivalent to the way we defined constant returns to scale in Chapter 8.

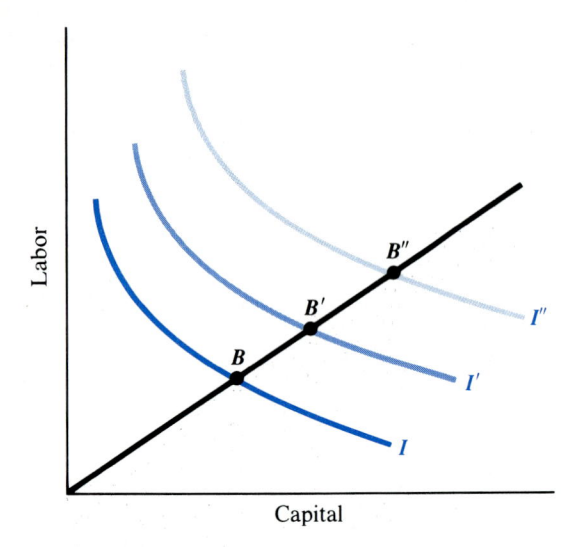

FIGURE 15A-2. An Isoquant Map. If many different input combinations can be used to produce any particular level of output, the isoquant connecting the corresponding points will be a smooth curve, such as I, I', and I''. Each of these curves shows the combinations of capital and labor that will produce a particular level of output. Output is higher on I'' than on I', which in turn corresponds to a higher level of output than I.

Economically, this means that as the firm moves to more capital-intensive techniques, each additional unit of capital used permits a smaller and smaller reduction in labor input if output is to be held constant.

Producing at Lowest Cost

Whatever level of output the firm chooses, it wants to produce at the lowest possible cost. Suppose the firm asks what production method gives it the highest output for a given cost, for example, $1000. (Compare the discussion of utility maximization with a fixed budget in the appendix to Chapter 6.) Assume that the hourly wage is $5 and that the rental rate of capital is $10 per hour. Then for $1000 the firm can employ 200 units of labor and no capital (point L_0 in Figure 15A-3) or 100 units of capital (point K_0 in Figure 15A-3) or any combinations of capital and labor on the straight line connecting points L_0 and K_0 in Figure 15A-3.

Line $L_0 K_0$ is an *isocost line* ("isocost" means "equal cost"), since all points on it correspond to input demands that cost $1000. It looks very much like the consumer's budget line. Its slope is equal to the rental-wage ratio, or the ratio of the cost of using 1 unit of capital to the cost of using 1 unit of labor.[14] In our example, the slope is equal to the ratio of the labor input at L_0, 200, to the capital input at K_0, 100—which is exactly the ratio of the rental rate ($10) to the wage rate ($5). The higher the rental rate relative to the wage, the more units of labor the firm has to give up using to be able to pay for another unit of capital.

To maximize output given total cost, the firm chooses the point of tangency, A in Figure 15A-3, between the isocost line and an isoquant. At any other point on the isocost line, for instance, point D, output is lower than it is at A. Points such as A' that correspond to higher levels

[14] Again we simplify by ignoring the fact that the slopes of isocost lines are negative.

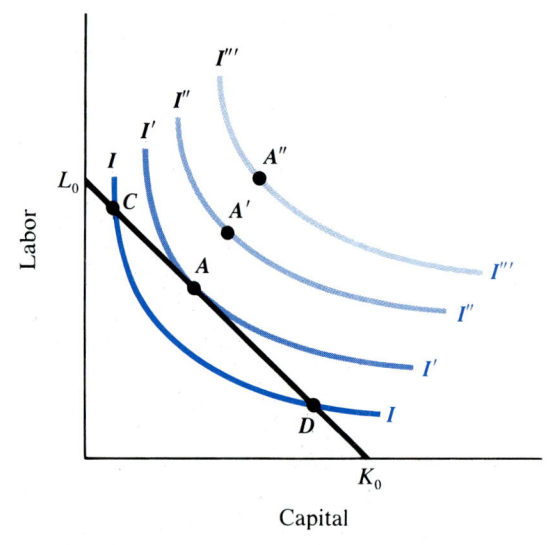

FIGURE 15A-3. Maximizing Output for a Given Level of Costs. Isocost line $K_0 L_0$ shows all combinations of capital and labor with the same cost. To produce the maximum output at this level of cost, the firm selects the inputs corresponding to point A, where the isocost line is tangent to an isoquant. It cannot produce more than the output level corresponding to isoquant I', since higher isoquants such as I'' and I''' do not touch the isocost line anywhere. It could produce less for the same cost, as at points C or D, but that would make no economic sense.

of output than at A cannot be reached without increasing costs.

The slope of the isocost line is the ratio of the rental cost of capital to the wage rate. The slope of the isoquant is the ratio of the marginal product of capital to the marginal product of labor. At A the two slopes are equal. Accordingly,

$$\frac{\text{Slope of}}{\text{isoquant}} = \frac{MPK}{MPL} = \frac{r_K}{w} = \frac{\text{slope of}}{\text{isocost line}} \quad \text{(A1)}$$

Multiplying both sides of this equation by MPL and dividing both sides by r_K, we obtain

$$\frac{MPK}{r_K} = \frac{MPL}{w} \quad \text{(A2)}$$

This is precisely the rule given by equation (6) in this chapter: In order to minimize cost, the firm must select levels of inputs such that the ratio of the marginal product of each input to the cost of using it is the same for all inputs employed. If a given set of inputs maximizes output, given cost, it also minimizes cost, given output.

A change in the relative prices of factors changes the slope of the isocost line. If the wage rises, line L_0K_0 becomes flatter, since the given $1000 outlay now buys less labor. As shown in Figure 15A-4, a wage increase causes the firm to move from a relatively labor-intensive method of production at point A to a relatively capital-intensive method at point C.

We cannot tell from the figures what level of output the firm should produce, because we cannot show the condition that the marginal revenue product of a factor be equal to the cost of that factor. But the isoquant-isocost diagram does show the fundamental condition for cost minimization, equation (A2), and also shows how changes in the relative costs of factors change the proportions in which the factors are used. In particular, the higher the wage, the more capital-intensive the technique of production used.

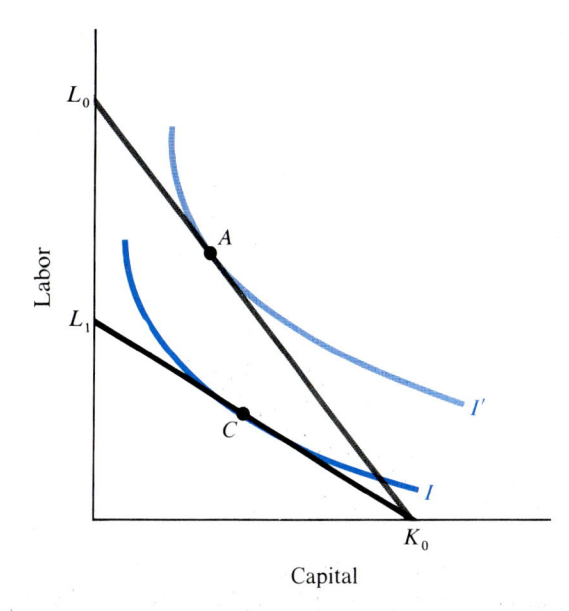

FIGURE 15A-4. The Effect of a Rise in Wages on the Choice of Technique. The firm is initially in equilibrium at point A. Then the wage rises, so that the maximum amount of labor that can be hired at the original cost level falls from L_0 to L_1. The firm now maximizes output given cost at point C, using more capital relative to labor than at point A. Thus a rise in wages has increased the capital-labor ratio.

Chapter 16
Labor Supply and Wage Determination

Why do the best baseball players earn over $1 million a year and the best engineers under $200,000? Why can college students majoring in engineering expect to earn more than equally smart students majoring in history? Why does an unskilled worker in a developed country earn more than an unskilled worker in a less-developed country?

The answer in each case is that earnings are determined by the supply and demand for the particular type of labor services. We studied the demand for labor in Chapter 15. In this chapter we discuss the supply of labor and then use supply and demand analysis to explore the determination of wages and other aspects of the operation of labor markets. Chapter 17 extends the analysis of these markets to take account of the effects of labor unions, as well as the effects of education and training that increase individual productivity in the long run.

We begin in the next section with some facts and observations about wage differentials among occupations and industries. We then look at individuals' labor supply decisions involving both how much to work and in what industry to work. Sections 3 and 4 analyze wage determination in perfectly competitive labor markets, first at the level of the industry and then for the economy as a whole. Section 5 applies this analysis to a discussion of the effects of the minimum wage. We conclude in section 6 by introducing and discussing the important concept of economic rent.

1. Wage Differentials

Table 16-1 presents some data on average earnings by industry. Similar differences exist in average earnings by occupation. Computer programmers earn about twice as much as messengers, for instance, and electricians and mechanics earn about twice as much as janitors.[1] Earnings differences among industries reflect in part differences in the mix of occupations employed in each. Welders earn more than clerks, for instance, and banks employ relatively more clerks and fewer welders than do firms in oil and gas extraction.

---

[1] Data on earnings by occupation are published by the Bureau of Labor Statistics in *Employment and Earnings* and the *Handbook of Labor Statistics*.

TABLE 16-1. Average Hourly Earnings of Production Workers in Several Sectors

Industry	Earnings, $/hr 1975	Earnings, $/hr 1984	% increase, 1975–1984 Earnings	% increase, 1975–1984 Employment	Statutory minimum wage, $/hr 1975	Statutory minimum wage, $/hr 1984
Oil and gas extraction	5.38	10.72	99.3	83.4	2.10	3.35
Banking	3.52	6.56	86.4	23.2	2.10	3.35
Leather	3.21	5.70	77.6	−24.9	2.10	3.35
Blast furnace and basic steel production	6.94	12.94	87.2	−40.2	2.10	3.35

Source: *Statistical Abstract of the United States, 1986*, Tables 694 and 710.

Should we expect wages to become equalized across industries and occupations eventually, as everyone moves toward the jobs with higher pay? Obviously not, for two main reasons. First, workers have different skills and abilities. Few of us know how to repair watches; few of us have the ability necessary to paint salable portraits even after lots of training.

Second, even if everybody could do every job, not all jobs are equally attractive. These differences are reflected in equalizing differentials in wages between jobs.

● An *equalizing* (or *compensating*) *differential* in wages is a difference in wages that compensates workers for the difference in the attractiveness of jobs.

One reason why wages in banking are lower than wages in oil and gas extraction, for instance, is that workers in oil and gas extraction lose on average almost 15 times as many workdays because of job-related injuries and illnesses as do workers in banking. Many people are willing to accept lower wages to work in a white-collar office job than in a blue-collar factory job. One reason why teachers' salaries are so low relative to those of many other college graduates is that teaching jobs have few dangers and offer long vacations.

But equalizing differentials are not the whole story. They do not explain, for instance, why in both 1975 and 1984 workers in the steel industry made more than twice as much as workers in the leather products industry. Table 16-1 also raises other issues. Why are banking wages closer to the wages in leather products than to the wages in oil and gas extraction? Do these differentials reflect differences in labor skills or the attractiveness of jobs, or do they reflect union activity or foreign competition? Why do employers ever pay any workers, in any industry, more than the minimum wage?

Consider next the percentage increases in average hourly earnings, which range from 78 percent in leather to 99 percent in steel. Since the consumer price index rose 93 percent from 1975 to 1983, *real earnings* (that is, earnings adjusted for inflation) actually fell in all these industries except oil and gas extraction. Note that there is no simple relationship between the rate of wage increase and the rate of employment increase in a sector. Although earnings increased fastest in the fast-growing oil and gas extraction industry, the second fastest rate of increase was in steel, where the work force shrank 40 percent in 9 years. What explains this pattern?

Questions of the sort posed here arise whenever one looks at data on employment and earnings across industries and occupations. In this chapter and Chapter 17 we develop the tools necessary to answer them.

2. The Supply of Labor

Utility-maximizing individuals and households, not profit-maximizing firms, are the sellers in labor markets. In the short run, on which we concentrate in this chapter, the total number of potential workers in the economy and their skills are given. There are then two issues, which we explore in this section. First, how do individuals decide *how much* to work? The answer to this question shows how the total supply of labor in the economy is determined. Second, how do individuals decide *where* to work? The answer to this question shows how the quantities of various types of labor supplied to particular industries are determined. In the next section we put the labor demand theory developed in Chapter 15 together with the analysis of labor supply given here to study the equilibrium wage and level of employment.

In the long run, of course, people can learn new skills. In the short run unskilled labor is a poor substitute for airline pilots for flying planes (although pilots are a good substitute for unskilled labor). Thus pilots will command a wage premium when air traffic demand increases suddenly. In the long run workers will acquire new skills as they seek better jobs. The premium for pilots will not last very long if teachers can be retrained to become pilots—so long as the pilots do not have a union that keeps the retrained teachers out. We devote Chapter 17 to the study of education, training, and the effects of unions.

The Individual's Labor Supply Decision

An individual's decision about whether and how much to work depends on the wage that may be earned and on many other factors, such as whether the person is in college, whether she has children or aged parents to support, and whether there is a car loan to be paid off. We concentrate here on the effects of the wage on the individual's labor supply decision. We ask first whether an increase in the wage increases or decreases the amount an individual wants to work. To start with, we assume that the individual is in the labor force and working and ask how many hours she will choose to work in each period in order to maximize utility.

Note that the amount an individual will want to work depends not on the dollar wage but on the real wage.

● **The *real wage*, or the dollar wage divided by the price level (W/P), measures the amount of goods the individual can buy with his or her wage earnings.**

The dollar, or nominal, wage is the number of dollars per hour the individual earns. People work to be able to buy goods, so that it is the real, not the nominal, wage that determines how much a person will want to work.[2]

[2] In Chapter 15 we noted that a perfectly competitive firm's demand for labor depends on *its* real wage, measured as the nominal wage divided by the price of its output. For the firm, the real wage is the ratio of the nominal wage to the price of what it *sells*; for the supplier of labor, the real wage is the ratio of the nominal wage to the prices of the goods she *buys*.

Figure 16-1 shows two possible labor supply curves. In (*a*) the labor supply curve is upward-sloping. The higher the real wage, the more the individual wants to work. In (*b*) the pattern is more complicated. At low real wages, the labor supply curve is upward-sloping, but at high wages, the curve has a negative slope. As the real wage rises above W_A, the individual begins to work fewer hours. The curve in Figure 16-1*b* is described as a *backward-bending labor supply curve*. Which of these possibilities better describes the facts?

The natural first guess is that the labor supply curve is upward-sloping. When the real wage goes up, the individual wants to work more; she wants to take advantage of the higher wage to earn a higher income. But then there is a second guess. When the real wage goes up, one can have one's cake and eat it too. That is, the individual can both work less and have more income than she did when the wage was lower. For instance, suppose that someone is working 40 hours a week at $10 per hour, earning $400 a week. Then the wage rises to $12. She can think of working only 35 hours, earning $420 (35 × $12) per week. Her total income is higher, and she works less. She can enjoy the extra 5 hours of leisure made possible by the higher wage and still have more income from work than she had before.

INCOME AND SUBSTITUTION EFFECTS. These two guesses suggest, correctly, that an increase in the real wage may either increase or reduce the amount an individual wants to work. Think of an individual who likes both leisure and consuming goods. When this person works more in order to consume more goods, he is thereby giving up leisure.

When the wage rises, every hour taken in leisure means that more income is given up. Since the income could be used to buy goods, the opportunity cost of leisure—the amount of goods that have to be given up to get 1 more hour of leisure—rises when the wage rises. This increase in opportunity cost in turn gives the individual an incentive to substitute consumption for leisure. This *substitution effect* leads the individual to work more, because work is now more rewarding.

But there is an offsetting *income effect*. It is now possible to consume both more leisure and more goods, because with a higher real wage the individual can earn more income while working less. The individual is thus

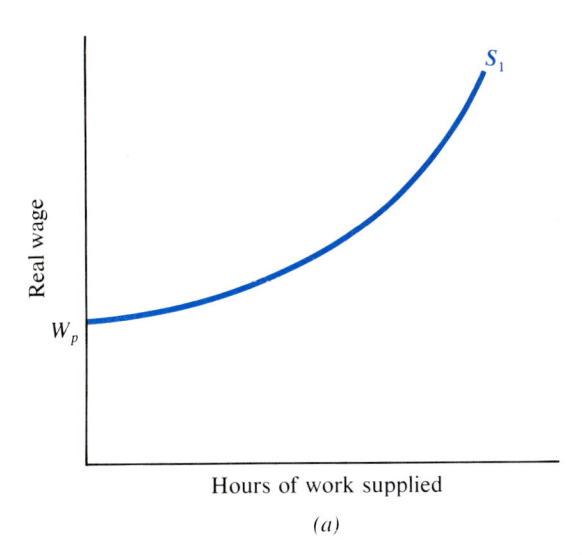

FIGURE 16-1. The Individual Labor Supply Curve. The individual labor supply curve shown in (a) describes someone who is always willing to supply more hours of labor when the real wage increases. The labor supply curve in (b) is described as backward-bending. When the wage is low, higher wages cause the individual described by this curve to supply more labor. But after the wage rises past W_A, he feels well enough off to work less when the wage increases further and to enjoy more leisure. In both panels, W_p is the lowest wage for which the individual will participate in the labor force; if the wage is below W_p, he is not interested in working at all.

better off when the wage rises and will probably decide to work a bit less hard as a consequence. Thus the income effect leads to a reduction in the quantity of labor supplied when the wage increases.

As we show explicitly in the appendix, using the graphic analysis developed in the appendix to Chapter 6, it is impossible without looking at the facts to know whether the income effect or the substitution effect generally wins out. It does seem plausible that most individual labor supply curves bend backward at very high wage rates. If the wage rate were $10,000 per hour, for instance, many of us would probably work less than we would at a wage of $10 per hour. After all, working full-time at $10,000 per hour would yield about $20 million per year, and it would be hard for most people to spend that much while working 40 hours a week. At very high wage levels—just how high varies a lot from person to person—the income effect probably comes to dominate the substitution effect, and further increases in the wage rate reduce the quantity of labor supplied.

What happens at the sort of wage rates most people actually earn? The evidence is that for men, the income and substitution effects just about cancel each other out.

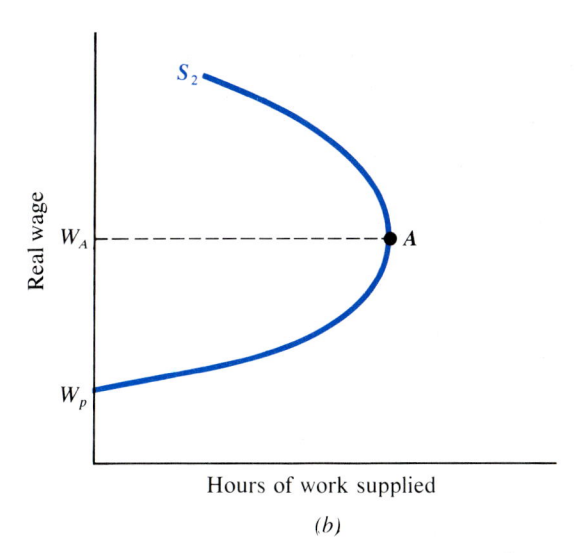

The labor supply schedule for mature men who are in the labor force is almost vertical, so that changes in the real wage do not have much effect on the amount they want to work. The evidence is that for women, the labor supply schedule slopes upward. Since men on average earn higher wages than women earn, this is broadly consistent with Figure 16-1b, with the data for men involving wages near W_A on average, and with the data for women reflecting their behavior at wages substantially below W_A.[3]

PARTICIPATION. So far we have examined the response to a change in the wage of someone who is already working. But much of the change in the labor supply of the United States and other economies has come from changes in labor force participation.

● The *participation rate* is the percentage of a given group who are in the labor force, either working or looking for work.

---

[3] A comprehensive but difficult overview of the theory and evidence on labor supply is provided by M. R. Killingsworth, *Labor Supply*, Cambridge University Press, Cambridge, England, 1983.

An increase in the wage the members of any group expect to earn should in theory increase the participation rate. That is because if someone is not working at all, not participating in the labor force, an increase in the wage does not make it possible to have a higher income by working the same amount: His income is zero unless he goes out to work. There is, therefore, no income effect, but there is a substitution effect. When the wage rises, every hour of leisure is more expensive in terms of forgone income, or income that is lost because the individual is not at work. Thus an increase in the wage will not cause anyone to leave the labor force. But a wage increase could well induce people to enter the labor force because it makes work more attractive relative to leisure—that is, because of the substitution effect.

This argument is reflected in Figure 16-1, since both of the labor supply curves slope upward at the point where the individual is doing 0 hours of work. This is the case because there is only a substitution effect at that point. If the wage had previously been below W_p (p for "participation") and now rises above it, the individual will enter the labor force. The exact value of W_p may vary considerably among individuals.

There have been major changes in labor force participation in the last two decades, about which Table 16-2 gives some details. The table shows the percentage of the population in each age-sex category who participated in the labor force in 1960 and 1984. Overall, male participation rates have dropped and female rates have risen. Looking first at the males, we see that the largest drop occurred in the 55–64 age group. This was a result of increasingly early retirement. Some evidence indicates that this in turn resulted at least in part from changes in the Social Security law that increased payments to those who retired early.

For females, the entire pattern of labor force participation has changed considerably. In 1960 in all age groups most women did not work. Furthermore, the participation rate was highest at ages 20–24 and then fell sharply. Women aged 25 to 34 were having children. Then after 35 some of them came back into the labor force. In contrast, in 1984 over half the women in all age groups up to 55 were working. Labor force participation fell very little at ages 25–34. Thus the female labor force participation data reflect the large change in the role of women in society that has taken place in the last 25 years.

Real wages for women have risen over the past 25 years. Careful studies do suggest that increased real wages have increased the labor force participation of women and thus account for part of the changing role of women in society. But the changing participation patterns shown in Table 16-2 probably also reflect other social changes, in particular changes in preferred family sizes and in attitudes toward working women.

HOURS OF WORK. We have drawn the labor supply schedule as if the individual could freely choose the number of hours to work, but we know that part-time jobs are not generally available on exactly the same terms as full-time jobs. Nonetheless, firms adjust to the hours of work their labor forces prefer—so long as it is not too expensive for them to do so. In manufacturing, where shift work is standard, the workweek has stayed at about 40 hours since World War II. In retailing, where it is easy to change the person standing at a cash register without bringing the operation to a halt, the average workweek has fallen from 40 to 32 hours since 1947. The percentage of the work force working part-time has increased from 11.4 percent in 1965 to 17.3 percent in 1984. Over half of workers aged 16 to 19 worked part-time in 1984.

The Supply of Labor to the Economy

The evidence is that the labor supply curve for the economy as a whole, which reflects the behavior of both men

TABLE 16-2. Labor Force Participation, 1960 and 1984

	Males		Females	
Age group	1960	1984	1960	1984
All	83.3	76.4	37.7	53.6
16–19	56.2	56.0	39.3	51.8
20–24	88.1	85.0	46.1	70.4
25–34	97.5	94.4	36.0	69.8
35–54	96.8	93.6	46.4	67.0
55–64	86.8	68.5	37.2	41.7
65 +	33.1	16.3	10.8	7.5

Source: Statistical Abstract of the United States, 1981, Table 636, and *1986,* Table 660.

and women, is upward-sloping. When the real wage rises, women want to work more and men do not reduce the amount they want to work. In total, therefore, a rise in the real wage leads to more work from the labor force.

Of course, if the real wage continued to rise, it is possible that the labor supply curve for the economy as a whole might eventually look like S_2 in Figure 16-1b. If in the year 2087 the real wage is five times its current level, people may feel that they want more leisure when the wage rises further. After all, if the wage were five times higher than its current level, workers could consume just as much as we do now by working only an 8-hour week. On the other hand, there will be many new goods and services available by then, and many of the things we now think of as luxuries will be considered necessities. In 1950, for instance, only 9 percent of households had television sets; today somebody who cannot afford a television set is very unlikely to feel so well off that he will work less when his wage rises.

The Supply of Labor to an Industry

So far we have been talking about the supply of labor to the economy in general. But the supply of labor to a firm or an industry is not the same as the supply to the economy. A small firm that is located in an urban area and that employs no specially trained workers will have a horizontal labor supply curve. It will be able to hire as many workers as it wishes at the going wage. Similarly, the labor supply curve facing an industry that is not a major employer in any particular area or of any particular type of labor services will be horizontal. But horizontal labor supply curves are the exception, not the rule, at the industry level.

Most large industries are important employers of at least some workers with special skills. The fishing industry is the only employer of those who know how to operate fishing boats, for instance, and steelworkers have skills that are used only in the steel industry. In addition, some industries are large employers in particular regions of the country; examples include logging in Oregon, oil production in Texas, and wheat farming in Kansas. For both these reasons, most industries are important buyers in at least some labor markets. They thus face upward-sloping supply curves of labor in the short run; more labor will be supplied to an industry the higher is its wage *relative* to the wages paid by other industries.

There is another reason why the labor supply curve for an industry is generally upward-sloping. As more and more workers respond to higher wages in that industry, they leave behind them sectors where labor is becoming increasingly scarce relative to capital. Accordingly, the marginal product of labor in other industries increases, and firms in those sectors are willing to pay higher wages. The positive slope of the labor supply schedule for an industry also reflects this rising *opportunity cost* for workers of leaving other industries.

In the short run, workers' skills and locations are fixed, and most workers are employed. In order to hire more workers of the types and in the locations it needs, any particular industry will have to pay more than the going wage. It will have to offer enough of a premium to make some workers leave jobs they like and perhaps even move from one area to another. Similarly, if its wages fall relative to those paid by other industries, it will not lose all its workers immediately.

An industry's long-run labor supply curve is flatter—that is, more elastic—than its short-run supply curve. In the long run, a given premium over the going wage elsewhere will attract more people than it will in the short run, since it takes time for people to learn that high-wage jobs are available, move to new areas, and acquire new skills. Households, the suppliers of labor, will adjust more fully to wage changes in the long run than in the short run, just as they adjust more fully in the long run to changes in the prices of the goods and services they consume. But even in the long run an industry's labor supply curve is likely to be upward-sloping. People differ in their willingness to work on auto assembly lines or in coal mines. The more workers any particular industry wants to employ, the higher the wage it will need to pay to overcome preferences for work in other sectors. Diving is a risky occupation, for instance, and only those with a high tolerance for risk are attracted to it now. In order to attract twice as many, even in the long run, the relative wage of divers would have to increase enough to attract people with a lower tolerance for risk.

Thus for most industries we expect the labor supply curve to be upward-sloping and more elastic in the long run than it is in the short run. The labor supply curve facing an industry looks like curve S_1 in Figure 16-1a, but the quantity of labor supplied is a function of the wage in that industry *relative to* wages in other industries.

3. Industry Labor Market Equilibrium

In Figure 16-2 we put together an industry's labor demand curve with the labor supply curve it faces. The labor supply curve, S_L, may refer to the short run or the long run; it is upward-sloping as drawn in either case.

Equilibrium in the labor market for the industry occurs at point E, where the quantity of labor demanded equals the quantity of labor supplied. The employment level is L_0, and the wage is W_0. The firms in the industry are all hiring the amount of labor they want to hire at that wage, and the workers in the industry are supplying the amount of labor they want to supply. Here and in general, we should think of the wage as the whole package of work compensation, including contributions to medical insurance, the pension fund, and other fringe benefits.

This supply-demand model of the labor market is easily used to study the effects of changes in the supply of or demand for labor. Suppose we are dealing with the labor market in the lumber industry, which we assume to be perfectly competitive.

First we examine the effects of a shift in the demand for labor. Suppose that there has been a fall in the demand for lumber because housing construction is down. The fall in the demand for lumber by consumers results in a lower price for lumber and thus, as we saw in Chapter 15, a downward shift of the labor demand curve for the firms in the lumber industry. The demand curve shifts downward to D'_L in Figure 16-2. The equilibrium point shifts from E to E', with a lower wage and a lower level of employment in the industry. Thus a decline in the demand for the good produced by an industry reduces the industry's derived demand for labor, reducing both the quantity of labor employed and the wage in that industry.

Consider next the effects of a shift in the supply of labor. Suppose that there has been an improvement in productivity in other sectors because capital investment has taken place there and that workers have become more productive. Wages in those sectors accordingly rise, and at each level of wages paid by the lumber industry there will now be a smaller quantity of labor supplied. What happens to wages and employment in the lumber industry, where there has been no investment in new machinery?

Figure 16-3 provides a graphic analysis. Less labor is supplied to the lumber industry at each wage, and this is shown as a shift of the labor supply schedule from S_L to S'_L. The equilibrium shifts from point E to E'. Accordingly, the equilibrium wage in the lumber industry rises—just as it has in other industries—but employment declines. The capital investment in other sectors leads to an expansion in output and employment there, to an economywide rise in wages, *and* to a fall in employment in the lumber industry.

The key assumption in this last example is that when

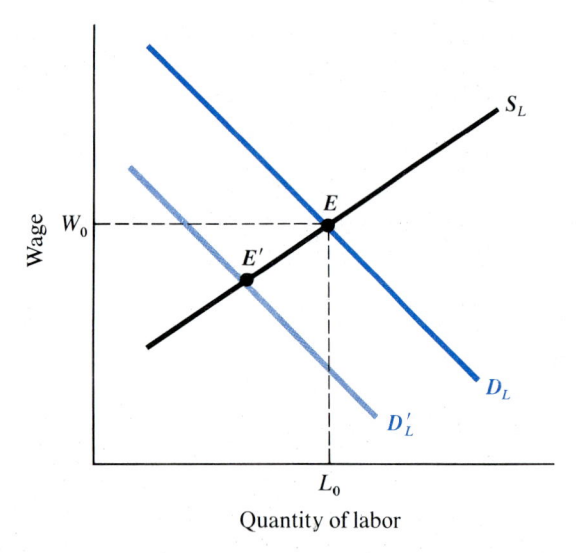

FIGURE 16-2. A Fall in the Price of Output. The industry depicted here faces an upward-sloping labor supply curve, S_L. The labor supply curve, D_L, is downward-sloping, reflecting diminishing returns to labor. The initial equilibrium is at point E, with wage W_0 and employment L_0. When the demand for the good produced by this industry falls, the price of output also falls. This shifts the labor demand curve downward to D'_L. In the new equilibrium at point E', the wage and employment levels are both lower.

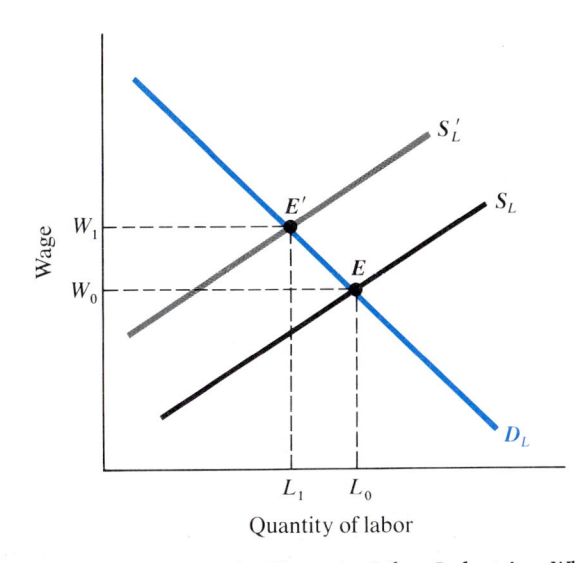

FIGURE 16-3. A Rise in Wages in Other Industries. When wages paid in other industries rise, workers leave this industry for better-paying jobs elsewhere. The labor supply curve in this industry accordingly shifts upward, from S_L to S'_L. As a result, the equilibrium point shifts from E to E', the wage rises from W_0 to W_1, and employment falls from L_0 to L_1. In this way, wage increases are spread throughout the economy.

TABLE 16-3 Comparative Wage and Employment Behavior, 1975–1984

	Production workers, percentage growth	
Sector	Hourly earnings	Employment
Total private sector	83.9	26.0
Oil and gas extraction	99.3	83.4
Banking	86.4	23.2
Leather	77.6	−24.9
Blast furnace and basic steel production	87.2	−40.2

Source: *Statistical Abstract of the United States, 1986*, Table 694.

wages elsewhere in an economy rise, some workers leave the lumber industry to work for the higher wages elsewhere. The key is thus the *mobility* of labor. If workers did not go off to try to obtain the higher wages elsewhere—that is, if they all refused to leave the lumber industry for some reason—they would not get higher wages.

This simple model of the labor market provides two powerful insights into the behavior of employment and economywide wage patterns. First, we see that the labor market is one of the chief links between various sectors of the economy. Second, if one sector does well and can afford to pay high wages to attract more labor, it must for that reason drive down production in other sectors. The very fact that a particular sector can and does increase wages means that it hires away from other sectors the labor with which to expand.

We can now analyze the pattern of changes in employment and wages shown in Table 16-1—and repeated for convenience in Table 16-3. For comparison, Table 16-3 also shows the growth in average hourly wages and employment of production workers in the entire private sector. Note first that wages in all the industries moved by roughly similar amounts, indicating links between different segments of the labor market.[4]

Concentrating on differences in wage growth, three industries support the analysis summarized in Figures 16-2 and 16-3. This analysis predicts that wages will rise faster in expanding industries than in contracting industries. The increase in employment and earnings in the oil and gas extraction industry between 1975 and 1984 was a result of the shift in the demand for labor in that industry—U.S. oil and gas employment rose sharply with the rise in the price of all fuels that started in 1973. Similarly, the lower rate of increase for wages in the leather industry along with the fall in employment in that industry resulted from the sharp competition that the leather industry faced from foreign producers. Banking expanded at about the average rate shown in the first row of the table, and wages in banking likewise grew at about the average rate for the private sector.

The blast furnace and basic steel industry, though, is far from conforming to the basic picture. Employment fell by about 40 percent as foreign competition made vast inroads on U.S. steel production, but steel wages still went up faster than average. The explanation is that this is a unionized industry. Unions were able to keep wages

---

[4] Since, as we have already noted, the consumer price index rose by 93 percent between 1975 and 1984, Table 16-3 also tells us that on average the real wages of production workers fell over this period.

moving ahead over this period despite the rapidly falling employment.[5]

This example raises a question about the effects of unions on wages, to which we turn in Chapter 17. But before we do that, we still have to ask what determines the average wage level in the economy as a whole.

4. The Determination of the Average Real Wage

So far we have explained how the wage in one industry is adjusted relative to the wages in other industries. But to understand the absolute level of wages in any industry, we must see what determines the average wage in the economy. The short answer is that the average wage is determined by the aggregate, or total, supply of and demand for labor—as we now show.

In drawing the aggregate labor supply curve, as in Figure 16-4, we take the skill-sex-education composition of the labor force as given and ask how the total amount of labor supplied to the economy changes with the real wage. We assume for simplicity that all real wages go up or down together. Of course, some workers get more than others, but we are not concentrating now on relative wages, which are assumed to remain constant as the average wage changes. Similarly, on the demand for labor side we are assuming that the wages paid by all industries go up or down together, with relative wages being given. Thus we focus on the determination of the average real wage rather than on relative wages.[6]

The labor supply curve for the economy as a whole is upward-sloping, as we saw in section 2. The labor demand curve of each industry slopes downward, and therefore the demand curve of all industries taken together also slopes downward. Thus we have aggregate labor supply and labor demand curves of the shape

[5] Colin Lawrence and Robert Z. Lawrence, in "Manufacturing Wage Dispersion: An End Game Interpretation," *Brookings Papers in Economic Activity*, Vol. 1, 1985, argue that the steel unions, seeing the decline of the steel industry as inevitable, pushed for high wages to make sure they got as large a share as possible of the revenues of the industry.

[6] Recall that the real wage is W/P, the nominal wage divided by the price level. It measures the amount of goods that can be bought with labor earnings.

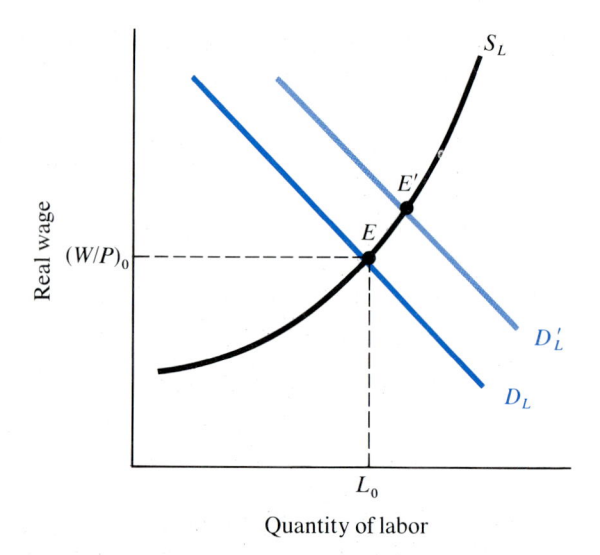

FIGURE 16-4. Determination of the Average Real Wage. The aggregate labor supply curve for the economy as a whole, S_L, is upward-sloping, and the aggregate demand curve for labor, D_L, is downward-sloping. The average real wage and total employment are determined at point E. When the demand for labor shifts from D_L to D'_L as a result of an increase in the capital stock, the equilibrium point shifts to E', and both employment and real wages rise.

shown in Figure 16-4. The aggregate labor supply curve may be very steep, and at some wage level it could even become backward-bending.

The determination of the average real wage is depicted by the intersection of the supply and demand curves at point E. On what does that wage depend? The position of the supply curve depends on the willingness of people to work, which in turn is influenced by their education, social customs, health, and similar factors. The position of the demand curve depends on the productivity of labor. In particular, the higher the level of the capital stock in the economy as a whole, the larger the quantity of labor demanded at any real wage. Thus if the capital stock increases, the demand for labor will increase. This would be shown as a shift of the aggregate demand curve for labor outward from D_L to D'_L. Accordingly, the equilibrium will shift to E', and the real wage will increase. It is partly because economies accumulate physical capital that real wages tend to rise over time.

The productivity of labor also depends on the skills the labor force has acquired. If the labor force is very skillful, there is a high marginal product of labor and firms are willing to pay more per worker. Economists refer to the skills of labor as the *human capital* of the labor force, as we discuss in Chapter 17. Increases in human capital over time also help account for increases in real wages over the course of decades and centuries.

Although we have drawn aggregate supply and demand curves for labor, we emphasize that there is no single market where all workers and all firms get together. The labor market is highly decentralized, and adjustments of wages in response to shifts in supply and demand take place in many markets and at different speeds. For this reason, we should think of the aggregate supply and demand curves for labor in Figure 16-4 as describing the average level to which the real wage tends to move over time. But the actual adjustments take place in many different firms and industries; they are not coordinated, and they may take a long time.

5. The Minimum Wage

Let us now apply the supply-demand analysis of labor markets to analyze the effects of an important government policy. The federal government imposes a minimum wage that may be paid to most workers. About 85 percent of the employees in private industry and 25 percent of those in government are covered. The minimum wage for the years 1975 and 1984 was shown in Table 16-1, and we asked why any worker receives more than the minimum wage.[7] Why don't employers force all wages down to the minimum legal level?

The answer is that the employers are competing in the labor market. Labor is productive, and the marginal revenue product of most workers is well above the minimum wage. Firms can earn profits by employing labor, even at wages above the legal minimum. If one employer succeeded in getting workers to work at a low wage, other firms could increase their profits by hiring those workers away and paying a slightly higher wage. Thus so long as firms are competing, the wage of labor will be driven to its marginal revenue product.

But this does not mean that the minimum wage has no effect on employment or wages, because one of the central facts of the labor market is that labor is not homogeneous. Not all workers have the same productivity. There are some workers for whom the minimum wage is above their marginal revenue product, such as young, unskilled workers.

Figure 16-5 shows the market for unskilled workers. The demand curve, D_L, slopes downward, and the supply curve, S_L, slopes upward. The minimum wage is W_{min}, which is above the wage at which quantity supplied equals quantity demanded, W_0. At the minimum wage, firms want to hire only L_d, while workers want amount L_s of work. The difference, the distance FG in Figure 16-5, is *unemployment* in the amount of $L_s - L_d$.

The minimum wage appears to be partly responsible for the very high unemployment rates among unskilled

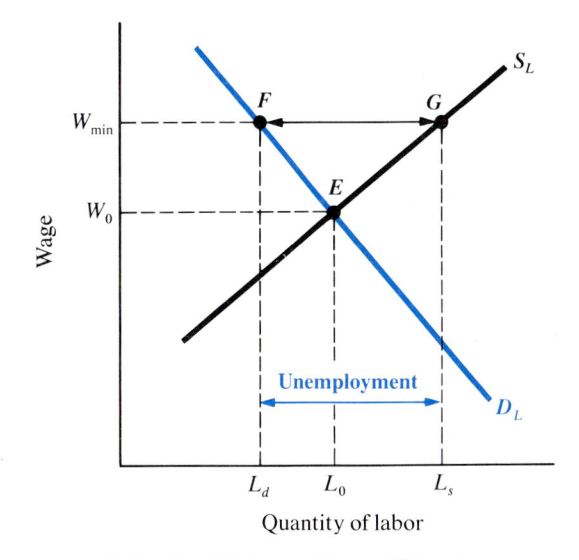

FIGURE 16-5. The Minimum Wage. Without a minimum wage, the labor market for unskilled workers clears at point E, with equilibrium wage W_0. When a minimum wage of W_{min} is imposed, firms seek to operate at point F on their demand curve, while workers would like to be at point G on their supply curve. As a result the quantity of labor supplied exceeds the quantity demanded by the distance FG, and the result is unemployment in the amount $L_s - L_d$.

---

[7] The minimum wage was unchanged at $3.35 per hour from the beginning of 1981 until 1987. It has thus fallen relative to market wages.

workers, particularly teenagers. In 1986, for instance, 19 percent of male workers aged 16 to 19 were unemployed. The unemployment rate for black males in this age bracket was 43.7 percent.[8] The questions that have to be raised are why legislators nonetheless vote for a minimum wage and why labor unions support it. A possible explanation is that the minimum wage damages only those who cannot get work as a result, while the people who remain at work get a higher wage. In Figure 16-5, the wage for those who remain employed increases from W_o to W_{min} as a result of the increase in the minimum wage. It may be that both the legislators and the unions are more concerned about those who keep their jobs than about those who lose them. This point can be put in a very different way by noting that many of those who are employed (not only the unskilled workers) probably have a somewhat higher wage because there is less competition from the workers who are unemployed as a result of the minimum wage.[9]

6. Supply Limitations and Economic Rent

Finally, we can use the analysis developed so far to discuss an often perplexing feature of labor markets—and to introduce a general concept that is useful in a wide variety of settings. The perplexing feature is the very high wages earned by some people. Most million-dollar-a-year baseball players are very happy to receive so much money to play a game in the summer sunshine. In fact, most are so happy that they would play ball for $500,000 a year, or probably even for $50,000, rather than do something else. Similarly, an acre of the best vineyard land would probably still be used for growing grapes even if the price of wine fell substantially. Economists use the concept of *economic rent* to analyze these and similar situations.

The basic reason the baseball star earns $1 million a year is that he is worth it to the team's owners. He controls a scarce resource in limited supply—his talent—and people are willing to pay more for the use of it than the minimum needed to get him to supply it. Accordingly, he earns an economic rent.

● An *economic rent* **is the amount of the payment to a factor of production that exceeds the minimum amount that would have to be paid to get that quantity of the factor supplied to this particular use.**

Figure 16-6 illustrates the concept of economic rent. Suppose we are dealing with a star who loves playing baseball so much that he would be happy to play baseball at any salary above W_A. This is shown by the supply curve, S. The demand curve for his services is shown by D. This is a derived demand curve; it depends on the

---

[8] These high teenage unemployment rates probably understate the problem, since teenagers who are so discouraged by the lack of jobs that they stop looking for work are not counted as unemployed.

[9] A second explanation rejects the analysis of Figure 16-5 and justifies the minimum wage as a means of increasing wages *and* employment. Recall from the analysis of monopoly that a price ceiling for a monopolist may lead the monopolist to *increase* production. Similarly, a *single* buyer of labor (a monopsonist in the labor market) may *increase* his hiring of labor if a minimum wage is imposed. It is sometimes argued that employers in effect get together in the labor market to act as a monopsony and that the minimum wage therefore improves the situation for all workers. We know of no evidence to substantiate this view, however.

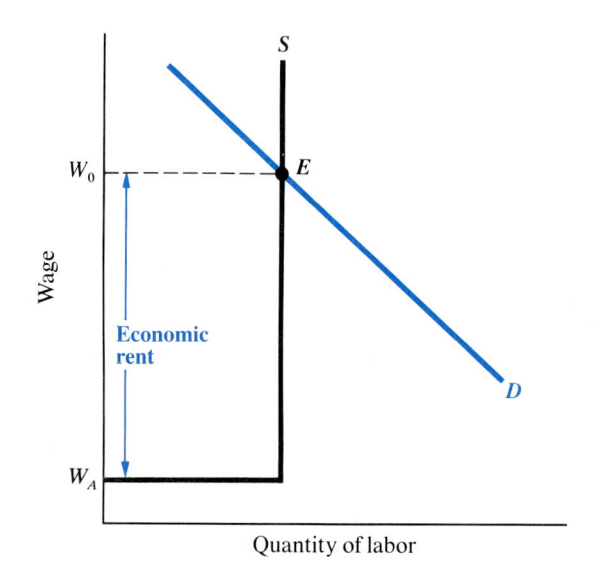

FIGURE 16-6. Economic Rent. The supply curve, S, shows the supply of labor (or any other factor of production) to a particular use. Supply is totally inelastic at wages above W_A, the lowest wage at which the factor will be supplied to this use. The wage paid is W_0, and the factor earns economic rent equal to the difference $W_0 - W_A$.

amount the player adds to his team's revenues. The baseball star sells extra seats; therefore, there is a derived demand for his services. The wage paid to the baseball player is shown by W_0.

The amount $W_0 - W_A$, the excess of the wage above the minimum amount needed to get the baseball player to play ball, is an economic rent. It is the payment that he receives by virtue of being the owner of the scarce resource that is his talent. It has nothing to do with his willingness to supply his services as a baseball player. It does depend on the fact that there is a limited supply of stars.

There are three points to be made about economic rents. First, the term is used because it was originally applied to the rent paid for land. The quantity of land is essentially fixed. The amount people are willing to pay for it depends on how productive the land is. But rent payments are not needed to induce the land to provide its services. They are there to ensure that the landowners put it to the most productive use. Subsequently, the term "rent" has been applied to other factors.

Second, rents exist only when there are limits on supply. If the supply curve of baseball stars were perfectly elastic, none of them would earn more than their opportunity costs. In many cases the limits that create rents are natural: There just aren't that many potential baseball stars born, and there are only a few acres capable of growing the very best wine grapes. In other cases, however, supply restrictions may be artificial. As we saw in Chapter 11, for instance, monopolies find it profitable to restrict the supply of their products. Accordingly, monopoly profits are sometimes called *monopoly rents* to emphasize the critical role played by supply restriction.

Third, rents exist because the demand for factors of production is a derived demand. This implies that the frequently heard complaint that the high salaries of baseball players are destroying the game should make us suspicious. The claim is that the owners can't afford to pay the salaries. But the high salaries are paid because the superstars bring in lots of extra dollars when they play. Thus, high salaries for baseball players are unlikely to ruin the game; more likely, the high salaries reflect the fact that the game is more prosperous than ever before.

A more sophisticated analysis might find some difficulties for the game in the high salaries the players receive. For instance, if one team has a larger market than the others have, the marginal revenue product of superstars in that city will be higher than elsewhere. This team will therefore be able to pay more for the superstars and it may end up with all the good players. Then the other owners may argue that the game is being ruined because the high salaries make it impossible for them to compete. The solution is to make sure that the revenues are spread around the league in a way that preserves competition between the teams.[10] Most sports leagues do spread revenues to some extent, though teams in large cities nonetheless on average win more games than do teams in small cities.

■ Is that all there is? Can we really understand everything about labor markets, in which most of us spend a large fraction of our lives selling services, using only the same basic supply-demand analysis that we used to analyze the fish market in Chapter 3? This chapter has, we hope, shown you that even though labor services and fish filets differ in fundamental ways, the tools of supply and demand can in fact be employed to explain a great deal of what goes on in labor markets. But we have so far ignored two obvious features of these markets: labor unions and investment in skills and education. Chapter 17 deals with these and related issues. We have also ignored discrimination and the question of whether the wages and other incomes determined in factor markets are fair in any sense. We return to these questions in Chapter 20.

---

[10] Nineteenth-century economists used to say that rent was not part of the cost of production of a good. Consider again the baseball player. Does it cost the United States $1 million to employ a baseball superstar in baseball? The answer is no. The cost to society is only the opportunity cost of using the labor in baseball rather than in its next best use, say, as a college algebra teacher. Thus the cost to society of using the baseball player in baseball is not $1 million but rather the $30,000 he could have earned by teaching algebra. Of course, the firm that hires the baseball player regards $1 million as the cost of using the player, and it is right to do so.

Summary

1 An individual's labor supply decision depends on her real wage: the nominal wage divided by the prices of the goods she buys. The higher the real wage, the more expensive it is to take leisure time. Thus the substitution effect of an increase in the wage causes an individual to work more. But there is also an income effect. When the real wage rises, the individual can take more leisure time and still have a higher income left with which to buy goods. These two effects work in opposite directions, and the overall effect is uncertain. However, for individuals not working, only the substitution effect is in operation, and a wage increase therefore leads to an increase in overall labor force participation.
2 The aggregate, or total, supply curve of labor is upward-sloping: An increase in the real wage leads to an increase in the quantity of labor supplied. The response of the overall quantity of labor supplied to the real wage is determined in part by a change in the participation rate.
3 The supply of labor to an individual industry is also generally upward-sloping and depends on the wage paid in that industry relative to wages paid elsewhere in the economy. It also depends on the workers' preferences for working in one sector rather than in another.
4 A rise in the wage paid in one sector will draw labor into that sector and therefore shift the labor supply curve for other industries. Wages will tend to rise in the other industries in response to the shift of labor out of those industries. Thus wage movements tend to be spread throughout the economy. An increase in the demand for labor in one sector because of increased exports or improved technology, for example, will spread throughout the labor market to other sectors, raising wages and reducing employment in those other sectors. In this way labor is freed for use in the expanding sector.
5 The average real wage is determined by the overall supply of and demand for labor. The aggregate demand for labor depends on the productivity of labor and thus on the amount of human capital and the amount of physical capital. Increases in either physical or human capital will lead to increases in the quantity of labor demanded at a given real wage and therefore to an increase in the real wage. Because the labor market is highly decentralized, shifts in the overall demand for or supply of labor take time to work their way through the many different industry labor markets.
6 The minimum wage increases the unemployment rate for unskilled labor while increasing the wage of those who remain employed.
7 Factors that earn more than the minimum needed to get them into their current use are earning an economic rent. The rent arises from the fact that the demand for the services of the factor is a derived demand and the supply is limited. The extremely high salaries paid to superstars in sports, entertainment, and related fields are largely economic rents.

Key Terms

Compensating (equalizing) differentials in wages
Real wage
Backward-bending labor supply curve
Labor force participation
Substitution effect
Income effect
Mobility of labor
Human capital
Minimum wage
Economic rent

Problems

1 A story in the *Boston Globe* (Feb. 28, 1987) reported that a plumber discovered while at work fixing a broken water main that he had just won $8 million in the state lottery. The plumber left work: "The guy had his water shut off, and I just said, 'Tough luck buddy,' and told him to find another plumber." What principle of individual labor supply does this illustrate?
2 Over the last hundred years, the real wage has risen and the length of the workweek has fallen. Does this tell you anything about the labor supply curve for individual workers? Explain the two effects that determine the shape of the labor supply curve for the individual.
3 Explain how an increase in the real wage can cause everyone who is now working to want to work fewer hours but still result in an increase in the total amount of work done in the economy.
4 Why should the labor supply curve to an industry slope upward even if the aggregate labor supply curve for the economy is not upward-sloping?
5 (*a*) Explain how foreign competition affects wages and the level of employment in an industry. (*b*) How does your explanation fit the pattern of wage and employment changes in the leather industry shown in Table 16-1? Name

at least one other industry for which the analysis is relevant.
6. In this chapter we argue that the rising participation rate of women both explains and is explained by the changing role of women in society. Some would argue that the changing role of women can be entirely explained by changing economic conditions. Develop arguments for or against the viewpoint that higher wages are the main force behind changing attitudes to childraising and other social changes relevant to women's role in the labor force, such as the availability of child care facilities.
7. (a) Consider the market for farm labor in California. Vigorous legislation is passed that severely restricts the inflow of migrant labor during the harvest season. Discuss in detail the effect on wages in the market for farm labor and the effect on the supply and price of California lettuce and grapes. (b) Does the legislation make everyone worse off?
8. Suppose that instead the California farmers are required to pay the minimum wage. (They do not do so now.) What are the effects on employment and on the supply and price of California lettuce and grapes?
9. Suppose a movie producer says that the industry is doomed because the stars are being paid such outrageous amounts for making each film. Evaluate the argument, being sure to use the concept of economic rent.
10. This chapter opened with three questions. It is time now for you to answer them. (a) Why do the best baseball players earn so much more than the best engineers? (b) Why can engineering students look forward to higher incomes than those of equally smart history students? (c) Why does an unskilled worker in the United States earn more than an unskilled worker in a less-developed country?

Appendix: Income and Substitution Effects of a Wage Increase

In this appendix we show geometrically the income and substitution effects of an increase in the wage rate on the quantity of labor supplied by an individual. We use the same methods developed to analyze consumer spending behavior in the appendix to Chapter 6.

Figure 16A-1 describes Sam's utility-maximizing labor supply decision. Sam derives utility from both consumption of goods and services, measured in dollars per month on the vertical axis, and leisure, measured in hours per month on the horizontal axis. We assume for simplicity that Sam needs 8 hours of sleep every night, so that he cannot increase total available hours by sleeping less, and that he spends his entire income on consumption.

If Sam does not work at all, he can enjoy T hours of leisure each month, but he will receive no income, and thus his consumption will be zero.[11] On the other hand, if he works every waking hour, his monthly consumption will be M, but he will have no leisure. His real wage is

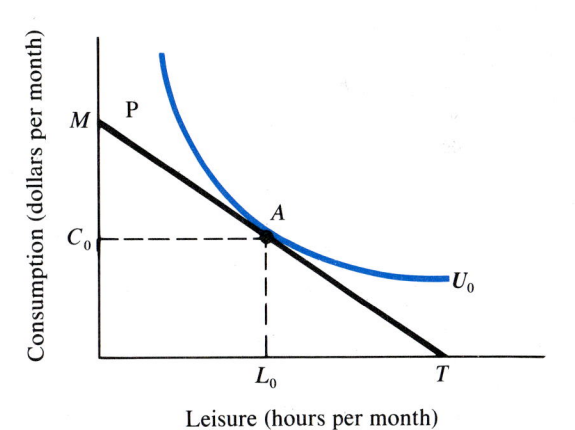

FIGURE 16A-1. An Individual's Utility-Maximizing Labor Supply. The individual faces a wage rate equal to the ratio of M, the maximum dollar amount he can consume each month, to T, the total number of hours he can work or enjoy as leisure. He chooses point A, where indifference curve U_0 is tangent to his budget line, MT. At this point his consumption is C_0, his leisure is L_0 hours per month, and he works the remaining $T - L_0$ hours each month.

---

[11] We simplify the analysis by neglecting welfare and unemployment insurance, which typically provide some income for those who do not work. These programs reduce the effective real wages of some low-income workers substantially, since the dollar gain from going to work is equal to wage earnings *minus* the welfare and unemployment insurance benefits that must be given up. We discuss these programs and their effects in detail in Chapter 22.

thus M/T, his earnings per hour worked. Given the wage rate he can earn, Sam can select any point on his budget line, MT. Movements to the left along this line, away from T, correspond to reductions in leisure—and thus to increases in the quantity of labor supplied.

Sam's utility-maximizing choice is represented by point A, where his budget line is just tangent to indifference curve U_0. At this point his income and consumption are C_0. In order to earn C_0 at the going wage, Sam must work $T - L_0$ hours, leaving him L_0 hours of leisure.

Now suppose the wage rate increases, so that Sam can earn M' in Figure 16A-2 if he works every waking hour. Figure 16A-2 shows his original budget line, MT, and his new budget line, $M'T$. Sam's original choice of labor supply (and consumption) is represented by point A on his original budget line. Line $M''T''$ is drawn through point A, parallel to $M'T$. We can usefully divide Sam's reaction to the shift in his budget line from MT to $M'T$ into two parts: his reaction to an initial shift from MT to $M''T''$ and his reaction to a second shift from $M''T''$ to $M'T$.

Sam's reaction to the initial shift from MT to $M''T''$ is the *substitution effect* of an increase in the wage. Sam can afford to stay at point A, but work has become more attractive relative to leisure. He will not react to this by working less, because that would involve choosing a point on the segment AT'', and he prefers A to all those points. (In fact, he chose A over all points between A and T, and these have more leisure for any level of consumption than do points between A and T''.) He will instead work more, and his utility-maximizing choice will be represented by a point such as B on $M''T''$. Thus the substitution effect of a wage increase on the supply of labor is positive.

Sam's reaction to the second shift, from $M''T''$ to $M'T$, is the *income effect* of an increase in the wage. This second shift does not involve a change in the wage rate; it enables Sam to enjoy more consumption and more leisure with no change in the relative price. If both consumption and leisure are *normal goods*, so that Sam consumes more of both when he becomes better off, his reaction to this second shift will involve the choice of a point between C and D on $M'T$. All these points involve the supply of fewer hours of labor (and the enjoyment of

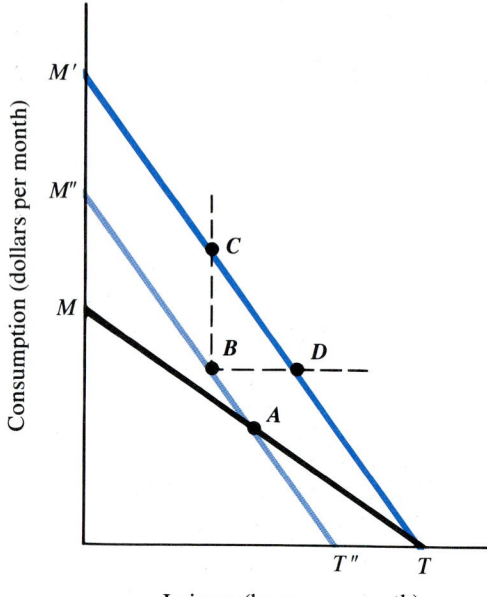

FIGURE 16A-2. Income and Substitution Effects of a Wage Increase. An increase in the wage rate shifts the individual's budget line from MT to $M'T$. Line $M''T''$ passes through the individual's original optimal point, A, and is parallel to his new budget line. When the budget line shifts from MT to $M''T''$, the individual's optimal choice will be described by a point such as B, to the left of A. This is the *substitution effect* of the wage increase. When the budget line shifts from $M''T''$ to $M'T$, the individual will opt for more consumption and more leisure—and thus will select a point between C and D along $M'T$ to the right of B. This is the *income effect* of the wage increase. If the substitution effect is larger, labor supply increases; if the income effect is larger, labor supply decreases.

more hours of leisure) than does point B, so that the income effect of a wage increase on the supply of labor is negative.

If Sam selects a point near C, to the left of A, the substitution effect dominates the income effect and the net effect of a wage increase on the quantity of labor services he supplies is positive. On the other hand, if Sam selects a point near D on his new budget line, to the right of A, the income effect dominates the substitution effect and a wage increase reduces the quantity of labor supplied. Either outcome is possible in theory.

Chapter 17
Human Capital and Unions

In 1984 manufacturing workers who belonged to unions earned 19 percent more than nonunion workers earned.[1] Male college graduates earned more than twice as much as men who attended only elementary school, and men aged 45 to 49 earned more than three times as much as those aged 18 to 24.[2] This chapter explores the effects of differences in skills and education and of labor unions on wages in the U.S. economy. Later, in Chapter 20, we consider wage differentials which arise from discrimination by sex or race.

The key feature on which we focus is that labor is not homogeneous. Chapter 16 discussed the fact that earnings differ among occupations; for instance, baseball stars earn more than professors, and workers in declining industries receive smaller increases than do those in growing industries. This chapter looks more closely at the facts to see what other characteristics of workers help explain actual pay differences. We look at the causes and effects of productivity differences and at the role of unions in wage determination.

We begin by introducing the concept of *human capital* and using it to examine the relationship between education and training, on the one hand, and differences in earnings and productivity, on the other. We then turn to the history of labor unions and their effects on wage differentials and the labor market in general.

1. Human Capital

The concept of human capital has been developed to explain why education and experience affect pay and what determines how much education people get.

---

[1] These figures, from Table 713 of the *Statistical Abstract of the United States, 1986*, are for median earnings. Median earnings in any group refers to the earnings level such that half the group earns more and half earns less. In general, the median of any set of numbers is the number in the middle, with half above and half below. By 1985 the differential between union and nonunion earnings had dropped to 16 percent (*Statistical Abstract*, 1987, Table 693).

[2] This comparison, based on data from U.S. Bureau of the Census, *Current Population Reports: Money Incomes of Households, Families, and Persons in the United States: 1984*, Table 34, involves mean earnings. The mean earning of any group is equal to the total earnings of group members divided by the number of persons in the group.

● *Human capital* is the value of the income-earning potential embodied in individuals. Human capital includes native ability and talent as well as education and acquired skills.

Normally, when we talk about capital, we refer to an asset (machinery, houses, factory buildings) with two features: It is the result of an investment, and it generates a flow of income over time. Similarly, human capital is created when a person (perhaps with his parents' help) invests in himself, paying for education and the acquisition of skills. Investments in human capital yield a payoff over time in the form of higher wages or the ability to do more satisfying work.

In this section we use the concept of human capital to analyze the impact of college education on earnings. In section 2 we then examine the economics of investment in college education and discuss on-the-job training and wages in sports and the performing arts. The analysis in these two sections assumes that wage differentials are entirely due to differences in the productivity of different types of labor. This is in accordance with the theory that was developed in Chapter 16, in which labor earns its marginal revenue product.

Education and Age-Earnings Profiles

We start from the observation that workers with more education have, on the average, higher incomes. Figure 17-1 shows how income changes with age and education. The figure shows the average age-earnings profiles for males in 1984.

● An *age-earnings profile* is the relationship between income and age for a particular individual or group of individuals.

Each profile shows how much individuals with a given amount of education earned at each age in 1984. The figure establishes two key facts. First, except for the

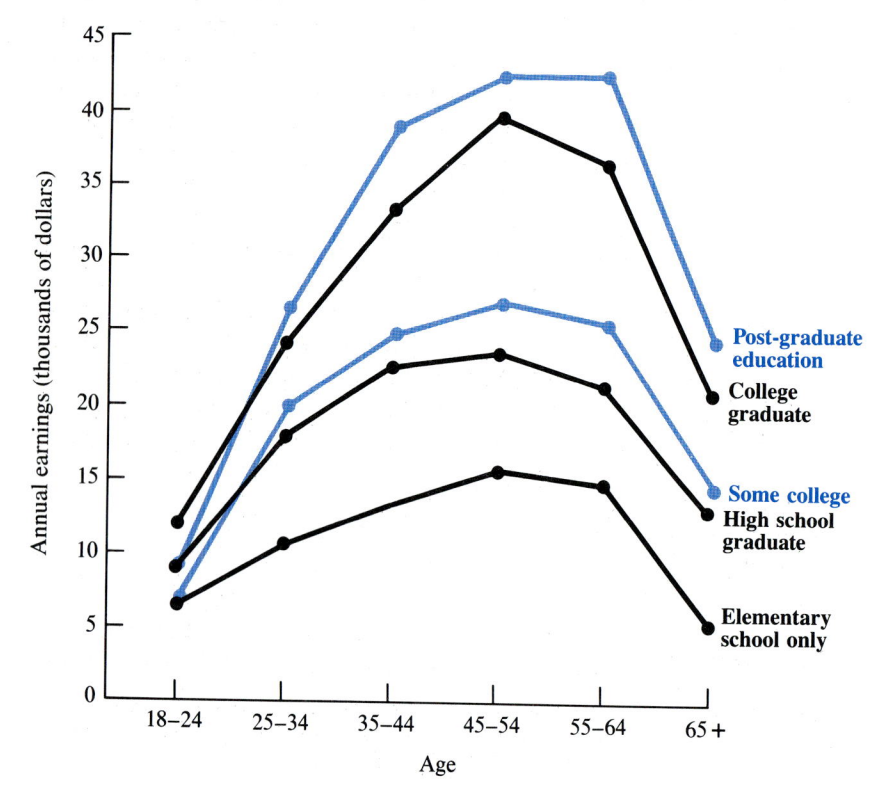

FIGURE 17-1. Age-Earnings Profiles of Males, 1984, by Education. The figure shows average earnings in the United States at different ages and years of education. Each level of education is represented by a separate curve. Earnings increase with education and, up to a point, with age. (*Source*: U. S. Bureau of the Census, *Current Population Reports*, Series P-60, *Money Incomes of Household, Families, and Persons in the United States: 1984*, Table 34.)

youngest workers, those with more education earn more on average. Second, the profiles rise very fast with age for younger people, especially those with more education, but then tend to flatten out. Some profiles actually decline toward retirement age.[3]

The most basic question raised by these data is why people with schooling should receive higher pay at all. There are at least two possible answers. First, perhaps the data simply reflect the fact that on average people with more ability have had more education. Second, perhaps schooling teaches special skills, such as reading, writing, and taking square roots, and also develops work habits that are useful in production.

There have been many attempts to see whether, holding ability constant, there is still an extra return to schooling. Studies that compare the earnings of individuals with the same measured IQ but different amounts of education find that increases in schooling increase earnings.[4] This doesn't prove that education increases productivity, however. The problem is that IQ scores don't measure all aspects of ability that translate into greater productivity on the job. Some people simply work harder than others, for instance, and IQ test scores don't reflect this. It is hard to look at the effects of education on earnings, holding ability constant, because it is hard to measure all relevant aspects of "ability."

Signaling versus Training

Building on these observations, some economists have argued that employers are willing to pay more for workers with more education mainly because education serves as a signal for aspects of ability that are difficult or impossible to measure directly.[5] The idea is that by attending college and passing exams, students signal to firms that they are good at doing certain things that are also useful at work, such as showing up on time and meeting targets. Similarly, good grades show a willingness to compete, and extracurricular activities show the ability to work with others. Diplomas, grades, and activities are signals that save firms the expense of evaluating job applicants for these and other skills. And going to college is a good idea for students because firms will be willing to pay a premium for college graduates.

The interesting implication of this argument is that students (and their parents) may make huge investments in education, and employers may pay educated people more, even if education does not in fact increase productivity. All this is rational as long as education *reveals* differences in productivity, whether or not it *increases* productivity. While spending on education may be rational for individuals, however, the resource expense of a college education is justified for society as a whole only if in fact it does increase productivity. Otherwise, society could save resources by finding a cheaper way of sorting out those with the skills that the marketplace rewards.

The available evidence indicates that the pure signaling argument is wrong: College education does raise productivity. But because native ability is so hard to measure, it is difficult to determine the precise extent to which education increases productivity. Nobody believes that college students learn nothing useful, if only because courses such as accounting and computer programming are directly job-related. On the other hand, it is also difficult to believe that education is not also used as a signal by employers. It seems reasonable to assume that education both increases and reveals productivity, and we make that assumption in what follows.

2. Education and Training

We begin by analyzing the economics of investment in college education and build on this analysis to discuss

---

[3] This observation has to be interpreted with care. The figure shows the earnings of individuals of *different* ages in a given year, 1984. It does not show how income changes with age for the *same* person. To see that, we would have to look at the amounts earned by the same person at different ages. Such profiles typically show income rising with age until the person retires. The difference between the profiles in Figure 17-1 and the age-earnings profile for a given person is that each generation earns, on the average, more than the previous one earned. Thus the generation going to college in the late 1980s has a profile with higher incomes at each age than does the generation of the 1970s.

[4] Of course, it is not just ability and education that show up in earnings. Certainly family background must also be taken into account.

[5] Michael Spence, *Market Signaling: Informational Transfer in Hiring and Related Screening Processes*, Harvard University Press, Cambridge, Mass., 1974, is the basic source.

the operation of the market for college-trained labor. We then consider the role of on-the-job training in the process of accumulating human capital and conclude with a discussion of human capital in the arts and professional sports.

Investing in Education

If education raises income, why doesn't everybody go to college? The decision to attend college rather than find a job is an investment decision, involving both costs and benefits. The major elements in this decision are the following:

1. There are *direct*, or out-of-pocket, costs for college (tuition, textbooks, etc.).
2. Going to college also involves *opportunity* costs: One enters the labor market later and thus gives up income that could have been earned for several years.
3. The *pecuniary* (dollar-value) benefits of college have already been discussed: College training, once completed, leads to permanently higher income.
4. A college education has *nonpecuniary* costs and benefits: Most people don't enjoy listening to (occasionally) boring lectures and taking exams, but many do enjoy broadening their horizons, meeting new people and being exposed to new ideas, watching and playing football, and doing whatever else students do. At least in retrospect, most people who graduate find that the nonpecuniary benefits of college outweigh the nonpecuniary costs.

These costs and benefits have to be weighed in making the investment decision about whether to get college training. Clearly, the greater the income increase a college diploma is expected to produce, the more attractive it is to invest in one and the more students will make the investment. On the other hand, an increase in tuition or other direct costs will tend to decrease the number of students attending college and thus lower the supply of college-trained people in a few years. Increases in the costs of college loans will similarly reduce enrollment.

In Figure 17-2, we show the important pecuniary elements in the investment decision by depicting the income pattern for a high school graduate entering the labor market at age 18 and the pattern for a college graduate who enters at age 22. The costs of going to college, represented by the gray-shaded area, are made up of direct costs and opportunity costs, the income forgone by not working between ages 18 and 22. The pecuniary benefits are given by the color-shaded income difference once the college graduate is in the labor market.

The Returns on Investment in College

Considering only pecuniary costs and benefits, is a college education worthwhile? To figure this out, we have to have some way of comparing the costs, represented by the gray area in Figure 17-2, with the benefits, represented by the area in color. The main difficulty in comparing these costs and benefits is that the costs occur earlier in time than do the benefits. Later benefits are typically worth less today than earlier benefits, and so we can't simply ask whether total benefits (in color) are larger than total costs (the gray area). We have to find some other way of determining whether a college education pays off.

The usual way of handling this problem is to treat the costs as an investment that pays off in the future in the form of the benefits received in later years. Then we ask what interest rate would be needed, given the amount invested, to produce the benefits actually seen in practice. As the appendix explains in detail, this is the *rate of return* on an investment in college education. The higher the rate of return, the more worthwhile it is, from a financial viewpoint, to go to college. To calculate whether college training pays off in narrow economic terms, we can consider the alternative of using the money invested in college education (corresponding to the gray area) instead in bonds or stocks. Would the return have been higher?

Studies in the 1960s showed that the real rate of return to education was more than 10 percent.[6] In the

---

[6] As Chapter 18 discusses in detail, a real rate of interest (or return) is an interest rate that is adjusted for inflation. If the interest rate is 12 percent and the inflation rate is 5 percent, the real rate of interest is 7 percent, that is, the return in terms of goods and services (rather than dollars with falling purchasing power) that can be bought as a result of making the investment.

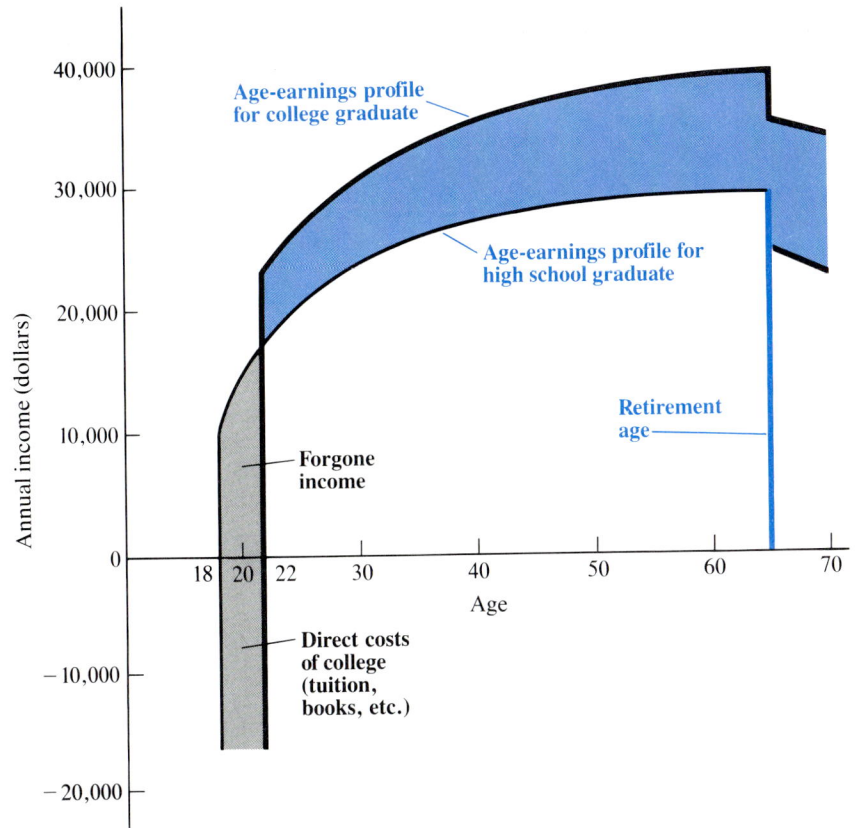

FIGURE 17-2. The Income Consequences of Going to College. The figure shows the effects of going to college on an individual's income. If she does not go to college, her income over her lifetime is as shown by the age-earnings profile for the high school graduate. If she does go to college, she has the profile shown for the college graduate. (We have ended the profiles at age 70, with a drop shown at the retirement age of 65. Of course, the profiles in practice continue beyond age 70.) Going to college costs an amount equal to the gray area in the diagram, which is made up of the loss of income from not working plus the direct costs of college. The benefits from going to college are shown by the colored area. This is the amount of the income for a college graduate that exceeds the income of a high school graduate after age 22, the age at which the college graduate is assumed to start work.

United States, the real return on stocks has averaged about 6 percent per year, and that on bonds about 2 percent. Any investment with a return of 10 percent looks very promising. In the 1960s, college was thus a very attractive investment indeed. But in the 1970s the real rate of return to college education fell well below 10 percent. This reduction was in part a result of an increase in the percentage of people going to college, as the subsequent analysis makes clear. Thus excess returns to education, over and above what could be earned on stocks, narrowed a lot.

The final element in the decision to attend college is the nonpecuniary, or consumption, part of a college education. Here people's tastes differ. Many people find college interesting and fun and would go to college even if it did not pay off financially. Others hate school and would not invest in college even if it paid very high pecuniary returns. To the extent that more productive people tend to enjoy college more, the decisions to attend college and to graduate send valuable signals to potential employers.

The Market for Educated Workers

Now that we have discussed the decision to acquire a college education, let us use the supply and demand model to analyze the market for college-trained personnel. In Figure 17-3 we have on the vertical axis the wage differential paid to college graduates, that is, the difference between the wage paid to college graduates and the wage paid to high school graduates. On the horizontal axis we measure the fraction of the work force with college training.

The curve labeled D is the demand curve for college-trained personnel. For each level of the wage differential, it shows the proportion of the labor force that firms want

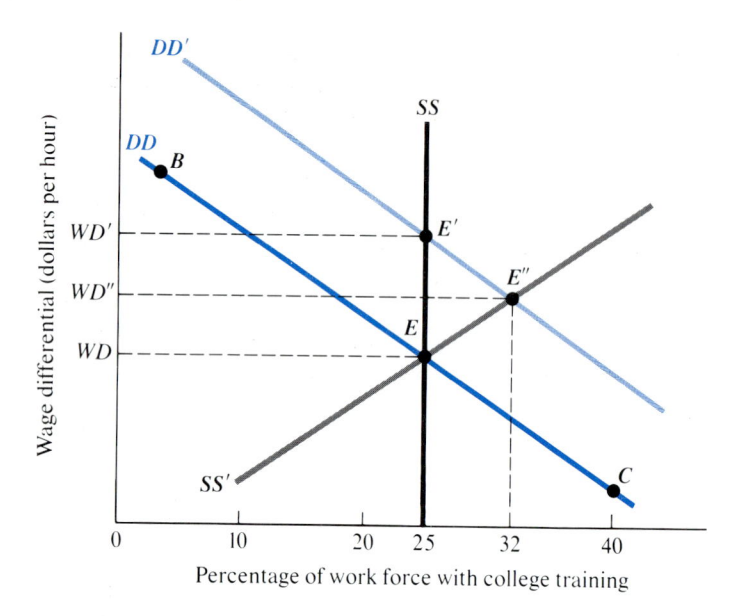

FIGURE 17-3. Wage Differentials and the Market for College-Trained Workers. The demand curve for college-trained workers slopes downward. The short-run supply curve, SS, shows the proportion of the labor force that has a college education at any given time. The S' curve is the long-run supply curve of college-trained persons. The greater the reward for college-trained labor, the larger the number of people who get college training. Equilibrium is initially at E. When the demand for college-trained workers shifts to D', the wage differential rises sharply to WD' in the short run. The higher wage differential attracts more people into college, and the long-run equilibrium shifts to E'', with wage differential WD'' and a larger fraction of the population with a college education.

made up of college-educated workers. For instance, at point B, where the wage differential is high, firms want only a small proportion of their labor force to be college-educated. At point C, though, where college-educated labor costs only about as much as labor with a high school education, firms want more of their workers to have a college education. The higher the wage differential, the more firms will be inclined to use non-college-educated workers instead of college-educated workers, who are assumed to be more productive on average. Hence the D curve slopes downward.

At any given time, the proportion of the labor force with a college education is fixed. Thus in the short run the supply of college-trained workers is fixed, and the short-run supply curve, S, is vertical. The location of this curve indicates how many people in the population have gone to college in the past. For instance, in the United States in 1984, only 19 percent of the population aged 25 or more had completed 4 or more years of college and another 16 percent had completed 1 to 3 years of college.

In the long run the percentage of the labor force with a college education can change. If the premium paid for a college education increased, more people would go to college to put themselves in line for the better jobs. Thus in the long run, we expect the supply of college-trained people to increase with the wage premium. We thus draw the *long-run* supply curve of college-trained workers, S', as upward-sloping.

In the short run, the equilibrium wage differential equates the quantity of college-trained labor demanded to the (fixed) quantity supplied. This equilibrium appears as point E in the figure, and the corresponding wage differential is equal to WD. Figure 17-3 is drawn on the assumption that the economy has been at this point for a while, so that point E is also on the long-run supply curve, S'. This means that with wage differential WD, 25 percent of potential students find it worthwhile to attend college.

Now suppose there is an increase in the demand for college-trained personnel, which is reflected in Figure 17-3 as a shift in the demand curve from D to D'. Such a shift may occur, for example, because the economy's mix of output changes from textiles and agricultural products to high-technology products, and college-trained personnel are more productive in firms that manufacture high-technology products. The short-run equilibrium point shifts from E to E', and the wage differential increases sharply in the short run, from WD to WD'. The increase is so large because, in the short run, there is no supply response at all. There is still only 25 percent of the population with a college education. People will have to go to college to be trained, and that takes years.

The next step in reacting to this demand shift is that more high school graduates decide to attend college. All those who had planned to get college training before the increase in pay for college graduates will certainly still go to college, but now some of the people who had opted for a job will have second thoughts and instead go to college. The long-run relative supply of college graduates will increase, as shown by the long-run supply schedule, S'. In the long run, therefore, the equilibrium is at point E'', with a pay differential of only WD''. The differential is reduced by the revision of the educational choices of new entrants in the labor market. In the long run, 32 percent of the work force ends up with a college education.

A similar analysis reveals the effects of a fall in the cost of attending college. In the short run, enrollment rises, but the supply of college-trained personnel is unaffected. In the long run, however, there will be more such people on the market for any given pay differential. This is depicted as a downward shift in the long-run supply curve. As should be clear from Figure 17-3, the fraction of the population with college degrees will rise and the pay differential will fall.

EDUCATION AND HOG CYCLES. The fact that a college education takes time results in delayed responses to changes in demand conditions. An upward shift of the demand curve raises pay differentials in the short run and increases the number of high school graduates who opt for college. But once they graduate, they will depress earnings and discourage others from obtaining college training. A drop in college enrollment will in turn reduce the future supply of college graduates; once again, earnings will rise, etc. If such a process, sometimes called a hog cycle or a cobweb, gets under way,[7] the short-run equilibrium supply and price (pay differentials and returns to education) will fluctuate around their long-run equilibrium values.

A good example of this type of cycle is provided by the market for scientists. After the Russians launched Sputnik, the first human-made satellite, in 1957, there was a science boom in the United States. This sharply increased the demand for scientists, thereby raising pay differentials and increasing entry into science training. Later the demand for scientists fell as firms and the government began spending less on research and development. Pay differentials collapsed, and enrollment dropped.

In terms of the demand and supply apparatus shown in Figure 17-3, this is illustrated as follows. First the demand curve shifts outward, and as a result, along the vertical short-run supply curve, the price (pay differential) increases. This increased price draws students into the sciences, slowly shifting the short-run supply curve to the right. But as the supply curve shifts, along the new demand curve, price declines and with it the incentive to enter the sciences rather than other occupations.

Table 17-1 shows the pattern of earnings growth for Ph.D. graduates in physics and, by comparison, for male professionals on average, along with the fraction of all Ph.D.s that were awarded in physics. We see clearly the post-Sputnik boom in earnings in the 1954–1962 period, followed by an increase in the proportion of Ph.D.s in physics in the 1962–1968 period. As the increased supply

---

[7] The process described here was studied initially in the hog market and other agricultural markets.

TABLE 17-1. The Growth of Relative Earnings in Physics

	1951–1954	1954–1962	1962–1968	1968–1970
Earnings growth*				
Physics Ph.D.s	9.2	67.7	22.3	8.8
Male professions	20.5	40.1	36.4	17.4
Ph.D. degrees in physics†, % of all Ph.D. degrees	5.9	5.4	5.6	5.1

* Richard Freeman, "Supply and Salary Adjustment to the Changing Science Manpower Market: Physics, 1948–1973," *American Economic Review*, March 1975.
† *Statistical Abstract of the United States*, various years.

of Ph.D. graduates (as a share of all Ph.D.s) enters the market, relative earnings drop (in 1962–1968), and then in the period 1968–1970 there are fewer Ph.D.s in physics.

On-the-Job Training and Age-Earnings Profiles

Education raises income, and there is therefore a payoff from investing in education. But time on the job also has a payoff. A worker with experience is worth more to his firm, and indeed to any firm, than is a worker who is new in the labor force. The difference between a new worker and a seasoned one is human capital acquired simply by holding a job—learning good work habits—or through on-the-job training. On-the-job training includes learning the routine customs of holding a job, cooperating in a production process, and acquiring specific skills. On-the-job training is a major reason for the initially steep portions of the age-earnings profiles in Figure 17-1. Workers with some experience on the job are more productive than is untrained labor; accordingly, pay rises along with experience.

All this raises an interesting question: Who pays for on-the-job training? If work experience gives workers useful skills, shouldn't we expect them to pay the firm for providing them with experience—by agreeing to work for low wages? In fact, many do just this.

To think clearly about who pays for on-the-job training, it is important to distinguish two types of skills. First, there is *firm-specific* human capital: knowledge of how to work in a particular firm. An important example is learning how to cooperate effectively with a particular set of coworkers. Firm-specific skills of this sort are of no significant value elsewhere. Second, there is *general* human capital: knowledge that can move with the worker and be used elsewhere.

We would expect firm-specific training to be mostly paid for by the firm that will benefit from it. Accordingly, the age-earnings profile for workers acquiring only firm-specific human capital would not necessarily start out at a very low level. But generalized on-the-job training will be paid for by the worker—in the form of a low starting wage and a steep age-earnings profile. Employers will have to pay high wages to those with generalized human capital or risk losing them to other firms where they would also be valuable. Since workers will receive the benefits from investment in general human capital, they also pay the costs.

CONTRARY EVIDENCE. The importance of experience and on-the-job training in determining the shape of the age-earnings profile has been questioned on the basis of the internal work records of a number of firms.[8] These records seem to show that older workers within a given rank are actually *less* productive than younger workers within the same rank. This evidence seems inconsistent with the view that productivity generally increases with experience.

But if productivity does not actually increase with experience, why do age-earnings profiles rise until workers reach their fifties, as shown in Figure 17-1? There are no definitive answers here, but there are two interesting suggestions. The first is that a rising profile may be a means of keeping employees interested in working hard. It is always difficult for a firm to measure a worker's effort. By having a rising earnings profile, the firm ensures that the worker will want to keep the job. The worker will want to earn the high incomes that are available only later, and so she will keep on working hard.

The second suggestion is that workers have a feeling that a rising profile is fair, that older workers deserve more than younger ones. This suggestion may well be right, but it is the type of explanation that makes economists uneasy. Economists prefer to think that customs or views of what is fair are at least not inconsistent with individuals' economic interests.

Human Capital in Arts and Sports

The idea of human capital which generates a return to skills is not limited to education or on-the-job training in ordinary industrial activity. It is also useful in the analysis of the economics of sports and the similar economics of music, dance, and theater.[9] All these activities are

---

[8] James L. Medoff and Katharine G. Abraham, "Experience, Performance, and Earnings," *Quarterly Journal of Economics*, December 1980.

[9] Roger Noll (ed.), *Government and the Sports Business*, Brookings Institution, Washington, D.C., 1974.

performed before audiences who purchase tickets and who value exceptional performance—as shown by their willingness to pay for tickets. As in football, in music and theater we find the need for extensive training of the performers, capital costs for setting up the performance, and the costs of managerial and backstage overheads.

There are, of course, huge differences in income between these fields. A good baseball player will make a substantially larger income than will a French horn player in a symphony orchestra. What accounts for the difference? Demand and supply. The good French horn player does not draw the same crowd as the good baseball player.[10]

3. Unions in the U.S. Economy

Labor unions have always been controversial. They are seen at one and the same time as organizations that protect workers against exploitation by powerful employers, as monopolies that inflate their members' wages, and as institutions that help modern industry run smoothly. We begin in this section with some data and historical background. In section 4 we consider how unions affect the operation of the labor market.

In 1985 almost 17 million U.S. workers, about 18 percent of all workers, were members of labor unions.[11] As Figure 17-4 shows, union membership as a percentage of the labor force has been falling for some time. Union membership doubled in just 2 years, between 1936 and 1938, during the Great Depression. It rose through World War II, with over one-third of the nonagricultural labor force being in unions at the end of that war. But the proportion of the labor force in unions has fallen steadily since 1955. A brief history of labor unions in the United States will help explain these trends.

---

[10] However, since the professional life of the baseball player will, on the average, be shorter than that of the French horn player, the individual with a choice might still want to become a French horn player.

[11] This includes members of employee associations, which are mainly in the government sector and operate much like unions.

FIGURE 17-4. Union Membership as Percentage of the Civilian Labor Force. (*Source*: B. Hirsch and J. Addison *The Economic Analysis of Unions: New Approaches and Evidence,* Allen & Unwin, Boston, 1986, Table 3.1.)

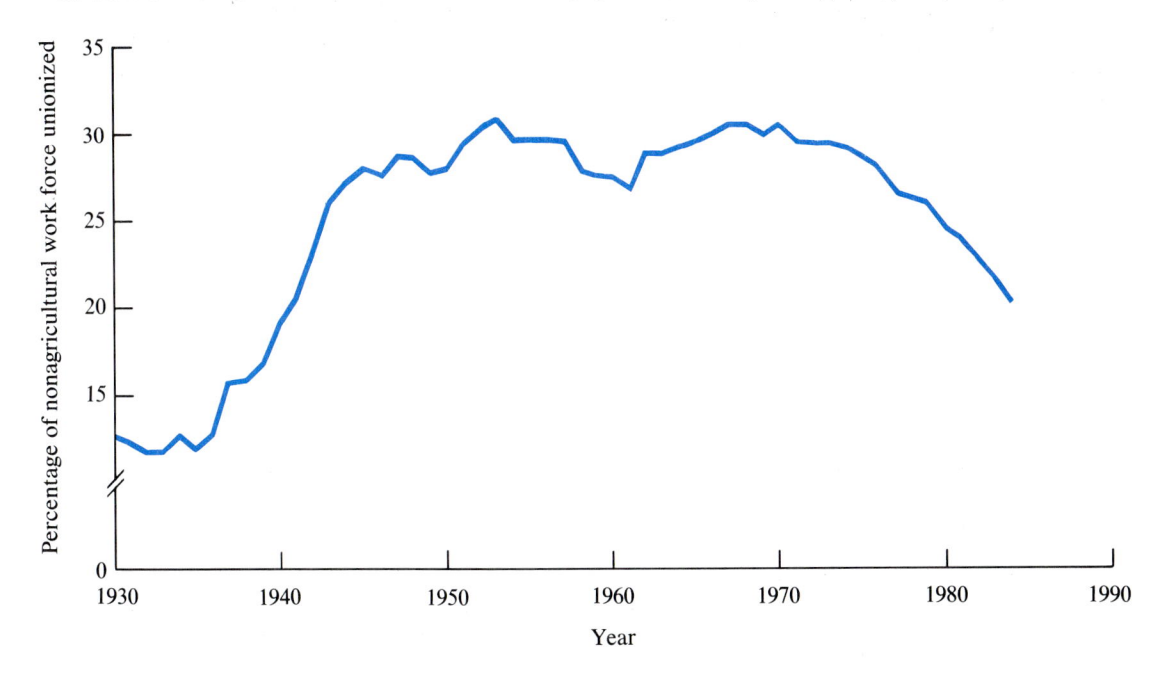

Origins of U.S. Unions

Trade unionism in the United States began to take its modern form in 1886, when the American Federation of Labor (AFL) was formed under the leadership of Samuel Gompers. Gompers established two key features of U.S. labor unionism. First, U.S. unions as they exist today work within the capitalist system; they do not seek to make radical changes in the U.S. economic system. Second, they have generally tried to stay out of political life, arguing that they can work with both political parties. In contrast, European labor unions have been much more political and have typically wanted to move their countries toward socialism. They tend to be directly affiliated with socialist parties. Unions in the United States sometimes support political candidates, but they are not formally affiliated with either of the major parties. They concentrate primarily on work-related issues.

Union membership grew fast during World War I but declined during the prosperous 1920s. The decline occurred in part because both business and government were antiunion and because the times were so good that there was little obvious role for unions. The major development of unionism came in the decade of the Great Depression, the 1930s.

The Great Depression and Legal Changes

Two changes that were largely responsible for the jump in union membership between 1936 and 1938 are reflected in Figure 17-4. The first was the founding in 1936 of the Congress of Industrial Organizations (CIO), which wanted to organize labor into unions based on the industries in which workers worked. Up to that time, the unions were mainly organized on craft lines: All people with the same specific skills belonged to the same union, no matter what industry they were in. But once unions were organized on industry lines, it became easier to unionize large numbers of workers, skilled and unskilled, in each industry.

The second major change was the passage of the *Wagner Act* in 1935. This act forbade employers to engage in unfair labor practices; in particular, it forbade discrimination against workers who were members of unions or who filed complaints against the company. Firms were not allowed to interfere with their workers' rights to form unions, and they had to bargain in good faith with a union that had been established by the workers.

The Wagner Act made it easier for unions to organize workers and made it possible for them to bring legal action against employers who objected to having the work force unionized. The rapid growth of unions was accompanied during and after World War II by a number of major strikes and, in reaction, by a growing feeling that the unions had been given too much power.

THE TAFT-HARTLEY ACT. This feeling led in 1947 to the passage of the Taft-Hartley Act, which cut back the power of unions. One important provision is that the so-called *closed shop*, an establishment in which the employer can hire only members of the union, is outlawed. A union shop, or an establishment in which anyone who is hired must become a union member within 30 days, is permitted, but states have the right to pass laws that outlaw the union shop. These so-called *right-to-work laws* weaken unions by providing that anyone who gets a job with a firm can keep it whether or not he joins the union. Twenty states, mainly in the south, southwest, and plains areas, have right-to-work laws.

A second important provision of Taft-Hartley gives the President the right to obtain a legal injunction delaying strikes for 80 days if they would threaten the entire economy. This 80-day period is supposed to allow the two sides to cool off and reach an agreement.

THE AFL-CIO. When the CIO was set up in 1936, its basis was a group that broke away from the AFL with ill feeling. In 1955 the two organizations got together again and formed the AFL-CIO. The AFL-CIO is the main labor organization in the United States, but it does not have much control over the unions that make it up. The unions do the bargaining for themselves, and the AFL-CIO has little to do with their day-to-day operation. Outside the AFL-CIO the Teamsters Union is one of the most powerful unions in the country.

Declining Union Membership

Why has the proportion of the labor force belonging to unions been declining from a peak level of more than 30 percent to less than 20 percent today? One important factor has been the changing pattern of production: The output of goods has risen less rapidly than has the output of the service sectors. While 25 percent of manufacturing workers belong to unions, only 7.2 percent of those in wholesale and retail trade, 6.6 percent of those in services, and 2.9 percent of those in finance, insurance, and real estate are union members. These differentials arise in large part because the service sectors employ more white-collar labor, and white-collar workers are harder to organize.

A second factor is that formal opposition to unions has strengthened. Firms have been moving into states with weak unions and with right-to-work laws. The states with strong unions are the old industrial states of the northeast.[12] The existence of right-to-work laws, which make it difficult for unions to organize, reflects a general public attitude toward unions that is less supportive than it used to be. Part of the public sees unions as getting more for their workers than is right and as inflicting costs on other people. For that reason, antiunion legislation has become easier to pass.

The one major area of growth for unions in recent years has been the public sector. In 1970, 11.2 percent of all union members were government employees at the federal, state, or local level.[13] By 1985, government employees accounted for 33.8 percent of union membership and 35.8 percent of government employees were unionized. Public-sector employees are not legally allowed to strike, but teachers' strikes have nonetheless become a common event. Early in the Reagan administration the professional air traffic controllers union (PATCO) went on strike illegally. To the surprise of the members of the union, they all were fired.

---

[12] See Richard Freeman, "The Evolution of the American Labor Market, 1948–1980," in Martin Feldstein (ed.), *The American Economy in Transition*, University of Chicago Press, Chicago, 1980.

[13] For an analysis of the increased unionization of the public sector, see Richard B. Freeman, "Unionism Comes to the Public Sector," *Journal of Economic Literature*, March 1986.

4. What Do Unions Do?

The traditional debate on this question[14] takes place between those who think unions exist to protect workers from employers' market power and those who think unions mainly exercise market power themselves. We begin by discussing the two sides of this debate and then consider more sophisticated views of the effects of unions that have been advanced in recent years.

Protection and Company Towns

Union members usually argue that their unions serve to offset the power of employers to dictate wages and working conditions. Of course, if labor markets are perfectly competitive, this makes no sense. In a competitive market, no single buyer or seller can "dictate" to any other; equilibrium wages and working conditions are determined by all buyers and sellers together, through the interaction of supply and demand.

The traditional union position makes sense under two sorts of conditions. If a worker has acquired specific human capital which will not do much for him in any other job, the firm is placed in a relatively strong position and the worker has little protection against some exploitation and arbitrary treatment. Unions can represent the interests of such individual workers by presenting a common policy on working conditions and wages. They give workers strength through numbers, because any firm knows that it would be expensive to replace its entire work force.

Unions may also provide protection in situations involving captive labor forces. Historically such situations have involved "company towns," where a single employer provides most of the jobs in an isolated area from which workers find it difficult to move. In such a situation the firm can exploit its monopsony position.

● **When a single buyer, of labor or anything else, faces many small sellers, the buyer is said to be a *monopsony*.**

---

[14] The authoritative book on this topic is Richard Freeman and James Medoff, *What Do Unions Do*, Basic Books, New York, 1984. See also the review symposium in *Industrial and Labor Relations Review*, January 1985.

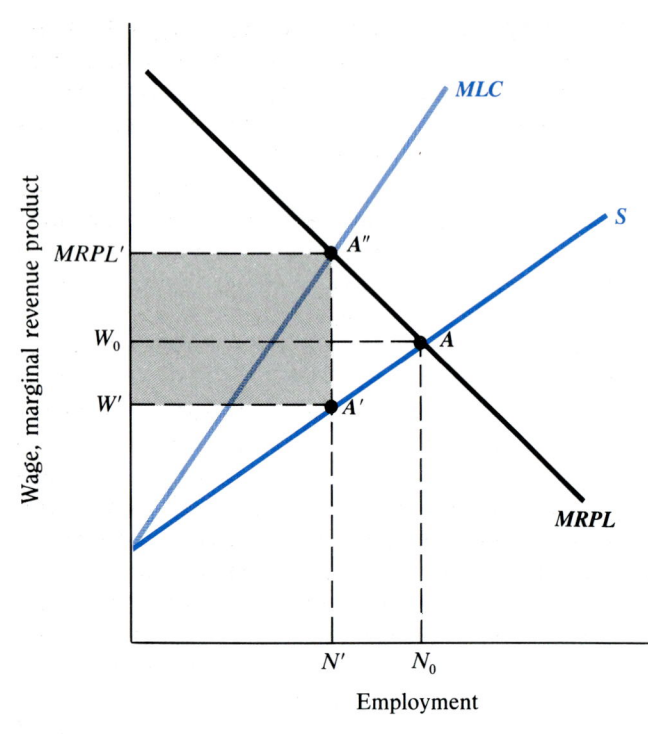

FIGURE 17-5. Monopsony in the Labor Market. The demand for labor comes from a single firm, which has a marginal revenue product schedule, *MRPL*. The labor supply curve is *SS*. A competitive labor market would settle at point *A*. But the monopsonistic firm maximizes profit by setting the marginal cost of labor, *MLC*, equal to *MRPL*. Equilibrium is at point A''. Employment is less than under competition, and the firm makes profits shown by the shaded rectangle.

What are the implications of monopsony for wage determination? Just as a monopoly creates profits by restricting supply, so a monopsonist creates profits by restricting demand. Figure 17-5 illustrates the analysis. The supply curve of labor facing the monopsony firm is *S*; it slopes upward to reflect the fact that the firm must pay higher wages in order to obtain more labor from its captive supply. The marginal revenue product of labor at different levels of employment is shown by the *MRPL* curve.[15] If the company took wages as beyond its control, thus behaving competitively, it would hire N_0 workers, so that the marginal revenue product of labor is equal to the wage rate, W_0.

But a monopsonist will not hire that many workers. Just as a monopolist recognizes that increasing output requires cutting price to all buyers, a monopsonist recognizes that as it increases employment, it must raise the wage it pays all its workers. It therefore looks at the marginal cost of hiring labor: the change in its total labor cost that would be produced by raising the wage enough to hire one more worker. The supply curve of labor represents the average cost per worker, and this supply curve is rising. Therefore, the marginal cost of labor must be above the average cost. Hence the marginal cost must be above the supply curve, just as a monopolist's marginal revenue curve is below the demand curve he faces. The schedule *MLC* shows the marginal cost of labor for this example.

The monopsony equilibrium is at point A'', where the marginal revenue product of labor (the addition to revenue from hiring one more worker) is equal to the marginal cost of labor (the addition to cost from hiring one more worker). The employment level is N', and the wage, read from the supply curve at point A', is W'. Hiring more than N' workers would require wage increases that would raise *MLC* above *MRPL* and would thus reduce profits. Note that monopsony involves both less employment (N' versus N_0) and lower wages (W' versus W_0) than does competitive behavior.

While company towns do exist, they are not a major

---
[15] See Chapter 15 for a discussion of this curve.

factor in the U.S. economy today. The main argument for unions' protective role is thus probably the existence of firm-specific human capital in many situations.

Unions as Monopolists

Once a union is established, it is likely to go beyond its protective function. It will try to raise members' wages. Union control over the firm's labor supply is essential to raising wages. Otherwise, whenever the union succeeded in raising wages for its members, the firm would go out to hire nonunion labor at a lower wage. Since right-to-work laws permit firms to do exactly this, they are valuable to management and hence threatening to unions.

We now analyze how unions raise wages by restricting supply, using Figure 17-6 to illustrate the argument. Suppose we are looking at the construction industry. The quantity of labor demanded at each wage rate is given by the downward-sloping marginal revenue product curve, $MRPL$.[16] The larger the labor force employed in construction, the lower the marginal revenue product. Suppose also that the wage that construction workers could be earning in other sectors of the economy is W_0. If the labor market for the construction industry were competitive, equilibrium would be at point E_0, with employment level N_0. The wage of construction workers would equal the economywide wage, W_0.

Now suppose that the construction industry becomes unionized. By restricting the supply of labor, the union can raise the wage of its members. Thus if the quantity of labor supplied to the construction industry is restricted to N_1, the equilibrium wage in construction is W_1, at point E_1 on the demand for labor schedule. The union has increased its members' wages, and it can make the gain in the relative wage stick because construction firms cannot get around using union labor by going into the labor market. Of course, it is also true that employment in the construction industry will be lower than it would be with a competitive labor market. Furthermore, with higher wages and hence higher construction costs, the relative prices of houses and structures will rise. Thus unions raise not only wages but also the relative cost and price of goods produced by unionized labor.

The analysis raises two questions. Note in Figure 17-6 that the union can raise the wage higher the more it restricts the supply of labor for the industry. The first question is, What determines how far the union will try to go in raising the wage at the expense of less employment? The second question is, What determines how much power unions have to control the supply of labor for particular industries?

We start with the first question. Assume, to begin with, that the union has full control over the supply of labor to the industry. In this case the union acts as a monopoly seller of labor to the firm. What should its objective be? We might think that a union, just like a product-market monopolist, should aim to maximize

---

[16] As we noted in Chapter 13, if the construction industry is perfectly competitive, this will be the industry's marginal value product ($MVPL$) curve.

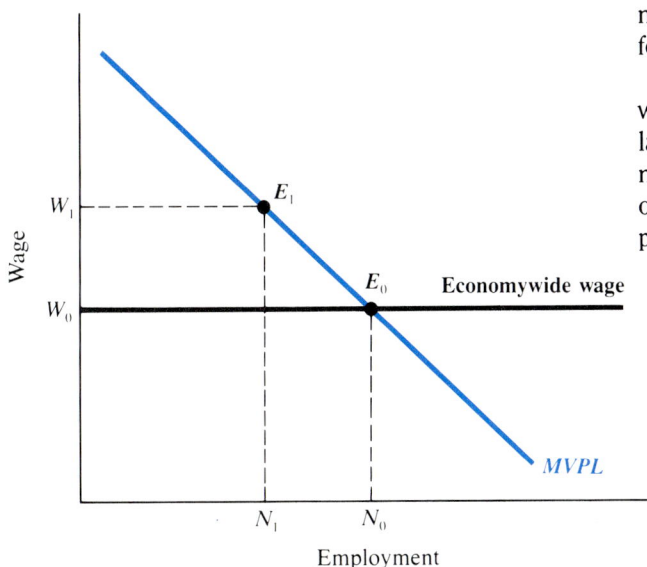

FIGURE 17-6. A Union's Effect on Wages and Employment. The $MRPL$ curve shows the demand for labor in a competitive industry. The economywide wage, W_0, is the wage that labor would be paid if there were no union. A union is able to control the quantity of labor supplied to the industry and thereby raise the wage above the competitive level. In the figure, the union raises the wage from W_0 to W_1 by restricting the quantity of labor supplied to N_1.

profits, or its income.[17] However, in the case of a union, it is far from clear what should be maximized. The union might want to maximize the income of its current members, or it might want to maximize the per capita income of the members who remain after it has raised the wage, or perhaps it is concerned with maximizing the size of its membership so that it can be sure of maintaining its power. These are all different objectives. Which one dominates depends largely on the extent to which the union is run in the interest of its officers, in the interest of its existing members, or in the interest of existing and potential members.

Restricting the supply of labor will work particularly well in raising relative wages when a small reduction in the labor supply yields a large increase in the relative wage. How successful a union can be in achieving a large increase in wages with only a small decline in employment depends on the elasticity of labor demand. In industries where the elasticity of labor demand is low, unions face a particularly favorable employment-wage trade-off.

We show the role of the elasticity of demand for labor in Figure 17-7. There are two possible demand schedules for labor, $MRPL$ and $MRPL'$. The demand curve $MRPL'$ is more elastic; any given change in wages generates a larger change in employment around point E_0. Suppose that under competition the equilibrium is at E_0 and that a union succeeds in reducing employment from N_0 to N_1. Along the demand schedule $MRPL$ the equilibrium wage rises to W_1, while along $MRPL'$ it rises only to W_1'. It is clear from the diagram that a given reduction in the labor supply raises wages more the less elastic the demand for labor is.

We can use Figure 17-7 to consider the effects of airline deregulation on the market for pilots. Traditionally, when there were few airlines and all were unionized, pilots commanded a high relative wage—high relative to the wages of other professionals. Assume that initially the demand for labor was $MRPL$, with E_1 as the initial equilibrium point. Deregulation opened up the possibility of new nonunion airlines entering into competition. As a result unionized carriers faced more elastic demand curves on the part of passengers, since passengers can substitute flights on nonunion airlines. Therefore, the schedule for the derived demand for labor becomes more like the elastic schedule, $MRPL'$. This change puts strong downward pressure on the union wage differential, since the airline companies can no longer afford to pay high wages without cutting back employment substantially. Of course, it is in the union's interest to expand its membership to the new airlines or to try to keep them out of business by lobbying for entry restrictions, for example. As always in a monopoly situation, the entry of new firms threatens monopoly profits,

---

[17] To get maximum revenue, as we saw in the discussion of the relation between demand elasticity and total revenue in Chapter 5, the union should set the wage at the level where the elasticity of demand for labor is 1.

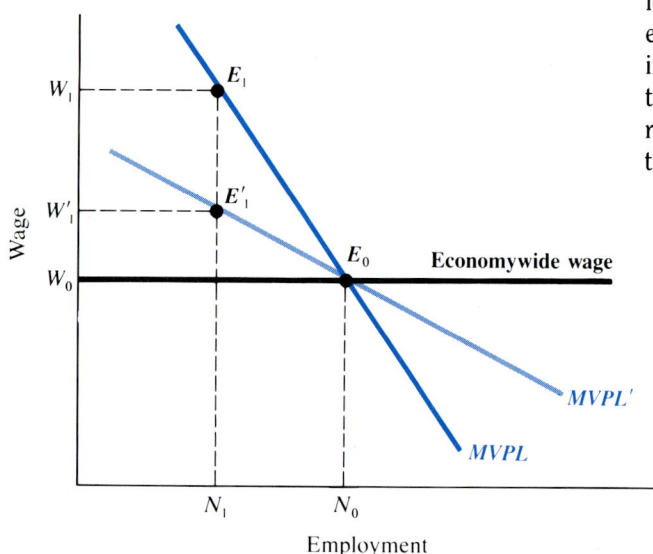

FIGURE 17-7. Wage Differentials and the Elasticity of Derived Demand. The effect of the union on wages and employment depends on the elasticity of the derived demand for labor, as shown by the $MRPL$ curve. The elasticity of derived demand is higher on $MRPL'$ than on $MRPL$. This means that a given restriction in the quantity of labor supplied produces a lower increase in wages for the union members on $MRPL'$ than on $MRPL$. The union prefers to face a low elasticity of $MRPL$. That way it gets large increases in wages with a small cutback in the level of employment.

which take the form of above-normal wages here. In this case, the wage differentials of unionized pilots are threatened by the entry of nonunion firms.

Another example, along much the same line, concerns the automobile industry. Suppose that automobile workers are unionized and command a high wage premium. Then foreign firms start competing in the home market. The demand for domestically produced cars becomes more price-responsive, and the derived demand for labor to produce cars therefore becomes more elastic. Car producers lose sales, and union employment falls. Unions lobby against imports, arguing that foreign cars are produced by cheap labor.

How effective are unions in raising wages?[18] In other words, how much difference does labor union membership make, holding constant worker characteristics such as skill, education, age, and experience? Most studies have put the union-nonunion differential at between 10 and 20 percent in recent years. The gap appears to widen when unemployment in the economy as a whole increases, since union contracts keep members' wages from falling. About 24 percent of blacks and 19 percent of Hispanics are union members, versus 17 percent of white workers. Thus unions tend to reduce the wage gap between whites and other workers. Indeed, unions may on balance reduce inequality in labor earnings.[19] Many studies find that rates of return to human capital investment are lower in unionized firms, for instance, and industrywide bargaining tends to reduce wage differentials for workers in different firms in a given industry.

Union Wages as Compensating Differentials

Some scholars have argued that unions in fact do not have much power to raise wages. They reason that observed wage differentials are in large measure simply compensation for the kind of labor performed by union workers. Union work has certain characteristics, "notably a structured work setting, inflexibility of hours, employer-set overtime, and a faster work pace."[20] These characteristics rather than the existence of unions might at least in part be responsible for higher union wages. There are two views about the link between wage differentials and working conditions.

The first view is that after a union has taken over and raised relative wages, employers respond by taking advantage of the presence of the union to raise productivity. Productivity is raised by establishing more standardized work patterns, which can be agreed upon and enforced in cooperation with the union. Because, other things equal, workers view these restrictions on the work pace and working time as costs, it is clear that the increase in their relative wage has in some way been eroded. They earn more, but they also work on relatively less attractive terms.

The other view is that unions are not primarily a means of restricting labor supply at all but rather organizations for effective communication between employers and workers regarding working conditions. We would expect unions to emerge in industries where there are gains to be derived from the establishment of structured working conditions. The union negotiates to reconcile the workers' dislike of restrictive working conditions with the firm's need for such terms. The wage differential is the compensation for the restrictive conditions.

Evidence for this view of union wage differentials as compensation for productivity and work conditions has emerged from a number of studies.[21] These studies have found that union labor has higher productivity, for example, because of lower quitting rates; that union labor accepts tighter working conditions; and so on. In sum, then, the union premium is not entirely a reflection of the union's monopoly restriction of the labor supply. Some of it represents a compensating differential. But the importance of the monopoly element in explaining union differentials remains.

---

[18] For a survey of studies of the effects of unions on wages, see C. J. Parsley, "Labor Unions and Wages: A Survey," *Journal of Economic Literature*, March 1980.

[19] See Richard Freeman, "Unionism and the Dispersion of Wages," *Industrial and Labor Relations Review*, October 1980.

[20] G. J. Duncan and F. P. Stafford, "Do Union Members Receive Compensating Differentials?" *American Economic Review*, June 1980, p. 355.

[21] See, in particular, R. Freeman and J. Medoff, *What Do Unions Do*, Basic Books, New York, 1984; and Duncan and Stafford, cited in footnote 20.

Unions and Profitability

If unions were merely an efficient means of organizing labor and the higher wage were merely compensation for higher productivity, firms would welcome unions. But firms resist unionization as if they expected to pay more in increased wages than they might expect to gain in labor productivity. The view that unions, all things considered, reduce corporate profitability emerges strongly from a study of the stock market reaction to attempts at unionization.[22]

The first step toward unionization is a petition for an election. The petition, if successful, leads to an election. If the union wins, it is certified as the recognized bargaining agent for its members. The study found that a petition for an election and a successful election both lead to a decline in the stock market prices of firms that face the threat of unionization. A successful organization attempt brings about on average a decline in the stock market value of the firm of $46,800 per worker. Even unsuccessful attempts produce a decline in the stock market value of $7,400 per worker. This represents quite dramatic evidence that unions turn profits into wages—at the expense of stockholders.

Bargaining and Strikes

When we think of unions, we probably think also of strikes. And, of course, strikes do sometimes disrupt major parts of the economy, such as the coal, steel, and trucking industries. How serious are strikes? Do they account for any significant losses of output in the economy?

Figure 17-8 shows the percentage of total working time lost in the United States as a result of work stoppages in the period since 1948. Strikes cost the U.S. economy very few workdays per year—much less than half a day per year per employee on the average. Moreover, the fraction of working time lost due to strikes has sharply declined in the past 10 years.[23]

Why are there strikes? One might think that a strike is the inevitable outcome of a bargaining situation in which the union and the firm are fighting each other. But it is important in thinking about unions to realize that the union and the firm have a common interest as well as opposing interests. The firm wants to make profits, and the workers want to earn income. Together they can achieve both. The workers need the firm to provide jobs, and the firm needs the workers to provide labor. Because

---

[22] See Richard S. Ruback and Martin B. Zimmerman "Unionization and Profitability: Evidence from the Capital Market," *Journal of Political Economy*, December 1984.

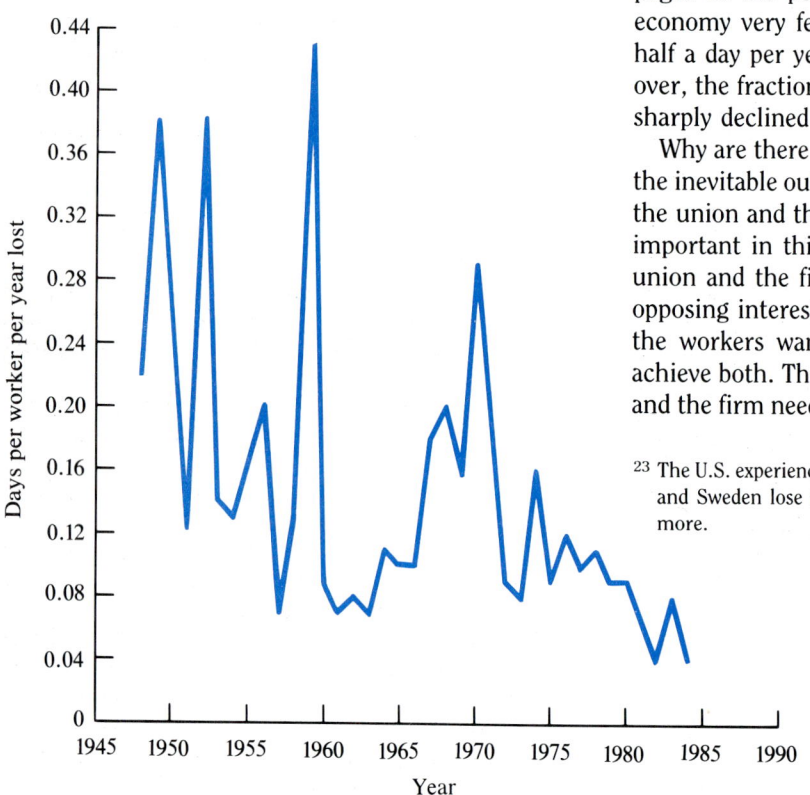

[23] The U.S. experience is about average on an international scale. Japan and Sweden lose fewer workdays, and Canada and Italy lose many more.

FIGURE 17-8. Working Time Lost Due to Work Stoppages (days per worker per year). (*Source*: *Handbook of Labor Statistics, 1985*, Table 123.

of these common interests the bargaining process between a firm and the union is usually completed without a strike. Indeed, the union and the firm are in continuing contact to operate the firm at times other than contract-negotiating time. Everyday issues between workers and management are settled routinely through daily union-management contact.

Sometimes a union and a firm will misjudge the other's strength or their own strength. A strike will take place, and one side or the other will give way eventually. Or sometimes a union or the firm will deliberately aim for a strike to show that it is tough enough to resist the demands of the other party. A strike is costly to both parties when it happens, but at least one side may believe that the strike will pay off in the long run because the other party will realize the seriousness of future threats and will be forced to make concessions.

On other occasions leaders of unions are forced into strikes by their members. The members may be very militant and demand a large wage increase. Even though the leadership may know that such an increase is not possible, it goes through with a strike to demonstrate its toughness to the membership and also so that the membership will eventually change its mind about the possibility of getting a higher wage.

Interesting as strikes are, they are not the usual means for reaching agreements between unions and firms. Typically the bargaining process concludes with a new contract that specifies working conditions, wages, and fringe benefits for the next year or two (or three), and the union does not go on strike.

■ We have seen that the labor market, which most of us rely on for most of our income, is a complex place. Individual workers must make investment decisions regarding human capital that are fully as difficult as the investment decisions made by business firms. Their earnings reflect talents and education, but also their ability to secure a job in a unionized industry. Unions are a declining force in the private sector but a growing power among government employees, and their impact on the labor market is complex. All this is fascinating both because of the subtlety of the interactions among the many factors involved in determining wages and incomes and because those forces determine the standard of living of each of us.

Summary

1. There are substantial differences in pay among workers. These reflect personal characteristics such as education, job experience, race, location, and union status. While pay differs from person to person, earnings on average increase with education, experience, and union membership.
2. Skills, or human capital, are the most important source of wage differentials among workers. Human capital is increased by both formal schooling and on-the-job training and experience. Other things equal, the more schooling and/or the more job experience a person has, the higher her human capital, productive potential, and (therefore) wages are.
3. The signaling hypothesis is another possible explanation of why a premium is paid for college-educated workers. It says that a college education does not itself add to a worker's productivity; it does, however, show that the worker is good at things that are useful to the firm.
4. Formal schooling, say, at the college level, involves not only direct costs (such as tuition) but also opportunity costs, or income that could be earned by working instead of going to college. The investment decision for human capital involves balancing the direct costs and forgone earnings associated with increased schooling against the prospective rewards from having more education.
5. There is some evidence that the shape of age-earnings profiles may not be due entirely to the greater productivity of more experienced workers. Rather, earnings may increase with age so as to encourage workers not to quit when quitting is costly for the firm.
6. Less than 20 percent of the workers in the United States belong to unions. Union membership increased sharply between 1936 and 1938 and reached a maximum as a share of the labor force at the end of World War II. The declining proportion of the labor force in unions reflects shifts in the pattern of demand for goods—demand has shifted away from goods produced by easily unionized labor—and a changing geographic pattern of production. Public sympathy for unions has also decreased.

7 Unions in the United States, as opposed to those in Europe, have as their main aim the improvement of the wages and working conditions of their members within the capitalist system. Foreign unions are more likely to be associated with socialist political parties.

8 Unions restrict labor supply for unionized establishments and thereby raise the wages of their members in relation to nonunion wages. The wage differentials vary across industries and occupations, with most being between 10 and 20 percent.

9 The wage differential that a union can achieve is larger the more effectively the union can control membership and the less elastic the demand for labor is. Union differentials will be higher or will cost less in terms of employment the less competition unionized firms face in the markets for their outputs.

10 Union labor tends to work under conditions that are more restrictive in terms of hours, overtime, and work pace than are the working conditions for nonunion labor. This has been interpreted as one reason for union differentials. While this view has merit, it does not invalidate the traditional view that unions create wage differentials chiefly by restricting labor supply.

Key Terms

Human capital
Age-earnings profile
Signaling
Rate of return to education
Firm-specific human capital
General human capital
Closed shop
Union shop
Right-to-work laws
Monopsony

Problems

1 Studies have shown that college-trained workers in the 1970s received a smaller wage differential than they did in the 1960s. (a) What effect would this have in the 1980s on the percentage of high school students going to college? Explain. (b) Suppose it was shown that going to college did not add at all to a person's lifetime income. Would anyone still go to college? Explain.

2 The energy shortage increased the demand for nuclear energy. Discuss in detail the labor market adjustment to the increased demand for nuclear engineers in the short run and in the long run.

3 Consider the following investment problem. A person with her existing skill can earn $20,000 a year for the next 40 years. Alternatively, she can enter a 3-year course of studies with direct costs of $7000 per year. If she could get an interest-free loan to finance the studies (so that the discount rate to be used is zero), what future income differential per year would make the investment in human capital worthwhile?

4 Suppose that economists form a union and establish certification procedures that specify who is qualified to practice economics. How would the move help raise the relative wage of economists? (a) What kinds of laws would help cement the monopoly? (b) How would the union restrict entry?

5 Apprentices are typically paid low wages. Using the concept of human capital, explain this observation.

6 Draw a demand schedule for labor. Assume that a union has a given number of members, N, that the economywide wage is W_0, and that the employment in this industry at that wage exceeds N. Illustrate the different targets that the union could pursue by manipulating the supply of labor to the industry: (a) maximize income, (b) maximize employment, (c) maximize wage.

7 Show in a diagram of the labor market how a policy of restricting flight time for pilots (to a maximum of, say, 40 hours per month) affects the wage differential of unionized pilots. Why is a restriction on the number of working hours an important part of the union's attempt to raise the wage differentials?

8 Draw two labor supply curves, one highly elastic and the other inelastic. In which market would a monopsonist earn higher profits?

9 It has been said that the entry of a union into an industry acts like a tax on the industry. Explain, using demand and supply curves for the good produced by an industry that becomes unionized.

10 Are there any conditions under which a firm might want to have a union organize the workers in the company?

Appendix: The Algebra of Present Values and Rates of Return

This appendix provides an algebraic treatment of the calculation of present values and rates of return.

Interest and Present Value

The *present value* of a stream of payments to be received in the future is the amount of money that would have to be invested today in order to finance those payments when they come due. In order to show how present values are computed, then, we must first see how investments grow over time.

Suppose that we invest a sum of K dollars today at an interest rate of r percent. For concreteness, assume that $K = \$100$ and that $r = 10$ percent, or 0.1 per year. What will the value of the investment be after 1 year? After a year we get back the initial investment, or the *principal* ($K = 100$), and we also receive the interest ($rK = \$10$). Therefore, we have the following pattern:

Present investment	Next year's value
$K	$K + $rK = $K(1 + r)

Now suppose that we ask how much we must invest today, $X, to have $R next year. We fill in the entries as follows:

Present investment	Next year's value
$X	$R = $X(1 + r)

The value of our investment next year will be our current investment plus interest, or $X(1 + r)$. For that to be equal to a given sum, say, $R = \$100$, we can write the following:

$$\$X(1 + r) = \$R \text{ or } \$X = \$R/(1 + r) = \$0.91R \quad (A1)$$

In equation (A1) we simply divided both sides by $(1 + r)$ to solve for the unknown current investment necessary to finance a payment of $R due 1 year in the future.

Equation (A1) is the general formula for the present value of a receipt in 1 year. Today's value is equal to next year's receipt ($R) divided by the term $(1 + r)$. We also call that division *discounting*. The term "discounting" refers to the fact that less than the face value of a future receipt is paid today for a claim on money in the future, as equation (A1) shows.

Now let us discuss the present value of a payment of $R to be received 2 years from now. Does equation (A1) help us price that payment? It does, so long as we apply it in two steps. First we have to calculate the value next year of the payment to be received the year after next. The answer is obtained with equation (A1). Then we have to calculate the value *this* year of that amount. Here are the steps in the calculation:

To be received in year 2:	$R
Value in year 1:	$R/(1 + r)
Value in year 0:	[$R/(1 + r)]/(1 + r)
	= $R/(1 + r)^2

Example: $100
$91 (at 10% interest)
$83

The process of valuing a distant payment, then, simply involves the *repeated* application of the price of a payment to be received *one* period hence. Using the logic of the table, we find that a payment of $1 to be received 3 years from now is worth

$$\frac{1}{1+r} \times \frac{1}{1+r} \times \frac{1}{1+r}$$

Similarly, the present value of a payment to be received 10 years from now is equal to the term $1/(1 + r)$ multiplied by itself 10 times. Any hand calculator will easily perform this computation.

More generally, let $PV_k(r)$ be the present value of a dollar to be received k years from now when the interest rate is r. Then we have the following:

Present value of a dollar k years from now	
$k = 0$	$PV_0(r) = \$1$
$k = 1$	$PV_1(r) = \$1/(1 + r)$
$k = 2$	$PV_2(r) = \$1/(1 + r)^2$
$k = 3$	$PV_3(r) = \$1/(1 + r)^3$
$k = 10$	$PV_{10}(r) = \$1/(1 + r)^{10}$
$k = n$	$PV_n(r) = \$1/(1 + r)^n$

These formulas indicate that the present value of a future dollar falls as the payment date becomes more distant. At 10 percent, a $1 payment to be received 10 years from now is worth only 39 cents today. Or, it takes 39 cents today, invested for 10 years at 10 percent interest, to arrive at a principal of $1.

So far we have looked only at the present value of a single payment. What about a stream of payments—for example, year 1: $100, year 2: $50, year 3: $200? The present value of this stream of future payments is simply the sum of the present values of each of the payments. If $\$R_k$ is the payment to be received in year k, the present value of the whole receipt stream is $PV_1(r) \times \$R_1 + PV_2(r) \times \$R_2 + PV_3(r) \times \$R_3$. If we use the numbers in the preceding example with $r = 0.1$, we find that the sum is $91 + \$41.32 + \$125.60 = 257.92$.

Perpetuities

Let us now consider the value today of a permanent stream of $\$R$ that is received year after year, from here to eternity, starting in year 1. Such a stream of income is called a *perpetuity*. In this case the present value is given by an infinite sum: $PV_1(r) \times \$R + PV_2(r) \times \$R + \ldots + PV_{100}(r) \times \$R + \ldots + PV_{2500}(r) \times \$R$, and so on. Even with the best computers we could not directly calculate the sum of the infinite number of individual terms.

Fortunately, there is a simple formula for calculating the present value:

$$\$V = \frac{\text{present value of a perpetuity}}{\text{of } \$R \text{ per year}} = \frac{\$R}{r} \quad (A2)$$

Since a perpetuity pays a constant stream of returns forever, it is as if the principal is never repaid. Each year's payment, $\$R$, is then equal to the interest on this constant principal, $\$rV$.

If $R = \$100$ and $r = 10$ percent, for instance, then the present value of *all* future receipts is $1000. A calculator shows that $PV_{50}(10) \times \$100 = \$0.85$, $PV_{100}(10) \times \$100 = \$0.0073$, $PV_{200}(10) \times \$100 = \$0.00000053$, and so on. Thus most of the present value of a perpetuity comes from payments in the near future, not from payments expected a couple of hundred years down the road.

These very distant payments are worth almost nothing today.

Rate of Return

The *rate of return* on any investment is the interest rate that makes the present value of the future returns from that investment just equal to its current cost. Suppose, for example, that a perpetuity costs $300 today and pays $15 per year. The rate of return on this investment is the value of r such that equation (A2) is satisfied:

$$r = \frac{\text{rate of return on a perpetuity that}}{\text{costs } \$V \text{ and pays } \$R \text{ per year}} = \frac{\$R}{\$V} \quad (A3)$$

In our example, the rate of return is $0.05 (= \$15/\$300)$, or 5 percent.

To take another simple case, suppose an investment costs $\$X$ today and pays $\$R$ in 1 year. The rate of return on this investment is obtained by solving equation (A1) for r:

$$r = \frac{\text{rate of return on an investment}}{\text{that costs } \$X \text{ and pays } \$R \text{ in 1 year}} = \frac{\$R}{\$X} - 1 \quad (A4)$$

Thus an investment that costs $100 and pays $110 in 1 year has a rate of return of $0.10 [= (110/100) - 1]$, or 10 percent.

More generally, the rate of return is calculated by searching (perhaps using a calculator or personal computer) for the interest rate that makes the present value of future payments exactly equal to the current cost of the investment.

Appendix Problems

1. How much should you be willing to pay today to increase your annual income by $5000 for the next 5 years if the interest rate is 3 percent? If the interest rate is 10 percent?
2. If a perpetuity pays $30 per year and costs $200, what rate of return would be earned by investing in it? What is the rate of return on an investment that costs $200 and pays $230 in 1 year?

Chapter 18
Tangible Wealth: Capital and Land

As the 1980s progressed, policymakers in the United States became increasingly concerned with our ability to meet foreign competition. Many argued that a key to regaining or maintaining our leading position in the world economy is to upgrade the economy's capital stock—for instance, to replace old-fashioned machinery in steel and automobile production with the modern technologies used in Japan and Europe.

● ***Physical capital*** **is the stock of produced goods that contributes to the production of goods and services.**

The economy's total stock of physical capital—its *capital stock*—includes the assembly line machinery used to make cars, factory and office buildings, the chairs in which we sit and the TV we watch while sitting,[1] houses that produce "housing services," railroad tracks, school buildings, airplanes, and so on. On a per person basis, rich economies have large capital stocks and less-developed economies have small capital stocks.

The capital stock is increased through the process of investment.

● ***Investment*** **occurs when part of current production is used to add to the capital stock.**

In order to modernize its capital stock, the United States (or any other economy) would have to invest in new automated equipment in the steel and automobile industries, for instance, or build up the new information processing industries. Beyond machinery and equipment, studies in the mid-1980s report that road, bridge, water, and sewer systems are deteriorating fast and that increased investment will be needed to maintain and improve those components of the physical capital stock.[2]

Physical capital is distinguished from land by the fact that it is produced, while the stock of land cannot be increased.

● ***Land*** **is a factor of production which, rather than being produced, is naturally available—but only in a fixed quantity.**

---

[1] Why are the chair and TV set capital? Because they contribute to producing the service "watching TV," which people value.
[2] Because the physical capital stock depreciates (wears out) through use and aging, some investment is needed each year just to prevent the capital stock from deteriorating.

In practice it is not always easy to separate land from capital. Much of the land in the United States owes its productivity to past investments made in clearing trees and rocks and in creating proper drainage. Thus part of what we call land is the result of past investments and is more like physical—produced—capital than a factor of production that is naturally available.

In Chapters 16 and 17 we discussed the supply and demand for labor, which earns about 75 percent of GNP and is thus the most important factor of production. In this chapter we analyze the supply and demand for land and physical capital. They are included in the same chapter both because land and physical capital are difficult to disentangle in practice and because the economics of capital and of land are basically the same.

Capital and land together make up the *tangible wealth* of the economy. This means that they are real, durable assets that directly yield valuable services over some period of time. Tangible wealth is different from but related to financial wealth. Someone who has 100 shares of General Motors stock owns financial wealth. Her stock certificates have value because they are ultimately a claim on tangible wealth, but they are not themselves tangible wealth—a stock certificate can't be used to produce automobiles.[3]

We begin with some basic data about tangible wealth in the U.S. economy. Section 2 then develops the implications of the fundamental principle that underlies the economics of both land and capital: *Because tangible wealth is durable, its value today depends on what it will produce in the future.* The rest of the chapter applies this principle to the factor markets for land and capital.

The theory of capital developed here applies to investment decisions that we all make. We have already seen in Chapter 15 how a student deciding to invest in college rather than take a job is buying human capital, the value of which depends on the future income it will generate. Someone deciding to buy a house or a car must consider the services it will provide in the future. Thinking about those examples will clarify the general principles outlined in this chapter.

1. Tangible Wealth: The Facts

In 1985, the total value of capital and land in the United States was estimated to be $12.5 trillion, or about $52,500 per person. Table 18-1 shows the composition of tangible wealth in the United States in 1950 and 1985.

The major categories of tangible wealth are shown in the first column. "Plant and equipment" includes buildings, machines, and tools owned by businesses. "Inventories" refers to finished goods, materials, and goods in process that are held by firms so that they can produce without running out of supplies and be sure that goods are available when customers want them.[4] "Residential structures" are houses and apartment buildings. "Consumer durables" include automobiles, refrigerators, TVs, and other tangible assets owned by households. The most striking point that emerges from the table is that the composition of the stock of tangible wealth has remained quite stable over the last 35 years.

Similar tables for other countries reveal some interesting differences. In agricultural countries, a larger fraction of national wealth consists of land and a lesser proportion consists of plant and equipment. Residential structures and especially consumer durables account for a larger share of wealth in rich countries than they do in poor countries.

---

[3] Similar to the distinction between tangible wealth and financial wealth is the distinction between physical capital and financial capital. A person about to open a business may say that he has capital of $10 million because he borrowed that much from the bank and his relatives. But this is financial capital: money and other paper assets. If the financial capital is used to buy office equipment and machinery, then the businessman has acquired physical capital, which is what this chapter is mainly about.

[4] Why are inventories part of the capital stock? Because they are a stock of produced goods that contribute to the production of goods and services.

TABLE 18-1. Composition of the U.S. Stock of Tangible Wealth (Percentage of Total Stock)

	1950	1985
Plant and equipment	26.5	30.3
Inventories	11.2	6.8
Residential structures	29.1	27.4
Consumer durables	12.6	11.1
Land	20.7	24.4

Source: Federal Reserve Board, *Balance Sheets for the U.S. Economy, 1946–85*, April 1986.

Chapter 18: Tangible Wealth: Capital and Land

TABLE 18-2. Tangible Wealth in the United States

	1950	1970	1985
Tangible wealth ÷ GNP	3.0	2.8	3.1
Share of land and capital in income*	35.2%	25.7%	26.2%
Plant and equipment used per worker†	$18.0	$29.2	$35.5

* National income minus compensation of employees as a fraction of national income.
† Thousands of 1985 dollars per worker, excluding consumer capital, owner-occupied housing, and household land holdings.
Source: *Economic Report of the President, 1986*, and Federal Reserve Board, *Balance Sheets for the U.S. Economy, 1946–85*, April 1986.

The role of tangible wealth in the U.S. economy is described by three numbers presented in Table 18-2. The first is the ratio of tangible wealth to GNP, or the value of all goods and services produced in the economy. The stock of wealth, measured at its market value, is equal to around 3 years' income. The second measure of the role of land and capital is their share of income produced in the United States. The table reveals that the income of land and capital—which is received as rents, interest, dividends, and profits—accounts now for about a quarter of income, having declined since 1950 from a level of about 35 percent.[5]

The third measure shown in Table 18-2 is the amount of plant and equipment per worker employed. In 1985, the average worker had about $35,500 worth of plant and equipment to work with; thus plant and equipment per worker nearly doubled between 1950 and 1985, revealing a large change in the way output is produced. Over time, the average worker has been able to cooperate with an increasing amount of capital; production has become more *capital-intensive*, which is one of the main reasons why workers have become more productive.

2. Rentals, Interest Rates, and Asset Prices

Tangible wealth is *durable*; today's factories, machinery, and land will help produce goods and services tomorrow

[5] Because of difficulties with the data, the share of land and capital in national income cannot be measured accurately.

as well as today. Thus time plays a central role in the economics of capital and land.[6] In this section we develop the basic economic principles that apply to all durable assets.

Stocks and Flows

The first step in understanding the demand and supply for capital is to understand the distinctions between the *stock* of an asset and the *flow* of services it yields over time and between a *rental payment* for services and an *asset price*. We make these points with the help of Table 18-3, discussing first the more familiar case of labor.

The commodity that is traded in the labor market is labor services, or hours of labor. The corresponding price is the wage per hour. We can think of the wage per hour as the price at which the firm rents the services of a worker, or the rental rate for labor. We do not have asset prices in the labor market because workers cannot be bought or sold in modern societies; they can only be rented. (In a society with slavery, the asset price would be the price of a slave.)

These concepts also apply to capital. Where a worker provides labor services, a machine provides machine services. For example, a dentist's drill may provide 1000 hours of drilling services per year, and a truck may provide 3000 hours of trucking per year.

● **The cost of *using* capital services is the *rental rate* for capital.**

The rental rate may be a quoted market price, the amount the firm pays to rent a piece of capital from its

[6] Because the future is always uncertain, risk and uncertainty also deserve star billing, as Chapter 19 demonstrates.

TABLE 18-3. Stock and Flow Concepts

	Capital	Labor
Productive contribution	Capital services (machine hours)	Labor services (labor hours)
Payment for service flow	Rental rate, $/machine hour	Wage, $/hr of labor
Asset price	Price of a unit of capital, $/machine	Only available in the case of slavery, $/slave

owner. For instance, there is a rental rate for hiring a moving van from U-Haul, equal to so many dollars per hour or day. But for some capital goods, such as dams and auto assembly lines, there is no actual rental market. In these cases the firm has to work out how much per hour or day it costs it to use its capital equipment, as we discuss in section 4.

Finally, in the case of capital, there is an asset price as well as a price for capital services.

● **The *asset price* is the price at which a drill or a truck or a house or any other piece of capital can be bought or sold outright.**

These concepts apply directly to land as well; the cost of *using* any parcel of land is a rental rate, while the price one must pay to *own* the land is the corresponding asset price.

Our next task is to understand the relationship that links asset prices and rental rates. The key idea here is that *the owner of an asset has the right to receive all present and future rental payments on that asset*. To show how the asset price includes the value of future rental payments, we must define and explain the concept of *present value*.[7]

Interest and Present Value

A dollar today is worth more than a dollar to be received a year from now. Why? Because a dollar received today can always be deposited in a bank account, where it will earn interest. Suppose that a deposit in a bank pays 5 percent per year in interest, or in other words, 5 cents for every dollar held in the account for a year. Then a dollar received today and deposited will grow to $1.05 in a year. Because of this, $1.05 to be received a year from now is worth $1 today.

What, then, is the value *today* of a dollar to be received 1 year from now? At a 5 percent interest rate, we would have to deposit 95.2 cents today to receive $1 a year from now. (Calculation: 5 percent interest on 95.2 cents = 4.8 cents; therefore, 1 year from now we would have the original 95.2 cents plus 4.8 cents interest, or $1.) It follows that at a 5 percent interest rate, the value *today* of $1 a year from now, or its *present value*, is 95.2 cents.

What about the more distant future? If we deposited a dollar and reinvested the interest every year, the value of the investment would grow over time at the rate of the interest, as shown in Table 18-4. In year 1 we have our inital investment plus 5 cents in interest, or $1.05. In year 2 we have the year 1 investment plus interest, or $1.05 + 5 percent of $1.05 = $1.1025, and so on. (The data in Table 18-4 are rounded to the nearest cent.)

The account grows rapidly because interest *compounds*: It is earned both on the *principal* (the original sum invested) and on the interest already earned. After 7¼ years at 10 percent, the value of the investment has already doubled;[8] after 20 years, it has accumulated to nearly seven times the initial investment. One dollar invested at 10 percent in 1776 would have grown to over $1.8 billion by the U.S. bicentennial in 1976.

Table 18-4 also shows the value today of a dollar received at various dates in the future. Suppose the

---

[7] The appendix to Chapter 17 presents an algebraic analysis of present value and related concepts.

[8] A useful rule of thumb is the *rule of 72*, which says that the time it takes to double your money is approximately equal to 72 divided by the interest rate (expressed as a percentage). At 5 percent, it takes about 14.4 years (72/5); at 10 percent, it takes about 7.2 years. The rule is good but not exact; the exact answers are 14.21 years at 5 percent and 7.27 years at 10 percent.

TABLE 18-4. Investment and Interest

	Year 0	Year 1	Year 2	Year 3	Year 20
Interest rate = 5%					
Value of $1 invested today in year	$1	$1.05	$1.10	$1.16	$2.65
Present value of $1 to be received in year	$1	$0.95	$0.91	$0.86	$0.38
Interest rate = 10%					
Value of $1 invested today in year	$1	$1.10	$1.21	$1.33	$6.73
Present value of $1 to be received in year	$1	$0.91	$0.83	$0.75	$0.15

interest rate is 10 percent. How much would we pay today for $1 a year from now? We would pay as much as we would have to deposit in the bank today, at an interest rate of 10 percent, to receive $1 a year from now. The answer is $0.91 (which yields 9 cents of interest a year from now plus the principal of 91 cents). In the same way we can calculate the value today of $1 to be received 2 years from now: $1/1.21 = $0.83. And a dollar 20 years from now is worth $1/6.73 = $0.15 today when the interest rate is 10 percent. In general, the value today, or the present value, of a payment to be received in the future is smaller the more distant the payment date.[9]

● The *present value* of a payment at any future date is the amount that would have to be invested today to produce exactly that payment on that date.

Table 18-4 shows how the level of the interest rate affects the relationships we have discussed. The higher the interest rate, the more rapidly the value of the initial investment grows. Compound interest works more

[9] Present value is sometimes called "present discounted value" to reflect the fact that the value of a payment to be received in the future is worth less today than it will be worth then.

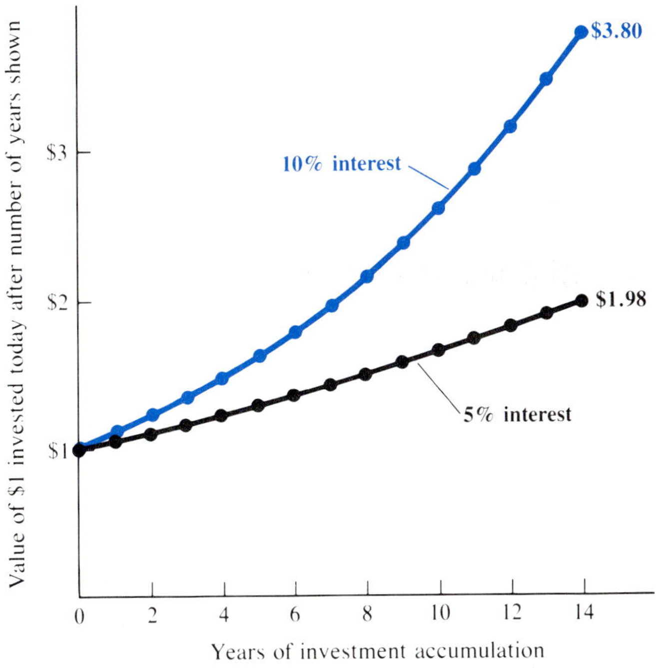

rapidly in our favor when interest rates are high. For instance, if the interest rate were 20 percent, our investment would increase nearly 40 times in 20 years. The other side of this coin is shown in the last row of the table. The present value of any future payment is higher at a 5 percent interest rate than it is when the interest rate is 10 percent. The reason for this is that to get $1 next year with only 5 percent interest, we have to invest $0.95 today rather than only $0.91. Therefore, we have to pay a higher price today to receive any given future payment the lower is the interest rate.

Figures 18-1 and 18-2 summarize the relationships we have discussed. For years 1 to 3, the points in Figures 18-1 and 18-2 correspond to the data in Table 18-4. Figure 18-1 compares the cumulative value of $1 invested at 10 percent with the cumulative value of $1 invested at 5 percent. This comparison shows that the higher the interest rate, the more rapidly a given investment grows. Figure 18-2 shows the present value of a $1 payment to be received in the future at these two interest rates. This figure shows that the present value is lower the more distant the payment date and the higher the rate of interest.

FIGURE 18-1. The Growth of Financial Capital through Compound Interest. The figure shows how $1 invested in year 0 grows in value over time if interest is reinvested. At an interest rate of 10 percent $1 grows to $3.80 after 14 years, but at an interest rate of 5 percent it grows to only $1.98.

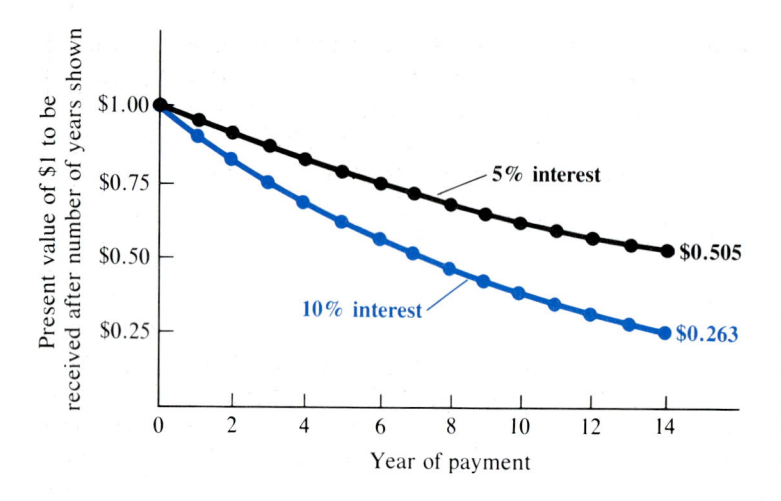

FIGURE 18-2. The Present Value of $1 to Be Received in the Future. The figure shows the amount that would have to be invested today in order to have $1 available at each date. This amount—the present value of $1 to be paid in the future—is lower the higher is the interest rate and the farther in the future is the date considered. To get $1 after 14 years, it is necessary to invest $0.505 today if the interest rate is 5 percent but only $0.263 if the interest rate is 10 percent.

Calculating the Value of an Asset

We can now state the basic principle that determines asset prices.

● **The price of any asset is equal to the present value of all present and future rental payments it will produce.**

Suppose that the Plush Limousine Service is thinking of buying a 1-year-old limousine that will yield a net rental (after deducting the costs of drivers, gasoline, and maintenance) of $4000 for 3 years and then can be sold for $10,000. With an interest rate of 10 percent, how much would Plush be willing to pay for this limo?

Table 18-5 presents the calculations that answer this question. The first two rows show receipts from rentals in each year and from the sale of the vehicle. The third row, taken from Table 18-4, shows the present value of $1 to be received in years 1, 2, and 3. The fourth row shows the present value of the receipts in each future year. For example, in year 1 we have $3640 (= $4000 × 0.91). This process is called *discounting* future payments; they are reduced to reflect the fact that payments are less valuable the farther in the future they will occur. The sum of the present values of each of the future payments plus the present value of the resale price is equal to the asset price. In our example, the asset price is $17,460; this is the maximum amount Plush would pay for the limousine.

Figure 18-2 implies that Plush would be willing to pay more for the limo if the interest rate were lower and less if it were higher. To see why, think of Plush borrowing in order to buy the limo. If it has to pay 10 percent interest rather than 5 percent, then more of its earnings go to pay the bank—and it will not come out at least even unless it pays less for the car.

In this example there is an actual rental market; Plush rents out its limos to people who like to travel in style. What about a firm considering the purchase of a machine to use itself rather than to rent to others? In this case there are no explicit rental receipts. In place of such receipts, the firm must use the increase in its revenues that the machine would produce, or its *marginal revenue product* as defined in Chapter 15. It is as if the firm

TABLE 18-5. A Present-Value Calculation

	Year 1	Year 2	Year 3	Asset price (= sum of all present values)
Rental receipts	$4000	$4000	$4000	
Resale value			$10,000	
Present value of $1 to be received in year*	$0.91	$0.83	$0.75	
Present value of receipts in year	$3640	$3320	$3000 + $7500	$17,460

* From Table 18-4; interest rate = 10 percent.

had two divisions; one buys durable inputs and rents them to the other, which in turn uses their services to produce output.

Plush is considering a relatively short-lived investment. What about a long-lived asset, such as a house or a piece of land? The calculations are the same, except that a house may yield services for 50 years or more, and land lasts forever. This suggests that computing the asset price of a house is difficult and computing the asset price of land is impossible.

However, as shown in the appendix to Chapter 17, there is a simple and useful formula for assets—called *perpetuities*—that yield a constant income per year forever. The present value of *all* future payments in this case is equal to the (constant) annual payment divided by the interest rate (expressed as a fraction).

$$\frac{\text{Present value}}{\text{of a perpetuity}} = \frac{\text{annual payment}}{\text{interest rate}} \qquad (1)$$

Thus an asset that yields $100 forever, with an interest rate of 10 percent, is worth $1000 ($100/0.1). If the interest rate were only 5 percent, the asset would be worth $2000 ($100/0.05).

We can understand equation (1) by manipulating it slightly to become

$$\text{Interest rate} = \frac{\text{annual payment}}{\text{present value of perpetuity}} \qquad (1a)$$

Suppose now that a perpetuity costs $100 and that the annual payment to its owner is $10. Then the interest rate earned on the perpetuity must be 10 percent. Or if the annual payment is $5, the interest rate must be 5 percent.

Equation (1) is exactly correct only for perpetuities, and they are rare.[10] But it yields a good approximation for assets with long, though finite, lives. It also indicates that the level of the current market interest rate has a very strong effect on the prices of long-lived assets such as houses and land. To understand why, think of a person borrowing to buy the asset. If the interest rate rises, the borrowing cost is higher and the borrower can afford to pay less for the asset. If the interest rate rises from 5 percent to 10 percent, the asset price of a perpetuity is cut by one-half. And—to show that equation (1) is a good approximation even for assets that merely have long but finite lives—the price of an asset yielding $100 each year for 50 years falls by 46 percent.

Real and Nominal Interest Rates

In order to complete our discussion of present value and asset price determination, we must deal with inflation. Most people would argue that one reason why a dollar next year is worth less than a dollar today is that prices are likely to be higher in the future, so that a dollar next year will buy fewer goods and services than a dollar today can. How should this be handled in computing present values?

In all the calculations we have made of present value, all the payments in this year and in future years were given in dollars. The interest rate we used was also expressed in dollars. When we say that the interest rate on bank deposits is 10 percent, we mean that next year we will receive 10 cents in interest for every dollar kept in the bank account for a year.

● **The interest rate expressed in terms of the increase in the dollar value of an investment is the *nominal* interest rate.**

The nominal interest rate tells us how much more in dollars we will have in the future if we invest dollars today. But we are usually more interested in what present and future dollars will buy—and thus more interested in the real interest rate than in the nominal interest rate.

● **The *real* interest rate measures the return on an investment in terms of the increase in the amount of goods and services that can be bought.**

Real and nominal interest rates differ substantially when there is rapid inflation. Suppose that the nominal interest rate is 10 percent but that prices will rise by 10 percent over the next year. Then a dollar invested today will become $1.10 in a year, but that $1.10 will buy exactly what $1 would buy today. The real interest rate is thus zero: After investing a dollar for a year, the investor

---

[10] The British government issues consols, which are perpetuities, promising to pay a given amount of pounds per year forever. The Canadian government also issued consols in the past.

can buy no more goods a year from now than she could have if she'd spent the dollar today. As this example suggests, the real interest rate can be quickly and reasonably accurately calculated as follows:

$$\frac{\text{Real}}{\text{interest rate}} = \frac{\text{Nominal}}{\text{interest rate}} - \text{inflation rate} \quad (2)$$

Rates of inflation cannot, of course, be precisely predicted in advance. If you lend money to the Plush Limousine Service at a 10 percent nominal rate of interest, the real rate of interest you will receive is uncertain. In deciding in advance whether to make the loan, you would use equation (2) to compute the *expected real rate* by subtracting the inflation you expect over the next year from the nominal interest rate. On the other hand, in deciding after the loan is repaid whether the investment was profitable, you would use equation (2) to compute the *actual real rate* by subtracting the actual inflation rate from the nominal interest rate. The difference between the expected real rate and the actual real rate is equal to the mistake you made in predicting inflation.[11]

Table 18-6 shows the nominal and actual real interest rates on high-quality corporate bonds in the United States over time. Until the early 1980s, actual real rates in the United States were quite low, on the order of 1 or 2 percent. Actual real rates were especially low in the 1951–1955 and 1971–1975 periods, mainly because rates of inflation exceeded expectations.[12] The inflation rate fell sharply in the early 1980s, and people probably overpredicted inflation. That is one reason for the high actual real rates in 1981–1985.

Why learn about the distinction between the real interest rate and the nominal interest rate? One reason is that in inflationary times, such as the 1970s in the United States, we can easily get a very wrong idea of the costs of borrowing if we look at the nominal interest rate. A nominal interest rate of 20 percent seems to be extremely high. But if the inflation rate is expected to be 19.5 percent, borrowing is in fact cheap. Similarly, anyone who thinks that he has a great deal if he can save at 20 percent when the inflation rate is likely to be 19.5 percent is making a big mistake, for after saving for a year he will hardly come out ahead. If the inflation rate is higher than expected, he may be worse off in real terms. For long periods in the 1970s many people were keeping their money in savings accounts at 5.25 percent per year and losing in real terms year after year as the inflation rate exceeded the nominal interest rate.

A second, related reason for learning about the difference between nominal and real rates of interest is that it is important to handle inflation consistently when calculating present values. So long as all payments are specified in dollars, a nominal interest rate can be used. But if future payments are expressed not in dollars of the future years but rather in *real terms* (that is, in terms of the purchasing power of this year's dollars), then a real interest rate must be used for the calculation.

Why Are Real Interest Rates Positive?

Why are borrowers willing to pay interest? There are two basic forces at work, one each on the supply and demand sides of the market for loans.

On the supply side, lenders are generally unwilling to lend funds that they could spend today unless they are compensated for postponing their spending until the

---

[11] If this makes you very nervous, of course, you could ask Plush to agree to pay you a fixed real rate of interest. The nominal rate of interest would then be approximately equal, from equation (2), to the agreed-upon real rate plus the actual inflation rate. Loans of this sort are relatively rare in the United States, but they are made in countries with high rates of inflation.

TABLE 18-6. Nominal and Actual Real Interest Rates on High-Quality Corporate Bonds in the United States

	Average interest rate, %	
Period	Nominal	Actual real
1951–1955	3.0	0.6
1956–1960	4.0	1.6
1961–1965	4.4	2.3
1966–1970	6.4	1.6
1971–1975	7.9	0.6
1976–1980	9.3	1.3
1981–1985	12.8	7.5

Source: *Economic Report of the President, 1986*, pp. 256 and 332.

[12] The high inflation associated with the Korean war was the culprit in the first period, and the inflation resulting from OPEC's increase in the price of oil was the big surprise in the second period.

loan is repaid. This means that the quantity of loans supplied will not be positive unless the price—the real interest rate—is also positive. On the demand side, borrowers are willing to pay interest to lenders because they expect to still come out ahead after paying the interest. Investment in physical capital is usually sufficiently productive to yield a profit even after paying back interest. These two important forces behind a positive real interest rate are summarized as impatience on the lenders' side and the productivity of capital on the borrowers' side.

3. Land Rents and Land Prices

In the remainder of this chapter we apply the general principles developed in section 2 to the analysis of supply and demand in the markets for land and capital. Since land and capital are factors of production, the demand for their services is a derived demand. We thus also employ the general principles of the derived demand for productive inputs developed in Chapter 15.

We begin in this section with the market for land. Since land is in essentially fixed supply[13] to the economy as a whole, the supply side of the land market is simpler than the supply side of the market for capital. The basic questions deal with what determines the rental rate on land and what determines the price of land.

Land Services

Figure 18-3 depicts the market for the *services* (or the use) of land. The supply of land—and thus the supply of land services—is perfectly inelastic, so the supply curve, ST, is vertical. The demand curve, DT, shows the derived demand for the services of land.[14] As we discussed in Chapter 15, the position and shape of this curve depend on the technologies of the industries that use land, the amounts of other inputs they employ, and the demands for their outputs.

---

[13] Why "essentially"? Because the quantity of land can be changed a bit through reclamation of land from the sea.
[14] Since both "land" and "labor" begin with an "l," it is standard to avoid confusion by using "t" (for "terra") to denote land.

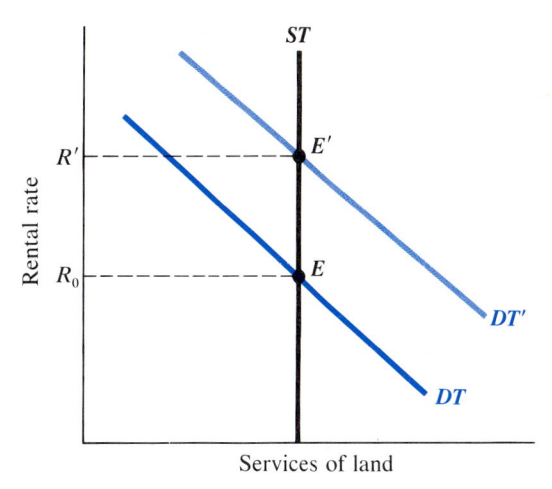

FIGURE 18-3. The Market for the Services of Land. The supply of land to the economy is fixed, as shown by the supply curve ST. The demand curve for land services, DT, is derived from the curves showing the marginal value product of land for individual firms. If the prices of agricultural products increase, the marginal *revenue* product of land rises for every firm. This is shown as a shift in the demand curve for land from DT to DT', and it produces a rise in the rental rate for land from R_0 to R'.

In particular, an increase in the demand for agricultural products will increase the marginal *revenue* product of land, which is equal to the marginal physical product of land times the price of output, and thus raise the quantity of land demanded at any given rental rate.

What happens to the *rental rate* for the services of land when the demand for farm products rises? The resulting increase in the demand for land services is shown as an upward shift in the demand curve to DT'. The rental rate per acre of land must increase from R_0 to R' so as to make the quantity demanded equal to the (fixed) quantity supplied. The rent is higher because the demand for agricultural products has risen.

Land Prices

What happens to the *prices* of individual parcels of land when the demand for farm products rises? We just saw that rental rates for land services increase. Since the price that anyone would be willing to pay for a given piece of land is equal to the present value of all future rental receipts the land will yield, it follows that land prices rise also. Since land lasts forever, equation (2) permits us to be a bit more specific: If the interest rate does not change, the percentage increase in land prices is exactly equal to the percentage increase in annual rentals. If rents double, so do land prices.

For a farmer who owns his own land and has no intention of leaving farming or expanding his acreage, none of this is visible; increasing land rents and land values do not affect his actual, out-of-pocket costs. Of course, he is earning more because the price of farm produce has risen. But now consider the economic position of the farmer who does not own but rather rents the land she works. She finds that the price of her output is higher, but at the same time the rent she has to pay has risen. Even though the demand for what she grows has risen and her output fetches a higher price, she may be no better off. She may well complain that the rent increase is making it impossible to earn a decent living by farming.

What accounts for the difference? Think of the farmer who owns his own land as being in two businesses: land ownership and farming. If his land business charges his farming business the going market rate for land services, his farming business will earn zero economic profits on average, since farming is a perfectly competitive industry. When the demand for farm products goes up, however, his land ownership business makes a profit because the value of its asset—land—rises.

Rents in General

Because land is traditionally thought of as *the* asset in fixed supply, the word "rent" is often used to describe the return to any factor that earns a return by virtue of being in limited supply.[15] Equivalently,

● **A factor earns a *rent* when it is paid more than the minimum amount needed to induce it to supply the given level of services.**

For instance, we say that opera singers and baseball players earn rents on their abilities. The baseball player receiving $2 million per year would happily play for $50,000 if that was the going price. The last $1,950,000 is a rent, which he obtains because the supply of players of his quality is inelastic.

The demand for the services of a baseball player is a derived demand, based on the revenue he generates for the club for which he is playing. Thus, as we saw in Chapter 16, when we are told that baseball tickets cost a lot because of the high salaries that have to be paid to baseball players, we should think again. Baseball salaries are high because baseball players enable clubs to sell many high-priced tickets.

Similarly, when there is an increase in the demand for food and food prices and agricultural land rents rise together, the land rents rise because food prices have risen. The food prices have not risen because the land rents are higher.

Often people buy land because they expect its price to go up, not because they expect to earn a profit by working the land or renting it out. They are speculating about what somebody else will be willing to pay for the land in the future. That potential buyer, in turn, or some buyer somewhere in the chain, will have to consider what renters of the land are willing to pay to use the land. Ultimately, the fundamental factor underlying the price of land is the amount people will be willing to pay to use the land in the future: The price of land is determined by the rentals that owners of land expect to receive.[16]

4. The Supply of Capital Services

We now shift our attention to capital. The demand sides of the markets for capital services and capital assets closely resemble the demand sides of the markets for land services and land that we just analyzed. But the supply of capital services is not fixed—new capital goods are produced every day. Accordingly, we begin in this section by analyzing the supply of capital services—

---

[15] This point was also discussed in Chapter 16.

[16] Is it possible for a long chain like this to keep going, with each person selling to someone else who has no intention of using the land, but only selling it to someone willing to pay more in the future, and so forth? In principle, yes, but only for a while. Speculative bubbles like this eventually burst when land prices become far out of line with expected future rentals.

asking, for instance, what determines the number of cars available for rent at each level of the rental rate. We then consider equilibrium in the market for capital services and, in section 6, in the market for capital assets.

Throughout this section and section 5 we talk about the supply of and the demand for the *services* of capital to emphasize that the analysis is about the *use* of capital, such as machines and buildings, independent of who owns the capital. Someone renting the services of a truck needs to use the truck itself in production, but he does not need to own it. But keep in the back of your mind the fact that most capital is acquired by firms that in effect rent it to themselves—just like a farmer who owns the land she uses.

Short-Run Supply

In the short run the total amount of physical capital in the economy is fixed. There are a given number of machines of each type, buildings, and stocks of raw materials. From the viewpoint of the economy as a whole, the short-run supply of capital services is thus perfectly inelastic.

But an individual industry may be able to vary the quantity of capital services it employs even in the short run. For instance, the quantity of services of trucks supplied to a particular industry can be changed in the short run by moving in trucks from other industries. For more specialized machinery such as blast furnaces, the quantity of services to an industry may be fixed in the short run. There are a given number of blast furnaces at any instant, and it takes a long time to build more.

Figure 18-4 shows the two possible types of supply curves for the services of capital for an industry in the short run. If the industry uses only specialized machinery, then the quantity of services supplied is constant in the short run, and supply curve S applies. The currently employed capital will be supplied to this industry no matter what the rental rate is, because it has nowhere else to go. If some of the capital used by the industry is not specialized and can be readily shifted from one industry to another, then the short-run supply curve for capital services will be upward-sloping, like S'.

Costs and Long-Run Supply

In the long run the total quantity of capital in the economy can be adjusted. New machines and factories can be built to increase the capital stock, and machinery can be allowed to deteriorate or fall out of use to decrease the capital stock. Not only can the total stock of capital be changed; so, too, can the amounts of services of capital supplied to particular industries. In the long run it does not matter that an industry uses very specialized machinery, since new machinery of that type can be built or the existing machinery can be allowed to deteriorate.

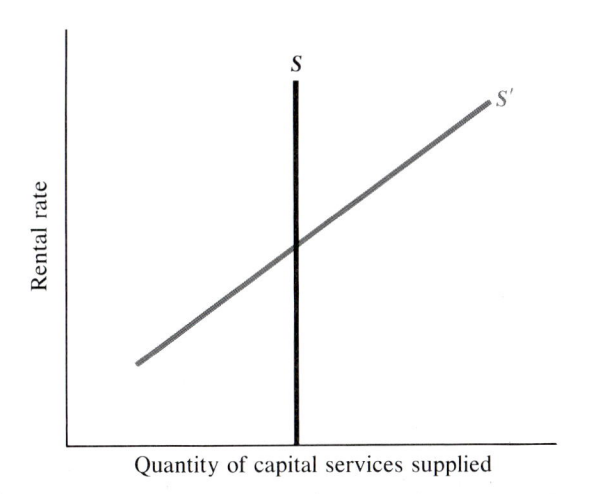

FIGURE 18-4. The Short-Run Supply of Capital Services to an Industry. If all the capital assets used by an industry can be used nowhere else, then the supply of capital services to the industry, as to the economy as a whole, is perfectly inelastic. This is shown by supply curve S. If some of the assets are not specialized and can be moved from industry to industry in the short run (such as trucks and typewriters), new capital will be brought into the industry in response to higher rental rates. An upward-sloping supply curve such as S' describes this case.

REQUIRED RENTALS. People will not supply wheat, basketballs, or socks in the long run if they cannot cover their total costs. The same principle governs the long-run supply of capital services.

● The *required rental* on a capital asset is the rental rate that allows the asset's owner to just cover the opportunity cost of owning the asset.

To understand the required rental, suppose you are considering borrowing $10,000 for a year to buy a new machine that you would rent to a business for 1 year and then sell. How much must you earn from that machine so as not to make a loss? Clearly you must at least cover the interest cost of the loan. Suppose the *real* interest rate is 5 percent. The real interest cost is then $500 ($10,000 × 0.05).

But interest is not the only cost you face. The real asset price at the end of the year will be less than $10,000 because the machine depreciates.

● ***Depreciation*** **is the reduction in value of a machine that occurs as a result of use and/or the passage of time.**[17]

Suppose the machine will be sold for $9000 at the end of the year. Then depreciation is $1000; in other words, the *depreciation rate*, (the ratio of depreciation to the value of the investment) is 10 percent.

Thus your annual costs for renting out a new machine in working condition are calculated as follows:[18]

$$\begin{aligned} \text{Annual cost} &= \text{interest cost} + \text{depreciation cost} \\ &= \text{value of investment} \\ &\quad \times (\text{interest rate} + \text{depreciation rate}) \\ &= \$10{,}000 \times (0.05 + 0.10) \\ &= \$1500 \end{aligned} \quad (3)$$

This annual cost is exactly the required rental that must be charged for the use of this machine if you are not to make a loss.[19] If you are considering using this machine yourself, it must increase your revenues by at least its annual cost or you shouldn't buy it.

---

[17] Economists define depreciation as the change in the asset price, that is, the change in the present value of the stream of services the asset will provide. Accountants use a variety of rules for calculating depreciation. As a result, economic depreciation only rarely equals accounting depreciation.

[18] This calculation does not take into account the maintenance that must be carried out during the year to keep the machine in working order. It is customary to deduct maintenance and other cash expenses from rental receipts rather than add them to the cost of capital services. (This is what we did in the example of the Plush Limousine Service in section 2.)

[19] Tax policy has important effects on the required rental for capital, which are studied in courses on taxation and corporate finance.

If the rental rate on a particular type of machine exceeds the required rental, it will be profitable to increase the quantity supplied of services of that type of machine. If an asset earns less than its required rental, it will not be maintained or replaced, and there will be a long-run reduction in the quantity of capital services supplied.

Equation (3) shows that the required rental rate, which is the cost of supplying capital services, is determined by three factors: the *price* of the capital good (the cost of the investment), the *real interest rate*, and the *rate of depreciation*. These are the three factors that determine the quantity of capital services supplied in the long run at each rental rate.

RATES OF RETURN. Practical investors often talk of rates of return rather than rental rates.

● **The *rate of return* on an investment is the profit from that investment, computed ignoring the interest paid to finance the investment, expressed as a percentage of the cost of the investment.**

For instance, suppose a machine costs $10,000 and is sold for $9000 at the end of the year and that the owner can rent out the machine for $2100 for the year. The profit for the year is $1100, or the rental of $2100 minus the depreciation of $1000. The machine costs $10,000. The actual rate of return—profits as a percentage of the cost of the investment—is 11 percent [= (1100/10,000) × 100 percent].

The required rate of return is the rate of return an investor has to earn to make a project worthwhile. This is just the rate at which the investor can borrow to finance the project. If the investor makes at least as high a rate of return as the cost of borrowing, then he comes out ahead and is willing to undertake the investment.

Required rates of return can be compared after the fact with the actual or realized rate of return on an investment. They are thus useful pieces of information for investors. If the required rate of return on one project is 7 percent and the investor expects to make 10 percent, she is likely to make the investment. If on another project the expected return is 12 percent and the required return is 13 percent, the investor will not undertake it.

Why would the required return be higher on one

project than on another? This is largely a matter of the riskiness of the project: The riskier the payoff, the higher the required rate of return. We bring risk and uncertainty into the analysis in Chapter 19.

The Long-Run Supply of Capital to the Economy

In the long run any given amount of capital services is supplied to the economy only if it earns the required rental. If it earns more than that, people go out to build more capital. If it earns less than the required rental, owners of capital let their assets deteriorate and go out of use. Thus the long-run supply curve of capital services shows the required rental on capital at each level of capital services supplied.

In Figure 18-5 we show two possible long-run supply curves for capital services. In the figure, we take the real interest rate and the depreciation rate as fixed. Thus only the third factor, the price of capital goods, affects the required rental. The perfectly elastic long-run supply curve, S'', is based on the assumption that the economy can produce as much physical capital as is demanded at a constant price. Then the required rental is constant in the long run, as equation (3) shows.

Supply curve S''' embodies the alternative assumption that the supply of capital services is not perfectly elastic, because capital is available only at a higher price as the quantity supplied increases. This means that the long-run supply curves of industries that produce capital assets, such as the construction industry, are upward-sloping. This seems to be a reasonable assumption. For instance, if construction were to increase by a large amount, it would be necessary to attract factors of production from other industries, thereby raising their prices and thus the price of output.

Accordingly, we assume that a long-run supply curve such as S''' applies at the level of the economy as a whole; more capital services will be supplied to the economy only at a higher price.

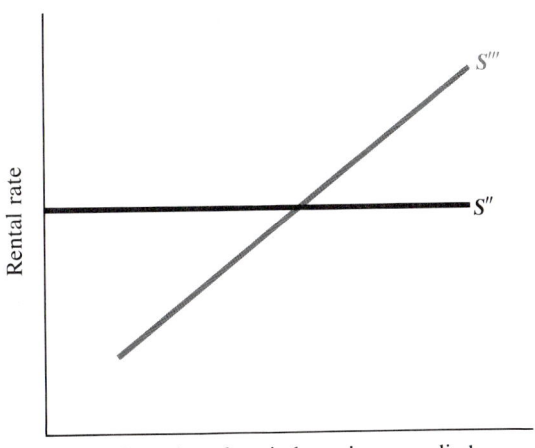

The Long-Run Supply to an Industry

We have exactly the same two possible supply curves for capital services for a single industry. If the industry is small relative to the economy as a whole, changes in its demand for capital services will not change the prices of the buildings and machinery it uses. Then the required rental will be constant, and the supply curve for capital services will be horizontal, S''. This is the case we shall assume in studying the market for capital services supplied to a single industry.

5. Equilibrium in the Market for Capital Services

In this section we show how the equilibrium rental rate on capital and the quantity of capital services used are determined by supply and demand in the market for capital services. We examined the supply side of the market in section 4; now we turn to demand.

Demand for Capital Services

As we saw in Chapter 15, a competitive firm will in the long run demand capital services up to the point where

FIGURE 18-5. The Long-Run Supply of Capital Services. The long-run supply curve of capital services describes the way the required rental rate changes as the amount of capital services supplied increases. We assume that the real interest rate and the depreciation rate are fixed, so that the required rental depends only on the price of capital goods. Then supply curve S'', which applies at the level of a single industry, implies that any amount of capital goods demanded will be supplied at a constant price. Supply curve S''', which applies to the economy as a whole, implies that the long-run supply curves of capital goods industries are upward-sloping.

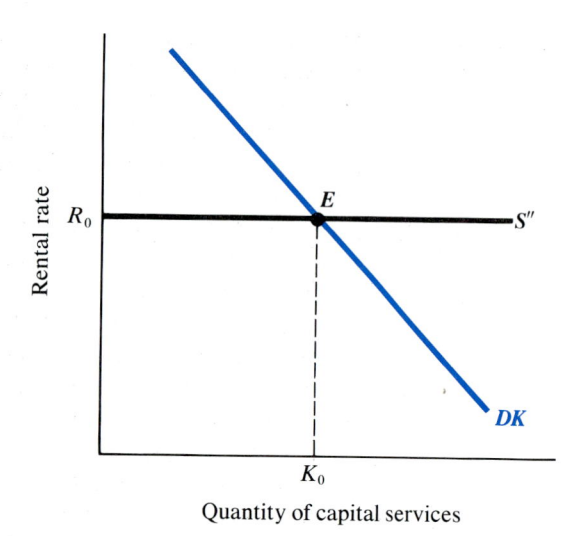

FIGURE 18-6. Long-Run Equilibrium in the Market for Capital Services. The long-run supply curve, S'', shows that any amount of capital services demanded will be supplied at a constant rental rate, R_0. The demand curve, DK, is derived from firms' marginal value product of capital schedules. Long-run equilibrium is at point E, with K_0 capital services used in production.

the marginal revenue product of those services equals their price, the rental rate. The marginal revenue product of capital services, and thus the demand for capital services, depends on the amount of capital employed, the price of the firm's output, and the amounts of other factors employed. Since the marginal revenue product of capital services is equal to the price of output times the marginal physical product of capital, an increase in the price of the firm's output increases its demand for capital services. The more labor employed in relation to capital, the higher the marginal physical product of an extra hour of capital services.[20] Therefore, an increase in the level of employment also raises the demand for capital services.

The industry's demand curve has the same general shape as the demand curve of each firm. Thus the industry's demand curve for capital services slopes downward, and it is shifted upward by an increase in the amount of the other factors being used by the firms in the industry. Finally, as Chapter 15 showed, an industry's demand curve for capital services will be more elastic the easier it is to substitute capital for labor and vice versa, the more elastic is the demand for the industry's output, and the more important is the cost of capital services relative to other costs.

Long-Run Equilibrium

Figure 18-6 illustrates long-run equilibrium in the market for capital services in a particular industry. For instance, this could be the demand for the use of truck services in the food industry. The market for capital services is in long-run equilibrium at point E. The demand curve, DK, shows the quantities of capital services demanded at various rental rates, and the quantities supplied in the long run are shown by S''. The equilibrium rental rate is R_0. Corresponding to that rental rate, amount K_0 of capital services is used in the industry. The quantity of services, K_0, is the amount such that capital in this industry earns precisely R_0, the rental required if the capital is to stay in the industry.

Short-Run Adjustment

To see how the market for capital services operates in the short run, let us consider the effects of an increase in wages on the amount of capital used in an industry and on the rental rate. Suppose the wage for truck drivers has risen because the union has succeeded in getting a high wage settlement. We first have to ask what the increase in wages does to the demand curve for truck services.

An increase in wages has two effects on the quantity of capital services demanded at any particular rental rate. First, because the cost of using labor has risen, the industry's supply curve of goods shifts to the left. This means that total industry output will fall because the product has become more expensive. The *cost effect* implies a reduction in output and therefore a reduction in the demand for capital services. But second, because the services of capital are now cheaper in relation to the services of labor, the firm will use more capital-intensive ways of producing output. This *substitution effect* tends to raise the demand for capital. The more elastic the

---

[20] Why? Because each unit of capital services has more workers to use it and is therefore more productive.

demand for the industry's output, the more output will fall as price increases, and the more important is the cost effect. On the other hand, the more substitutable capital and labor are, the more important is the substitution effect. Either effect may dominate in theory.

Consider the example of the increased wages of truck drivers. Firms may react by increasing the ratio of capital to labor by using larger trucks (there is more truck per driver). This substitution effect increases the demand for the services of capital (trucks). But because the cost of getting food to market has risen, the price of food rises and the quantity of food demanded falls. This cost effect reduces the demand for truck services.

Figure 18-7 shows the case where the cost effect dominates, leading to a fall in the quantity of capital services demanded at every rental rate. Given the downward shift of the demand curve for capital services from DK to DK', what happens to the rental and the quantity of capital services employed? In the short run, we assume that the quantity of capital services supplied is fixed, so that the supply curve of capital services is vertical at level K_0, as shown by the curve labeled S. The shift in demand for capital services thus moves the industry to point E' from point E. The rental rate for capital services in the industry falls substantially, from R_0 to R'.

The rise in wages thus is achieved in part at the expense of consumers, who pay more for the final good, and in part at the expense of the owners of the capital used by this industry, who receive less for the services of their capital. Since most capital is owned by the firms that use it, this generally means that firms' profits decline in the short run when the cost of labor rises. The actual rate of return on capital in this industry falls below the required rate of return.

Adjustment in the Long Run

Because payments for capital services do not cover the costs of supplying those services in the short-run equilibrium illustrated in Figure 18-7, the firms supplying capital services to this industry no longer find it worthwhile to keep up the capital stock in the face of wear and tear. They do not replace existing capital as it wears out. As the quantity of capital services supplied is reduced, the rental rate rises. Over time the equilibrium point moves up the DK' curve with a rising rental rate and declining use of capital services, as shown by the arrows along that curve. The long-run equilibrium is at point E'', where the suppliers of capital services again receive (just) the required rental rate.

When the supply of capital services to the industry is completely elastic, as on supply curve S'', the industry's long-run adjustment in the market for capital services is accomplished entirely through a change in the quantity of services employed.

These conclusions, it should be emphasized, would be the same if we were talking about labor or any other factor. If a factor can easily be shifted to other industries, its long-run earnings will not be affected by demand conditions in a specific industry. Earnings will change only in the short run—for as long as it takes the factor to

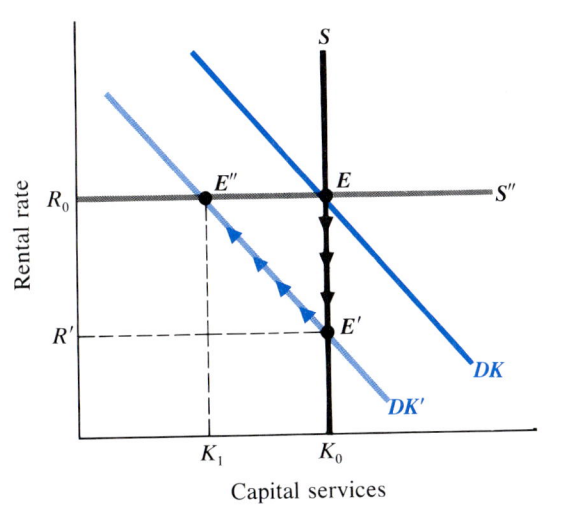

FIGURE 18-7. The Impact of a Rise in Wages on the Market for Capital Services. An industry is initially in long-run equilibrium at point E. An increase in wages reduces the marginal revenue product of capital at all levels of capital services; this is shown as a downward shift in the demand curve for capital services from DK to DK'. the short-run supply curve is S, since capital is fixed in the short run. Thus in the short run the actual rental rate falls R_0, the required rental rate, to R'. Because actual rentals are below required rentals, capital leaves the industry in the long run, and the industry moves along the DK' curve from point E' to point E'', the new long-run equilibrium. Capital services fall from K_0 to K_1 in the long run.

move out when demand for its services falls or move in when demand rises.

RENTS AND QUASI RENTS. The earnings of capital assets are often called *quasi rents*. This term serves to emphasize the difference between the short run and the long run in the market for capital services. In the short run, if the supply of capital services to an industry is inelastic, payments for those services are like rents to land. In this case, capital, like land, will continue to be supplied in the short run even if rentals fall to nearly zero; firms will continue to produce as long as their variable costs are covered. In the short run under competition, high profits, like high land rentals, are the result of high prices, not the cause.

But the "quasi" in "quasi rents" reminds us that in the long run capital and land are very different. If the earnings of capital are below the required rate of return, the quantity of capital supplied will be reduced in the long run, while the long-run supply of land is perfectly inelastic. In the long run under competition, profit rates are equal to the required rate of return on capital.

Capital and Rates of Return in the U.S. Economy

We saw in Table 18-2 that tangible assets per worker in the U.S. economy almost doubled over the 1950–1985 period. Over that same period the ratio of wages per worker to rentals per unit of land and capital more than doubled.[21] A number of studies have found that the rate of return on capital assets in the U.S. economy has been relatively stable over time. Pretax rates of return have generally been a bit above 10 percent; returns after payment of corporate income taxes have generally been between 6 and 8 percent. Thus the rise in the wage-rental ratio mainly reflects the general rise in real wage rates over time.

[21] *Technical footnote*: There is no published series for the wage-rental ratio. We approximated this ratio by multiplying tangible assets per worker by the ratio of labor income to nonlabor income. (Both ratios were taken from Table 18-2.) To see the idea behind these calculations, let r be rentals per unit of tangible assets, K the tangible assets used in production, w the wage rate, and L the amount of labor employed. Then tangible assets per worker is K/L, the ratio of labor to nonlabor income is wL/rK, and the product of these two quantities is w/r. Alternative estimation methods yield broadly similar results.

Box 18-1. Taxation of Rents and Profits

The American economist Henry George (1839–1897) argued that the government should raise all its revenues by taxing rents on land. The case for such a policy in regard to economic efficiency is as follows. Since land is in perfectly inelastic supply, taxing land rents will not restrict the supply of land services to the economy as a whole. The only effect will be to lower the price received for those services by landowners. But this means that the tax would produce no net loss for the economy; money would simply be transferred from landlords to the government. (Recall the analysis of who pays a tax in Chapter 4.)

No government has ever adopted George's proposal. Why not? First, as we noted at the start of the chapter, it is difficult to separate land from capital. It is probably impossible to devise a tax that affects only land rents. Second, land rents are just not important enough in modern economies. Even if the government received all the land rents in the U.S. economy, it would not come close to balancing its budget.

Third, there is an implication that rents perform no function in an economy. But differences in rents do attract land into different uses. If all rents had to be paid as taxes, differential rents would give landowners no incentive to find the best use for their land.

What about taxing profits instead? A tax on *economic* profits would have many of the desirable features of George's proposal. Suppose the government took 50 percent of economic profits. Then if any decision increased before-tax profits, it would also increase after-tax profits. A tax on economic profits, like a tax on land rents, would produce no net loss for the economy as a whole, since it would not change any decisions regarding resource use.

Many countries, including the United States, have taxes on profits—but they are taxes on accounting profits, not economic profits. If the government takes 50 percent of rental payments for capital services, the owner of a capital asset must receive twice as much before tax in order to earn the required rental after paying taxes. In the short run, since the supply of capital is perfectly inelastic to the economy as a whole, a tax on accounting profits has no effect on the supply of capital services. But in the long run it can have important effects on the supply of services—and thus on the allocation of resources.

The increase in both tangible assets per worker and the wage-rental ratio is typical of economies in the course of long-term growth. This pattern can be interpreted as follows. Over time the economy has increased its capital stock at a rate faster than the growth in the labor force. Therefore, the economywide capital-labor ratio has increased. The increase in the economywide capital-labor ratio in turn, in combination with technological improvements, has raised the productivity of labor, and thus the wage rate has risen relative to the rental rate for capital services.

6. The Price of Capital Assets

So far we have taken the prices of machines and other capital assets as given. It is now time to ask what determines the prices at which different types of capital goods are sold. We are concerned here with the *asset price* rather than the rental price of capital—the price of a house or a truck or a machine rather than the cost of using or renting it.

The value of any asset to its current owner or any potential buyer is equal, as we saw in section 2, to the present discounted value of the future returns it will yield. The first step in calculating the present value of a piece of machinery or a building is to work out how much revenue it brings in each year (in the form of either rentals or increases in output) and to subtract maintenance expenses and any other costs of ownership. This gives the amount the asset returns to the owner each year. Then, to obtain the value of the asset and the price at which it will sell, we use the methods presented in section 2 to calculate the present discounted value of the stream of returns.

The present discounted value of the stream of rentals on an asset—and thus the price of the asset—can change for two reasons. First, the interest rate at which those future rentals are discounted may change. An increase in the real interest rate reduces the present value of future payments—and thus reduces the value of the asset.

Second, the future rentals may change. Suppose, for instance, that the wage in the shoe-making industry rises because there has been a general increase in wages in the economy. Suppose also that, as in Figure 18-7, the wage increase reduces the demand for capital services in the industry. As a result, the rental rate for capital shoe making falls in the short run.

The fall in the rental rate in turn causes a corresponding fall in the asset price of capital used to make shoes. Whoever owns the capital will now get a lower price for it, because for some time it will not generate much income for the owner. Shoe-making machinery becomes less valuable. If a corporation owns the capital it uses, the corporation becomes less valuable to its owners, and the value of its stock falls.

But capital goods are produced; there is a supply side to the market for capital assets. So long as used machines are available for less than it costs to build a new machine, no one in the industry will buy new machines to replace those wearing out.[22] As the old machines wear out, less capital is being used in production, and the rental rate on capital begins to rise toward the required rental rate. New machines begin to be ordered, and eventually the asset price of the machines in use in the industry will rise to the long-run equilibrium levels.

In long-run equilibrium, the price of any capital asset (a machine or a building) must be equal to the cost at which the good can be produced. If the asset price were above the cost at which the machine or building could be produced, then more of the capital good would be produced. Builders would increase the number of houses built, and firms would make more machines. If the asset price were less than the cost at which the equipment could be produced—as was the case with the shoe-making machinery discussed in this section—then the existing capital would be left to wear out, and the result would be a smaller capital stock.

Thus, because capital moves into (or out of) an industry when rentals exceed (or fall short of) the required rental, the price of a capital asset in long-run equilibrium is equal to both the cost of producing the asset *and* the present discounted value of the rentals received by the owner of the asset. Because land cannot be produced, only the second of these conditions holds in the market for land.

---

[22] Because new machines generally incorporate improvements, it will not literally be the case that no new machines will be built until the old ones wear out. Rather, there will be a fall in demand for new machines while the old ones are available at a low price.

■ In this chapter we have generally neglected the effects of uncertainty. This has permitted us to focus on the implications of the durability of capital and land and on the role of time and interest rates in linking markets for services and markets for assets. The assumption of perfect certainty which we have made here is, like the assumption of perfect competition, both useful and almost never exactly correct. In order to understand fully how investors decide whether to buy or to build long-lived capital assets and many other aspects of economic life, it is necessary to take into account the effects of uncertainty. Chapter 19 analyzes those effects.

Summary

1. Physical capital falls into four broad categories: consumer durables, plant and equipment, residential structures, and inventories. Physical capital and land together make up tangible wealth. Tangible wealth yields a flow of services that is useful in production and in consumption.
2. The role of tangible wealth in the U.S. economy is described by three numbers. In 1985 the ratio of tangible wealth to national income was about 3, the share of the national income going to the owners of tangible wealth used in production was about one-quarter, and the value of production capital per worker was about $35,000.
3. A rental rate is the rate paid for the use of land or capital. The rental rates for capital and land are determined by the supply and demand for their services. Demand for the services of capital and land, like the demand for labor, is a derived demand. The asset price of a parcel of land or a capital good is the price that must be paid to buy (as opposed to rent) the asset.
4. Factors of production earn *rents* when they receive more than the minimum amount needed to induce them to supply their services. Rents are earned by factors in fixed supply, such as land. Factors, for example capital, earn quasi rents when they are in fixed supply for the short run, but the quasi rents disappear as the quantity of factors employed is adjusted.
5. Present-value calculations allow us to translate receipts accruing in future time periods into current values. Because investments earn interest, a dollar to be received tomorrow is worth less today than a dollar in hand today. The higher the rate of interest, the smaller the present value of a dollar tomorrow.
6. The present value of a perpetuity is equal to the ratio of the annual rental to the rate of interest.
7. The nominal interest rate indicates how much more *money* will be received (or paid) in the future as a result of saving (or borrowing). The real, or inflation-adjusted, interest rate is a measure of the extra *goods and services* that can be bought as a result of saving. The real interest rate is approximately equal to the nominal interest rate minus the inflation rate.
8. The supply of land to the economy as a whole is fixed in both the short run and the long run. The price of land in both the short run and the long run is equal to the present value of the services it will provide in the future.
9. In the short run, the quantity of capital services supplied to the economy as a whole is fixed and the supply to particular industries is inelastic. In the long run, the supply of capital to the economy as a whole and to individual industries is highly elastic.
10. The required rental on a capital asset is the opportunity cost of operating that piece of capital. It is greater the higher the price of the capital asset, the higher the real interest rate, and the higher the depreciation rate. In long-run equilibrium in the market for capital services, the actual rental equals the required rental.
11. The rate of return on a capital asset is equal to profits made from owning and renting out that asset (ignoring the cost of borrowing to finance the purchase of the asset) expressed as a percentage of the purchase price. The required rate of return is equal to the cost of borrowing for the firm. In long-run equilibrium, actual rates of return equal required rates of return. A rise in the wage rate raises the marginal cost of production and therefore reduces equilibrium output. This cost effect reduces the employment of both capital and labor. But there is also a substitution effect that raises the demand for capital; an increase in the wage rate makes it profitable to substitute capital for labor. The cost effect is stronger the more important is capital relative to other inputs and the more elastic is the demand for the final product. The substitution effect is stronger the easier it is to substitute capital for labor.
12. In long-run equilibrium, the price of capital assets will be equal to the cost at which they can be produced. This will also be equal to the present discounted value of the rentals

they earn. In the case of land, which cannot be produced, the asset price is just equal to the present discounted value of all future rentals.

Key Terms

Physical capital
Financial capital
Tangible wealth
Financial wealth
Rental rate
Depreciation rate
Required rental rate
Required rate of return
Rent
Quasi rent
Asset price
Compound interest
Present (discounted) value
Perpetuity
Nominal interest rate
Real interest rate

Problems

1 Explain why rich countries tend to have a relatively large share of their capital stocks in the form of consumer durables. What is the value of your consumer durables? (To be consistent with the official data, don't count clothing or shoes.)

2 In the United States in 1985 the average member of the labor force cooperated with $35,000 worth of capital. Does this sound high or low? Can you think of three industries in which capital and land per worker are likely to be higher than average? Lower than average?

3 We count the stock of consumer durables—cars, TVs, washing machines, etc.—as part of the capital stock. But consumer durables do not generate any cash income for their owners. (*a*) Is it appropriate to regard them as part of the capital stock? (*b*) Consider an individual who is deciding whether to buy a washing machine or continue using a Laundromat. The cost of using the Laundromat is $3 per week. The washing machine costs $400, the interest rate is 10 percent, and other expenses of using the washing machine (including electricity and depreciation) amount to $2 per week. Does it make sense to buy the washing machine?

4 Using a calculator or computer, calculate the value in 1, 2, 3, and 20 years of $1 invested at compound interest when the rate of interest is 20 percent. Repeat the calculation for an interest rate of 2 percent. Use the results to construct the equivalent of Table 18-4.

5 A bank offers you $1.10 next year for every 90 cents invested today. What is the rate of interest implicit in the deal?

6 It is possible for a firm to purchase a machine for $10,000. The machine will increase the firm's revenues by $3600 for 2 years and can be sold at the end of the second year for $9000. Use the data in Table 18-5 to determine whether the machine is worth buying if the firm faces an interest rate of 10 percent.

7 Gasoline stations near the off ramps of interstate highways tend to charge higher prices than do stations located far from major roads. They also tend to occupy more expensive land. Which (the correct answer could be either, neither, or both) of the following is correct, and why? (*a*) Stations near interstates must charge higher prices in order to cover the rentals on their more expensive land. (*b*) Land rents near interstates are higher because gasoline stations located there can charge higher prices.

8 Discuss in detail how the following two events affect the rental rate and capital stock in an industry in the short run and in the long run. (*a*) The nominal interest rate increases from 5 percent to 10 percent while the expected inflation rate increases from 3 percent to 8 percent. (*b*) The nominal interest rate increases from 5 percent to 10 percent while the expected inflation rate remains at 3 percent.

9 In the short run the price and quantity of a good supplied by a perfectly competitive industry both increase, and the industry's profits also rise. (*a*) Explain why the increase in profits did not cause the rise in price. (*b*) Using supply and demand curves, explain what did cause the rise in price. (*c*) What is likely to happen to price and the rate of return on capital invested in the industry in the long run?

10 In what ways are the earnings of capital assets—quasi rents—like the earnings of land—rents? In what ways are they different?

11 In the text we asserted that in long-run equilibrium the present value of rentals on any capital asset must equal the cost of producing it. (*a*) Consider a machine for removing the fuzz from peaches that would cost $100,000 to build. It would yield rentals of $1000 per year forever, and the real interest rate is 10 percent. What is the asset price of the machine? (*b*) Will the machine be built? (*c*) Does the assertion in the text apply to all *conceivable* capital goods or only to those which are actually produced?

Chapter 19
Uncertainty in Economic Life

The only certainties, it is said, are death and taxes. But nobody knows when she will die—this is why there was $5.5 trillion in outstanding life insurance in the United States in 1984—or exactly how much tax she will owe in the future. Every action we take that affects the future has an uncertain outcome. When we add to a savings account, we do not know how much the money will buy when we want to use it, because the rate of inflation between now and then is uncertain. The value tomorrow of stocks bought today is uncertain, as are the economic returns from alternative possible majors in college. An oil company never knows for sure what—if anything—a new well will produce. Because land and capital derive their value from the returns they will generate in the future, the economics of capital, on which we focused in Chapter 18, and the economics of risk and uncertainty are closely linked.[1]

In this chapter we concentrate on two fundamental questions. First, how does the existence of uncertainty affect individuals' behavior? We answer in section 1 that people generally dislike risk, all else equal, and are willing to pay to avoid bearing it. This answer raises the second question: In a market economy, how is risk bearing allocated among individuals? We answer this question by examining the operation of three sets of markets that are critical to the allocation of risk in developed modern economies.

We begin in section 2 with insurance markets, which deal primarily and directly with risk. We discuss the central roles of *risk pooling* and *risk spreading* in the operation of these markets. We then turn to capital markets, which deal with both risk and (as we stressed in Chapter 18) time. Section 3 shows how the relation between rental payments and asset prices is modified when there is risk, describes the roles of risk pooling and risk spreading in capital markets, and considers whether the stock market mainly provides a place for rich people to gamble or plays an important role in guiding the allocation of resources in efficient directions. We conclude in section 4 with a discussion of the use of *hedging* to reduce risk in futures markets.

---

[1] In the discussion here, "risk" and "uncertainty" are synonymous, though a distinction is sometimes made between them in advanced analyses.

1. Individual Attitudes toward Risk

Economists describe attitudes toward risk by defining three types of consumers: those who are *risk-averse*, those who are *risk-neutral*, and those who are *risk lovers*. How are these types defined, and which is the most common?

Suppose we are tossing a fair coin, defined as one that has an even chance of coming up heads or tails. Suppose heads wins $1 and tails loses $1. Who would take the gamble? A risk-neutral person cares only about the average payoff. Since that is zero, he is indifferent between taking the bet and not taking it. If the payoffs were $1000 rather than $1, he would still be indifferent, since the average payoff would still be zero.

A risk lover, on the other hand, would prefer to take the bet since it provides risk, which he likes. He would be *more* eager to bet if the stakes were $1000 rather than $1, since the outcome would be riskier. In fact, he would still take the bet if heads payed $1000 but tails cost a bit more than $1000—so that the average payoff was negative—precisely *because* the outcome would be uncertain. A risk lover is willing to give up something in terms of average return for the pleasure of bearing risk.

Most people would rather not take the $1 bet, and they would be even more reluctant if the stakes were $1000 rather than $1. These people are risk-averse. A risk-averse person does not like to bear risk and will do so only if she is compensated. She will only take bets that are slanted in her favor. If heads pays $4, for instance, while tails costs $1, the expected payoff becomes $1.50 [= (1/2) × ($4) + (1/2) × (−$1)].[2] The outcome is still uncertain, but the average payoff is probably high enough to compensate most risk averters for the risk involved and thus to make the gamble attractive to them.

The usual assumption in economics is that most people are risk-averse. They will devote resources—by buying insurance, for instance—to reduce the risk they bear. And they will undertake risky ventures—such as the gambles we have been discussing—only if the average payoff is attractive enough to compensate them for bearing the risk involved. We will see these two principles in operation throughout the rest of this chapter.

But if this assumption is correct, why do people gamble? In 1983, for instance, state lotteries took in about $4.7 billion and paid only $2.4 billion in prizes. Thus the average payoff to a lottery ticket is well below its cost, *and* the payoff is uncertain. Why, then, does anybody buy lottery tickets? One answer is that some people are risk lovers, even though most are not. Another answer is that even people who are generally risk-averse sometimes enjoy spending a few dollars for the excitement of having a (small) chance of winning a lot of money—just as some people who choose low-risk office jobs enjoy skiing a few days a year. Insurance, though, is bought for serious matters, such as the possibility of being hospitalized or having to pay for damage caused in a car accident. In 1983, almost $270 billion—about 8 percent of GNP—was spent on insurance premiums. People seem to spend much more to reduce risk through insurance than to increase it through gambling.[3] Various other sorts of evidence—such as the fact that high wages must generally be paid to attract workers to very risky jobs—also indicate that people are generally risk-averse when they make important decisions.

2. Insurance Markets

Insurance is one of the main ways individuals and businesses reduce the risk they bear. If someone faces the prospect of having his car stolen, he may choose to pay a *premium* of, say, $400 to an insurance company in exchange for an insurance policy that obligates the company to buy him a new car if his car is stolen. He thus bears no risk but has paid $400 to have the insurance company bear it instead. The main question we address here is how insurance companies can cover all their costs and still sell policies at prices buyers find attractive.

---

[2] As the calculation in brackets shows, the expected payoff is the probability that the coin comes up heads (1 in 2) times the payoff in that case ($4) plus the probability that the coin comes up tails (1 in 2) times the payoff in that case (−$1).

[3] Since many common forms of gambling are either illegal or otherwise difficult to measure—poker games among friends, for instance—we can't know for sure how much is spent on gambling. On the other hand, some forms of gambling, such as poker games and football pools among friends, seem to be valued for social reasons more than because they make life riskier.

Risk Aversion

A first—illuminating but incomplete—answer to this question begins by noting that, as we have just argued, most consumers are risk-averse. To see what this implies about insurance, consider Dick, who owns a car that would cost $6000 to replace and that has a 1 in 20 chance of being stolen this year. With no insurance, his average or expected loss from theft is $300 [= $6000 × (1/20)]. How much would Dick pay for auto theft insurance to eliminate this risk?

Suppose first that Dick is risk-neutral. In this case, since he cares only about average gains or losses, he would pay no more than $300—his average loss without insurance—for insurance against theft. Now consider the Ajax Insurance Company. If it agrees to compensate Dick if his car is stolen, its average payout will be $300, so it must charge at least $300 for this policy. But Ajax has other costs as well: It must write the policy, keep track of payments, and verify that cars have really been stolen, among other things. If Ajax's marginal costs per policy are, say, $100, it will not be willing to insure Dick for less than $400. If Dick is risk-neutral, he will not be willing to pay this much, and he will not buy insurance.

Now suppose that Dick, like most of us, is risk-averse. Then he will be willing to pay more than $300 to eliminate the risk of auto theft that he bears. If he is risk-averse enough, he will be willing to pay at least $400, and he and Ajax can do business. Individuals thus purchase insurance at rates that permit insurance companies to break even because they are risk-averse; they would not be willing to pay more than their expected losses if they were risk-neutral.

However, as we noted previously, this answer is incomplete. The owners of Ajax Insurance are probably also risk-averse. Why, then, are they willing to accept only $300—$400 from Dick minus $100 in costs—to bear the risk that Dick's car will be stolen, when Dick is willing to pay up to $400 to get rid of that risk? The answer in this case rests on the mechanism of *risk pooling*.

Risk Pooling

To see most clearly how risk pooling works, let us shift our attention from insurance against auto theft to life insurance. Suppose that we ask, as people in the life insurance business must, what percentage of people of a given age will die in the next year on average. This information is conveniently available in mortality tables, data from which are shown in Figure 19-1. For instance, according to the data, on average only about 1 percent

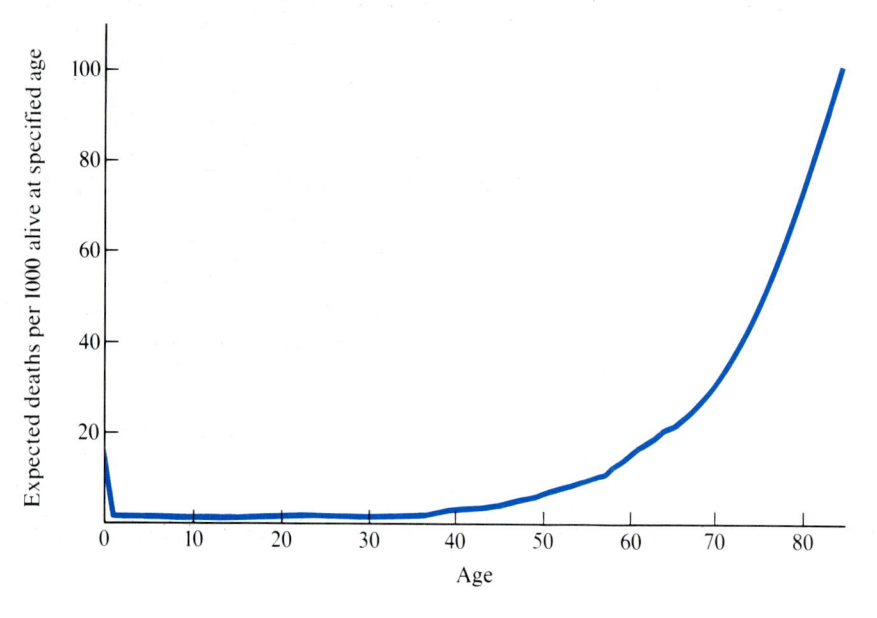

FIGURE 19-1. The U.S. Mortality Table, 1982. The graph shows the probability—expressed as the expected number of deaths per 1000 people—that someone alive at each age specified on the horizontal axis will die in the next year. It is based on actual U.S. data. (*Source: Statistical Abstract of the United States, 1986*, Table 108.)

(10 people per 1000) of those aged 56 will die during the next year. Life insurance cannot do much about an individual's risk of death, of course, but it can help people reduce the risk that they will die and leave their families without adequate financial resources.

Now let us take 100 people aged 56 without knowing much about their particular health conditions. According to the mortality table, we should expect 1 percent of them—one person—to die within the next year. How certain can we be that exactly one person will die rather than zero or two? Not very certain at all. Accidents and illnesses happen, and it is quite possible that none or two or more will die. But suppose we have 1 million people aged 56. How sure can we be now that the percentage of deaths will be very close to 1 percent? We can, in fact, be virtually certain that the percentage of deaths will be very close to 1 percent.

To get a sense of why, consider flipping a fair coin. On average, heads should come up half the time. But if you flip it only once, the proportion of heads will not be close to 50 percent—you will get either one head (100 percent) or zero heads (0 percent). If you flip it twice, however, these extreme outcomes become less likely; the chance of getting all (that is, two) heads is 1 in 4, as is the chance of getting all tails. The more often you flip the coin, the more likely it is that the fraction of heads observed will be close to ½. If you flip it 10 times, for instance, the probability of getting between 40 percent and 60 percent heads is .66; if you flip it 20 times, this probability rises to .74; and if you flip it 100 times, the probability becomes .95.

Uncertainty about the proportion of people who will die within the next year similarly becomes very small as the group insured becomes larger. The low level of uncertainty about mortality in large groups makes life insurance possible, even though life insurance companies are owned by risk-averse people.

A life insurance company sets up an arrangement in which those who wish to leave money to family or friends pay premiums to the insurance company in exchange for the company's promise to pay out a much larger amount if the insured person dies. The insurance company can make these promises with a high degree of certainty because it pools the risks that many individuals will die.

This risk pooling makes its payouts virtually certain, since the fraction of its policyholders who will die in any period is virtually certain. It will charge a little bit extra because of the paperwork involved and also because it inevitably bears some small remaining amount of risk—it cannot be absolutely certain that only the expected number of people and not more will die each year. And buyers will pay a little bit extra because they are risk-averse.[4]

INDEPENDENT RISKS. Under what conditions does risk pooling work? The essential condition is that the risks faced by the individuals insured must be substantially *independent*. The causes of death in the 57th year of life in the United States reflect mainly individual circumstances and thus are substantially independent across individuals. If one person dies of a heart attack, that does not increase the likelihood that someone else will die.

It would be different if epidemics were a serious problem. Suppose, for instance, contrary to the facts, that the 1 percent probability of death at age 57 means there is a 1 percent chance that a plague will strike and wipe out all 57-year-olds over the next year. If there is no plague, everyone lives. In this case an insurance company cannot be at all certain that almost exactly 1 percent of 57-year-olds will die—in fact, it knows that either none will die or all will die, no matter how many people it has insured.

Other insurance, such as fire and automobile insurance, also depends on risk pooling. In each case, the insurance company pools a large number of independent individual risks. The fraction of insured homes that will burn or of insured cars that will be stolen is then nearly certain, so that the insurance company's costs are nearly risk-free. Thus insurance covering these risks can be profitably offered by risk-averse insurance companies because they in fact bear very little risk. As in the case of life insurance, risk-averse buyers will pay more than their average losses in order to avoid risk.

---

[4] Does this mean that the business of selling life insurance is hugely profitable? It probably would be if there were only a single seller of insurance—a monopoly. But in fact competition among insurance companies generally serves to keep premiums close to costs, including as always a normal return on the capital invested by the owners of insurance companies.

Risk Spreading

Not all insurance covers risks—such as the risks of death or auto theft—that can be effectively pooled. For instance, it is possible to buy earthquake insurance in California. It is not true that each year the percentage of Californians suffering from earthquake damage more or less averages out. In most years there is very little damage, but when there is a major quake, damages can be huge. Similarly, owners of oil tankers can buy insurance that will pay any damages caused by oil spills, even though there are not many tankers over which risk can be pooled and oil spill damages can be many millions of dollars.

This sort of insurance is made possible by *risk spreading*: the division of a single risk among many different people. When Lloyd's of London sells insurance to the owners of an oil tanker that covers the risk of an oil spill, for instance, a large number of insurance companies that are members of Lloyd's divide the coverage. That is, each company gets a given fraction of the premium paid by the tanker's owners and in turn agrees to pay the same fraction of the damages, if any. The huge risk of an oil spill, which could easily bankrupt a large shipping company, has thus been spread over many insurance companies so that none will suffer a large loss if a spill occurs.

At this stage, risk pooling comes into play. Over the years, the members of Lloyd's provide insurance against many different types of risks. Since these risks are generally independent, the insurance companies' total payouts are, as before, relatively predictable.

There are also cases where risk spreading will not work. These are cases where the event against which people want insurance protection will have large effects on the entire economy. Consider, for example, nuclear war. No doubt we would all be willing to pay a small amount for an insurance policy that would pay off in the event of nuclear war. But an insurance company selling insurance that will pay off if there is a nuclear war would have a hard time persuading people that it would actually be able to meet its commitments. All survivors who had bought the insurance would be trying to collect at the same time, and it is unlikely that the company would have enough assets left to cover all the claims.

Moral Hazard and Adverse Selection

Even when risk pooling and risk spreading are possible, it may be impossible for insurance companies to make money insuring some risks. There are two reasons. First, in some cases having insurance affects individuals' behavior in a way that increases the insurance company's costs. This is the problem of *moral hazard*. Somebody with insurance that will pay for a new car if her old car is stolen, for instance, has little incentive to lock her car. But if most insured cars are stolen every year as a consequence, the cost of theft insurance to the insurance company will be close to the cost of a new car, and it is unlikely that anybody will buy insurance at a price high enough to cover this cost. One way of dealing with this problem is to offer only partial coverage, so that if a car is stolen, the owner will receive something less than the cost of a new car. This provides some incentive to lock one's car, but it also leaves the car owner bearing some risk that she cannot eliminate by taking out insurance.

A second problem, *adverse selection*, arises because the people who want to buy insurance against a particular loss are those most likely actually to collect the payoff. Suppose that as a matter of unbreakable habit some people never lock their cars. Theft insurance will clearly be more attractive to these people than to others who are more careful. But this means that people who buy theft insurance are a bad (adverse) selection from the general population from the insurance company's point of view: They are less careful than average, and their cars are more likely to be stolen. If the insurance company raises its rates to allow for this, it will make theft insurance less attractive to those who lock their cars. It may be impossible for careful people to buy insurance at a reasonable price—relative to the chance that *their* cars will be stolen—simply because the insurance company cannot tell that they are in fact careful.

Insurance companies do generally try to avoid selling to especially risky individuals. Life insurance policies generally do not pay off in the case of suicide, since otherwise suicidal people would buy them, and are generally not issued without a medical examination, for instance. But like the problem of moral hazard, adverse selection can rarely be completely eliminated.

3. Risk and Capital

Capital markets, like insurance markets, permit individuals to reduce risk. Unlike insurance markets, however, capital markets can also be used to increase risk—as when somebody invests everything she owns in a stock on which she has received a hot tip.

In Chapter 18 we argued that the price of a capital good or tract of land must equal the present discounted value of the future returns it will yield. We assumed there that the future returns were known. We begin this section by asking how this rule must be modified when future returns are uncertain.

We then show how the markets for *financial* capital permit the risks associated with *physical* capital to be spread over many people and also allow individuals to pool risks through diversification. Thus the mechanisms of risk spreading and risk pooling are important in capital markets as well as in insurance markets. We conclude this section with a discussion of the *efficiency* of the stock market, the most important market for financial capital. Are the stock market gyrations reported on the news every day driven by basic economic forces or do they just reflect gambling and speculation?

Risk and Return

Consider two machines, both of which will be worth $90 at the end of 1 year. Machine A will yield revenue of $20 during the year for certain, but machine B may yield revenue of either $10 or $30. If both outcomes are equally likely, the average return from holding machine B for a year is $110—$90 plus the average of $10 and $30—exactly the same as the certain return from machine A. If the interest rate is 10 percent, how much is each machine worth today?

We saw how to answer this question for machine A in Chapter 18. The present value of $110 to be received 1 year in the future is $100 when the interest rate is 10 percent, and this must be the value of machine A.

Since machine B has the same average return, does it have the same value? Not for a risk-averse individual, since he is made worse off by bearing risk. Machine B, which is equally likely to return $100 or $120, is less attractive to a risk-averse individual than is machine A, which returns $110 for certain. A risk-averse individual will thus pay something less than $100 for machine B. This example illustrates a general principle:

● **The price of an asset with uncertain returns will usually be lower than the present value of its average future returns.**

The difference will be greater the riskier the returns and the more risk-averse the individual.

Let us now consider the average rate of return that would be earned by purchasing either of these machines. As we discussed in Chapter 17 (and spelled out in detail in that chapter's appendix), when the returns on an asset are certain, the rate of return on the asset is the interest rate that makes the present value of future returns equal to the asset's price. When returns are uncertain, we compute the average rate of return by using the average returns. Thus if r is the rate of return on a machine that costs P, is expected to be worth V at the end of a year, and yields an average revenue of R, we have

$$P = \frac{V + R}{(1 + r)} \qquad (1)$$

Multiplying both sides by $(1 + r)$, subtracting P from both sides, and dividing by P yields the following general formula:

$$r = \frac{R + (V - P)}{P} \qquad (2)$$

For both machines A and B, $R = \$20$ and $V = \$90$. For machine A, $P = 100$, and equation (2) tells us that $r = 0.10$ ($= 10/100$), or 10 percent. We argued previously that machine B costs less than $100. Suppose it costs $90. Then equation (2) implies that the average rate of return from buying machine B is 0.22 ($= 20/90$), or 22 percent. Machine B sells for less than machine A and yields a higher average rate of return than does A because the returns to B are risky. This difference is what compensates a risk-averse investor for bearing the risk involved in owning machine B. The general principle illustrated by this comparison is the following:

● **Riskier investments yield higher average rates of return than do less risky investments.**

SOME EVIDENCE. To illustrate this last principle, we consider the real (inflation-adjusted[5]) rates of return on stocks and Treasury bills (short-term government bonds). These are financial assets, not tangible assets such as machines and tracts of land, but they are still investments that pay returns in the future. Thus our earlier discussion indicates that if stocks are riskier than Treasury bills, investors in stocks should earn a higher average rate of return than investors in bills earn.

There are two components of the return on stocks: dividends and capital gains. *Dividends* are payments that a company makes to stockholders each year. A company does not have to make a dividend payment if it decides not to, but large corporations typically make regular dividend payments. The *capital gain* is the increase in the value of a stock. Both dividends and capital gains provide a return to the purchaser of the stock; they correspond to R and $(V - P)$, respectively, in equation (2).

A sample calculation of the real rate of return on a stock follows. Suppose the following events occur: The stock was bought at the beginning of the year for $45; during the course of the year the company paid out $2 in dividends; and at the end of the year the stock is worth $52. Suppose also that prices of goods have gone up 5 percent during the year. The real rate of return on the stock is calculated as follows:

$$\begin{aligned}\text{Real rate of return} &= \frac{\text{dividend} + \text{capital gain}}{\text{purchase price}} - \text{inflation rate} \\ &= \frac{2 + (52 - 45)}{45} - 0.05 \\ &= \frac{9}{45} - 0.05 = 0.15 = 15\% \end{aligned} \quad (3)$$

The formula used here is basically equation (2) with the addition of an adjustment for the decline in the purchasing power of money during the year.

---

[5] Real rates of return were introduced in Chapter 17 and discussed in detail in Chapter 18. A real rate of return is the rate of return in dollars adjusted for changes in the price level. Thus if the money value of your stocks goes up 17 percent but prices have gone up 8 percent, the real rate of return on your stocks is 9 percent—this is the increase in the purchasing power of the money you invested.

In the case of a Treasury bill, which is a promise to pay, say, $100 at the end of the year in exchange for $92 at the beginning of the year, the real rate of return is just the nominal rate of return, 8.7 percent ([(100 − 92)/92] × 100 percent), minus the inflation rate (5 percent), or 3.7 percent in this case.

Figure 19-2 shows how much more the real rate of return on stocks has fluctuated than the real return on Treasury bills, especially in the period since World War II. The annual real rate of return on stocks has on several occasions been more than 40 percent and also sometimes less than *minus* 30 percent. Since movements in the stock market are notoriously difficult to predict,[6] there is clearly considerable uncertainty about the real rate of return that will be earned by buying stocks. There is also uncertainty about the real rate of return on Treasury bills, because we cannot predict the inflation rate exactly, but real returns on stocks are clearly riskier than are real returns on Treasury bills.

Table 19-1 gives average real rates of return on stocks and Treasury bills over the period 1926–1985. On average, the real rate of return for stocks was a healthy 6.6 percent per annum. Treasury bills barely kept up with inflation and yielded an average real rate of return of just 0.3 percent. This difference is exactly in line with the principles we have developed.

Someone who is very risk-averse and invests in Treasury bills has to pay for certainty by expecting to earn a

---

[6] In fact, we argue subsequently that if stock markets function well, they must be essentially impossible to predict.

TABLE 19-1. Average Annual Real Rates of Return on Stocks and Treasury Bills, 1926–1985

	Period, %			
	1926–1985	1926–1952	1953–1985	1967–1981
Stocks	6.6	7.0	6.3	1.3
Treasury bills	0.3	−0.5	0.9	−0.3

Note: For calculating real returns, inflation is measured by the consumer price index.

Source: Roger G. Ibbotson and Rex A. Sinquefield, *Stocks, Bonds, Bills, and Inflation: The Past and the Future*, Financial Analysts Research Foundation, Charlottesville, Va., 1982, updated by the authors.

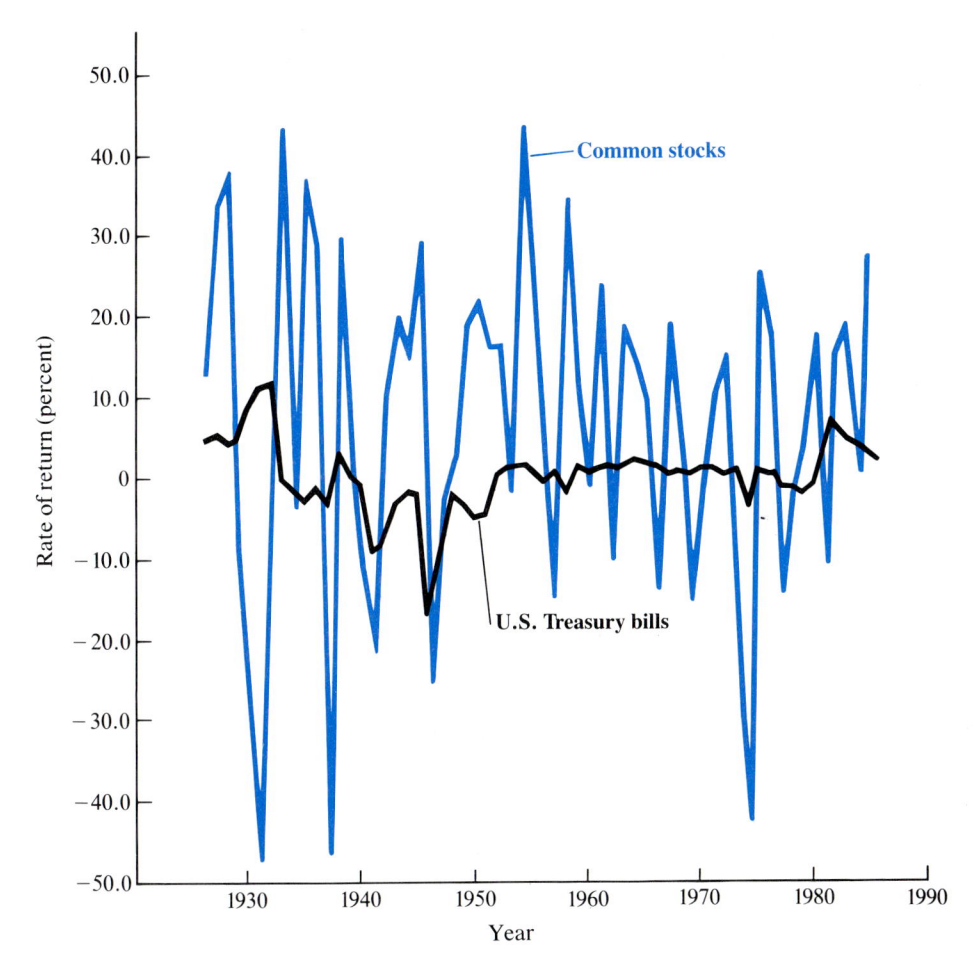

FIGURE 19-2. Annual Real Rates of Return: Stocks and U.S. Treasury Bills, 1926–1985. (*Source*: Roger G. Ibbotson and Rex A. Sinquefield, *Stocks, Bonds, Bills, and Inflation: The Past and the Future*, Financial Analysts Research Foundation, Charlottesville, Va., 1982, updated by the authors.)

lower (indeed, virtually zero) real rate of return. A less risk-averse individual who is willing to buy stocks is, *on average*, rewarded for bearing greater risk by earning a higher return. But the risk is real: The stock investor could lose a lot of money. Someone buying stocks at the beginning of 1973 and selling them 2 years later, for instance, would have lost almost half the value of her investment. Even over the long period 1967–1981, stocks yielded an average real rate of return of only 1.3 percent. Of course, investors in Treasury bills over this same period earned a negative real rate of return—their dollar investments grew more slowly than did the price level.

Risk Spreading in the Capital Markets

We used data on financial assets rather than physical assets in the preceding illustration because there are well-organized markets for financial assets in which many individuals and institutions participate and about which detailed information is published. We now argue that because many people participate—directly or indirectly through pension funds and other institutions—in markets for financial assets, these markets perform a risk-spreading function much like that of Lloyd's of London in the insurance markets.

Suppose you invest all your savings to buy a cookie shop. If consumers like your cookies, you may use the profits your business produces to buy the equipment and rent the space necessary to produce and sell your cookies at other locations around town. As we discussed in Chapter 7, if your cookies are popular enough, you may even decide to form a partnership so that you can raise money from others (your new partners) in order to expand your business rapidly. And if your cookies are a huge success, you may form a corporation and sell stock to many different individuals, each of whom then becomes a part owner of the business.

In general, as businesses grow, they acquire more owners: partners or shareholders. One reason for this, which we stressed in Chapter 7, is that no single individual or small group is likely to be wealthy enough to supply all the financial capital needed by a large, rapidly growing firm. But there is another reason that has to do with risk.

Suppose you have $1 million in stocks, bonds, and other assets—just enough to finance the new cookie shops you would like to open. In this case is there any reason to seek partners or to form a corporation and sell stock? There may be. If you remain the sole owner and invest every cent you have, you alone bear all the risk associated with your business. If people decide to exercise more and eat fewer cookies or if somebody comes up with a better cookie than yours, you may lose everything. If you are confident enough that nothing of this sort will ever happen, you may want to invest the whole $1 million yourself; the high returns you expect will then compensate you for the risk you are bearing. But if you are not supremely confident, or if you are very risk-averse, you may want to share some of the risk with others. When you bring in additional owners, you, like Lloyd's of London, engage in risk spreading. If 100 people each buy 1 percent of the cookie business, each bears a much smaller risk than you would have borne if you had remained the sole proprietor.

The absolute dollar risk associated with very large corporations such as IBM and General Motors is enormous. The earnings of these firms can change unpredictably from one year to the next by hundreds of millions of dollars. But IBM and GM, like most large firms, are organized as corporations, and they have millions of owners. These include individuals who directly own IBM or GM stock, those whose pensions will be paid by institutions that own shares of these firms, and those who own shares of mutual funds that hold IBM or GM stock. A mutual fund buys stocks (or bonds or other financial assets) with money supplied by its clients and divides the returns on those stocks among its clients in proportion to the amounts they have invested. Thus if you invest $1000 in a mutual fund that in turn invests 1 percent of its total assets in IBM stock, you have in effect invested $10 ($0.01 \times \$1000$) in IBM. The value of your investment in IBM will change over time as IBM's earnings change, but you do not bear much risk as a consequence.

Thus by spreading large risks among many people, the capital markets make it possible for firms to make enormous, risky investments in physical capital—like those made by IBM and GM every year—even though no single individual would be willing to bear a large share of the risk involved.

Risk Pooling and Diversification

As in insurance markets, risk pooling is also an important function performed by the capital markets. To see this, let us look more closely at buyers of financial assets. A risk-averse consumer (or investor) prefers a higher average return on the portfolio of financial assets he holds but dislikes higher risk. Because consumers are risk-averse, they have to be compensated for risk by receiving a higher return when they bear more risk. We look first at the investor's choice between risky and safe assets. We then argue that risk-averse investors will engage in risk pooling, much as life insurance companies do, by holding a diversified portfolio containing many different risky assets.

PORTFOLIO RISK. Suppose first that there are only two assets, one riskless and the other risky. A consumer can choose the fraction of his wealth that he invests in each. As we argued previously, the risky asset will pay a higher rate of return on average to compensate for its riskiness. At one extreme, the investor could hold all his wealth in the risky asset, earning a high average return and bearing the maximum possible risk. Alternatively, he could hold all his wealth in the riskless asset, sacrificing some return on average in exchange for getting rid of all risk. Or he could hold some of each asset, earning an intermediate rate of return with some, but not maximum, risk.

Unless the consumer is completely risk-averse, he will choose to hold some of the risky asset and some of the riskless asset. In general, the fraction of his wealth invested in the risky asset will be higher the less risk-averse he is, the less risky the risky asset is, and the greater the difference between the average returns of the two assets. This difference is the reward for risk bearing, and the consumer will thus bear more risk the more he is rewarded for doing so.

PORTFOLIO DIVERSIFICATION. Let us now take into account the fact that investors can choose among many different risky assets. We show that it will in general be in the consumer's interest to diversify his portfolio—that is, to hold many different risky assets (stocks, say) rather than only one. The basic logic is the same as in the discussion of risk pooling by life insurance companies.

Suppose that there are two risky assets available: oil stocks and bank stocks. Each has two possible returns: $4 in good times and $2 in bad times. Good times are as likely as bad times in each industry, and good times in one industry are entirely unrelated to good times in the other, so that the returns in the two industries are independent. Suppose that the stocks cost the same and that the investor has decided to buy two shares. Should she put all her money in oil stock, put it all in bank stock, or diversify her portfolio of risky assets by buying one share of each?

To answer this question, suppose first that the investor buys two shares of the bank stock. There is a 50 percent chance that things go well for banking, in which case the investor earns $8. Or things go badly for banking, and she earns only $4. Similarly, if she buys two shares of the oil stock, she will earn either $8 or $4, and both outcomes are equally likely. In both cases the average return is $6.

Now suppose she diversifies by acquiring one share of each stock. In Table 19-2 we show the payoffs from this diversified portfolio. Each combination of events shown

TABLE 19-2. Payoff on a Diversified Portfolio

		Banking	
		Good times, $	Bad times, $
Oil	Good times	8	6
	Bad times	6	4

in Table 19-2 is equally likely. There is thus a 25 percent chance that both the oil industry and the banking industry will do badly, a 50 percent chance that one will do well and the other badly, and a 25 percent probability that both will do well. Now there is only a 25 percent chance each of earning $4 or $8 and a 50 percent probability of earning $6. The average return is $6—just as if everything had been invested in oil stock or in bank stock—but the investor bears less risk if she diversifies. Thus *any* risk-averse investor will prefer the diversified portfolio to either of the specialized alternatives.

It is of course possible in this example for both industries to have a good year or both to have a bad year. But there is also some chance that a good year in one will offset a bad year in the other, thus tending to stabilize the overall return. In this example and in general, this possibility is exactly what makes diversification attractive to investors.

- *Diversification* **is the strategy of reducing risk by spreading investment across several risky assets.**

The principle of diversification is that of not putting all your eggs in one basket.[7]

What happens if more stocks are available that have the same return structure as oil and banking stocks and whose returns are also independent of each other? Just as

---

[7] When Professor James Tobin of Yale received the Nobel prize for economics in 1981 for, among other things, his work on portfolio choice, reporters asked him to summarize as simply as he could what his work was about. He replied that it showed that it was not wise to put all your eggs in one basket. This reply resulted in several cartoons in which people were given Nobel prizes for other discoveries, such as "A stitch in time saves nine." Of course, Tobin's work went well beyond the simple eggs-in-one-basket example and showed precisely what trade-offs are involved in making portfolio choices and what portfolios the consumer will end up choosing.

in the discussion of life insurance, the more independent risks that can be pooled, the more predictable the overall outcome. In this case, the chance of getting returns much different from $6 falls as the number of industries represented in the portfolio is increased. Not only should one not put all one's eggs in one basket, the more baskets the better.

CORRELATED RETURNS. So far we have assumed that asset returns are independent of each other. This means, for instance, that if one stock has a high return, it is no more or less likely that others will also. But in fact stock returns do move together to some extent. When there is good economic news, most stocks tend to rise; when there is bad news, most stocks tend to fall.

Asset returns are *correlated* when they move together. If returns on two assets tend to move in the same direction, they are *positively correlated*. If the returns usually move in opposite directions, the two assets are *negatively correlated*. Positive and negative correlations have different implications for the effects of diversification in reducing risk. Suppose two assets move together in exactly the same way and in the same direction. When stock A is high, so is stock B, and vice versa. In this case there is no gain at all from diversification. There is no difference between buying 2 units of either and buying 1 unit of each. Thus diversification achieves nothing.

Diversification can achieve much more when asset returns are negatively correlated. Table 19-3 gives an extreme example. There are three possible macroeconomic events that determine the returns on two stocks: boom, slump, and normal times. The returns on stock A follow the economy as a whole very closely. When times are good, the stock pays a high return of 16 percent, but it does poorly when there is a slump. Stock B, on the other hand, does well when the economy is in trouble, earning 22 percent during a slump, but it earns only 4 percent when times are good. Each stock taken by itself is risky. But if we divide our portfolio evenly between the two stocks, our actual return will be absolutely riskless, as shown in the third row of the table. Because of the negative correlation of their returns, the two stocks exactly compensate for each other.

In general, a stock that is negatively correlated with others is very useful in helping to reduce the uncertainty of the return on one's overall portfolio, even if its return is highly variable. A stock that is positively correlated with others provides less in the way of useful diversification, even if its return is relatively stable. This suggests, correctly, that when assembling a portfolio, one must look at the effect of buying an asset on the riskiness of overall portfolio returns rather than the riskiness of the asset's returns in isolation.

The idea of diversification is important in many situations besides the consumer portfolio problem, though the principle is the same everywhere. For instance, an individual farmer will be anxious not to rely too much on a single crop. She will try to have different products in case the market for one of them or the crop itself is bad one year. Then she can always turn to the other products and hope that they have a good year. Risk is reduced by diversification.

Efficient Markets

There are two basic images of the stock market. One is that of a casino where Lady Luck and the better gamblers reign supreme. In this view stock pricing is based on speculation with no rational basis. The second view—the theory of *efficient markets*—is that the stock market is a sensitive processor of information, responding quickly to each new piece of information bearing on the right price that should be paid for stocks. Those who hold the second view recognize that stock prices fluctuate a lot but argue that these fluctuations are the appropriate responses to changing information.

Why does it matter? Stocks are claims on the income that is generated by the activities of different firms. All else equal, the higher the price of a company's stock, the easier it is for that company to raise financing for new

TABLE 19-3. Negatively Correlated Stock Returns

Stock	Returns, %		
	Boom	Normal	Slump
A	16	6	−2
B	4	14	22
$\frac{A + B}{2}$	10	10	10

investment. If a firm has 100 shares of stock outstanding, for instance, and sells 50 new shares, those who buy the new shares now own one-third of the firm. By selling stock, the original owners obtain money that can be invested to yield future returns, but they give up a fraction of those returns to the new owners. The higher the price of the firm's stock, the more money is obtained by selling those 50 shares and the greater the future returns the original owners will enjoy.

If the stocks of firms with good investment opportunities sell for high prices, those firms will be encouraged to raise money and make productive investments. But if stock prices are mainly determined by the whims of gamblers, there is no reason to think that the most productive investments will be encouraged in this fashion. Thus it matters whether the stock market is efficient, because this sets the terms on which firms can invest. If the stock market does not reward the good firms, with good prospects, by making it easy for them to sell stocks to raise financing for their investments, the economy will allocate capital badly. The stock market plays an important role in determining the allocation of investment in the economy.

What are the arguments for the two views of the stock market: the view that the stock market is a casino with no fundamental economic forces determining stock prices versus the view that the stock market is a finely tuned machine that responds to every important economic signal and responds correctly?

Typical of the arguments on the irrationality side are those of the great English economist John Maynard Keynes.[8] Keynes argued that what really dominates in the stock market is gambling about the price at which stocks can be sold in a few days. He contended that investors are simply trying to figure out what other investors will be willing to pay for a stock in the near future; they pay attention neither to the returns the firm's existing assets will produce nor to its investment opportunities. These arguments led him to a gloomy conclusion: "When the capital development of a country becomes the by-product of the activities of a casino, the job is likely to be ill-done."[9] Keynes has more claim to be believed than most, since he himself was a successful stock market investor (gambler?).

Efficient-markets theorists, on the other hand, argue that if stock prices don't correctly reflect all available information, there is easy money to be made. If a stock's price is too low, shrewd investors will buy more of it, thus driving up its price; the same investors will drive down the price of overpriced stocks by selling them. Thus stock prices will be driven to levels that reflect the future returns each company will produce. This view has been tested by seeing whether there is evidence that stock pricing ignores available information. If this had happened, it would have been possible for investors to make money by using that information.

Early tests suggested that it was not possible to make better than average returns by using publicly available information. The most common test of whether the market neglects information is to ask if, using the past history of prices, you can find a rule that yields high rates of return on average. For instance, perhaps a rule such as "Buy a stock when it has risen 2 days in a row and sell it if it falls more than 3 days" would be the secret to success. However, rules such as this appear not to work.

But the most recent research has uncovered some anomalies. For instance, there is a "January effect" in the stock market: On average, stock prices of small companies rise more than normally early in January. Efficient-markets theory would say that people should be aware of this effect and buy in December. This would raise prices at the start of January and eliminate the effect. There is also some evidence suggesting that the stock market fluctuates "too much" relative to fluctuations in the profits earned by firms. These anomalies have reopened the issue of the efficiency of the stock market.

4. Hedging and Futures Markets

Futures markets are an important institution for dealing with uncertainty about prices. There are organized markets for the future delivery of many commodities and assets, among them corn, wheat, soybeans, pork bellies (bacon), coffee, sugar, copper, heating oil, plywood, British pounds, and Treasury bills. The prices of all these

---

[8] John Maynard Keynes, *General Theory of Employment, Interest and Money*, Harcourt, Brace, New York, 1936, pp. 154–158.

[9] Keynes, ibid., p. 159.

things are subject to large, unpredictable fluctuations. There was rapid development of futures markets in the late seventies and early eighties. Futures markets for Treasury bills, some bonds, stock indexes, and heating oil are among the markets that were added.

The economic reason for setting up futures markets is to make it possible for interested individuals and institutions to reduce the risks they bear because the prices at which they will buy and sell in the future are uncertain. When this uncertainty diminishes or other methods of reducing risk appear, futures markets disappear, and many have done so over the years.

If you look at the financial pages in a newspaper (if not in your local paper, certainly in the *Wall Street Journal*), you will see prices quoted for the delivery of, say, wheat on several future dates, which may range over a year and a half ahead. The standard wheat contract specifies a quantity of wheat (usually 5000 bushels) and a date in the future. When that date arrives, the issuer of the contract—the original seller—is obliged to provide the specified quantity of wheat to whomever owns the contract at that time.

Hedgers and Speculators

Who trades in the futures markets, and why? There are two basic types of participants in these markets: hedgers and speculators. *Hedgers* are people who use a market to reduce the risks they face. In the wheat market, hedgers are people whose main business is related to wheat; they grow it, process it, or sell it. Such people use the market to get themselves some certainty about the dollar prices they will be receiving or paying for wheat in the future. A farmer who will have wheat to sell at harvest time is uncertain now about the price he will get then. He may decide to reduce the risk facing him by selling some of the crop ahead of time, in the futures market, for delivery after the harvest is in. On the other side of the market, a baker or miller may want to lock in future supplies at a known dollar price, and so she will buy wheat today at a given price for delivery later.

As described so far, the trading in futures markets could be entirely between future suppliers of the good and future demanders, both of whom use the market to reduce their risks. In fact, most trading in futures markets occurs among people who have never seen wheat and would certainly not know what to do with it if it arrived on their doorsteps. These traders are *speculators*, individuals who are active in the market but are thereby not reducing any of their own wheat-related risk. Such people are speculating by promising to sell wheat they do not have now or buy wheat they will not use. They are in the market because they expect to earn profits for taking risks.

Table 19-4 shows what two speculators in the wheat market might have in mind. Speculator A believes that wheat will sell for more in 6 months' time than today's futures price, $2.70 per bushel. The price he is speculating on is the future *spot price*, the ordinary price for the immediate ("on the spot") purchase and sale of wheat. He is concerned with the spot price of wheat that will exist 6 months from now, compared with the present futures prices for wheat to be delivered in 6 months. If speculator A's beliefs in Table 19-4 are right, then every bushel of wheat he buys today for future delivery will cost him $2.70 and can be resold in the spot market in 6 months' time for $3.10. Thus speculator A will be able to clear 40 cents on each bushel. Speculator B believes that in 6 months the spot price will be lower than the current futures price. She therefore sells a contract obliging her to deliver wheat in the future. If her expectations are right, she will make 30 cents on every bushel.

TABLE 19-4. Expectations of Wheat Prices and the Futures Price

	Wheat price in dollars per bushel		
	Today's price for delivery in 6 months	Spot market price expected today to exist in 6 months	Decision
Speculator A	2.70	3.10	Buy wheat today for delivery in 6 months
Speculator B	2.70	2.40	Sell wheat today for delivery in 6 months

Futures Prices as Forecasts

This last example generalizes. Whenever somebody—hedger or speculator—thinks that the spot price at some future date will be above the going futures price, she has an incentive to buy wheat on the futures market for delivery at that date, since if she is right she can resell it immediately and make a profit.[10] If many people think this way, there will be an increase in demand in the futures market, and the futures price will rise. Similarly, if many people think that the future spot price will be below the current futures price, they will sell on the futures market and drive down the futures price. The observed futures price at any instant thus has the property that roughly as many people think it is above the future spot price as think it is below the future spot price. Thus economists and others sometimes say that the futures price respresents the market's forecast of future spot prices—where by "the market" they mean an average view of market participants.

An example illustrates this point. Table 19-5 shows futures prices for oats on the Chicago Board of Trade on February 26, 1987. Note that the futures price falls until September 1987. This occurs because the new crop begins slowly to come in after March and will be almost all in by September. Thus the quantity supplied on the spot market will be rising, and the spot price can be expected to fall. There are no new supplies through the following May. Any oats sold after September will have been stored. Because storage is costly, it is easy to forecast that the spot price will be higher in December than it will be in September, and the December futures price is accordingly above the September price.

Do futures prices generally provide good forecasts of future spot prices? No and yes. No in the sense that they often differ substantially from the actual spot prices that prevail. This mainly reflects the inherent uncertainty and variability of the corresponding spot prices—the fact that led to the setting up of futures markets in the first place. Yes in the sense that futures prices are not systematically wrong. That is, on average they are neither above nor below the spot price they forecast, but there is a lot of variation around the average. This is consistent with the efficient markets theory, since it implies that there is no way to make money by betting that spot prices will generally be above or below futures prices. Speculators, by putting their money on the line, help ensure that the futures price well reflects available information about what the spot price will be in the future.

■ We began this chapter with the observation that everything is risky and followed by arguing that most people dislike bearing risk. It is thus not too surprising that institutions have been created to permit individuals to reduce the risk they bear through risk pooling, risk spreading, and hedging. The insurance market and the markets in which risky assets are traded are very large. Still, there are many risks that cannot be eliminated by these mechanisms. One cannot buy insurance against nuclear war or failing an examination; it is difficult to buy bonds that pay a riskless real rate of return; and a farmer can guarantee the price at which she sells her output but cannot guarantee that she could not have sold for more if she had not hedged.

---

[10] This simplifies a bit, since future spot prices are uncertain and even speculators are generally risk-averse. They thus typically diversify their portfolios and don't bet all they own on movements in future spot prices.

TABLE 19-5. Future Prices for Oats, February 26, 1987

Date of delivery	Price per bushel, $
March 1987	1.5400
May 1987	1.4800
July 1987	1.3450
September 1987	1.2925
December 1987	1.3350

Summary

1. Uncertainty pervades economic life. Individuals appear both to enjoy some risk, as shown by widespread gambling, and to be risk-averse, as shown by the purchase of insurance. Risk aversion is said to exist when individuals require better than even odds to accept a risk. Risk aversion is more prevalent than risk loving in major economic activities.
2. The prevalence of risk aversion means that individuals try to find ways of reducing uncertainty and that individuals who bear risk are, on average, compensated for doing so.
3. Insurance is one of the main means for reducing risks faced by individuals. Some risks that individuals face are not risks to society as a whole, in that the overall level of risk for society is much lower than that for individuals. Insurance schemes involving many different people effectively *pool* individual risks. Examples are life, property, and health insurance.
4. Other insurance schemes operate by spreading risk across many individuals who are not themselves at risk to begin with. An example is earthquake or other disaster insurance.
5. Most insurance programs suffer from problems of adverse selection in that the people who want the insurance are those most likely to collect payments. Moral hazard is another problem of insurance. It occurs when the existence of insurance makes people behave in ways that increase the likelihood that they will have the accident against which they are insuring.
6. Historically, there has been a large difference between the returns earned on risky assets such as stocks and the returns earned on safer assets such as Treasury bills. The average real return on stocks over the past 50 years has been 6.6 percent, while that on Treasury bills has been about zero. But stock returns fluctuate much more.
7. The riskiness of a portfolio can be reduced through *diversification*, or spreading risk over many different investments. As long as the returns on the assets vary independently of each other at least a little, the riskiness of a portfolio is reduced by being spread over more stocks.
8. The risk that an asset contributes to a portfolio is not measured solely by the variability of the asset's own returns. Also important is the *correlation* of returns on an asset with returns on other available assets. An asset that is negatively correlated with other assets may actually reduce the overall riskiness of a portfolio, even though its own returns are risky.
9. In equilibrium, risky assets earn higher rates of return because portfolio holders have to be compensated for bearing extra risk. The equilibrium rates of return are established by supply and demand in the markets for assets.
10. In an efficient market, assets are priced in a way that reflects the risk and returns associated with the incomes they produce. Efficiency of the assets markets matters because the allocation of investment depends on asset prices giving the right signals to investors. There is much evidence that asset markets are reasonably efficient and some evidence that asset prices fluctuate too much for markets to be efficient.
11. Futures markets are markets where a price is established today for the future delivery of goods. Such markets enable those active in the industry to *hedge*, reducing uncertainty about future receipts or payments by making some contracts now. Speculators are also active in the futures markets. They try to profit by differences that they expect between the futures prices and the *spot price* that will exist in the market at the time of delivery. The futures price is likely to be close to the price that is expected by market participants to exist in the spot market in the future.

Key Terms

Risk-neutral consumers
Risk-averse consumers
Risk lovers
Risk pooling
Risk spreading
Moral hazard
Adverse selection
Average rate of return
Diversification
Correlation of returns
Efficient markets
Futures markets
Hedgers
Speculators

Problems

1. Characterize the following individuals as risk-averse, risk-loving, or risk-neutral. Each has been offered a bet in which a fair coin (with an even chance of coming up heads or tails) is tossed. If it comes up heads, the individual wins a dollar. If it comes up tails, he or she pays a dollar. Individual A is indifferent whether she plays the game or not. Individual B is willing to pay 2 cents to play. Individual C will play only if

he receives 5 cents to do so. Which of the individuals would you expect to want insurance against car theft?

2. Explain why there is no social risk in the outcome of a lottery, even though each individual ticket holder in the lottery faces risk.

3. Are individuals who both gamble and buy insurance being inconsistent?

4. It is sometimes said that the family is one of the main forms of insurance available in society. In what sense is this true?

5. You hear on the radio a commercial for life insurance for anyone aged 45 and above, with no medical examination required to receive the insurance. (*a*) Do you expect the rates charged for such insurance to be high, low, or average? (*b*) Why?

6. In which of the following are risks being pooled? (*a*) life insurance, (*b*) insurance for Boulder Dam, (*c*) insurance for an opera star's voice.

7. Why might an individual be willing to add to his portfolio a risky asset with an expected rate of return of only 0 percent?

8. Someone successfully sets up a firm to counsel unemployed people on the best way to use their time. Will the stock of this firm be expected in equilibrium to earn a rate of return of more or less than 6.6 percent? Why?

9. Why did the stock market fall sharply in response to the news that President Kennedy had been shot?

10. Someone gives you a tip that a company has invented a fine new product. (*a*) What do you do about it if you are active in the stock market? (*b*) Why do securities laws try to prevent insider trading, where people who run a firm buy and sell stock in that company on the basis of private information? (*c*) Why does it matter whether asset markets are efficient?

11. Sometimes, just before the harvest comes in, the futures price of wheat is below the *current* spot price. For example, the futures price for delivery in 3 months might be $3.00 per bushel and the current spot price $3.25. (*a*) How can this be? (*b*) (This is a difficult question.) Suppose that there is absolutely no cost for storing a good. Is it possible for the futures price to be substantially above the current spot price?

Chapter 20
Inequality, Poverty, and Discrimination in the United States

In earlier chapters we studied how wages and the rates of return to capital and land, and thus incomes, are determined in the factor markets. In this chapter we examine the overall picture, discussing the distribution of income and of wealth in the United States, the extent of poverty, and its causes.

The distribution of wealth and of income in the United States and in most other countries is extremely uneven. The richest 0.05 percent of households own 35 percent of all personal wealth in this country, while the combined wealth of the bottom 90 percent of households amounts to less than 30 percent of the total. At the bottom of the economic ladder, more than 34 million people, or 14.4 percent of the U.S. population, live below the official poverty level.[1] A great deal of debate on public policy is concerned, directly or indirectly, with the reasons for inequality and poverty and with the appropriate response on the part of government.

During the 1930s and again in the 1960s the federal government assumed increased responsibility for those deemed underprivileged and developed an array of programs to wage war on poverty. In the 1960s many, including President Johnson, argued that much poverty resulted from current and past discrimination, not differences in abilities, and equal opportunity legislation was passed to reduce poverty by reducing discrimination. By 1984 government spending on antipoverty programs amounted to 10 percent of GNP. Yet poverty, hunger, and homelessness are far from conquered, and a larger fraction of the population is below the poverty line than was the case a decade ago.

In the late 1980s, many ask whether the war on poverty declared in 1964 by Lyndon Johnson has been counterproductive, increasing poverty rather than reducing it. In *Losing Ground*, Charles Murray echoes widespread skepticism about government policies to combat poverty when he writes: "We tried to do more for the poor and produced more poor instead. We tried to remove the barriers to escape from poverty, and inadvertently built a trap."[2] In this chapter we focus on the measurement and

---

[1] The wealth data refer to 1983, and the poverty data refer to 1984. The definition of poverty and more details about the extent of poverty follow later in this chapter.

[2] Charles Murray, *Losing Ground: American Social Policy 1950–1980*, Basic Books, New York, 1984, p. 9

determinants of inequality and poverty, paying special attention to the economics of discrimination. Chapter 22 considers government antipoverty policies and their effects in more detail.

We begin in section 1 with an analysis of the functional distribution of income.

● The *functional distribution* of income describes the distribution of income among different factors of production, in particular the shares of income received by capital and labor.

The functional distribution helps us understand the distribution of income among individuals based on their characteristics as workers or owners of tangible wealth (capitalists). But while this distinction is useful, it is not true in modern economies that those who own property receive no income from labor or that those who earn salaries and wages receive no income from capital. Most people who own stocks and bonds also work; many retired workers receive income from stocks and bonds held by a pension fund.

For this reason, we turn to the personal distribution of income in section 2.

● The *personal distribution* of income is the breakdown of aggregate income among individual economic units: persons, families, or households.

The personal income distribution describes how income is distributed among you, us, the Du Ponts, and others. It reflects how society answers its "for whom" question at each point in time. In section 3 we expand the discussion to ask how individuals' positions on the economic ladder vary over their lifetimes and about the relations between parents' and children's incomes.

Section 4 considers the effects of discrimination on individual earnings and income inequality. Section 5 concludes with a discussion of poverty in the United States.

1. The Functional Distribution of Income

In this section we consider the division of total national income between suppliers of labor and suppliers of capital. We begin by developing the general principles involved and then turn to the facts. To avoid unnecessary complications we consider only two factors of production, capital (which includes land here) and labor, and we proceed as if both factors were homogeneous.

The Theory

In Figure 20-1, L_D is the economywide demand curve for labor at some point in time. Its location reflects the technology and capital stock available to the economy. The downward-sloping L_D curve shows that the quantity of labor demanded rises when the real wage falls. The lower the real wage, the more attractive it is to firms to use labor-intensive production processes.

The economy's labor supply schedule is shown in Figure 20-1 as L_S. We assume for simplicity that the quantity of labor supplied is independent of the real wage.[3]

[3] In fact, as we discussed in Chapter 16, higher wages cause households to supply more labor. But we lose nothing important by assuming the supply elasticity to be zero here.

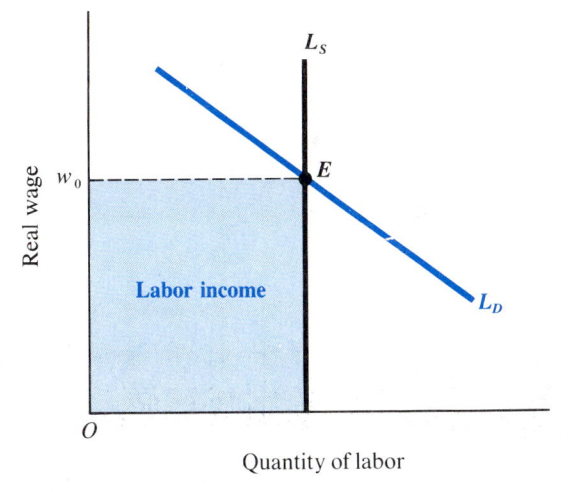

FIGURE 20-1. Equilibrium in the Labor Market Determines the Real Wage and Labor Income. For given technology and a given capital stock, the schedule L_D represents the economywide demand for labor. The lower the real wage, the more labor-using the techniques firms wish to use, and hence the larger the quantity of labor demanded. With a given labor supply L_S, the equilibrium real wage is w_0. Labor income is equal to the shaded rectangle, or the wage rate times the quantity of labor employed.

The intersection of L_D and L_S at point E determines the equilibrium real wage, w_0. In the equilibrium at E, labor income is equal to the shaded rectangle—the real wage times the quantity of labor employed.

Since we consider only two factors of production, capital and labor, any income that does not go to capital must accrue to labor. Conversely, if we know that labor's share of income is, say, 70 percent, we also know that the remainder, 30 percent, must be the share of capital.

$$\text{Labor's share of income} = \frac{\text{labor income}}{\text{total income}} \quad (1)$$

$$= \frac{\text{wage rate} \times \text{employment}}{\text{total income}}$$

We will now see how labor's share is affected by changes in the supply of labor, changes in the capital stock, and changes in technology.

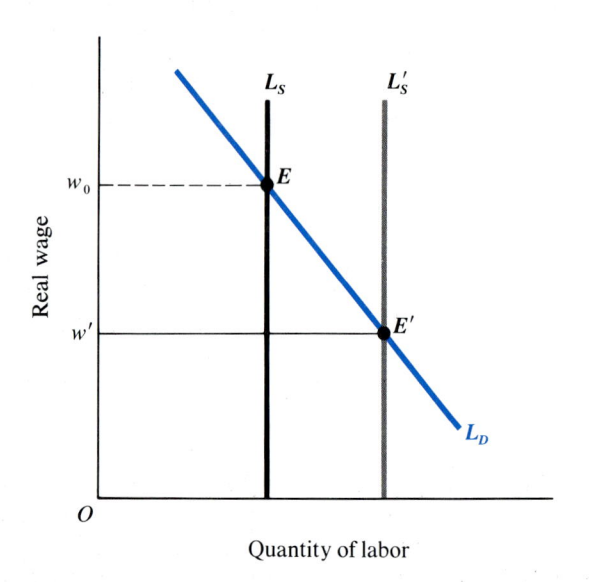

FIGURE 20-2. The Effect of an Increase in the Supply of Labor. A shift in the labor supply schedule to L'_S lowers the equilibrium real wage at which the labor force will be employed. Firms have to be induced to employ more workers per unit of capital by a decline in the relative cost of labor — a fall in real wages. Total labor income may rise or fall depending on the elasticity of the labor demand schedule. With demand inelastic, labor income must fall.

AN INCREASE IN LABOR SUPPLY. An increase in the supply of labor (perhaps because of immigration or a change in attitudes toward work) is represented as a shift in the labor supply schedule to L'_S in Figure 20-2. Given the capital stock, firms will hire more workers only at a lower real wage. As an increased labor force makes a larger number of workers compete for jobs, the real wage therefore is driven down to w'.

What can be said about labor's share of income? With unchanged capital and technology and higher employment, the economy produces more output. Therefore, the denominator of equation (1) will rise with labor supply growth. What happens to labor's share then depends on the behavior of labor income. There are more workers, so employment increases, but we also saw that the real wage declines. Hence labor income, which is the wage times employment, may rise or fall. As we learned in Chapter 5, the elasticity of labor demand determines the outcome. If the demand for labor is *inelastic*, an increase in the quantity of labor supplied will lower total spending on labor—which is just labor income. Conversely, if labor demand is *elastic*, an increase in labor supply will raise labor income.

What determines the elasticity of demand for labor? One important determinant is the ease with which labor and capital can be substituted for each other in production. At one extreme, the capital-labor ratio is nearly fixed by technology, as it is when people dig ditches with shovels, for instance. In this case an increase in the number of workers per unit of capital (shovel) does not increase output much. Then an increase in the labor supply will bring about a relatively large decline in the real wage, since with a given capital stock there is no incentive to employ more workers unless the real wage falls sharply. If capital and labor are poor substitutes, then, an increase in the supply of labor leads to a fall in labor income and thus in labor's share of total income.

At the other extreme, if capital and labor are easily substitutable (imagine people and robots working side by side, performing the same tasks), the demand for labor will be highly elastic. In this case wages may fall very little when the quantity of labor supplied rises. If capital and labor are good substitutes, so that the demand for labor is elastic, an increase in the supply of labor will lead to an increase in labor income. If the demand for labor is elastic enough, labor income will rise more than total income, and labor's share will increase.

AN INCREASE IN THE CAPITAL STOCK. Since there are only two inputs, exactly the same analysis applies to an increase in the capital stock, holding constant the supply of labor. With more capital for firms to employ, there will be an excess supply of capital and an excess demand for labor at the initial wage and rental rates. An increase in the capital stock increases the marginal product of labor, and this is shown in Figure 20-3 as a shift in the labor demand curve to the right from L_D to L'_D. The real wage will rise as firms compete for labor to operate the now abundant capital. The shift in labor demand leads to a rise in the real wage from w_0 to w' and therefore to a rise in labor income. Thus an increase in the capital stock must raise the real wage and labor income.

Whether labor's share of total income (which is again higher) rises or falls when the quantity of capital increases depends again on the ease of substitution between labor and capital. If substitutability is high, relative factor prices change very little, and labor's share falls. If substitutability between factors is very low, however, it takes large changes in factor prices to induce firms to change production techniques. In this case labor may gain both absolutely and relatively.

Because the analysis of changes in capital and labor is entirely symmetric, we can talk about changes in the ratio of capital to labor rather than changes in the labor force and changes in the capital stock separately. Table 20-1 summarizes the discussion in those terms. The table shows the effect on income distribution and factor incomes of an increase in the amount of capital per worker, or the capital-labor ratio. An increase in the capital-labor ratio always raises the real wage and lowers the real rental of capital; these changes are larger the less

TABLE 20-1. The Effects of an Economywide Increase in the Amount of Capital per Worker

Substitutability	Real wage	Real rental of capital	Labor income	Capital income	Labor's share of income
High	+	−	+	+	−
Low	+	−	+	−	+

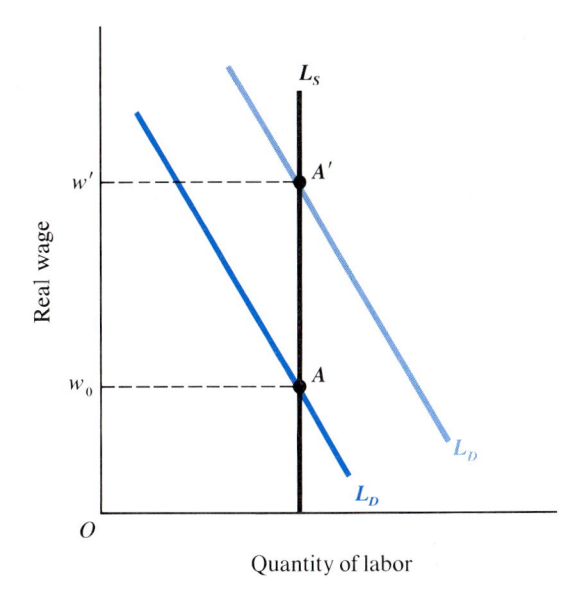

FIGURE 20-3. An Increase in the Capital Stock Shifts the Demand for Labor. An increase in the capital stock raises the marginal productivity of labor, since each worker now has more capital to work with. The demand curve for labor moves to the right, from L_D to L'_D. The real wage therefore rises. The increase in the real wage is larger the less substitutable are capital and labor.

substitutable are these two inputs. Thus labor's share rises when the two inputs are poor substitutes but falls when they are good substitutes—in the latter case the change in the amount of capital per worker outweighs the changes in the earnings per unit of the two inputs.

CHANGES IN TECHNOLOGY. Technological change may raise the productivity of capital and labor equally, or it may favor increased use of one at the expense of the other.[4] We will not discuss the various possibilities in detail but simply note that changes in technology can raise or lower labor's share of total income.

---

[4] Often workers oppose the introduction of new machinery because in the short run it reduces the number of jobs in the firms in which they work. But for the economy as a whole, new machinery leads to growth and higher productivity. Thus total employment has continued to grow even though for decades workers have complained that automation eliminates jobs.

The U.S. Experience

How has the functional distribution of income changed historically in the U.S. economy? We start in Table 20-2 with estimates of the growth of the capital stock and labor input over the past 96 years.

In both the period 1889–1929 and the period since 1929, capital grew on average more than a percentage point per year faster than did labor. Thus the long-term experience is that capital per worker has increased. The theory we have developed predicts that this would lead to a rise in the real wage and a fall in the rental on capital. The change in labor's share would depend on the ease of substitutability between capital and labor and on the nature of technological change over the period.

Unfortunately we do not have exactly the right data with which to evaluate these predictions. Table 20-3 shows the distribution of income among three factors: labor (compensation of employees in the form of wages and salaries), income from property (corresponding to income from capital in terms of this section), and proprietors' income. This last category is the source of the trouble. It shows the income of unincorporated businesses (farms, owner-operated shops, self-employed people such as dentists and artists). But these unincorporated businesses yield an income that is partly a return on the capital used in the business (the farmland and livestock, the shop, the dentist's drill) and partly a return to the labor supplied by the owner. We therefore cannot tell what part of proprietors' income to lump with employees' compensation as labor income and what part to lump with income from property as capital income. The lack of a more complete division of proprietors' income makes it difficult to develop a precise historical perspective on the shares of capital and labor income.

TABLE 20-2. Growth Rates of Capital and Labor Input, 1889–1985
(Average Annual Percentage Growth Rates)

Period	Capital	Labor	Capital-labor ratio
1889–1929	3.1	2.0	1.1
1929–1985	2.3	1.0	1.3

Source: U.S. Department of Commerce, *Long-Term Economic Growth, 1860–1970*, Federal Reserve System, *Balance Sheets for the U.S. Economy, 1946–1985*, and *Economic Report of the President, 1987*.

TABLE 20-3. Shares of National Income (Percent)

	1929	1950	1960	1970	1985
Compensation of employees	60.3	65.2	70.9	75.5	73.9
Proprietors' income	17.7	16.3	11.4	8.2	7.6
Property income	22.0	18.5	17.7	16.3	18.6

Source: *Economic Report of the President, 1987*, Table B-23.

Even so, the data in Table 20-3 are of interest. Employee compensation has risen substantially since 1929, from 60 to about 75 percent of national income. Property income (dividends, interest, rent on land) by contrast declined from 1929 to 1970, although there has been a recent increase. Do these data support the view that the increase in the capital-labor ratio since 1929 (seen in Table 20-2) raises the real wage and labor's share of income?

Suppose first that all of proprietors' income is simply labor income. Labor's share is then the sum of the first two rows in Table 20-3. We would then conclude that labor's share has risen from 78 percent to 81.5 percent over the period. Conversely, suppose that all of proprietors' income is income from capital. This assumption implies that labor's share has increased from 60.3 percent to 73.9 percent. Thus, unless the share of proprietors' income derived from capital rose a lot over the period, the data indicate that labor's share of income over the period 1929–1985 increased substantially. Since the capital-labor ratio rose over the period, this means that substitutability between capital and labor was low and/or that technical progress favored labor.

2. The Personal Distribution of Income

We now turn our attention from factors of production to individuals and families—who may supply both labor and capital. Do a few families receive most of the income in the United States, or is there actually little inequality? Is the distribution of income more or less unequal in the United States than it is in other nations? To answer these questions, economists generally use the Lorenz curve to measure the extent of inequality in the personal distribution of income.

The Lorenz Curve

Data are available for the distribution of total income among families in the U.S. economy.[5] The data for 1960 and 1984 are summarized in Table 20-4. They indicate that the personal distribution of income has not changed much since 1960.

We read the table as follows. In 1960 the poorest (lowest) fifth (20 percent) of families received only 4.8 percent of total U.S. income. In 1984 their share was 4.7 percent. By contrast the richest (top) 20 percent of families received more than 40 percent of total income in both years. The table thus gives some indication of the inequality of the distribution of incomes. For instance, the top 20 percent of families receive more than eight times as much income as the bottom 20 percent receive. We often hear of a widening gap between the rich and the poor. The data in Table 20-4 show that in the United States this is not the case; the income distribution has not changed dramatically in the last 25 years.[6]

The data for 1984 in Table 20-4 are presented graphically in the *Lorenz curve* shown in Figure 20-4. This curve is designed to answer at a glance such questions as, What share of total income goes to the bottom 60 percent of families? On the vertical axis we plot percentages from zero to 100 percent, representing shares of total income. On the horizontal axis we also plot percentages

[5] Separate data are available on the distribution of income by persons and by families. The data on distribution by families report direct evidence from surveys. The data on distribution by persons are estimates.
[6] The distribution of wealth between families *has* changed. In 1963, for example, the top 1 percent of families owned 32 percent of all wealth; by 1983 their share had increased to 42 percent.

TABLE 20-4. Distribution of Aggregate Money Income among Families

	Percentage of total income received by familes in					
Period	Lowest fifth	Second fifth	Third fifth	Fourth fifth	Top fifth	Top 5%
1960	4.8	12.2	17.8	24.0	41.3	15.9
1984	4.7	11.0	17.0	24.4	42.9	16.0

Note: Money income is income before deduction of income and Social Security taxes.
Source: *Statistical Abstract of the United States, 1986*, Table 754.

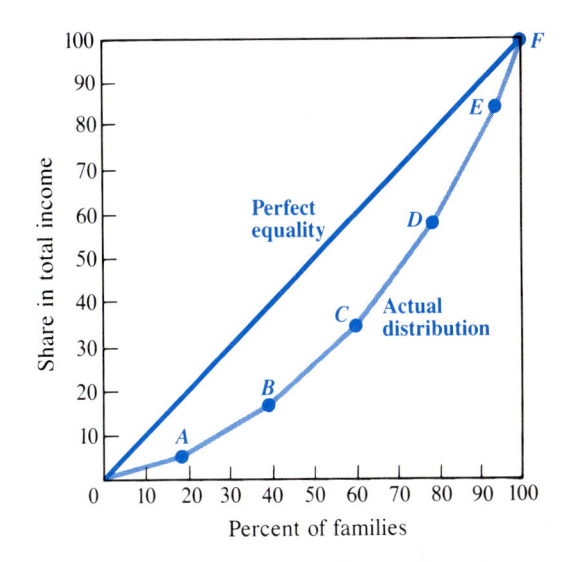

FIGURE 20-4. The U.S. Lorenz Curve, 1984. *Note*: Money income of families and unrelated individuals. (*Source: Statistical Abstract of the United States, 1986*, Table 759.)

from zero to 100 percent, representing fractions of the total number of families. Points farther to the right on the horizontal axis correspond to families with higher incomes.

The curve labeled "actual distribution" is then constructed by adding across the columns in Table 20-4 from left to right to obtain the fraction of income received by the poorest 20 percent of the population, the poorest 40 percent, the poorest 60 percent, and so on. Table 20-4 shows directly that the poorest 20 percent of families in 1984 received 4.7 percent of income. This observation is plotted as point A. Adding the first two columns in Table 20-4, we find that the poorest 40 percent of families had 15.7 percent of income. This information is shown as point B. Continuing similarly, the poorest 60 percent of families received 32.7 percent ($= 4.7 + 11.0 + 17.0$) of income, and this enables us to plot point C. Point D shows that the share of the bottom 80 percent is 57.1 percent ($= 32.7 + 24.4$). Finally, since the top 5 percent of all families receive 16 percent of total income, the share of the bottom 95 percent must be 84 percent, and this is shown as point E. Connecting all the points, we have the Lorenz curve $0ABCDEF$ for the U.S. economy. Each point on the curve shows the share of total income received by the corresponding fraction of the poorest families.

The shape of the Lorenz curve summarizes the extent of inequality in the personal distribution of income. Two extreme cases make this clear. Suppose first that a tiny fraction of families receives all income. In this case the Lorenz curve will coincide with the horizontal axis and then run up to 100 percent of income near 98 or 99 percent of families. (Draw such a schedule for yourself to better visualize it.) Alternatively, suppose that all families have the same income so that the bottom 20 percent of families have 20 percent of income, the bottom 40 percent of families have 40 percent of income, and so on. In this case, the Lorenz curve would be the straight line labeled "perfect equality" in Figure 20-4. The actual Lorenz curve for the U.S. economy, and for all other economies, is somewhere between these extremes. It is below the diagonal line 0F because there is some inequality, but it is not nearly as far away from the diagonal as it could be.

The Lorenz curve gives a simple way of looking at equality. The closer the actual Lorenz curve is to the diagonal, the more equal the income distribution. Figure 20-5 makes the point by comparing the income distributions of the United States and Mexico. In neither country is distribution either perfectly equal or extremely unequal. However, it is clear that in the United States the distribution is more equal—the Lorenz curve is closer to the line of perfect equality—than is the case in Mexico.

Qualifications

We are interested in the personal income distribution because income represents purchasing power over goods and services and thus gives some indication of the relative welfare or well-being of people. Of course, money income may be a very crude indicator of well-being, and as we discussed in Chapter 6, there is no scientific way to compare the happiness of different individuals. Even so, the distribution of income is one of the few available indicators of relative well-being, and it is widely used to analyze inequality. However, there are important qualifications that must be taken into account when using Lorenz curves based on government data.

The income distribution reported in Table 20-4 comes from the U.S. Census. The income recorded by the Bureau of the Census includes income both from current work effort and from property as well as cash transfers received. These transfers include Social Security payments, unemployment benefits, retirement benefits, and public assistance. But the income measure does not include income in kind (such as the services provided by owner-occupied housing) or transfers in kind (such as food stamps and free medical care). A more comprehensive concept of income that includes income and transfers in kind would give a more accurate picture of inequality.

A second qualification concerns taxes. The income measures we have considered here include transfers but do not deduct personal income taxes or Social Security taxes. These taxes affect the distribution of income. In particular, the personal income tax is slightly progressive (people with higher incomes tend to pay a larger fraction of their incomes) and is thus designed to reduce inequality. Available estimates indicate that this effect is small: The share of after-tax income received by the top 20 percent of familes is only about 2 percentage points below their share of before-tax income.[7] The tax system

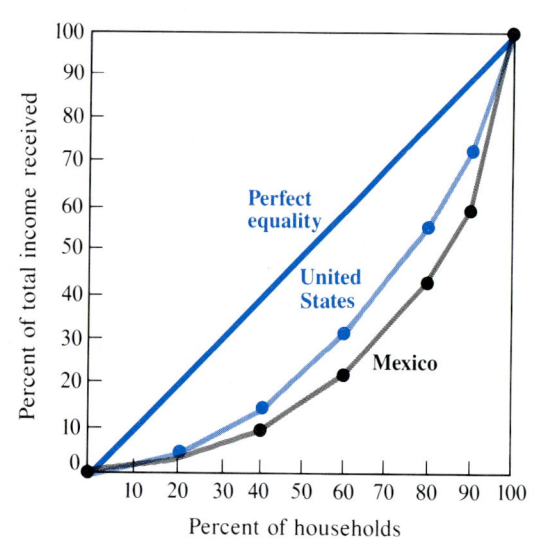

FIGURE 20-5. The Lorenz Curves for the United States and Mexico. (*Source: World Development Report,* 1985, Table 28.)

[7] See Joseph A. Pechman, *Who Paid the Taxes, 1966–85*, Brookings Institution, Washington, D.C., 1985, p. 5.

does redistribute income, but it has little impact on inequality.

A third problem with the income distribution data arises because families are of different sizes, and it costs more to provide a large family with food and other necessities. At the high end of the income distribution, the number of persons per family is nearly a third higher than at the bottom end—3.7 versus 2.9 persons per family. The smaller average size of low-income families reflects in part the fact that they are families of old people or very young people (college students, for example) who have not yet had children. In addition, high-income families tend to have more earners per family than do those with low incomes. The ratio of earners to nonearners is nearly 2 at the high-income end and only 0.3 at the low-income end. Thus the large share of income accruing to the top 20 percent of families is partly accounted for by the larger number of people working per family and overstates differences in well-being because of the larger size of upper-income families.

Adjustments for the number of earners and the number of people per family must be used with care, however. To some extent, the number of family members reported reflects peculiarities of the tax and transfer systems. Rich families are encouraged to claim children in college as dependents and report them as family members living in the household. Poor families, by contrast, can claim more welfare payments if there is only one parent in the household.

The Distribution of Wealth

Data on the distribution of wealth exist but are less reliable than those on the distribution of income. The data show the amounts of wealth (excluding the value of human capital) owned by different people and display extraordinary disparities in wealth.

According to a 1986 study by the Joint Economic Committee of the Congress, the richest 5 percent of families owned 35 percent of the nation's wealth in 1983. A Census Bureau study showed that the median white family in 1986 had 10 times the nonhuman wealth that the median black family had—with most of the wealth of each being in the family house. However, even for white families the median wealth level was under $40,000 in 1983.

Because human capital makes up most of the wealth of most people, these data, impressive as they are, overstate differences in standards of living within the country. They nonetheless indicate extraordinary differences among families.

3. Economic Mobility

To what extent does economic status—being rich or being poor—persist within a family over time or from one generation to the next? Do the poor stay poor, without much possibility of escaping into the middle class or even moving to the top? Of course, we know plenty of stories of people who have risen to great wealth from humble origins, but perhaps there is a much larger number of people with real potential who could not escape from the poverty in which they grew up.

● **Economic mobility refers to the ease with which a person or family can move up or down the income distribution ladder.**

We first deal with issues of measurement and then discuss the interpretation of the available data on mobility.

Measuring Mobility

Table 20-5 suggests a way of thinking about economic mobility. Suppose we have two equally large income groups: the poor and the rich. In the first column we place the status of parents, and in the next two columns we show the status of their children. In each of the cells we show the percentage of children with each background that reach a given status. In the table we show a

TABLE 20-5. Hypothetical Economic Mobility Table

If parents were	Probability of child being	
	Poor, %	Rich, %
Poor	90	10
Rich	10	90

case of low social mobility: A child with poor parents has a 90 percent chance of staying poor and only a 10 percent chance of moving into the rich group. Likewise, the children of the rich have a 90 percent chance of staying rich and only a 10 percent chance of becoming poor.

Suppose, at the other extreme, that there were perfect mobility. Then all people would have the same chance of being rich or poor, regardless of the economic status of their parents. In this case, with the same number of rich and poor people, every cell in Table 20-5 would show 50 percent. A child born into a poor family would have an even chance of staying poor or becoming rich.

The probabilities in the economic mobility table will be more like 90 percent to 10 percent than 50 percent to 50 percent if income depends mainly on inherited wealth and connections. But the table will show greater mobility if personal motivation and willingness to work hard are important. Which of these better describes the facts of economic life in the United States?

Table 20-6 presents data indicating that mobility in the United States is quite high, closer to the 50/50 pattern than to the 90/10 pattern. These data are based on a long-term study in which the economic fortunes of a large group of individuals have been followed year by year since 1968. The income data for the young adults in the table are for 1981. The table shows in each row the percentage of young adults in different parts of the income distribution. For instance, 59 percent of the children of parents in the lowest 40 percent of the income distribution were themselves in the lowest 40 percent. Equivalently, as many as 41 percent of the children of the poorest 40 percent of the parents were in a higher part of the income distribution than were their parents. At the other end of the income distribution of the parents, 25 percent of the children of parents in the top 40 percent of the distribution were themselves in the lowest 40 percent.

Family, Merit, and Luck

What lies behind data such as those in Table 20-6? We can separate out three factors: family background, achievement, and luck. Unfortunately, we do not have much to say about luck and therefore concentrate on the other two factors. Family background enters in three separate ways in determining economic status. First, heredity may play a role. To the extent that the children of smart or talented parents tend to be smart or talented, they will tend to be more successful than will other children.

Second, the family environment may affect how an individual develops and uses his inborn abilities. Growing up in a hardworking, middle-class family may give a child motivation and drive that would not be developed by a child growing up in a family so rich that no one works. Third, differences in family wealth directly affect children's opportunities. Children of rich people almost always attend college, regardless of their ability, while only the most able children from slums go beyond high school. This third channel also involves less-well-defined but very real benefits such as connnections and access to opportunities on the basis of family ties and background. Being in the club definitely helps. Similarly, it is often argued that the United States has developed a culture of poverty in the past two decades, as children who grow up in families dependent on welfare themselves become dependent.

The other important determinant of socioeconomic success is personal achievement—the result of motivation and hard work. Of course, personal achievement is hard to measure and even harder to separate from inherited ability and the effects of family background. Because there are few good alternatives, educational achievement remains one of the most-used indicators of ability and potential in our society. Indeed, even if one learns noth-

TABLE 20-6. Economic Mobility between Generations in the United States

Parents' income in	Probability (in %) of young adult being in		
	Lowest 40%	Middle 20%	Top 40%
Lowest 40%	59	18	22
Middle 20%	34	23	43
Top 40%	25	20	55

pendence across Generations," *Economic Outlook*, Summer 1983, p. 61, Table 1. "Income" in the table is the ratio of income to needs in the original source. Sums may not total 100 because of rounding.

ing in college, graduation demonstrates motivation to potential employers, as we discussed in Chapter 17. And we, at least, like to think that education really does enhance ability. Therefore, programs that provide access to education for people from poor family backgrounds are one of the main mechanisms for making the race for economic status fairer and the odds of success more equal.

The data in Table 20-6 do suggest that despite the many forces that tend to make children's incomes similar to those of their parents, there is still considerable economic mobility in the United States.[8] But because the data involve only a very broad view, it is possible that they conceal a significant problem of long-term welfare dependence.[9]

There is also evidence available on the economic mobility of families over relatively short periods of time rather than between generations. Table 20-7 shows that one-third of the families that were in the bottom 40 percent of the income distribution in 1971 had risen

[8] Evidence of high mobility goes back a long way. James R. Kearl and Clayne L. Pope, "Intergenerational Effects on the Distribution of Income and Wealth: The Utah Experience, 1850–1900," National Bureau of Economic Research, Cambridge, Mass., Working Paper No. 754, 1981, examined incomes and wealth of fathers and sons in Utah in the late nineteenth century. They found that high-income fathers tended to have sons with higher income and wealth than average but that the effect was not large. What effect there was came from the fathers passing on their wealth at death rather than from the sons earning higher incomes on their own.

[9] Hill and Ponza in the article that provided the data in Table 20-6 conclude, however, that their evidence does not support "the culture-of-poverty, underclass, and welfare-dependence theories" (p. 64). We return to this issue in Chapter 22.

TABLE 20-7. Family Economic Mobility in the United States

If family income in 1971 was in	Probability (in %) of family income in 1978 being in		
	Bottom 40%	Middle 20%	Top 40%
Bottom 40%	67	16	18
Middle 20%	37	31	33
Top 40%	15	20	66

Source: Greg J. Duncan, *Years of Poverty, Years of Plenty*, University of Michigan, Ann Arbor, 1984, Table 1.1. Rows do not total 100 because of rounding.

TABLE 20-8. Median Weekly Earnings by Sex and Race, 1984 (Index, White Males = 100)

	Men	Women
White	100	66
Black	75	60
Hispanic	71	56

Source: *Statistical Abstract of the United States, 1986*, Table 713.

higher in the distribution 7 years later. Similarly, about a third of those who were in the highest 40 percent in 1971 had slipped lower within 7 years.

4. Discrimination

While there is considerable economic mobility—between generations and over shorter time periods—in the United States, it is possible that there would be even more but for the effect of discrimination. Some have argued that discrimination also accounts for much of the poverty and income inequality in this country.

Table 20-8 shows relative earnings by race and sex in 1984. Female workers and nonwhite workers on average earned much less than white males earned. In this section we examine the role of discrimination in creating these differences, see how they have changed over time, and discuss government policies to aid disadvantaged groups.

There are two main sources of inequality in economic status between different groups in the labor force. First, there are differences in the share of good jobs held by each group. Second, there may be differences in the pay received for the same job. We begin with the first of these.

Who Has the Good Jobs?

Table 20-9 shows the pay and the fraction of each group in each of several occupations. It is clear that a large fraction of the pay differentials in Table 20-8 arises from differences in the mix of jobs held by the members of each group. Women, blacks, and Hispanics are more likely than average to have jobs that pay poorly. For

TABLE 20-9. Selected Occupations: Relative Pay and Distribution of the Labor Force

Occupation	Relative earnings*	Percent of group employed			
		All	Women	Black	Hispanic
Managers	100	10.7	7.9	5.4	5.8
Professionals	93	12.7	14.0	8.7	6.0
Operators, fabricators, and laborers	61	16.0	9.7	24.1	25.0
Administrative support	57	16.3	29.7	16.8	15.4
Service workers	45	13.7	18.9	24.5	25.0

* Index of median weekly earnings of full-time workers, managers 100.

Source: *Handbook of Labor Statistics, 1985*, Table 17; *Statistical Abstract of the United States, 1986*, Table 704. Data refer to 1983.

example, while 10.7 percent of all workers have jobs as managers, only 5.4 percent of blacks work as managers. Similarly, women, blacks, and Hispanics are more likely than other workers to have service jobs, which on average pay less than half as well as managerial jobs. The only surprising exception to this pattern is the large fraction of women with jobs classified as "professional." But this classification is broad, including both physicians (16 percent women) and prekindergarten and kindergarten teachers (98 percent women).

The best jobs do more than pay well. Managerial and professional jobs also tend to be steadier than others. While the overall unemployment rate in 1983 was 9.6 percent, for instance, unemployment in these top categories was only 3.3 percent. This low share of good jobs also helps explain why the unemployment rates for blacks (21.0 percent in 1983) and Hispanics (16.3 percent) are generally well above average.

Why do a higher percentage of white males have good jobs? Why do white women have an edge over blacks in getting managerial jobs? Three types of discrimination, past and present, have helped shape these patterns.

PREJUDICE. The most obvious source of discrimination is blatant prejudice: racism or sexism. If a white male is deciding between two equally qualified applicants for a good job, another white male and a black female, the white man is probably going to be hired. This may reflect the decision maker's own prejudices, or it may be a response to the prejudices of customers or other workers. As long as white males control most jobs and prefer to work with or be supervised by other white males, women, blacks, and Hispanics will not get their share of good jobs for which they are qualified.

STATISTICAL DISCRIMINATION. Suppose an employer is choosing between two new graduates from the same college, with identical grades. One is black and one is white, but neither the employer nor her customers nor the other workers care whether a white or a black is hired. Discrimination can nonetheless occur, even without prejudice, if the employer believes that blacks on average have poorer work habits than do whites. Then skin color provides information, and the employer will hire the white applicant because, taking skin color into account, he is believed to be more productive.

This sort of discrimination can develop into a self-fulfilling prophecy. If access to good jobs is based in large part on inherited attributes, such as sex, skin color, and family background, individuals discriminated against have much less incentive to invest in acquiring education or developing good work habits. As groups initially *believed* to be less qualified respond by reducing their investments in skills, they *become* less qualified in fact, and group membership becomes a better predictor of actual productivity.

ACCESS TO EDUCATION. The third way in which discrimination creates unequal shares of good jobs and economic status is through the unequal provision of good education and skills. Table 20-10 shows the strong differences in educational attainment by race that have prevailed historically.[10]

Thirty years ago the typical black worker had only an elementary school education, while the typical white worker had finished high school. In 1959, a black worker was only 48 percent (25.5 percent versus 52.6 percent) as likely as a white worker to have finished high school.

[10] While male workers have historically obtained more years of education on average than have female workers, the differences between all men and all women are much smaller than those shown in the table.

TABLE 20-10. Percentage of Workers Having Completed High School and College

Year	High school			College		
	White	Black	Hispanic	White	Black	Hispanic
1959	52.6	25.5	NA	10.3	4.1	NA
1974	70.9	45.5	44.7	15.7	9.3	5.7
1984	81.6	71.6	55.2	21.6	11.6	8.3

NA = data not available.
Source: *Handbook of Labor Statistics*, 1985, Table 61.

Since then, high school graduation rates of blacks and Hispanics have increased more rapidly than has the rate for whites. In 1984, a black worker was 88 percent as likely as a white worker to have finished high school. But Hispanics still lag far behind, and since poor communities can generally afford only poor schools, it is unlikely that blacks and Hispanics receive the same quality of education in elementary and high school as do whites.[11] Moreover, the educational gap at the college level has not narrowed much. In 1959 a black worker was 40 percent as likely as a white worker to have finished college; by 1984 this figure had risen to only 54 percent, and a Hispanic worker was only 38 percent as likely as a white worker to have a college diploma.

COSTS OF DISCRIMINATION. Discrimination in hiring is economically costly. It is obviously costly to those who are discriminated against; their incomes are lower. It may also be costly to those who discriminate. If an employer's prejudice causes him to hire less productive workers, his profits will be lower. Finally, discrimination imposes costs on the economy as a whole. It prevents an efficient allocation of workers to jobs and causes disadvantaged groups not to invest in human capital, resulting in inefficient production and lost output. Quite independent of moral considerations, there are strong economic arguments against discrimination.

[11] There is some evidence that improvements in the relative quality of schools attended by blacks in the last 20 years have reduced the differences between the earnings of blacks and whites with equal numbers of years of education. See the articles by John Akin and Irv Garfinkel; Finis Welch; and Charles Link, Edward Ratledge, and Kenneth Lewis in the *American Economic Review*, March 1980.

Equal Pay for Equal Work?

The second type of discrimination is discrimination on the job, which results in unequal pay for equal work. In the absence of any kind of discrimination we would expect that for the same kind of work performed, men and women or white and Hispanic workers would receive the same pay. But this may not occur, and such discrimination may be hard to detect because of differences in titles and positions that do not reflect differences in work. On-the-job discrimination occurs, for instance, if a female secretary does a lot of computer programming in an automated office but is paid much less than a male programmer.

While this kind of discrimination is harder to prove, there is little doubt that it has been pervasive. A recent study estimated that, holding constant experience, education, industry, and job responsibility, women earn about 30 percent less than men.[12]

Equal pay for women has become a public issue under the heading of *comparable worth*.[13] Carolyn Shaw Bell has summarized the issue as follows:

> Men's wage rates are higher, the pay in male-dominated jobs exceeds that for female-intensive jobs, women are more concentrated in women's jobs than are men in men's jobs, and earnings differ even after all possible corrections for ability, experience, time worked, age, education, and anything else that can be controlled for.[14]

These facts have led some people to propose legislation that requires pay to be geared not to conditions in the labor market but rather to an objective classification of the characteristics and skill requirements of each job. The argument is that schoolteachers, generally women, should not be paid less than auto mechanics, generally men, simply because women have historically been limited by their parents or society to a narrow set of occupations.

[12] Marianne A. Ferber, Carole A. Green, and Joe L. Spaeth, "Work Power and Earnings of Women and Men," *American Economic Review*, May 1986.
[13] For a discussion of the comparable worth issue, see the symposia in *Contemporary Policy Issues*, April 1986, and *Monthly Labor Review*, December 1986.
[14] See C. Shaw Bell, "Comparable Worth: How Do We Know It Will Work?" *Monthly Labor Review*, Dec. 1985, p. 11.

Critics of comparable worth doubt the possibility of "objectively" classifying jobs (is it really harder to teach first grade than to tune a Porsche?) and note that if wages are not responsive to supply and demand, unemployment will rise sharply in some occupations and shortages will appear in others. These critics argue that limitations on womens' job choices should be addressed directly, not rectified by distorting the wage structure.

Toward Equal Opportunity

There has been substantial progress in the United States in the past 20 years in reducing discrimination and inequality in economic status by race and sex. Table 20-11 gives some measure of the relative progress that nonwhite members of the labor force have achieved. While in 1967 the median wage of a nonwhite worker was only 70 percent of a white worker's wage, it is now 80 percent. For nonwhite women the catch-up has been larger. Their median wage rose from less than 60 percent of that of white women to more than 90 percent in 1978.[15]

The table also shows that the same sort of progress is apparent in the holding of white-collar jobs, even though it is still true that a smaller fraction of nonwhites than whites have good jobs. The fraction of nonwhites who hold managerial, administrative, and professional jobs has increased substantially. For example, between 1972 and 1983 this share increased from 13 to 21 percent.

What accounts for this progress? Three factors are especially important. The first is a general reduction in prejudice throughout the labor market. The second is the effort, through the Civil Rights Act of 1964 and associated legislation, to use the powers of the federal government to eliminate discrimination against nonwhite and female workers. The third factor, in part a result of the previous two, is an improvement in the education and skills of nonwhite people. They have better access to education and a greater motivation to improve their skills; thus they are able to get better jobs.

While everyone agrees that some progress has been made, some argue that government programs have done more to create the illusion of progress than to advance the welfare of women and nonwhites.[16] During the sixties and seventies there was an expansion of public employment and government welfare programs. These programs either took people out of the labor force by putting them on welfare, which required that they not work, or took them out out of the private labor market by giving them public employment. In general, the people in public employment programs were paid poorly and given little training for better jobs.

There were two effects on the relative wages of nonwhite workers. First, the lowest-paid nonwhite workers were no longer in the labor force; therefore, the average pay of those left in the labor force rose. Second, because there were fewer nonwhite workers in private-sector jobs (as a result of some dropping out of the labor force and some working for the government), the relative wages of nonwhites rose. The overall effect, it is argued, was the appearance of a reduction in inequality and of an increase in the relative pay of nonwhite workers. These arguments make it clear that it is not only important but difficult to devise and evaluate effective antidiscrimination programs.

---

[15] For more data see R. Freeman, J. Dunlop, and R. Schubert, "The Evolution of the American Labor Market: 1948–80," in M. Feldstein (ed.), *The American Economy in Transition*, University of Chicago Press, 1980.

TABLE 20-11. The Economic Catch-Up of Nonwhites in 1967–1982

	Nonwhite Percentage of Employment			Relative earnings, nonwhite % of white
	White-collar	Blue-collar	Services	
1967	5.4	12.5	25.2	69.9
1982	9.1	13.1	19.7	80.5

Source: *Handbook of Labor Statistics, 1980*, Table 60; *1983*, Table 16; and *1985*, Table 41.

[16] See Richard B. Freeman, "Changes in the Labor Market for Black Americans, 1948–72," *Brookings Papers on Economic Activity*, vol. 1, 1973; and Richard Butler and J. Hekman, "Industrial Impact of the Labor Market Status of Black Americans: A Critical Review," in Leonard J. Hausman et al. (eds.), *Equal Rights and Industrial Discrimination*, Industrial Relations Research Association, University of Wisconsin, Madison, 1977.

5. Poverty

An important issue in thinking about the distribution of income is whether our main concern is with inequality or with poverty. To see why the answer matters, suppose that everyone agrees that any family with an income below $15,000 is poor. If 95 percent of families have incomes of $16,000 and 5 percent of families have incomes of $100,000, we have no poverty but considerable inequality. Alternatively, with the same average income, suppose that half the families have incomes of $14,000 and half have incomes of $26,400. In this case there is less inequality, but half the population is poor. Which is the better society? Which do we, or should we, really worry about more, poverty or inequality? This is a question of values which each person must answer for himself or herself. Economics can do no more than make the distinction clear.

In this section we turn our attention to poverty in the United States. We begin by considering the definition of poverty. We then discuss changes in the incidence of poverty for particular individuals and in society as a whole.

Relative and Absolute Poverty

Figure 20-6 describes the distribution of family incomes in the United States in 1984. It shows the percentage of total families with incomes in each of the indicated ranges: less than $5,000, between $5,000 and $10,000, and so on. The figure indicates that more than half of U.S. families had incomes in excess of $20,000 and that 13 percent even had incomes of more than $50,000. But a third of all families had incomes of less than $15,000, and 20 percent of all families had incomes of less than $10,000. Who, among all these different families, are the poor? Where is the line between the families we call "poor" and those above the poverty line?

The official definition of *absolute poverty* was developed in the 1960s.

● **A family is defined as poor if its income is less than three times the Department of Agriculture's estimate of the cost of an "economy food program" for the family.**

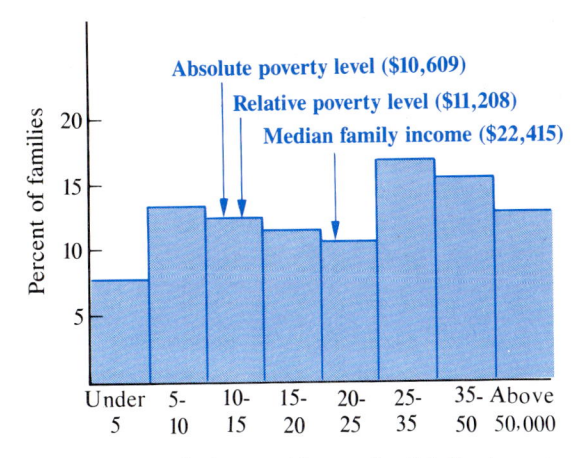

FIGURE 20-6. Distribution of Family Income and the Poverty Level, 1984. (*Source: Statistical Abstract of the United States, 1986,* Tables 742 and 743.)

The reasoning behind this definition starts from the fact that low-income families spend about one-third of their income on food. The Agriculture Department each year estimates the cost of an economy food program that is supposed to be just adequate to provide a nutritious diet. That cost is multiplied by 3 to obtain the official estimate of the poverty line.[17]

The median family income in 1984 was $22,415: this means that 50 percent of families in the United States had incomes below $22,415 and 50 percent had incomes above that number. By comparison, the official poverty line for a nonfarm family of four was $10,609, or 47.3 percent of the median income. Families (nonfarm with four or more members) with incomes below $10,609 thus could not afford the economy food basket, the poverty line standard of living. In Figure 20-6 we indicate both the absolute poverty line and the median income. It is apparent that a sizable fraction of U.S. families were in poverty in 1984.

An alternative definition of poverty recognizes that the quality of life is affected not only by the sheer ability to

---

[17] The estimates of the poverty level of income are also adjusted for family size and a number of other factors that determine the cost of food for a family.

survive physically through adequate nutrition, housing, and health care but also by not having to suffer emotional deprivation from occupying too low a relative income position in society. We can imagine an extremely affluent society (like the United States, people in less-developed countries would say) where even the low-income families can afford all the necessities of life. Yet the low-income families may not be able to afford many of the amenities—entertainment, vacations, an occasional splurge—and certainly none of the luxuries that those around them visibly enjoy.

This leads to another definition of poverty, namely, *relative poverty*. Some families not in absolute poverty—and thus able to survive physically—may still be deprived emotionally if their income is too far below the median. In practice relative poverty has come to be set at one-half the median family income level; thus in Figure 20-6 the relative poverty level is defined by a family income of $11,208 (= 0.5 × $22,415). There is nothing special about this fraction; it simply strikes many observers as a plausible way to make operational the idea that someone can be poor even if he can afford food, shelter, and health care. Of course, relative poverty in the United States is a far cry from the poverty in poor countries that leads to starvation.

The Incidence of Poverty

In 1984, 33.7 million persons, or 14.4 percent of the U.S. population, had incomes that placed them below the absolute poverty line. Table 20-12 shows the incidence of poverty among various population groups. Poverty is most prevalent among members of minority groups, children, and persons living in families headed by women.

The data show starkly that poverty strikes blacks and Hispanics disproportionately. This is probably due to long-standing patterns of discrimination, which are reflected in lasting inequality of opportunity, education, quality of jobs, seniority, and all the attributes that lead to high incomes. For all groups, children are more likely to be living in poverty than are adults, and nearly half of black and Hispanic children live in poor families. The difference between children and adults reflects in part

TABLE 20-12. The Incidence of Poverty, 1984 (Percent of Indicated Group)

	All races	White	Black	Hispanic origin
All persons	14.4	11.5	33.8	28.4
Children*	21.0	16.1	46.2	39.6
Female householders†	34.0	n/a	n/a	n/a
Children‡	54.0	n/a	n/a	n/a
Aged 65 and Over	12.4	10.7	31.7	21.5
Unrelated§	24.2	n/a	n/a	n/a

* Aged 16 and under for Spanish origin, 18 and under otherwise.
† Persons living in a family with a female householder, no husband present.
‡ Children living in a family with a female householder, no husband present.
§ Persons aged 65 and over not living with any relatives.
n/a = data not available.
   Source: *Statistical Abstract of the United States, 1986*, Tables 767, 768, and 769.

the fact that large families have a harder time making ends meet than do smaller families. The high incidence of poverty among children has disturbing implications for the future.

The incidence of poverty is also particularly high for households headed by women, with no husband present. Over half the children in such families live in poverty. This problem arises in part because it is still hard for women to get high-paying jobs. Moreover, the need to care for small children prevents some female family heads from working at all.

In the past, old people were especially likely to be poor. In 1959, for instance, 35.2 percent of persons aged 65 and above lived in poverty, compared with 22.4 percent of the population as a whole. In 1979, these numbers were 15.2 percent and 11.7 percent, respectively. Recent increases in Social Security payments have lifted many senior citizens out of poverty. But, the incidence of poverty among older people not living with relatives is still quite high. Society is not kind to those who have lost the ability to earn an income and cannot obtain financial support from relatives.

As the pattern in Table 20-11 suggests, the probability of poverty for some more narrowly defined types of families is much higher than the numbers shown there. For example 56 percent of black families headed by a female in 1982 were poor.[18]

Figure 20-7 shows how the overall incidence of absolute poverty in the United States has changed since 1960. Two features of the graph are striking: the decline in the 1960s and the upturn beginning in 1978. As we shall discuss in Chapter 22, both these changes partly reflect government decisions regarding tax and transfer programs. In the mid-1960s the Johnson administration began to wage a "war on poverty." In the early 1980s the Reagan administration began a serious attack on the Johnson programs, charging that they were wasteful and inefficient.

Note, though, that the behavior of the poverty rate from 1978 to 1985 in Figure 20-7 reflects the macroeconomic behavior of the economy as well as government transfer programs. The poverty rate rose through 1983 as the economy went into a deep recession and then began to fall as the economy swiftly recovered from that recession.

Debates on how and how much to aid the poor have raged periodically in the United States since at least the 1930s, and we can expect them to continue in the future.

The Poverty Pool

In any year many people—currently about 14 percent of the population—have incomes below the poverty line. But it makes a large difference to the way we view the poor whether the composition of this group changes very much from one year to another or whether, on the contrary, the same people stay poor year after year. Is there economic mobility across the poverty line?

Some people are poor only for a short time after they suddenly lose a job. For others, poverty may become a permanent status, starting with being born into a poor family and continuing for a lifetime. Individual experiences will differ depending on the age and background of the person who becomes poor. For old people who are poor, especially if they are unrelated individuals, there is very little chance of ever escaping from poverty again. Great economic opportunities do not appear for old people. The opposite is true for young people. A married student couple may have an income below the poverty level but then may earn well above the median income within a year of graduation.

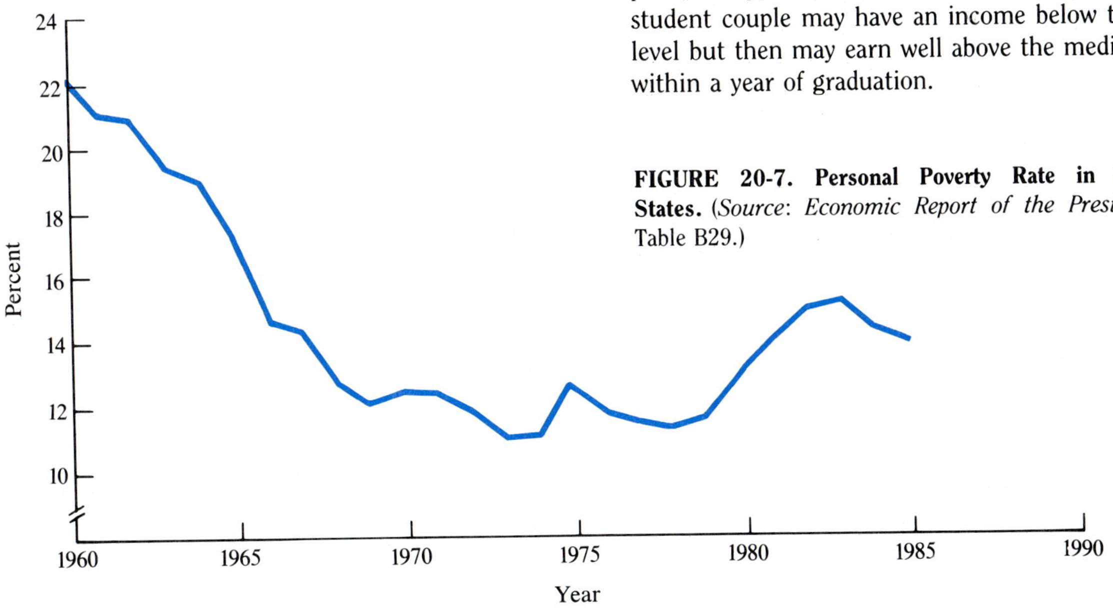

[18] See William Julius Wilson and Kathryn M. Neckerman, "Poverty and Family Structure: The Widening Gap between Evidence and Public Policy Issues," in Sheldon H. Danziger and Daniel H. Weinberg (eds.), *Fighting Poverty*, Harvard University Press, Cambridge, Mass., 1986.

FIGURE 20-7. Personal Poverty Rate in the United States. (*Source*: *Economic Report of the President, 1987*, Table B29.)

Research shows that only a small fraction of those *becoming* poor at any time will remain poor for long. But of the people who *are* poor at any time, people who are chronically poor account for a large share.[19] These two statements may seem contradictory, but they aren't. The probability that a person who falls below the poverty line (and thus *becomes* poor) this year will be out of poverty within 2 years is 60 percent. But taking all those who *are* currently poor as a group—and thus including some who have been poor for many years—we find that the probability of anyone in that group leaving poverty within 2 years is only 18 percent. These findings are, of course, strongly affected by the fact that old people have little chance of getting out of poverty once they fall into it.

If we want to attack poverty intelligently, we must deal with differences among the poor. The appropriate policies are entirely different for old people and for students, for job losers in an economywide recession and for job losers in a permanently depressed area of the country.

They are also different for female heads of households with dependent children. The unemployed need jobs to recover from poverty. People in depressed areas need to move elsewhere or acquire new skills. Women with dependent children require child support and/or day care centers so they can search for and take jobs.

■ Income inequality and poverty are controversial in part because they have many sources, the relative importance of which is hard to sort out. Few doubt that discrimination exists, for instance, though its importance as a source of poverty and inequality remains uncertain. But serious, long-lived controversies usually involve values more than facts, and this area is no exception. Everyone agrees that hardworking, bright people should be rewarded, but how much? And if hard work should be rewarded, how much should laziness be punished? Should parents be allowed to accumulate wealth to pass on to their children, or does inheritance give some an unfair advantage in life? Different people with different values and beliefs will give different answers to questions like these.

[19] This discussion follows Mary Jo Bane and David T. Ellwood, "Slipping into and out of Poverty: The Dynamics of Spells," NBER Working Paper No. 1199, September 1983.

Summary

1. The functional distribution of income deals with the distribution of national income between different factors of production. The personal distribution deals with the income distribution among individuals or families.
2. Theory predicts that movement in the relative shares of capital and labor over time depends on three factors: changes in the economywide capital-labor ratio, the degree of substitutability between capital and labor in production, and the nature of technical progress.
3. In the United States the capital-labor ratio has risen substantially over time, and labor's share of national income also appears to have risen substantially.
4. The personal distribution of income is unequal in all countries. The Lorenz curve summarizes the degree to which the distribution is uneven by showing what fraction of income is received by each fraction of the population, moving from the poorest to the richest people. The Lorenz curve allows comparisons of the degree of inequality across times or across countries; the farther away from the diagonal the curve lies, the less equal is the personal distribution of income.
5. In the United States the top 5 percent of families receive about 16 percent of all income while the poorest 20 percent of families receive only 5 percent of all income. The Lorenz curve of the U.S. economy has not changed much in recent decades. These data neglect income and transfers in kind, taxes, and differences in family size and number of earners.
6. Economic success is determined by an individual's family background, achievement, and luck. The relative importance of these factors remains controversial, but data do show that children have a good chance of being in a different part of the income distribution than their parents are.
7. Female and nonwhite workers receive, on the average, lower wages and incomes than do white male workers. The wage differentials reflect the fact that female workers and nonwhite workers are more heavily concentrated in relatively poor jobs (service workers rather than managers) and that within given jobs they receive less pay for identical

work and have less of an opportunity for advancement.
8. Equal opportunity policies seek to eliminate the impact of discrimination on the economic status of nonwhites and women. There has been a sizable improvement in the relative position of nonwhite workers in the last decade, but it is not clear to what extent this reflects reduced discrimination and to what extent it reflects withdrawal of the lowest-paid workers from the labor force.
9. Improved education, in terms of both quality and duration, seems to be narrowing the wage differences between white workers and nonwhite workers of the same age group.
10. There are two common definitions of the line between poverty and nonpoverty. The absolute poverty line is a level of income below which a family cannot maintain a specified subsistence level of food and other necessities. The relative poverty line, usually set at one-half the median income level, reflects concern for the economic status of people who are not threatened by starvation but who are poor among the rich.
11. About 14 percent of the U.S. population lives in absolute poverty. This fraction fell sharply during the 1960s but rose from the late 1970s before beginning to fall again with the recovery of the U.S. economy in 1983. Poverty is highly concentrated among particular groups: blacks, Hispanics, children, families headed by women, and older people not living with relatives.
12. Only a small fraction of those becoming poor at any time will remain poor long. But people who are chronically poor represent a large fraction of those who are poor at any time.

Key Terms

Personal income distribution
Functional income distribution
Lorenz curve
Economic mobility
Discrimination
Comparable worth
Poverty versus inequality
Absolute and relative poverty lines

Problems

1. Use Figure 20-2, which develops the equilibrium in the labor market, to show the effect on the functional income distribution of an increase in the labor supply accompanied by an increase in the capital stock that leaves the capital-labor ratio unchanged. (*a*) What happens to wages, capital income, and the shares of capital and labor in income? (*b*) How would your answers differ if the labor force increased proportionately more than the capital stock?

2. Until the middle 1930s there was a firm belief that labor's share in income tended to be stable and nearly constant over time. Does the U.S. experience in the last 20 years support or contradict that belief?

3. The accompanying table shows income distribution data for the United Kingdom for two years, 1949 and 1979. (*a*) Draw in one graph the Lorenz curves for both years. (*b*) Which year shows more equality?

	Bottom 50%	51–60%	61–70%	71–80%	81–90%	Top 10%	Top 1%
1949	26.5	9.5	10.5	11.9	14.5	27.1	6.4
1979	26.2	9.3	11.3	13.5	16.3	23.4	3.9

Source: Central Statistical Office (U.K.) *Economic Trends*, May 1978 and February 1981.

4. The accompanying table shows data for the before-tax and after-tax income distribution in the United Kingdom. (*a*) Draw the Lorenz curves for both series in the same diagram. (*b*) Does the U.K. tax system increase or reduce equality?

Before-Tax and After-Tax Income Distribution in the United Kingdom

	Bottom 20%	2d 20%	3d 20%	4th 20%	Top 20%	Top 1%
Before-tax	5.9	10.3	16.5	24.7	42.6	5.3
After-tax	7.0	11.5	17.0	24.8	39.7	3.9

Source: Central Statistical Office (U.K.), *Economic Trends*, May 1978 and February 1981.

5. Consider the economic mobility table, Table 20-6. Discuss three public policies (legal arrangements or specific government programs) which would make mobility more nearly perfect. Discuss three that would have the opposite effect.

6. What is the relevance, if any, of Table 20-6 to the question of whether income is mostly determined by heredity or by environment?

7. Who benefits from economic discrimination against women? Explain.

8. The government enacts a minimum wage law that requires firms to pay at least $5 per hour of labor. (*a*) What are the

effects on unskilled workers who were earning only $4 per hour before the enactment of the law? (*b*) If firms discriminate against nonwhite workers in that they are willing to pay a 20 percent premium for white workers, do you think that nonwhite workers will be particularly hurt or helped by the minimum wage?

9 Which do you think is more important, poverty or inequality, and why?

10 Discuss why in an economy where everybody has adequate food and shelter there may still be a poverty problem.

11 It has frequently been argued that the market-determined distribution of income should be accepted and not tampered with. Discuss this argument, keeping in mind that a competitive market economy produces an efficient allocation of resources.

12 Students, even though they may earn high incomes in the future, and old people, even though they may have earned high incomes in the past, are often counted among the poor. Is this appropriate? If not, how should people of different ages be treated differently in compiling poverty statistics?

**PART FIVE
TAXES, TRANSFERS,
AND GOVERNMENT
SPENDING**

Chapter 21
Taxes and Government Purchases

The year 1986 saw the most radical federal tax reform in the United States since the end of World War II. The 1986 Tax Reform Act was the culmination of well over a decade of public dissatisfaction with the complexities and perceived unfairness of the tax system.

Advocates of tax reform argued that taxes were not only unfair, with some wealthy people managing through one legal method or another to avoid paying taxes altogether, but also too high. They pointed out that while in 1929 less than 1 hour of each day's work went to pay taxes, in 1981 $2\frac{3}{4}$ hours of each day's work went to pay the government. The tax revolt led in several states to laws to limit the government's right to raise taxes. There has been a movement to amend the U.S. Constitution so as to limit taxes and require a balanced budget.

The tax revolt led to federal tax cuts from 1981 to 1984, which preceded the large budget deficits of the 1980s. The tax cuts of the early 1980s and the tax reform of 1986 raised a host of issues that are at the heart of controversies over the role of government in the economy and its effects on the allocation of resources.

"Taxes are what we pay for civilized society," said Oliver Wendell Holmes, meaning that many of the government's functions are essential, and so therefore are taxes. But taxes, as we know from Chapter 4, create distortions and affect patterns of production; for instance, by taxing wage earnings the government may make people want to work less, or by taxing gasoline the government may make people want to drive less. One of the main questions in this chapter is how to tax best, or equivalently, how to minimize the distortions in the economy that taxes inevitably create.

The level of taxes is largely determined by the level of government spending. The second major question we take up in this chapter is, What determines desirable levels of government spending? Does positive economics have anything to say about this, or is it all a matter of normative economics, with the answer depending on political preferences? The answer is, of course, somewhere in between.

In discussing taxation and government spending in this chapter, we expand the discussion of the role of government in the mixed economy that began in Chapter 4. We briefly review the reasons for government intervention in the economy that were given there. In theory there is a case for government intervention to stabilize the business cycle, provide public goods, reduce externalities in production or consumption, improve the flow of information, regulate private markets that are monopolized or imperfectly competitive, and redistribute income. We leave discussion of the business cycle for the macroeconomics section of this book. Government regulation of industry, which covers imperfectly competitive markets, externalities, and issues of information, was taken up in Chapters 13 and 14. In Chapter 22 we will focus on government transfer payments and welfare programs. Here we concentrate on the tax system and on government purchases of goods and services.

1. Taxation in the U.S. Economy

We start with tax facts. Governments in the United States—federal, state, and local—between them collect in taxes nearly one-third of GNP. This is a smaller share than that of government in most industrialized countries, as the data in Table 21-1 show, but it is a much larger share than the government in the United States took during peacetime in any period before World War II.

Table 21-2 shows the sources of government revenue in the United States. A small part of government revenue comes from fees and charges for government services, but most comes from taxes. Most of the taxes (62 percent) are collected by the federal government, which redistributes some of these revenues to state and local governments.

TABLE 21-1. Government Revenue as a Percentage of GNP, 1983

Country	Taxes/GNP, %
Sweden	60
Belgium	45
Germany	45
Italy	45
United Kingdom	42
Canada	39
Australia	33
United States	32
Japan	30

Source: OECD Economic Outlook, December 1986, Table R9.

TABLE 21-2. Sources of Government Revenue in the United States, 1985
(Percentage of Total Net Government Revenue)

Source	Federal government	State and local government	Total
Taxes on income and property			
Personal income tax	26.7	5.7	32.4
Social Security	24.6	3.5	28.1
Corporate profits tax	5.8	1.4	7.2
Property taxes	—	8.5	8.5
Taxes on goods			
Excise and sales taxes	2.8	13.3	16.1
Customs duties (tariffs)	1.0	—	1.0
Other (including non-taxes)	1.3	5.4	6.7
Total	62.2	37.8	100.0
Federal grants to state and local governments	−7.8	+7.8	—

Source: Survey of Current Business, December 1986.

The three chief sources of government revenue are the personal income tax, Social Security contributions, and excise and sales taxes. The latter are the largest source of revenue for state governments. The Tax Reform Act of 1986 reduced personal tax rates and increased taxes on corporations; even so, the personal income tax, introduced in 1913, will continue to be the government's largest source of revenue.

Over a quarter of government revenue comes from Social Security taxes. These taxes are contributions which entitle the payer to receive retirement pay and disability payments. Because payments to the Social Security system are not voluntary, we call them a tax rather than an insurance premium. The Social Security system is made compulsory on the argument that people may not be sufficiently farsighted to provide for their own needs in retirement and in case they become disabled.

Sales and excise taxes, which are next in order of importance, are taxes levied on the sale of specific goods. At the federal level there are excise taxes on liquor and tobacco as well as on automobiles, telephone calls, and airplane tickets. At the state and local levels, general sales taxes (often with some goods exempted) are an important source of revenue.

TABLE 21-3. Composition of Tax Revenue in the United States
(Percentage of Total Tax Revenue)

	Income tax, Social Security	Corporate profits	Sales, excise, customs	Property	Other
1902	—	—	30.3	41.8	27.9
1927	7.8	11.1	12.8	38.8	29.5
1985	60.5	7.2	17.1	8.5	6.7

Source: *Historical Statistics of the United States, 1970*, p. 1119 and Table 21-2.

The corporate profits tax is levied on the accounting income (defined in Chapter 7) of corporations. Corporate profits taxes produced nearly 25 percent of federal government revenue in 1949, but that share fell to less than 10 percent by 1985.[1] The 1986 Tax Reform Act raised corporate income taxes to about 13 percent of federal revenue. The corporate income tax has been highly controversial. Economists point out that corporate profits are taxed twice. First they are taxed when the corporation earns the profits. Then, when the corporation pays out the profits as dividends to stockholders, they are taxed again. Despite this criticism, the 1986 tax bill actually increased corporate taxes.

The U.S. tax structure, like the tax structures in other countries, has changed radically in this century. In 1902, as shown in Table 21-3, most tax revenue came from property, sales, and excise taxes and from customs duties (tariffs) on imported goods. There was no tax on personal income or corporate profits. Not only was the structure of taxation different, so was the amount. Total tax revenues in 1902 were only 8 percent of total income (GNP), compared with more than 30 percent today. Of course, government did much less in those days. Well over half the small budget was devoted to defense and to veterans' benefits; there was very little in the way of social welfare expenditures.

The VAT

One major tax is not used in the United States, the *value-added tax* (VAT), which is an important source of government revenue in many other countries, especially in Europe. The VAT is equivalent to a general retail sales tax levied at a common rate on all goods sold in the economy. The VAT is collected at every stage of production. At each stage what is taxed is not sales but *value added*: the sales price minus the cost of purchased inputs. Thus a car manufacturer who buys steel and tires from other firms is charged VAT on the value of the cars he sells minus the value of the purchased inputs of steel and tires. A car retailer in turn is charged tax on the value of her sales minus the price she pays the manufacturer for the cars. Adding up the taxes collected at each stage, we see that VAT comes to the same thing as an outright retail sales tax.

With the facts on government revenue set out in this section, we can now move on to discuss both the effects of taxation on the allocation of resources and the principles of good taxation. We will discuss what is a good (or least bad) tax, which taxes should be avoided, and why.

2. Principles of Taxation

Given the many actual and imaginable types of taxes, how should a government finance itself? The first criterion is *fairness*, or equity. The second is *efficiency*. Efficient taxes are those which minimize adverse effects on resource allocation. We now consider these two issues—though of course in discussing fair and efficient taxes, we do not imply that real taxes are fair or efficient.

How to Tax Fairly

Government taxes and spending affect the distribution of income, imposing burdens on some and conferring benefits on others. Economists, to say nothing of taxpayers, have long been concerned about how the benefits and the

---

[1] Alan Auerbach and James Poterba, "Why Have Corporate Tax Revenues Declined?" *NBER Tax Policy Annual 1987*, explain the decline in the relative importance of corporate taxes as a result of both lower corporate profits and changes in the tax laws.

burdens should be spread. Two main ethical precepts are widely accepted.

● *Horizontal equity* **says that equals should be treated equally by the tax laws.** *Vertical equity* **says that unequals should be treated unequally.**

Suppose two people both work 40 hours a week, one earning wages at a regular job and the other working in his own business, say, a restaurant. Suppose the profits the owner of the restaurant makes are exactly equal to the wages of the worker. Horizontal equity suggests that each person should be taxed the same amount. If the tax system taxed profits at a different rate than it taxed wages, horizontal equity would be violated in this example. Vertical equity implies that someone who earns more should be taxed more, even if somehow her reported (taxable) income is artificially low.

But exactly how should unequals be treated? This is mainly an ethical question. The oldest principle in public finance is that taxes should be based on *ability to pay*. This suggests that taxes should be based on income or wealth. An alternative is to base taxes on *benefits received* from government activities. Before discussing these principles, we must ask how "equals" should be defined.

DEFINING EQUALS. A natural starting point is the argument that those with equal levels of current income should be treated equally by the tax system. But current income is really not a good measure of how well off a person is. A medical student earning the same income as a janitor is better off than the janitor, for the medical student has the higher lifetime income. Perhaps we should define equals by their lifetime incomes.

Even if we could reliably estimate lifetime income (some medical students flunk out, after all), difficult issues would remain. Consider two people, each of whom had the same lifetime income. Both are now retired. One saved while young and now lives well. One had a good time while young and lives very poorly now. Are they equals? Or consider two people, each working in the same factory, doing the same work, and getting the same pay. One of them has five children to support. Are they equals? The issues are ethical, and unfortunately the principle of horizontal equity does not give concrete answers in these cases. In practice the issue is settled by legislators, who probably have a principle like horizontal equity in mind when voting on taxes but who certainly have many other political considerations and pressures in mind too.

ABILITY TO PAY VERSUS BENEFITS. Vertical equity deals with an issue on which there is much room for dissent, namely, how unequals are to be treated unequally. The ability-to-pay principle clearly takes the view that government should redistribute income, since it says payments for government services should be higher for the richer and lower for the poorer in society. The benefits principle, which says that people should pay according to the benefits they receive, would not redistribute income. Those applying the benefits principle to all taxation either see the current distribution of income as appropriate or at least believe the government should not set out to redistribute income. Such a view is typically put forward by conservatives.

Whether the benefits principle appears fair depends on the purpose of government spending. Consider, for instance, paying for police protection. Since crime rates tend to be highest in low-income areas, one can argue that the poor benefit more from police protection than do the rich. The ability-to-pay principle says the poor should nonetheless pay lower taxes. The benefits principle would say that the poor should pay more, since they benefit more. In this case the benefits principle will strike most people as unfair. But consider instead highway use. Many have no trouble with the argument that highway users should pay more than others toward the building and maintenance of roads. And they do, for the highway system is financed in part through gasoline taxes.

The benefits principle cannot be applied to public goods,[2] because we do not know how to measure the benefit of the public good to each person. Nor is the benefits principle consistent with government transfer payments. Should a person receiving unemployment compensation pay the government for it in proportion to the benefit? In that case, people who received the trans-

---

[2] Recall from Chapter 4 that national defense is the classic example of a public good.

fers would pay by giving them back to the government, and there would be no transfers.

PROGRESSIVE AND REGRESSIVE TAXES. Returning now to the ability-to-pay principle, the key question is how much taxes should change with the ability to pay, however defined. This question addresses the desirability of a progressive tax structure.

● **A tax structure is *progressive* if it reduces the after-tax inequality of economic well-being. It is *regressive* if it increases after-tax inequality.**

Income is used to measure well-being only because no better measure is available. A tax system is progressive if the Lorenz curve for after-tax income shows a more equal distribution of income than the Lorenz curve for before-tax income.[3] Figure 21-1 illustrates how progressive taxes reduce income inequality. Equivalently, a tax structure is progressive if the rich pay a larger share of their income in taxes than do the poor.

For a long time the popular view has been that taxes should be progressive. This is a value judgment, a judgment about what is fair, that is built into the tax structure. The federal tax schedule up to 1986 was sharply progressive, with the marginal tax rate rising with income.

● **The *marginal tax rate* is the rate at which an extra dollar of income is taxed. The *average tax rate*, in contrast, is the ratio of taxes to income.**

When the marginal tax rate rises with income, the average tax rate also rises with income.[4]

The federal tax schedule up to 1986 had 14 different marginal rates, with the rate rising with income. Although it was apparently very progressive, various deductions, tax loopholes, and special features reduced the effective progressivity. On balance, the U.S. tax system was slightly progressive.[5] As we discuss in Chapter 22,

---
[3] The Lorenz curve was introduced in Chapter 20. See particularly Figures 20-4 and 20-5.
[4] Remember the general relationship between average and marginal from Chapter 8.
[5] For a good discussion, see Joseph A. Pechman, *Federal Tax Policy*, 4th ed., Brookings Institution, Washington, D.C., 1983. The fifth, 1987, edition of this classic work describes the post-1986 tax system.

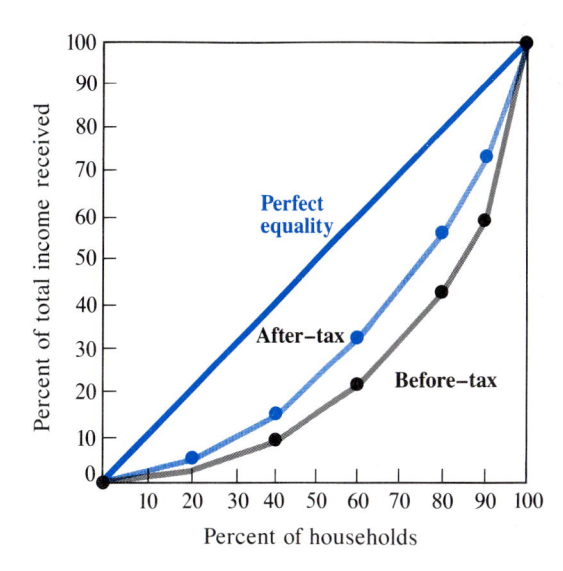

FIGURE 21-1. Progressive Taxes Reduce Inequality. The Lorenz curves show that progressive taxes make the distribution of after-tax income (the colored curve) more equal than that of before-tax income (the black curve).

taxes and transfers (including food stamps and other welfare payments) combined have a large progressive effect on the distribution of income.

The tax structure was simplified (though even the simplified structure is extraordinarily complicated) in the 1986 Tax Reform Act, which has two basic tax rates, 15 percent and 28 percent.[6] It might seem that having so few tax rates would make it difficult to make the tax system progressive, but the tax system can be made progressive with just one marginal tax rate and an exemption level.

Figure 21-2 shows how. Suppose first that taxes are made proportional to income, as in (*a*). Taxes are the distance between the 45° line and the after-tax income line. With taxes proportional to income, after-tax incomes are proportional to before-tax incomes and the tax system is neither progressive nor regressive. In (*b*) no taxes at all are paid until income reaches the exemption level Y_0. Thereafter each extra dollar of income pays the same marginal tax rate. The average tax rate, or the ratio

---
[6] As we explain in the next footnote, the statement made by politicians that the system has only two tax rates is slightly misleading.

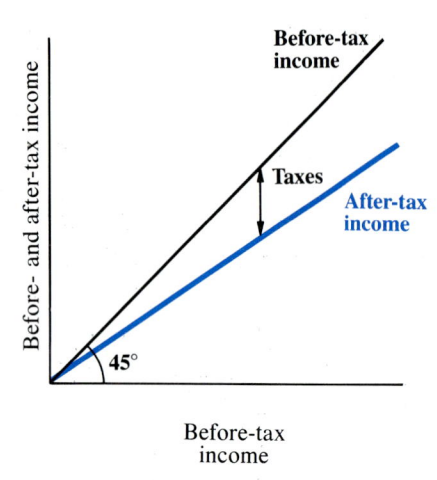

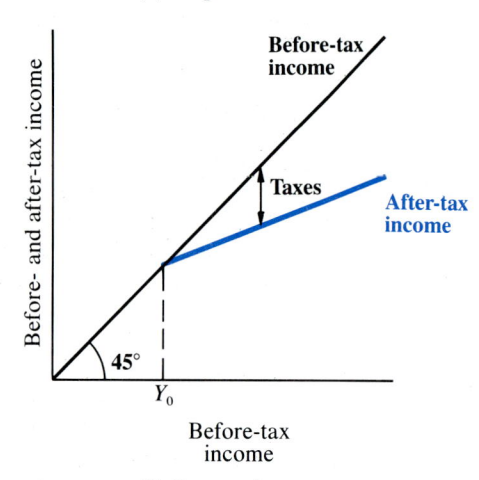

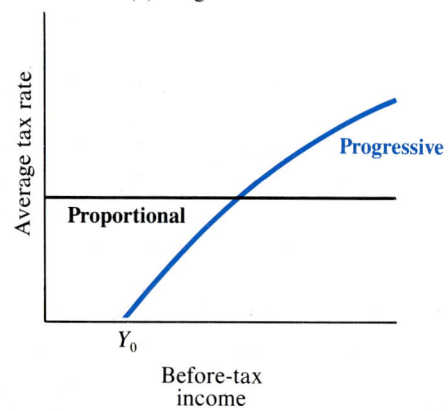

FIGURE 21-2. Proportional and Progressive Taxes. Taxes are proportional to income in (*a*), so that the ratio of after-tax income to before-tax income is the same at all income levels. With income up to level Y_0 exempt from taxes in (*b*) and a constant marginal tax rate thereafter, taxes are progressive. The average tax rate rises with income. In (*c*) the average tax rates corresponding to (*a*) and (*b*) are shown.

of taxes to income, is zero up to income level Y_0 and then gradually rises in (*b*) as income rises. The average tax rates from (*a*) and (*b*) are shown in Figure 21-2*c*.

The U.S. income tax, both before and after the 1986 tax reform, includes an exemption level such as Y_0 below which income is not taxable. Thus the current system is progressive even though it has only two tax rates. Under the 1986 Tax Reform Act, though, progressivity stops at a high income level. Once a taxpayer's average tax rate reaches 28 percent, each extra dollar of income is also taxed at 28 percent, ensuring that the average tax rate continues to be 28 percent.[7]

Taxation, Efficiency, and Waste

The second criterion for taxation—efficiency—involves the waste that is created as people try to avoid taxes. We discussed the example of cigarette taxation in Chapter 4. Because the analysis is essential to understanding the allocative effects of taxes, we present another example in Figure 21-3. This time we examine the important issue of the effects of the income tax on the labor market.

The question is, What effect does income taxation have on the amount of work done in the economy? Should we expect higher taxes to reduce work effort, with people preferring to substitute leisure for work when the after-tax compensation for working declines?

Schedule *D* is the economywide demand curve for labor, and schedule *S* shows the supply of labor. As in Chapter 16, the labor demand curve is downward-sloping

---

[7] The careful student will ask the following question. If there are only two marginal tax rates, 15 percent and 28 percent, and an exemption level, how can the average ever get up to 28 percent? The answer is that the tax rate structure under the Tax Reform Act is more complicated than the official claim that there are only two rates—15 percent and 28 percent—suggests. In fact, there is a middle range of incomes for which the marginal tax rate is 33 percent.

because as the real wage declines, firms are willing to substitute labor for capital, using more labor-intensive production processes. The supply of labor is upward-sloping, reflecting the assumption that in response to higher real wages workers are willing to supply a larger number of work hours. The quantity of labor supplied increases when the real wage rises both because workers already on the job are willing to work more and because people not previously working want to find jobs. The initial equilibrium is at point E.

Suppose now that the government imposes a tax on wages, or labor income. All workers have to pay the government 20 cents for every dollar of wages they earn. This shifts the supply schedule of labor upward. Previously it took only \$4 of wages paid by the employer to get workers to supply a given amount of labor. Now that there is a tax, it will take a before-tax wage of \$4.80 to leave the workers with take-home pay equal to the \$4 required to induce them to supply that much labor. Similarly, to have, say, an \$8 take-home pay, they need a before-tax wage of \$9.60. Thus the imposition of a 20 percent tax on wages shifts the supply schedule of labor upward to S', by exactly the amount such that the *after-tax* wage is equal at each level of labor supply to the wage on the original supply curve.

The new equilibrium in the labor market is at point E'. The imposition of the tax has reduced the amount of hours worked. It has *raised* the before-tax wage to W' from W, and it has *lowered* the after-tax wage to W'''. The difference, $E'A'$, represents tax payments, or the *wedge* which the tax drives between the value of a worker to the firm and the amount received by the worker for working 1 more hour.

When the tax is imposed, workers will continue working the same amount only if they are compensated for the taxes by receiving a higher before-tax wage. But firms' demand for labor is negatively related to the wage. If the wage were to rise, firms would not want to hire as much labor as before. The market reaches a new equilibrium when employment has declined to the point where the marginal productivity of labor rises enough so that firms are on their demand curves for labor, willing to pay a higher before-tax wage (W') than before (W) and workers are working less, or enjoying more leisure, at a lower after-tax wage (W''') than before (W).

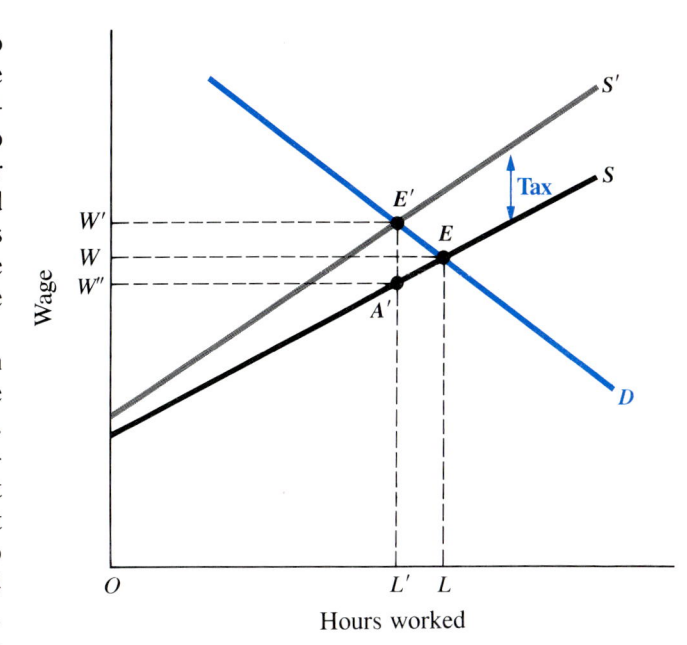

FIGURE 21-3. A Tax on Wages. A tax on wages reduces take-home pay at each market wage. Therefore, the labor supply schedule shifts up, from S to S'. The tax moves the market equilibrium from E to E'. The number of hours worked declines, the before-tax wage increases to W', and the after-tax wage falls to W'''.

In Figure 21-4 we show the same schedules that are in Figure 21-3 and focus on two areas. The triangle $EE'A'$ represents the waste (of consumers' and producers' surplus) created by the tax,[8] and the area $W'E'A'W'''$ shows the government's tax collection. We now explain these areas.

The labor market now clears at the before-tax wage of W'. At this wage the amount of hours worked has fallen from L to L'. The tax therefore reduces work effort. At level L' of work there is a wedge between the value of work to a firm, given by point E' on the demand for labor schedule, and the cost or disutility of work to workers,[9]

---

[8] We discussed waste (the loss of consumers' and producers' surplus) in Chapters 10 and 11.

[9] The decision to work an extra hour is also the decision to reduce leisure by an hour. We can thus talk interchangeably about the marginal cost of an extra hour's work to the worker and the loss of marginal utility from reducing leisure by 1 hour.

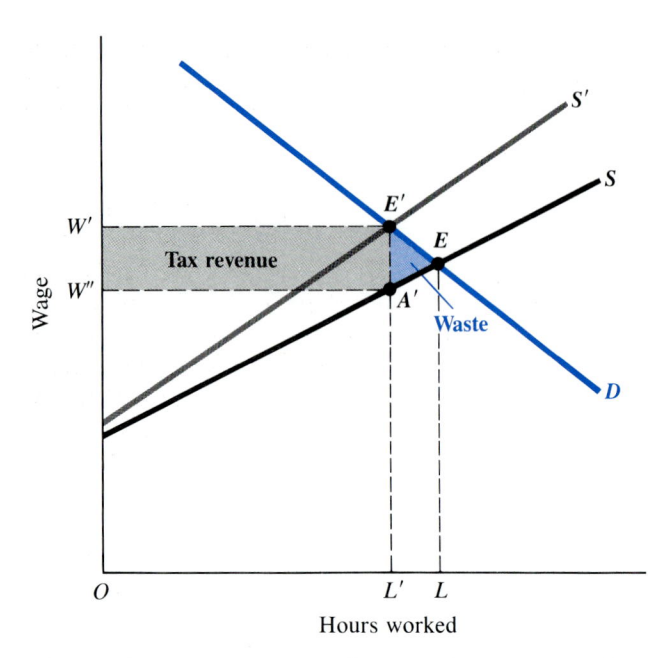

FIGURE 21-4. Tax Revenue and Waste. The imposition of a tax shifts the supply schedule to S'. The before-tax wage rises to W', and the number of hours worked drops from L to L'. Triangle $EE'A'$ represents the social waste or deadweight loss arising from the discrepancy between the marginal valuation by firms of an extra hour of work and the marginal cost of another hour of work to workers. The area $W'E'A'W'''$ is the total amount of revenue collected by the government. Taxes drive a wedge, $E'A'$, between the productivity of labor and the marginal cost of extra work for labor; they are a disincentive to work.

their after-tax wage, W'''. The marginal cost of 1 more hour of work to firms (W') exceeds the marginal cost to workers of working the extra hour (W'''). Therefore, the tax has introduced a *distortion*. Such a distortion is also called a *tax wedge* since the tax drives a wedge between prices paid and prices received.

What exactly is the distortion? Suppose all markets are perfectly competitive. With the wage paid by firms above that received by workers, the marginal value product of labor exceeds the marginal cost of work to the workers. If they worked 1 more hour, society would gain the amount W', the marginal value product of labor. The cost of that extra hour of work to the suppliers of labor, and thus to society, is the smaller amount, W'''. But because the tax puts a wedge between the cost of labor to the employer and the wage received by the worker, that extra hour of work does not get done.[10]

The tax acts as a disincentive to work so that, as a result, too little work is done. The total waste is equal to the triangle $EE'A'$, the loss of consumers' and producers' surplus. The government collects in tax revenue the shaded rectangle equal to $(W' - W''') \times L'$, which is equal to the amount of hours worked, L', times the wage tax per hour.

Deadweight Burdens and Efficient Taxation

Figure 21-4 shows that it is costly to raise government revenue. Besides the cost to the workers who have to share their wages with the government, there is a net waste associated with tax collection, equal to the area of the triangle. The government's tax revenue ultimately benefits someone, perhaps the very workers who pay the tax. But the triangle represents a net waste of resources due to misallocation.

● **The *deadweight burden* of a tax is the waste or loss of consumers' and producers' surplus that arises from the distortion of the allocation of resources created by the tax.**

The existence of waste makes it important to ask what design of the tax system would interfere least with efficiency or create the least waste. A simple and important case will further understanding of the deadweight burden of taxation. Suppose, as in Figure 21-5, that the quantity of labor supplied is equal to L at any wage. Thus labor supply is totally inelastic with respect to the wage.

In this case, as can be seen from the figure, the imposition of a tax will not affect the number of hours of work supplied, and therefore the equilibrium remains at E. The full adjustment to the tax takes place through a fall in the after-tax wage. But because labor supply is unresponsive to the wage, there is no adjustment at all in hours worked. In this special case there is no waste

---

[10] Check back to Chapter 10 for conditions for the optimal allocation of resources.

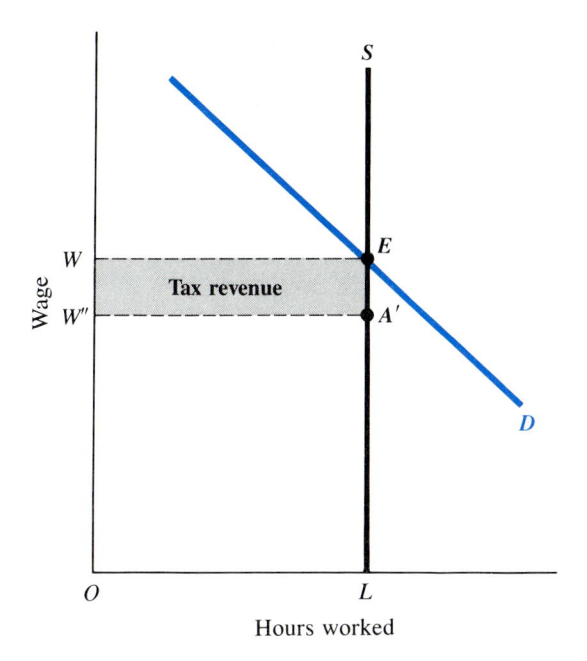

FIGURE 21-5. A Tax on a Factor in Inelastic Supply. If the labor supply is *entirely* inelastic or unresponsive to the wage, the supply schedule is vertical. A tax leaves the before-tax wage unchanged at W and reduces the after-tax wage by the full amount of the tax. In this special case there is no waste at all.

because workers continue to work exactly the same amount whatever wage they receive.[11] Problem 3 at the end of this chapter asks you to show that there is also no waste if the demand for labor is perfectly inelastic.

We thus have the following general principle: Any tax on a good or factor that is in completely inelastic supply (or demand) will create no waste because there is no reduction in the taxed activity. The general rule is to concentrate taxes where they will produce the smallest reductions in output.

● **To raise a given amount of revenue most efficiently, the government should minimize output reductions by taxing most heavily those goods for which supply or demand is least elastic.**

---

[11] Technical warning: In advanced courses, it is shown that there is no deadweight burden of a tax in this case only if the labor supplier is compensated for the loss of income the tax causes.

Heavy taxation of cigarettes and liquor, for which the demand is inelastic, accords with this principle. These are examples of "sin taxes"—sin is probably also in inelastic demand.

THE WELFARE COST OF TAXES. Does the U.S. tax system cause a lot of waste, or is our previous discussion only of theoretical interest? One careful estimate of the effects of the income tax on work effort suggests the following.[12] Because taxes reduce the after-tax wage, a person who earned $10,000 under the pre-1986 tax system reduced labor effort by 9 percent compared with the amount he would have worked if taxes had been zero. This is a very significant labor supply response, certainly in line with Figure 21-4, not with Figure 21-5.

There are also estimates of the waste per dollar of taxes imposed. The numbers here are around 30 cents of waste for every dollar of taxes the government collects. Again, this is a very large number, and it certainly drives home the point that taxation has important side costs in the form of waste.[13]

Should we conclude that because a dollar of taxes costs an extra 30 cents in waste, taxes are too high? Not without considering the benefits of government spending on, for example, welfare programs and defense. The marginal benefits per dollar of spending could be much larger than $1.30.

TAX INCIDENCE. In Box 4-1 we discussed the question of tax incidence: Who really bears the burden of a tax? Recall that the answer is not that whoever sends the check to the government bears the burden. Rather, the burden is borne by whichever side of the market suffers a loss in its after-tax profit or utility.

Typically, the burden is borne by both the supplier and the demander, as we show using Figure 21-4. There we observe that the before-tax wage increases somewhat and

---

[12] Jerry Hausman, "Labor Supply," in Henry J. Aaron and Joseph A. Pechman (eds.), *How Taxes Affect Economic Behavior*, Brookings Institution, Washington, D.C., 1981.

[13] A range of estimates is provided in Edgar K. Browning, "The Marginal Cost of Raising Tax Revenue," in Phillip Cagan (ed.), *Essays in Contemporary Economic Problems, 1986*, American Enterprise Institute, Washington, D.C.

the after-tax wage falls somewhat. Because the after-tax wage falls by less than the full tax, the tax is only partly borne by workers; it is also borne by firms that have reduced profits or by consumers of the final good, who pay more.

In the special case when a factor is inelastically supplied, that factor bears the entire burden of a tax. This can be seen in Figure 21-5, where the after-tax wage falls from W to W''', an amount equal to the tax. In general, the incidence is split between the supply and demand sides of the market. The more inelastic supply is relative to demand, the larger the part of the tax that is borne by suppliers.[14]

3. Tax Reform

The Tax Reform Act of 1986 followed major changes in the tax law in 1978, 1981, and 1982 and intense discussion and analysis of the tax system within the economics profession.[15] It is quite certain that further tax reforms will follow, for several major issues in tax reform were not settled by the 1986 act. In this section we discuss three major tax reform issues which were discussed in 1986 and will continue to be on the tax reform agenda.

Income versus Consumption Tax

The first issue is whether to tax income or consumption. The existing system taxes mainly income, which reflects a person's production, or what she puts into the economic pie. An often proposed alternative is to tax consumption, that is, what people buy,[16] or take out of the economic pie.

The difference between consumption and income is saving. Thus taxing consumption is equivalent to exempting from income tax any amounts saved. In fact the tax system had been moving in the direction of exempting saving from income tax over the years with the establishment of tax-exempt forms of saving such as individual retirement accounts (IRAs). Each person was allowed to contribute up to $2000 per year to an IRA and deduct the contribution from taxable income.[17]

The basic argument in favor of taxing consumption rather than income is that otherwise saving is taxed twice: first when the income that is saved is earned, and second when that saving in turn generates income (for example, interest) for the saver. In addition, recall the argument in section 2 that it might be fairer to tax people on the basis of lifetime income rather than current income. In fact, consumption is more closely related to an individual's lifetime income than to her current income.[18] Thus basing taxation on consumption is closer to taxing people on the basis of lifetime income than on the basis of current income.

One way of taxing consumption is through a sales or value-added tax. Then people pay taxes on their purchases. An alternative is to calculate consumption by subtracting saving from income. The individual fills out her regular income tax forms, calculates how much of the income was saved, and is taxed on income minus saving. This method has the advantage that the tax can be made progressive, with the marginal tax rate rising with the level of consumption.

In the event, the 1986 Tax Reform Act was a mixture. Basically it taxes income, but some forms of saving are not taxed.

Corporate Income Tax

The pre-1986 decline of the corporate income tax as a revenue source for the government meant that the relatively unpopular personal income tax was bearing a larger share of the tax burden. The declining amount of corporate taxation was not primarily the result of a reduction in the formal rate of taxation but rather the

---

[14] You can experiment with the slopes of supply and demand curves to see what determines whether the before-tax or after-tax wage does most of the adjusting.

[15] See, for example, David F. Bradford and U.S. Treasury Department Tax Policy Staff, *Blueprints for Basic Tax Reform*, Tax Analysts, Arlington, Va., 1984; Robert E. Hall and Alvin Rabushka, *The Flat Tax*, Hoover Institution Press, Stanford, Cal., 1985; and Joseph A. Pechman (ed.), *The Promise of Tax Reform*, Prentice-Hall, Englewood Cliffs, N.J., 1985.

[16] Consumption excludes the purchase of assets, such as houses, stocks, and bonds.

[17] IRAs continue after 1986 and still offer benefit to some savers, but their tax treatment is complicated.

[18] This is because people tend to save when their incomes are high relative to lifetime average income and dissave when income is low relative to lifetime average income (for example, when they are retired or when they are students).

result of inclusion of a host of special tax allowances, especially for investment.[19] The "three-martini lunch" came in for special publicity: Businesses could deduct as an expense the costs of entertaining customers. Many critics argued that there was no reason to subsidize lunchtime drinking by making all such costs deductible.

Special tax allowances not only reduced the total amount of corporate tax revenue but also introduced many distortions into the tax system. Calculations showed that tax rates differed widely across industries, without any apparent economic rationale. For instance, air transportation was taxed at a rate of *minus* 13 percent (i.e., it was subsidized) while petroleum and coal production was taxed at 31 percent.[20] With different tax rates, investment would tend to be high in the low-tax industries and low in the high-tax industries—and with such wide divergences in tax rates, the distortions from too much investment in some industries and too little in others were calculated to be large.[21]

The 1986 reform made taxation more uniform across industries by reducing and standardizing allowances for investment and depreciation.[22] The formal corporate tax rate was reduced from 42 percent to 35 percent. But because investment and depreciation allowances were reduced and made more uniform, total corporate taxes increased. Three-martini lunches are 80 percent deductible, and dividends are still taxed twice—first as corporate profits and then as individual income.

Tax Simplification

Politically, the most powerful appeal of the 1986 tax reform was the claim that it would simplify the tax system. Simplification proposals before 1986 centered on two elements: the ending of many deductions that it was thought were being abused and a reduction in the number of different marginal tax rates. Among the deductions that could be taken from income before the tax reform were charitable contributions, payments for state and local taxes, mortgage interest, medical expenses, and payments for child care. Most of these remain as deductions.

The plain fact is that many of the complicated features of the tax system are there because many people want them. Homeowners are a potent political group, and Congress would not have been able to pass a tax bill without their support. People believe it only fair that medical expenses be deductible from income in computing taxes. Thus, although people complain about the complexities of the tax system, it is unlikely that a simple system will be seen any time soon.

However, two significant simplifications were accomplished in 1986. Many of what were seen as abuses in the tax system originated in the different tax rates for ordinary income and *capital gains*. Because capital gains were taxed at a lower rate than was ordinary income, anyone who could find a way of earning income through buying and selling assets could expect to pay lower taxes. The Tax Reform Act makes the tax rate on capital gains the same as that on ordinary income.

Second, the Tax Reform Act did reduce the variety of marginal tax rates. The shift in the range of marginal tax rates from 11 percent to 50 percent to only 15 percent and 28 percent[23] was possible for two reasons: Corporate taxes went up, so that the total taken from individuals could fall, and many loopholes were closed, so that marginal tax rates on individuals could be cut.

4. Government Purchases

From taxes we turn to government spending, both the facts and the economic theory of government purchases. However, as we noted in Chapter 4, the government does not confine its intervention in the economy to precisely those conditions in which economic theory says there is a theoretical case for intervention. In practice, govern-

---

[19] See Alan J. Auerbach, "The Corporation Income Tax," in Joseph A. Pechman, (ed.), *The Promise of Tax Reform*, Prentice Hall, Englewood Cliffs, N.J.

[20] These data are presented in the article by Alan Auerbach, ibid.

[21] Subsequently, some economists showed skepticism about the importance of those distortions. See, for example, Lawrence Summers, "Should Tax Reform Level the Playing Field?" National Bureau of Economic Research Working Paper, 1987.

[22] Firms are allowed to deduct from their revenue the depreciation of their machinery, or the loss of value that the machines suffer during the course of the year. These allowances had generally been set too high, thus enabling the firms to subtract more from their income than real depreciation warranted.

[23] Recall from footnote 7 that there are actually three marginal rates: 15 percent, 33 percent, and 28 percent.

ment intervenes when politicians see a way of improving the lot of their constituents.

Provision of Public Goods

A public good is one that, even if it is consumed by one person, is still available for consumption by others. The classic examples are national defense and clean air. Radio programs and the views in national parks are other public goods. In discussing public goods we shall assume that it is impossible to exclude anyone from consumption of the good. Exclusion may indeed be possible. For instance, before cable television it was not possible to exclude viewers in a given area from watching TV programs, and the TV signal was thus a public good. With cable TV, nonpayers can be excluded and the signal becomes a private good. This is not the sort of public good we are discussing. We are considering public goods such as defense and clean air, where exclusion of others from consumption of the good is impossible.

Private markets cannot be expected to produce the right amount of a public good, because individuals have no incentive to reveal the value of the good to them by buying it or volunteering to pay a share of the cost.[24]

How much of a public good should be produced? Here we use the general principle, which also applies to ordinary private goods, that society should produce up to the point where the marginal cost to society is equal to the marginal social benefit from more production.

We start by developing the demand curve for public goods, which gives the marginal social benefit. Suppose that the public good is public safety and that there are two people in the society. The valuation placed on the amount of public safety by a single person is shown by the demand curve for safety as a function of price in Figure 21-6. That is how much safety she should buy if

[24] It may help clarify the nature of public goods if we assume that there are strong externalities in the consumption of such goods. Externalities exist when actions by one person or firm affect the welfare of others without any action on the part of those affected. Your purchase of a public good certainly affects my welfare, since it automatically increases my consumption of that good. Since you don't receive the total benefits from purchasing the good (as you do in the case of a hamburger, for instance), you will spend less on it than would be optimal for society as a whole.

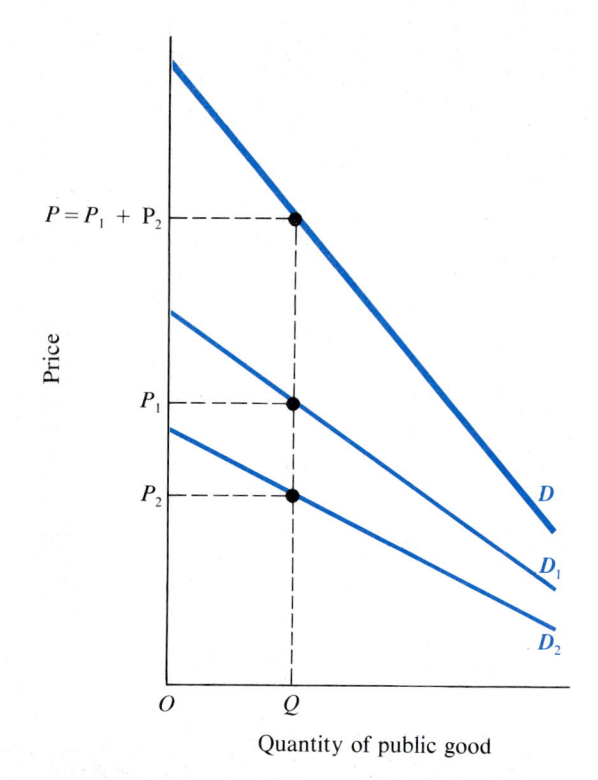

FIGURE 21-6. The Demand for a Public Good. There are two people, with demand curves D_1 and D_2, respectively, for the public good. What is the value that the group places on an additional unit of output? At each level of output we add *vertically* the price that each is willing to pay for another unit. Thus at output Q we add P_1 and P_2 to arrive at the total valuation of another unit of the public good. In this way we generate the demand schedule D. The demand schedule is special because consumption by one person does not preclude consumption of the same good by the other.

price were given and she were telling the truth. Thus D_1 is the demand curve of one person in the group. D_2 is the demand curve of the second person.

Society's demand curve for public safety is shown by D, which adds up the prices that each person in society is willing to pay for the given amount of safety. For instance, at amount of safety Q, the first person is willing to pay P_1 and the second is willing to pay P_2. Since each gets the total amount of safety produced, society, consisting of the two of them, is willing to pay P_1 plus P_2. This sum is the value that society places, at the margin, on that amount of safety. This is shown by the corresponding price, *P*, on society's demand curve for safety, *D*.

The total demand curve for a public good differs from that for a private good. With a public good, we add the demand curves *vertically*. At each level of output, we add the prices that all the individuals in the economy taken together are willing to pay. That is because each person gets to consume *all* of the public good that is produced. With a private good, we add the demand curves *horizontally*.[25] The total amount of a private good supplied has to be split up among all the people in society, each equating the marginal benefit of consuming his portion to the amount he pays, or the price. The difference between the demand curves occurs because there is excludability in the consumption of private goods, meaning that when someone consumes a private good, she thereby excludes other people from also consuming it. That is not possible with a public good.

In Figure 21-7 we combine the demand curve (*D*) for the public good, say, safety, with the supply schedule. The supply schedule is given by the marginal cost of producing safety. The way we have drawn the *MC* schedule, there is an initial phase of declining *MC*, but ultimately *MC* is rising. The social optimum is at point *E*. At that point the marginal social valuation of an extra unit of safety (which is equal to the value all people together place on an extra unit) is equal to the marginal cost. If output of the public good were any lower, society would gain by an expansion.

REVELATION OF PREFERENCES. How would a government find out how much to spend on public goods? Why not ask people how much they would be willing to pay for different levels of output of the public good? In other words, ask people to reveal their demand curves, such as D_1 in Figure 21-6. The problem here, as discussed in Chapter 4, is that if taxes to pay for the good will be imposed according to the announced demand curve, individuals will have an incentive to lie. If everyone else tells the truth about her willingness to pay for national defense, say, $1000 each per year, then we are not going to have appreciably less defense if I say I am willing to pay only $20 or, for that matter, zero. I become a *free rider*, enjoying the benefits without paying the costs. But if everyone thinks that way, it will be very hard to get the truth.

What if we separate the demand for public goods from the requirement that people pay for the public good? If the amount people have to pay is unaffected by the amount of the public good they say they would like, they may announce a quantity demanded that corresponds to the case where the price is zero. If the city asks whether I want safer streets, at no cost to me, I am for it—the safer the better so long as I don't have to pay. Thus this approach is also flawed.

In practice decisions about the amount of public goods to provide are made through the political process. We do

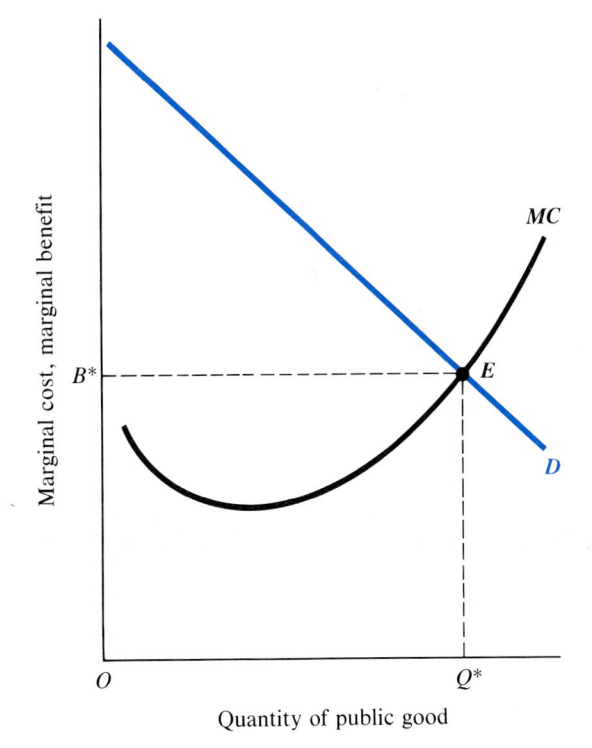

FIGURE 21-7. The Optimal Supply of a Public Good. Schedule *MC* shows the marginal cost of supplying an extra unit of the public good. *D* is the demand schedule; it shows society's marginal valuation of each unit. The social optimum is at *E*, where marginal cost equals marginal benefit.

---

[25] This is the process by which the market demand curve was derived in Chapter 6.

not know whether the political system tends to provide the right amount, too much, or too little of public goods.

Government Provision of Goods

Governments in the United States provide health services, national defense, the Library of Congress, the services of the FBI and CIA, the national parks, state liquor stores, education at state universities, and much more. Table 21-4, reproduced from Chapter 4, shows the composition of government spending.[26]

Table 21-4 shows that while the government does provide public goods, not all the goods that it provides are public. National defense and police, which account for nearly 20 percent of total government spending, are indeed public goods. The national parks are a mixed case, since enjoyment of the views in the parks is a public good but use of the eating and camping facilities is not. Liquor sales (which are included in the "other" category) are not a public good, and liquor could perfectly well be sold through private markets, as it is in most states. In the middle are some categories, such as education and health spending (which account for 17 percent of total government outlays), that have some aspects of a private good and some of a public good.

---

[26] In this chapter we focus on purchases of goods and not transfers; welfare payments are examined in Chapter 22.

TABLE 21-4 The Composition of Government Spending in the United States, 1983
(Percentage of Total Government Spending)

Function	Federal	State	Local	Total
Total	58.2	17.3	24.6	100.0
National defense and international relations	16.9	—	—	16.9
Education	0.9	3.3	8.8	13.1
Health and hospitals	0.9	1.5	1.7	4.2
Transportation and highways	0.4	1.6	1.4	3.4
Police	0.2	0.2	1.1	1.5
Social Security, welfare, etc.	20.3	6.4	1.4	28.2
Interest on debt	8.0	0.8	1.0	9.8
Other	10.6	3.5	9.2	22.9

Note: Components do not sum to totals because of rounding.
Source: *Facts and Figures on Government Finance, 1986*, p. 18, Tax Foundation, Inc., Washington, D.C.

Cost-Benefit Analysis

Suppose that the government—federal, state, or local—is deciding whether to undertake a particular project. The project may be the building of a dam, a tunnel or highway, or perhaps a school. How can the government decide whether the project makes sense from an economic viewpoint?

The analytic tool for deciding is essentially no different for a government than it is for a private firm. It is to try to evaluate the benefits from the project and then compare them with the costs. If the benefits exceed the costs, the project should be undertaken. A private firm makes the decision on the basis of how the project affects its profits. The government should take a broader view, making the decision by comparing the *social* benefit of the project with the *social* cost.

Take as an example the analysis of whether to build a third tunnel under Boston Harbor. At present there are two tunnels on the main route to the airport. Travel to and from the airport, particularly at rush hour, is painfully slow, and many people waste time sitting in their cars or in taxis or buses when they could instead be working or, for that matter, relaxing at home. The possibility of building a third tunnel has often been discussed, and indeed funds for the project have been voted by the Congress.

The first step in the analysis is to lay out, year by year, the costs of the project and the benefits from it. The costs of a new tunnel would of course include the direct costs of construction: the workers, machinery, and products needed to build the tunnel. We would also need to take into account other costs which are not paid for in cash. The main nonmonetary (economists say "nonpecuniary") cost results from the increased congestion caused by the heavy equipment using the roads around the construction project during the 4 years it would take to build the tunnel. The cost of that congestion is estimated first by calculating the total amount of extra time motorists traveling in that area would spend on the roads (for example, 10 minutes per day for 50,000 motorists) as a result. The cost of congestion would then be the number of hours times the value of motorists' time, which is often taken as the average after-tax wage. Other congestion costs would include gas, and perhaps some estimate of the costs imposed in other parts of the city by the diversion of traffic to those areas, as well as the inconvenience to local residents.

The benefits from the tunnel come mainly in the saving of time for motorists. Once the tunnel is in operation, after 4 years, motorists, many of them on their way to and from the airport, will be making the trip much more rapidly. The value of the time and gasoline they will save counts as a benefit of the tunnel.

Now the costs and benefits in the different years have to be added up, and a final decision must be reached. In this project, as in most investments, the costs occur before the benefits. Recall from Chapter 17 that a future receipt or outlay generally has a lower value today than it will have in the future. For instance, suppose we have to pay $1 a year from now. We can put aside less than $1 today and be in a position to pay out $1 a year from now. Specifically, if the interest rate is 5 percent, by putting aside 95.2 cents today and earning 5 percent on that amount, we will have $1 a year from now. For this reason future costs and benefits are *discounted* back to the present.

Once all the costs and benefits are put on a present-value basis, the benefits and costs are each added. If the costs outweigh the benefits, the economic analysis says the project should not be undertaken. If the benefits outweigh the costs, the project should—from the economic viewpoint—be carried out.

No cost-benefit analysis can be perfect, because not all the costs and benefits can be calculated. For instance, it is quite possible that providing an extra tunnel to the airport will lead to more air travel and more congestion for travelers as planes have to line up to take off and circle the airport before landing. Furthermore, the correct prices to use are not always clear. Just how much is 10 minutes less travel time per day for the average traveler worth to society?

Most important in such calculations is the interest rate that should be used in calculating the present values. Considering that the benefits are further in the future than the costs, a high interest rate will reduce benefits relative to costs.[27] For this reason proponents of a project often claim that the relevant interest rate for that project is very low.

---

[27] Be sure you understand why. If necessary check back to Chapter 17. We ask you to explain this in Problem 8.

PROFITS VERSUS BENEFITS. In the analysis of the tunnel project, we nowhere discussed the fact that the government might charge a toll for the use of the tunnel. That is because government receipts do not affect the *social* desirability of the project. If a toll were charged, it would be paid by people because they saved time using the tunnel—and the value of the time saved has already been taken into account in Table 21-4.

It is quite possible that the tunnel could be a commercial success. That is, the tunnel authority could borrow the amount it needs to pay for the construction and then receive enough in tolls to meet the interest and maintenance costs and eventually pay off the debt.

But this would not necessarily imply that the tunnel should be built. It could be that the cost of congestion caused during the construction was so large as to make the social costs outweigh the benefits. Those congestion costs are an *externality* of the tunnel project—a cost inflicted on people that does not show up in market prices.

On the other side, it could be desirable to build the tunnel even if it would not be commercially viable. Suppose that much of the social benefit comes from time saved by motorists who, after the tunnel is built and many drivers have started coming into town through the tunnel, face less congestion than before on other routes into the city. The tunnel authority could not charge for those gains. These too provide an externality—people are benefiting from the tunnel and not paying any extra for doing so.

It is the presence of the externalities—costs and benefits that are not priced through the market, and in this case not captured by the builders of the tunnel—that make the social cost-benefit analysis necessary.

5. Local Government

Although state government revenue exceeds the direct revenue of local governments, local governments (cities and towns) spend more than state governments spend. As Table 21-4 shows, local governments account for 25 percent of total government spending, and state governments only 17 percent. Local governments can spend more than they receive in direct revenue from property and other local taxes because the state governments make large transfers to them.

In this section we first discuss some consequences of the fact that individuals can choose which local government will serve them.[28] We then discuss education, the largest single category of local expenditure. Cities and towns provide a host of other services, including water, sanitation, police, and, in some cases, electricity.

Zoning and the Invisible Foot

It is clear that the ability of consumers (and businesses) to move from one place to another creates a sort of competition among local governments. Economists have in fact argued that the market for public services provided at the local level operates efficiently, because competition among different cities enables consumers to choose the optimal package of local services. This is called the *Tiebout hypothesis*.[29] If there are many local government units, each providing a different package of services—crime prevention, education, parks, and so on—each family can come close to obtaining its optimal package. The argument is sometimes called the *invisible foot*—people vote with their feet by moving to the community that provides the optimal basket of taxes and benefits. The invisible foot operates to bring about a good allocation of resources through competition among local governments.

But since people are free to move, how does a suburb that offers, say, a better educational system keep out people who might be able to give their children a good education by moving a huge family into an apartment or small house, thus not paying their share of taxes? The answer to that is *zoning*.

Zoning is the regulation of land use by local authorities. For instance, most cities and towns do not allow factories or supermarkets in residential areas, and many suburbs ban apartments and require that houses be built on large lots. Such zoning regulations deal with externalities (air pollution from factories, traffic congestion from supermarkets, the unsightliness of slums), but they also keep out the poor.

Is it fair to exclude the poor from wealthy suburbs? On the one hand, if it is acceptable for there to be differences in income among people, then there will be differences among their consumption levels. As an economic matter, small, exclusive suburbs—with exclusion based on one's inability to pay the local taxes—are an efficient means for controlling access to some goods, just as prices are a means for limiting access to other goods. On the other hand, there is an argument that access to some services, such as the education of children, should not be determined purely by the parents' income.

Education

Education is provided by the government in all countries. In many countries schooling is controlled by the central government rather than by local government, as in the United States. And despite the existence of private schools in most countries, most education is government education.[30] Given the fact that people who obtain an education earn higher incomes, why should the government involve itself in education at all? Doesn't the fact that the economic returns to education are reflected in market prices—namely, wages—mean that individuals can see the value of an education and that private markets could therefore do a good job of producing the right amount of education?

There are several reasons for government involvement in education. The first is that it is widely believed that an educated citizenry is a public good, contributing to the general level of civilized living within a society. The second reason is redistributive. Many believe that everyone deserves an even break, that children with potential should be able to realize it and not be penalized because their parents are poor. The government, by providing education, ensures that everyone receives a given minimum standard. This is probably the main reason for government intervention. A third reason is that children are not sufficiently well informed to choose the optimal

---

[28] The same applies to state government and even to the country in which people live, but the choice is most obvious in the case of local government, where people choose a local government by deciding in which town or suburb to live in a given metropolitan area.

[29] Charles M. Tiebout, "A Pure Theory of Local Expenditures," *Journal of Political Economy*, October 1956, is the original (nonmathematical) reference.

[30] This is true of school education, though not of college education in the United States. In many countries, most colleges are either government-operated or at least heavily funded by the government.

level of education for themselves and that it is not certain that their parents will do so either. The parents may not have the means to provide the education or, if they are selfish, may not be willing to provide enough education for their children.

Even if we agree that it is desirable for the government to require that all children receive a basic education, questions remain about how that education should be provided. One possibility is for the government merely to specify the level of education that each child should have. Private schools could then compete to provide that education. The state or some private body would certify schools to ensure they met government standards. But what if the parents could not afford to send children to school? Milton Friedman and others have suggested that parents be given *education vouchers* that could be used to pay for schooling.[31] There have been local experiments with education vouchers, but given the long history of local government-provided schooling, a major shift to a system without government production of elementary and high school education is unlikely

[31] See Christopher Jencks and others, *Educational Vouchers*, Center for the Study of Public Policy, Cambridge, Mass., 1970.

■ The political process, which reflects both pressure groups and the public's notions of fairness, ultimately determines the role of government in the economy, but this is not a reason to ignore the economics of taxation and government spending. Economic analysis can be used to examine the effects of different types of taxes on the allocation of resources, the deadweight burdens associated with taxes, and the design of efficient tax systems. Economics can also be used to analyze which types of spending are best left to public decisions and which to the market. Although the role of government in the economy has grown rapidly this century, continued growth is not inevitable, and some reduction of the role of government is entirely possible.

Summary

1. Government revenues in the United States amount to nearly one-third of GNP. This is less than in most industrialized countries but much more than in the past. The federal government collects over 60 percent of the taxes but transfers some of the revenue to state and local governments.
2. The two largest sources of government revenue in the United States are the income tax and Social Security taxes. Corporate taxes were raised by the 1986 Tax Reform Act. The value-added tax, or VAT, a national sales tax levied at each stage of production on value added at that stage, is widely used in other countries.
3. Principles of vertical and horizontal equity are used in designing and evaluating tax systems. Horizontal equity says that equals should be treated equally. Vertical equity says that unequals should be treated unequally. One view about how unequals should be treated is that people should pay taxes according to their ability to pay. This suggests that the wealthier should pay more. If they pay proportionately more than do the poor, i.e., pay a higher proportion of their income or wealth, the tax system is progressive; it is regressive if they pay proportionately less.
4. Taxes on the scale levied in modern economies inevitably create distortions in the allocation of resources. The taxes open up a wedge between buyers' and sellers' valuations of goods and factor supplies. For instance, when wages are taxed, the value of the marginal product of labor is higher than the take-home wage of the worker and therefore higher than her valuation of leisure.
5. The tax wedge between buyers' and sellers' valuations leads the economy away from an undistorted equilibrium and affects the allocation of resources. Taxation creates deadweight losses in that the cost of taxation to the economy is greater than the amount of revenue raised by the government. The amount of the deadweight loss increases with the elasticities of supply and demand in the market where the tax is imposed. If either supply or demand is perfectly inelastic, there is no net loss. The total waste of taxation is minimized by taxing relatively heavily those goods whose demand or supply is relatively inelastic.
6. A perennial issue in designing a tax system is whether to tax income or consumption. A consumption tax does not tax saving and therefore tends to encourage it. The United States has basically an income tax system, but with some exemptions for saving.
7. Society is producing the optimal amount of a public good

when the marginal cost of production is equal to the sum of the amounts individuals are willing to pay for the public good. Demand curves for a public good should be added *vertically*, since one person's consumption of the good does not reduce the consumption of others.

8 Government decisions on how much of a good to buy or produce should be informed by cost-benefit analysis. The analysis includes all the social costs and benefits, not only those for which explicit payments are made. To make it possible to add costs and benefits in different years, an interest rate has to be used to calculate present discounted values.

9 Local government purchases more goods and services than does state government. The biggest single local government expenditure is for education. The Tiebout hypothesis suggests that competition among local governments may produce an optimal allocation of resources with respect to the services provided by local government.

10 There is extensive government intervention in education. This occurs to some extent because education is a public good but more because society agrees that children should be given an opportunity to reach their potential. In practice governments produce much education—through local schools and state colleges and universities—though in principle the law could require people to receive education while leaving private schools and colleges to produce it. Education vouchers have been suggested as a means of ensuring that parents could pay for the education that the law requires.

Key Terms

Value-added tax (VAT)
Vertical and horizontal equity
Ability-to-pay principle
Benefit principle
Progressive and regressive taxes
Marginal tax rate
Average tax rate
The tax wedge
Waste, or deadweight burden
Consumption tax
Public goods
Cost-benefit analysis
The Tiebout hypothesis and the invisible foot
Zoning
Education vouchers

Problems

1 Table 21-4 shows which goods the government buys. Using the table, speculate on why the role of government in the economy has increased so much since the beginning of the century.

2 How would you apply principles of horizontal and vertical equity in deciding how much to tax two individuals? Each is healthy and capable of the same work, but one chooses to devote more time to suntanning and therefore has a lower income.

3 Show, using supply and demand curves, why the effects of taxes on resource allocation are minimized when either the supply curve or the demand curve is vertical.

4 In Chapter 4 we argued that taxation affects the amount of cigarettes consumed. Under what circumstances would this not be true? What would you deduce about the desirability of taxing cigarettes—from the viewpoint of economic efficiency—in that case?

5 Suppose a simplified tax system is enacted, with an exemption level and thereafter a constant marginal tax rate. The exemption is for $10,000, and beyond that a marginal tax rate of 20 percent applies. (a) Calculate the average tax rate (taxes divided by total income) at income levels of $10,000, $20,000, $100,000, and $1,000,000. (Then check your answer for consistency with Figure 21-2.) (b) How does the level of the exemption affect the progressivity of the tax? (c) Would the tax be more progressive if the exemption were only $5,000?

6 Explain how you would determine how much of a public good should be produced if you knew everyone's demand function for public goods. Then explain why it is difficult to discover what demand functions really are.

7 Here is a very simple potential government project to evaluate using cost-benefit analysis. The costs all occur in year 1 and are $100 million. There are benefits of $50 million in year 2 and $80 million in year 3. Is the project worth doing if (a) the interest rate is 15 percent, (b) the interest rate is 10 percent?

8 Explain, using the harbor tunnel project in section 4, why it may make sense to undertake a project even if it would not make a profit for a private operator. Then explain why that conclusion does not necessarily imply that the government should actually run the project.

9 Which activities that are provided by local government in Table 21-4 could as well be provided by the private market? Can you see any reason why they are provided by the government instead?

10 Why does society try to make sure that every child receives an education? Discuss different ways this could be done and reasons for choosing one method rather than another.

11 In the discussion of the efficiency of competitive markets we showed that the price system works like an invisible hand to optimally allocate resources. Here we discussed the role of the invisible foot. Are these the same mechanisms? If there are differences, where do they stem from?

Chapter 22
Welfare Programs, Poverty, and Income Distribution

Transfer payments account for over a third of government spending in the United States, nearly 12 percent of GNP. Over the quarter century from 1960 to 1985, transfer payments were the fastest growing component of government spending. From less than 6 percent of GNP in 1960 they rose to double that amount 25 years later.[1]

The growth in transfer payments, particularly welfare payments, was highly controversial. In 1964, the year that President Johnson declared war on poverty, the *Economic Report of the President* said (p. 55):

> There will always be some Americans who are better off than others. But it need not follow that the "poor are always with us." In the United States we can see on the horizon a society of abundance free of much of the misery and degradation that have been the age-old fate of man. Steadily rising productivity, together with an improving network of private and social insurance and assistance has been eroding mass poverty in America. But the process is far too slow. It is high time to redouble and to concentrate our efforts to eliminate poverty.

In that year 19 percent of the population was below the official poverty level.

In 1973, following a rapid expansion of poverty programs, the proportion of the population below the official poverty line reached a minimum at 11.1 percent (see Figure 20-7). Since then the proportion below the official poverty line has increased in recessions and decreased in recoveries, but it still was 14.0 percent in 1985, after 3 years of recovery from recession. Officially measured poverty was not eliminated after 1965 and indeed made a comeback after 1973. Some blame the war on poverty for its return:

> While government transfer programs have improved the standard of living for some of the poor through increased benefit levels and relaxed eligibility requirements, they have also stifled the incentives for the poor to improve their own economic status and for the nonpoor to avoid poverty. They have introduced a perverse incentive structure, one that penalizes self-improvement and protects individuals against the consequences of their own bad choices.[2]

---

[1] Interest payments on the national debt are the other major category of transfer payments. In both 1960 and 1980 they were equal to about 1.3 percent of GNP; by 1985 that proportion had doubled.

[2] James Gwartney and Thomas S. McCaleb, "Have Antipoverty Programs Increased Poverty?" *Cato Journal*, Spring/Summer 1985, p. 7.

In Chapter 20 we examined poverty and the distribution of income in the United States. Market economies do not succeed in keeping everyone out of poverty. Private charitable groups have always taken some part in helping the poor. So have governments, most markedly in the United States since the Great Depression and Lyndon Johnson's "great society."

This chapter studies government's role in reducing the extent of poverty and affecting the distribution of income in the United States.[3] That role is shaped by a fundamental trade-off between equity and efficiency, which we discuss in section 1. Section 2 describes welfare programs in the United States and their effects on poverty. Section 3 takes up an issue dear to the hearts of political conservatives: the effects of welfare programs on incentives and the supply of labor. Alternatives to the current welfare system are discussed in section 4. Finally, section 5 draws together many of the issues discussed in this chapter and Chapter 21 by summarizing the evidence on the net effect of taxation and transfer payments on the distribution of income.

1. The Equity-Efficiency Trade-Off

Redistribution of income is costly. In order to redistribute income, taxes must be levied to take resources from some people so that they can be given to others. As Chapter 21 demonstrated, taxes generally cost society as a whole more than the government takes in in revenue. Transfers also generally produce distortions, as section 3 in this chapter discusses. Specifically, an individual's incentive to work is reduced when he is assured that his basic needs will be taken care of, particularly if he will lose his welfare and unemployment benefits by taking a job. In addition, taxation and transfer programs are expensive to run: Welfare programs employed over 400,000 government workers in 1984. The implications have been put most clearly by Arthur Okun:

> ... we can transport money from rich to poor only in a leaky bucket.... Given (1) a social preference for equality (or at least for more equality than market-determined incomes provide), and (2) a cost of altering the market-determined distribution, society faces a trade-off between equality and efficiency. The resulting optimum will normally be a compromise.[4]

How big are the leaks from Okun's bucket? That depends critically on how much higher taxes and transfer payments reduce the supply of labor. The key variable in determining the effects of programs that impose taxes in order to make transfers to the poor is the elasticity of labor supply with respect to after-tax wages. If this elasticity is high, then the higher taxes needed to pay for income redistribution will substantially reduce the supply of labor of those paying the taxes and thereby will reduce output significantly; at the same time, if the elasticity of labor supply is high, then providing income for those who don't work will reduce their labor supply substantially.

Research on this question has not yet produced definitive results. One controversial study concluded that using income taxes to increase the income of the poorest 40 percent of the population by taxing the top 60 percent would produce a net loss of $2.50 for every dollar transferred.[5] That is, those at the top would lose $3.50 for every dollar those at the bottom gained.

Income redistribution and poverty programs could nonetheless be worthwhile. In the first place, the study we just mentioned assumes an elasticity of labor supply higher than most economists find plausible—its estimated cost per dollar transferred is almost certainly too high. More fundamentally, the social value of income redistribution depends entirely on the preferences of society's members. Those who value equality highly might well be willing to spend $3.50 to give a dollar to the poor if there were no cheaper way to make the transfer.

Waste and distortions in social welfare programs and the disincentive effects of taxation—the leaks in Okun's bucket—as well as simple aversion to sharing with the poor, who may be viewed as lazy and undeserving rather than unfortunate, have led to recurrent moves to reform welfare programs and the tax structure. Such an attempt has been made in the 1980s. Tax rates were reduced in

---

[3] Government welfare and redistributional programs are more extensive in many European countries than they are in the United States.

[4] "Further Thoughts on Equality and Efficiency," in Joseph A. Pechman (ed.), *Economics for Policymaking, Selected Essays of Arthur M. Okun*, M.I.T. Press, Cambridge, 1983.

[5] Edgar K. Browning and William R. Johnson, "The Trade-Off between Equity and Efficiency," *Journal of Political Economy*, April 1984.

1981 and again in 1986, and eligibility rules for welfare programs were tightened in the early eighties.

The decisions to cut taxes and tighten welfare eligibility provide a clear example of society making a choice to tolerate increased inequality in the expectation that tax and government spending cuts would reduce waste and distortions in the economy. Opponents of the tax and welfare cuts claimed that the distortions had been exaggerated and that the main effect of the Reagan administration's economic policies would be to increase inequality. Proponents of the policies replied that the improvements in the economy—growth, innovation, and investment—would do more for the poor than any amount of public programs. We turn now to those programs and attempts to measure their impact.

2. Welfare Programs in the United States

In this section we describe the major government transfer programs in the United States and their effects on measured poverty. In the next section we examine evidence on their incentive effects. Section 5 shows how these programs, together with the tax system discussed in Chapter 19, affect inequality in the distribution of income.

The large number of public assistance and transfer programs in the United States can be grouped by recipients and by type, as in Table 22-1.[6]

Welfare recipients are classified into elderly, totally disabled, and others, with the last group being made up of people in a variety of unfortunate or undesirable circumstances, such as being unemployed (and therefore receiving unemployment insurance) or being a child in a poor family (AFDC).

The programs are classified as social insurance, cash assistance, and in-kind benefits. Social insurance programs provide benefits only to those who have made contributions in the past; because benefits are not exactly matched to past contributions, social insurance programs redistribute income. Table 22-2 gives data on the sizes of the different programs for 1960 (before the

[6] This follows the classification by David T. Ellwood and Lawrence H. Summers, "Poverty in America: Is Welfare the Answer or the Problem?" in Sheldon H. Danziger and Daniel H. Weinberg (eds.), *Fighting Poverty*, Harvard University Press, 1986.

TABLE 22-1. Government Public Assistance and Social Insurance Programs, United States

Recipients	Social insurance	Cash assistance	In-kind benefits
Elderly	Social Security Old age and survivors Public employee and railroad retirement Medicare	Supplemental Security Income	Medicaid Food stamps Housing
Totally disabled	Social Security disability Medicare	Supplemental Security Income	Medicaid
Others	Unemployment insurance Workers' compensation	Aid to Families with Dependent Children (AFDC) General assistance (GA)	Medicaid Food stamps Housing

war on poverty) and for 1980. By far the largest programs are social insurance, especially old age and survivors' benefits in the Social Security system, and the public employee (including the military) and railroad pensions. The first two rows in Table 22-2 account for over 50 percent of the total in 1980. The old age component of Social Security payments is for those who retire, and the survivors' component consists mainly of payments to surviving spouses.

Government Retirement Programs

The data show that the government in the United States (as in most countries) operates massive pension schemes. However, individuals could provide for their own retirement through private saving. Why, then, is there always government involvement in retirement programs? Social Security was started in the United States during the Great Depression, when it was clear that many people's private savings for retirement had been inadequate to provide them with a socially acceptable standard of living. Society was not then, and would not now, be willing to make people live with the consequences of their own past mistakes and lack of foresight by telling those who had not saved that they had to starve.

TABLE 22-2. Spending on Welfare Programs

	(billions of 1980 dollars)		(% of GNP)	
	1960	1980	1960	1980
Programs for the elderly	43.5	192.5	3.0	7.0
Social Security, old age and survivors	29.2	104.7		
Public employee and railroad retirement	9.7	44.3		
Medicare	0.0	29.1		
Medicaid	0.0	8.7		
Other	4.6	5.7		
Programs for the totally disabled	2.3	31.9	0.2	1.2
Social Security, disability	1.6	15.4		
Medicare	0.0	4.5		
Supplemental Security Income	0.7	5.0		
Medicaid	0.0	7.0		
Other	16.1	67.2	1.1	2.5
Unemployment insurance	8.4	18.9		
Workers' compensation	3.6	13.6		
AFDC	2.8	12.5		
GA	0.9	1.4		
Medicaid	0.0	7.5		
Food stamps	0.0	8.6		
Housing	0.4	4.7		
Total	61.9	291.6	4.3	10.7

Source: David T. Ellwood and Lawrence H. Summers, "Poverty in America: Is Welfare the Answer or the Problem?" in Sheldon H. Danziger and Daniel H. Weinberg (eds.), *Fighting Poverty*, Harvard University Press, 1986, p. 85. Ratios of GNP added.

But once people know that they will be provided for even if they do not save, a problem arises that economists call *moral hazard*. The hazard in this case is that by providing for people who do not save, society reduces the incentive to save. There are two approaches to solving this problem. Society can either have programs to help the elderly poor, but with sufficient strings attached so that people will prefer not to use these programs unless they have to, or make savings compulsory. Programs with strings attached exist (in the form of private charities and Supplemental Security Income), but given the possibility that large sums would still have to be provided to the old who had not saved, all countries rely mainly on compulsory savings.

A compulsory savings program can be run by the government, as in almost all countries, or the government can simply require people to show each year that they have saved the required amount. The compulsory government-run program has the advantage that there is no need to check that each person has done the required amount of saving that year and no need to check on the soundness of the bank or mutual fund or other institution in which savings have been deposited. It has the disadvantage that the program is entirely in the hands of the government and therefore is subject to political manipulation of various sorts. A compulsory government scheme is also under no competitive pressure to offer savers convenient and innovative methods of saving.

In a private savings scheme, individuals would make their payments, the interest would accumulate, and then, on retirement, people would get out what they paid in, with the interest they had earned in the meantime.[7] Social Security in the United States is a *transfer program*, not a savings scheme. The amounts contributed in

---

[7] A person who has saved in a private savings scheme can obtain an *annuity* when he or she retires. The annuity pays a fixed amount each year that the person is alive. One gap in private markets in the United States is that it is not possible to receive an *indexed* annuity, one that will pay a fixed *real* amount each year that the person is alive. Social Security payments to the retired are indexed, so that a retired person does not have to worry about the possibility that inflation will reduce the purchasing power of her payments.

any one year are not directly saved by the government. Rather the scheme is "pay as you go," meaning that the government uses its revenues from Social Security (or payroll) taxes each year to pay the people drawing Social Security benefits *that year*. Furthermore, there is no tight link between payments and later receipts. If Congress decides just before an election that Social Security benefits should be raised, they are.

Other Social Insurance

Social Security makes payments for disabled and sick workers as well as for the retired. The disability component of Social Security rose especially fast between 1960 and 1980. Medicare covers most of the medical care of the elderly and disabled—it is counted as social insurance although it could also be thought of as an in-kind benefit, since it provides medical care, not cash.

Medicare was established in 1966 and rapidly became a major program. It is now the third largest of the public assistance programs. The growth of Medicare payments was associated with a rapid increase in the costs of medical care. One of the major initiatives of the Reagan administration was to try to control the growth of medical costs. The effort has been reasonably successful—and the medical profession is unhappy at the outcome.

Medical insurance, like pensions, could be provided privately. However, as in the case of pensions, governments in most countries are heavily involved in the provision of medical care or at least in paying for it. Access to medical care is seen as a merit good, something people have a right to consume regardless of their economic status. Most people sympathize with the plight of a poor person unable to afford medical insurance and therefore without medical care. Medicaid provides access to medical care for the poor, both elderly and nonelderly.[8]

The growth in Social Security payments has been associated with a steady decline in the percentage of the elderly who fall below the poverty line. In 1960, 35 percent of the elderly fell below the poverty line (compared with less than 22 percent of the nonelderly). By 1978 only 14 percent of elderly people lived in poverty. Since then the proportion of the elderly in poverty has stayed around 14 to 15 percent; by 1983, for the first time a greater proportion of the nonelderly than the elderly were living in poverty.

In Chapter 20 we noted that poverty may be a temporary phase for many, who can expect to leave poverty within a year or two when they find a job or return to health. Poverty is far more likely to be permanent among the elderly. The decline in poverty among the elderly is thus an especially significant achievement for which Social Security deserves much of the credit.

Cash Assistance

Cash assistance is available to some poor people, including the aged, the disabled, and single-parent families with young children. The largest cash assistance program is AFDC, which makes payments to poor single parents who have children living with them. In 1985, 16 percent of all families were headed by a female in a household with no adult male present. Over 40 percent of black families fell into this category, and more than half of those families lived below the poverty line. Thus the problem addressed by AFDC is a very large one.

AFDC is among the most controversial welfare programs. Critics assert that by providing payments for unmarried mothers, AFDC encourages unmarried women to have children. By providing the aid to single-parent families, AFDC makes it advantageous for one parent to move out. Furthermore, children growing up in families that receive welfare, particularly AFDC, are introduced early to the possibility of living without work; this is the supposed source of the "culture of poverty" in which children follow their parents into welfare dependency.[9]

Real spending on AFDC has not increased since the mid-1970s, and according to budget projections it will be cut back slowly through the 1980s.

---

[8] We leave it to the reader to work out the argument over whether government should merely require the elderly to have medical insurance or should provide that coverage itself. The argument follows closely the lines of our discussion of Social Security retirement provisions.

[9] Charles Murray, in *Losing Ground,* Basic Books, New York, 1984, notes that AFDC was introduced in the 1930s to provide for widows with small children. He provides an extensive review of the charges against AFDC.

In-Kind Benefits

In-kind benefits are provided by Medicaid, food stamps, and subsidized housing. Medicaid covers the medical expenses of the poor among the elderly, the disabled, and those in single-parent families. Food stamps are vouchers that can be used to purchase food.

In-kind benefits show the greatest rate of growth in Table 22-2. There were practically no in-kind programs in 1960, whereas in 1984 they accounted for $66 billion, or 1.7 percent of GNP. Food stamps, like AFDC, have attracted special attention as being responsible for the culture of poverty.

Benefit levels per person in the food stamp program have remained constant in real terms since 1971. Government spending on the program nonetheless increased rapidly during the 1970s, because an increasing number of eligible people took advantage of the program.

The Safety Net

● **The *safety net*, or low-income benefit programs, is the set of welfare programs that provide benefits to the poor on the basis of their poverty.**

As the name suggests, safety net programs are there to protect those who for one reason or another do not earn enough in the market economy to support themselves at the standard of living that the programs provide.

The safety net consists of AFDC, Supplemental Security Income, public housing, food stamps, Medicaid, and some other programs. The Reagan administration promised to maintain the safety net programs, those which protect the genuinely poor, as it attempted to reduce the size of welfare programs in the 1980s.

Effects on Poverty

The official count of the percentage of the population below the poverty line (see Figure 20-7 and the data quoted in the introduction to this chapter) does not include in-kind transfers in income. Thus the official measure of poverty does not take into account any reductions in poverty brought about by food stamps or Medicaid, for instance. These programs do contribute to reducing *actual* poverty, but they do not contribute to reducing *measured official* poverty.

We show in the last two columns of Table 22-3 the large impact of in-kind transfers on poverty. In the last column the value of in-kind transfers is added to each individual's income, and the poverty rate is recalculated using that definition of income. Taking account of in-kind transfers would have reduced the official poverty rate by one-third in 1983. The effect is especially strong for blacks, those living in a household headed by a female, and the elderly.

Table 22-3 shows that actual poverty has indeed fallen substantially since 1964 and that in-kind payments have played a big role in that improvement. The table also shows the significant differences in poverty rates among

TABLE 22-3. Percentage of Persons in Poverty

Group	Official measure, 1964	Official measure, 1983	Adjusted for in-kind transfers, 1983*
All	19.0	15.2	10.2
White	14.9	12.1	8.6
Black	49.6	35.7	21.2
Hispanic		28.4	20.2
Living with female household head†	45.9	40.2	24.7
Elderly (65+)	28.5‡	14.1	3.3
Children (18−)	20.7‡	22.2	15.6

* In-kind transfers are valued at market prices.
† No husband present.
‡ Data are for 1966.

Source: Sheldon H. Danziger, Robert H. Haveman, and Robert D. Plotnick, "Antipoverty Policy: Effects on the Poor and the Nonpoor," in Sheldon H. Danziger and Daniel H. Weinberg (eds.), *Fighting Poverty*, Harvard University Press, 1986, p. 56.

different demographic groups. Most remarkable is the virtual eradication of poverty among the elderly once in-kind payments are taken into account.

Changes in poverty rates are not due only to changes in poverty programs. The poverty level is fixed in real terms. Thus if the distribution of income remains the same, rising average incomes should reduce the poverty rate. And indeed the poverty rate does tend to fall as median family incomes rise. The rapid progress against poverty in the 1960s seen in Figure 20-7 was accompanied by an increase in real median family income of 34 percent. In the seventies real median family income increased by less than 0.05 percent. Indeed, from 1973 to 1980, real median family income fell 6 percent. Thus the slowdown of progress in the war on poverty in the seventies was in part due to the reduction in the growth of the entire economy.[10]

The Return of Poverty

Was the increase in official poverty in the first half of the 1980s a result of the recessions of 1980 and 1981–1982 or was it primarily a reflection of the Reagan administration's attack on welfare programs? The administration described its efforts as being to *target* welfare payments to the genuinely poor so that it could cut total spending on welfare without harming those who needed the safety net.[11]

Spending on welfare programs increased sharply through the 1970s. In his last budget, President Carter planned to cut the *growth*, though not the *level*, of welfare spending. President Reagan's first budget proposed a significant cut in real welfare spending by 1984. Table 22-4 shows budget outlays on programs for the poor.

In fact, real welfare spending by 1984 was higher than it had been in 1981 and even higher than planned by the Carter budget, but it was well above the level planned in the original Reagan budget. Congress did not approve all the cuts the administration wanted to make. The fact that welfare programs were being cut by the Reagan administration is most evident in Table 22-4 in the decline in actual budget outlays for low-income programs from (fiscal year) 1981 to 1982, as the economy went into recession.

Cutting benefits during a recession certainly added to an increase in poverty that the recession would have caused by itself. The Reagan welfare cuts thus contributed to the increase in poverty from 1980 to 1983, even though the recession must receive primary blame. At the same time there is some evidence that the administration was able to improve the targeting of welfare payments, so that a larger fraction of each dollar went to the poor.[12]

---

[10] Rebecca M. Blank and Alan S. Blinder, "Macroeconomics, Income Distribution, and Poverty," in Sheldon H. Danziger and Daniel H. Weinberg (eds.), *Fighting Poverty*, Harvard University Press, 1986, examine the effects of macroeconomic conditions on poverty rates. They estimate that an increase in the prime-age male unemployment rate of 2 percent lasting for 2 years would increase the poverty rate by 0.9 percent.

[11] John C. Weicher, "The Reagan Domestic Budget Cuts: Proposals, Outcomes and Effects," in Phillip Cagan (ed.), *Essays in Contemporary Economic Problems, 1986*, American Enterprise Institute, Washington, D.C., provides a careful discussion.

[12] Ibid.

TABLE 22-4. Real Outlays for Low-Income Benefit Programs, 1960–1984 (Fiscal Years, 1980 Dollars)

	1960	1970	1980	1981	1982	1983	1984
Actual outlays	10.0	19.8	50.1	53.8	51.4	55.3	55.4
Carter budget (Jan. 1981)				52.1	52.0	54.4	54.6
Reagan budget (March 1981)				51.8	47.5	47.6	46.1

Source: John C. Weicher, "The Reagan Domestic Budget Cuts: Proposals, Outcomes and Effects," in Phillip Cagan (ed.), *Essays in Contemporary Economic Problems, 1986*, American Enterprise Institute, Washington, D.C., 1986, Tables 1-1 and 1-2. The federal government's fiscal year runs from October 1 and, like automobile model years, is named for the later year.

3. Disincentive Effects of Transfers

The taxes needed to finance government transfer programs create distortions and social waste, as described in Chapter 21. In addition, the programs themselves may have distortionary or disincentive effects. We examine these effects in this section, starting with Social Security.

Social Security

The first charge made against the Social Security system is that it reduces the nation's overall rate of saving because it is a "pay-as-you-go" scheme. If there were no Social Security system, everyone would have to save for retirement privately. Some of these savings would be deposited in banks, which would lend them to firms that want to invest.

Now suppose that the Social Security system has just been invented and that each person is required to save exactly as much as he or she did before. Instead of sending a check to the bank, the saver sends it to the government. The government in turn passes on the proceeds to Social Security recipients, who spend them. Under the Social Security system the individual's saving goes to make transfer payments, whereas with private savings the individual's saving ends up financing investment. The capital stock will thus be higher with private saving than it is under Social Security. The size of this effect has been difficult to estimate, but given that social insurance payments received by the government in 1985 exceeded $350 billion (over 9 percent of GNP) and gross private saving was nearly $700 billion, the existence of Social Security could have a major impact on total saving.[13]

Social Security appears also to affect the date of individuals' retirement and thus to affect the supply of labor to the economy. There is a bunching of retirement at ages 62 and 65, which are the ages at which the Social Security system provides early retirement and regular retirement benefits, respectively. There has been a gradual reduction in the labor force participation of men in their sixties, some of which may be attributable to the availability of Social Security. Of course, that is not necessarily socially undesirable. It may have been that men in their sixties were working before only because they had not had the foresight to save enough for retirement earlier and that Social Security, far from distorting the choice individuals would optimally make, provides people with the opportunity to retire at the right age.

The 1970s saw rapid growth in disability payments and the number of individuals retiring as totally disabled under the Social Security system. This trend also suggested that the existence of the program was reducing the supply of labor. Evidence on this issue has been inconclusive; a major problem is to decide whether individuals who receive disability payments from the government are actually totally disabled or, as the hypothesis that people take advantage of the provision of disability insurance implies, merely faking it. Since individuals are supposed to be totally disabled to receive this type of payment, it is difficult to see how faking can be a major factor.

Medicaid and Medicare payments are believed to have been at least partly responsible for the jump in medical costs in the seventies. Many elderly people who had been too poor to visit the doctor could now afford medical care. This implied an outward shift of the demand curve for medical services, which would lead to higher prices.

Unemployment insurance also creates a moral hazard problem. If the costs of being unemployed are reduced, workers are more likely to quit their jobs or engage in behavior that gets them fired. Similarly, they are more likely to stay unemployed as long as insurance benefits are available. A recent study found that the latter effect is reflected in large jumps in the rate at which the unemployed find jobs around the date that unemployment insurance benefits run out.[14] It is not only workers

---

[13] There has been controversy over the effects of Social Security on saving. Harvard University's Martin Feldstein has argued that Social Security significantly reduces the amount individuals save for themselves. Others contend that people understand that Social Security is just a transfer program and that it therefore does not affect their saving. The issue has been remarkably difficult to settle by studying the data.

[14] Lawrence Katz, "Layoffs, Recall and the Duration of Unemployment," Working Paper 1825, National Bureau of Economic Research, Cambridge, Mass., January 1986.

whose incentives are distorted: Firms are more likely to lay off workers when unemployment insurance is available than when it is not, since workers will object less.

Thus all the social insurance programs,[15] with the possible exception of disability, reduce the incentive to work. This means that the good they do in reducing hardship comes at a social cost greater than the budgetary cost of the programs.

Welfare Programs

The most controversial charge against welfare programs is that they encourage the breakup of the family. AFDC has been singled out for special blame here. The charge is that by providing aid only for children living with a single parent, AFDC encourages the other parent to move out or never to move in.

There is no question that an increasing percentage of children are being raised in female-headed, single-parent households. Whereas in 1970, 12 percent of children were raised in female-headed households, by 1982, the figure was up to 19 percent. While many find this trend disturbing, very little of the increase in the 1970s can be attributed to AFDC, since the percentage of children raised in households receiving AFDC was about 11 percent in both 1972 and 1982. Furthermore, AFDC payments vary widely across states, but states with more generous AFDC benefits do not have more than their share of children living with a single parent. Nor is there much evidence that AFDC significantly reduces the work effort of recipients.[16]

Most AFDC recipients are in the program for only a short time. Nonetheless, most AFDC spending goes to very long term welfare-dependent recipients. It is not clear what can be done about this problem, since as Ellwood and Summers observe, "there are just two routes to self-sufficiency for single mothers, work and marriage, and both of these can be hampered by the presence of young children."[17] As Table 22-3 shows, 40 percent of female-headed households are below the poverty line. Even after counting in-kind benefits, nearly one-quarter of such families, with about 4 million children under age 18, live in poverty.

Some blame welfare programs for the fact that unemployment rates among black teenagers have been at least twice as high as those among white teenagers in recent years. In 1984, for instance, 42.6 percent of black males aged 16 to 19 who were in the labor force were unemployed, compared with 16.8 percent of white males. But unemployed youths, black or white, do not receive many welfare benefits; food stamps are the main resource. Yet food stamps do not seem to provide an adequate explanation of the large and persistent black youth unemployment problem.

The minimum wage determined by the government is also sometimes blamed for high black youth unemployment. Economic analysis indeed implies that the minimum wage will increase unemployment, particularly among those who would otherwise have received a lower wage.[18] But the minimum wage has not been raised since 1981; it has therefore fallen relative to market wages, but there has been little improvement in the rate of employment among black youth. The high level of black youth unemployment is both a social problem and a phenomenon that is difficult to explain.

Welfare and the Tax System

In the pre-1986 U.S. income tax system, the marginal tax rate rose with income from 15 percent for low-income households to 50 percent for those at the top. It turns out that the U.S. welfare system is structured so that the poor often face marginal tax rates higher than those which apply to the very rich.

Table 22-5 illustrates the problem, using the post-1986 tax rates. Suppose someone who earns no income receives benefits of $5000. The amount provided by food stamps and other welfare payments falls as outside income rises. Thus for every dollar earned in the market, a welfare recipient receives *net* less than an extra dollar of income. In Table 22-5 we assume that the welfare recipient loses 50 cents of benefits for every dollar of outside income earned. When his or her income rises to $10,000, that person receives no more benefits.

---

[15] The social insurance programs are defined in Table 22-1.

[16] Ellwood and Summers, op. cit., review the evidence on the effects of AFDC.

[17] Ibid., p. 97.

[18] See Chapter 16 for the analysis.

TABLE 22-5. Welfare and Marginal Taxes

Income, $	Benefits, $	Income + benefits, $	Taxes, $	−Income + benefits − taxes, $	Marginal tax rate, %
0	5,000	5,000	0	5,000	50
5,000	2,500	7,500	0	7,500	50
10,000	0	10,000	0	10,000	15
30,000	0	30,000	4,500	25,500	15
1,000,000	0	1,000,000	280,000	720,000	28

Note: Marginal tax rates from $10,000 up are those in the 1986 Tax Reform Act. From $0 to $10,000, it is assumed that recipient loses 50 cents of welfare benefits for every dollar of income earned and that that individual pays exactly zero taxes up to an income of $10,000.

We also assume that that person's deductions are such that he or she pays no income tax on income of $10,000 but thereafter faces first a 15 percent marginal tax rate and later a 28 percent rate.[19]

Because the individual in Table 22-5 is losing welfare benefits fast as earned income rises, the marginal tax rate on the first $10,000 of income is a high 50 percent. In fact, the marginal tax rate on outside income can be much higher when the loss of benefits from several programs is taken into account. There are even examples of people in specific programs and places who are "taxed" (by losing benefits) more than 100 percent on outside income.[20] These high marginal tax rates strongly reduce work incentives for individuals who are on the fringes of the labor force in the first place.

Unfortunately, high marginal tax rates are unavoidable if benefits are to be paid mainly to the poor. This follows from basic arithmetic. Suppose the poverty line is an annual income of $10,000 for a family consisting of a single mother with two small children. And suppose that society decides that this family should receive $8000 in cash and in-kind transfers, probably enough to avoid malnutrition, if the mother earns no income. How much should the family have to live on if the mother takes a job paying $10,000 per year? If the answer is $10,000, the marginal tax rate is 80 percent: An increase of $10,000 in before-tax income raises the after-tax income (including benefits) of the family by only $2000. The tax takes the form of an $8000 (80 percent of $10,000) fall in benefits.

Looking at the problem in another way, let us ask how high a marginal tax rate is acceptable. If the answer is 50 percent, the highest rate specified in the pre-1986 income tax system, the working mother in our example will lose only $5000 in benefits because she earns $10,000 in income. Her after-tax income (including benefits) when she earns $10,000 will be $13,000: $10,000 in earned income and $3000 in welfare benefits. But if the marginal tax rate never goes above 50 percent and if $8000 is the basic level of benefits, she will continue to receive welfare benefits as long as she earns less than $16,000. Thus in this example all nonpoor families earning up to $16,000 receive welfare benefits. When the marginal tax rate was 80 percent, only families earning up to $10,000 received welfare benefits.

By reducing the marginal tax rate in this example from 80 percent to 50 percent, we have made work more attractive to poor people. This is likely to increase the efficiency of the economy. But the consequence is that welfare payments must be made to many nonpoor families, and the workers whose taxes finance those payments may well resist. Once again we see the equity-efficiency trade-off in operation.

4. What Can Be Done?

The current welfare system, with its host of programs and multitude of laws and regulations, offends those who value simplicity. It also offends many who are concerned with equity and efficiency. Some people who are not poor

---

[19] As pointed out in Chapter 21, there is a middle range with a 33 percent marginal rate.

[20] Gwartney and McCaleb, op. cit., present an example of a single mother of two children in Pennsylvania whose marginal tax rate for market incomes up to $10,000 is above 50 percent at all incomes and above 100 percent between $4000 and $6000. This means that such a mother would actually have lower total income if she received a raise in a job in which she was earning $4000.

receive substantial welfare payments, while others who are poor receive nothing—in some cases because they don't understand the system and are unaware that they are eligible for benefits. The system confronts welfare recipients with high marginal tax rates and requires raising the income tax rates paid by others; both create disincentives to work.

How can these problems be solved? Some call loudly for abolishing the entire system—although they quickly exclude programs for the elderly and the truly needy. As we have discussed, these exclusions cover most welfare expenditures. Others call for a return to traditional values. But while many problems would be solved if everyone strongly valued work and self-sufficiency, we do not know how to instill those values. Three other proposals deserve more extended discussion, though they too are not panaceas.

Workfare

One way of reducing the adverse effects of the current welfare system is through *work requirements*, or *work fare*. Several states have experimented with this approach, requiring those who receive benefits to work or at least look for work. But we probably do not want *all* welfare recipients to be in the labor force; for instance, it may not be a good thing to force single parents of small children to work full-time away from home.

Workfare programs encounter a number of problems in practice. Many of the poor lack skills and work habits that command a high price in the labor market, and the welfare system makes the payoff from landing a low-paying job very small indeed. It may be easy to force somebody to go through the motions of looking for a job; it is impossible to force somebody to look hard for a job she doesn't want. The government can give jobs to the poor, but this requires raising taxes, and government jobs reserved for the poor have not proved to be good training for employment in the private sector. Nonetheless the success of workfare in some states suggests that this idea will be pushed further in the future.

The Negative Income Tax

Both liberal and conservative economists have supported replacing all existing welfare programs with a negative income tax. The negative income tax has two basic components. First, each household would receive a check from the government, probably once a month, large enough to cover basic necessities. These checks, called *demogrants* in one proposal, could place each household above, on, or below the poverty line, depending on the design of the program. The demogrants would replace all welfare programs. This is the "negative" component of the income tax: Everyone receives a payment from the Internal Revenue Service. But second, all income (wages, salaries, dividends, interest, rents, and so on) would be subject to taxation at the margin. Every extra dollar of income would be subject to tax, and at some income level the amount of taxes paid would exactly offset the demogrant. Of course, tax rates might have to be raised considerably in order to pay for the demogrants.

Figure 22-1 illustrates before-tax and after-tax income under a negative income tax system. In the example shown, each person starts with a demogrant of $6000, paid by the government, and is thereafter taxed at a marginal rate of 40 percent. The demogrant plus a flat

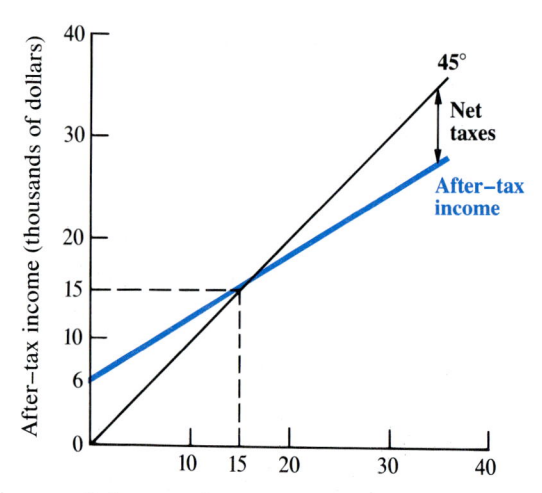

FIGURE 22-1. A Negative Income Tax. Each individual receives $6000 from the government, even if before-tax income is zero. Thereafter there is a constant marginal tax rate of 40 percent. Up to before-tax income levels of $15,000 the individual is on balance receiving a transfer from the government; at higher income levels on net he makes payments to the government.

marginal tax rate gives the tax system substantial progressivity (compare Figure 22-1 with Figure 21-2*b*). Up to $15,000 of outside income, this plan's *break-even level*, the individual on balance receives net payments—negative taxes—from the government. At $15,000, taxes equal to 40 percent of income are just equal to the $6000 initial cash payment by the government. Thereafter the worker's after-tax income is below before-tax income: Net income taxes are positive.

The major advantage of the negative income tax is that by replacing welfare programs with a check from the Internal Revenue Service it would reduce paperwork, bureaucracy, and the complexity of the current welfare system. But there are two major problems with this approach. The first is that marginal tax rates would have to be increased dramatically in order to pay for demogrants at or near poverty line levels. If every U.S. household had been given a demogrant equal to its poverty line income in 1980, the total cost would have been about $527 billion.[21] Even if all the transfer programs shown in Table 22-2 had been abolished at the same time, government spending would have been $235 billion higher. An increase of about 60 percent in personal income and payroll taxes would have been required to pay for this change. From an ability-to-pay perspective this would not be nearly as bad as it seems, since the average household would have had an extra $6250 with which to meet its tax bill. But most individuals would face higher marginal tax rates, and the effects on work incentive, labor supply, and national output could be serious.

The second problem is more political than economic. Most existing welfare programs are aimed at groups for which substantial sympathy exists (old people, the sick and disabled, and children) or provide necessities (food, housing, and medical care). Proposals to abolish these programs and instead simply write checks to all who are poor, for whatever reason, give rise to worries about lazy people who will spend their demogrants irresponsibly. For these two reasons, the negative income tax has been dropped from the discussion of alternative approaches to welfare reform, at least for the time being.

---

[21] This is based on *Statistical Abstract of the United States, 1986*, pp. 40 and 430.

Private Charity

Is there any economic reason to go beyond charitable giving in dealing with problems of poverty? Shouldn't we just allow the market to work, with people who have money making the transfers to the poor that they wish to make? There are two arguments for going beyond private charity. First, there is no particular reason to think the market necessarily generates the socially best precharity distribution of income and therefore no good reason to think that whoever is rich will make the best decisions for society about how much to redistribute income. Individuals' different views about a desirable income distribution cannot be excluded from the political process.

Second, there is a free-rider problem in the provision of private charity. My own individual donation makes essentially no difference to the amount of poverty in society. I may abhor poverty and be willing to contribute to reducing it if others do so, but there is no point in my doing so alone. There is thus a public good problem, and the market is unlikely to produce the right amount of charitable donations. Compulsory participation in alleviating poverty through taxation may well produce a better outcome for society, as all countries have decided.

At the beginning of the 1980s, the Reagan administration argued that private charity would replace many of the welfare programs that the government was seeking to reduce. More than other countries, the United States has a long tradition of private giving. In 1984 charitable contributions amounted to $74 billion, over 2 percent of GNP. Nearly half the total was given to religious institutions and organizations; educational institutions and hospitals were other major recipients. Beyond donations in money, individuals donate their time by volunteering to work in hospitals, museums, and other institutions.

Recall that total government transfers to the nonelderly, nondisabled in Table 20-2 amounted to 2.5 percent of GNP. Could it be then that charitable giving could substitute for substantial parts of the welfare system? To some extent it already does; about 10 percent of total charitable contributions go for social welfare purposes. But much of charitable giving does not; most support for museums, public libraries, universities, and churches does not go to the poor. The share of giving for welfare purposes would have to rise remarkably if private charity were to become a serious substitute for government welfare programs.

Besides, charitable contributions do affect the government budget. Every charitable contribution that goes to a recognized charity is tax-deductible and therefore reduces the government's revenues as people get to pay lower taxes. Even private charity has a component that is given by the government.

Studies have been made of the price and income elasticity of charitable giving by individuals.[22] Estimates of the price elasticity are around 1, while income elasticities appear to exceed 1. The income elasticity indicates, not surprisingly, that the rich give a larger share of their income than do the poor. In calculating the price elasticity, the price of giving is taken to be the net after-tax cost to the individual of giving away $1.

Assuming that the price elasticity of charitable contributions is 1, we can calculate how a change in tax rates affects giving. Suppose an individual's tax rate is 40 percent. Then for every dollar she gives to charity, she loses only 60 cents of after-tax income. The price of a $1 charitable donation is then equal to 60 cents. A price elasticity of unity means that a reduction in that price of, say, 6 cents (i.e., 10 percent of the price) would increase charitable giving by 10 percent—if the individual's after-tax income remained the same. If the tax rate rose to 46 percent, then indeed the price of giving away $1 would fall to 54 cents, or by 10 percent. Thus, holding income constant, an increase in the tax rate on individuals from 40 percent to 46 percent would raise charitable giving by 10 percent. Of course, in this example the increased tax rate reduces after-tax income, thereby tending to offset the price effect of the tax increase.

Thus tax policy should be expected to have powerful effects on charitable contributions. The perhaps surprising point to note is that a cut in the marginal tax rate *increases* the price of charitable giving and thus tends to reduce giving. Why? Because when the marginal tax rate is reduced, the tax reduction an individual receives for making a charitable donation is reduced. It follows that a "revenue-neutral" tax reform of the 1986 type, one that reduces marginal rates while keeping total taxes constant, would reduce charitable giving: The price effect reduces donations, and there is no income effect because total taxes are unchanged.

5. Government and Income Distribution: The Results

Much of government activity is concerned with alleviating poverty and with the distribution of income. The welfare and transfer programs analyzed in this chapter are almost entirely redistributive. In Chapter 21 we considered the progressivity of the tax system. Now we draw the discussion of redistribution to a close by asking the bottom-line question: What net effect does government activity have on the distribution of income?

The question can be asked at two levels. Ideally, we would take into account the incentive effects of taxes and transfers on labor supply and on saving and calculate what the income distribution would be with government and without it. And we would consider the distribution of the benefits of government purchases of goods and services across the population. But this is a virtually impossible task, if only because debates still rage about the importance of the various incentive effects we have discussed.

A simpler question has, however, been answered. Given the incomes actually earned in the economy, how different is the after-tax and after-transfer income distribution from that before taxes and transfers? The answer is that taxes make almost no difference to the distribution of income—that is, the tax system is essentially neither progressive nor regressive. But transfers do have a major redistributive effect, reducing the inequality of income and also, as we saw in Table 22-3, significantly reducing poverty.[23]

The effects of taxes and transfers on the distribution of income are shown in the Lorenz curves in Figure 22-2. Recall from Chapter 20 that the closer the Lorenz curve is to the diagonal, the more equal is the distribution of income. The fact that taxes make essentially no difference is shown by the virtual coincidence of the Lorenz

---

[22] Charles T. Clotfleter, *Federal Tax Policy and Charitable Giving*, University of Chicago Press, 1985.

[23] Joseph A. Pechman, *Who Paid the Taxes, 1960–85*, Brookings Institution, Washington, D.C, 1985.

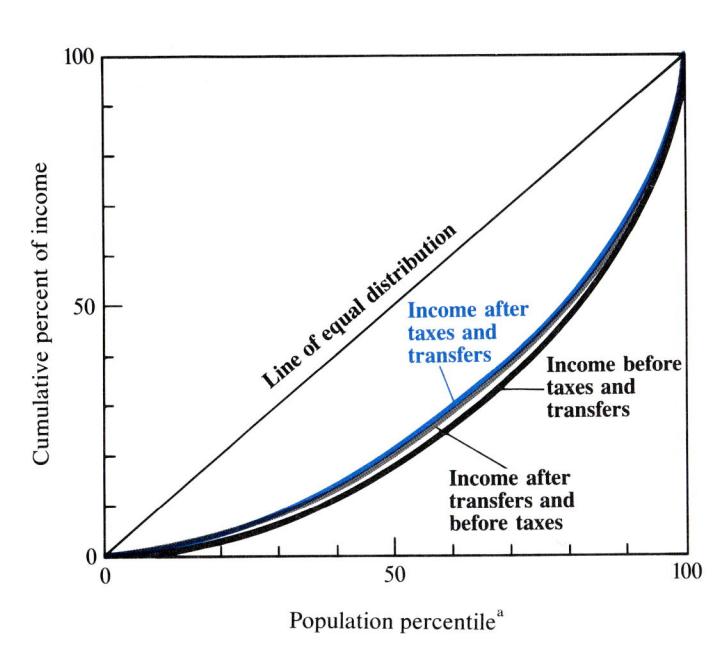

FIGURE 22-2. The Effects of Taxes and Transfers on the Distribution of Income: Lorenz Curves. (*Source*: Joseph A. Pechman, *Who Paid the Taxes, 1960–85*, Brookings Institution, Washington, D.C., 1985.)

curves for "income after transfers and before taxes" and "income after taxes and transfers," respectively. But the clear daylight showing between those curves and "income before taxes and transfers," which lies closer to the diagonal, shows that transfers indeed redistribute income in a way that reduces inequality.

■ This chapter and Chapter 21 have analyzed the microeconomic effects of government taxation, purchases of goods and services, and transfer payments. No simple summary is possible; the taxing and spending decisions made at the federal, state, and local levels have profound and diverse effects on the economy and on society. In Chapters 13 and 14 we considered government's other microeconomic role—as regulator of private decision making. There too the government's role in the economy is varied and widespread. Our economy is indeed "mixed"; both public and private decisions, operating through markets and through the political process, shape our economic life.

Summary

1. Government transfer programs amount to nearly 12 percent of GNP and were for the quarter century to 1985 the fastest growing component of government spending.
2. The official poverty rate reached its minimum of 11.1 percent in 1973 and has risen since then to the range of 14 to 15 percent. The rise has been largely due to a growth slowdown and also to some extent to reduced welfare spending and tightened eligibility requirements.
3. Redistribution of income creates an equity-efficiency trade-off, summarized in Okun's leaky bucket analogy. The main leaks are administrative costs and the adverse incentive effects of higher taxes and welfare programs themselves.
4. The major transfer programs can be classified into social insurance (only those who have paid in are eligible for benefits), cash assistance, and in-kind benefits. The major categories of recipients are the elderly, the disabled, and other poor people.
5. Social insurance is the largest category of transfer programs. Social Security payments do not go primarily to the poor. In absolute terms, increases in retirement benefits accounted for the largest share of the growth of transfer programs from 1960 to 1980.

6 In relative terms, in-kind benefits—Medicaid, food stamps, and public housing—increased most rapidly in that period. These programs, along with cash assistance, particularly AFDC, are the most controversial.
7 The official measure of poverty does not include in-kind benefits in measured income. Taking such benefits into account shows that government welfare programs have significantly reduced actual poverty.
8 The social welfare programs all have real disincentive effects on work and on saving. Social Security, because it is on a pay-as-you-go basis, reduces total saving in the economy; its retirement provisions encourage retirement at particular ages. Welfare programs encourage parents to stay single, may break up families or prevent their forming, and may produce a culture of poverty in which people grow up learning to rely on welfare.
9 The equity-efficiency trade-off is inherent in the provision of welfare and transfer programs. Benefits must fall sharply with increased income, or significant payments must be made to those who are not poor. If benefits fall sharply, as they do in the current system, the poor may face higher marginal tax rates than do the rich.
10 The negative income tax would replace many welfare programs with a simple tax system that would provide a minimum amount of income to everyone. Such a scheme would require a large increase in total tax revenue and would raise marginal tax rates for many people. Instead, the current approach to welfare is to try to limit total welfare spending by targeting the benefits to the poor and needy and to experiment with work requirements of various sorts.
11 Over 2 percent of GNP is given in the form of private charity each year in the United States. Tax incentives have a substantial effect on the amount of giving. Since elimination of poverty is a public good, private charity faces a free-rider problem.
12 On balance, the tax system has virtually no effect on the distribution of income. But transfers substantially reduce income inequality.

Key Terms

Okun's leaky bucket
Equity-efficiency trade-off
Social insurance
Pay-as-you-go Social Security
In-kind benefits
Cash assistance
Safety net
Targeting of programs
Aid to Families with Dependent Children (AFDC)
Work requirements
Workfare
Negative income tax.

Problems

1 It has frequently been argued that the market-determined distribution of income should be accepted and not tampered with. Present and evaluate arguments for and against this view.
2 Suppose that it costs society (a) $3.50 or (b) $1.30 to transfer $1 to each person living in poverty. Discuss the desirability of making transfers in each case, explaining how you are dealing with the equity-efficiency trade-off.
3 Explain why, politically, programs for the nonelderly, nondisabled have been the most unpopular social welfare programs. Name specific programs if you can (use Tables 22-1 and 22-2). Relate this to the current lack of interest in the negative income tax.
4 Using data presented in this chapter, discuss the claim that programs to deal with poverty among the elderly have been the most successful of all transfer programs.
5 Is it desirable for the government to (a) require people to save for their retirement and (b) run that saving program itself? You may want to refer here to individual retirement accounts, which were discussed briefly in Chapter 21.
6 Explain why Social Security retirement payments may reduce both the economy's capital stock and its supply of labor.
7 "Transfer recipients should not be allowed to use children as hostages in order to blackmail society. No disadvantaged child is undeserving. However, we must find ways of helping children that will not be used by undeserving, irresponsible adults." (This quote is from James Gwartney and Thomas McCaleb, "Have Antipoverty Programs Increased Poverty?" p. 15, cited in footnote 2.) Explain the difficulty of finding methods of doing what is suggested here and discuss the authors' suggestion of work requirements for adults and transfer programs aimed directly at children.
8 (a) A negative income tax provides a payment of $8000 to each person and has a marginal tax rate of 35 percent. At what income level does a person pay zero net taxes? (b) Show why reducing the break-even level of income requires either raising the marginal tax rate or reducing the initial

payment (demogrant). A picture may help. (c) Discuss the benefits of the negative income tax compared with more carefully targeted programs.

9 A person has before-tax income of $30,000, a price elasticity of charitable donations of unity, and an income elasticity of 1.5. He is giving $2000 to charity. Now the government imposes a flat rate tax of 25 percent on that person. How is the amount he donates affected?

10 (a) Explain why we do not have a complete picture of the effects of government taxes and transfers on the economy. (b) Summarize in words the results shown in Figure 22-2.

PART SIX
THE WORLD ECONOMY

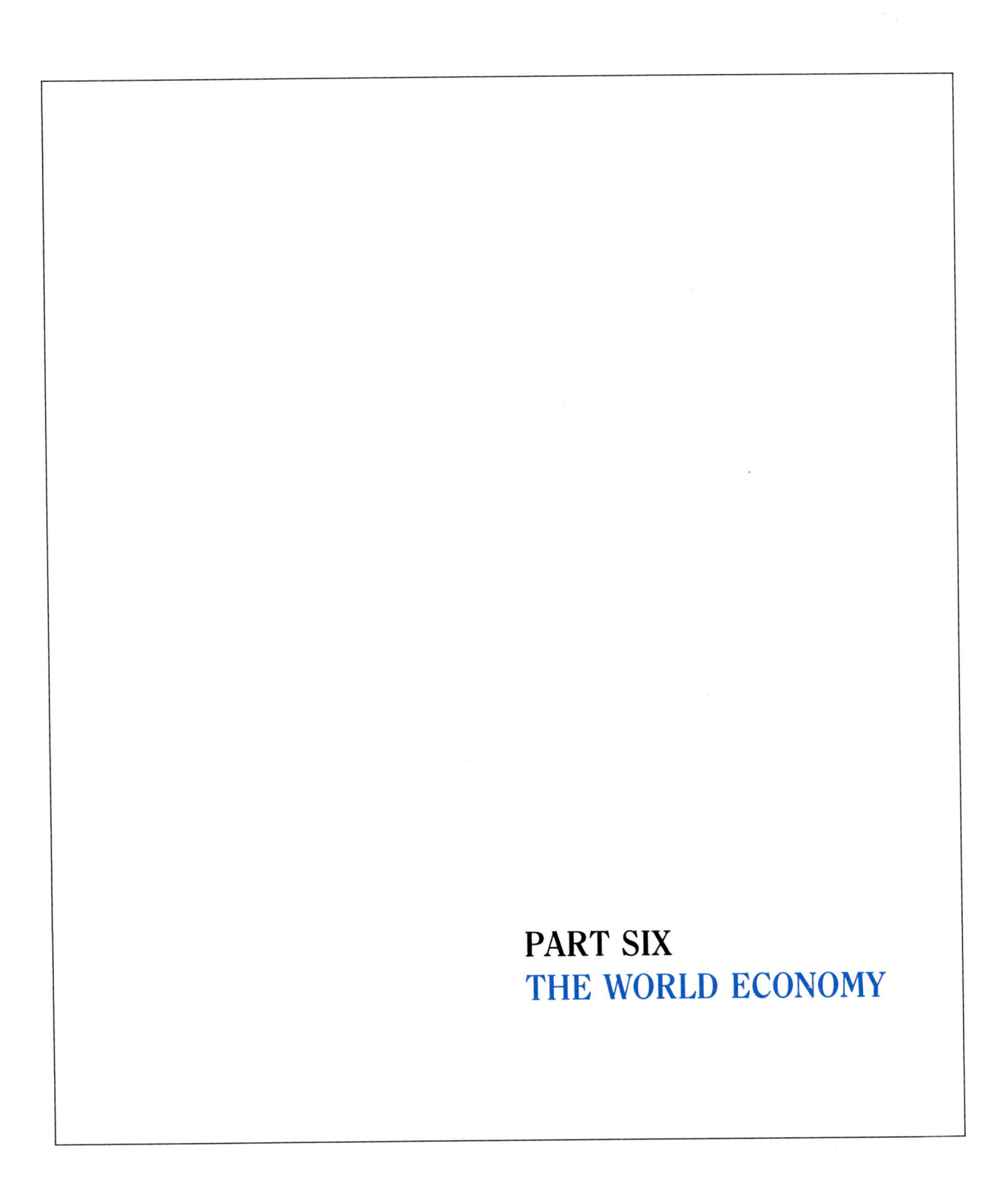

Chapter 23
Gains from Trade and Problems of Trade

In this chapter we discuss why countries trade and examine the gains they obtain by doing so. At the simplest level, countries trade because they can buy some goods more cheaply abroad than at home. It seems obvious that this must make them better off than they would be if they cut themselves off from trade entirely.

But things are a bit more complicated because trade is a two-way street: To be able to import, a country must export. As has been argued, countries cannot indefinitely borrow or sell assets to pay for imports. International trade involves *specialization* and *exchange*. A country that trades with others specializes by producing more of some goods than is demanded in the home market. The excess is exported in exchange for goods desired by domestic residents but not produced in sufficient quantity at home.

Specialization and exchange allow a country to increase its standard of living in two ways. First, trade exploits international differences in costs. These arise from international differences in technology and in the availability of raw materials or other factors of production. For example, cold areas are poorly suited to growing wine, and equatorial areas do poorly at producing wheat. International trade enables countries to specialize in producing what they can produce most cheaply and to buy abroad what it would be costly to produce at home. Second, trade makes it easier to exploit economies of scale, that is, to lower costs by increasing output. There is no better way to increase the volume of production than to use the entire world as a market. These sources of gains from trade are analyzed in detail in sections 1 through 3 of this chapter.

Even though international trade raises standards of living, it also creates problems and friction between countries. While countries are on balance better off if they trade, some people may lose—especially in the short run as the economy adjusts to changing trade conditions. American consumers are made better off when Japanese automobile production becomes more efficient, for instance, but automobile workers in Detroit are not. Section 4 provides some additional examples. Because foreign competition may make life difficult for some voters, governments are frequently under pressure to reduce imports, for example, by imposing tariffs. In sections 5 through 8 we discuss the policies with which governments react to trade problems and consider arguments for and against imposing tariffs and otherwise restricting international trade.

1. Comparative Advantage and Gains from Trade

We start by showing the gains from trade when there are international differences in the available techniques of production that lead to differences in costs. We use a model first presented by the great English economist David Ricardo (1772–1823).[1]

● **The Ricardian model demonstrates the *law of comparative advantage:* Countries specialize in producing goods they can make at a *relatively* lower cost than other countries.**

The precise meaning of this law will become clear as we develop the model.

We assume that there are only two countries in the world: the United States and France. Two goods can be produced: cars and textiles. Labor is the only factor of production, and there are constant returns to scale. Table 23-1 shows the assumptions made about production.

Note that labor in France is less productive in both industries. However, the difference is not uniform.

American labor is *relatively* more productive at making cars than at making textiles. It takes France twice as many hours to produce a car as it takes the United States, but for textiles the ratio is only 8 to 5. As we show in the rest of this section, these relative productivity differences are the basis for trade. French labor will not be unemployed because it is less productive, but it will earn lower wages.

We assume that there is perfect competition in both industries. This implies that prices must equal unit labor costs. Table 23-1 shows these unit labor costs for the two goods in each of the two countries. For example, in the United States it takes 300 labor hours to produce a car at a cost per hour of W. Thus the unit labor cost of an American car is $300 \times W$. If the wage were \$20 per hour, this would amount to \$6000 per car.

In the absence of international trade, the prices of each good in each country would be determined by their labor costs. Since it takes 300 hours to build a car and 5 hours to produce a yard of textiles in the United States, 60 (= 300/5) yards of cloth would cost as much as one car in the absence of trade. In France a car would cost as much as 75 (= 600/8) yards of cloth. Thus in France cars would be *relatively* more expensive than in the United States, while in the United States textiles would be *relatively* more expensive than in France.

Who Produces What under Free Trade?

Suppose now that the United States and France can trade freely with each other.[2] Competition then guarantees that goods will be produced wherever they can be made most cheaply. If it costs more to produce textiles in France than it does in the United States, citizens of both countries will buy only U.S. textiles, and none will be produced in France.

RELATIVE COSTS. The United States will be the lower-cost producer of automobiles if the U.S. unit labor cost, $300 \times W$, is less than the unit labor cost in France, $600 \times W^*$. We can rewrite this criterion as an inequality:

---

[1] Ricardo was a successful stockbroker before retiring at the age of 40 to become a Member of Parliament and an economist. His great book was *The Principles of Political Economy and Taxation*, published in 1817. Ricardo was a pioneer in the careful development of economic models; he stated his assumptions clearly and deduced their consequences rigorously.

[2] By this we mean that there are no tariffs or other barriers to trade of the sort discussed later in this chapter. We also assume for simplicity that it costs nothing to transport cars or textiles between the United States and France.

TABLE 23-1. Production Techniques, Wages, and Prices

	United States	France
Wage per hour	W	W^*
Hours required per unit of output		
Cars	300	600
Textiles	5	8
Unit labor costs		
Cars	$300 \times W$	$600 \times W^*$
Textiles	$5 \times W$	$8 \times W^*$

| U.S. is lower-cost car producer if | $300 \times W < 600 \times W^*$ | (1) |

or, dividing both sides by 300 and by W^*, we obtain the following:

| U.S. is lower-cost car producer if | $W/W^* < 600/300 = 2$ | (1a) |

Equation (1a) tells us that the United States produces cars more cheaply provided that it has less than twice the wage prevailing in France. It shows that *who is the lower-cost producer depends on differences in both technology and wages.*

Similarly, if U.S. unit labor costs in textiles, $5 \times W$, are lower than French unit labor costs, $8 \times W^*$, the United States will be the lower-cost producer.

| U.S. is lower-cost textile producer if | $5 \times W < 8 \times W^*$ | (2) |

or, dividing both sides by 5 and by W^*,

| U.S. is lower-cost textile producer if | $W/W^* < 8/5 = 1.6$ | (2a) |

Table 23-2 summarizes the implications of inequalities (1a) and (2a). If the U.S. wage is less than 1.6 times the French wage (region I), the United States is the lower-cost producer of both goods. In this case competition ensures that the prices of both goods equal the U.S. costs. At the other extreme, if the U.S. wage is more than double the French wage (region III), France is the lower-cost producer of both autos and textiles, and both prices equal French costs. In between (region II), the United States is the lower-cost producer of autos and France is the lower-cost producer of textiles.

RELATIVE WAGE DETERMINATION. We now show that the relative wage, W/W^*, must settle in region II of Table 23-2 or at one of its boundaries. It cannot be in region I or region III. Suppose, on the contrary, that the relative wage settled in region I. The United States would then be the lower-cost producer of both goods. Because French producers would not be able to afford to compete in either good, all French labor would be unemployed. French workers would prefer to work at lower wages than not to work at all, and wages would fall at least to the point where French labor became sufficiently cheap to be competitive in textiles. Conversely, if the relative wage were in region III, the United States would not be able to compete in any line of production. Unemployment would force down U.S. wages at least to the level $W/W^* = 2$ where the United States would become competitive in automobiles.

● The *equilibrium relative wage* is the wage that achieves full employment in both countries. At the equilibrium relative wage each country can produce at least one good.

With this definition in mind, the equilibrium relative wage must settle somewhere between 1.6 and 2, including these two extremes. For example, if the relative wage settles at $W/W^* = 2$, the United States produces cars and France produces both cars and textiles. At the other extreme, if $W/W^* = 1.6$, the United States produces both goods and France produces only textiles. In between, the United States produces only cars and France produces only textiles.

TABLE 23-2. Wages, Costs, and Prices

	Region I, $W/W^* < 1.6$	Region II, $1.6 < W/W^* < 2$	Region III, $W/W^* > 2$
Production	United States is lower-cost producer of both goods	United States is lower-cost for cars; France is lower-cost for textiles	France is lower-cost producer of both goods
Prices			
Cars	$300 \times W$	$300 \times W$	$600 \times W^*$
Textiles	$5 \times W$	$8 \times W^*$	$8 \times W^*$

EQUILIBRIUM PRODUCTION PATTERNS. Figure 23-1 shows three possible patterns of production. In all cases France exports textiles and the United States exports cars, and in each case at least one of the countries specializes in production. But what determines which pattern actually is established?

That depends on the relative sizes of the countries and on the tastes of their residents for the two goods. In case

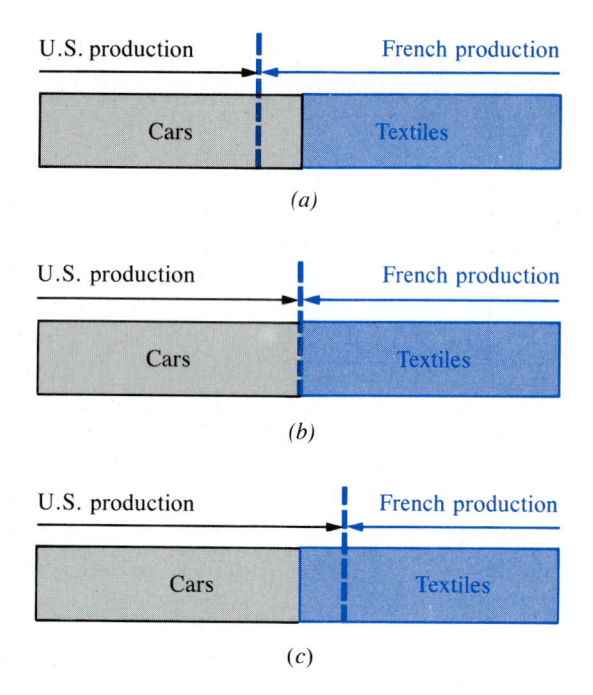

FIGURE 23-1. Patterns of Trade and Production. (*a*) Cars cost the same to produce in both France and the United States, and they are produced in both countries. Textiles are produced only in France, where it is cheaper to produce them. (*b*) Cars are cheaper to produce in the United States, and textiles are cheaper to produce in France. Both countries accordingly specialize. (*c*) Textiles cost the same to produce in both countries and are produced in both. Cars are cheaper to produce in the United States and are produced only there. Note that in all cases, the United States exports cars and France exports textiles.

(*a*) in Figure 23-1, the United States produces only cars but cannot produce enough to satisfy the total demand for cars from both countries. In this case the French must produce both cars and textiles, and W/W^* must equal 2. The other extreme case, case (*c*), corresponds to a situation in which the United States is much larger than France. Here French production of textiles is not adequate to meet total world (U.S. plus French) demand, and the United States must produce some textiles as well as all the automobiles for both countries. It follows from our previous discussion that $W/W^* = 1.6$ in this case. If U.S. auto production and French textile production are both just adequate to meet total demand in both nations, we have case (*b*) in Figure 23-1.

COMPARATIVE ADVANTAGE. This example demonstrates the law of comparative advantage, which asserts that each country will produce (at least) the good for which its cost advantage—measured as a ratio—is greatest or its cost disadvantage is least. In our example, the ratio of U.S. to French costs in automobiles is $(1/2)(W/W^*)$; the corresponding ratio in textiles is $(5/8)(W/W^*)$. Since 1/2 is less than 5/8, the United States has a comparative advantage in automobile production at all wage rates and thus will always produce autos at the equilibrium relative wage, as we saw previously. Similarly, France has a comparative advantage in textiles (since 8/5 is less than 2/1) and will thus always produce textiles in equilibrium.

The idea that the location of production should be determined by *comparative* advantage is at first sight surprising. If the United States has higher productivity in *both* goods, why won't it always produce both goods? How can the United States benefit by trading with France if France is less productive in both industries?

An example shows why comparative, not absolute, advantage is the correct guiding principle. Consider two economists writing a book. The first takes 30 minutes to type a page and 20 minutes to draw a figure, and the second takes 60 minutes to type a page and 30 minutes to draw a figure. The second is relatively faster at drawing diagrams, though absolutely she is slower at both tasks. How should the two of them divide up the work of drawing figures and typing text? Obviously, if the faster economist both typed and drew diagrams, the slower professor's labor would go to waste. The slower professor should also do her share, and it is more efficient for her to do diagrams than to type. That way she can be thought of as saving relatively more of the speedy professor's time for typing.

Looking back to the United States/France example, if we focus on the fact that labor is more productive in both lines in the United States, we tend to forget that the French labor is also a scarce resource and that the world should use it to produce goods as well.

Gains from Trade

In this model, we saw that opening trade between countries will lead at least one of them to specialize. Each country will export the good in which it has a comparative advantage and import the good of which it is the relatively less efficient producer. Now we ask whether anyone gains from allowing trade. The answer is yes. A country that specializes will be better off, and a country that does not will be no worse off. Thus the world as a whole benefits from trade, and nobody is harmed.

We begin by showing that the residents of a country that specializes under trade can purchase more of the imported good with their labor time than they could produce themselves. Suppose the relative wage settles at $W/W^* = 2$ so that the U.S. wage is twice the French wage. As we saw previously, in this situation the United States produces cars and France produces both cars and textiles. Now let us ask whether a U.S. worker has a higher standard of living with trade or without. In the absence of trade he has to work 300 hours to earn enough to buy a car and 5 hours to buy a yard of textiles. With trade it still takes 300 hours of work to buy a car. But now 4 hours of U.S. labor buys 8 hours of French labor (since the U.S. wage is twice the French wage), and it takes exactly 8 hours of French labor to produce a yard of textiles. Thus with only 4 hours of work, instead of the 5 required without trade, the U.S. worker can buy a yard of textiles. The U.S. clearly gains from trade.

Are French workers correspondingly worse off? Not at all. Since France produces both cars and textiles, a French worker must put in 600 hours to earn enough to buy a car and must work 8 hours to buy a yard of textiles—exactly as if there were no trade. Since a country that specializes must gain and a country that does not specialize does not lose, trade is clearly a good thing in this model.

Many Goods

The United States/France example with only two goods illustrates the basic principles of comparative advantage and gains from trade. The same principles continue to hold when there are many goods. Suppose that in addition to cars and textiles, trade may also occur in TV sets, shoes, ceramics, and computers. Table 23-3 lists the unit labor requirements for each industry in the two countries as well as the relative (United States relative to France) unit labor requirements.

The idea of a relative unit labor requirement was already noted in Table 23-1. There we saw that in the United States it takes 300 hours to produce a car, versus 600 hours in France. The relative unit labor requirement is simply the ratio of these two numbers, or 1/2. Table 23-3 shows hypothetical hours of labor in the United States and in France for different goods. The last row shows the relative unit labor requirement which, in combination with the relative wage, guides the pattern of specialization.

The United States is relatively most efficient at producing computers, needing only one-sixth as much labor time as France. France is relatively most efficient at producing shoes. The table shows the U.S. comparative advantage decreasing from left to right, from computers to shoes. French comparative advantage decreases in the opposite direction, from shoes to computers.

Who will produce which goods? Since every country must produce at least one good, the United States will certainly produce computers and France will certainly produce shoes. The United States will produce the goods listed on the left in Table 23-3, and France will produce the goods on the right. Just where the dividing line between them falls again depends in part on the sizes of the two countries and the levels of demand for all products. Figure 23-2 shows a possible pattern of production.

In the case shown in Figure 23-2 both countries gain from trade, since both are specialized to some extent. Each is importing some of the goods it used to produce

TABLE 23-3. Unit Labor Requirement: The Many-Goods Case (Hours of Labor per Unit of Output)

	Computers	Cars	TV sets	Textiles	Ceramics	Shoes
United States	200	300	50	5	7	15
France	1200	600	90	8	6	10
United States/France relative unit labor requirement	1/6	1/2	5/9	5/8	7/6	3/2

| Computers | Cars | TV sets | Textiles | Ceramics | Shoes |

U.S. production ⟶ ⟵ French production

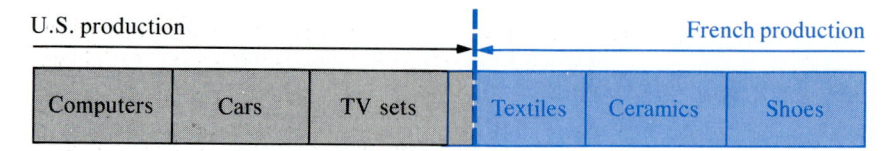

FIGURE 23-2. Patterns of Production with Many Goods. The goods are arranged in order of decreasing U.S. comparative advantage (and increasing French comparative advantage) from left to right. The pattern of production is determined by the position of the dividing line. The United States produces goods to the left of the line, and France produces goods to the right of the line. Each country imports the goods it does not produce. The position of the line is determined in large part by the relative sizes of the countries.

domestically. This means that those goods are now being produced relatively more cheaply than before, and therefore consumer buying power has increased in both countries.

2. Differences in Factor Endowments

In the Ricardian model discussed in the previous section, differences in the relative productivity of labor led to differences in relative costs, or comparative advantage. Differences in relative costs in turn gave rise to international trade and to gains from trade. Now we extend our analysis to consider other reasons for international trade and for gains from trade.

Relative costs of producing goods are determined not only by differences in technology but also by the relative amounts of factors of production (or the factor endowments) a country has. To take the simplest example, Saudi Arabia has a comparative advantage in producing oil because it has a larger stock of oil in the ground than other countries do. Saudi Arabia can produce oil relatively cheaply compared to other countries, just as Chile and Zambia can produce copper relatively cheaply. These countries therefore produce and export those minerals.

Differences in Capital-Labor Ratios

Differences in raw material endowments are one reason why relative costs of production differ among countries. But so are differences in countries' endowments of other factors of production, for instance, capital (machines, buildings, computers, and so on), and labor.

Consider, for instance, the United States and Mexico. The United States has both more capital and more labor than Mexico because it is a bigger country. But the United States also has relatively more capital. That is, the capital-labor ratio, or the amount of capital per worker, is larger in the United States than it is in Mexico. In the absence of trade, the rental rate on capital in the United States would be relatively lower, because the United States has relatively more capital. U.S. labor would be relatively more expensive.

We will continue with the example of cars and textiles, but now we assume that both capital and labor are required to produce cars or textiles. Automobile production is assumed to be relatively capital-intensive in both countries. This means that more capital is used per worker in making cars than in making textiles. Table 23-4 summarizes the relevant information. The United States has twice as much capital per worker as does Mexico, so that the United States is a capital-rich country compared to Mexico.

With no trade, these two countries would have very different relative prices. In the United States, where there is a lot of capital relative to labor, cars could be produced at a lower cost relative to textiles than in Mexico. Thus the price of cars relative to textiles would be considerably lower in the United States than in Mexico. The United States has a comparative advantage in

TABLE 23-4. Hypothetical Capital-Labor Ratios

	Endowments (capital per worker)	Technology Cars	Textiles
United States	$5000	Capital-intensive	Labor-intensive
Mexico	$2500	Capital-intensive	Labor-intensive

capital-intensive automobiles, and Mexico in labor-intensive textiles.

Because cars are relatively cheaper in the United States, the opening of trade would lead the United States to produce and export cars and Mexico to produce and export textiles. Comparative advantage continues to be the basic explanation of trade patterns: Countries export the good in which they have relatively lower costs of production. In the Ricardian model, comparative advantage depends on labor productivity. In this extended model, it also depends on the relative availability of capital and labor. Capital-rich countries export relatively capital-intensive goods and import relatively labor-intensive goods.

Some Evidence on Factor Endowments and Trade Patterns

The preceding discussion suggests that countries that have an abundance of capital relative to labor compared with other countries will export goods that require relatively more capital than the goods they import. Figure 23-3 offers some evidence on this theory.

The horizontal axis shows the capital-labor ratio, measured in thousands of U.S. dollars per worker, for different countries. The vertical axis shows the capital-labor ratio of exports compared to imports. A number like 0.5 means that exports are only half as capital-intensive as imports. The data clearly suggest a positive relationship between the relative amounts of capital and labor and the pattern of trade. This confirms in a broad way the comparative advantage theory based on relative supplies of capital and labor.

Comparative advantage, or lower relative costs of production, is one of the fundamental reasons for international trade. Cost differences may occur either because countries differ in productivity or because the relative supplies of factors of production differ. Countries then specialize in producing the goods in which they have a comparative advantage.

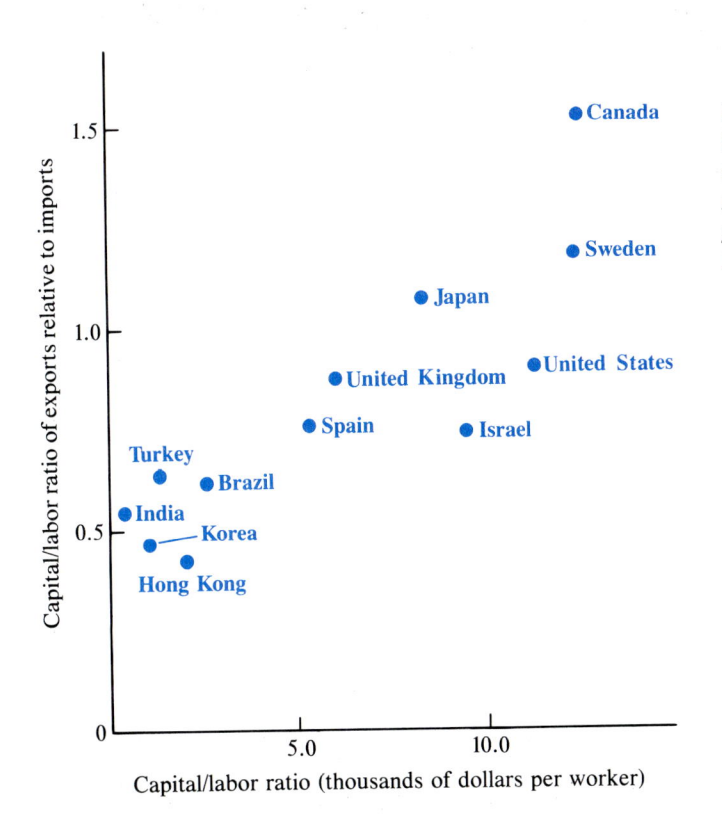

FIGURE 23-3. Economywide Capital-Labor Ratios and the Capital-Intensity of Exports Relative to Imports. The data are from U.S Department of Labor, *Changes in the International Pattern of Factor Abundance and the Composition of Trade,* Economic Discussion Paper 8, June 1980, and are explained in the text.

3. Intra-Industry Trade

A striking fact that emerges from trade statistics, or from looking around a parking lot or department store, is that specialization is relatively rare. The United States, like many other countries, both imports and exports automobiles, refrigerators, clothes, chemicals, and many other products. Intra-industry (within an industry) trade is extensive.

● *Intra-industry trade* **occurs when a country both imports and exports goods produced by a single industry.**

Much of the high volume of trade among the industrialized countries is intra-industry trade.

Three forces interact to determine the extent of intra-industry trade. First, consumer preferences for diversity create a demand for a broad range of similar goods. Consumers do not all want exactly the same types of cars, shirts, or radios. Second, there are economies of scale in the production of many goods. Thus a firm that specializes in the production of a particular product variety, such as luxury automobiles or very small radios, and sells them worldwide will have a cost advantage over firms that produce only for their home markets. These two factors tend to produce intra-industry specialization, with different countries specializing in different varieties of the same broadly defined good. The third force, transportation costs, works against this tendency. If two countries are producing goods at roughly the same cost, then high costs of transporting the goods between the two countries will ensure that each produces for its own market unless scale economies are very significant.

The observed pattern of intra-industry trade is the outcome of these three forces. In Figure 23-4 we show the relative significance of intra-industry trade for several U.S. industries. We define an index that is 0 when trade in a particular commodity is entirely one-way: The country only exports or only imports the good. The index takes a value of 1 if there is complete two-way trade in the sense that the country imports as much of a particular good as it exports.[3]

At one extreme, there is little two-way trade in fuels; the United States imports fuel but exports very little. At the other extreme, two-way trade is very important in office and telecommunications equipment, where the index is about 0.84. That is, imports of this equipment are equal to 84 percent of exports. Various other goods lie in between. In general, the more undifferentiated the commodities are (fuel, iron and steel), the more we expect comparative advantage to dictate trade patterns. As we move toward finished manufactures, product differentiation becomes dominant and comparative advantage loses some of its overriding role. Thus intra-industry trade takes place, for example, in automobiles and office equipment.

Intra-industry trade reflects economic integration among countries. The more closely markets are integrated and the lower the obstacles to trade—in terms of

---

[3] More precisely, the index is defined as the ratio of the smaller of imports and exports to the larger of these two values.

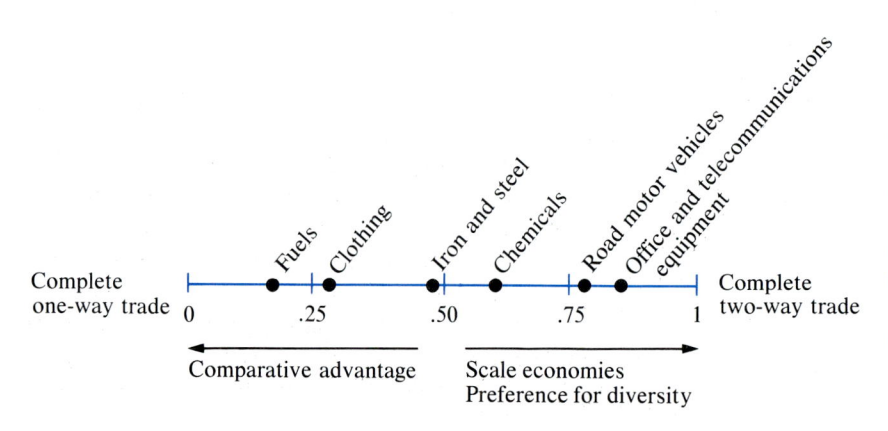

FIGURE 23-4. The U.S. Index of Intra-Industry Trade for Selected Commodities. When there is no intra-industry trade, so that a good is either only exported or only imported, the value of the index is zero. When the values of imports and exports of a good are equal, the index is 1, and then trade is dominated by intra-industry trade. The figure shows considerable variation in the importance of intra-industry trade among the selected goods. (*Source*: GATT, *International Trade, 1978/1979*, Geneva 1979.)

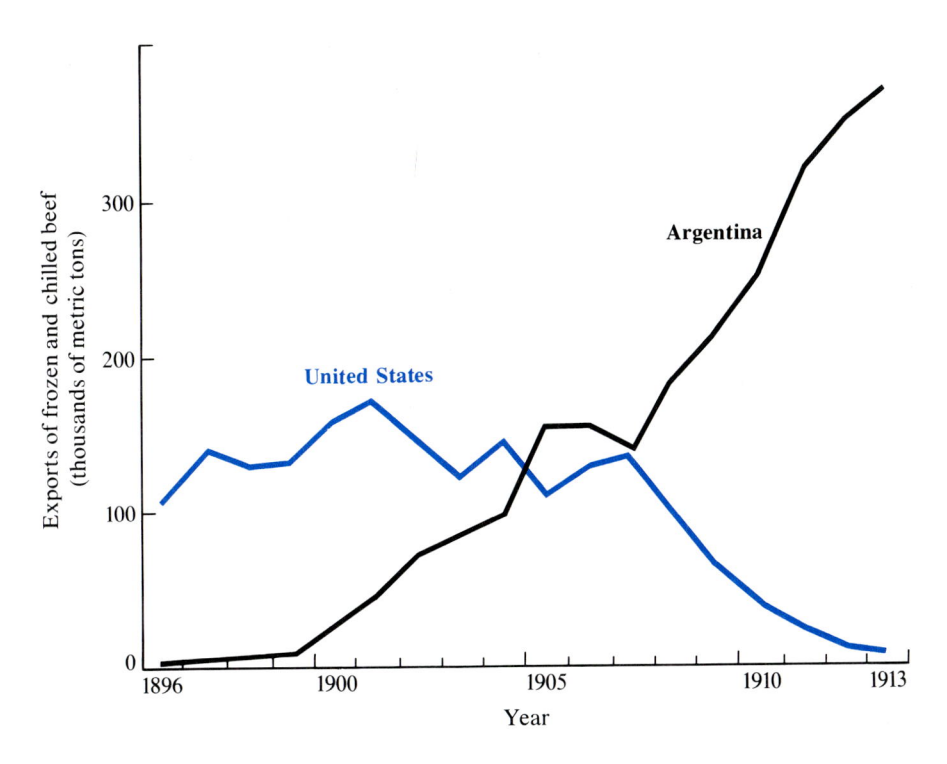

FIGURE 23-5. Refrigeration Enables Argentina to Become a Major Exporter of Beef. (*Source*: League of Nations, *The Network of World Trade,* Geneva, 1942, p. 86.)

both distance and tariffs—the more intra-industry trade we would expect to observe. For instance, intra-industry trade is extensive among the countries of the European Economic Community.[4] Japan, by contrast, imports primary commodities and exports virtually nothing in this category and exports manufactures but imports very little in that category. Accordingly, the index of intra-industry trade for Japan is small for most goods.

Intra-industry trade comes into its own particularly when close proximity and the absence of restrictions to trade create very integrated markets. These characteristics also describe trade among different regions of the United States—although Detroit, like Japan, would have almost complete one-way trade in automobiles. The gains from such trade are that consumers are able to consume a more diverse group of commodities at lower cost than they could if producers were not able to take advantage of international markets to produce on a large scale.

[4] Germany, France, Italy, Netherlands, Belgium, Luxembourg, United Kingdom, Denmark, Spain, Portugal, and Greece.

4. Gainers and Losers

We have shown why countries trade and why there are on balance gains to opening an economy to trade rather than avoiding exchange with the rest of the world. But it does not follow that international trade always makes everyone affected better off. We now look at two examples of the conflicts and problems that can be created by international trade.

Refrigeration

Figure 23-5 shows the frozen and chilled beef exports of the United States and of Argentina in the period 1900–1913. At the end of the nineteenth century the discovery of mechanical refrigeration made it possible for Argentina to become a supplier of frozen meat in the world market. Exports that had been nonexistent in 1900 rose to nearly 400,000 tons by 1913 as the new technology was used to ship meat to Europe. The United States had been an exporter of beef, but U.S exports dwindled from their 100,000-ton level to virtually zero.

TABLE 23-5. Argentinian Beef Exports Made Possible by the Invention of Refrigeration: Gains and Losses

	United States	Europe	Argentina
Producers of beef	−	−	+
Other producers	0	0	−
Consumers	+	+	−

Sharply rising Argentinian beef exports—and similar increases in meat exports from Australia and New Zealand—provide a good example of the conflicts of interest that international trade raises. Table 23-5 shows who gained (+) and who lost (−). In Argentina the possibility of exporting implied a major change in the production structure of the entire economy. Cattle grazing and meat exporting attracted resources. Owners of cattle and land gained; other users of land (small farmers, for instance), whose costs increased, lost out. Argentinian consumers found their steaks becoming more expensive as meat was shipped abroad. Thus even for some Argentinians the possibility of exporting was a mixed blessing.

In the United States and Europe the main effects were on consumers and beef producers. Beef producers lost because beef prices fell, and consumers gained for the same reason. The effects on producers of other goods were slight.

Did the world gain on balance from refrigeration that allowed trade in meat? If gainers and losers are given equal weight, then gains and losses are added together, and the answer is yes. But if losers were for some reason given a larger weight than gainers, the calculation might change. One might, for example, have more sympathy for the losers (including small farmers in Argentina and small ranchers in the United States) than for the winners (including large ranchers in Argentina and wealthy steak eaters in the United States). But such a weighting would be a personal value judgment.

The U.S. Automobile Industry

More than a quarter of the cars now sold in the United States are imported, mostly from Japan. Following a sharp increase in imports over the 1978–1980 period, U.S producers pressured the government to prevent further increases in imports.

The restriction on imports took the form of a *voluntary export restraint* administered by the Japanese government. Under this policy the Japanese government agreed that Japanese firms would not increase their car exports to the United States by more than a specified number of cars.

Again there were gains and losses. Restriction of imports of cars from Japan raised the prices of Japanese cars to American consumers and probably increased the prices of other cars as well. The reason is that U.S. producers could afford to raise their prices because foreign competition had been limited. Restrictions also cost jobs, or at least reduced growth in incomes, in Japan. On the other hand, more American automobile workers could keep their jobs, and people who owned stock in domestic automobile companies gained.

There are also both gainers and losers in other contexts where trade is restricted. The restrictions might take the form of limits on exports of particular goods, perhaps for strategic reasons (the United States tries to prevent exports of sophisticated computers to the Soviet Union, for instance), limits on lending to countries that violate human rights, limits on wheat exports to the Soviet Union, or limits on all trade with a particular country as a measure of economic warfare.

These and other measures that affect international trade produce both winners and losers. To measure their gains and losses, we next develop in detail the analysis of a tariff and then apply this analysis to other instruments of commercial or trade policy.

● *Commercial policy* **is government policy that influences trade through taxes, subsidies, and direct restrictions on imports or exports**

5. The Economics of Tariffs

The most common type of trade restriction is a tariff, or import duty. A tariff usually requires the importer of a good to pay a specified fraction of the import price to the government. With a tariff at the rate of 20 percent on automobiles, for example, and a world price of $6000, the duty would be $1200 (= 0.2 × $6000). The importer's costs now include both his payments to foreign producers ($6000) and the duty he pays to the government ($1200).

Neglecting other costs for simplicity, the minimum domestic price at which the importer would be willing to sell is equal to the world price plus the duty. Since the duty is equal to the tariff rate times the world price, this minimum price is also equal to the world price times (1 + the tariff rate):

Domestic price = world price × (1 + tariff rate) (3)

Even if competition forces the importer to charge his minimum price, the tariff raises the domestic price of an importable commodity above the world price, in the car example, from $6000 to $7200. In doing so it provides protection for domestic producers of the same or substitute commodities, and it taxes consumers—as we now demonstrate in detail.

The Free-Trade Equilibrium

The standard of comparison is the free-trade equilibrium that would prevail with no tariff. Suppose a country faces a given world price, say, $6000 per car, and domestic and foreign cars are identical, or perfect substitutes. Figure 23-6 illustrates the home market for automobiles. The

Given the domestic demand curve in Figure 23-6, domestic consumers demand Q_d cars at a price of $6000. Their consumption of cars is described by point G on the demand curve. Domestic firms produce only Q_s units at this price, at point C on their supply curve. The difference, Q_d minus Q_s, would be made up by imports. At the prevailing world price, part of home demand is satisfied by domestic production, and part by imports.

Equilibrium with a Tariff

Figure 23-7 shows the effect of imposing a 20 percent tariff on automobiles. The tariff raises the price at which an importer is willing to supply cars in the home market. At a price of $7200—$6000 foreign cost plus $1200 duties—importers are willing to sell any quantity in the home market. Hence the new tariff-inclusive price that

[5] Note that by drawing a supply curve for automobiles we are assuming that the domestic automobile industry is approximately perfectly competitive. This serves to simplify the analysis but is not essential for the conclusions.

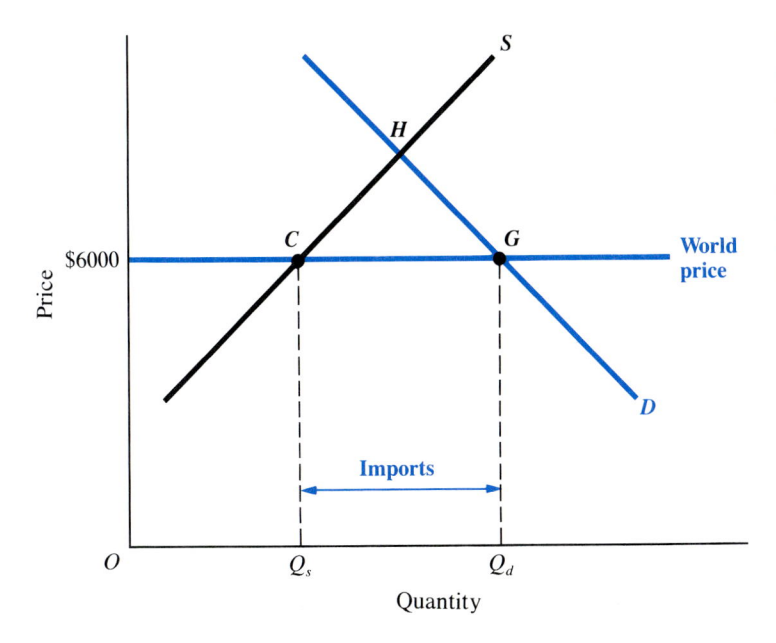

FIGURE 23-6. Production, Consumption, and Imports under Free Trade. D is the demand curve of domestic residents for automobiles; S is the supply curve of domestic auto producers. Automobiles are available in the world market for $6000. Therefore, with free trade, the domestic price of automobiles must be $6000 as well. At this price domestic demand is Q_d, domestic supply is Q_s, and the difference, $Q_d - Q_s$, is made up by imports.

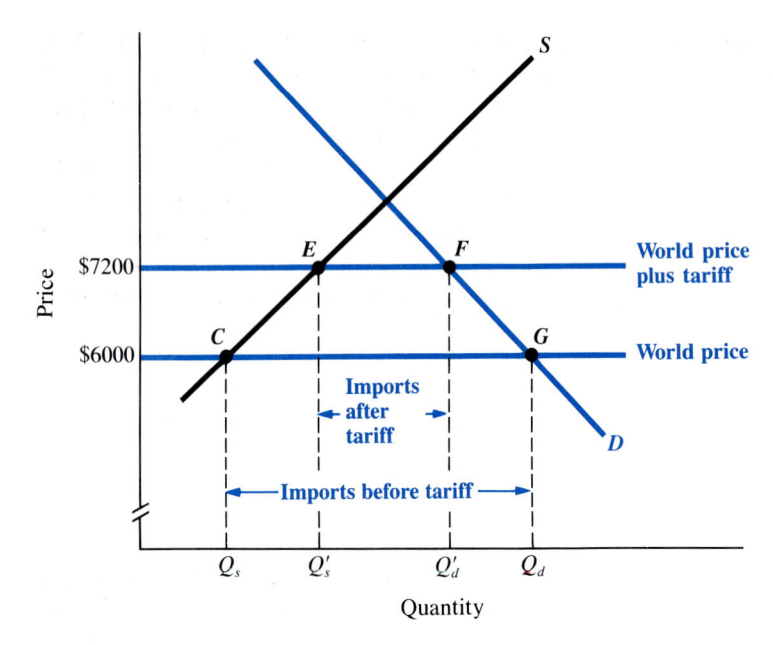

FIGURE 23-7. The Effects of a Tariff. The imposition of a 20 percent tariff raises the price at which cars can be imported from $6000 to $7200. Quantity demanded falls from Q_d to Q'_d as a consequence, and domestic production increases from Q_s to Q'_s. Imports accordingly fall.

will prevail in the home market is $7200, as shown by the dashed horizontal schedule. The tariff raises the domestic, or tariff-inclusive, price above the world price.

What are the effects of the tariff on consumption and production? Because the tariff raises domestic prices of imports, it encourages domestic production. Domestic firms increase their output from Q_s to Q'_s. The tariff provides protection by allowing home firms to produce at a marginal cost above the world price. At point E on the supply schedule, the domestic marginal cost is equal to $7200 and thus exceeds the world price of $6000. This is possible only because domestic producers do not have to pay the tariff and therefore can afford to be less efficient than their competitors in the world market. On the production side a tariff thus discriminates in favor of domestic producers. It acts like a subsidy to the domestic production of cars.

On the demand side the price increase induces consumers to reduce their total purchases of cars. In total they will buy fewer cars, but more will come from domestic producers and fewer from foreign producers. Quantity demanded falls from Q_d to Q'_d; consumers move along the demand curve from point G to point F. For consumers the tariff is clearly a bad idea. It is exactly like a tax on cars. And as Figure 23-7 shows, the combined effect of higher domestic production and lower domestic demand is a fall in imports.

Costs and Benefits of a Tariff

Figure 23-8 and Table 23-6 together provide a detailed accounting of the costs and benefits of this tariff. We begin by noting that consumers pay more for the goods they continue to purchase. The increased cost is $1200 times the quantity Q'_d, equal to area $LFHJ$ in Figure 23-8. Where does this money go?

Part goes to the government as tariff revenue. Tariff revenue is equal to the quantity of imports ($Q'_d - Q'_s$) times the tariff ($1200), or the rectangle $EIHF$. The tariff revenue represents a transfer from consumers to the government.[6] It does not represent a cost to society as a whole because the government uses the revenue. For example, the government could increase defense or welfare spending or return the revenue to consumers by cutting income taxes.

Increased consumer payments also go in part toward higher profits for domestic firms. This transfer corre-

---
[6] Recall that a transfer is a payment for which no goods or services are directly exchanged.

sponds to the area *ECJL*. Firms receive higher prices for their initial output (Q_s) and pocket the difference between price and marginal cost on the increased output ($Q'_s - Q_s$) induced by the tariff. For firms these profits or rents are a main attraction of tariffs, but to society they are not a net benefit. They are rather a transfer of income from consumers to producers. (Remember, as a group consumers own the firms and hence they receive the profits that a tariff creates for the firms.)

The shaded area *EIC*, labeled *A*, does correspond to a social cost. Part of the increased payment of consumers supports inefficient domestic production. Inefficient production means that it costs more to produce a unit of the good domestically, at the margin, than it would cost to buy it in the world market. The total excess of the domestic marginal cost over world price—the triangle *A*—is a social cost or waste induced by the tariff. Consumers and society pay for waste when a tariff is imposed

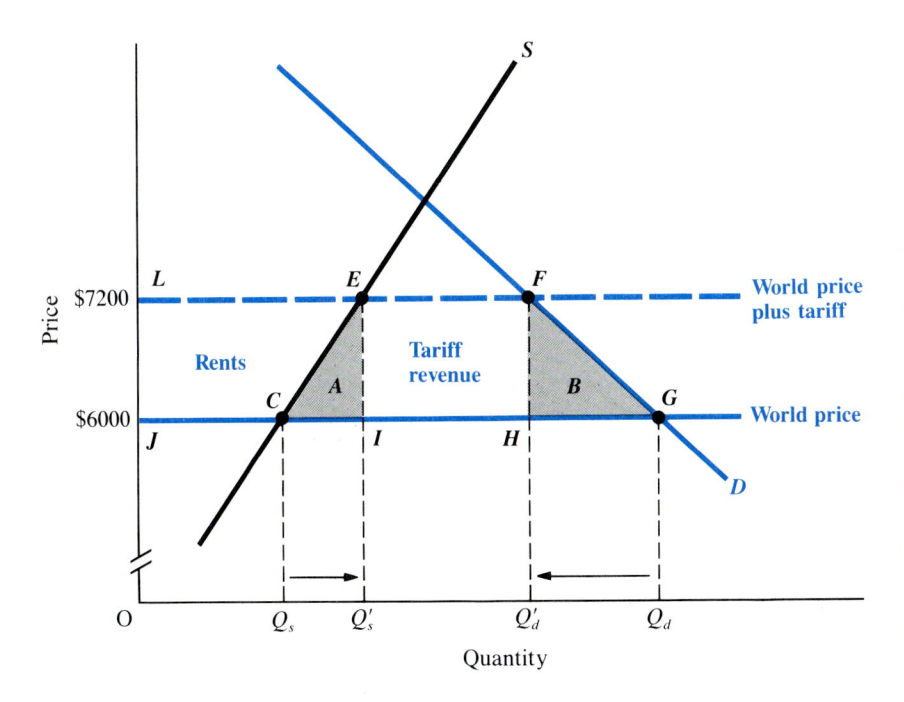

FIGURE 23-8. The Welfare Costs of a Tariff. When the tariff raises automobile prices, the total cost to consumers is the area *LFGJ*. Of this total, *LECJ* goes to domestic producers in the form of rents (higher profits) and *EFHI* goes to the government as tariff revenue. This leaves areas *A* and *B* as the net social cost of the tariff. Area *A* represents the excessive cost of producing cars at home rather than buying them on the world market. Area *B* represents the consumers' surplus lost because consumption is inefficiently restricted.

TABLE 23-6. Costs (−) and Benefits (+) of a Tariff

	Consumers	Domestic firms	Government	Society
	Pay tariff revenue −*EIHF*		Collects tariff +*EIHF*	0
	Pay rents to firms −*ECJL*	Receive rents +*ECJL*		0
	Pay excess cost of domestic production −*EIC*			−*EIC*
	Lose surplus −*FGH*			−*FGH*
Net	−*LFGJ*	+*ECJL*	+*EIHF*	−(*FGH* + *EIC*)

because the resources drawn into the industry protected by tariffs could have been used more efficiently in other sectors.

Rectangle *LFHJ* in Figure 23-8 corresponds to the first three lines in Table 23-6. But there is an additional cost to consumers, area FGH in Figure 23-8, labeled *B*. This is the loss of consumers' surplus caused by the reduction in consumption from Q_d to Q_d'. The marginal value of each additional car to consumers is given by the demand schedule. The marginal cost to society is given by the world price. When the marginal valuation exceeds marginal cost, reducing consumption is wasteful and gives rise to a loss of consumers' surplus. This is a cost to society just like the waste on the production side. The shaded areas *A* and *B* in Figure 23-8 thus represent the net social costs of a tariff.

TRANSFERS AND COMPENSATION. Of course, as we noted in the preceding section, net costs and benefits are not all that matters. Even though society as a whole loses from the tariff, some people will almost certainly gain. This group is likely to include owners of domestic automobile firms and those who will benefit most from the government spending of its tariff revenue. If these revenues are spent on missiles, for instance, managers of missile-producing firms may gain from the tariff—even though they must pay more for the automobiles they drive to work.

The net social loss shown in Table 23-6 means that the dollar value of gains from protection are less than the dollar value of losses. This means that, potentially, the losers could bribe the gainers from protection not to lobby for tariffs. Equivalently, if the economy moved to free trade, the gainers could compensate the losers and still come out ahead. This shows that free trade *potentially* can be made to benefit everyone. In practice, though, the compensation payments from gainers to losers are not usually made. This is one important reason why free-trade arguments are not surefire political winners.

6. Arguments for Tariffs

The model used in the preceding section is of course unrealistic. Many proponents of tariffs have argued that more complex models of reality and the recognition that avoiding waste is not society's only goal support the view that tariffs can be on balance good for society as a whole. We evaluate the main arguments of this sort in this section.

Second-Best Arguments

The starting point for testing any argument for a tariff is the recognition that a "good" tariff must fulfill a double test. First, the tariff must work in the sense of bringing about a socially desirable objective. Second, it must do so at a lower cost, in terms of waste, than any other available method. Most popular arguments for tariffs fail the second half of this test because other methods—consumption or production subsidies or taxes—solve the problem more cheaply. Arguments that fail the second half of the test are thus *second-best* arguments, since they show only that a tariff can be used to achieve a desirable goal, not that it is the best way of achieving that goal. Let us consider some examples.

WAY OF LIFE. Society may want to protect the livelihood of inefficient farmers or craftsmen, perhaps because it feels that these people, with their traditional, stable way of life, serve to stabilize and enrich the community. Therefore, it is argued, tariffs should be imposed to protect these people against foreign competition.

This is a second-best argument because there is a better way of protecting the traditional way of life, at a lower cost to consumers. A tariff both discourages consumption and protects producers. But we can protect producers directly by giving them a production subsidy and not affect consumption. A production subsidy can keep wheat farmers in business, for instance, without also taxing bread.

LUXURIES. To take another second-best example, suppose society frowns on conspicuous consumption of luxuries (Rolls-Royce cars, golden toothpicks). Should it use a tariff to discourage luxury consumption or is a consumption tax on luxuries the better way? A tariff in effect both taxes consumers and encourages domestic producers of luxuries. If we are interested in reducing the consumption of luxuries, there is no reason to encourage domestic production. A consumption tax is the right tool.

INFANT INDUSTRIES. The infant industry argument is one of the most common arguments for a tariff. It begins with the observation that firms often learn how to produce efficiently by actually producing. But if at the outset domestic firms have no experience and thus incur high costs, how can they ever sell enough to learn to produce more cheaply than foreigners? Thus, it is argued, young, or infant, industries should be given tariff protection until they grow up and can compete on equal terms with more experienced foreign producers.

There is indeed a case for investing in infant industries under these conditions, but there are two reasons why a tariff is not the best way to achieve the goal. First, a production subsidy is better than a tariff. There is no reason consumers should be taxed while domestic producers are learning how to produce; this just shrinks the domestic market. Second, in practice there is a great danger in building up industries that never grow up in the sense of becoming competitive, and for that reason it will always be difficult to get rid of tariffs or subsidies once they are introduced. Once the industries are set up, whether or not they are competitive, reducing their protection will result in a loss of jobs that politicians are reluctant to cause. Thus infant industry protection, whether by subsidies or by tariffs, is a very difficult issue. The theory is tempting, but practical experience has often been very disillusioning.

REVENUE. In the eighteenth century most government revenue came from tariffs, because tariffs were easy to collect at the ports through which goods were imported. At that time tariffs were an efficient way for governments to raise revenue. Indeed, even today in countries where the administrative system is underdeveloped, tariffs may be a good way of raising revenue. But in modern economies with developed accounting and administrative systems, there is little to be said for the tariff as an efficient method of raising revenue. It is no harder to collect general sales taxes on all goods sold than to collect taxes on imports. And such general taxes are much less inefficient than raising revenue via tariffs.

Cheap Foreign Labor

It is frequently argued that home producers require protection because foreign countries use cheap labor. But that argument is superficial. First, foreign labor is cheap per hour worked. But part of the reason for this is usually that it is also less productive. It probably takes more foreign labor than domestic labor to produce 1 unit of the imported good. Thus the cost of foreign labor per unit of output may not be lower than the unit labor cost of domestic production.

But arguing about how much foreign labor costs misses the point that a major reason to trade is that there are international differences in factor endowments. Trade is a way to exploit our production and endowment advantages by exporting goods we can produce relatively cheaply and using our exports to buy those goods which foreign countries can produce relatively cheaper. Some foreign countries have more and cheaper labor or more and cheaper raw materials. We can gain from this by allowing them to produce the goods in which they have a comparative advantage. If we do not import from them, we cannot export the goods in which we have a competitive advantage, and we lose the benefits of trade.

The problem is not that foreign labor is unfairly cheap but that some domestic labor is producing goods that should be made abroad. If the domestic industry has lost comparative advantage, then it should be closed down. Its workers might then be given assistance to relocate to other industries and areas. Indeed, the United States does provide adjustment assistance to workers in industries suffering from foreign competition. Such assistance helps workers at far lower costs to society as a whole than providing tariff protection.

Foreign Subsidies and Dumping

Foreign governments sometimes subsidize their producers, who can then export more cheaply. Domestic producers say that this is unfair, because the foreign government is giving the foreign firms an advantage, and that is true. But should we oppose the practice?

If the foreign governments are providing the subsidy permanently and we can rely on its continuing, then we should take advantage of it. If some foreign government wants to make it cheap for us to consume televisions or golf balls, that is fine. In this case there is no objection to the subsidy, although there may be a case for providing adjustment assistance to domestic workers who are harmed.

But in practice subsidies are often temporary. They are an attempt by foreign governments to help out producers who are having short-run difficulties. In that case, there is an argument for some restriction, such as a duty. A countervailing duty would offset the foreign subsidy, thus neutralizing its effect on the prices faced by consumers. Otherwise, as prices of subsidized imports decline, domestic producers first have to reduce production when the low-priced foreign goods arrive and then have to increase it again when the subsidy is removed. If subsidies are temporary, they are likely to disrupt our industry—and there is an economic case for preventing this.

The subsidy issue is closely related to that of dumping.

● *Dumping* **takes place when firms sell abroad at a price below cost.**

Dumping typically takes place in recessions, when an industry does not want to cut back production but cannot sell at home. The industry then turns to foreign markets, disrupting foreign production in order to stabilize its own production.

The objection to dumping is that it is bound to be temporary. If foreigners want always to sell at a price below cost, then we should be eager to import from them. But a private firm cannot afford to sell below cost in the long run. U.S. laws provides for antidumping duties to avoid such disruption of U.S. industry; see Box 23-1 for details.

Exploiting National Market Power

The soundest argument for tariffs is based on the exploitation of a nation's power in world markets. Individual households or firms usually behave competitively in making decisions to consume or produce, taking prices as given. But a large country as a whole may face a downward-sloping demand curve for some of its exports or an upward-sloping supply curve for some of its imports. It then has monopoly power in export markets or monopsony power in import markets.

In either case there is a national gain from restricting trade by reducing exports or limiting imports. A tariff that reduces imports will lower the world price we pay. If the nation as a whole has market power, it can exploit foreigners by making them in effect pay part of the tariff.

Box 23-1. How the United States Deals with Trade Problems

U.S. trade laws provide for action in two broad areas: *unfair* foreign trade and *fair but troublesome* trade.

UNFAIR FOREIGN TRADE
The U.S. government is charged to intervene when foreign exporters gain access to the U.S. market by means of unfair practices or advantages. The chief examples are foreign dumping, foreign subsidies to exports, and foreign infringement of U.S. trademarks or patents. Private parties hurt by foreign exports can initiate a fact-finding procedure that, if it substantiates the claim, leads to offsetting measures imposed by the U.S. government. If it finds dumping or foreign subsidies, the government will impose antidumping, or "countervailing," duties that offset the unfair advantage gained by foreign suppliers and enable domestic firms to compete on "an even playing field."

Authority to offset foreign "unfair, unreasonable or discriminatory" practices constitutes a broad authority for the U.S. government to impose restrictions on foreign countries' exports to the United States when these countries are found to limit U.S. imports in their own markets. For example, Brazil's restriction of access by foreign companies to its computer market is the kind of violation that would allow the President to retaliate by restricting Brazil's access to the U.S. market.

FAIR BUT TROUBLESOME TRADE
The President has authority under the trade laws to grant *temporary* relief from imports under "safeguard" or "escape clause" provisions whenever domestic industries are injured by imports, even though those imports are not entering the U.S. market as a result of unfair trade advantages or practices. Escape clause protection can be provided whenever increases in imports are the main source of serious injury to a U.S. industry. The relief can take any of a number of forms: tariffs, quotas, or foreign voluntary export restraints (VERs).

U.S. protectionism over the past 10 years has gained vigor in implementing the existing law's provisions for countervailing duties, enforcement of fair trade practices, and escape clause action. U.S. producers claim this is at most barely adequate to restore a level paying field. Foreign producers argue that the U.S. market is being closed to them.

Note, though, that such a tariff serves only the *national* interest; from a world point of view it represents a misallocation of resources just like any other exercise of market power. And it may invite retaliation—in the form of higher tariffs abroad—that can erase even the national gains.

National Defense

One of the oldest arguments for tariffs is that a country may want to protect domestic industries that produce strategic materials, so that it does not become excessively dependent on foreign sources of supply that may be cut off in an emergency or war. This argument has some validity; a country could not, for instance, rely on its main potential enemy for the supply of ammunition. Nonetheless, here too countries have to consider carefully whether there are other policies that can better achieve the goals for which tariffs are being considered.

For instance, it is often argued that for strategic reasons the United States should protect the domestic oil industry in order to encourage oil production and render the country less vulnerable to a foreign oil embargo. But oil is a depletable resource, and it is not clear that the United States reduces its long-run vulnerability to foreigners by encouraging the production of domestic oil. Rather, it should encourage attempts to increase supplies that are potentially available in the case of a foreign shutoff of oil—for instance, by subsidizing exploration and development of oil wells though not their actual use.

7. Other Commercial Policies

Tariffs are not the only form of commercial policy. Three other ways in which governments interfere with free international trade deserve attention: quotas, nontariff barriers, and export subsidies.

Quotas

Under a tariff importers are free to purchase any amount of foreign goods provided that they pay the duty. Under a quota, or quantitative restriction, by contrast, the government limits the quantity or sometimes the value of imports that are allowed. Thus the government might restrict car imports from Japan to not more than 2 million units or shoe imports from Brazil to not more than 500,000 pairs.[7]

Quotas, like tariffs, restrict imports. Because quantity supplied is thus reduced, domestic prices rise above those prevailing in the rest of the world. Quotas differ from tariffs in two important ways. One is that quotas eliminate any impact of foreign competition on domestic prices. For instance, if world market prices fall because foreign firms reduce their costs, imports will rise and the domestic market price will fall under a tariff. But there would be no effect on the domestic market under a quota, since imports cannot rise.[8]

The second difference is that quotas provide certainty about the quantity of imports. While this is often an advantage from the viewpoint of policymakers, it is in practice one of the shortcomings of quotas. They remove domestic producers entirely from the threat and discipline of foreign competition. With an effective quota, foreigners cannot even give away their products free in the home market if these imports would exceed the quota. Indeed, quotas were widely introduced in the 1930s precisely to prevent foreign competitors from entering home markets by means of sharp price-cutting.

We noted previously that in the late 1970s the U.S government arranged with Japan a *voluntary export restraint*. This is simply a quota imposed by a foreign country on its exports to us. Two differences between a quota imposed by us and a foreign voluntary export restraint are worth noting. First, a foreign voluntary export restraint is a less directly visible trade restriction and thus is less obvious to domestic consumers than is a tariff or a quota.[9] It has the same effect of reducing

---

[7] Quota permits are allocated in one of two ways. The government may auction them to the highest bidder, meaning the company willing to pay most for a permit. Or they can be administratively allocated to firms, often on the basis of past levels of imports or as political favors. Quota permits are valuable because they allow the holder, without competition, to buy low in the world market and resell at a high price in the protected market.

[8] Since the gap between the domestic price and the world price would rise, those allowed to import would make higher profits, however.

[9] Many LDCs complain that the voluntary export restraints they are persuaded to impose on their strongly growing exports are not altogether voluntary: LDCs feel they must choose between limiting their exports through voluntary quotas and facing even more serious restrictions by the importing countries.

foreign sales in our markets, but our government is not seen imposing the trade restriction and hence will not be blamed by consumers. Second, foreigners can charge higher prices than they could if we imposed the quota and auctioned the rights to the highest bidder. Thus they are at least in part compensated for reduced sales. In fact, it has been argued that the voluntary export restraint on Japanese cars raised the profits of Japanese auto producers by in effect allowing them to restrict sales and raise prices, as a cartel would.

Nontariff Barriers

● **Nontariff barriers are administrative regulations that discriminate against foreign goods and in favor of home goods.**

These regulations can take many forms. A government buying policy that stipulates that at equal—or even higher—prices domestic products must be given preference ("Buy American!") is a nontariff barrier, for instance. American firms have charged that this form of discrimination is routinely practiced in Japan. The Japanese counter that American firms have not learned to do business in Japan and are less than successful for that reason.

Nontariff barriers may also arise in regulatory standards (for pollution equipment or safety, for instance) or in taxation that tends to fall particularly heavily on foreign-type products. Progressive road taxes in some countries, for example, fall heavily on relatively large cars that tend to be American. Sanitary restrictions prohibit trade in certain agricultural commodities (fruit into California, for example) or in food and beverages (beer into Germany). While they may have a good sanitary justification, these restrictions clearly act at the same time as a convenient instrument of protection for local producers.

Export Subsidies

We have so far looked only at restrictions on imports, but there are also commercial policies directed at exports. Countries attempt to promote their exports of industrial goods by outright subsidies, by exempting the exported goods from certain domestic taxes, or by providing particularly cheap credit.

An export subsidy increases exports, but it does so at a social cost. With the subsidy in place, firms produce goods at a marginal cost above what foreigners are paying for the goods. The government, and ultimately the taxpayer, gives firms a subsidy that makes up the difference between what the goods cost them to make and what foreigners pay. On the consumption side there is a cost because we are selling goods abroad for a price below what they are worth to home consumers. Just like a tariff, an export subsidy involves waste. Just as in the case of a tariff, there is rarely a first-best argument for an export subsidy.

8. Why is There Protection?

Tariffs, quotas, nontariff barriers, and export subsidies all have in common that they impose excess costs or waste for society as a whole. For over a century, economists have argued that there are few if any valid arguments in favor of these protective policies.

On the contrary, protection is expensive. For instance, a recent World Bank study reported that

> For each job saved in clothing, for example, the U.S. economy as a whole sacrificed about $169,600 to protect a worker earning about $12,600. Clearly the resources wasted in the process could have been better used in other activities and in retraining and reallocating the affected workers.[10]

The World Bank also estimates that each job saved by automobile import restrictions costs $47,000, and that each job protected in steel costs $71,000 to the economy as a whole.

In light of all this, why is protection so common? To answer this question we begin with a look at history and then consider how economics and politics interact to determine commercial policies.

Protection over Time

Figure 23-9 shows the history of tariffs in the United States over the past 165 years. The United States traditionally had high tariffs, but since World War II (indeed,

[10] World Bank, *World Development Report, 1986*, p. 23.

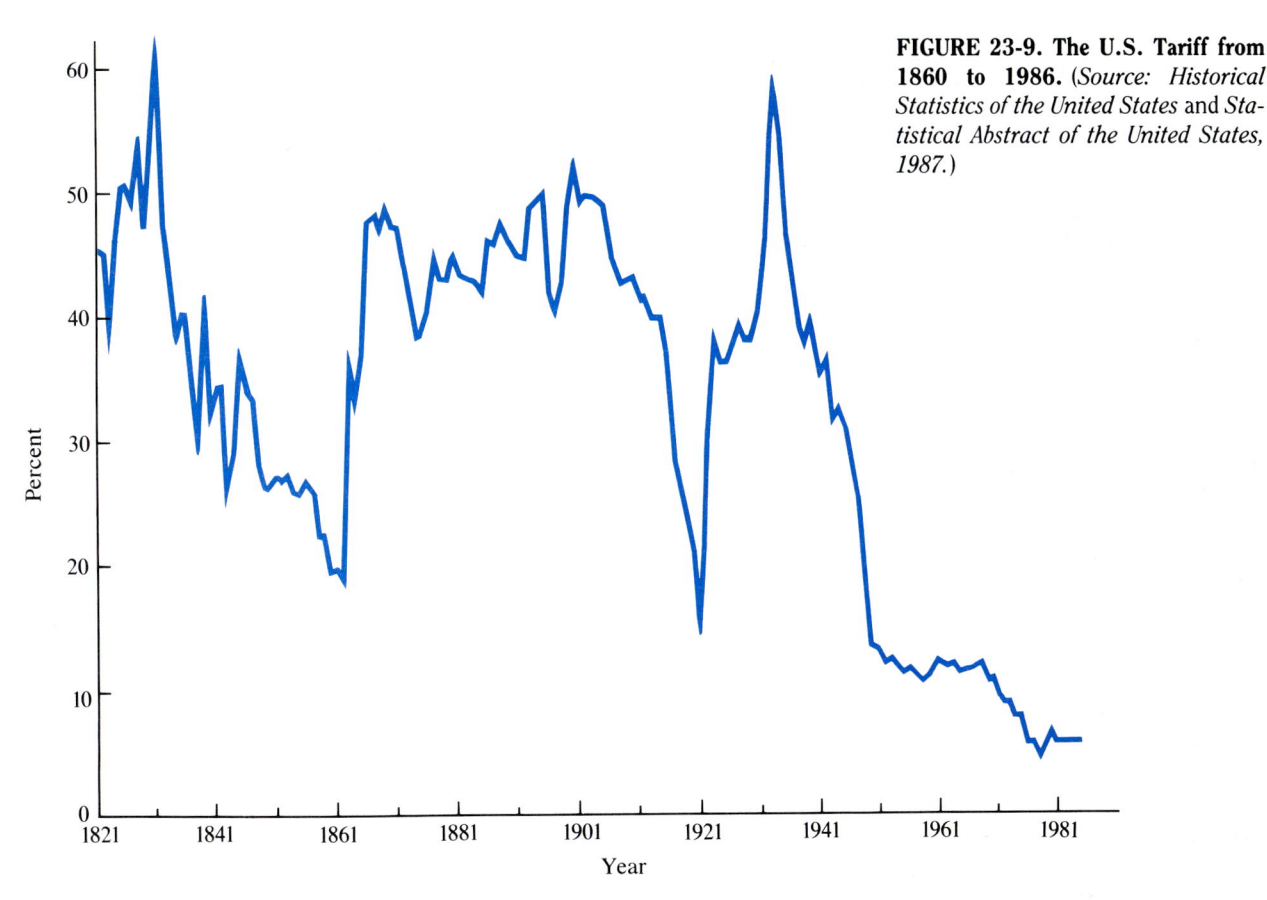

FIGURE 23-9. The U.S. Tariff from 1860 to 1986. (*Source: Historical Statistics of the United States* and *Statistical Abstract of the United States, 1987.*)

starting in the 1930s) tariffs have come down and have never been lower than they are now. The same trends apply in the rest of the industrialized world. Figure 23-10 shows tariff rates for the main groups of goods. Tariff rates are very low; world trade has probably never been freer than it is at present.

The gradual reduction of tariff rates over time has been due to multilateral trade negotiations in the context of *GATT*, the General Agreement on Tariffs and Trade. In successive rounds of negotiations, all member countries have cut their tariff rates to today's low levels. At the same time they have agreed on a *code of conduct* that severely limits their ability to impose trade restrictions.

But against this trend of *generalized* trade liberalization runs a growing countercurrent of *selective* trade restrictions. Here protection is on the rise. Countries with strong export performances, particularly Japan and the NICs, have been persuaded to adopt voluntary export restraints in areas such as textiles, automobiles, and machine tools. The importing countries felt that selective protection would avoid a much wider and destructive move toward broad import restrictions. In the depression of the 1930s, international trade collapsed as governments raised tariffs in a vain attempt to protect domestic jobs at the expense of foreigners. The memory of these destructive trade wars still makes governments nervous about adopting broad trade restrictions. Exporters, on the other hand, believed that some protection was inevitable and that it would be better to accept selective restrictions instead of a broad and possibly dramatic shift toward protection.[11]

An especially interesting case of trade restriction is the

---

[11] For details on recent protective measures, see the *Annual Report of the President of the United States on the Trade Agreements Program*; OECD, *Costs and Benefits of Protection*, 1985; and the annual report by GATT, *International Trade*.

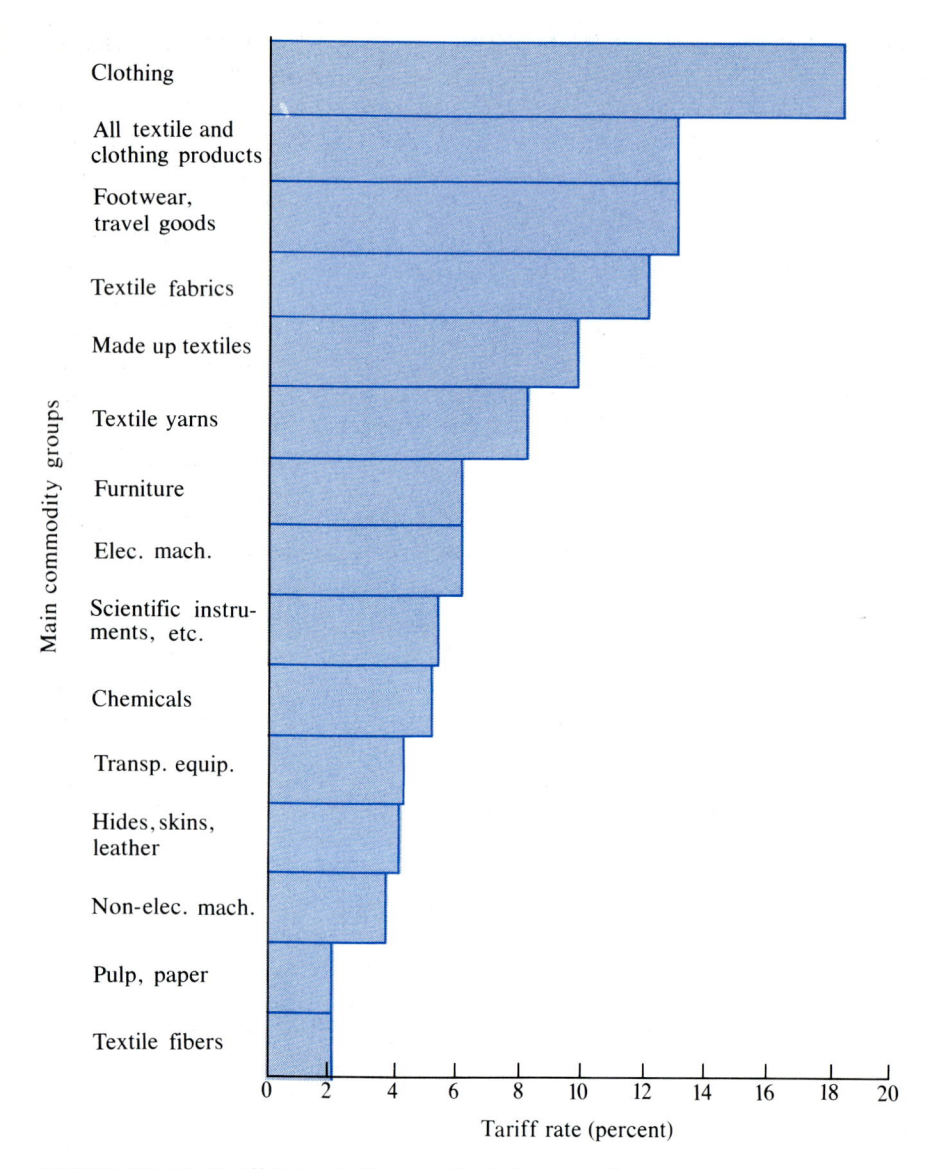

FIGURE 23-10. Tariff Rates in Industrialized Countries for the Main Commodity Groups. (*Source*: OECD, *The Costs and Benefits of Protection*, 1985.)

1986 semiconductor agreement between the United States and Japan. To protect U.S. producers against low-cost imports of semiconductor chips from Japan, an agreement between the United States and Japan set minimum prices for Japanese sales in the U.S. market. When Japanese firms broke the agreement in 1987, the United States responded with a large tariff on a selected list of Japanese goods.

Politics, Economics, and Protection

Three primary arguments have been advanced to explain the increasing political attractiveness of protection despite its generally high costs to society as a whole. First, those who would gain from protection are better organized than those who would lose. Second, those who would lose may not understand what is at stake. Third, tariffs represent disguised subsidies and are thus more attractive than direct, visible handouts. We now discuss these in turn.

CONCENTRATED BENEFITS, DIFFUSE COSTS. Consider the American losers and gainers from Japanese competition in the automobile industry. The losers were the autoworkers and the owners of stock in U.S. auto companies, and the gainers were the purchasers of Japanese cars.

Restriction of trade would benefit the autoworkers and the companies and would hurt the car-buying public. The autoworkers are a clearly defined group, with efficient union representation. Management too knows its way around the political arena. But the millions of buyers of cars are not well organized. The benefits of being able to buy Japanese cars are not so large that buyers are likely to organize themselves into a lobbying group to fight the producers. Because the benefits from restricting trade typically go to a well-defined group and the costs from restricting trade are borne by a larger, less organized group, the political system tends to accommodate the pressures of the organized group by imposing restrictions. This is the concentrated benefits, diffuse costs explanation for trade restrictions.[12]

CONSUMER IGNORANCE. An additional reason for the lack of organized opposition to protection may be that many people simply do not understand its effects. When in 1985 a poll asked, "Do you think the United States should limit imports from Japan to protect American industry?" an astonishing 70 percent of the respondents answered, "Yes."[13] That is a reasonable reply for autoworkers. But most U.S. citizens would be affected mainly as consumers of Japanese goods, not as producers of competing U.S. products, and they would accordingly be harmed by protection. The fact that public opinion shows strong—if possibly irrational—support for trade restrictions encourages legislators to implement protection.

[12] This general argument was discussed in Chapter 4.
[13] The Wall Street Journal and NBC News Poll, reported in the *Wall Street Journal*, Oct. 11, 1985.

HIDDEN SUBSIDIES. Even given the ability of concentrated interests to achieve their goals, why do they prefer tariffs or quotas to domestic production subsidies? And why do governments go along? This is surprising, because as we have argued, subsidies are usually a more efficient means than tariffs to achieve the same ends.

There are two main reasons why governments frequently use tariffs when from an economic viewpoint they would do better to subsidize production. The first reason is that the tariff solution somehow seems the natural answer to a trade problem. Japanese cars are the problem for Detroit producers. The direct solution looks simple: Forbid Japanese cars.

The second reason for using tariffs is that it is less clear who is doing what for whom with a tariff than with a subsidy. A producer receiving a subsidy explicitly takes money from the taxpayers. A tariff appears mainly to harm foreigners and indeed brings in money for the government. In fact, however, under a tariff consumers are paying higher prices directly to the producers, but that is less obvious than the producer actually getting checks from the government. Tariffs don't look like a giveaway, while subsidies do.

In practice, however, protection is more likely to be supported by the concentrated benefits, diffuse costs argument than because society has made a fully informed decision to accept its costs as an acceptable price for some social goal. Production subsidies are most likely to be rejected because they make the costs of providing concentrated benefits visible to all. Thus the economist's basic attitude toward tariffs is opposition and skepticism—conceivably they are appropriate, but more likely the arguments for them come down to self-interest at the expense of others, dressed up in fancy talk.

■ The argument that free trade benefits society as a whole is one of the oldest in all economics and one of the most heavily challenged. Businessmen and trade unions say that it simply ignores reality, which is the invasion of U.S. markets by foreigners. U.S. industry is losing out; jobs are disappearing. How can economists continue to say that trade must remain free for the benefit of all? Part of the reason economists are misunderstood reflects the fallacy of composition: Individual industries *can* benefit from protection, but only at the expense of the rest of the economy. It is the second part which is of little interest to firms that are confronting trade problems and hence is deliberately overlooked. But the government can't subsidize everything; subsidies in the form of protection are particularly expensive. The debate is bound to continue. It has been heated up recently by rapid changes in the competitiveness of domestic industries brought about by dramatic fluctuations in the value of the dollar relative to other currencies.

Summary

1. Countries trade because they can buy goods more cheaply from other countries. Differences in costs of production arise because of differences in methods of production and in factor endowments. In addition, scale economies make it efficient to specialize in production.
2. Ricardian trade theory shows that a country will produce those goods in which it has a comparative advantage. These are the goods it produces *relatively* cheaply. Countries benefit from trade even if one of them is more efficient than the other in making all goods.
3. Under the simplifying assumptions made by Ricardo, countries specialize in production and in importing and exporting. The dividing line between the goods they import and export depends mainly on their relative sizes.
4. Countries gain from trade if they specialize. In effect they are using their resources, embodied in the goods they export, to produce the goods they import, and they are using less labor than they would have to if there were no trade. The opening of trade benefits at least one of the trading partners and harms neither.
5. The extension of trade theory to more than one factor of production emphasizes *relative* factor abundance. A country that has a relatively high capital-labor ratio will export capital-intensive goods and import labor-intensive goods. The relative abundance of raw materials such as oil is another major factor explaining patterns of world trade.
6. Intra-industry trade occurs because of scale economies and consumer preferences for diversity. By producing for the world market, firms enjoy lower production costs. Consumers benefit from having a choice between imported and domestic products. Intra-industry trade accounts for a large share of trade in Europe and the United States.
7. World trade creates conflicts between the interests of consumers and the interests of producers. Cheap imports benefit the consumer but hurt the domestic producer. Export subsidies benefit the producer but hurt the consumer.
8. A tariff raises the domestic price of imported goods subject to the tariff; this discourages consumption but increases domestic production. Imports are reduced because total consumption of the good falls and because domestic production increases.
9. Part of the losses a tariff imposes on consumers are offset by the government's tariff revenue and increased profits for domestic firms. But there is a net cost to society: Losses to consumers exceed the gains to other sectors. This net cost arises from overproduction by firms—marginal cost exceeds world price—and underconsumption by consumers.
10. Few arguments for tariffs stand up to close scrutiny. In most instances the same goal can be achieved with less waste by means of a production subsidy or a consumption tax.
11. U.S. tariffs and those in other countries have fallen substantially since World War II and are now at their lowest levels ever. The reduction in tariffs is in part a response to the disastrous collapse of world trade when tariffs rose sharply in the 1930s. But there is an upsurge of protectionism in the form of quotas and "voluntary" export restraints.
12. The persistent pressure for protection is largely explained by the fact that producers have more at stake (per head) than consumers and therefore find it more profitable to organize political support for their position and the fact that the costs of tariffs are less visible than the costs of direct subsidies.

Key Terms

Unit labor requirements
Unit labor cost
Comparative advantage
Gains from trade
Intra-industry trade
Commercial policy
Tariff
Quota
Nontariff barriers
Export subsidy

Dumping
GATT
Voluntary export restraint

Problems

1. "A country that is absolutely less productive in every industry than its trading partners cannot compete in world trade and therefore can only lose by opening itself up to foreign competition." Discuss this assertion in detail.
2. Consider the case of Table 23-3, where there are many goods. Suppose that in the initial equilibrium the United States produces computers, cars, and TV sets and France produces the remaining goods. Suppose now that a large number of workers move from France to the United States. What do you think will happen to the pattern of specialization and trade?
3. Consider Table 23-3 and suppose again that initially the United States produces computers, cars, and TV sets and France produces the remaining goods. Suppose now that in France the unit labor requirement for TV sets falls from 90 hours to 30, or that the ratio of U.S. to French labor requirements for TVs rises from 5/9 to 5/3. (*a*) What happens to the order of goods in terms of comparative advantage in Table 23-3? (*b*) What will happen to trade patterns?
4. In the text we showed that where there are only two goods (automobiles and textiles), U.S. residents benefit from trade if the United States specializes in production. This takes place if $W/W^* = 2$. Show that when $W/W^* = 1.6$ and France specializes, French residents benefit from trade.
5. Explain in words why a country that is relatively capital-rich will tend to export goods that are relatively capital-intensive in production and import goods that are relatively labor-intensive.
6. "The system of world trade condemns poor countries to produce goods that use unskilled labor. Therefore, they are precluded from good jobs and the potential for progress." Discuss this statement and indicate what parts are correct and what parts are incorrect and why.
7. Consider five goods: stereo equipment, wine, cotton shirts, computers, and steel beams. Which of these goods do you think have a high index of intra-industry trade for the United States, and which have a low index? Explain your reasons.
8. It has been argued that a tariff does not impose costs on society because it just moves money from one pocket to another—from consumers to businesses and the government. Comment carefully on this argument.
9. Society has decided that preservation of the national artistic heritage is important. For that purpose a complete ban on the export of any U.S. artistic product is imposed. (*a*) Do you think such a quota is preferable to an export tax? (An export tax is the opposite of the export subsidy studied in section 7.) (*b*) Who gains and who loses from the ban? (*c*) Do you think the ban will encourage young artists to stay in business?
10. Certain activities—agriculture, weapons development, the manufacture of basic materials—are essential to the national defense and military preparedness. Should a tariff be imposed to maintain these activities in the face of foreign competition? Evaluate the pros and cons carefully.
11. The accompanying table shows wages in the automobile industry and in manufacturing in general in the United States and Japan in 1985.

Hourly Compensation, 1985

	United States	Japan
Motor vehicles	$19.21	$8.03
Manufacturing	12.97	6.45

Source: U.S. Bureau of Labor Statistics.

(*a*) On the basis of these data and the analysis in this chapter, do you think the United States should protect the automobile industry with a tariff, with a quota, or not at all? (*b*) Is there any argument for providing temporary relief for the automobile industry, for example, by imposing a tariff for a few years only?

Glossary

Adverse selection. Occurs because the people who buy insurance against a particular loss are those who know that they are more likely on average actually to suffer that loss.

Age-earnings profile. The relationship between income and age for a particular individual or group of individuals.

Antitrust policy. Attempts to protect and enhance competition by making it harder to create, exercise, or protect monopoly power.

Asset price. The price at which a unit of financial capital (such as a share of stock) or physical capital (such as a truck or a house) can be bought or sold outright.

Average fixed cost (*AFC*). The ratio of fixed cost to output.

Average product (*AP*). The ratio of output produced to the amount of some particular input employed.

Average tax rate. The ratio of total taxes to income.

Average total cost (*ATC*). The ratio of total cost to output, equal to average fixed cost plus average variable cost.

Average variable cost (*AVC*). The ratio of variable cost to output.

Balance sheet. Shows the assets (what is owned), liabilities (what is owed), and net worth (assets minus liabilities) of a particular firm or other entity at a particular time.

Barriers to entry. Keep potential competitors from entering industries in which established sellers are earning positive economic profits.

Bracket creep. Occurs when the *share* of taxes in a given amount of real income increases as the price level increases because households are pushed into higher tax brackets.

Break-even price. The price at which a firm just breaks even, equal to the minimum level of average total cost.

Budget constraint. Specifies the combinations of goods a consumer or household or any other economic unit can afford to buy.

Budget deficit or surplus. A deficit is the excess of government outlays over its receipts. When the government is running a deficit, it is spending more than it is taking in. When it is running a surplus, receipts exceed outlays.

Business cycle. The more or less regular pattern of expansion (recovery) and contraction (recession) in real output around the economy's average or trend growth path.

Capital gains. Are earned when an asset, such as a share of stock, is sold and the seller receives more than she originally paid for the asset.

Capture hypothesis. The view that regulators serve the interests of regulated firms (who have captured them through the political process), not the interests of consumers.

Cartel. A formal agreement among rival sellers to raise price and restrict output.

Cashflow. The net amount of money a firm or other entity actually receives in a given period.

Closed shop. An establishment in which the employer can hire only union members.

Collusion. An explicit or tacit agreement among firms in an industry to fix prices and restrict outputs or otherwise limit rivalry among themselves.

Command economy. An economy in which all resources are allocated by central direction.

Commercial policy. Government policy that influences trade through taxes, subsidies, and direct restrictions on imports or exports.

Comparable worth. The notion that wages should be based on the inherent worth or difficulty of the job performed rather than the market wage.

Comparative advantage. A major determinant of the pattern of international trade. According to the theory of comparative advantage, countries export the commodities for which they have the lowest *relative* cost.

Complements. Goods are complements if an increase in the price of one lowers the quantity demanded of the other.

Constant returns to scale. Exist when long-run average cost is independent of the level of output.

Consumers' surplus. The difference between the maximum amount consumers would be willing to pay for the quantity of a good they demand and the amount they actually pay. It is measured as the area between the demand curve and a horizontal line at the market price.

Corporation. An organization legally permitted to carry on certain activities, such as running a railroad or producing a newspaper. The owners of a corporation are liable only for their investments in the corporation, even if these are not sufficient to cover the losses it incurs.

Cost-benefit analysis. Evaluates a project by comparing its benefits to society as a whole with the costs of undertaking it.

Costs. A firm's expenses of producing the goods or services sold during a particular period; equal to fixed costs plus variable costs. Accounting and economic costs typically differ.

Cross price elasticity of demand. The percentage change in the quantity of a good demanded when the price of another good increases by 1 percent.

Cross section data. Measurements of a variable for different economic units (such as households, firms, states, or nations) at the same point in time.

Deadweight burden of a tax. The waste (the net fall in consumers' plus producers' surplus) that arises from the distortion of the allocation of resources created by the tax.

Demand curve. Shows graphically the quantity of a good demanded at each price, with other factors that affect quantity demanded held constant. The demand curve is typically downward-sloping.

Demand schedule. The relationship between the quantity of a good demanded and the price of that good, with other factors that affect the quantity demanded held constant.

Depreciation. The reduction in value of a machine or building that occurs as a result of use and/or the passage of time.

Derived demand. Firms' demands for productive inputs, which ultimately depend on—are derived from—the demands for final goods and services.

Diminishing marginal utility. Is derived from a good if each extra unit of the good consumed adds less to total utility than the unit before.

Discouraged workers. Those who leave the labor force because they believe they cannot find a job.

Diseconomies of scale (or decreasing returns to scale). Occur when long-run average cost rises as output increases.

Diversification. The strategy of reducing risk by spreading investment across several risky assets.

Dividends. More or less regular (usually quarterly) payments made by a corporation to its stockholders.

Dumping. Takes place when firms sell abroad at a price below cost.

Econometrics. The branch of economics that uses and develops statistical methods to measure relationships among economic variables.

Economic data. Facts, most often expressed as numbers, that provide information about economic variables.

Economic efficiency (or Pareto efficiency). Occurs when it is impossible to reallocate resources so as to make one person better off without also making another person worse off. In regard to production, economic efficiency implies production at least cost.

Economic mobility. The ease with which a person or family can move up or down in the income distribution.

Economic profit. The difference between total revenue and total economic cost (including the opportunity cost of owner-supplied capital) in a particular period.

Economic regulation. Government regulation concerned with prices, entry, and qualities in particular industries, such as electricity supply.

Economic rent. The amount of payment to a factor of production that exceeds the minimum that would have to be paid to get that quantity of the factor supplied to the particular use.

Economic variable. Anything that influences the "what," "how," and "for whom" decisions with which economics is concerned or that describes the results of those decisions.

Economics. The study of how societies, with limited, scarce resources, decide what gets produced, how, and for whom. Positive economics seeks objective or scientific explanations of the workings of an economy; it deals with what is or could be. Normative economics offers prescriptions for action based on personal value judgments; it deals with someone's views of what should be.

Economies of scale (or increasing returns to scale). Are present when a firm's long-run average cost falls as output increases.

Elasticity of demand (or price elasticity of demand). The percentage increase in quantity demanded that occurs as a result of a 1 percent reduction in price, holding constant all other factors that affect quantity demanded. Demand is said to be elastic if the price elasticity of demand is greater than 1. Demand is inelastic if the price elasticity is less than 1. Demand is unit-elastic if the elasticity equals 1.

Elasticity of supply. The percentage increase in the quantity supplied of a good produced by a 1 percent increase in its price, holding constant all other factors that affect quantity supplied.

Employment rate. The percentage of those in a given group who are working.

Equalizing (or compensating) differential. A difference in wages that compensates workers for the difference in the attractiveness of jobs.

Equilibrium price. The price at which the quantity demanded is equal to the quantity supplied.

Equilibrium quantity. The quantity supplied and demanded at the equilibrium price.

Equity. Ownership shares in a firm. Also used as a synonym for fairness.

Equity, horizontal. Says that equals should be treated equally by the tax laws.

Equity, vertical. Says that unequals should be treated unequally by the tax laws.

Exports. Sales of domestically produced goods and services to foreigners.

Export subsidy. A subsidy on exports designed to encourage firms to export more.

Externality. Exists when the production or consumption of a good directly affects businesses or consumers not involved in buying and selling it and when those spillover effect are not fully reflected in market prices.

Factors of production. The inputs—including labor services, land, machines, tools, buildings, and raw materials—used to produce goods and services.

Federal trade commission (FTC). An expert body that, along with the Department of Justice, enforces the U.S. antitrust laws.

Fixed Costs (*FC*). Costs that in the short run do not depend on how much the firm produces. These are the costs of its fixed inputs.

Fixed inputs (or fixed factors). The quantities of a firms' fixed inputs that cannot be changed easily or quickly and are thus constant in the short run.

Free-market economy. One in which the government plays no role in allocating resources.

Functional distribution of income. The division of national income among different factors of production, in particular the shares of income received by capital and labor.

Futures markets. Organized markets for the future delivery of many commodities and assets.

Gross national product (GNP). The market value of the goods and services produced within a given period by domestically owned factors of production, wherever they are located. Nominal GNP measures the value of production in the prices of the period of production; real GNP measures the value of production using a fixed (base year) set of prices, thereby providing a measure of aggregate output that is not affected by inflation.

GNP deflator. A measure of the price level based on all the goods and services produced in the economy, calculated as the ratio of nominal GNP to real GNP.

Growth rate. The percentage rate of increase per year of any variable (often real GNP) over a specified period of time.

Hedgers. People who use futures markets to reduce the risks they face.

Human capital. The value of the income-earning potential embodied in individuals. It includes native ability and talent as well as education and acquired skills.

Imperfect competition. Markets in which either buyers or sellers are individually able to affect the price at which they buy or sell.

Imports. Goods and services bought by domestic residents from foreigners.

Income effect. The portion of a consumer's reaction to a price change that reflects the corresponding change in his real income.

Income elasticity of demand. The percentage change in the quantity of a good demanded caused by a 1 percent increase in income.

Income statement (or profit and loss statement). Shows the revenues, expenses, and profit (or net income) for a particular firm for a particular period.

Individual proprietorship. A business owned by an individual, who is fully entitled to the profit earned by the business and fully responsible for any losses it incurs.

Inferior good. A good for which quantity demanded falls when income rises. Equivalently, a good for which the income elasticity of demand is negative.

Inflation rate. The percentage rate of increase of the general price level per year over a specified period of time.

Interest rate. The payment, expressed in percent per year, made by a borrower to a lender in exchange for the loan of a sum of money. The nominal interest rate is expressed in terms of the money payments made on a loan. The real (or inflation-adjusted) interest rate is expressed in terms of goods and services; it is approximately equal to the nominal rate minus the inflation rate.

Intermediate product. A nondurable produced good or service used as an input in production.

Intra-industry trade. Occurs when a country both imports and exports goods produced by a single industry.

Invention and innovation. Related aspects of the development of technical knowledge. Invention is the discovery of new knowledge; innovation is the development of methods for applying existing knowledge.

Inventories. Goods held in stock by a firm for use in future production or for future sales.

Kinked (oligopoly) demand curve. Exists if a firm believes that if it cut price all its rivals would match the cut, while if it raised price none would follow along.

Labor force. Those 16 years of age and over who are employed plus those who are unemployed and looking for work.

Land. The factor of production which, rather than being produced, is naturally available—but only in fixed quantity.

Law of demand. The proposition that an increase in price lowers the quantity demanded. For normal goods, this law is implied by the economic theory of consumer behavior. As an empirical matter, it also holds for inferior goods.

Law of diminishing returns. The proposition that if the quantities of some factors are fixed, then the marginal product of any variable factors (such as labor) will, beyond some level of use of that input, decline as the input of that factor is increased further.

Logrolling. When groups get together to decide how they will vote on a package of issues rather than taking one issue at a time.

Long run. A period of time long enough for a firm to be able to vary all its factors of production or for a firm or household to adapt fully to a price change.

Long-run average cost curve (*LAC* curve). A curve that shows the lowest cost of producing any given level of output, allowing all factors of production to vary optimally to minimize cost.

Long-run break-even price. The lowest price at which a firm can just break even in the long run. It is the firm's minimum long-run average cost, the lowest point on its *LAC* curve.

Long-run marginal cost curve (*LMC* curve). The increase in cost due to an extra unit of output when the firm is free to vary all inputs optimally to minimize costs.

Long-run supply curve. Shows how quantity supplied depends on price when firms have had time to adjust fully to price changes.

Lorenz curve. Measures the extent of inequality in the personal distribution of income.

Lump-sum taxes. Taxes fixed by the government independent of income or purchases.

Luxury. A good or service that has an income elasticity of demand greater than 1.

Macroeconomics. The study of the operation of the economy as a whole.

Marginal analysis. Seeking the optimal value of some variable by comparing the costs and benefits that would be produced by small changes in that variable. Underlies the economic theories of consumer demand and firm supply.

Marginal cost (*MC*). The increase in total cost a firm must incur to produce 1 more unit of output.

Marginal product (*MP*). The addition to a firm's output obtained by employing an additional unit of some particular variable input.

Marginal rate of substitution (*MRS*). The *MRS* of good A for good B (MRS_{AB}) measures how many extra units of good B a consumer must receive to compensate him for giving up 1 unit of good A—or, equivalently, how many units of good B the consumer would give up to get 1 more unit of good A.

Marginal rate of transformation (*MRT*). The *MRT* of good A for good B (MRT_{AB}) is the increase in the output of good B that can be obtained by reducing the output of good A by 1 unit—or, equivalently, the reduction in the output of B necessary to permit the output of A to increase by 1 unit.

Marginal revenue (*MR*). The change in a firm's revenue obtained by selling 1 more unit of output.

Marginal revenue product (*MRP*). The increase in a firm's revenue resulting from using 1 extra unit of some particular variable input. Under perfect competition, when marginal revenue equals the fixed market price, it is generally called the marginal value product (*MVP*).

Marginal tax rate. The fraction of an extra dollar of income that has to be paid in taxes.

Marginal utility. The increase in total utility that is obtained by consuming an additional unit of some particular good.

Market. A set of arrangements by which buyers and sellers of a good or service are in contact to trade that good or service.

Mean. The sum of a set of numbers divided by the number of numbers in the set; one form of average.

Median. When a set of numbers is ordered from highest to lowest, the median is the number in the middle; a form of average not affected by extreme values.

Merit goods. Goods that society thinks people should consume or receive, no matter what their incomes are.

Microeconomics. The branch of economics concerned with the behavior of firms, households, and other economic units; the operation of markets; and the overall efficiency of resource allocation.

Minimum efficient scale. The output level at which a firm's long-run average cost first falls to approximately its minimum value.

Minimum wage. The lowest wage that can legally be paid to a particular group of workers.

Mixed economy. In a mixed economy both the government and the private sector (businesses and consumers) play important roles in answering the "what," "how," and "for whom" questions for society as a whole. All real economies are mixed.

Model or theory. A simplified description of reality or an exact description of a simple imaginary economy.

Monopolistic competition. A market structure in which a large number of firms produce products that are close but imperfect substitutes for each other.

Monopoly (or monopolist). The only seller of a particular good or service in a market.

Monopoly power (or market power). The ability of a seller or group of sellers acting together to raise price above the competitive level by restricting its own output.

Monopoly profits. Profits that exceed the opportunity cost of capital supplied by a firms' owners and that reflect the firm's ability to raise price above marginal cost.

Monopsony. The only buyer of a particular good or service in a market.

Moral hazard. The tendency of somebody with insurance that covers a particular risk to take less care to avoid that risk.

Natural monopoly. An industry in which any level of output is more cheaply produced by one firm than by two or more.

Necessity. A good or service with an income elasticity of demand less than 1.

Negative income tax. A proposed replacement for the current welfare system that involves taxable cash payments to all households, along with increases in income tax rates.

Nontariff barriers. Administrative regulations that discriminate against foreign goods and in favor of home goods.

Normal good. A good for which the quantity demanded at every price increases when income rises. Equivalently, a good for which the income elasticity of demand is positive.

Okun's leaky bucket. Redistribution of income involves administrative costs and the adverse incentive effects of higher taxes and welfare programs themselves.

Oligopoly. A market in which most sales are made by a few firms, each large enough to affect the market price by its own actions.

Opportunity cost. The opportunity cost of any good or service is the amount of other goods or services that must be given up to obtain it.

Optimal positive output. The level of output that maximizes a firm's profit under the assumption that it is not going to shut down.

Participation rate. The percentage of a given group who are in the labor force, either working or looking for work.

Partnership. A business jointly owned by two or more people who share its profit. Each of the owners (or partners) is jointly responsible for any losses the business incurs.

Patent. A patent gives an inventor exclusive rights to the use of her invention for a limited time—17 years in the United States.

Perfectly competitive firm. A firm that takes the price of its output as given and unaffected by the amount it sells.

Perfectly competitive market. A market in which all sellers are perfectly competitive and there are many buyers, each well informed about sellers' prices, small relative to the market, and acting independently.

Perpetuity. A security that yields a constant income per year forever.

Personal distribution of income. The breakdown of aggregate income among individual economic units—persons, families, or households.

Physical capital. The stock of produced goods (such as machinery, equipment, and buildings) that contributes to the production of goods and services.

Poverty. A family is defined as poor if its income is less than three times the U.S. Department of Agriculture's estimate of the cost of an "economy food program" for the family. Some families that are not poor in this absolute sense may experience the emotional deprivation of relative poverty because their income is far below the median.

Predatory pricing. The (relatively rare) practice of cutting price in order to drive a rival seller from the industry.

Present value. The present value of a payment to be received at any future date is the amount that would have to be invested today to produce exactly that payment on that date.

Price discrimination. The practice (common in imperfect competition) of charging different prices to different consumers on the basis of differences is demand elasticities.

Price index. One hundred times the ratio of the dollar cost of a specified collection of goods and services (the market basket) in a given period to the cost of the same collection in a specified base period.

Price level. A weighted average of the prices of different goods and services in the economy, with more important prices receiving larger weights: usually measured by a price index.

Price makers versus price takers. Perfect competitors are described as price takers because they take the market price as given and beyond their control; monopolists are often described as price makers because they determine the market price.

Primary factors of production. Labor, capital, and land used to produce goods and services.

Private good. A good, such as an ice cream cone, that if consumed by one person, cannot be consumed by another.

Producers' surplus. The cumulative excess of price over the marginal cost of production. It is measured as the area between the supply curve and a horizontal line at the market price.

Product differentiation. A situation in which buyers consider the products of competing sellers to be close but imperfect substitutes.

Production function. Gives the maximum amount of output that can be produced using any specified amount of inputs.

Production possibility frontier (PPF). Shows the maximum possible output of some specified good or service that can be produced by a particular economy, given the resources and knowledge it has available and the amounts of all other goods and services it also produces.

Profit (or net income). The excess of revenue over costs.

Progressive tax structure. A tax structure that reduces the after-tax inequality of economic well-being.

Public good. A good, such as national defense, that if consumed by one person, is still available for consumption by others.

Quantity demanded. The amount of a good or service that buyers are willing and able to buy in some particular period; depends on the price of the product and on other factors, including the prices of other goods and buyers' incomes and tastes.

Quantity supplied. The amount of a good or service that sellers are willing to sell in some particular period; depends on the price of the product and on other factors, primarily the prices of the inputs used in production and the techniqes of production available to sellers.

Quota. A government-determined limit on the quantity (or sometimes the value) of imports of a particular product in a particular period.

Real income. The value of income measured in terms of the goods it will buy—as opposed to nominal income, which is measured in dollars.

Real price. The real price of any good or service is its dollar price relative to the price level, that is, its price measured in constant (base period) dollars.

Real wage. For a worker, the real wage is her dollar wage divided by the price level and thus measures the amount of goods she can buy with her wage earnings. For a firm, the real wage is the dollar wage it pays divided by the price of its output.

Regressive tax structure. A tax structure that increases after-tax inequality in economic well-being.

Relative price. The price of good or service A relative to the price of some other good or service B is equal to the ratio of the price of A to the price of B.

Rent. The difference between a factor's earnings and the minimum amount needed to induce it to supply the given level of services. Also used to describe the cost of using land.

Rental rate (of capital). The cost of using the services of a particular piece of capital. The required rental rate is the minimum rate that allows the owner of a particular piece of capital to just cover the opportunity cost of owning that asset.

Retained earnings. The part of a corporation's earnings that are kept in the firm rather than being paid out to stockholders as dividends.

Revenue. The amount a firm receives from the sale of goods or services during a given period.

Right-to-work laws. State laws that provide that anyone who gets a job with a firm can keep it whether or not he joins the firm's union.

Risk-averse behavior. Most consumers are risk-averse; they are willing to pay to avoid bearing risk. Risk lovers are willing to pay to bear risk, and risk-neutral consumers are indifferent to bearing risk.

Risk pooling and risk spreading. Mechanisms used to make insurance economical by combining large numbers of independent risks (pooling) and dividing large risks among many individuals (spreading).

Safety net. The set of welfare programs that provide benefits to the poor on the basis of their poverty.

Scatter diagram. A graph showing values of two economic variables for several different economic units or time periods.

Seller concentration. The extent to which sales in a market are concentrated in the hands of one firm or a few firms.

Short run. A period of time during which some of a firm's inputs cannot be varied or in which a firm or household has not fully adapted to a price change.

Short-run average total cost (*ATC*). The cost per unit of output during the short run; equal to average variable cost (*AVC*) plus average fixed cost (*AFC*).

Short-run marginal cost (*MC*). The increase in variable cost that would occur if output were increased by 1 unit in the short run.

Short-run shutdown price. The lowest value of the market price for which a perfectly competitive firm will continue in operation in the short run; equal to the minimum value of its average variable cost.

Short-run supply curve. Shows how quantity supplied depends on price in the short run, when the quantities of some inputs are fixed.

Social cost of monopoly. The net loss to society caused by monopoly output restriction; measured by the total of the differences between the value consumers place on each unit of lost output and its marginal cost of production.

Social insurance. Transfer programs that provide benefits only to those who have made contributions in the past.

Social regulation. Government regulation concerned with preservation of the environment, workplace risks, consumer protection, and related issues.

Speculators. Traders in securities or futures markets who increase the risk they bear in hopes of earning high returns.

Stabilization policy. Government actions that attempt to control the economy in order to keep GNP close to its potential level and to maintain low and stable rates of inflation.

Substitutes. Two goods are substitutes if an increase in the price of one raises the quantity demanded of the other at every price.

Substitution effect. The substitution effect of a price change is the adjustment of quantity demanded to the change in relative prices.

Sunk costs. Fixed costs that cannot be avoided even by going out of business; generally, costs that cannot be avoided or recovered and that thus should not affect decisions.

Supply curve. Shows graphically the quantity of a good supplied at each price, with other factors that affect quantity supplied held constant. The supply curve is typically upward-sloping.

Supply schedule. The relationship between the quantity of a good supplied and its price, with other factors that affect the quantity supplied held constant.

Tangency equilibrium. The long-run equilibrium under monopolistic competition in which each firm's demand curve is just tangent to its average cost curve.

Tangible wealth. Real, durable assets that directly yield valuable services over some period of time; capital and land as distinguished from paper assets (financial wealth).

Tariff. A tax on imports of particular goods or services; usually requires the importer of a good to pay a specified fraction of the import price to the government.

Technical efficiency. A method of production is technically efficient if there is no other method that uses less of at least one input and no more of any other input to produce a given level of output. Technical efficiency is required for but does not imply least-cost (economically efficient) production.

Technical progress. Occurs whenever it becomes possible, with given input prices, to produce a given level of output at lower cost. Produces increases in productivity.

Theory of efficient markets. The view that the stock market is a sensitive and accurate processor of information, responding correctly to each new piece of information bearing on the right price that should be paid for stocks.

Tiebout hypothesis (or invisible foot). The argument that by choosing among local governments providing different mixes of taxes and services, consumers can come close to obtaining the optimal mix.

Time series. A collection of measurements of a variable at different points or intervals of time.

Total condition (or profit check). Specifies that a firm should produce its optimal positive output only if revenues at that output level are at least equal to its variable costs.

Total product (*TP*) curve. Shows the relationship between the input of a variable factor and the resulting level of output produced.

Transfer payments (or transfers). Are made without a corresponding provision of goods or services by the recipient.

Two-part tariff. A price system in which users pay a fixed sum for access to a service and then pay a variable charge for each unit of the service they consume.

Unemployment benefits. Unemployed people who lose jobs that they have had for some time are entitled to collect unemployment insurance or benefits for a specified period as long as they can show that they are looking for work.

Unemployment rate. The percentage of the labor force who are out of a job and looking for work.

Union shop. An establishment in which anyone who is hired must become a union member within a specified period of time.

Utility. The pleasure or happiness a household derives from the goods and services it consumes.

Value added. The value of a firm's sales minus the value of the materials and other intermediate goods used in producing the goods sold.

Value-added tax (VAT). Equivalent to a general retail sales tax levied at a common rate on all goods sold in the economy but collected at every stage of production.

Variable costs (VC). Costs that depend on the level of the firm's output. These are the costs of its variable inputs—and thus its total cost in the long run.

Variable input (or factor). A firm can adjust the amount of a variable input that it uses at will, even in the short run. All inputs are variable in the long run.

Workfare. Welfare reforms that involve imposing work requirements on benefit recipients.

INDEX

Key terms appear in **boldface** type.

Aaron, Henry J., 385n.
Ability-to-pay principle, 380
Above-normal profits, 170
Abraham, Katharine G., 308n.
Absolute advantage, 418
 (*See also* Comparative advantage, law of)
Absolute changes, 32–33
Absolute poverty, 369–371
Accounting costs, 135–136
Accounting depreciation, 332n.
Accounting income of corporations, 379
Accounting profits, 131–136, 336
Accounting values of assets, 134–135
Achievement in economic status, 364–365
Actual real interest rates, 328
Ad valorem taxes, 63n.
Adams, Walter, 217
Addison, J., 309
Advantage:
 absolute, 418
 comparative, law of, 416–421
Adverse selection, 344
Advertising as nonprice competition, 229–230
AFDC (Aid to Families with Dependent Children), 398–400
AFL (American Federation of Labor), 310
AFL-CIO (American Federation of Labor–Congress of Industrial Organizations), 310
After-tax wages, 383–384
Age:
 and poverty, 370, 371, 400, 401
 in transfer payments, 72–73
 (*See also* entries beginning with the term: Social Security)
Age-earnings profiles, 302–303, 308–309
 defined, 302
 (*See also* Income; Wages; *entries beginning with the terms:* Income; Wage)
Aggregate output:
 dollar value of, 29–30
 quantity of, 30–31
Agricultural land prices, 329–330
Agricultural price supports, 72, 167–168
 in price elasticity of demand, 86
Aid to Families with Dependent Children (AFDC), 398–400
Air traffic controller strike, 311

Airline industry:
 deregulation of, 248–249
 price-fixing in, 257–258
Akin, John, 367n.
Allen, Jeremiah, 246
American Airlines, 257–258
American Federation of Labor (AFL), 310
American Federation of Labor–Congress of Industrial Organizations (AFL-CIO), 310
American Telephone and Telegraph Company (AT&T), 251, 258, 259
American Tobacco Company, 255, 258
Animal and Plant Health Inspection Service, 244
Annuities, 399n.
Antitrust law, 204, 238n., 251, 255–256
 court interpretation of, 257–259
 enforcement of, 256–259
 and mergers, 217, 258–260
 (*See also specific entries, for example:* Clayton Act; Robinson-Patman Act)
Antitrust policy, 234, 252–255, 259–262
 defined, 252
Arc elasticity of demand, 100
Argentinian beef exports, 423–424
Arrow, Kenneth, 70n.
Arts, human capital in, 308–309
Asset prices, 326–327, 337, 345
 defined, 324
Assets:
 defined, 133
 depreciation of, 131, 132, 134, 136, 332
 riskiness of, 348–350
 stocks of, 323–324
 types of: capital (*see* Capital assets)
  durable, 322–323
  durable productive, 53
  financial, 346–347, 350
  intangible, 134
  tangible, 336–337
 value of, 134–135, 326–327
  market, 134–135
AT&T (American Telephone and Telegraph Company), 251, 258, 259
Auctions, 221
Auditors, 131n.
Auerbach, Alan J., 379n., 387n.
Automobile industry, 173, 245
Average cost curves, long-run, 149–151
Average cost pricing, 264

Average costs, 147–149
 long-run, 149–151
Average fixed costs, 147–148
 defined, 147
Average price levels (*see* Price levels)
Average product, 143–144
Average real rate of return, 346–347
Average real wages, 294–295
Average tax rates, 381
Average total cost, 147–148
 defined, 147
Average variable costs, 147–148
 defined, 147
Averages, 26

Backward-bending labor supply curves, 288, 289
Bailey, Elizabeth, 248
Balance sheets, 133–134
 defined, 133
Balanced budget amendment, 73
 (*See also* Constitutional reform to deal with inflation)
Bane, Mary Jo, 372n.
Barriers to entry, 197, 208, 216, 218, 225–226
Barriers to trade, 71–72, 424–435
Barten, A. P., 89
Baumol, William J., 240, 241
Beer industry, 217
Before-tax wages, 383–384
Behavior (*see specific entries, for example:* Consumer behavior; Oligopolies, behavior of)
Bell, Carolyn Shaw, 367
Bell operating companies, 258
Belongia, Michael T., 168
Benefit-cost ratios, 186
 (*See also* Cost-benefit analysis)
Benefits:
 social, of government projects, 390–391
Benefits principle, 380–381
Berle, Adolf A., Jr., 130n.
Blank, Rebecca M., 402n.
Blinder, Alan S., 402n.
Boards of directors, 127n., 130
Bower, Blair T., 241n.
Bradford, David F., 386n.
Braniff International, 257–258
Break-even level in negative income tax, 407

449

Break-even prices, 164–165, 169
Breakfast cereal firms, 223
Brown Shoe Co., Inc. v. United States, 262
Browning, Edgar K., 385n., 397n.
Buchanan, James, 64, 70n.
Budget constraint, 103–104, 116–119
  defined, 103
Budget deficits, 61–62
  and defense spending, 5–6
  effects of, 73
  reducing, 73
Budget line, 116–119
Burdens of taxes, 384–386
Burtless, Gary, 37n.
Business cycles:
  defined, 62
  and rate of return on stocks, 350
  stabilization of, 62, 66
Business decisions and marginal products, 143
Business organization, forms of, 125–129
Businesses (*see* Firm-specific human capital; Firms)
Butler, Richard, 368n.
Buyers:
  consumers and households as, 101–103
  firms as, 101n.
  large, 198
  spending by, 83–87
    (*See also* Consumers, spending by)
  (*See also* Consumers; Demand; *entries beginning with the term:* Demand)

CAB (Civil Aeronautics Board), 235n., 237, 248–249
Cagan, Phillips, 385n., 402
Capital:
  productivity of, 359
  types of (*see* Financial capital; Human capital; Physical capital)
Capital assets:
  depreciation of [*see* Depreciation (of assets); Depreciation rates]
  earnings of, 336
  prices of, 324, 326–327, 337, 345
  rate of return on, 336–337
  real interest rates on, 332
  required rental rates on, 331–332
Capital gains, 128–129, 346
  defined, 128
  taxation of, 387
Capital-intensive production, 323
Capital-labor ratios, 277, 337, 358, 360

Capital-labor substitution, 277–278, 358–359
Capital markets, risk in, 345–351
  pooling of, 348–350
  spreading of, 347–348
Capital services, 323–324
  demand for, 333–334
  market equilibrium in, 333–337
  supply of, 330–337
Capital stock, 321, 358–360
Capitalism, Socialism, and Democracy (Schumpeter), 211
Captive labor forces, 311–313
Capture hypothesis, 236–237
  defined, 237
Cartels, 221–223, 226
  (*See also* Organization of Petroleum Exporting Countries)
Carter administration:
  deregulation by, 247, 248
  welfare spending by, 402
Cash flow, 132
Cash transfer payments, 362, 398–400
Celler-Kefauver Act, 256, 258
Cellophane market, 204
Chamberlin, Edward H., 197n., 226n.
Charities, private, 407–408
Choice, 3–4
  and costs, 9
  defined, 3
  at the margin, 9
  public, 70–71
  trade-offs in, 4
Cigarette producers, 223–224
CIO (Congress of Industrial Organizations), 310
Circular flow diagram, 23–26
  firms in, 24–25
  households in, 24–25
  markets in, 24–25
Civil Aeronautics Board (CAB), 235n., 237, 248–249
Civil Rights Act of 1964, 368
Clayton Act, 255–258, 262
Closed shops, 310
Clottleter, Charles T., 408n.
Coal prices, 54–55, 96–97
Cobb-Douglas production function, 140n.
Cobwebs (hog cycles), 307–308
Coca-Cola, 260
Collective bargaining, 316–317
  (*See also* Strikes; Unions; Wage agreements; *entries beginning with the term:* Union)

Collusion:
  defined, 218
  in oligopolies, 218–225
    explicit, 218, 219, 221–223, 257–258
    tacit, 218, 219, 223–225, 257–258
Command economies, 12, 14
  defined, 12
Common stock, 127n.
Company towns, 311–313
Comparable worth, 367–368
Comparative advantage, law of, 416–421
  defined, 416
Compensating differentials in wages, 287, 315
Competitive firms, 158–159
Competitive fringes, 209–210
Competitive industries, 179–181, 187–188
  (*See also* Perfect competition)
Competitive market economies, 181
Competitive markets (*see* Imperfectly competitive markets; Perfectly competitive markets)
Complements, 48–49
  defined, 48, 89
Completely inelastic demand, 87
Composition, fallacy of, 86
Compound interest, 324–326
Concentrated interests, 71–72
Concentration ratios, 215–216, 260, 261
Conglomerate mergers, 258
Congress of Industrial Organizations (CIO), 310
Conscious parallelism, 257–258
Consols, 327n.
Constant dollars, 30
Constant returns to scale, 152
  defined, 151
Constitutional reform to deal with inflation, 73
Consumer behavior, 108–109, 187
Consumer durables, 322–323
Consumer income (*see* Income)
Consumer preferences (*see* Preferences)
Consumer price index (CPI), 28–29, 31, 33
Consumer Product Safety Commission (CPSC), 244
Consumers:
  as buyers, 101–103
  in demand, 49, 52
  income of (*see* Income)
  price responses of, 54, 55, 107–108

Consumers (*Cont.*):
  risk attitudes of, 341–343, 345–349
  as sellers, 101*n.*
  spending by, 101–114, 116–122
    (*See also* Buyers, spending by)
Consumers' surplus, 111–114, 181–184
  defined, 112, 182
Consumption bundles, 103
Consumption efficiency, 189
Consumption taxes, 386
Contestable markets, 221*n.*
Control Data Corporation, 258
Corporate earnings, 127–129
  retained, 128–129, 133, 134
Corporate income taxes, 60, 378, 379, 386–387
  (*See also* Corporate profits taxes)
Corporate profits, 131–136, 336
  (*See also* Profit checks; Profit maximization; Profits)
Corporate profits taxes, 336, 379
  (*See also* Corporate income taxes)
Corporations, 125, 127–129
  boards of directors of, 127*n.*, 130
  defined, 127
  limited liability of, 129
  mergers of (*see* Mergers of firms)
  shareholders of, 127, 348
  stocks of (*see* Stock certificates; Stock markets; Stocks, of corporations)
  takeovers of, 128
Correlated returns, 350
Cost-benefit analysis:
  of government regulation, 247
  of government spending, 390–391
  social, 391
  (*See also* Benefit-cost ratios)
Cost conditions, changing, 149
Cost curves, long-run average, 149–151
Cost effect, 334
Cost minimization, 265, 276, 284
  (*See also* Profit maximization)
Cost of living index (consumer price index), 28–29, 31, 33, 424
Costs:
  and choice, 9
  defined, 131
  short-run, 144–149
  types of (*see specific entries, for example:* Average costs; Opportunity costs; Social costs)
  (*See also* Benefit-cost ratios)

Council on Wage and Price Stability (COWPS), 113
CPI (consumer price index), 28–29, 31, 33
CPSC (Consumer Product Safety Commission), 244
Crandall, Robert L., 257–258
Crandall, Robert W., 233*n.*, 242*n.*, 245*n.*
Cross price elasticity of demand, 88–89
  defined, 88
Cross price elasticity of supply, 92*n.*
Cross section data, 35
Current dollars, 30
Curves in graphs (*see* Graphs, curves in)

Dairy price supports, 167–168
Danziger, Sheldon H., 371*n.*, 398*n.*, 399, 401, 402*n.*
Deadweight burdens of taxes, 384–386
  defined, 384
Decreasing returns to scale (diseconomies of scale), 151, 153–154
Defense, national, 385, 431
Defense spending, 5–6
Delaney amendment, 245
Demand:
  adjustments in, 93–94
  consumers in, 49, 52
  elasticity of (*see* Price elasticity of demand)
  income in, 49, 50, 52
  law of, 102–103, 110–111
  in monopolies, 198–199, 202–203
  preferences in, 49–50
  prices in, 42–44, 48–52, 87–88
  and supply (*see* Supply and demand)
  types of (*see specific entries, for example:* Capital services, demand for; Inelastic demand)
  (*See also* Quantity demanded)
Demand curves, 42–44
  for competitors, 158
  defined, 44
  factors affecting, 48–50
  movements along, 51
  shapes of, 99–100
    kinked, 224–225
  shifts in, 48–52, 95
  slopes of, 109–111
    downward, 226–227
    individual, 101–103
    industry, 280–281
    labor, 274, 275, 280–281, 357

Demand curves, slopes of (*Cont.*):
  long-run and short-run, 93
  market, 101–103
Demand schedules, 43–44
  defined, 43
Demogrants, 406–407
Department of Transportation, 235*n.*
Depreciation (of assets), 134, 136
  defined, 131, 132, 332
Depreciation rates, 332
Depressions (*see* Great Depression; Recessions)
Deregulation, 235, 247–249
  (*See also* Government regulation)
Derived demand, 271–281, 314
  defined, 271
Derthick, Martha, 247*n.*
Diminishing marginal rate of substitution, 121
Diminishing marginal utility, 105–106
  defined, 105
Diminishing returns, law of, 142–143
Disability payments, 403
Discounted value (*see* Present value)
Discounting (of future payments), 319, 326
  (*See also* Present value)
Discounts, 208*n.*
Discrimination:
  economic, 365–368
  employment, 310, 365–368
  price, 208–209, 255–257
  racial, 365–368, 370
  sexual, 365–368, 370
  wage, 367–368
Diseconomies of scale, 151, 153–154
  defined, 151
Diversification (portfolio), 349–350
  defined, 349
Dividends, 133, 346
  defined, 128
  double taxation of, 379, 387
Dollar amount:
  of aggregate output, 29–30
  as economic variable, 27
Dollars:
  current versus constant, 30
Dominant firms, 209–210
Downward-sloping demand curves, 226–227
Dr. Pepper, 260
Dunbar, Frederick C., 243
Duncan, Greg J., 315*n.*, 365
Dunlop, J., 368*n.*
Du Pont, 204

Durable assets, 322–323
  productive, 53
Durable goods, 93n.

Earnings:
  of capital assets, 336
  of corporations, 127–129
    retained, 128–129, 133, 134
  of individuals (see Age-earnings profiles; Income; Wages; entries beginning with the terms: Income; Wage)
Econometrics, 36–37
  defined, 36
Economic activity, circular flow of (see Circular flow diagram)
Economic choices (see Choice)
Economic data, 26–27, 34–35
  defined, 23
  graphs of, 34–37
  nonexperimental, 37–38
Economic decisions, 140
Economic depreciation, 332n.
  [See also Depreciation (of assets)]
Economic deregulation, 235, 247–249
  (See also Government regulation)
Economic discrimination, 365–368
  (See also Discrimination)
Economic efficiency, 176–190
  defined, 139
  (See also Efficiency)
Economic jargon, 14–15
Economic laws, 34–38
  (See also entries beginning with the term: Law)
Economic mobility, 363–365
  defined, 363
Economic models:
  of consumer behavior, 109
  and theories, 22–27
Economic profits, 131–136, 336
  defined, 131
  (See also Profits)
Economic ratios, 31–32
Economic regulation, 233–249, 251, 262–265
  (See also Government regulation)
Economic rent, 296–297
  defined, 296
Economic stabilization, 62, 66
Economic status, 363–365
  inequality in, 365–368
  (See also Poverty; Wealth)

Economic systems, 11–14
  (See also Economies, types of)
Economic variables:
  comparing, 31–38
  defined, 22–23
  measuring, 27–31
Economics:
  defined, 3
  as dismal science, 4–7
  econometrics in, 36–37
  as science, 4–7
  types of:
    micro-, 14, 415
    normative, 5–7
    positive, 4–7
    welfare, 186
  understanding in, 37–38
Economies:
  defined, 7
  (See also Inflation rates)
  models of, 7–11
  types of (see specific entries, for example: Market economies; Mixed economies)
Economies of Imperfect Competition, The (Robinson), 197n.
Economies of scale, 151–154
  defined, 151
  in market concentration, 216–218
  of monopolies, 207
  in trade, 415, 422
Educated workers, market for, 305–308
  (See also Education)
Education:
  and age-earnings profiles, 302–303
  and economic discrimination, 366–367
  and economic status, 365
  government in, 392–393
  and hog cycles (cobwebs), 307–308
  and income, 302–305
  interest rates on, 304–305
  investment in, 304–305
  and labor productivity, 303
  and training, 303–309, 657
  and wage differentials, 302–308
Education vouchers, 393
Efficiency:
  and competition, 176–190
  and consumer behavior, 187
  and equity, 177–178, 184–186, 397–398
  and market concentration, 217
  of market equilibrium, 183–184
  and price systems, 179–181
  in resource allocation, 10–11, 177–190

Efficiency (Cont.):
  in taxation, 382–386
  types of: consumption, 189
    economic, 139, 176–190
    exchange, 188–189
    Pareto, 177–190
    production, 10–11, 187–189
    technical, 139
  and value judgments, 178–179
  and waste, 10, 11, 382–386
Efficient markets, 350–351
Efficient production, 10–11, 187–189
Efficient scale, minimum, 154, 216–218
Elastic demand, 83–85, 87
  defined, 83
Elastic supply, 92
Elasticity of demand (see Price elasticity of demand)
Elasticity of supply (see Price elasticity of supply)
Electrical equipment cartels, 221
Electricity prices, 149
Ellwood, David T., 372n., 398n., 399, 404
Elzinga, Kenneth G., 217
Empirical graphs, 17
Employee associations, 309n.
  (See also Unions; entries beginning with the term: Union)
Employees [see Worker(s)]
Employment:
  discrimination in, 310, 365–368
  equal opportunity for, 368
  levels of, 274
  and output, 272–274
  and output prices, 278–279
  retirement from, early, 403
  (See also Retirement programs; entries beginning with the term: Social Security)
  [See also Occupations; Training; Work; Worker(s); entries beginning with the terms: Job; Work]
Employment Act of 1946, 62
Engel, Ernst, 90n.
Engineering decisions, 140
Engineering standards, 241, 246–247
Environmental Protection Agency (EPA), 233, 241–243
Equal employment opportunity, 368
Equalizing differentials in wages, 287
Equilibrium:
  in international trade, 425–426
  under monopolistic competition, 226–227

Equilibrium (*Cont.*):
  overshooting, 94
  in perfectly competitive economies, 186–190
  types of: free-trade, 425
    long-run, 226–227, 334
    market (*see* Market equilibrium)
    short-run, 226, 227
    tangency, 227
Equilibrium prices, 46–47
  defined, 46, 179
Equilibrium production patterns, 417–418
Equilibrium quantity, 46
Equilibrium relative wages, 417
Equipment, 322–323
Equipment cartels, 221
Equity:
  and efficiency, 177–178, 184–186, 397–398
  horizontal and vertical, 380
  in taxation, 379–382
Equity-efficiency trade-off, 397–398
Essay on the Principle of Population (Malthus), 4*n.*,
Essential resources in monopolies, 207–208
  (*See also* Resource allocation; Resources)
European Economic Community, 423
Excess demand, 45–47
Excess supply, 45–47
  (*See also* Surpluses)
Exchange efficiency, 188–189
Exchanges, stock, 350–351
Excise taxes, 63–65, 378
Exclusive dealing arrangements, 256
Expected income, 50
Expected prices, 50
Expected real interest rates, 328
Expenditures (*see* Spending)
Experience and productivity, 308
  (*See also* Training)
Explicit collusion, 218, 219, 221–223, 257–258
Export restraints, voluntary, 424, 430–433
Export subsidies, 432
Externalities, 388*n.*, 391
  defined, 67, 238
  in market failure, 234–235
  and pollution control, 238–243

Factor markets in circular flow, 24–25
Factors of production, 138–139
  defined, 24

Factors of production (*Cont.*):
  in international trade, 420–421
  in long run, 149–154
  in short run, 141–149
  taxes on, 384–386
  types of: primary, 271–272
    variable versus fixed, 141
  (*See also* Capital; Labor; Land)
Fair but troublesome international trade, 430
Fairness (*see* Equity)
Fallacy of composition, 86
Family background in economic status, 364
Family income distribution, 360–369
  (*See also* Personal distribution of income; Personal income)
Farming (*see* entries beginning with the term: Agricultural)
FCC (Federal Communications Commission), 237, 259
FDA (Food and Drug Administration), 235, 243–245
Federal budgets (*see* entries beginning with the term:* Budget)
Federal Communications Commission (FCC), 237, 259
Federal Trade Commission (FTC), 233, 248, 255, 256, 259–262
Federal Trade Commission Act, 255
Feldstein, Martin, 311*n.*, 368*n.*, 403*n.*
Ferber, Marianne A., 367*n.*
Final products, 271
Financial assets, 346–347, 350
Financial capital, 126, 135, 322*n.*, 324–326
Financial statements, 131–134
Financial wealth, 322
Firm-specific human capital, 308, 311–313
Firms:
  as buyers, 101*n.*
  in circular flow, 24–25
  demand by (*see* Input demand)
  in economy, 123–125
  elements of (*see specific entries, for example:* Managerial goals; Production; Profits; Wages)
  mergers of (*see* Mergers of firms)
  owners of, 129, 135
    (*See also* Shareholders)
  supply curves of: long-run, 169–170
    short-run, 164–165
    (*See also* Supply curves)
  supply decisions of, 168–169

Firms (*Cont.*):
  types of: corporate (*see* Corporations)
    dominant, 209–210
    imperfectly competitive, 158
    partnership, 125–127
    perfectly competitive, 158–159
    sole proprietorship, 125–126
  (*See also* entries beginning with the term: Business)
Fixed costs, 144–145
  average, 147–148
  defined, 144
Fixed factors of production, 141
Flows of services, 323–324
  (*See also* Circular flow diagram)
Food and Drug Administration (FDA), 235, 243–245
Food stamps, 398, 399, 404
Foreign government subsidies, 429–430, 432
Foreign labor, cheap, as tariff argument, 429
Foreign voluntary export restraints, 424, 430–433
Four-firm concentration ratios, 215–216
Free-market economies, 12–14, 55–56
  defined, 13
Free-rider problem, 66, 72, 389, 407
Free trade, 71–72
Free-trade equilibrium, 425
Freeman, Richard B., 307, 311*n.*, 315*n.*, 368*n.*
Friedman, Milton, 64, 393
FTC (Federal Trade Commission), 233, 248, 255, 256, 259–262
Functional distribution of income, 357–360
  defined, 357
Futures markets, 351–353

GAF Corporation, 128
Gambling, 341
Garfinkel, Irv, 367*n.*
GATT (General Agreement on Tariffs and Trade), 433
Geis, Irving, 35*n.*
General Agreement on Tariffs and Trade (GATT), 433
General Electric, 257
General human capital, 308
General price levels (*see* Price levels)
George, Henry, 336
Giffen, Sir Robert, 111*n.*
Giffen goods, 111

454 Index

GNP deflator, 30–31
Gompers, Samuel, 310
Goods:
  transformation of, 188–189
  types of (*see specific entries, for example:*
    Complements; Final products; Normal
    goods; Substitutes)
  (*See also* Goods and services; Product
    curves; Product differentiation;
    Production)
Goods and services:
  demand for (*see* Demand; *entries
    beginning with the term:* Demand)
  government involvement in, 60, 66–67,
    387–391
  (*See also* Government spending)
  opportunity costs of (*see* Opportunity costs
  problems involving, 3–4
  supply of (*see* Supply; *entries beginning
    with the term:* Supply)
Government:
  decision making by, 69–73
  in economic stability, 62, 66
  in education, 392–393
  in gross national product, 61–62, 72–73,
    124–125, 378, 379
  in income distribution, 408–409
    (*See also* Income redistribution;
    Transfer payments; Welfare
    programs)
  in legal framework, 59–60
  local, 391–393
  in market economies, 64, 66–69, 71–72
  in mixed economies, 59–74
  in resource allocation, 63–64
  taxation by (*see* Taxation; Taxes; *entries
    beginning with the term:* Tax)
  transfers by (*see* Transfer payments)
  (*See also entries beginning with the term:*
    Public)
Government deregulation, 235, 247–249
  (*See also* Government regulation)
Government employees in unions, 311
Government intervention, 64, 66–69, 71–
    72, 377–378
  (*See also* Government regulation)
Government policy:
  for monopolies, 207–208
  on trade, 424–435
  types of: antitrust, 234, 252–255, 259–
    262
    stabilization, 62, 66
Government production, 60, 66–67

Government purchases, 60, 387–391
Government regulation, 60
  of monopolies, 207–208, 251–265
    natural, 253, 262–265
    (*See also* Antitrust law; Antitrust
    policy)
  reform of, 246–247
  standards in, 244–246
  types of: economic, 233–249, 251, 262–
    265
    local, 392
    social, 233, 235, 237–247, 251
  (*See also* Government deregulation;
    Regulatory lags)
Government regulatory agencies, 235–
    238
  (*See also specific entries, for example:*
    Environmental Protection Agency;
    Food and Drug Administration)
Government retirement programs, 398–400
  (*See also* Individual retirement accounts;
    entries beginning with the term:
    Social Security)
Government revenues, 60–61, 378–379,
    426, 429
  (*See also* Taxation; Taxes; *entries
    beginning with the term:* Tax)
Government sales, 60, 66–67
Government spending, 60–62, 72–73, 387–
    391
  composition of, 390
  cost-benefit analysis of, 390–391
  on defense, 5–6
  local, 391–393
  on public goods, 388–390
  on welfare programs, 398, 399
  (*See also* Budget deficits; Taxation; Taxes;
    entries beginning with the term: Tax)
Government subsidies, 429–430, 432, 435
  (*See also* Subsidized housing)
Grabowski, Henry G., 245*n*.
Graham, David R., 248*n*.
Gramm-Rudman-Hollings Act of 1985, 73
Graphs, 16–21
  axes, origins, and intercepts of, 17–18
  curves in, 19–21
    movements along, 51
    shifts of, 48–52, 54
    slopes of, 18–21
    steepness of, 18–19
    (*See also specific entries, for example:*
    Demand curves; Indifference curves;
    Supply curves)

Graphs (*Cont.*):
  defined, 17
  drawing, 17–18
  of economic data, 34–37
  types of, 17
  variables in, 17–21
Green, Carole A., 367*n*.
Growth rates of economic variables, 33–
    34
  defined, 33
Gruenspecht, Howard K., 233*n*., 245*n*.
Gwartney, James, 396*n*., 405*n*.

Hall, R. L., 244*n*.
Hall, Robert E., 386*n*.
Hankow Shipping Conference, 226
Hartford (Conn.) Steam Boiler Inspection
    and Insurance Co., 246
Hausman, Jerry, 385*n*.
Hausman, Leonard J., 368*n*.
Haveman, Robert H., 37*n*., 401
Hedgers in futures markets, 352
Heinlein, Robert, 11*n*.
Hekman, J., 368*n*.
Herfindahl index, 260
Heyman, Samuel J., 128
HHI (Hirschman-Herfindahl index), 260
Hill, Martha S., 364, 365*n*.
Hirsch, B., 309
Hirschman-Herfindahl index (HHI), 260
History of Economic Analysis (Schumpeter),
    152*n*.
Hitch, C. J., 224*n*.
Hog cycles (cobwebs), 307–308
Holmes, Oliver Wendell, 377
Holsendolph, Ernest, 251*n*.
Horizontal axes of graphs, 17–18
Horizontal equity, 380
Horizontal mergers, 258–260
Hostile takeovers, 128
Hot money, 724
Households:
  as buyers, 101–103
  in circular flow, 24–25
Housing, subsidized, 398, 399, 401
Houthakker, H., 88, 90
Huff, Darrell, 35*n*.
Human behavior, 38
Human capital, 295, 301–309
  in arts and sports, 308–309
  defined, 302
  types of: firm-specific, 308, 311–313

Index 455

Human capital, types of (*Cont.*):
  general, 308
  in wealth, 363

Ibbotson, Roger G., 346*n*., 347
IBM (International Business Machines), 251, 258
ICC (Interstate Commerce Commission), 235
Imperfect competition, 195–211
  (*See also specific entries, for example:* Monopolies; Oligopolies)
Imperfect information, 235
Imperfectly competitive firms, 158
Imperfectly competitive markets, 196–198
  defined, 195
  (*See also* Monopolies; Monopolistic competition; Oligopolies)
Import competition, 173, 424
In-kind transfer payments, 362, 398–401
Incentives:
  in government regulation, 244
  and transfer payments, 403–405
Income:
  in budget line, 117–119
  circular flow of (*see* Circular flow diagram)
  in demand, 49, 50, 52
  and education, 302–305
  from labor, 357–360, 442
    (*See also* Wages)
  and output, 25
  types of: accounting, 379
    expected, 50
    in-kind, 362, 398–401
    money, 361
    national (*see* National income)
    net (*see* Profits)
    nominal, 29
    ordinary, taxation of, 387
    personal (*see* Personal income)
    real, 29, 110
    Supplemental Security, 398, 399, 401
Income distribution:
  and economic mobility, 363–365
  of families, 360–369
    personal, 357, 360–368
  government in, 408–409
    (*See also* Income redistribution; Transfer payments; Welfare programs)

Income distribution (*Cont.*):
  in Pareto efficiency, 189–190
  and taxes, 408–409
  types of: functional, 357–360
    personal, 357, 360–368
    (*See also* Income inequality)
Income effect, 118, 119, 288–290, 299–300
  defined, 110
Income elasticity of demand, 89–90
  defined, 89
Income inequality, 361–362, 365–368
  versus poverty, 369–372
  and taxation, 380–382
Income redistribution, 68, 397–398, 408–409
  (*See also* Taxes; Transfer payments; Welfare programs)
Income statements, 131–133
  defined, 131
Income taxes:
  on capital gains, 387
  on ordinary income, 387
  types of: corporate, 60, 378, 379, 386–387
    negative, 406–407
    personal, 60, 362–363, 378, 386, 387
    Social Security, 60, 362–363, 378, 400
  and welfare programs, 404–405
Increasing returns to scale (*see* Economies of scale)
Incremental costs, 146*n*.
Indexation, 399*n*.
Indexed annuities, 399*n*.
Indifference curves, 119–122
  defined, 120
Individual demand curves, 101–103
  defined, 102
Individual demand schedules, 102
Individual labor supply, 299–300
Individual labor supply curves, 288–289
Individual labor supply decisions, 288–290
Individual proprietorships, 125–126
  defined, 126
Individual retirement accounts (IRAs), 386
Indivisibilities in production, 151–152
Industries:
  capital per worker in, 277
  concentration in, 215–218
  demand of, 279–281
  demand curves of, 280–281
  dominant firms in, 209–210
  in economy, 123–125
  labor market equilibrium in, 292–294

Industries (*Cont.*):
  marginal cost curves of, 172
  supply to: of capital services, 331–333
    of labor, 291–292
  supply curves of, 165, 172
  types of: competitive, 179–181, 187–188
    infant, 429
  wages in, 286–287, 291–294
  (*See also* specific entries, for example: Airline industry; Steel industry)
Inelastic demand, 83–85, 87
  defined, 83
Inelastic supply, 92
Inequality (*see* Income inequality; Wages, inequality in)
Infant industry tariff argument, 429
Inferior goods, 89–90, 111
  defined, 49, 89
Infinitely elastic demand, 87
Inflation rates, 33–34, 327–328
  defined, 33
Information:
  imperfect, 235
  in social regulation, 243–247
Information-related problems, 67–68
Injunctions against unions, 310
Input demand, 275–276, 278–279
  of firms, 272–279
  of industries, 279–281
Input markets, 271
Input prices, 274, 278
Inputs:
  quantity of, and profit maximization, 275–276
  types of (*see specific entries, for example:* Productive inputs; Variable inputs)
  (*See also* Production; *entries beginning with the term:* Production)
Insurance:
  as risk pooling, 342–343
  risk spreading with, 344
  risks unacceptable in, 344
  life, 343, 344
  social, 398–400
    (*See also entries beginning with the term:* Social Security)
  unemployment, 403–404
Insurance markets, 341–344
Insurance premiums, 341
Intangible assets, 134
Intercepts of graphs, 18

Interest:
    on investment, 319–320, 324–329
    on national debt, 396n.
    types of: compound, 324–326
Interest expenses, 133
Interest rates:
    calculating, 327
    on education, 304–305
    and present value, 319–320, 324–329, 391
    types of: actual, 328
        expected, 328
        nominal, 327–328
        real, 327–329, 332
Interests, concentrated, 71–72
Intermediate products, 271
International Business Machines (IBM), 251, 258
International trade:
    barriers to, 71–72, 424–435
    (*See also* Tariffs)
    capital-labor ratios in, 420–421
    equilibrium in, 425–426
    factors of production in, 420–421
    gains from, 415–418
    government policy on, 424–435
    labor productivity in, 416–419
    patterns of, 420–421
    problems of, 423–435
    refrigeration in, 423–424
    relative costs in, 416–417
    types of: fair but troublesome, 430
        free, 71–72, 425
        intra-industry, 422–423
        unfair, 430
Interstate Commerce Commission (ICC), 235
Intra-industry trade, 422–423
    defined, 422
Inventories, 132–133, 322–323
    defined, 132
Investment:
    defined, 321
    in education, 304–305
    interest on, 319–320, 324–329
    (*See also* Interest rates)
    rate of return on, 304–305, 320, 332–333, 345–347
    value of, 319–320
Invisible foot argument, 392
Invisible hand of Adam Smith, 12–13, 160, 176
IRAs (individual retirement accounts), 386
Isocost lines, 284

Isoquant maps, 283, 284
Isoquants, 282–285

James, Simon, 4n.
"January effect" in stock markets, 351
Japan:
    in international trade, 424
Jencks, Christopher, 393n.
Job training, 308–309
Johnson, Lyndon, 356, 396
Johnson, Samuel, 4
Johnson, William R., 397n.

Kahn, Alfred, 248
Kaplan, Daniel P., 248n.
Katz, Lawrence, 403n.
Kearl, James R., 365n.
Keeler, Theodore E., 233n., 245n.
Kelman, Steven, 247n.
Keynes, John Maynard, 351
Killingsworth, M. R., 289n.
Kinked demand curves, 224–225
Klass, Michael W., 233n., 236, 243n., 247n.
Kneese, Allen V., 241n.
Korean war, 328n.

L-shaped LAC curves, 154
Labor:
    cheap foreign, as tariff argument, 429
    marginal product of, 272–277
    marginal revenue product of, 272–274, 278–279
    marginal value product of, 273
    mobility of, 293
    (*See also* Capital-labor ratios; Capital-labor substitution)
Labor costs, unit, 416–417
Labor demand:
    and capital stock, 358–360
    elasticity of, 358–359
    and labor supply, 292–297
    optimal, 273–274
    and productivity, 279
    and unions, 313–314
    and wages, 292–296
    (*See also* Labor markets; Labor supply)
Labor demand curves, 274, 275, 280–281, 357
    (*See also* Labor supply curves)

Labor force:
    captive, 311–313
    unemployed in, 430
    (*See also* Employment; Unemployment)
Labor force participation rate, 289–290
    defined, 289
Labor income, 357–360
    (*See also* Income; Wages)
Labor market equilibrium, 292–294, 357–360
Labor markets:
    monopsonies in, 311–313
    supply limitations in, 296–297
    and wages, 295–296, 357–360
    (*See also* Labor demand; Labor supply)
Labor practices, unfair, 310
Labor productivity, 143–144, 295
    and education, 303
    and experience, 308
    relative, in international trade, 416–419
    technical progress in, 359
    and unions, 315
Labor requirements, unit, 419
Labor services, 323
Labor supply, 287–292, 357–360
    and capital stock, 358–360
    to economy, 290–291
    elasticity of: and taxation, 384–386
        and transfer payments, 397
    individual, 299–300
    to industries, 291–292
    and labor demand, 292–297
    limitations on, 296–297
    and Social Security, 403
    and unions, 313–314
    and wages, 286–300
    (*See also* Labor demand; Labor markets)
Labor supply curves, 288–292
    (*See also* Labor demand curves)
Labor supply decisions, individual, 288–290
Labor unions (*see* Unions; *entries beginning with the term:* Union)
Land:
    versus capital, 322
    defined, 321
    prices of, 329–330
    use of, zoning in, 392
Land rents, 296–297, 329–330
Land services, market for, 329
Lave, Lester B., 233n., 245n.

Index

Law of comparative advantage, 416–421
    defined, 416
Law of demand, 102–103, 110–111
    defined, 111
Law of diminishing returns, 142–143
Lawrence, Colin, 294n.
Lawrence, Robert Z., 294n.
Laws:
    economic, 34–38
        (See also entries beginning with the term: Law)
    government (see Government regulation; specific entries, for example: Clayton Act; Robinson-Patman Act)
Lazear, E., 88, 90
Leaky bucket analogy of Arthur Okun, 397
Leonard, Thomas M., 113
Lewis, Kenneth, 367n.
Liabilities:
    defined, 133
Liability, limited, 129
Life expectancy, 342–343
Limit pricing, 225
Limited liability, 129
Linear relations in graphs, 17–19
Link, Charles, 367n.
Living standards, 415
Lloyd's of London, 344
Loans:
    by banks, 409
Local government, 391–393
Logrolling, 70–71
Long run, 140–141
    defined, 140
    factors of production in, 149–154
Long-run adjustments in capital services market, 335–336
Long-run average cost curves, 149–151
    defined, 150
Long-run average costs, 149–151
Long-run break-even prices, 169
Long-run demand curves, 93
Long-run equilibrium, 226–227, 334
Long-run marginal cost, 150–151
Long-run marginal cost curves, 150–151
    defined, 150
Long-run production costs, 149–154
Long-run rent controls, 185–186
Long-run supply:
    of capital services, 331–333
    and demand, 92–97
Long-run supply curves, 94–95, 168–174
    defined, 95

Long-run supply curves (Cont.)
    of firms, 169–170
    of markets, 170–172
    shifts of, 172, 173
Long-run supply decisions of firms, 168–174
Lorenz curves, 360–362, 381, 408–409
Losing Ground (Murray), 356
Lotteries, 341
Low-income benefit programs, 401, 402
    (See also Welfare programs)
Luck and market concentration, 217
Luxuries, 90–91, 428
    defined, 90

MacAvoy, Paul W., 236n., 259
McBride, Mark E., 153
McCaleb, Thomas S., 396n., 405n.
Majority voting, 70–71
Malthus, Thomas, 4n.
Managerial diseconomies of scale, 153
Managerial goals, 130
Manual of Political Economy (Pareto), 177n.
Margin, at the, 9, 107
Marginal conditions, 160–163, 168, 202
Marginal cost curves, 150–151, 172, 179–180
Marginal cost pricing, 263–264
Marginal costs, 145–151
    defined, 146
    and prices, 160–161
    in profit maximization, 276
Marginal principle, 163, 164
Marginal product, 141–144
    defined, 142
    of labor, 272–277
        (See also Marginal revenue product, of labor)
Marginal rate of substitution, 187–189
    defined, 187
    diminishing, 121
Marginal rate of transformation, 188–189
    defined, 188
Marginal revenue, 198–201, 203, 276
    defined, 198
Marginal revenue product, 272–273
    of labor, 272–274, 278–279
Marginal revenue product curves, 274
Marginal tax rates, 381–382, 387, 404–407
    defined, 381

Marginal utility, 104–108
    defined, 105
    diminishing, 105–106
    ratios of, 108
Marginal valuation, 179–180
Marginal value product, 276
    of labor, 273
Market concentration, 215–218, 260, 261
Market definition, 258
Market demand, 101–114
Market demand curves, 101–103
    defined, 102
Market demand schedules, 101–102
Market economies:
    competitive, prices in, 181
    free-, 12–14, 55–56
    government in, 64, 66–69, 71–72
Market equilibrium:
    for capital services, 333–337
    efficiency of, 183–184
    in supply and demand, 45–48
    types of (see specific entries, for example: Labor market equilibrium)
Market failures, 234–235, 244, 246–247
    government intervention in, 64, 72
Market power (see Monopoly power)
Market value, 134–135
Markets:
    in circular flow, 24–25
    defined, 11
    entry into, barriers to, 197, 208, 216, 218, 225–226
    with large buyers, 198
    monopolization of, 255, 258, 259, 261–262
    in resource allocation, 11–14
    in supply and demand, 42
    supply curves of: long-run, 170–172
        short-run, 165–166
    types of (see specific entries, for example: Labor markets; Perfectly competitive markets)
Markham, Jesse W., 255n.
Marshall, Alfred, 3
Masson, R. T., 154
Means, Gardiner C., 130n.
Means (of numbers), 26
Medians (of numbers), 26
Medicaid, 398–401, 403
Medicare, 398–400, 403
Medoff, James L., 308n., 311n., 315n.

Mergers of firms:
  and antitrust law, 217, 258–260
  government guidelines for, 260
  and monopolies, 255, 256
Merit in economic status, 364–365
Merit goods, 68–69
  defined, 68
Michael, R., 88, 90
Milk price supports, 72
Miller, J. C., III, 113
Minimum efficient scale, 154, 216–218
Minimum wage, 6–7, 295–296, 404
Minority groups, poverty in, 370
  (*See also* Race; Racial discrimination)
Mixed economies, 13–14
  defined, 13
  government in, 59–74
Mobility:
  economic, 363–365
  of labor, 293
Models (*see* Economic models)
Money income, 361
Monopolies, 68
  in cellophane, 204
  defined, 196
  demand in, 198–199, 202–203
  economies of scale of, 207
  government regulation of, 207–208, 251–265
    (*See also* Antitrust law; Antitrust policy)
  as imperfect competition, 195–211
  and mergers, 255, 256
  and monopoly power, 196–197
    (*See also* Monopoly power)
  optimal positive output for, 201–202
  versus perfect competition, 197
  price changes in 202–203
  price discrimination in, 208–209, 255–257
  problems of, 252–254
  reasons for, 206–208
  in resource allocation, 203–206
  social costs of, 205–206, 252
  and technical progress, 210–211
  types of: natural, 154*n.*, 253, 262–265
    unnatural, 252, 254–255
  Monopoly Competition (Chamberlin), 197*n.*
Monopolistic competition, 196, 197
  defined, 214
  versus perfect competition, 228

Monopolistic competition (*Cont.*):
  theory of, 226–230
Monopolists:
  defined, 68, 158*n.*
  profit maximization by, 201–203
  unions as, 313–315
Monopolization of markets, 255, 258, 259, 261–262
Monopoly losses, 252–254
Monopoly markets, 198–211
  dominant firms in, 209–210
  prices and output in, 203–205
  revenue in: marginal, 198–201
    total, 199–201
Monopoly power, 68, 196–197, 251–254
  defined, 197
  in market failure, 234
  national, as tariff argument, 430–431
Monopoly profits (rents), 202, 264, 265, 297
Monopsonies, 198, 311–313
  defined, 311
Moral hazards, 344, 399, 403–404
Morgan, J. Pierpont, 254
Morrison, Steven, 249*n.*
Mortality statistics, 342–343
Mueller, Willard, 204
Multiple variable inputs, 275–278
Murray, Charles, 356, 400*n.*

National defense, 385, 431
  spending on, 5–6
National Highway Traffic Safety Administration (NHTSA), 233, 244, 245
National income, 357–362
National market power as tariff argument, 430–431
Natural monopolies, 154*n.*, 253, 262–265
  defined, 207
Natural oligopolies, 216
Necessities, 90
Neckerman, Kathryn M., 371*n.*
Negative income taxes, 406–407
Negative slopes of graphs, 19
Negatively correlated returns, 350
Nelson, Ralph L., 255*n.*
Net income (*see* Profits)
Net worth, 133, 134
NHTSA (National Highway Traffic Safety Administration), 233, 244, 245
Noll, Roger, 308*n.*

Nominal GNP, 29–31
  defined, 29
Nominal income, 29
Nominal interest rates, 327–328
  defined, 327
Nonexperimental economic data, 37–38
Nonlinear pricing, 208*n.*
Nonlinear relations in graphs, 19–21
Nonprice competition, 228–230
Nontariff barriers to international trade, 432
  (*See also* Trade barriers)
Normal goods, 89–90, 111, 300
  defined, 49, 89
Normative economics, 5–7
  defined, 5
Northern Securities Company, 254

Oates, Wallace E., 240, 241
Occupational Safety and Health Administration (OSHA), 233, 237–238, 244–246
Occupations:
  and unemployment rates, 366
  wage differentials in, 365–368
  (*See also* Employment; *entries beginning with the term:* Job)
OECD (Organization for Economic Cooperation and Development), 62, 72–73
Oil prices:
  deregulation of, 247–248
  increases in, 54–55, 79, 80, 92–93, 328*n.*
  world, 222–223
Okun, Arthur, 397
Oligopolies, 196–198, 214–230
  barriers to entry into, 225–226
  behavior of, 221–226
    collusive (*see* Collusion, in oligopolies)
    noncollusive, 225
  defined, 214
  kinked demand curves of, 224–225
  natural, 216
  nonprice competition in, 228–230
  rivalry in, 218–219
Oligopolists' dilemma, 219–220
Oligopoly pricing theory, 224–225
Oligopsonies, 198
On-the-job training, 308–309
OPEC (Organization of Petroleum Exporting Countries), 54–55, 79, 80, 92–93, 96–97, 222–223, 328*n.*

Opportunity costs, 8–9, 135–136
　in budget constraint, 104
　defined, 8
　and marginal rate of transformation, 188
Optimal labor demand, 273–274
Optimal positive output, 160, 162, 201–202
Optimal regulation, 238–241
Optimality:
　Pareto, 177–190
　social, 180–181
Ordinary income, taxation of, 387
　(*See also* Income taxes)
Organization for Economic Cooperation and Development (OECD), 62, 72–73
Organization of Petroleum Exporting Countries (OPEC), 54–55, 79, 80, 92–93, 96–97, 222–223, 328n.
Origins of graphs, 17–18
OSHA (Occupational Safety and Health Administration, 233, 237–238, 244–246
Output:
　in competitive markets, 203–205
　and cost minimization, 276
　and employment, 272–274, 278–279
　and income, 25
　maximizing, 284–285
　in monopoly markets, 203–205
　prices of, 278–279
　　aggregate (total) (*see* Aggregate output)
　　optimal positive, 160, 162, 201–202
　　(*See also* Production; *entries beginning with the term:* Production)
Output effect, 278, 281
Outstanding bills, 131–132
Overshooting, 55, 94
Owners of firms, 129, 135
　(*See also* Shareholders)

Paradox of voting, 70, 71
Pareto, Vilfredo, 177
Pareto efficiency (optimality), 177–190
Parsley, C.J., 315n.
Participation rate in labor force, 289–290
　defined, 289
Partners, 126
Partnerships, 125–127
　defined, 126
PATCO (professional air traffic controllers union), 311
　(*See also* Air traffic controller strike)

Patents, 210, 430
Paternalism by regulators, 245
Pay (*see* Wages)
Pay-as-you-go Social Security, 400
Payroll (Social Security) taxes, 60, 362–363, 378, 400
Pechman, Joseph A., 362n., 381n., 385n.–387n., 397n., 408n.
Peck, Merton J., 234n.
Pepsi-Cola, 260
Percentage changes, 32–34, 81–82
　(*See also* Price elasticity of demand)
Perfect competition, 176–190
　versus monopolies, 197
　versus monopolistic competition, 228
　in resource allocation, 203–206
　supply under, 157–174
Perfectly competitive economies, 186–190
Perfectly competitive firms, 158–159
　defined, 158
Perfectly competitive markets, 159–160, 183–184, 203–205
　defined, 159
Perfectly contestable markets, 221n.
Perfectly elastic demand, 87
Perfectly elastic supply, 92
Perfectly inelastic demand, 87
Perfectly inelastic supply, 92
Performance standards, 241
Perl, Lewis J., 243
Permits, tradable, 243
Perpetuities, 320
　defined, 327
Personal achievement in economic status, 364–365
Personal distribution of income, 360–368
　defined, 357
Personal income:
　disposable, 29n.
　money, 361
Personal income taxes, 60, 362–363, 378, 386, 387
　(*See also* Income taxes)
Physical capital:
　defined, 132, 321
　versus financial capital, 322n.
　versus land, 322
Plant and equipment, 322–323
Plotnick, Robert D., 401
Pollution control, 233, 238–243
Pollution taxes, 240–243
Ponza, Michael, 364, 365n.

Pope, Clayne L., 365n.
Portfolio diversification, 349–350
Portfolio risks, 348–349
Positive economics, 4–7
　defined, 4
Positive output, 160, 162, 201–202
Positive slopes of graphs, 19
Positively correlated returns, 350
Posner, Richard, 204
Postal Service, 262, 265
Poterba, James, 379n.
Poverty:
　and age, 370, 371, 400, 401
　culture of, 364, 365n., 400
　incidence of, 370–371
　and income distribution of families, 369
　versus income inequality, 369–372
　official measure of, 396, 401–402
　pools of, 371–372
　and race, 307, 401, 404
　and sex, 401, 404
　types of: absolute, 369–371
　　relative, 370
　and unemployment, 371–372
　war on, 356, 396
Poverty programs (*see* Welfare programs)
PPF (production possibility frontier), 7–11
Pratten, C. F., 153
Predatory pricing, 225–226, 258
　defined, 225
Preferences:
　in demand, 49–50
　in intra-industry trade, 422
　for public goods spending, 389–390
　revealed, 108
Preferred stock, 127n.
Prejudice in discrimination, 366
Premiums, insurance, 341
Present value:
　calculating, 319–320, 337, 391
　in cost-benefit analysis, 391
　defined, 325
　and interest rates, 319–320, 324–329, 391
Price ceilings on rent, 185–186
Price changes:
　in budget line, 118–119
　effects of: income, 110, 118, 119, 288–290, 299–300
　　substitution, 110, 118, 119, 278, 288–290, 299–300, 334–335

Price changes (*Cont.*):
  in indifference curves, 122
  for inputs, 278
  in monopolies, 202–203
  for outputs, 278–279
  value of, 111–114
  (*See also* Price levels)
Price discrimination, 208–209, 255–257
  defined, 208
Price elasticity of demand, 80–83, 99–100
  defined, 81
  extreme cases of, 87
  for inputs in industries, 281
  for labor, 358–359
  for monopolies, 202–203
  for primary commodities, 739
  and seller revenue, 83–87
  and substitutes, 87–88
  types of: arc, 100
    cross, 83–89
    derived, 314
    income, 89–90
Price elasticity of supply, 91–92
  cross, 92*n*.
  defined, 92
  of labor, 384–386, 397
Price-fixing, 221, 255–258, 260–261
Price indexes, 28–31, 33
  defined, 28
Price leaders, 224
Price leadership, 223–225
Price levels, 27–28
  defined, 28
  and GNP deflator, 30–31
Price makers, 158–159, 202
Price supports, 72, 167–168
Price systems, 51
  and efficiency, 179–181
  and resource allocation, 55–56
Price takers, 158, 202, 209
Price wars, 221
Prices, 27
  and costs, 160–161
  in demand, 42–44, 48–52
    in quantity demanded and supplied, 46–47
  in market economies, 181
  in markets: competitive, 203–205
    monopoly, 198–202, 203–205
  overshooting by, 55, 94
  in Pareto efficiency, 189
  percentage changes in, 80–83

Prices (*Cont.*):
  (*See also* Price elasticity of demand)
  in quantity demanded and supplied, 46–47
  ratios of, 108
  in resource allocation, 11–14, 55–56
  responses to: consumer, 54, 55, 107–108
    producer, 54–55
  in short run, 164–165
  in supply, 42–44, 53
    in quantity demanded and supplied, 46–47
  types of: break-even, 164–165, 169
    equilibrium, 46–47, 179
    expected, 50
    real, 32, 274, 279
    relative, 31–32, 107–108
  (*See also specific entries, for example:* Asset prices; Oil prices)
Pricing:
  average cost, 264
  limit, 225
  marginal cost, 263–264
  natural monopoly, 263–265
  nonlinear, 208*n*.
  oligopoly, 224–225
  predatory, 225–226, 258
Primary factors of production, 271–272
  (*See also* Capital; Factors of production; Labor; Land)
Principal, 319, 324
Prisoners' dilemma, 220
Private charities, 407–408
Private goods, 66–67
  defined, 66
Private regulation, 246–247
Private sector, 124–125
Producers, price responses of, 54–55
Producers' surplus, 181–184
  defined, 183
Product curves, total, 141, 142
Product differentiation, 197, 218
  defined, 214
Production, 124–125
  capital-intensive, 323
  costs of, 138–154
    in long run, 149–154
    in short run, 141–149
  and derived demand, 271–281
  factors of (*see* Factors of production)
  indivisibilities in, 151–152
  in international trade, 416–420

Production (*Cont.*):
  of natural monopolies, 264, 265
  patterns of, equilibrium, 417–418
  specialization in, 152, 415, 419
  (*See also* Supply; *entries beginning with the term:* Supply)
Production efficiency, 10–11, 187–189
Production function, 141–144
  defined, 140
Production methods, 139–141
Production possibility frontier (PPF), 7–11
  defined, 7
Production techniques, 282–285
  (*See also* Technical progress)
Productive assets, durable, 53
Productive inputs, 271
Productivity:
  and labor demand, 279
  technical progress in, 359
  (*See also* Technical progress)
Products:
  final, 271
  intermediate, 271
  (*See also* Goods)
Professional air traffic controllers union (PATCO), 311
  (*See also* Air traffic controller strike)
Profit and loss statements (income statements), 131–133
Profit checks, 162, 163, 168–169, 202
Profit maximization, 129–131
  and input quantity, 275–276
  marginal costs in, 276
  marginal revenue in, 276
  by monopolists, 201–203
  short-run supply decisions in, 160–164
  (*See also* Cost minimization; Production, costs of)
Profits, 129, 134
  defined, 131
  in government spending, 391
  taxation of, 336, 379
  (*See also* Income Taxes)
  types of: above–normal, 170
    accounting, 131–136, 336
    corporate, 131–136, 336, 442
    economic, 131–136, 336
    monopoly, 202, 264, 265, 297
  and unions, 316
  (*See also* Retained earnings)
Progressive taxes, 381–382
Property taxes, 60
Proportional taxes, 382

Proprietorships, 125–126
Protectionism, 71–72, 424–435
Proxy fights, 128
Public assistance programs, 398–401
  (*See also* Welfare programs)
Public choice, 70–71
Public goods, 66–67, 380, 388–390, 407
  defined, 66
Public utilities, 262–265
  (*See also* Natural monopolies)
Putnam, Howard, 257–258

Qualls, P. D., 154
Quantity:
  of aggregate output, 30–31
  as economic variable, 27
  equilibrium, 46
Quantity bought, 42, 47–48
Quantity demanded, 42–44, 46–48
  defined, 42
  percentage changes in, 80–83
  (*See also* Price elasticity of demand)
Quantity discounts, 208n.
Quantity sold, 44
Quantity supplied, 44–47
  defined, 44
Quasi-rents, 336
Quirk, Paul J., 247n.
Quota permits, 431
Quotas in international trade, 71–72, 424, 430–432

Rabushka, Alvin, 386n.
Race:
  and poverty, 370, 401, 404
  and unemployment rates, 404
Racial discrimination, 365–368, 370
Racism in discrimination, 366
Rates of return:
  on assets: capital, 336–337
    financial, 350
  on investment, 304–305, 320, 332–333, 345–347
  real, 304–305, 346–347
Ratios (*see specific entries, for example:* Concentration ratios; Economic ratios; Prices, ratios of)
Ratledge, Edward, 367n.
Reagan administration:
  and air traffic controller strike, 311
  and antitrust law, 257

Reagan administration (*Cont.*):
  deregulation by, 248
  and mergers, 259, 260
  on private charities, 407
  welfare programs of, 401, 402
Real GNP, 30–31
  changes in, 32–35
  defined, 30
  and inflation, 35–36
Real input prices, 274, 279
Real interest rates, 327–329, 332
  defined, 327
Real prices, 274, 279
  defined, 32
Real rate of return, 304–305, 346–347
  defined, 346n.
Real wages, 274, 294–295
  defined, 288
  and labor market equilibrium, 357–360
  and labor supply, 288–291, 299–300
Red dye #2 ban, 245
Refrigeration in international trade, 423–424
Regressive taxes, 381
Regulation (*see* Government regulation; Government regulatory agencies; Private regulation)
Regulatory lags, 265
Related goods, prices of, 48–49
Relations in graphs, 17–21
Relative costs in international trade, 416–417
Relative labor productivity, 416–419
Relative poverty, 370
Relative prices, 31–32, 107–108
  defined, 31
Relative wages, 416, 417
Rent:
  defined, 330
  taxation of, 336
  types of: economic, 296–297
    land, 296–297, 329–330
    monopoly, 202, 264, 265, 297
    quasi-, 336
Rent control, 185–186
Rental rates, 323–324
  on capital assets, 331–332
  defined, 323
  (*See also* Wage-rental ratio)
Required rate of return, 332–333
Required rental rates, 331–332
  defined, 331
Residential structures, 322–323

Resource allocation:
  efficiency in, 10–11, 177–190
  government in, 63–64
  markets in, 11–14
  monopoly versus competition in, 203–206
  prices in, 11–14, 55–56
Resources:
  defined, 3
  scarcity of, 3, 4
Retained earnings, 128–129, 133, 134
  defined, 128
Retirement, early, 403
Retirement programs, 386, 398–400
  (*See also* entries beginning with the term: Social Security)
Return(s):
  correlated, 350
  diminishing, law of, 142–143
  to factors of production (*see* Rent; Rental rates)
  rates of (*see* Rates of return)
  to scale, 283
    constant, 151, 152
    decreasing (diseconomies of scale), 151, 153–154
    increasing (*see* Economies of scale)
Revealed preferences, 108
Revenue, 131–132
  defined, 131, 132
  government, 60–61, 378–379, 426, 429
    (*See also* Taxation; Taxes; *entries beginning with the term:* Tax)
  marginal, 198–201, 203, 276
    (*See also* Marginal revenue product)
  seller, 83–87
  tariff, 426, 429
  total, 85–87, 199–201
Ricardian model of international trade, 416–420
Ricardo, David, 416
Right-to-work laws, 310
Risk-averse consumers, 341–343, 345–349
Risk lovers, 341
Risk-neutral consumers, 341
Risk pooling, 342–343, 348–350
Risk spreading, 344, 347–348
Risks:
  attitudes toward, 341
  in capital markets, 345–351
  economics of, 340–353
  and rates of return, 345–347
  regulation of (*see* Government regulation; Private regulation)

Risks (*Cont.*):
   types of: independent, 343
      portfolio, 348–349
   (*See also* Insurance)
Rivalry in oligopolies, 218–219
Robinson, Joan, 197*n*.
Robinson, Kenneth, 259
Robinson-Patman Act, 255–256
Roosevelt, Theodore, 254, 256
Ruback, Richard S., 316*n*.
Rule of 72, 324*n*.
Rule of two-thirds, 152

Saccharin ban, 245
Safety net welfare programs, 401, 402
   defined, 401
   (*See also* Welfare programs)
Sales taxes, 60, 63*n*., 378, 386
Salop, S. C., 256
Samuelson, Paul, 108*n*.
Saving:
   and Social Security, 403*n*.
   and taxation, 386
Savings programs, compulsory, 399–400
Scale:
   defined, 151
   returns to [*see* Return(s), to scale]
Scales of axes, 18
Scarcity, 3, 4
Scatter diagrams, 35–36
   defined, 35
Scherer, F. M., 217
Schubert, R., 368*n*.
Schumpeter, Joseph, 152*n*., 211
Scientists, market for, 307–308
Sealed-bid auctions, 221
Second-best tariff arguments, 428–429
Securities (*See specific entries, for example:* Stocks, of corporations)
Seller concentration, 215–218
Sellers:
   consumers as, 101*n*.
   revenue of, 83–87
   (*See also* Supply; entries beginning with the term: Supply)
Service economies, 125
Services:
   flows of, 323–324
      (*See also* Circular flow diagram)
   and goods (*see* Goods and services)

Service economies (*Cont.*):
   types of (*see specific entries, for example:* Capital services; Land services, market for)
7-Up, 260
Sex:
   and poverty, 370, 372, 401, 404
Sexism in discrimination, 366
Sexual discrimination, 365–368, 370
Shareholders, 127, 348
Shares:
   economic, 30
   of stock (*see* Stocks, of corporations)
Shaw, George Bernard, 4
Sherman Act, 255–258
Shipping cartel, 226
Short run, 140–141
   defined, 140
   factors of production in, 141–149
Short-run adjustments in capital services market, 334–335
Short-run break-even prices, 164–165
Short-run costs, 144–149
Short-run demand curves, 93
Short-run equilibrium, 226, 227
Short-run output and employment, 272–274
Short-run prices, 164–165
Short-run production costs, 141–149
Short-run production function, 141–144
Short-run rent control, 185–186
Short-run shutdown prices, 164
Short-run supply:
   of capital services, 331
   and demand, 92–97
Short-run supply curves, 94–95, 164–165
   defined, 95
   of markets, 165–166
   shifts of, 166–168
Short-run supply decisions, 160–164
Shortages, 45–47
Shutdown prices, short-run, 164
Signaling, 303
   (*See also* Education)
Sinclair, Andrew, 254*n*.
Sinquefield, Rex A., 346*n*., 347
Slopes of graphs, 18–21
Smith, Adam, 13, 64
   invisible hand of, 12–13, 160, 176
   on specialization, 152
Smith, Richard Austin, 221
Smith, Vernon L., 37*n*.

Social benefits of government projects, 390–391
Social cost-benefit analysis, 391
Social costs:
   of government projects, 390–391
   of monopolies, 205–206, 252
Social insurance, 398–400
   (*See also entries beginning with the term:* Social Security)
Social objectives of firms, 130
Social optimality, 180–181
Social regulation, 233, 235, 237–247, 251
Social Security payments, 73, 400
   indexation of, 399*n*.
Social Security system, 398–400, 403–404
Social Security taxes, 60, 362–363, 378, 400
Soft drink market, 260
Spaeth, Joe L., 367*n*.
Specialization, 152, 415, 419
Specific taxes, 63*n*.
Speculators in futures markets, 352
Spence, Michael, 303*n*.
Spending:
   by buyers, 83–87
   by consumers, 101–114, 116–122
Sports, human capital in, 308–309
Spot prices in futures markets, 352, 353
Stabilization policy, 62, 66
Stafford, F. P., 315*n*.
Standard Oil Trust, 255, 258
Statistical discrimination, 366
Steel industry, 173
Steepness of graphs, 18–19
Stigler, George J., 236*n*.
Stock certificates, 127
Stock markets, 350–351
Stockholders, 127, 348
Stocking, George, 204
Stocks:
   of assets, 323–324
   of capital, 321, 358–360
   of corporations, 127–129
      dividends on (*see* Dividends)
      prices of, 350–351
      rate of return on, 346–347, 350
      types of, 127*n*.
Straight-line relations in graphs, 17–19
Strikes, 311, 316–317
   (*See also* Collective bargaining; Unions; *entries beginning with the term:* Union)
Subsidies, 429–430, 432, 435

Subsidized housing, 398, 399, 401
Substitutes, 48–49
   capital-labor, 277–278, 358–359
     (*See also* Capital–labor ratios)
   defined, 48, 89
   in demand, prices of, 50–52, 87–88
Substitution:
   marginal rate of, 187–189
     diminishing, 121
Substitution effect, 118, 119, 278, 288–290, 299–300, 334–335
   defined, 110
Sugar prices, 113
Sultana explosion, 246
Summers, Lawrence H., 387n., 398n., 399, 404
Sunk cost fallacy, 163, 164
Sunk costs, 144, 163
Supplemental Security Income, 398, 399, 401
Supply:
   adjustments in, 94–95
   in competitive industries, 187–188
   and demand (*see* Supply and demand)
   durable productive assets in, 53
   elasticity of (*see* Price elasticity of supply)
   in labor markets, 296–297
   under perfect competition, 157–174
   prices in, 42–44, 53
   technical progress in, 53, 166–167
   types of (*see specific entries, for example:*
     Capital services, supply of; Inelastic supply; Labor supply)
   (*See also* Production; Quantity supplied; entries beginning with the term: Production*)*
Supply and demand:
   in competitive industries, 179–181
   long-run and short-run, 92–97
   market equilibrium in, 45–48
   markets in, 42
   prices in, 42–44
   taxes in, 63–64
   (*See also* Demand)
Supply curves, 44–45, 52–54
   defined, 44
   of industries, 165, 172
   shifts in, 54
     responses to, 93–94
   types of (*see specific entries, for example:* Labor supply curves; Short-run supply curves)
Supply decisions, 160–164, 168–169

Supply schedules, 44
Surpluses, 45–47
   consumers', 111–114, 181–184
   producers', 181–184
Sweezy, Paul, 224n.

Tacit collusion, 218, 219, 223–225, 257–258
Taft-Hartley Act, 310
Takeovers of corporations, 128
Tangency equilibrium, 227
Tangents to curves, 20–21
Tangible assets, 336–337
Tangible wealth, 321–337
   (*See also* Capital; Land)
Targeting of welfare payments, 402
Tariffs, 424–428
   arguments for, 428–431
   costs and benefits of, 426–428
   defined, 113
   history of, 432–434
   revenue from, 426, 429
   two-part, 263
   (*See also* Taxes)
Tastes (*See* Preferences)
Tax cuts:
   by year, 377, 397–398
Tax-deductible charitable contributions, 408
Tax incidence, 384–385
Tax rates:
   average, 381
   marginal, 381–382, 387, 404–407,
Tax Reform Act of 1986, 60, 377–379, 381, 382, 386–387, 405
Tax simplification, 387
Tax wedges, 383–384
Taxation, 378–387
   costs of, 397
   efficiency in, 382–386
   fairness (equity) in, 379–382
   principles of, 379–386
   of rents and profits, 336
   (*See also* Government revenue; Government spending)
Taxes, 60–62
   deadweight burdens of, 384–386
   in demand and supply, 63–64
   on factors of production, 384–386
   and income distribution, 408–409
   types of: ad valorem, 63n.
     capital gains, 387

Tax wedges, types of (*Cont.*):
   consumption, 386
   corporate income, 60, 378, 379, 386–387
   corporate profits, 336, 379
   excise, 63–65, 378
   income (*see* Income taxes)
   payroll (Social Security), 60, 362–363, 378, 400
   pollution, 240–243
   progressive, 381–382
   property, 60
   proportional, 382
   regressive, 381
   sales, 60, 63n., 378, 386
   specific, 63n.
   value-added, 379, 386
   on wages, 382–383
   (*See also* Income taxes)
   (*See also* Tariffs)
Taylor, L., 88, 90
Teamsters Union, 310
Technical economies of scale, 152
Technical efficiency, 139
Technical progress, 172, 173
   defined, 172
   and monopolies, 210–211
   in productivity, 359
   in supply, 53, 166–167
Telephone industry:
   deregulation of, 247–248
   regulation of, 251, 258, 259
Tender offers, 128
Theoretical graphs, 17
Tiebout, Charles M., 392n.
Tiebout hypothesis, 392
Tietenberg, Thomas H., 243n.
Time series data, 34–35
   defined, 34
Tobin, James, 349n.
Total conditions, 162, 163, 168–169
Total cost, 144–147
   defined, 144
Total output (*see* Aggregate output)
Total product curves, 141, 142
   defined, 141
Total revenue, 85–87, 199–201
Total utility, 104–108
Trade:
   economies of scale in, 415, 422
   types of: foreign (international) (*see* International trade)

Trade, types of (*Cont.*):
   free, 71–72, 425
   intra-industry, 422–423
Trade barriers, 71–72, 424–435
Trade-offs:
   in budget constraint, 104, 117
   defined, 4
Trade patterns, 420–421
Trade secrets, 210
Tradeable permits, 243
Trademarks, 430
Trading in future markets, 352
Training:
   and education, 303–309
   vesus signaling, 303
Transfer payments, 68, 396, 397, 399–400, 408–409
   and benefits principle, 380–381
   defined, 60
   disincentive effects of, 403–405
   to elderly, 72–73
     (*See also* entries beginning with the term: Social Security)
   and labor supply elasticity, 397
   types of: cash, 362, 398–400
     in-kind, 362, 398–401
Transformation, marginal rate of, 188–189
Transportation costs, 422
Transportation Department, 235*n*.
Treasury bills, 346–347
Truman, Harry, 15
Trusts, 255, 258
Two-part tariffs, 263
Tying contracts, 256

U-shaped average cost curves, 148
Ubell, Earl, 246
Uncertainty as inflation cost
   (*See also* Risks; entries beginning with the term: Risk)
Unemployment:
   and minimum wage, 404
   and poverty, 371–372
Unemployment insurance, 403–404
Unemployment rates:
   by occupation, 366
   and race, 404
   and wages, 295–296
Unfair international trade, 430
Unfair labor practices, 310
Union Carbide Corporation, 128
Union membership, 309–311

Union shops, 310
Unions, 309–317
   antitrust cases against, 256
   functions and effects of, 311–317
   history of, 310
   and labor demand and supply, 313–314
   as monopolists, 313–315
   and profitability of firms, 316
   and wage differentials, 311–316
Unit-elastic demand, 83–85, 87
   defined, 83
Unit labor costs, 416–417
Unit labor requirements, 419
U.S. Postal Service, 262, 265
U.S. Steel Corporation, 209, 210, 255
Unnatural monopolies, 252, 254–255
Upward-sloping labor supply curves, 290–292
Utilities, public, 262–265
   (*See also* Natural monopolies)
Utility:
   and consumer behavior, 108–109
   consumer spending without, 116–122
   defined, 103
   in indifference curves, 120
   marginal (*see* Marginal utility)
   total, 104–108
Utility function, 104
Utility-maximizing labor supply, 299–300
Utility meters, 103
Utility possibility frontier, 177–178
Utils, 103

Value:
   types of: market, 134–135
     present (*see* Present value)
   (*See also* Marginal value product)
Value-added taxes (VAT), 379, 386
Value judgments and efficiency, 178–179
Variable costs, 144–145
   defined, 144
Variable factors of production, 141
Variable inputs:
   multiple, 275–278
   prices of, 53
   single, 272–274
Variables:
   economic (*see* Economic variables)
   in graphs, 17–21

Variety as nonprice competition, 228–230
VAT (value-added taxes), 379, 386
VCRs (videocassette recorders), 54, 55
Vernon, John M., 245*n*.
VERs (voluntary export restraints), 424, 430–433
Vertical axes of graphs, 17–18
Vertical equity, 380
Vertical mergers, 258
Videocassette recorders (VCRs), 54, 55
Viscusi, W. Kip, 245*n*.
Voluntary export restraints (VERs), 424, 430–433
Voting:
   majority, 70–71
   paradox of, 70, 71

Wage differentials, 286–287
   and education, 302–308
   and elasticity of derived demand, 314
   by occupation, 365–368
   types of: compensating, 287, 315
     equalizing, 287
   and unions, 311–316
Wage discrimination, 367–368
Wage-rental ratio, 336–337
Wages:
   industry-wide, 291–294
   inequality in, 367–368
   and labor demand, 292–296
   and labor markets, 295–296, 357–360
   and labor supply, 286–300
   in monopsonies, 312
   and on-the-job training, 308–309
   taxes on, 382–383
     (*See also* Income taxes)
   types of: before- and after-tax, 383–384
     minimum, 6–7, 295–296, 404
     real (*see* Real wages)
     relative, 416, 417
   and unemployment, 404
   and unemployment rates, 295–296
   and unions, 315
   (*See also* Marginal revenue product, of labor)
Wagner Act, 310
War on poverty, 356, 396
Waste:
   and efficiency, 10, 11, 382–386

Waste (*Cont.*):
  in taxation, 382–386
  in welfare programs, 397–398
Water-diamond paradox, 107
Way of life tariff argument, 428
Wealth:
  distribution of, 363
  types of: financial, 322
    tangible, 321–337
    (*See also* Capital; Land)
  (*See also* Economic status)
Wealth of Nations, The (Smith), 13, 64, 152
Wedges, tax, 383–384
Weicher, John C., 402
Weinberg, Daniel H., 371*n*., 398*n*., 399, 401, 402*n*.
Weiss, Leonard W., 154, 233*n*., 236, 243*n*., 247*n*.
Welch, Finis, 367*n*.
Welfare economics, 186

Welfare programs, 396–409
  dependence on, 364, 365*n*.
  government spending on, 398, 399
  problems of, 404–408
  safety net, 401, 402
  size reduction of, 401, 402
  and taxes, 385, 404–405
  waste in, 397–398
  (*See also* Transfer payments)
Western Electric, 258
White, Lawrence, J., 233*n*., 256
White sales, 221
Wilson, James Q., 237*n*.
Wilson, William Julius, 371*n*.
Winston, Clifford, 249*n*.
Work:
  equal, and equal pay, 367–368
  hours of, 290
  (*See also* Employment; Right-to-work laws)
Work requirements (workfare), 406

Work stoppages, 316–317
  (*See also* Strikes)
Worker(s):
  tangible assets per, 336–337
  types of:
    educated, market for, 305–308
    government, in unions, 311
Workfare (work requirements), 406
Working conditions, 315
Workweeks, 290
Worth:
  comparable, 367–368
  net, 133, 134

Yamey, B. S., 226*n*.
Yandle, B., 113
Youth Employment Opportunity Wage, 6–7

Zimmerman, Martin B., 316*n*.
Zoning, 392